Oliver Tap

(IN)VISIBLE

Out-of-Body Experiences

and

Explorations into the Afterlife

The Monroe Method

Cover Design: Oliver Tappe
Photo of the Author: Jürgen Reisch www.jurgenreisch.com
Editors: Anna-Barbara Tietz, Olaf Arlt
Translators: Martina Lammers, Oliver Tappe

www.olivertappe.com
www.facebook.com/oliver.tappe
Instagram: @oliver_tappe

Published by:
Creative Energetics, Inc.
4550 Via Marina #307
Marina del Rey, CA 90292
USA

ISBN-13: 9798864800607

About the Author

Oliver Tappe's inaugural visit to the Monroe Institute in Virginia in 2000 proved transformative. It prompted him to reevaluate everything he previously understood about his own existence. Following this momentous visit, the former TV journalist and tour guide has continued to explore realms beyond the visible through countless Out-of-Body Experiences. In 2010, Oliver became a certified outreach trainer for the Monroe Institute, conducting workshops across Europe, Canada, and the United States. In his book (IN)VISIBLE, Oliver shares deeply personal and captivating experiences that have strengthened his conviction that humans are much more than just their physical bodies.

Oliver is also a certified yoga instructor who has studied trance mediumship at Arthur Findlay College in England. In addition to this, he is an intuitive artist with a passion for abstract painting. In 2018, he further expanded his skill set, becoming a certified NeuroGraphica® Specialist. His love for painting and communicating with spirit guides has blossomed into a unique art form. Oliver channels supportive messages and guidance from the other side.

In 1992, Oliver relocated to Los Angeles, where he currently resides with his wife Anna-Barbara, and their cherished dog Lottie.

CONTENTS

I dedicate this book to all those
who still believe that their life ends with death.

1

IT BEGINS WITH A FAREWELL

"We are not human beings having a spiritual experience. We are spiritual beings having a human experience."
Pierre Teilhard de Chardin, French Philosopher and Jesuit Priest

I find myself in an unfamiliar room, bearing witness to my mother's final moments. Her body, once full of life and strength, has carried her through the trials and joys of life. Now it is time to go home.

I feel a gentle touch on my shoulder, light as an angel's. When I turn around, I'm greeted by the face of a woman in her mid-twenties, her smile full of encouragement.

"It's okay," she whispers.

She motions towards the frail, nearly lifeless body on the bed.

"That's not me," the young woman insists. "That's the expression of my fear and pain, a minute part of my entire self."

Her voice is all too familiar. As a child, her melodies lulled me to sleep, her words guided, comforted, and sometimes admonished me.

My gaze shifts back to the tired eyes of the woman on the sickbed, eyes that look at me apathetically.

"How can I let you go without forgetting you?" I find myself asking.

The answer comes even before I finish my last word.

"I will always be with you. At all times, in all places. I am the flower, the tree, and the sky. I am wherever you want to see me."

The young woman behind me gently strokes my hair as only a mother could.

As a teenager, I pushed away this hand in embarrassment.

Typical of a boy.

Today, I welcome her touch. It could be the last time, the final moment to feel her so close.

Turning back to her, she grants me another smile. Her love is unconditional. Complete. This youthful woman is my mother. Just as I knew her when I was a little boy – without fear, without pain, and without wrinkles. She will leave those behind on her sickbed when she is ready to go.

As if through a veil, I see the young and the old merging. Her breath is so shallow; I can hardly perceive it anymore.

I sit here, watching my mother's passing.

The hospital room recedes from my awareness, replaced by a highway stretching out before me. It extends straight into the horizon, bordered by desert on both sides. It's a Friday afternoon, and I'm en route from Las Vegas to Los Angeles.

Years ago, I would have dismissed this as a daydream. But now, I recognize it as an excursion, a journey far beyond the constraints of time and space.

I pull off at the next exit, park the car, and dial my parents' number. Hearing their voices, even though they are aged and not in the best of health, brings a sense of relief. They are still alive, and I find comfort in knowing that they will forever be present whenever I seek their presence or guidance in this dimension or another.

Following two decades of extensive consciousness exploration and profound personal experiences, I've come to understand that humans are multidimensional beings. Each one of us is an expression of universal consciousness, focused on the physical plane and manifested as individuals. We aren't possessors of consciousness; rather, consciousness possesses us.

One facet of our multidimensional existence is the innate ability to transcend the limits of the physical dimension. We can learn to expand our awareness and focus our attention on *non-physical dimensions.* What initially seems like a daunting task is a process that can be learned in a few steps. The prerequisites are as simple as the techniques themselves: curiosity, a sense of adventure, and an open mind—in whichever order you prefer.

One method to uncover your multidimensionality and broaden your personal spectrum of perception is to practice Out-of-Body Experiences (OBEs). This approach has provided me with insights into questions I have grappled with throughout my life. Consciousness exploration through OBEs is an ongoing journey where each answer I discover leads to more questions.

The primary one that has intrigued prophets and philosophers for centuries remains: Is there life after death?

However, not everyone exploring Out-of-Body Experiences is necessarily interested in the afterlife. I regularly encounter people who, while they are deeply fascinated by astral travel (or astral projection), choose not to delve into their mortality or interact with otherworldly dimensions.

For me, the process was the exact opposite. From a young age, I was profoundly curious about what happens after we die.

Today, an increasing number of scientists worldwide who seek answers are open to alternative theories and concepts previously dismissed as esoteric musings of marginal groups. Renowned researchers at esteemed universities have contemplated the possibility that our soul—regardless of its precise definition—persists beyond our physical death.

Opinions remain divided, but some bold pioneers have emerged in the meantime. One of them is Professor Hans-Peter Dürr, a former director of the Max Planck Institute for Physics in Munich, Germany, who clearly stated his conviction:

"What we term this mortal world is essentially material, the tangible. The afterlife represents everything else—the all-encompassing reality, the broader aspect. The body dies, but the spiritual quantum field persists. In that sense, I am immortal."

Though this view is considered radical for a scientist, leaders of world religions have been preaching this for millennia. Hoping to fill churches and collection plates, Christianity, for example, describes heaven and hell, angels, and purgatory. Religions entice people with promises of eternal peace and warnings of damnation. Their followers often need to choose the "one" true religion—given they have the privilege of living in a society that doesn't mandate a specific faith.

My grandmother once said, "But you must believe in something, or you have no foundation."

"Do I really?" Even as a child, I questioned myself and resolved to unearth my own truth. But first, my parents had me don a suit for confirmation and recite the Lord's Prayer.

"Or you'll burn in hell!"

And who wants that?

Even though I received the blessing, my lack of confidence in organized religion did not change. I found it challenging to listen to the dull sermons of our small-town preacher, who, instead of speaking plainly, used parables and waved his cassock in a threatening manner. His wide sleeves reminded me of large, black, ominous crows' wings.

Little of what he preached from the pulpit resonated with my inner voice. My ears perked up only when he showered the congregation with words like *death* and *resurrection*. The day of my confirmation marked the end of my brief tenure as a devout churchgoer.

What persisted was my fascination with death and dying. During school vacations, I often spent hours in the cemetery adjacent to my grandmother's property. I moved from grave to grave, captivated by the inscriptions on strangers' monuments and gravestones.

"Where are they now?" I continuously pondered.

I found it challenging to accept the concepts of heaven and hell. However, I had an inherent sense that there was more beyond the visible and tangible. Guided by my intuition, I began searching for new leads at a young age.

In an era when the internet was still a futuristic concept and esoteric information was scarce, I believed my only option was to communicate with the spirits of the deceased. To get my questions answered, I was willing to explore all avenues.

So, I scoured the local library for books with guidance on reaching the afterlife. Too embarrassed to borrow the books, I discretely removed the relevant pages and pocketed them. My curiosity surpassed my fear of being caught.

At home, I secluded myself in my room and practiced the art of necromancy. For hours, I stared into the flame of a candle, hoping to catch a glimpse of *the other side*—unfortunately, to no avail. I tried divination by glass moving and using a pendulum. After my home-made Ouija board also failed to initiate a conversation with the dead, I finally gave up, disheartened and frustrated.

Years later, my interest reignited when I stumbled upon a book by Robert A. Monroe in a German bookstore: *Journeys Out of the Body*. A brief look at the back cover filled my heart with excitement.

Monroe wrote that anyone could have a conscious OBE. The notion that the soul could leave the body and safely return to it captivated me immensely.

With some trepidation, I brought my precious find to the check-out counter. Would the store clerk smirk at my interest in the esoteric? Little did I know how purchasing this book would redefine my life and set it on an entirely new path.

Today, approximately 30 years and hundreds of OBEs later, I am convinced that our physical incarnation is merely a minuscule, perhaps insignificant, part of our overall existence. It serves the evolutionary development of a multi-tiered system.

Death is simply an energetic shift. We relinquish our physical form and once again become fully aware of our soul's original source—the "great" consciousness. It's as if we're returning home. However, in truth, we never completely left our source. Our perception is merely limited during our brief sojourn on planet Earth.

Our awareness of daily life is focused on our physical reality. The system as a whole exists outside this restricted perspective.

This book's objective is not to answer humanity's questions regarding life and death. Instead, its aim is to inspire the reader to explore the subject themselves. What I describe in the following pages is based solely on my experience and subsequent beliefs.

How did I come to my insights?

Of course, I read numerous books by and about individuals who, in various ways, made contact with the afterlife. These included psychic mediums, people with near-death experiences, spiritual healers, and hypnosis therapists. Many of these accounts have reinforced my belief in life after death.

However, it's important to note that *belief* does not equate to *knowing*. True knowledge can only be acquired through direct personal experience. And I was determined to travel down that road, regardless of the cost.

On November 11, 2000, inspired by Robert Monroe's books, I set off to a six-day workshop at the Monroe Institute in Virginia. My luggage was filled with the hope of encountering something similar to what the institute's founder describes in his fascinating reports about Out-of-Body Experiences.

"It doesn't matter what religion you belong to or what faith you practice," said Monroe, whose Gateway Voyage program has been taught in its original form at the institute since the 1970s. "Simply be open to the possibility that you may be more than just your physical body."

I appreciated Monroe's emphasis on debunking old doctrines without replacing them with new ones. The foundation of the *Gateway Voyage* program lies in the Hemi-Sync audio technology developed by Monroe. It enables individuals to achieve altered states of consciousness and sustain them. This, in turn, provides an ideal basis for Out-of-Body Experiences and perceptions.

Only six days and nights later, my previous worldview had been completely transformed. What I experienced during the *Gateway Voyage* program profoundly influenced my life from that point onward.

For the past twelve years, I have been an outreach trainer for the institute in Europe, Canada, and the United States, delivering lectures and organizing workshops. During this time, I have also developed my own programs inspired by the Monroe Method. In my workshops, I focus on providing participants with a safe space to make their own unique experiences.

Likewise, I want to encourage the readers of this book to embark on a journey of gaining new insights and perhaps even developing a completely new worldview.

This book is not a step-by-step guide on how to achieve an OBE. There are already plenty of those available. Instead, I describe my personal journey as a traveler between worlds and the challenges I faced. My intention is to facilitate the path to conscious OBE for others.

Expressing supernatural experiences can be challenging, as

they require a supernatural vocabulary. Despite this obstacle, I place great importance on remaining as close as possible to the essence of my experiences.

I also recount the experiences of other individuals, changing some names and locations to respect their anonymity.

While I consciously avoid imparting any form of dogma, I have drawn certain conclusions from my encounters and experiences in non-physical realms, which I will share with my readers. These conclusions are based on circumstances I have observed in non-physical regions and interactions with non-physical beings. It is essential to understand that my conclusions are not absolute truths. Rather, they serve as guidance and navigation aid for the reader's own explorations.

I deliberately refrain from presenting comprehensive syntheses or theories that may require revision as I gain further knowledge and experience.

My fascination with exploring the afterlife has grown tremendously over the years. Nothing is more exciting than meeting and communicating with those who have passed away.

While the departed can perceive us at any time, it's often difficult for the living to perceive them. Nevertheless, the deceased patiently attempt to contact us, often to reassure us that they are doing well or to express their love for us. Sometimes, they even have valuable information to share.

Unfortunately, in our loud and busy world, the subtle signals from our non-physical friends are often lost. To connect with our loved ones, we must learn to adjust our vibrational frequency accordingly. And that comes more easily to some people than others.

I believe those who embark on this learning process will be rewarded in many ways. Once the connection between the two worlds is established, both sides experience delight. And as a welcome side effect, the fear of death, which haunts many individuals from a young age, diminishes.

The afterlife is not our final destination and is not as far away as we might think. Most people perceive it as distant because their limited perspective, rooted in their daily lives, allows them only to glimpse fragments of that world.

Those who thoroughly study the subject, train, and refine their perception will discover that the dimension we call the afterlife can be found all around us and alongside us in this life.

Some individuals struggle to abandon old doctrines and embrace a new understanding of the world. We naturally hold onto what we know, as our thoughts and actions are dominated by habits that provide a sense of security and orientation. We often disregard new impulses and ideas that don't align with the profoundly ingrained worldview we've been taught or that challenge the accepted reality defined by most of our social and family circles.

Many people believe that they have already learned everything there is to know about the nature of humanity and the world through their studies in biology, geography, and religion. Changes could entail unexpected, possibly unpleasant consequences.

Here's some good news for those whose curiosity outweighs their commitment to their profoundly ingrained worldview: Anyone can visit the afterlife and communicate with the departed. If you're willing to open your heart and overcome self-doubt, you'll find it easy to transcend the limitations of the physical dimension, and your friends on the other side will be grateful.

Join me on a journey that could bring you closer to your destination than you ever thought possible. Expect plenty of surprises along the way.

Have a great trip!

2

GATEWAY VOYAGE – A JOURNEY THROUGH THE PORTAL OF REALIZATION

"And those who were seen dancing were thought to be insane by those who could not hear the music."
Friedrich Wilhelm Nietzsche, Philosopher

November 11, 2000

My legs tremble as I disembark from the propeller plane at Charlottesville airport. Dazed from the turbulent hour-long flight, I'm relieved to be back on solid ground.

The fresh autumn air in Virginia provides a delightful contrast to California's consistent and mild climate. Seeing the deciduous trees along the highway fills me with joy, and I can't seem to get enough of the vibrant leaves.

The taxi ride to my accommodation takes less than 20 minutes. Since the flight has already strained my travel budget, I choose to spend the night at a cheap motel located on the city's outskirts, next to a busy road. I've waited for this day for five months. I took a week's vacation and traveled across the continent from the west coast to the east coast, hoping to learn more about the Out-of-Body Experiences described by Robert Monroe.

The room at the motel is run-down and has a musty smell, with paper-thin walls. I can hear someone showering next door, and the TV blares loudly. I feel restless, excited, and uncertain. After all, I have no idea what to expect from the *Gateway Voyage* in the upcoming days.

The constant background noise keeps me awake until the early hours, so I decide to buy two cans of beer and a pack of cigarettes from a minimart nearby. I actually did quit smoking several weeks earlier, but beer without cigarettes doesn't work, and cigarettes without beer certainly doesn't, either.

"I'll definitely put an end to this nonsense tomorrow!" I promise myself, not for the first time.

The noise persists throughout the night, with flushing toilets, slamming doors, and squeaking beds. I'm already wide awake when the alarm goes off at seven. Suddenly, doubts creep in. The thought of spending six days with a group of strangers on an isolated campus in the middle of nowhere scares me. I'm not one to fit in easily. What if I don't get along with the other participants? Or if nothing significant happens and I've wasted more than two thousand dollars? My mind races with these thoughts.

At half past ten, the shuttle bus from the Monroe Institute arrives at the motel. There's no turning back now. Mike, the driver, greets me warmly as if we're old friends. The other four passengers turn out to be participants who were picked up from the airport before me. They bombard me with questions.

"Where are you from?" Dianne from Toronto asks.

"I'm originally from Germany," I reply, "but I've been living in California for many years!"

"Is this your first visit to the institute?"

I nod. The elderly lady throws her head back and laughs.

"Nothing will ever be the same again when you get back on this bus six days from now."

Dianne has already attended three courses at Monroe. This time, she's traveled all the way from Canada to participate in the *Lifeline* program, which runs parallel to the *Gateway Voyage.*

"You'll be staying at the Nancy Penn Center," she explains.

"Our program takes place about a mile away in Bob Monroe's

former residence."

I'm impressed. I'm already familiar with Monroe's home from reading his books. I'd love to ask Dianne a few questions, but I don't have a chance to get a word in. The drive from Charlottesville takes 45 minutes, and only a few miles into the journey, my ears start ringing.

This is my first time in Virginia, and I'm surprised by the sparsely populated, hilly landscape. Occasionally, we pass a farm or a few modest wooden houses off the highway.

"Look over there!" Mike exclaims, pointing ahead.

"That's the house that inspired Earl Hammer to create the TV show *The Waltons*. Remember John-Boy and Jim-Bob?"

Everyone gets excited. The Waltons! Of course, who could ever forget them?

We leave the highway and turn onto a narrow, winding road that ascends steeply. The closer we get to our destination, the more my anticipation builds.

"Perhaps we'll meet again at the airport next week!" Dianne shouts after me when I unload my suitcase at the institute's parking lot. "I can't wait to hear what you have to share!"

I'm filled with awe as I gaze at the wooden front door of the Nancy Penn Center. This is the place I've read so much about, where Robert Monroe pursued his extrasensory studies, secluded from civilization amidst meadows and forests. The institute's cornerstone was laid 26 years ago, and five years have gone by since Monroe passed away.

My thoughts are abruptly interrupted by one of the other participants tugging at my sleeve.

"Let's go!" exclaims Ben, a rather big and tall guy in his mid-fifties from Kansas City, appearing hyper and impatient. "I'm sure they have food waiting for us."

Tammy, one of the institute's staff, welcomes us into the lobby.

"You are in number 19," she says, pointing me in the right direction. "Your roommate's name is Phil. He's already checked in."

Tammy leads me through a long corridor with dark wood paneling, giving the building the feel of an oversized ski lodge.

Curiously, I step into the small room. Next to the two desks and two clothes rails, there are wooden cubicle enclosures on both sides of the door, each adorned with a heavy, dark curtain. Behind each curtain lies a twin-size mattress.

"That's your CHEC Unit," Tammy explains, pointing to the left. "CHEC stands for Controlled Holistic Environmental Chamber. This is where you'll do your exercises."

I'm intrigued.

"And where are the bedrooms?" I cautiously inquire.

Tammy laughs.

"The CHEC Unit is also your bed."

I wonder how long it will take before I get claustrophobic inside the 35-inches-wide and just under 80-inches-long enclosure. But I decide not to voice my concern.

After Tammy leaves the room, I take a closer look at my CHEC Unit. There are headphones on the pillow, with most of the cable hidden inside the wall. Loudspeakers are set into the sides on the left and right. Above the foot of the mattress hang three colorful lightbulbs, reminiscent of the light organ in small-town discos from my youth in the eighties.

Apart from three tiny desk drawers and the clothes rail, there's nowhere to place my personal belongings. Now I understand why they advised us to bring as little as possible.

I begin exploring the long hallways. There are no private bathrooms, but ample showers and toilets along the corridor. A staircase leads from the accommodation wing to a kind of foyer.

"This is the Fox Den," I hear Tammy say from behind. "Bob's wife Nancy was very fond of foxes, as you can see from the decorations."

Hesitant, I descend the stairs and notice a group engaged in a lively discussion.

"Come and join us," an elderly man invites me, gesturing towards a vacant chair beside him.

The conversation revolves around paranormal perceptions and supernatural experiences. Bill from Texas wants to know if I've encountered any. All eyes are on me. I spontaneously recall an event from my younger years, but before I can speak, everyone suddenly turns their gaze toward the stairway. Bill jumps up and raises both arms.

"Laurie!" he exclaims with delight.

"William!" the woman on the stairs shouts back, her voice rough and scratchy, akin to a chain smoker's.

They embrace, and then Laurie addresses the group.

"Welcome to the Monroe Institute! I'm glad you found us."

Robert Monroe's daughter sits down beside me, filling me with awe. Laurie has been the institute's director since her father's passing. She's delighted to learn that I'm from Germany.

"We have many visitors from Germany, more than from any other European country."

Laurie and I converse for half an hour, discussing her father, the institute, and even my home country. After our chat, she heads to work and hugs me like an old friend.

"I've got a hunch that we'll be seeing more of you here in the future, Oliver," she says, leaving me amazed. "And my instincts are never wrong," she adds with a wink.

Throughout the afternoon, more workshop participants from various countries, including Great Britain, Australia, Canada and Kuwait, as well as Alaska, Hawaii, and other states, arrive at the Fox Den. Many of them seem visibly exhausted after long flights.

Despite their different cultures, the group members maintain a surprisingly informal atmosphere.

The animated conversations halt when our two trainers, Karen Malik and John Cahill, enter the room. They announce that they would like to speak to each of us individually before dinner.

I'm the first one called.

John leads me to a spacious couch in the adjacent room, wasting no time on small talk.

"Why did you choose the *Gateway Voyage*?" he asks. "What are your expectations for the program?"

Having been introduced to the subject of Out-of-Body Experiences through Robert Monroe's books, I tell him want to have an OBE like many first-time visitors to the institute.

"Your expectations may be too narrow," John cautions. "While it's good to have a specific goal, focusing solely on one aspect of the program could cause you to miss out on other, even more valuable experiences. The *Gateway Voyage* offers much more than just OBEs."

Although I don't fully grasp John's message, I simply nod, deciding to take things as they come and remain open to whatever unfolds.

Returning to the Fox Den, I sit next to Ann from Seattle. Attending the Monroe Institute has been her dream for years.

"I am here to prepare myself for the next stage of my journey," she says, her voice weak and frail, making it difficult to hear her clearly.

"What journey are you talking about?" I inquire.

"I'm still feeling very well. But that can soon change at my age," she replies.

The 86-year-old takes a deep breath and clasps my left hand. "I'm not afraid of dying. In fact, I'm excited about it because I've long known that I am more than just my physical body. However, it would be nice to explore the path to the afterlife beforehand."

Uncertain how to respond to her candidness, I'm both impressed and startled. Ann tightens her grip on my hand.

"Let's be friends," she suggests, looking at me expectantly.

"I would like that very much," I reply.

Ann's bony hand gently caresses my forearm. We sit together in silence for a short while before her head slumps forward. Seconds later, I hear her soft snoring. My new friend has dozed off.

After dinner, Karen and John await us at the entrance of the assembly room, politely requesting each participant to deposit their wristwatch into the baskets they are holding.

"This week, we want you to forget about linear time," Karen announces. "We will wake you early in the morning and ring the big bells in the Fox Den and on the porch to indicate the start of each new program activity."

Spending a week without knowing the time doesn't particularly appeal to me. It's only now that I realize there are no wall clocks anywhere in the building. Hesitant, I place my watch into the basket, remove my shoes, and enter the room.

The floor is adorned with a thick, fluffy white carpet. We begin with an introduction to the Hemi-Sync technology, followed by information about the preparatory steps integral to each exercise. This process involves several elements.

"First, you will hear the sound of waves, which serves as the starting signal," John explains. "Next, we have the energy conversion box, where you envision a lockable crate to contain any distracting thoughts. Then we proceed with the resonant tuning, which involves vocalizing vowel sounds to stimulate energy exchange within the physical body."

Once back in my room, I cautiously enter the CHEC Unit for the first time and immediately feel a sense of claustrophobia. The wooden enclosure is even narrower than it appeared from the outside, providing barely enough space to lie comfortably without touching its sides. I don't dare to fully close the heavy black linen curtain.

Through the speaker system, John instructs us to put on our headphones and activate the Ready Light. The small red lamp indicates to the trainers in the control room that everyone is in place and ready for the upcoming exercise. Shortly after, I hear the soothing sound of ocean waves.

Here we go!

Robert Monroe's voice is dull, reminiscent of a radio announcer from the 1950s. I struggle to contain my interfering thoughts in the imaginary crate. Then, a choir signals the start of the resonant tuning. I am drowning out my thoughts by chanting vowels.

A few minutes later, the choir ceases, and Monroe recites his famous Gateway affirmation:

"I am more than my physical body. Because I am more than physical matter, I can perceive that which is greater than the physical world.

Therefore, I deeply desire to expand, to experience, to know, to understand, to control, to use such greater energies and energy systems as may be beneficial and constructive to me and to those who follow me.

Also, I deeply desire the help and cooperation, the assistance, the understanding of those individuals whose wisdom, development and experience are equal or greater than my own.

I ask their guidance and protection from any influence or any source that might provide me with less than my stated desires."

I attempt to follow the guided relaxation, but my heart beats louder and louder. *Why on earth am I feeling so excited?*

Bob slowly counts from 1 to 10. I feel a slight pressure in my skull. My right hand begins to tingle as if it has fallen asleep. It's unpleasant, but there's nothing I can do about it. I'm unable to move my hand. The heaviness I now perceive is more dominant than the desire to stop the tingling.

For a moment, I feel as if I'm sinking. Before I can delve deeper into this sensation, Monroe's voice continues through my earphones, sounding muffled:

"Focus 10. You are now in Focus 10, the state where your body is deeply relaxed, and your mind is fully awake."

Unexpected images flash in my mind's eye, constantly changing within fractions of a second. They're so fleeting that I can't grasp any of them.

The tingling sensation in my hand subsides, and suddenly, my body feels as heavy as lead. I'm momentarily frightened. Thoughts race uncontrollably through my mind. This must be what it feels like to be paralyzed.

3

FIRST EXPERIENCES WITH HEMISPHERIC SYNCHRONIZATION

"I believe Hemi-Sync has enabled me to return to a realm similar to that which I visited deep in coma, but without having to be deathly ill. But just as in my dreams of flying."
Eben Alexander, Author of
"Proof of Heaven: A Neurosurgeon's Journey into the Afterlife"

Those who've ventured into the realm of meditation know that there are many styles and schools. Each variant presents unique techniques and methodologies.

The goal and purpose of meditation can also significantly differ, mainly hinging on the underlying philosophy.

Many people turn to meditation to achieve relaxation or boost self-love, while some aim for grander goals like human augmentation or even enlightenment—all while perched on their cushions.

My understanding of meditation was pretty rudimentary before the *Gateway Voyage*, limited to brief meditative moments at the end of my yoga sessions.

It was only through my engagement with Hemi-Sync, an audio technology pioneered by Robert Monroe, that I started exploring alternative approaches to meditation. Today, I find it hard to imagine life without my regular practice. I need the quiet to regroup, heal, and more importantly, find refuge from the daily grind.

Hemi-Sync still forms a crucial component of Monroe Sound Science, a sound technology created by the Monroe Institute. It enables the practitioner to fall into a deep meditative state within minutes and maintain it over a prolonged period.

Monroe Sound Science has evolved significantly over the past 50 years, consistently enhancing its capabilities through ongoing research and advancements in audio technology.

To explain the technology in detail would go beyond the confines of this book. Therefore, I'll stick to its crucial principles.

The human brain responds to rhythmic sounds by generating specific brainwave patterns. Thus, consistent drumming can induce relaxation in listeners. Slow, rhythmic music has a similar impact.

Scientists have been fascinated by the influence of varying sound and tone patterns for centuries. However, one doesn't need a scientific background to perceive the effect of sound and rhythm on the brain.

Consider, for instance, two tuning forks calibrated to slightly distinct pitches – say, one to 400 Hz and the other to 405 Hz. When struck simultaneously, these sounds amalgamate in the air to form a third sound, a so-called monaural vibration of 5 Hz.

Musicians, especially those playing string instruments like the guitar or violin, are very familiar with these vibrations because they constantly tune their instruments. The monaural vibration disappears only when the tuning fork aligns with the relevant string.

However, when the two different sounds are separately channeled into each ear via headphones, the brain constructs a third sound from the 5 Hz difference, which is known as a phantom sound or binaural beat. The right and left hemispheres of the brain adjust to this new frequency to establish equilibrium. This phenomenon results in hemispheric synchronization, a harmonized state of the brain.

In most individuals, the brain's left hemisphere manages logic, reasoning, and analytical thinking, while the right hemisphere operates intuitively, visually, emotionally, and in a less coordinated manner. When the brainwaves in the right and left hemispheres synchronize, the heart and mind operate as a single unit.

Hemi-Sync provides a straightforward yet incredibly efficient method to modify our brainwaves. Over its extended development phase, the technology was fine-tuned to such a degree that the head of a Zen Buddhist temple in Vancouver, British Columbia, was astonished after spending a few days at Monroe. He declared that Gateway students could achieve meditative states within a week that had taken him years of dedicated practice to reach.

Monroe developed a spectrum of specific frequency compositions to support various meditative states and designed a kind of map to facilitate easy navigation through the different levels of consciousness for the user.

He dubbed the altered states he explored as Focus levels, or "F" for short, and assigned each a number between 10 and 35. However, he referred to waking consciousness as C1. Monroe never clarified why he opted for the letter C, although it's likely shorthand for consciousness.

One of the primary objectives of the *Gateway Voyage* program is to educate participants about and enable them to differentiate between Focus levels 10 through 21.

I am experiencing firsthand how distinctively the brain reacts to the Hemi-Sync technology's frequency combinations while I lie still, flat on my back. At this moment, I am unable to move even my little finger.

To prevent panic onset, I focus on breathing—a technique I learned through yoga. Inhale. Exhale. Fear cannot find room in the present moment. Inhale. Exhale. Here and now.

It works. I start to calm down and relax. I barely sense my body. It feels as if my mind has separated from it. I am enveloped in profound stillness.

That is until the sound of someone snoring breaks in. The noise irritates me, and I attempt to locate its source. Is it Phil, my roommate? Or is it coming from the individual on the other side of the CHEC Unit's wall? I am clueless as the direction of the sound keeps shifting.

The snoring becomes increasingly annoying, and I feel almost relieved when Monroe's voice comes through the headphones.

"It is now time to return to waking consciousness!"

Bob slowly counts down from 10 to 1. As he reaches 1, I am surprised at how effortlessly I can move my arms and legs again.

Following the trainers' instructions, I jot down my observations in a notebook and head to the meeting in the White Carpet Room—the designated gathering area.

My experience with Focus 10 aligns with most participants' accounts. Monroe's description of this state as "body asleep—mind awake" couldn't be more precise.

Only Ann's experience of Focus 10 diverged significantly:

"Body asleep—mind also asleep," she shares, inciting amusement in everyone.

"I remember the affirmation, and then I must have dozed off. I only woke up when the exercise was over."

My first night in the CHEC Unit passes surprisingly well without any claustrophobic feelings.

The calming sound of waves emitted from the speakers, situated at the head of the wooden enclosure, combined with Hemi-Sync frequencies, fosters a soothing sleep rhythm. After six hours, I feel well-rested, rejuvenated, and energized.

It's still dark when I step onto the porch outside the Nancy Penn Center. The air is crisp; the setting couldn't be more picturesque. Moonlight softly illuminates the Blue Ridge Mountains and casts a radiant glow on the monumental Brazilian quartz crystal situated at the edge of the institute's expansive grounds.

I'm compelled to examine this colossal crystal up close. Only when I'm standing directly in front of it can I grasp its immense size. Carefully, I press my body against the crystal, which towers over me. Its surface is icy cold, but surprisingly, I begin to feel warmth after just a few minutes. I can undeniably sense its powerful energy.

Before breakfast, the first chime of the day signals the beginning of the optional yoga class. I'm in. After all, I've been practicing yoga for many years. Shaaron Honeycutt, an instructor of Iyengar Yoga, is quite candid and straightforward. According to her, comprehending one's body is paramount before attempting to leave it.

Later in the dining room, over scrambled eggs and toast, she admits to me that she actually finds Out-of-Body Experiences somewhat overhyped.

Shaaron quickly noticed my good grasp of the different asanas.

"Have you ever thought about becoming a yoga teacher?"

I shrug my shoulders, but secretly, I've repeatedly entertained the idea. My work as a television journalist and tour guide lost its charm some time ago.

"I'm over 30," I say, "and nowhere near as flexible and fit as a yoga teacher should be."

Shaaron disagrees.

"It doesn't matter if you can tie your legs together behind your head. You'll inspire many people when you love what you're doing and possess the necessary knowledge and sensitivity."

I can't stop pondering her words. Is Shaaron right? Am I selling myself short? Should I start from scratch at my age? Especially now that I'm doing well financially.

The sound of the bell interrupts my thoughts. Like the other 23 participants, I can hardly wait to return to the CHEC Unit and put on my headphones.

Today's first exercise involves the final step in Monroe's preparation process: activating the REBAL, the Resonant Energy Balloon.

We start by revisiting the elements of preparation we already know. Then, I am asked to visualize energy erupting from my head, enveloping my physical body, and reentering it through the soles of my feet. Next, the energy needs to rise and burst out from my head again until a stable cycle is established.

I find this challenging since I don't have a particularly vivid imagination. The more I attempt to conjure images in my head, the more chaotic it becomes. A few minutes later, I'm wide awake again and incredibly frustrated.

I try once more, only to fail a second time.

It feels like I've lost control over my mind. Random thoughts drift through my head, and I clearly struggle to master the exercise. My REBAL begins to resemble a whirlwind more and more.

However, once the Hemi-Sync frequencies begin to kick in, it doesn't take long before I experience the first signs of Focus 10. This time, it feels much easier. Like last time, my right hand tingles, and the physical heaviness is almost familiar.

I'm slowly becoming irritated when someone starts snoring again. I try my best to ignore the sound, but I can't. After what feels like forever, I hear Bob say:

"It's now time to return to waking consciousness."

I'm already awake. Irritated, I open my eyes and stare into the dark inside the CHEC Unit.

I lift my left arm to flip the light switch, which sits approximately three feet above the mattress on the enclosure's interior wall. But my fingers can't grasp the switch. Instead, my hand and forearm glide through the solid wooden wall.

I distinctly perceive the texture of the wood, inch by inch. When I realize what's happening, my arm springs back, and my body goes limp. I'm so startled that I don't dare to breathe.

What on earth just happened?

My left arm is still in the same position I had put it at the beginning of the exercise: underneath the bed cover. My heart is racing like crazy. I can't come up with a rational explanation.

How could my hand have passed through the wall when it is under the cover at the same time?

When I share my experience with the group and the trainers, they deduce that I had experienced a so-called partial projection. This is a type of OBE where your consciousness only partially separates from the physical body.

I'm captivated and continue to ponder this phenomenon hours later.

During the next exercise, I find it challenging to relax as I persistently try to recreate what happened earlier. I'm eager to experience a full astral projection. But because it doesn't come naturally, I grow restless.

I was told that you can't force an Out-of-Body Experience. Yet, the more I try to surrender, the more I find myself clinging to my aspiration of soaring through the air with my energy body.

In the late afternoon, I seek advice from John.

"What exactly do you hope to achieve with an OBE?" he inquires.

I can't answer his question. I was so enraptured by the prospect of learning to leave my physical body that I hadn't considered what might happen next.

John suggests that I reevaluate my approach.

"Carefully consider what you would do if you achieved an OBE. Ask yourself what truly matters to you, and then articulate your explicit intention. Writing it down often clarifies the mind," he advises.

John takes a deep breath and pauses for a moment before continuing.

"Remember our conversation from yesterday? If you cling to a certain expectation, you only get in your own way."

John's suggestions prompt me to reassess the situation. Had I been too naive or impulsive? Should I have been more prepared before traveling all the way to distant Virginia?

I take a long walk to gather my thoughts and decide to focus less on having an OBE and instead follow the program without a personal agenda.

Before introducing another exercise, Karen reviews the individual components of the preparation process.

"The steps remain consistent for each exercise. That's why memorizing the process is crucial," she emphasizes. "From now on, you'll be responsible for your own preparation."

Since I struggled significantly with visualizing the REBAL during the previous exercise, I ask Karen for guidance. Surprisingly, other participants express similar concerns.

"Each of you must discover your own non-physical channels of perception," Karen explains. "For some, these may be more visual, while for others, they might be more intuitive or emotional."

A hands-on exercise follows to reinforce our understanding of energies. The trainer pairs us off and demonstrates how to sense the other person's energy field with our hands.

I'm fortunate to have Karen as my partner. Under her direction, I distinctly perceive the energy field around her, which immediately boosts my confidence in my own abilities.

Back in the CHEC Unit, our next task is to construct an energy tool, a universal aid that allows us to purposefully direct energy in the non-physical realm.

The concept of an energy tool is completely foreign to me, and I have no idea how to create something out of nothing. Regardless, I strive to maintain an open mind.

Closing my eyes, I almost immediately sink into deep relaxation. When Robert Monroe's voice begins to flow from the headphones, I am already busy activating the energy field around me. This time, I avoid forcing visual impressions, instead opting to "sense" the energy ball enveloping me.

There's no whooshing sensation around me, yet I can perceive a faint pulsation. Eventually, I clearly feel the energy field around me stabilizing, cloaking me like a coat, and my physical awareness fades.

A gentle, pleasurable vibration follows this pulsation. Even though I can't feel my physical body, this vibration seems to permeate every single cell.

I lie there, observing. The vibration gradually intensifies until Monroe's voice halts it. He instructs us to visualize a spark of light gradually forming into a rod of glowing energy. I'm supposed to mentally hold it in my energy hand and project different colors onto it.

When this doesn't immediately work, frustration bubbles up. I can't imagine the light rod, let alone the hand to hold it. My left, analytical brain hemisphere takes over, my inner critic whispering, "What nonsense."

But I try to ignore this doubter, taking deep breaths.

Don't give up!

Once again, I shift my focus to the Resonant Energy Balloon. To my surprise, I sense the field immediately. A few seconds later, I refocus on the energy rod.

"How would it feel to hold a glowing rod in my hand?" I ponder.

No sooner have I posed the question than a completely unexpected, angelic female figure appears in my mind's eye. She has long, dark hair framing her exotic face, wearing brown shorts and a yellow T-shirt instead of angelic attire. She holds a glowing light rod.

"Here, Oliver, take my energy bar tool! I don't need it anymore," she smiles, offering it to me.

I am so bewildered that I immediately return to waking consciousness. The abrupt transition leaves me feeling dizzy, my thoughts a chaotic jumble.

Unable to relax enough to complete the exercise, I reach for my notebook.

John and Karen have frequently suggested jotting down every perception, as experiences outside waking consciousness can be as fleeting as dreams. As I scribble down notes, I recall the image of the entity. Was it merely a figment of my imagination? A delusion? Was it my wishful thinking that led to this perception?

During the group's gathering in the assembly room to discuss the exercise, I sit in the first row opposite the trainers, eagerly listening to the other participants' enviable accounts.

Most have no problem at all visualizing. In fact, some even report that their mentally generated images rapidly take on a life of their own, transporting them into what seems like a movie. I'm far from achieving that.

As I'm about to express my disappointment over the failed exercise, a participant at the back of the room speaks up.

"Well, I found it very easy to create the energy tool, and it only took a few seconds. Then I thought I'd check on the others. I first sensed Ann; she was standing there, doing nothing. When I tried to get her attention, she didn't react."

Ann, seated diagonally behind me on a couch, claps her hands in amusement.

"I slept through the entire exercise, start to finish."

The group laughs.

"That explains it," the lady at the back of the room comments.

"But that's not all," she continues. "Next, I saw Oliver. He seemed distraught. He found it hard to create the energy rod, so I simply gave him my tool."

The room falls silent. I feel everyone's gaze on me. Did I hear right?

I jump up and look around.

"You are Oliver, aren't you?"

The woman's voice carries a note of uncertainty. I nod and hold up my notebook.

"I'm Maya," she introduces herself.

The yellow T-shirt, the khaki shorts, the long, dark hair—everything matches.

"What you've just described is written in this notebook, Maya. I don't know how you did it, but I saw you clearly."

The other participants begin to whisper excitedly. I turn to the trainers, who nod at me with encouragement.

"How is that possible?" I ask aloud when I'm alone in my room later. "And where was I when Maya found me, if not in this CHEC Unit?"

At dinner, I pose these questions to John, hoping for a sensible explanation. But John isn't ready to provide the answers. Instead, he suggests I find them myself.

"When he was alive, Robert Monroe stressed: 'Don't believe anything I tell you. Search for yourself and gather your own experiences.' He gave us a map, but we must undertake the journey ourselves."

Reluctant and unwilling to embark on this journey alone, I try talking to Maya. She seems experienced enough to potentially help me.

But the woman from Hawaii merely shrugs.

"Just let it sink in," she suggests. "I think we are going to see a lot more in the coming days. And perhaps the answers will just come to you."

I envy her composure.

"How did you even find me?" I probe.

Maya tilts her head and smiles mischievously.

"I asked my spirit guides to lead me where I was needed most."

Her reply raises more questions.

"Who are these spirit guides?"

"I don't really know. All I can say is they're always there when I need their help."

Spirit guides? Sounds like a wild fantasy to me. But I also can't disregard our shared experience. Maya and I definitely met. There must be an explanation. But spirit guides…?

As if she can read my thoughts, Maya suggests a new approach.

"Why don't you try to perceive your own spirit guides? Just like you experienced your energy field during the last exercise."

"Are you saying I have spirit guides, too?"

"Absolutely. Everyone has helpers in the spirit world. And everyone perceives them differently. Some see angels. Some see religious figures. Shamans work with power animals."

"How do you do it?"

"I see very clear images," Maya tells me. "One of them is an old medieval monk. Another one appears as a man with a wolf's head."

I can't hide my skepticism and shake my head doubtfully. But Maya remains persistent.

"Why don't you give it a shot and see what comes up? You've nothing to lose."

I recall Monroe's books. He also wrote about his encounters with entities who guided and accompanied him. But if I truly have spirit guides, wouldn't they have made contact before?

Everything is new and confusing. Only three days ago, I had no experience of the subject at all. And now I'm supposed to close my eyes and look for my spirit guides? Every halfway normal person, including my past self, would think I'm crazy.

On the other hand, Maya is right. I've nothing to lose.

Before I can start looking for my guides, Karen and John introduce us to another level of consciousness: Focus 12. Robert Monroe described this level as a state of expanded awareness. In the upcoming exercise, we will explore the differences between Focus 10 and Focus 12.

This time, the preparatory process goes off without a hitch and I immediately perceive the REBAL. The more I relax, the more I feel the vibration. It's not just within me, but also around me. I am part of the vibration. I am the vibration!

The clarity of this thought, which I didn't consciously formulate, amazes me. It just arose. And with it came the sudden realization: I am part of the vibration. I am energy. And that energy can move.

Now, I clearly feel the movement, knowing that my physical body is lying there, asleep. But suddenly, my consciousness is part of another state, one that transcends physical matter.

I experience this state intensely, even if only for a few moments. Shortly thereafter, I reunite with my physical body.

When I immerse myself in the vibration again, my awareness of my body disappears. For the first time, I experience what Monroe describes in the Gateway Affirmation:

"I am more than my physical body."

I want to reach for my notebook but don't dare to interrupt this special moment of insight for a mundane act such as writing. To clear my mind, I focus on my breathing.

And there it is again. More pronounced and louder than before: the snoring. The incredibly annoying snoring. I decide to bring it up with the trainers. Maybe I can switch rooms.

I listen intently and am now sure that the snorer is in the next room. It's hard to move my head, but I want to press my ear to the wall to be absolutely certain.

When I manage to turn my head to the side, I hear a loud gurgling sound, then silence. No more snoring. Suddenly, it hits me like a ton of bricks: I am the one snoring! I have been listening to myself snoring and didn't even realize it.

Wow! My body was truly asleep while my mind was wide awake.

Armed with this new understanding, I refocus on the exercise. Thanks to the Hemi-Sync signals, it doesn't take long for the familiar heaviness of Focus 10 to set in.

Then Robert Monroe instructs us to count from 10 to 12 to change our level of consciousness. A loud hissing sound from the audio carrier, reminiscent of an overhead jet plane, signals the adjustment of the tone frequencies.

My breathing halts, and I struggle for air as my chest expands. Then tranquility.

I'm no longer breathing; I'm being breathed. Something breathes me. As air escapes from my lungs, my awareness also expands. It's as if my brain suddenly sends antennas out in all directions.

My head feels as weightless as a helium balloon whose thin skin can be stretched indefinitely. Unlike in Focus 10, I feel nothing but a pleasant lightness. I float and expand far beyond the limits of my physical body.

Monroe's voice interrupts my bliss with the instruction to return to Focus 10. I really don't want to, but the Hemi-Sync signals facilitate the change, and a few moments later, I feel a sort of external pressure.

It's like someone trying to cram a large gob of cotton candy into a tiny can. My head grows heavier and heavier. I can feel my physical body but can't move it.

A short while later, Monroe guides us again from Focus 10 to Focus 12. This time, I also struggle to breathe.

Once my breath returns, my awareness noticeably expands, and I experience extreme lightness and infinite vastness again.

I focus my attention on my ethereal environment. Snapshots appear in my mind's eye. But the images are too transient to interpret. They disappear as quickly as they appear in the expanse of Focus 12.

I let myself drift without any clear intentions. I float. I glide. It's neither dark nor light. Rarely have I felt such euphoria.

The phrase "I am more than my physical body" now carries a new and profound meaning. My experience has transformed what was once only a premise into a fact. Into a new truth which irrevocably changes my understanding of the world.

I'm jolted when the curtain of my CHEC Unit is drawn aside, and Phil, my roommate, peeks in.

"Are you okay?" he asks worriedly, raising his eyebrows.

It takes me a moment to sit up.

"That exercise was quite intense."

My voice sounds as if I'm intoxicated. Phil laughs.

"I felt the same," he replies. "I was fully out."

"What do you mean by fully out?"

"Out of body! I found myself flying over the Nancy Penn Center and the crystal, over the trees and the hills," he tells me excitedly, spreading his arms as if he were in flight. "I saw a shoe lying on the roof."

"Why should there be a shoe on the roof? That's absurd."

"I have no idea. But let's go and check."

I'm somewhat reluctant as I climb out of the narrow CHEC Unit to follow Phil through the long corridor, which ends at the staircase of a tower-like annex. With an energy that's incomprehensible to me, Phil dashes up the spiral staircase to the rooftop terrace.

The view is breathtaking. I inhale the crisp autumn air, feeling increasingly alert and grounded. The unobstructed vista, the colorful foliage, the absolute tranquility —it's downright heavenly.

Phil taps my shoulder and points at something.

"Check it out, man!" he exclaims, pointing his finger. "There's a shoe back there."

I'm just as astonished as he is. Indeed, Phil had an Out-of-Body Experience and flew over the institute's roof. I struggle to hide my envy.

"How did you do it?" I ask him.

He shrugs.

"I wish I knew. It just happened. I can hardly believe it myself."

When we reenter the assembly room, several participants already discuss their experiences in Focus 12.

"Such vastness!" exclaims Melinda, a nurse from New York.

She spreads her arms out so wide that she accidentally clips her neighbor. I can understand her euphoria all too well. But what, I wonder, can I do in —or with —that vastness?

"Focus 12 is extremely well-suited for nonverbal communication," Karen explains. "This level of consciousness allows us to make contact with our spirit guides, for example.

My ears perk up.

"But some of us already did that in Focus 10," I interject.

"That's true."

Karen goes into more detail. "In Focus 10, our body is asleep while our mind is fully awake. However, the mind does have the ability to proceed to another level from Focus 10. Hemi-Sync aids our intention but doesn't confine us to a specific level. Therefore, it's not particularly surprising when the mind takes its own path."

Phil asks what could have triggered his OBE.

"An Out-of-Body Experience in the classical sense can happen anytime you're in a state of deep relaxation, even without a specific intention," John explains. "OBEs often occur when we least expect them and aren't holding onto a fixed idea."

Unfortunately, the trainer doesn't want to delve any deeper into the subject at this point. Instead, he invites those who haven't yet had a chance to speak to describe their impressions of Focus 12.

Many echo my sentiments. They relished the boundless expanse but had no other expectations beyond that.

John suggests we use the next exercise to ask questions and receive answers.

We often receive symbols, scents, physical sensations, or brief image sequences to decipher.

"Who provides these? Where do they come from?" The woman beside me quizzes him.

"That's another question you can ask when you're in a state of expanded awareness," John says. "Just stay open-minded. And those of you who've already established a connection with your spirit guides can use the exercise to strengthen that connection."

Back in the CHEC Unit, I follow the sound signals, first into Focus 10, then into Focus 12. Again, I experience a notable shortness of breath followed by the overwhelming sensation of the vastness—this time, even more intense than before. My mind extends its antennas. I've arrived in Focus 12.

"Ask your first question," Robert Monroe's voice instructs. "Trust that you will receive an answer in a way you can easily understand."

To simplify the process, I heed John's advice and initially pose a question that requires a clear Yes or No answer.

"Should I train to become a yoga teacher next year?" I mentally ask, feeling slightly ridiculous.

Nothing. I wait, but there's no response. After an entire minute, I repeat the question. "Should I train as a yoga teacher next year?" My left leg twitches, but still no answer.

Robert Monroe's voice comes in again:

"You can now ask another question or repeat the first one if the answer needs more clarification."

"Should I train as a yoga teacher next year?" I ask for the third time. Even before I finish formulating the question in my mind, my left leg twitches again.

Didn't John mention something about physical signals earlier?

"Is that the answer?" I spontaneously ask. And again, I feel the sensation in my left leg.

When Monroe's voice prompts me once more to pose my question, I rephrase it.

"Should I wait until 2002 to train as a Yoga teacher?"

This time, my right leg twitches.

If the twitching of the left leg signifies a Yes, then the movement of the right leg must mean No. But wouldn't that be too simple?

I decide to dismiss my inner skeptic this time. At least I've found a method that I might be able to refine. I feel a slight sense of accomplishment.

Phil pulls back the curtain of his CHEC Unit and looks at me.

"So?" I ask, intrigued.

"I don't even know where to start," he confesses. "I met my spirit guide. He presented himself as a bear and showed me many interesting things. I didn't need to ask him anything. He already knew what I wanted and provided detailed answers. It was simply amazing! What about you? How did you do?"

I take a deep breath.

"My legs twitched."

Phil tilts his head.

"And?"

"Nothing. That was it. First the left leg and then the right."

Phil bursts into laughter.

"You better not say anything," I warn him, "or I'll find a different roommate."

I can't help but wonder why Phil is having these incredible experiences and I'm not.

Could I be doing something wrong?

4

SPACE WITHOUT TIME AND THE BRIDGE TO THE AFTERLIFE

"One's destination is never a place but a new way of seeing things."
Henry Miller, Author

My self-doubt gnaws at me as I head to the assembly room, but Karen tries to lift my spirits.

"Everyone's journey is unique. Being able to differentiate your perceptions is a big step. You're on the right track and far ahead of many others."

Her words offer little comfort.

However, hearing about other participants' experiences lifts my spirits. Only a handful had experiences similar to what Phil encountered.

Ann, as it turns out, slept through the entire exercise once more, and found it amusing. It becomes apparent that most of the group members are struggling to trust their perceptions.

When I share my experience with my twitching legs, Melinda chimes in enthusiastically.

"Thank you, Oliver! Thank you!" she exclaims, raising her arms in jubilation. "I was so frustrated because I didn't receive any answers to my questions. But my arms kept jerking. I shrugged it off as random muscle spasms."

Melinda looks relieved.

"That's exactly why we gather here after each exercise," John explains. "Each person who shares their experience with the group contributes enormously and inspires the others."

Although I remain skeptical about this new form of communication between me and my supposed spirit guides, I decide to give the process a chance and explore its possibilities further.

More exercises in Focus 12 follow. Gradually, I allow myself to trust the physical signals and accept them as answers. However, not every question can be addressed with a simple Yes or No.

"You shouldn't shy away from complex questions," Maya advises, "or you'll stagnate and cease progressing."

She urges me to listen to my inner voice and trust my intuition.

"Do you remember Robert Monroe's writings about sudden insights and 'thought balls' being passed to him?"

I recall Monroe's works very well. But not everything he wrote makes sense to me.

"I'm sorry, Maya, but the term 'thought ball' doesn't mean much to me."

"Monroe came up with the term because there was no existing word to describe the phenomenon. He likely wanted to avoid leading the reader to incorrect assumptions. Don't get hung up on the terminology. Try looking at all of this as a playground of consciousness."

And this is exactly how I approach the next exercise called "Five Messages". The objective is to seek messages while in the state of expanded awareness. It is about discovering what is essential for my further development at this point in my life.

I let go of the expectation of meeting my personal spirit guides, and the idea of receiving as many as five messages during one exercise seems overly ambitious. I would be content with just one.

So, I'm even more astounded when I do indeed receive clear and comprehensible impressions during all five stages of the exercise. However, the content of the messages surprises me the most.

In response to the question, "What is the fifth most important message?" I see a mental image of an endless hiking trail winding its way through valleys and hills. I intuitively understand that the message is: The journey is the destination.

For the fourth most important message, I hear music and see a joyful couple twirling around a dance floor. The scene carries a dual meaning for me. I need to step out of my comfort zone, and I should perceive the process as a dance to be enjoyed.

Message number three presents me with a skull. The image unsettles me. But before I can dwell on it, the second most important message appears. It is once again intuitive, but this time in the form of a complete sentence: "You cannot change other people!"

This is a significant issue in my life. Although the message is not exactly comforting, it clearly shows me that something outside of my conscious thinking is taking place. I would never have willingly dredged up that sentence from the depths of my mind.

The most important message presents me with a clear exclamation mark and five letters, which I quickly jot down: "! RTSTU."

Following the exercise, I take time to absorb each individual message. The image of the skull increasingly troubles me, particularly as I'm confident that it was not a product of my imagination.

Symbols such as a skull often represent suppressed or hidden fears that inhibit our development," Karen explains during dinner. "When we're in a state of expanded awareness, these blocks often manifest themselves symbolically. We can then consciously release the fear without necessarily identifying the specific issue we're dealing with."

Seeing the expression on my face, Karen realizes that while I've heard her, I don't fully grasp what she's saying.

"Sometimes, you just have to trust the process," she advises before moving on to another participant.

Yet one mystery remains: the letter sequence "!RTSTU," the most significant of the five messages. I ponder its meaning.

Later in the evening, still clueless, I seek Phil's help. One look at my notes gives him the solution. He rearranges the letters on a blank page. "!RTSTU" transforms into "TRUST!

A warm shiver runs down my spine. The message couldn't be more fitting.

The *Gateway Voyage* program is very structured and intense. It leaves little time for a breather.

I feel just about reasonably sure that I can navigate Focus 12 when the trainers introduce Focus 15.

"F15—the state of No Time," Karen writes on the board.

She doesn't explain further. Instead, we're all asked to gather impressions and share them with the group after the exercise.

Transitioning from Focus 10 to Focus 12 is now relatively easy, and I relish the familiar vastness. But when Bob Monroe counts up from 12 and shortly after welcomes me in Focus 15, I find myself enveloped in complete darkness.

Everything around me is black, and I feel like I'm in a barrel of thick black ink.

"Where am I?" I shout mentally.

My words disappear into the darkness. This state bears no resemblance to the lightness of Focus 12. It's neither pleasant nor unpleasant. It simply IS. Here in this space, I AM. Nothing more.

I am on the threshold between infinite calm and encroaching fear. It feels unfamiliar, yet familiar. Intuition tells me that I've been here before. But I can't recall when or why.

I focus on my breath to keep the rising fear at bay. From a distance, I hear the thumping of my heart, though I don't feel my body at all. The more I surrender to the silence, the safer I feel. Secure and supported. I am.

"OLIVER!" A sudden voice screams in my ear so loud that it physically hurts. I'm instantly on high alert. My heart races. I'm wide awake. The exercise ends abruptly for me.

Shaking, I reach for a pen and paper to record the experience.

Who shouted my name?

I wait patiently until Phil draws back the curtain of his CHEC Unit.

"Did you hear that too?" I ask him.

He shakes his head.

I'm stunned because, in my perception, the voice was so loud that Phil must have heard it clearly.

Neither John nor Karen has an explanation. However, Karen mentions that other participants have reported similar experiences in the past. While this doesn't provide a concrete answer, it does provide a bit of reassurance. At least I know I'm not losing my sanity.

Ann believes that my spirit guides might have contacted me and called out my name. I find the idea somewhat appealing but lack any proof. And why would they want to frighten me like that?

"Your spirit guides can't get through if you continue to doubt," says Ben from Kansas, suggesting that I accept any information received during meditation without judgment.

"You're receiving all these puzzle pieces so you can eventually assemble them. But that only works if you give each piece a chance. Otherwise, the puzzle will never be complete."

Most of the other participants describe their experience of the intense darkness of Focus 15 similarly to mine. Only a few had distinct and detailed perceptions.

When I use the subsequent F15 exercises to explore the darkness in more detail, I soon discover that my thinking in this timeless space is significantly clearer than in my waking consciousness. Visualization becomes astonishingly easy. The images that flickered fleetingly and incoherently in my mind's eye in Focus 10 and Focus 12 solidify in Focus 15.

They are accompanied by thoughts I don't consciously generate. They simply emerge and line up like pearls on an invisible string. Each thought has its place, and I can effortlessly move back and forth between them without confusing or forgetting any of them. Had I possessed this ability as a child, school would have been much easier.

"The boy simply doesn't concentrate," the teachers said. "He's intelligent but lazy."

For the first time, at the age of 34, here at the Monroe Institute, I experience what it feels like to follow complex thought processes from start to finish.

The deeper I immerse myself in the darkness, the clearer the information I bring back into waking consciousness becomes. My fear of losing myself in the infinite expanse of F15 fades with each exercise.

All I must do is ask for an image, and it immediately materializes in my mind. Suddenly, I can visualize, a skill I find extremely challenging in my waking consciousness.

"Everything is possible – nothing is a must! The source of all potential is here in Focus 15."

I can't identify the origin of these words. They are just there. I don't hear them with my physical ears. And yet, I understand them clearly.

Despite the insights gained and the increasing clarity of my perceptions, doubts linger. I discuss this with John who thinks I need to trust the process even more.

"That's all well and good," I explain to him during a break, "but unless I get some tangible proof that my perceptions are real and not delusions, it doesn't really help."

During the concluding meditation in Focus 15, Robert Monroe instructs me to visualize a place on Earth that makes me feel especially good. I pick the island of Corsica where I lived for two years as a young man and of which I have wonderful memories.

Soon enough, I find myself standing barefoot on a beach, the pleasantly cool spray of the sea washing over my feet. I can even feel the wet sand.

Following Monroe's instructions, I imagine myself growing taller. I expand until I can easily see the ocean from an aerial perspective. Soon after, I notice the earth's curvature on the horizon. Fascinated, I turn around and gaze down at the island. I grow even taller. Now I can clearly see Sardinia, the Italian boot, and even the North African coast.

And still, I continue to grow. The earth beneath me rapidly shrinks until I'm floating through the universe, surrounded by absolute silence.

The planet is now at eye level, and I watch as the earth slowly rotates on its own axis.

When I intuitively reach out for the globe with my right hand,

John, our trainer, appears out of nowhere on the opposite side. As fast as lightning, he grabs the planet with both hands and smiles at me.

"Here, Oliver, catch!" he shouts.

Before I can respond, the earth hurtles toward me, striking my forehead. The jolt makes my entire body tremble, and I'm instantly jolted back to waking consciousness.

It takes a few minutes for me to regain my composure. The experience felt more tangible than a lucid dream, so I carefully document every detail in my notebook. Not wanting to disturb Phil, I quietly sneak out of the room.

The fresh air outside feels grounding. Still, even minutes later, I can't shake off the sensation of hovering a few inches above the ground. On impulse, I lay down in the meadow next to the massive crystal in the institute's garden.

The earth is moist from the rain. My eyes trace the clouds slowly drifting across the sky above me.

"I was up there!" I whisper to myself.

"You're nuts," my mind retorts.

Could I possibly have experienced an OBE? How do you even define an Out-of-Body Experience? Who can answer my barrage of questions?

At this point, I understand it's not the trainers' responsibility to interpret participants' experiences. Though I'm certain there's a valid reason for this, I'm yearning for someone's insights to help me make sense of my unexpected voyage into outer space.

By the time I return from my walk, lively discussions are already underway in the assembly room. John catches my eye and gestures to an empty seat near him.

As I settle into my cushion, Ann excitedly shares that she managed to stay awake this time. The group reacts with applause.

I feel genuinely happy for the elderly woman who has become my favorite among all the participants.

"It was incredibly beautiful," Ann chokes out between sobs, wiping away a few tears.

"I met my deceased son. He showed me his new home."

Everyone in the room is mesmerized by the 86-year-old's narrative.

"I've waited 20 years for this moment," she continues, her voice shaking. "Twenty long years... Knowing that Samuel is doing well means so much to me."

Ann pauses momentarily.

"My son took his own life. No one knows why. He didn't even leave a suicide note."

Deeply touched by Ann's story, I struggle to hold back my own tears.

Her account is followed by more equally striking stories. I don't share my own experience because it feels unspectacular compared to theirs.

There's no response when Karen asks if anyone else has anything to contribute before we move on to a new topic. I find myself lost in thought, staring blankly.

Why do everyone else's experiences seem so much more extraordinary than mine?

As I look up, John's voice sounds like it's coming from a great distance.

"Here, Oliver, catch!" he shouts, throwing a large ball of fabric my way. It unexpectedly hits my forehead.

A little dazed, I pick up the ball. I can hardly believe what I see: The ball has a world map printed on it and looks like a globe.

"That's... that's... exactly what I experienced in Focus 15!" I exclaim to the group. "I was in the universe, and you, John, threw the globe at me."

John doesn't appear to be particularly impressed.

"You wanted proof," he comments dryly, "didn't you?"

I feel my head spin. I struggle to comprehend what happened. It simply doesn't make sense. Did I have a clairvoyant premonition? Or does John possess some unsuspected paranormal abilities?

One thing is certain, something occurred that my rational mind cannot grasp. On one hand, it's exciting; on the other, it unnerves me. I begin to realize that this program involves far more than what I initially imagined classic Out-of-Body Experiences to be like.

Although I'd love to stay in Focus 15 for the remaining two days, John and Karen have different plans for us. We're about to visit Focus 21.

Robert Monroe describes this stage as the bridge between physical and non-physical energy systems—a threshold between physical reality and the levels outside time and space. At first, this doesn't make much sense to me.

And it becomes even more abstract. Karen and John explain that there's a café near the bridge. This café is a thought construct, created by the many thousands of *Gateway Voyage* participants who have met and exchanged their experiences there over the years.

According to John, "Among other things, the café serves as a launch point for shared excursions into non-physical realities. It's kind of a base camp where you can agree to meet. And after the exercise, you can discuss your observations."

Sounds exciting. But I'm unsure how to find this café. As if reading my mind, Karen explains the process.

"When you want to explore a certain place in a non-physical realm, you must program your inner GPS accordingly. You do this by setting a clear intention."

So, I set my navigator to "café at the bridge" in Focus 21 and allow the sound frequencies to take me there. Monroe's voice guides us through a color spectrum, the so-called Miranon colors.

Miranon is an entity that conveyed critical information about certain qualities of the non-physical to Bob Monroe through a human medium.

According to Miranon, each level between Focus 15 and 21 is associated with a certain color: blue (F15), red (F16), yellow (F17), rose (F18), green (F19), purple (F20) and white (F21).

Step by step, I delve into the colors that are supposed to transport me from one Focus level to the next, and soon lose all sense of time in the process. I can't determine if I spend seconds or minutes on each level.

I have a hard time visualizing the first three colors. Only when I reach Focus 18 do I get a distinct impression of rose. The color envelops me like a dense fog.

"We will meet again here," a soft voice whispers out of nowhere.

Before I can respond, Monroe begins to count again. I find myself floating above a green cloud, then a purple one. This cloud seems bigger and wider than the others, its color is also far more intense.

Slowly, but surely, I drift through the purple until a bright white glow becomes visible in the distance, drawing me to it like a magnet.

Instead of seeing colors, I now sense and taste nothing but light. It's brighter and clearer than any light I've ever seen. It's dazzling, yet it doesn't blind me.

A wonderful sense of comfort washes over me. I am bathing in the light. At this moment, nothing else matters. I could stay here forever.

Very reluctantly, I follow Monroe's instruction to return to my familiar surroundings.

Upon finding myself back in waking consciousness, I realize that tears are streaming down my face. I can't move my physical body and I remain motionless in the CHEC Unit for a few minutes after the exercise.

As I walk towards the White Carpet Room, I can already hear the excited chatter of the other participants from the staircase.

"I met Maya at the café," Phil exclaims as I enter the room. "She looked at me and we crossed the bridge together."

I am astonished to hear that others had similar experiences. Many participants perceived each other and are enthusiastically sharing their observations.

But this time, I don't feel envious. Although I didn't make it to the café, my experience was still incredibly profound and will resonate for quite some time.

Suddenly, I remember the voice in Focus 18: "We will meet again here," it had said. I have no idea where it came from or who said it.

During another venture into Focus 21, I let myself drift without any sensation of my physical body, hoping for encounters. But it does not come to that.

All I see is light, extending infinitely as far as my mind's eye can see. Linear time and the concept of space have no meaning here. Everything is unified. I am part of the light. The light is within me, surrounding me. I am light!

Initially, I manage to hold on to the energy of Focus 21. But then, some kind of tension builds up. My awareness stretches like a rubber band that threatens to snap at any moment.

When I get back to One, I hear Monroe's voice in the far distance.

"You will be wide awake, and all your senses will function perfectly. Five... Four..., Three..., Two..., One! One!"

The tension becomes unbearable. The bright light recedes. I rush through what feels like a tunnel, and an unpleasant jolting sensation pierces my physical body, which suddenly feels very alien to me.

I slowly open my eyes, lift my left hand, and examine it in the semi-darkness of the CHEC Unit. It appears as it always does. Yet, I can't shake the feeling that it doesn't belong to me.

It takes a few hours before I feel grounded again. My thoughts continually orbit around the light and the energy in Focus 21. I don't know why, but I yearn to return to this place that isn't really a place by definition and about which I essentially know nothing.

The week has passed all too quickly. But before we deal with mundane issues like travel arrangements, the trainers have a surprise for us.

"This is a small preview of what awaits you beyond Focus 21," John reveals, writing "Focus 27 – The Park" onto the wall chart with a black marker.

I'm already familiar with the Park from Monroe's detailed descriptions in the books I read before coming to Virginia.

It is the place or, more precisely, the level of consciousness that can be described as the afterlife in worldly terms.

I am simultaneously curious and cautious. Although the concept of the afterlife has intrigued me since childhood, the idea of willingly traveling there now seems absurd.

Besides, I'm still trying to assimilate what I experienced in Focus 21. Consequently, I only half-heartedly participate in the exercise without any particular expectations.

As I head to my room, I try to recall Monroe's writings about Focus 27. He talked about a healing and rehabilitation center in the Park, a planning center, a library, and, naturally, a reception area where newcomers meet old friends and family members who have passed from physical life before them.

As with every exercise, I make myself as comfortable as possible in my CHEC Unit. After five days and nights in this confined wooden enclosure, I am longing for the spacious comfort of my bed back home.

The moment Monroe's voice reaches my ears through the headphones, along with the now familiar sense of physical heaviness, I am overcome by a mental fatigue that I cannot shake off. So, I simply fall asleep.

When I come to, I find myself in a French street café, sitting at a round outdoor table with a sugar bowl and a glass of water in front of me.

A little confused, I scan the strange surroundings. Nothing is familiar, apart from the ambiance reminiscent of my numerous trips to France. My lack of orientation leaves me feeling embarrassed. As hard as I try to remember how I got here, I draw a blank.

All the tables around me are occupied with people deeply engrossed in conversation. Yet no one seems to notice me.

I strain my ears to listen in on the conversation happening at the table beside me. However, I fail to recognize the language they are speaking. All I can perceive is a muffled and unintelligible sound, as if I were submerged underwater.

Only now do I realize that there are no people or vehicles on the street or the sidewalk in front of me.

Where can I possibly be?

I dare not leave my seat. Where would I go, anyway? I wonder if I've ordered anything and whether I've already paid. But no matter how hard I try, I do not remember. Panic begins to set in when a young man sits down at my table without being invited.

"My apologies for keeping you waiting," he unexpectedly and clearly says. "There's a lot happening today."

I stare at him and don't even dare to ask who he is or if we know each other.

"I'd love to show you the Park now," he continues and points to the right. "They are expecting you."

In an instant, my memory returns: Monroe Institute, CHEC Unit, Focus 27, the Park…

"Okay," I respond, getting up from my chair, when I suddenly hear another voice.

"Express your gratitude to those who supported you on your journey to the Park, and say goodbye for now," I hear through the headphones. "It's time to return to waking consciousness."

Startled and disappointed by the sudden end to this intriguing encounter, I open my eyes with a curse on my lips. Every time it gets interesting, Robert Monroe brings me back to physical reality! My first visit to the afterlife ends abruptly before it even truly began.

I'm amazed at how quickly my week at the institute passes. As we prepare to leave, the trainers advise us to be patient with ourselves in the days ahead.

"You may experience spontaneous emotional outbursts, and difficulty concentrating is also common," Karen explains. "After all, your brain has been stimulated in an entirely new way over the course of this past week."

John advises us to wait at least 30 days before making any life-changing decisions.

"Some participants feel a strong urge to radically overhaul their lives after this program, but it's not advisable," he cautions. "Allow the new experiences to sink in first. If the desire for change persists after a month, then you can take the necessary steps."

The urgency I detect in John's voice alarms me a little although I know he isn't addressing me personally. But apparently there have been participants in the past who have spontaneously separated from their life partners, quit their jobs, or sold their homes after their *Gateway Voyage*.

At this point, I don't anticipate my life taking such a drastic turn.

However, exactly 30 days after returning home, I make the decision to leave my job as a tour guide and TV journalist. I plan to move to Australia for a year and embark on yoga teacher training.

5

IN SEARCH OF MY SPIRIT GUIDES

"The intuitive mind is a sacred gift and the rational mind is a faithful servant. We have created a society that honors the servant and has forgotten the gift."
Albert Einstein, Physicist

My year in Australia was challenging and often pushed me to my physical and emotional limits.

However, the breathtaking landscape in the northern region of New South Wales and the mentality of the Australians made it all worthwhile. Their refreshing outlook on life provided a much-needed break from the demanding yoga schedule.

The training itself was tough, as it exposed me to dogmas, rituals, and doctrines that conflicted with my personal beliefs.

To my surprise, the school in Byron Bay, where I pursued my teacher training, was not very receptive to alternative spiritual approaches. It strictly adhered to ancient traditions, and the only accepted truth was that which was dictated by the old masters.

It provided little opportunity to integrate the experiences I had gathered at the Monroe Institute. Most of my 29 fellow students showed little interest in conversations and discussions about Out-of-Body Experiences and perceptions. Their primary focus was on contorting their physical bodies according to the rules of Ashtanga yoga, often leading to injuries. I quickly realized that while yoga theoretically aims to dissolve the ego, the practice itself yielded something quite different.

A sense of competition emerged over the months, with everyone striving to be the best, to achieve the most extreme poses.

It became an individualistic struggle, and I allowed myself to be drawn into it.

After the year of rigorous training, I suffered from intense back and joint pains for several months.

Four hours of physical yoga practice per day, six days a week, took a toll on my body that couldn't be healed overnight. During this time, my body became my greatest adversary, especially because it could no longer meet the demands imposed by my ego.

Due to the demanding schedule, the use of Hemi-Sync fell by the wayside. The packed timetable, including theory modules on history, philosophy, and anatomy alongside asana practice, left little time for other interests. I would spend the few free hours we were granted walking on the beach, swimming in the ocean, or exploring the nearby rainforest. Sundays were often dedicated to rest, as my body would be screaming out for it.

Therefore, I was delighted to have the opportunity to spend an additional week at the Monroe Institute upon returning to the United States. I had maintained a close connection with Shaaron Honeycutt, and during my darkest moments, I confided in her and always found her support.

At this point, Shaaron had already completed all the institute's programs and recommended that I take the *Guidelines* program to enhance my intuition further and establish conscious interaction with my spirit guides.

A few days after landing in Los Angeles, I traveled to the East Coast without any specific expectations. I hadn't thoroughly reviewed the agenda for the upcoming week, which perhaps made it easier for me to fully engage with the process during my second week at the institute.

During that week, I did encounter quite a few stumbling blocks, but they no longer discouraged me. One of the challenges I had to face daily came in the form of Click Outs during the Hemi-Sync exercises.

Click Out is Monroe's jargon for a gap in awareness where any sense of time and memory is lost.

Over the years, experienced Monroe trainers have collected and shared their insights and perceptions of the phenomenon. According to these, a Click Out could have the following causes and meanings:

In a non-physical environment, our brain doesn't always find the reference points to translate certain experiences into a physical frame of reference. Neither verbal language nor symbols familiar to us are found there.

When a brain lacks the words or images to express the quality of an experience, it cannot provide a translation, resulting in a Click Out—a distinct state different from sleep.

While those who sleep are generally aware that they have slept, experiencing a relative sense of time and lingering drowsiness upon waking, Click Outs lack these characteristics. They simply occur, and we recognize their significance.

Some trainers have reached the conclusion that a Click Out can also be caused by a substantial information download the brain cannot process in real time.

This information, which comes from our higher selves, is integrated into our consciousness gradually in a way that is meaningful to us based on our individual capacities, development, history, and culture.

I had the privilege of being trained by Karen Malik once again, with the assistance of Lee Stone, another experienced facilitator. I felt extremely well supported and guided by both throughout the program.

While many participants were able to quickly develop a stable bond with their spirit guides in the early stages of the workshop, my own process consisted of experiences that unfolded rather unexpectedly and did not initially seem to be related to the actual topic. Here is an excerpt from my *Guidelines* diary dated January 27, 2002:

I barely complete the preparatory process when I can clearly feel the now familiar vibration in my body. This time it seems even more intense than before. As if someone has connected me to an electric circuit.

However, unlike usual, the vibration shows no signs of diminishing.

As I glide from Focus 10 to Focus 12, it intensifies noticeably once again. Soon after, I struggle to hear Monroe's voice and can no longer follow his instructions.

My ears are suddenly filled with muffled sounds. They are so unpleasant and distracting that I consider taking the headphones off and ending the exercise.

Then follows a Click Out.

When I come to, I find myself in a desert. My first impulse: I am on a bus tour in the southwest of the United States. (Note: This is my brain's interpretation, based on my years of experience as a tour guide in this part of the country.)

When I look around and see no other people in my surroundings, I feel uneasy and desperately try to remember where the bus is parked. But no matter where I look, all I see is sand.

Despite the glaring sun and flickering air before my eyes, I feel cold. Looking at my feet, I realize that I'm not wearing any shoes or socks. I carefully raise my right leg. It unexpectedly soars up, and the next moment I'm floating about nine feet above the desert sand.

Just thinking about my tour bus catapults me lightning-fast from the desert into urban surroundings, right into the middle of a busy boulevard. Totally disoriented, I try to escape from the traffic onto the sidewalk as unscathed as possible.

Just before reaching the curb, I get hit by a truck. To my own amazement, I find myself unhurt on the pavement. When I ask a pedestrian for help, he just walks through me.

Only now do I realize I am dead!

Strangely, this insight comforts me. Perhaps because it explains my ethereal state.

But how did I die? And where is my physical body?

Before I am even able to gather clear thoughts, I feel a strong pull and perceive a loud whooshing sound in my ears.

When I open my eyes, I'm back in my CHEC Unit, just as disorientated and confused as I was seconds earlier.

It took a few minutes before I fully regained consciousness and could think clearly. All indications suggested that I just had a spontaneous Out-of-Body Experience.

"Spontaneous and uncontrolled," Sarah, a psychologist from New York, commented. She had been familiar with OBEs since her early childhood, as they had become a refuge for her after enduring physical and mental abuse in an orphanage.

I came to appreciate Sarah's sober perspective on things. Unlike many of our fellow students, she never tried to shine with her experiences during the sharing circles.

According to Sarah, the classical OBEs, like the one I had experienced, were only a small part of a broad spectrum of extrasensory experiences.

She advised me that if these types of OBEs were to become more frequent in the future, I should learn how to control them, or else they might cease being enjoyable.

Sarah proved to be right. I had four more uncontrolled OBEs, which, in retrospect, were fascinating, but in the moment of experiencing them, they were rather uncomfortable.

I would have wished to perceive the separation from my physical body more consciously, allowing me to have at least some orientation during the experience.

However, the sequence remained the same: relaxation, vibration, Click Out, coming to in a strange location, and an abrupt return into my physical body.

While I was grateful for the Out-of-Body Experiences I had, they also hindered me from fully focusing on the objective of the *Guidelines* program—to meet my spirit guides.

Despite my efforts, I didn't receive clear perceptions of these supposed allies. There were no introductions, visual impressions, or names.

Looking back at my diary entries and audio recordings, I now realize that I did gain significant impressions. I had discounted them due to their perceived vagueness or lack of alignment with my expectations.

Breaking through the barrier between the non-physical and

physical levels is not easy for our spirit guides. And even when they succeed, our ego is always ready to dismiss any signs.

Doubt often outweighs trust. However, a fruitful relationship between the physical and spirit world can only be built through the path of trust. First and foremost, it is essential to learn to give as little space as possible to the ego and to follow one's own intuition.

The Monroe Institute's *Guidelines* program offers valuable methods to strengthen the connection to the spirit world. Success or failure clearly depends on how quickly the individual can let go of old patterns.

I gave my inner doubter too much room for too long, accompanied by a lack of self-confidence that took a while to overcome.

Recognizing and accepting spirit guidance remains a lifelong process for me. Like any interpersonal relationship, we must listen to each other to make progress as a team. I intentionally use the term "team" because that's how I perceive my spirit guides—as a group or collective of individuals or entities working together for the common good.

The path to gaining this insight and establishing solid communication with my team was rather tumultuous, and I take full responsibility for that.

*

As part of the *Guidelines* program each participant gets to experience a session called Personal Resource Exploration Program (PREP). During this session, each participant spends approximately an hour in a soundproof chamber equipped with a waterbed at Monroe's research lab.

An experienced technician monitors the session and transmits individually adjusted sound frequencies through headphones.

The soundproof chamber is equipped with a microphone that allows live communication of the experience. Additionally, the participant wears sensors to measure and record vital signs such as body temperature, pulse rate, and brainwaves.

Participants are provided with audio recordings and a printout of the data as a memento.

In cases where there are many participants, the PREP sessions are spread out over the week, with the order determined by a random draw.

The prospect of the PREP session was both exciting and anxiety-inducing for me. I felt a certain pressure to succeed and was stressed by the knowledge that a technician would monitor my every movement.

When my name was one of the first to be drawn from the lottery drum, I wanted to run away. However, I understood the importance of this experience and was determined to face the challenge.

When the first two participants of the group shared their successful experiences the next day, my confidence was completely shaken. I would have preferred to postpone the session by one, or even better, two days, but the trainers believed it was important to honor the sequence.

"That's also a part of your spiritual guidance," Karen explained. "There must be a reason why you are number 3 and not number 22."

My old friend, doubt, protested silently. However, I had no choice but to comply with the rules. I was called to the lab in the late afternoon of the second day, right after my first Out-of-Body Experience.

Skip Atwater, who would monitor and guide my session, fitted me with the electrodes and sensors.

In 2000, Skip served as the institute's Director of Research. He had met Monroe in 1977 through his work with a secret U.S. Army unit, and they soon became friends.

I had already read extensively about Skip, as he had been the head of Project Stargate, the military's secret Remote Viewing unit during the Cold War and was well known in relevant circles.

Contrary to my expectations of someone of his position, Skip turned out to be an extremely sensitive and kind-hearted man. He not only noticed my nervousness but also knew how to alleviate it.

The pleasant temperature of the waterbed already suggested a sense of weightlessness even in a waking state of consciousness.

"I will now close the door and switch off the light," Skip informed me. "Should you start feeling unwell, you can use the microphone to let me know."

My heart raced as the door locked. Of course, Skip Atwater could observe this on his monitor.

"Take your time and relax, Oliver," I heard his sonorous voice through the headphones. "It may help if you start with the preparatory process. I give you a few minutes before I bring in the first set of frequencies.

I recalled a calming breathing technique I had learned in my yoga studies.

"From this point onward, everything you say will be recorded," Skip explained, "and I will intervene if I don't hear anything from you for a while or if it seems like you've fallen asleep."

It took a few minutes until I found my inner peace and was able to silence the continuous flow of thoughts in my head.

"I'll now guide you to Focus 10 and then on to Focus 12."

Shortly after, I could already feel the effects of the frequencies. First, the weightiness of Focus 10, followed by the boundless expanse of Focus 12.

Mentally, I reached out to my spirit guides for support, although I had no idea who they were at that point.

After a considerable amount of time passed without me saying anything, Skip kindly asked me to describe my perceptions. However, apart from some colorful light flashes and glimpses of unfamiliar faces, nothing remarkable occurred.

"You might want to direct a question to your spirit guides," Skip suggested. "My monitor clearly shows that you are stable in Focus 12. It's a good prerequisite for communicating with them."

To this day, I cannot adequately explain what happened next. The audio tape later revealed that I started talking, but I had no conscious recollection of what I said.

It was only when Skip shifted the sound frequencies into the Beta range to bring me back to waking consciousness that my self-awareness became more pronounced again. I vividly remember the moment when the lights came on inside the chamber, and Skip released me from the electrodes and sensors.

"Take as much time as you need and join me when you're ready. I've got some water here for you."

It took a few minutes before I managed to lift my sluggish body from the large waterbed. I felt like a seal struggling against the current, trying to crawl to shore.

Dazed and unsteady on my feet, I exited the chamber.

"That was pretty wild," Skip chuckled and pointed at his monitor. "Check it out."

While Skip printed out the data from our session, he explained the different graphs.

"It's interesting that you initially spoke in English in Focus 12. Once I sensed that you were traveling steadily and having encounters, I brought you up to Focus 21. There, you suddenly started speaking in German. Unfortunately, I could no longer guide you because I don't understand the language."

His statement took me by surprise. At that moment, I wasn't even aware that I had spoken during the session.

"You can listen to the recordings later." Skip handed me an audiotape and a lengthy printout of the measured data.

I had neither the time nor the desire to listen to the tape at the institute using an ancient Walkman. Instead, I stowed it away in my suitcase with the intention to thoroughly analyze it at home.

However, one thought kept circling through my mind: I had no conscious memory of what had happened during the session. On the other hand, Skip had heard my voice. This raised the question for me of whether I might be constantly experiencing events on different levels of consciousness that my brain is unable to transport into my waking mind.

Over the years, I have continued to ask myself this crucial question. The definitive answer is: Yes!

Perceptions in states of expanded awareness are akin to our nocturnal dreams. Often, we know that we have dreamt but cannot recall the exact details of the dreams.

Therefore, after the *Guidelines* program, I began verbally describing my perceptions into a recorder while I was doing the exercises.

The following days proved to be very meaningful for me. Karen and Lee had done an exceptional job of directing me onto a promising path that left little room for doubt.

I learned to accept that I had spirit guides who didn't want to tell me their names or show themselves to me. Instead of constantly searching for personified entities displaying physical characteristics, I began to put more effort into sensing their presence intuitively.

By the end of the week, I felt I had made a significant breakthrough. With my intensive Hemi-Sync training, I could now transition from waking consciousness to Focus 12, the state of expanded awareness, within seconds. This opened the door to heightened intuitive perception and communication with my spirit team.

Focus 12 not only allowed me to perceive my own guides but also enabled me to observe other non-physical beings and phenomena that would have otherwise remained hidden.

Who or what are these so-called spirit guides?

Much like Robert Monroe, I believe that everyone should embark on their own search for answers. As a teacher and trainer, it is not my role to dictate what people should do. Instead, I strive to create a safe space where individuals can have their own experiences and share them if they choose to do so. I also share my own experiences for inspiration without claiming to possess universal truths.

Personally, I have come to the conclusion that my team is part of a consortium that made an agreement before my incarnation into this physical life. This agreement, sometimes called a soul contract, governs the tasks of all team members, including my own.

I see myself as an equal member of a collective with no definitive hierarchy. Instead, each link in this chain carries specific responsibilities.

On the physical level, I seek the assistance of a mechanic when my car breaks down, consult an accountant for financial advice, and rely on medical or alternative practitioners for my physical well-being.

Similarly, on the non-physical level, I have experts who are familiar with my life plan and help me to manifest it for the greater good of all.

Over time, I have come to accept that nobody within my team emphasizes their individuality. No one seeks the spotlight or takes center stage. We function as a unified whole, working together towards our common goals. This understanding has led me to believe that my guides do not introduce themselves individually or adopt earthly names. Instead, they prefer to be addressed and acknowledged as a collective entity.

Through patient inquiry and attentive listening for answers, I have learned a great deal about my team. This includes significant evidence of shared incarnations.

In 2018, during an OBE workshop, I spontaneously asked these entities why they chose to be my guides in this life. The following excerpt is taken from my journal:

I have barely posed the question when I feel a powerful tug at the soles of my feet. The ground beneath me starts to vibrate, and I soar upwards.

In a split second, I catch a breathtaking bird's-eye view of the seminar room and the participants inside lying flat on their mats.

The next moment I find myself in the middle of an old ruin of what seemed to have been a monastery or abbey of some sort. Surprisingly, my perception is vividly visual.

I am standing in a circle alongside a group of Franciscan monks, all dressed in their distinctive dark brown cowls. Strangely, none of the monks have heads, although some have pulled up their hoods.

I try to absorb every detail: the weathered and partially ruined walls, the tall grass, the clear blue sky. The scent of grass and flowers fills the air. I intuitively know that we are a tight-knit religious community.

"We are brothers," it echoes through my head.

Those words come from the monks. I am part of an order and have been chosen to complete a quest.

"Why me?" I inquire.

"Because you have the skill to do it," comes the collective response.

The number 1786 enters my thoughts. I understand that it signifies the year 1786.

"What is the quest that you want me to complete?"

"You know what you have to do."

"Yes," I respond mentally. "I know what I need to do."

The circle disperses, and one by one, the monks vanish without a trace from my field of perception until I am left alone amidst the ruins.

I take a moment to carefully observe my surroundings. I realize that I am familiar with this place: the distinctive Mediterranean tree and the sturdy walls. Everything feels intimately known.

"We are brothers," the voice echoes once more.

Then the scene fades away, replaced by a roaring sound in my physical ears. Within seconds, I become aware of my physical body lying on the mattress. The room remains quiet.

I hardly dare to breathe as I recall the scene again before I grab a pen and paper to record my experience.

"I know what I need to do."

I utter these words with absolute certainty, as though I truly understand what transpired in that location. Yet, I have no conscious access to the information.

As I turn to my side, I notice tears streaming down my cheeks.

It wasn't until several days later, once I had regained emotional composure following the intense experience, that I sat down at my desk and began my research.

Within minutes, I stumbled upon two significant locations: the Couvent d'Orezza on the island of Corsica and the old Spanish Mission in Santa Barbara, California.

The ruins of the monastery in Corsica aligned with about 90 percent of my visual impressions. During my meditation, I had distinctly perceived its tall bell tower. Furthermore, I had felt a strong attraction to Corsica from a young age and had lived on the island for a couple of years in my early twenties.

However, back then, I had no knowledge of these specific ruins. I had never ventured that far inland, and as a 22-year-old, exploring monastic ruins had not been one of my primary interests.

On the other hand, I instantly felt a connection to the mission in Santa Barbara, where I had frequently guided groups of German tourists. On each visit, I felt a pull towards a particular area of the garden that closely resembled the surroundings in my vision.

My heart skipped a beat when I discovered that the mission was founded by Spanish priests, led by Father Fermín Lasuén, in 1786. He succeeded Father Junipero Serra, who had constructed several missions in California under the direction of the Spanish Crown and had passed away in 1784.

Another intriguing detail caught my attention. I had spent the winter months of 2008 and 2009 on the Spanish island of Mallorca, where my accommodations were situated on Avenida California, at the intersection of Avenida Junipero Serra. Coincidence?

Although these events occurred some time ago, I now also consider the possibility that my visual perceptions may have been metaphoric or inaccurately interpreted by my brain.

Nevertheless, the core message remains unchanged: There is a task to be solved or a topic to be dealt with, of which I do not even have a vague idea to this day.

It was truly remarkable to have such a vivid visual perception of the collective consciousness that comprises at least a portion of my spirit team.

However, my guides seldom reveal themselves in distinct forms or as defined beings, such as the faceless monks I encountered. Whenever such visions do occur, they are always accompanied by a sense of urgency.

Each of us has a team with whom we can consciously connect when we open ourselves to it. I experience daily how enriching this connection can be, even though in my case, it mostly exists on an intuitive level.

For most individuals, having a name, a form, or at least a symbol for their spirit guides is important. I have encountered many who seem to have a clear understanding of who their guides are and what they are called.

In the early stages of my exploration of consciousness, I used to envy them. However, I have since come to terms with how I perceive my team. In fact, I am grateful because not knowing their specific identities has allowed me to develop trust in the unseen.

When I visited Arthur Findlay College in England in 2019 to attend a course on trance mediumship, I received a wonderful confirmation of this trust.

My teacher, trance medium and artist Lynn Cottrell, creates impressive portraits of individual spirit guides, as well as entire teams, among other works.

Participants at the college get the opportunity to book private sessions with their teacher during break times.

I got to know Lynn as a fascinating medium, and I felt privileged to have the chance to learn from and be inspired by her. The messages Lynn transmitted from the spirit world felt authentic and incredibly accurate. Never mind her fun and uplifting attitude.

Since working in a trance state was a new experience for me, I asked Lynn for a one-on-one session. I hoped to gain more clarity about my personal development at that time.

Lynn explains her process as follows: She connects with the spirit guides of her counterpart and receives information about the abilities that would be beneficial to develop further. At the same time, she channels the energy of the spirit guides into a highly detailed drawing. The portraits that Lynn creates with pastel chalk at an incomprehensible speed are incredibly expressive, beautiful, and deeply moving.

As I made my way to our session, I felt a mixture of excitement and apprehension about the drawing Lynn would create for me. I had been connecting with my guides without relying on visual cues, and now Lynn would suddenly bring them to life on paper.

I saw our session as perhaps my only chance to see them visually, but a part of me was hesitant. Did my team truly want to be represented in that way?

Despite my reservations, I decided to go with the flow and let events unfold naturally.

Lynn was already waiting for me with a large sketch pad and

her pastels. She explained that she would first transmit information from my guides for the initial ten minutes or so before commencing the drawing.

Anxiously, I sat across from my teacher, observing as she entered a light trance. Within seconds, she began to speak, pouring forth a wealth of information at a speed I had never witnessed before. After a few minutes, she abruptly stopped and looked at me with wide-open eyes.

"By the way, I won't draw anything for you," Lynn unexpectedly declared.

She seemed taken aback by her own words.

"Your team says it's not necessary. You don't need a picture."

Most people might have been disappointed by this news, but I couldn't have been happier. The message that I didn't need a picture was the most profound confirmation I could receive.

Lynn used the remaining 20 minutes to transmit even more information, and I eagerly absorbed every word, knowing that she was undeniably connected to my team.

For instance, Lynn described intricate details about my ability to work across different levels of consciousness and offered helpful suggestions on how to enhance my processes.

These small yet significant moments of verifiable experiences provide us with confirmation and renewed motivation. Secretly, we all yearn for proof, and I firmly believe that everyone will receive it once they are ready to trust.

In 2012, ten years after my PREP Session at the Monroe Institute's laboratory, I came across the long-forgotten audio tape again while moving into my new apartment.

In the end, I hadn't listened to the recording after returning from the *Guidelines* program. Back then, I couldn't find a Walkman, never mind a cassette tape deck. It was the digital age and CD players had long replaced the old recorders.

Consequently, the envelope containing the audio tape had been stored away with a box of old letters.

This time, I made a point of acquiring a cassette player and eagerly listened to my own voice. I was deeply moved by the words I had spoken, despite having no recollection of them. Among other things, I vividly described how I would transition from being a tour guide, leading groups to earthly sites, to guiding them to the astral plane.

One particular sentence from the recording has stayed with me to this day:

“We can show you the path, but only you can clear the way by following your true calling.”

6

THE JOURNEY INWARDS

"What was said to the rose that made it open
was said to me here in my chest."
Jalal al-Din Rumi, Persian Sufi Mystic

Two years passed after my *Guidelines* program in 2002 before I made my return to the Monroe Institute a third time.

Guidelines had sparked a profound period of transformation and integration for me. Back then, I could clearly feel how much the work with the Monroe Method and my time in Australia had shaped me anew.

Following my return from Virginia, I no longer felt at ease in the bustling city of Los Angeles. I yearned for a more serene environment where I could try my hand at teaching yoga. Therefore, when an unexpected job offer came my way in the alpine village of Verbier, located in French-speaking Switzerland, I eagerly accepted.

The summer spent amidst the mountains proved to be incredibly nourishing for me. I taught yoga sessions in the early mornings and late afternoons, leaving plenty of time to delve into consciousness research and further practice Out-of-Body Experiences.

I stayed in a cozy 270-square-foot cabin nestled among towering conifers situated near the village center. It was the ideal abode for relaxation and meditation. In this humble dwelling, I deliberately opted for a life devoid of television or internet access, relying instead on the handful of books I had brought with me from the United States. These books were cherished OBE classics, providing me with ample entertainment and knowledge during my tranquil stay.

But the more I read, the less progress I made in practical terms. My mind became overwhelmed with numerous explanations, different approaches, and instructions from renowned OBE masters like William Buhlman, Robert Bruce, and Jurgen Ziewe.

Reflecting on it now, I realize that my intensive studies were actually counterproductive. Instead of finding my own path, I was merely emulating the experiences of others.

I longed to experience what Monroe and his peers had gone through—in the exact same manner. I held a clear and specific notion of how an OBE should manifest, and I was determined to pursue it without any hindrance. Realistically, who could have possibly stopped me? After all, there was nobody in the vicinity with whom I could have engaged in discussions about this matter.

Consequently, I diligently practiced every single day using various Hemi-Sync recordings, constantly yearning for that one significant OBE.

By late summer, consistent training had brought me to the point where I could successfully leave my physical body, or at least that was my perception. Through mental anchoring, I could now reach and remain in Focus 10 within a matter of minutes, even without relying on Hemi-Sync.

During my practice, I would visualize my energy body moving from right to left in a rocking motion. This visualization was sometimes accompanied by vibrations or a loud swooshing sound in both ears. On average, every third attempt yielded the desired outcome.

However, there were instances when I would sink through the mattress beneath the bed and find myself unable to move in any direction.

Additionally, after vigorous rocking, I occasionally fell sideways out of bed, bouncing uncontrollably like a rubber ball.

Unfortunately, my OBEs were short-lived, lasting only seconds before the gravitational pull of my physical body drew me back like a magnet. I would regain consciousness, breathing heavily, often accompanied by a powerful jerk or muscle twitching.

There were also occasions when I consciously perceived leaving my physical body. But those instances were immediately followed by a Click Out.

On certain days, I would click out even during the relaxation phase, and I would only regain consciousness once I was already outside of my physical body, often finding myself in strange and unfamiliar locations. I frequently felt uncertain whether these experiences were lucid dreams or actual Out-of-Body Experiences.

As my OBEs became more frequent, my life began to mirror the chaos within them.

In the early days of fall, my role as a yoga teacher in Verbier ended, disrupting my daily routine.

Over the following months, my meditation practice dwindled as I prioritized other activities, traveling through Europe and reconnecting with old friends. My pursuit of the perfect Out-of-Body Experience temporarily took a back seat.

Interestingly enough, I experienced several spontaneous OBEs without any preconceived intention. These astral travels consistently occurred in the early hours of the morning. They shared a common trait: I never recalled the moment of leaving my physical body, only regaining consciousness in realms beyond the physical reality.

Here is an excerpt from my journal dated February 2003:

An icy draft blows across my face, causing me to instinctively reach for the blanket to cover my ears. However, my hands grasp at nothing. I feel disoriented, and panic sets in.

Around me, I perceive fog-like swirls that generate a chilling wind. I attempt to shield myself by covering my face with my hands. But I have no hands—and no body either.

Before I can comprehend my peculiar state, I am seized by a vortex that propels me into a tunnel, spiraling on its axis.

Moments later, I shoot out of the structure at breakneck speed like a cannonball and fly towards a housing settlement. Guided by an unseen force, my journey concludes right in front of a garden gate.

I immediately recognize the house beyond the gate. It holds precious memories from my childhood. The house belongs to my Uncle Heini and Auntie Anna. Auntie Anna was my grandmother's closest friend. Both passed away long ago.

Flooded with memories, I cautiously traverse the small front yard and approach the door.

Click Out.

Now, I find myself on the house's second floor, specifically in Auntie Anna's kitchen. Right in front of me sits a bucket filled with LEGO bricks. Auntie Anna is seated at the table, and upon noticing me, she claps her hands and smiles. When I shift my gaze, I see my grandmother.

"How wonderful of you to visit us," her words resonate clearly.

Grandma takes hold of my hands. I realize that I suddenly do have hands again.

"My boy..." she says, and tears well up in my eyes. "I'm living here with Auntie Anna now. I'm staying on the first floor."

Slightly bewildered, I contemplate why my grandmother doesn't reside in her own house.

"We get along wonderfully," she explains. "How lovely of you to visit us," she repeats, enveloping me in a warm embrace.

"Where is Grandpa? And why are you not with him?" I ask.

"Oh, don't you worry, my boy," she comforts me and goes on to explain that Grandpa is residing on a different vibratory level.

Grandma can sense my confusion.

"He does come to visit, though" she says softly and with a smile on her face.

Before I can ask another question, I feel a pull.

"It is time," an unfamiliar voice whispers.

Reluctantly, I disengage from my grandmother's embrace. She waves at me.

"Everything is all right," she reassures. "Auntie Anna and I are doing well."

As the force of the pull intensifies, my perception begins to blur. Suddenly, darkness engulfs me, a deep and profound darkness. I feel overwhelmed by emotions. With a powerful jolt, I regain awareness of my physical body.

When I open my eyes, I find myself lying in bed, unable to move. It takes several minutes before I regain my composure and think clearly again.

During that time, I lacked the ability to categorize the experience. However, now I understand that what occurred was a visit to *The Park* in Focus 27.

Little did I anticipate that in the years to come, I would develop a strong affinity for that realm and return to it frequently to reunite with friends and relatives or to explore its wonders.

Towards the end of 2003, I felt a strong desire to delve back into the realm of OBEs with renewed vigor. It was time to revisit the Monroe Institute again and seek fresh inspiration.

Shaaron Honeycutt suggested that I take the *Heartline* program, and without much hesitation, I followed her advice. Trusting Shaaron's expertise as a fellow yoga teacher and knowledgeable individual on all things Monroe, I believed this choice would propel my progress.

Thus, in the spring of 2004, I found myself once again journeying to Virginia's Blue Ridge Mountains. Shaaron and her husband, A.J., graciously invited me to stay at their home near the institute for a few days before the program officially commenced. This opportunity allowed me to delve deeper into the history of the Monroe family, immersing myself in their fascinating legacy.

A.J., the only boy in a blended family of six children, shared a special bond with his stepfather.

When A.J.'s mother, Nancy Penn Honeycutt, passed of cancer

in 1992, Robert Monroe was deeply affected. The loss shattered his world, prompting him to retreat from public life and minimize his involvement at the institute.

As Bob's health deteriorated and he became incapable of caring for himself, A.J. and Shaaron made the decision to move back into the family villa. They took on the responsibility of looking after Bob until his passing in 1995.

Over long walks and evenings spent in front of the fire with me, A.J. recounted the institute's beginnings and shared stories about the diverse and fascinating individuals who had visited over the decades. Among them was Elisabeth Kübler-Ross, the renowned pioneer in near-death studies. Bob had invited her to his laboratory, where she experienced her first conscious OBE under his guidance. Monroe and Kübler-Ross maintained a close friendship until his death.

In collaboration with the psychologist and parapsychologist Charles Tart, Monroe and Kübler-Ross created the Hemi-Sync series titled *Going Home*. This set of guided meditations was designed to facilitate a smooth transition for the dying and bring comfort to their loved ones and companions.

For A.J. Honeycutt, Out-of-Body Experiences were something normal even as a child. While his peers played in the fields and meadows, A.J. went to the lab with his stepfather and developed an interest in his research at a young age.

His sisters were also deeply involved in Monroe's work. Each family member contributed to the institute's development and the production of sound recordings in some capacity.

My in-depth conversations with A.J. about OBEs and other paranormal phenomena motivated me to resume my practice more seriously. It was my deepest desire to be able to leave my body at will and explore unknown dimensions. I eagerly anticipated how the *Heartline* program would facilitate this.

Penny Holmes, A.J.'s sister, developed the program shortly after Bob's passing and has been training it ever since.

Shaaron and A.J. preferred not to disclose any details before the program began, ensuring that I didn't build up unrealistic expectations and spoil the element of surprise. I was eager for new experiences and curious about what lay ahead.

To my surprise, on the first day of the program, A.J. drove past the Nancy Penn Center and took me to the family's villa, known as Robert's Mountain Retreat.

After Monroe's death, the impressive house had been transformed into a secondary retreat center. The lounge serves as a meeting room, and the family's former sleeping quarters are now equipped with CHEC Units instead of regular beds.

"Apart from that, not much has actually changed," A.J. remarked as he gave me a tour of the house. "The kitchen, the TV room, the pool—everything is just as it was when my parents were still alive."

The unchanged original decor exudes distinctive Southern charm. The walls boast a peach-colored hue, and floor-length drapes with floral patterns adorn the windows. Magnificent chandeliers hang from the ceilings, adding to the ambiance. The property is incredibly spacious, with the dining room comfortably accommodating 20 individuals.

A.J. spread his arms wide, saying, "Mom and Dad always emphasized the importance of having a large house. They loved welcoming and entertaining guests."

I was thrilled to spend the week in this historically rich place. A.J. had graciously arranged for me to stay in the most exquisite room of the old villa all by myself.

The opening meditation of the workshop had the sole purpose of providing relaxation and allowing the 18 participants to reacquaint themselves with Focus 10.

However, I craved more, and I wanted it immediately. I had arrived with a firm intention to refine my OBE skills. I verbalized this intention as an affirmation, stating it clearly before the first exercise.

I was wholly committed to adhering to my strict agenda.

And thus, I was bound to fail. That evening, I wasn't even able to enter the "mind awake, body asleep" state. I remained wide awake and tense, to the point where my muscles began to ache after only a few minutes. A cramp in my right calf was the final straw. I removed the headphones and abruptly halted the exercise.

Feeling disappointed and annoyed by my profound failure, I grounded myself in my CHEC Unit for the remainder of the evening. Perhaps I simply needed to settle down, acclimate to the new surroundings, and get a restful night's sleep.

Tomorrow is a new beginning.

By late evening, the muscle pain had subsided, and I had managed a solid six hours of sleep. I woke up in the morning feeling rested and full of drive.

After breakfast, Penny and her co-trainer John Kortum, outlined the plan for the rest of the week. As implied by the name *Heartline,* the program primarily centers around heart energy.

I was somewhat skeptical of the concept, and when Penny started discussing self-love and self-acceptance, I considered packing up and heading home.

What on earth am I doing here?

It seemed that I may have breezed through the program description a bit too quickly before signing up. I certainly hadn't noticed the terms self-love and self-acceptance. Why on earth had Shaaron recommended this course?

Somewhat frustrated and miffed at the thought of spending my money on a self-help program, I went back to my room. As I climbed the stairs, I had an idea. I could simply place the heart energy issue on hold and remain true to my own objectives.

I settled comfortably in my CHEC Unit, eager to leave my body and begin an exhilarating journey.

I had barely finished the preparatory process and mentally phrased my affirmation when my physical body began to cramp in several areas. At first, I thought this was an intense version of the familiar vibrations heralding an upcoming OBE.

My joyful anticipation quickly faded when my muscles' spasmodic movements intensified and caused significant discomfort.

In a panic, I removed the headphones and massaged my arms and legs. Suddenly, everything hurt.

What the heck is going on with me?

It seemed pointless to continue the exercise in my current state, so I rolled out my yoga mat next to the CHEC Unit to gently stretch my aching muscles. It worked. Just a few minutes later, the tension in my body began to ease.

However, the pain came back soon after I returned to the CHEC Unit.

The morning devolved into psychological and physical torment, and I couldn't focus on the meditations. Even a long walk through the woods during the lunch break didn't help. My mood worsened with each passing hour.

I was hesitant to burden the trainers with my issue. If I, as a certified yoga instructor, couldn't determine the root of my problem, how could Penny or John possibly be of help?

So, I set a deadline for myself: If I didn't feel better by the morning, I would withdraw from the program.

I spent a restless night tossing and turning on the mattress, unable to find sleep. By the early hours of the morning, the pain had become so severe that I couldn't remain lying down. I rose and packed my belongings. In a state of desperation, I knocked on Penny's door before breakfast.

"I can't continue," I confessed, tears welling up in my eyes. "I need to go home."

Penny urged me to remain calm.

"Go back to your room, Oliver. I'll be there in a minute."

Soon after, she arrived at my door carrying two cups of tea.

"Let's figure this out," Penny declared, gesturing towards the CHEC Unit. "Why don't you lie down and tell me when the pain began."

She drew up a chair and sat next to me.

"It started during the first exercise in the evening, the day before yesterday," I relayed in a shaky voice, providing details about the recurring discomfort. Penny listened intently.

"What are you hoping to gain from this program?" she asked. "Why did you come here?"

I felt caught out.

"I... I'm not sure," I stuttered.

I didn't want to bring up Shaaron and A.J. since they were related to Penny. And nobody had coerced me into enrolling in the course. The decision had been entirely mine.

"I don't think this program is a good fit for me," I admitted cautiously. "I didn't realize it wouldn't include OBEs, and I was hoping to improve those skills."

Penny nodded understandingly.

"I think I know what the problem is. And it's completely fine if you decide not to continue with the *Heartline* program. You are an adult, after all. "

She took a deep breath.

"Your body seems to be reacting to your intention of wanting to leave it. Whatever that may imply. But your body doesn't appear to be in resonance with your intent."

Penny suggested I reflect on the idea that each body cell is imbued with consciousness and that separating the body's consciousness and the soul's consciousness isn't necessarily in the body's best interest. After all, the body's duty is to host the soul aspect and its consciousness during our lifetime.

"Your body has a role," she stated.

I'd never considered that. But her words struck a chord.

"And it wants to fulfill that role, regardless of anything else," I added.

"Perhaps you could try communicating with your body," Penny suggested, "and invite your body's consciousness into a mental dialogue. You could ask it to journey with you rather than attempting to separate." She paused for a moment. "I'm not suggesting that this will solve your problem. But it's worth a shot, don't you think?"

Penny's approach resonated with me, and I appreciated her suggestion to communicate with my body. I probably should have considered this much earlier. Why hadn't I, a yoga instructor, thought of it myself?

After giving me a comforting hug, Penny left. I decided to follow her advice. Nonetheless, I left my packed bag at the door, just in case.

After breakfast, the trainers introduced the first Hemi-Sync exercise of the day. My muscles ached as much as before, and it was a struggle to climb into the CHEC Unit.

I donned the headphones, closed my eyes, and tuned in to my body. I could distinctly feel its resistance. But how, I wondered, does one communicate with one's body?

I envisioned each cell being infused with consciousness and performing its role as part of a larger collective.

An overwhelming sense of gratitude washed over me. Then, quite spontaneously, I questioned why I wanted to leave my body.

This body carries my mind and a portion of my soul through a world entirely inaccessible without it.

"I want to discover what it means to be a multidimensional being," I whispered into the darkness of the CHEC Unit. "I have a profound need to understand who I am, where I came from, and where I am going."

Then, I mentally invited my body's consciousness to join me in these explorations.

Another surge of profound gratitude coursed through me. And when Penny introduced the upcoming exercise with a beautiful poem by Rumi, tears welled up in my eyes. A torrent of emotions rose from deep within me.

I wept until a sense of tranquility enveloped me. A beautiful, healing tranquility. And for the first time in my life, I felt complete.

The pain began to recede from my body. It wasn't entirely gone by the time the exercise was over, but I intuitively knew that it was only a matter of hours or days before my body-mind system would regain its balance.

Despite diminishing pain, *Heartline* still represented a huge challenge for me. But after my cathartic emotional release, I understood there was a reason for my participation in the program.

It was new territory for me to confront and share my emotions with others. It wasn't easy, but I wanted to take advantage of the opportunity.

I began to grasp the importance of self-love and cultivating a healthy sense of self-worth. Unconditional love and acceptance of oneself are not only vital to successful interpersonal relationships. Self-love also enables us to resonate with what exists beyond physical reality because the fundamental substance of "all that is" vibrates at the frequency of unconditional love.

Heartline offered me a safe space to release emotional baggage and recalibrate as a person. I learned more about myself that week than I had in the previous 38 years of my life.

Inspired by Penny, I cultivated a new relationship with my body and gained a fresh perspective on OBEs.

I was now deeply motivated to stop attempting to replicate others' experiences and, instead, to uncover my own truth. Just as Robert Monroe had done.

This was the beginning of a new era for me.

*

After my stay at the Monroe Institute, I felt the urge to travel to Europe. My intention for the following months was to delve deeper into the anatomy and energetic structures of the physical body.

What I experienced, thanks to Penny's advice, felt like a true miracle to me. My body had responded noticeably to the intentional signals my mind had sent. To me, this was a clear indication that there must indeed be a cellular consciousness with the ability to communicate.

During my initial research, I stumbled upon the work of Dr. Bruce Lipton, an American developmental biologist noted for his views on epigenetics. Lipton formulated the theory that gene expression can be swayed not only by environmental factors but also by individuals' attitudes and thoughts.

I avidly followed Lipton's work, struck by the fact that he wasn't some fringe theorist but a respected scientist blending Western medicine with revolutionary thinking. Here was a man capable of articulating how body cells react to each person's internal dialogue in a way that's easy to comprehend.

Lipton's writings helped me understand what must have happened during my numerous attempts to separate body and mind within my own system.

2004 was a year of further transformations for me. After attending a lecture about Dr. John Veltheim's BodyTalk-System™ in Hamburg, Germany, I felt I needed more in-depth study of the subject.

The BodyTalk-System™ integrates the knowledge and practices of Western and traditional Chinese medicine, applied kinesiology, Advaita philosophy, and quantum physics.

In a four-day basic training program, I learned to communicate with the physical body using a muscle test and a sophisticated protocol to rectify imbalances within the body-mind system.

I also trained as a massage therapist to expand my knowledge of anatomy and gain more insight into the human body.

To my own surprise, and although I initially found it challenging to touch the bare bodies of total strangers, I very much enjoyed the work.

Rather than just massaging my clients, I learned to "read" their bodies with my hands while in a state of expanded awareness, in other words, Focus 12. My clients' positive feedback confirmed my perceptions, and my appointment book was full to the brim in only a matter of months.

However, the intensive treatments also took their toll on me. I was physically exhausted when I came home from work at night. Some days, I performed massages for six or seven hours without a break. I expended more energy on my clients than was beneficial for my own health, and my well-being began to deteriorate. I rarely found the time to meditate or practice OBEs anymore.

The constant stress manifested itself as neurodermatitis. Ironically, my hands, the most crucial tools for my work, were severely affected by incessant itching and weeping eczema. A nightmare for a massage therapist.

Since I could accept fewer and fewer appointments due to my symptoms, I quickly got into a spiral of negative thoughts and general existential worries. This worsened my situation, pushing me further into victimhood and inciting resentment toward the universe.

Why me, of all people? And why my hands?

Looking back, I understand now that such questions were unhelpful. During that challenging period, I had lost my sense of direction and inner balance.

I now realize I should have reached out to my spirit team and sought guidance to discern if my current activities were aligned with my true calling and purpose.

It was essential for me to reconnect with my authentic self and find my way back to a path that resonated with my soul's journey.

7

A NEW UNDERSTANDING OF OUT-OF-BODY EXPERIENCES

"This body is not me. I am not limited by this body. I am life without boundaries. I have never been born, and I have never died."
Thich Nhat Hanh, Buddhist Monk

In the spring of 2005, I returned to California, hoping to avert a financial disaster. The shift in climate and reduction of stress soon alleviated my symptoms.

Having firmly decided against returning to my career as a TV journalist, I once again turned to tourism, guiding German tourist groups across the United States. Although I didn't see this job as my ultimate vocation, it did afford me the luxury of taking time off during the winter months.

The season was lucrative. When I bid farewell to the last group in October, I had saved enough for the winter—five long months that I planned to spend on both physical and non-physical journeys of my choice.

By this point, it had been a significant while since I had regularly practiced Out-of-Body Experiences. I was resolute in my determination to uphold the promise I had made to myself – to no longer be swayed by other people's experiences. So, I declared my inner conflict, which had peaked during the *Heartline* program, to be resolved.

Aside from attending an OBE workshop by William Buhlman, which provided me with valuable inspiration and pointers for my future growth, I practiced on my own and intentionally avoided any literature on the subject.

I heeded Bill's advice to cultivate a certain discipline and practice each day at set times. He suggested that the early hours of the morning were particularly ideal, as our minds are alert and clear, but our bodies are still relaxed.

This new routine showed its effectiveness after just a few weeks, and the quality of my experiences increased. When I practiced in the morning, my Out-of-Body state was unquestionably more stable than what I had been accustomed to from my afternoon or evening practices.

I was especially thankful to Bill for recommending that we experiment with commands such as "clarity now!" or "front door now!" The former is used to intervene when an emerging OBE threatens to fail due to a lack of clear perception. The latter can help overcome immobility or consciousness bouncing back into the physical body.

These commands worked incredibly well for me, especially when I encountered a state of sleep paralysis, which happened quite often. This phenomenon is common among OBE practitioners and can be very frightening for those who aren't familiar with it.

My first experience with sleep paralysis occurred in the mid-nineties, well before my first visit to the Monroe Institute. I can still recall the unsettling memory of that morning when I woke up to find myself completely immobilized.

My mind was lucid and alert, yet my body was utterly paralyzed. Despite my best efforts, I found myself unable to move even a single finger.

Lying on my side, I felt the presence of an entity at the foot of my bed. I was convinced this being harbored malevolent intentions.

A chilling thought crossed my mind: "If it touches my foot, I'll die!"

I tried to pull my foot under the covers, but I was unable to. With my heart pounding, I rapidly succumbed to a profound fear for my life.

I can't accurately recall how long the paralysis lasted, but those terrifying minutes seemed to stretch on before the stiffness finally dissipated and the presence of the entity faded away.

Since then, I've experienced sleep paralysis multiple times. Essentially, this condition is nothing more than an intensely heightened state of Focus 10, where part of your awareness already extends beyond the physical body. The strange entity I had sensed at the foot of the bed was a partial projection of my own consciousness.

Now, thanks to Bill's advice, I know how to extract myself from this unsettling state. Using clear commands gives me the choice to either fully return to my body or to initiate a total detachment of consciousness from the body.

But sleep paralysis was never the main problem for me. It was rather that I struggled with clumsy immobility after reaching the Out-of-Body state. As I've already mentioned, I often slid under the mattress or the couch and felt trapped there.

The commands helped in these situations as well. They allowed me to project my consciousness to another place successfully.

However, I still couldn't master navigating between dimensions.

This caused me immense frustration. Although I was able to move out of my body consciously, I kept getting stuck in physical matter reality or, rather, an energetic impression of it.

Even though colors, shapes, and materials in my surroundings didn't entirely match what I knew from waking consciousness, I usually recognized where I was. From a certain point on, traveling around the world in an Out-of-Body state became easy. I just had to think about a specific place; a moment later, I would find myself in Paris, New York, or Sydney.

What probably sounds exciting at first becomes surprisingly dull quite fast. For starters, in the energetic state, I was unable to interact with physical reality. Additionally, I was constantly a traveler.

Yet, I was never alone. I kept encountering entities who seemed to be floating around apathetically. My explanation for this is that those were sleepers—people having an unconscious OBE while they were asleep or unconscious for other reasons.

Only rarely did I encounter beings who were clearly aware of their experience and willing to communicate.

In March 2006, I was meditating in the early morning hours. After reaching the vibrational state, I decided to roll out of my body sideways. As often happens, I ended up under the bed. Then, I was taken by surprise:

It takes three attempts before I manage to maneuver into the hallway. I notice that I am walking on a hardwood floor instead of the carpet that should be there. I'm also puzzled by the blue walls that should actually be white.

I pause for a moment. Did I end up in someone else's apartment? I investigate the kitchen and dining area. The furniture is definitely mine.

I decide to leave physical reality and explore other dimensions. I immediately ascend, speeding through the roof and flying rapidly through the air. It's quite difficult to slow down. Then, I start approaching the ground again. I have no idea where I am.

As I try to get my bearings on the landscape below me, I notice a female figure to my right. She seems just as amazed by my presence as I am by hers. We communicate telepathically.

"Are you real?" she asks.

"What do you mean?"

"I've never met anyone like you before," she continues.

Her comment surprises me. Looking down at myself, I notice that I have an upper body but no hips or legs.

Her body is complete, however. I even notice distinct female curves. I wonder if the woman may be dead and I'm dealing with some kind of ghost.

No," she replies unexpectedly. "Why should I be dead? I'm doing just fine."

I feel exposed. She can evidently read my mind. How disconcerting. Annoyed, I turn away and use the command "physical body now!"

There is a pull from behind, and I immediately jolt back into my body.

To this day, I don't know who that woman was. Looking back, I'm frustrated that I didn't ask her more questions.

Many such encounters ended abruptly in the early years because I could not make rational decisions or act deliberately during my excursions. Instead, I allowed myself to be guided by impulses, often driven by fears or insecurities.

In the above-mentioned case, I was unsettled because the other person could read my mind while I was having a telepathic conversation with her. But back then, I hadn't fully grasped the rules of communication in the non-physical.

In general, I'm profoundly grateful for all the experiences I've had so far. In their sum, they have led me to the profound realization of being more than physical matter. And each step along the way provided significant learning potential.

In the meantime, I understand that each dimension or consciousness level has its own physical, spatial, temporal, and/or energetic laws. For us on planet Earth, relatively stable basic framework conditions like time, gravity, and verbal language are a given.

In the non-physical other "environmental" conditions apply. An astral traveler must first become familiar with these.

Especially the ability of controlled navigation requires practice and experience.

As evidenced by my encounter with the woman, movement in the non-physical requires neither legs nor wings. Consciousness is transported only by clear intentions. These can unfold tremendous powers and manifest instantly.

To prevent spiraling uncontrollably through the matrix, one should have a specific goal in mind. Those who get stuck during the journey or don't know how to proceed can learn to use available resources. This includes the support of our spirit guides and other intelligent beings.

Without external assistance, one quickly reaches their limits in uncharted non-physical territory, and many paths remain blocked. Not every area is inherently open to visitors.

I like to compare the various non-physical environments with different levels of a video game where you must master one level before reaching the next, and the player is constantly presented with new challenges.

In the spring of 2006, before starting another season as a tour guide, I spent a few weeks in Germany visiting friends and family.

I was driving from Kassel to Frankfurt on the Autobahn on a Friday afternoon when suddenly, a lady I'd met in 2002 during the *Guidelines* program popped into my mind. We'd stayed loosely in touch over the years.

At that time, Mara and her husband lived in Denver, Colorado. She was part of a group that met once a week to exchange paranormal experiences. Mara emailed me sporadically with interesting and sometimes bizarre stories from her circle.

That afternoon on the Autobahn, I had an overwhelming sensation that she was with me, not just in thought, and I kept glancing at the passenger seat. For several minutes, I couldn't shake the feeling that Mara was sitting in my car, right next to me.

Only an alert about a traffic jam on the radio made me drop the thought. The perception vanished, and I refocused on the traffic.

By the time I reached Frankfurt, I'd already forgotten the incident. That night I partied with friends and, unusually for me, went to bed way past midnight.

When I woke up the following morning, I found an email from Mara in my mailbox:

"Hi, Ollie. I had a lot of fun with you on the German Autobahn yesterday. Don't drive too fast. Love, Mara."

"Unbelievable!" was my first thought.

I glanced at the clock. I would have loved to call Mara straight away, but I had to wait a few hours due to the time difference. After several unsuccessful attempts, I eventually reached her in the early evening.

"Finally!" I exclaimed into the phone and excitedly told her what had happened during the car ride from my perspective.

Mara laughed.

"So, you really did sense my presence!" she said with relief. "I gave it my all."

"How did you manage to do that?" I asked her.

Mara explained that she had initiated an Out-of-Body Experience with the intention of finding me at six o'clock in the morning her time.

"But how did you even know that I'm in Germany?"

"I didn't," she replied, "but that's not important. The intention alone matters. Instead of heading for a specific place, I let myself be guided to you."

"By whom?"

"My spirit guides, of course," she explained as if this were completely normal.

I was curious how Mara had managed to capture my attention and infiltrate my thoughts. During any of my Out-of-Body Experiences, I had never successfully interacted with another person who was awake.

"I guess the circumstances were just right. I had a clear intention, and you were in a state of expanded awareness at the right moment. This happens automatically when we drive along the highway and don't have to concentrate too much," she explained.

Mara touched on an important point. While driving, I let my thoughts wander and switched to autopilot.

This created an optimal basis for perceiving subtle impulses akin to the state of expanded awareness.

"How are you doing with your OBE practice?" I asked Mara. "What are your biggest challenges?"

Unlike me, she didn't encounter many obstacles, as I learned.

We shared our respective experiences and how they shaped our understanding of Out-of-Body Experiences. Our lengthy conversation gave me a lot to ponder and prompted me to reevaluate the knowledge I had previously gathered from the relevant literature.

Mara had come to the realization that the foundational theories explaining and describing Out-of-Body Experiences were no longer current.

"Don't waste your time with those silly exit techniques," she advised me that evening.

Like most people interested in exploring Out-of-Body Experiences, I delved into many books on the subject when I commenced my experiments.

Early works often suggested that the soul is tethered to the physical body and can disengage from it as a sort of energy body through appropriate exercises. According to these accounts, this energy body is linked to the physical body via a "silver cord."

The theory states that the cord connects the body and soul from birth, serving as a safety tether during an OBE, ensuring that the soul always finds its way back into the body. If the silver cord severs, life ends.

Mara viewed the traditional explanation of the interplay between the soul and body as too restrictive and outdated.

"Those ideas are over a hundred years old," she stated.

In her understanding, the nature of human consciousness was much more complex than a simple interplay between body and soul.

Her words struck a nerve. Despite years of experimentation and countless successful OBEs, I had never clearly discerned my supposed energy body. Nor had the silver cord ever been a feature.

But how is it that so many people report experiencing exactly that phenomenon?

Mara suggested the possibility that the energy body and the silver cord might be manifestations of those individuals' expectations. Today, I share a similar viewpoint, understanding that non-physical environments are responsive to thought and react instantaneously. This also explains why individual reports of perceptions in an out-of-body state vary greatly.

My conversation with Mara was a catalyst. I began to realize that notions such as energy bodies or silver cords were mere beliefs as long as I couldn't corroborate them with my own experiences. Until then, I had never questioned the explanations and mechanisms I had read about.

It's never easy to discard old belief systems, especially those delineating and upholding your worldview. But perhaps it was time to open myself to new impulses and opportunities if I wanted to advance.

It's not without reason that Robert Monroe consistently emphasized: "Don't believe anything I tell you. Go out there and find out for yourself."

By now, I have taken those words to heart. While it's vitally important and beneficial to draw inspiration from other people and their experiences, only your own direct experiences can lead to sustainable personal growth.

I could read ten books that mention a silver cord. But if I don't perceive the cord, my reality differs from those ten authors. That doesn't make my experience less significant. Quite the contrary. If I remain true to my own reality, I respect and honor my personal journey.

At the outset of his explorations, Robert Monroe also believed that a second body detaches from the physical body during an OBE. He reassessed this theory later, considering the phenomenon more as a kind of projection. Monroe suggested that people identify with their physical form due to lifelong conditioning, even when in an out-of-body state.

With the realization that he didn't have to go through all the trouble of detaching himself from the physical body, Monroe developed a method he called Quick Switch Technique. He would extend his consciousness or awareness like a rubber band and make a connection to where he wanted to go. Then he would let go at the starting point, snapping himself to the destination.

The process of "making a connection" refers to the intention setting and the focusing of the mind on the specific destination, creating a direct mental link. The destination could be a physical place, a different plane of existence, or even another person.

The act of "letting go at the starting point" is about releasing the connection to the physical body or the current state of awareness, allowing the consciousness to be "snapped" to the destination in the same way a stretched rubber band will snap back to its original form when let go. This way, Monroe could instantly transition his consciousness from one location to another.

He later called this process Phasing.

The term Phasing originates from the field of physics and conceptualizes consciousness as a form of oscillation or waveform that aligns with physical reality but can also remove itself from it. This happens fluidly or in stages.

According to Monroe, trance, hypnosis, meditation, and even OBEs are merely manifestations of a single phenomenon where consciousness focuses beyond physical reality in different ways and to varying degrees.

The individual's intent determines the destination of the journey. A clear intention can transition an individual from the confined state of physical waking consciousness to other, more expansive levels of awareness.

I was already familiar with the Phasing technique, having explored it at the Monroe seminars. My experiences with it had been quite intriguing. But are Phasing and Out-of-Body Experiences truly one and the same?

This sparked new questions: What exactly constitutes an OBE? What occurs when I leave my body? Do I really exit my physical form?

Even today, there are no definitive answers, but there is no shortage of opinions, personal accounts, studies, theories, and research findings.

An OBE is generally characterized as an event that involves a sensation of floating outside the physical body and perceiving one's own form from a bird's eye view.

Particularly, those who have had a spontaneous OBE often describe this sensation. Individuals who have undergone near-death experiences report similar perceptions.

However, those who deliberately train to induce an OBE often struggle to replicate such experiences. Only a few successfully perceive their physical bodies, yet many remain determined to achieve this, viewing the above-mentioned universal assumption as proof of a successful OBE.

One possible explanation could be that the prerequisites for each circumstance are vastly different. Personal expectations, belief systems, and unconscious fears can influence the desired outcome.

From my own experience, I can say that every conscious attempt I made in this direction failed and led to an abrupt end of the OBE.

Nowadays, I regard such endeavors as a waste of time. If I want to see my own body, all I need to do is stand in front of a mirror. There's no need to spend months practicing.

At this point, I would like to emphasize that the classic out-of-body exercises described in detail in the relevant literature, although outdated, are still important as an approach to practicing OBEs. I see them as tools that the practitioner can use until they become obsolete.

I too, spent years working with these exercises; they were an integral part of my own evolutionary process.

My intention is not to judge which method is superior. I advocate for everyone to test the available methods and draw conclusions. I aim to share my personal experiences in hopes of inspiring others.

Ultimately, the goal is to achieve an astral projection. The way it is initiated doesn't matter as much. The primary concerns should be a clear intention and the results produced by the chosen method or approach.

Personally, I could only progress to a certain point with the traditional exercises to exit the body. However, the experience I gained through this process is invaluable, not least because I learned a lot about myself.

Yet, I don't want to dismiss the existence of an energy body outright. While I do perceive an energy field, I wouldn't classify it as a separate body. For me, the concept of an energy body is an analogy for a non-physical phenomenon that is worth exploring.

Drawing upon the discoveries of numerous physicists, quantum physicists, philosophers, and consciousness researchers, we can hypothesize that consciousness is not a product of the brain and, thus, not anchored in the physical body. It exists independently of space and time.

From my perspective, the idea of leaving the physical body during an OBE doesn't quite hold up, even if this perception is achieved under certain circumstances.

Nowadays, I view consciousness as a fundamental intelligence that has manifested various environments in the interest of its own evolutionary process, of which our physical reality is just one of the infinitely many realities within a complex matrix.

Practicing the Phasing technique was my next logical step after talking to Mara.

If I effectively sidestep the process of leaving my physical body and aim to focus my consciousness directly on another location, I first need to establish a state of profound mental calm. While it's not absolutely necessary to also relax the body completely, it can be beneficial when practicing until a certain level of confidence in using the method is established.

Achieving a stable Focus 10 is, therefore, an optimal starting point. But not everyone finds it easy to quiet down both the mind and body. Those who have already established a regular meditation practice definitely have a head start.

I've made it a habit to meditate for at least 20 minutes every morning. When I find my thoughts intruding, I resort to a simple mantra, mentally reciting the words: "I am" or "here and now" in rhythm with my breath.

Once I establish a state of complete internal tranquility, I reach a point where I no longer engage mentally with physical reality. My brain no longer processes any information. I become one with everything and experience pure existence.

Physicist and consciousness researcher Thomas Campbell aptly labels this state as Point Consciousness.

Strictly speaking, an OBE already begins at this stage. Ideally, I also lose any perception of the physical body in this state. My individual consciousness is free to focus elsewhere within the vast expanse of collective or universal consciousness.

As always, it's crucial to form a clear intention before the meditation begins. Those who work with the Monroe Method commence each exercise with a preparatory process, which includes a specific affirmation as well as supportive energy work.

Monroe's Focus level scale, a map of sorts for the consciousness matrix, offers a variety of non-physical environments that can be accessed from Point Consciousness. Hemi-Sync frequencies or frequencies used by Monroe Sound Science assist in maintaining a stable focus effortlessly.

Depending on one's personal intention, Phasing can assume different degrees.

Consciousness is essentially able to focus on more than one place simultaneously. Proper training allows me to control my awareness in a way that facilitates parallel perception and even interaction.

This implies, for instance, that I can perceive sounds from my physical surroundings while simultaneously communicating with someone in Focus 27. The key is not to be distracted by the physical sounds. The moment I react, I quickly slide back toward waking consciousness.

In our everyday lives, we constantly shift our attention from one point to another without much consideration or questioning the process. I can play a game on my cellphone and watch television at the same time. Sometimes I focus on the TV set and, at other times, on the phone in my hand. To some degree, I can follow both the game and the movie simultaneously in this state of divided or parallel awareness.

Consciousness knows no limits. We simply need to recondition our physical apparatus and eliminate beliefs that constrain us.

One belief frequently appearing in esoteric literature, and one I had unconsciously adopted, is that our physical body houses the soul.

But what if the opposite is true, and the body exists within the soul? A consideration that can flip our inner and outer worlds upside down.

To sum up, it can now be stated that Out-of-Body Experiences are a refocusing of consciousness beyond the physical body.

We interrupt the information flow from one reality to plug into the information flow of another reality.

The greatest challenge is that each level operates under its own rules, which can greatly differ from those of our physical reality.

One example is lucid dreams, dreams where we are entirely aware that we're dreaming and can act according to our decisions. During a lucid dream, we can, for instance, fly, while gravity prevents us from doing so in our physical reality.

To me, lucid dreams also belong to the category of OBEs. The difference is that we first fall asleep before we regain consciousness, while a classical OBE is generally initiated from waking consciousness.

8

PERCEPTION AND NON-PHYSICAL SENSES

"Thought is so cunning, so clever,
that it distorts everything for its own convenience."
Jiddu Krishnamurti, Indian Philosopher

"I am more than my physical body" – this phrase served as Robert Monroe's creed. It underpinned his research into consciousness and stands as the starting point for all Monroe Institute courses. They are the first words of the Gateway Affirmation, integral to the preparatory process for every classic Monroe meditation.

Many people don't doubt that there is something more. Something that goes beyond the biological aspects of our being. For example, by firmly believing that they have a soul.

Through decades of research, Robert Monroe expanded and refined his understanding of what it means to exist beyond our physicality. Though challenging to measure and seemingly intangible for many, this concept continued to fascinate him.

Monroe began his quest for evidence and explanations without the burden of religious ideologies or the dominant scientific and cultural norms. His efforts culminated in a groundbreaking, complex model of the manifestations and laws that govern our existence in the non-physical realm.

Countless Out-of-Body Experiences left Monroe convinced that the physical dimension is merely a tiny fragment of an enormous matrix. Our human perspective is extremely limited and makes it difficult, if not impossible, to comprehend the full extent of this structure in its entirety. But this didn't deter Monroe from asking questions and searching for answers. And, in my opinion, he developed very helpful tools for this exploration with his Hemi-Sync exercises.

The Monroe Method enables us to explore at least parts of the matrix.

Those who engage with the process don't only broaden their personal but also our collective horizon, and this doesn't require years of meditation or the use of psychedelic drugs.

However, these explorations into the non-physical come with their own set of challenges. It's not as simple as playing a Hemi-Sync recording and closing your eyes, only to return an hour later with a comprehensive report from your journey into the matrix's depths. Utilizing this method demands a certain level of discipline and training.

While Hemi-Sync supports us in accessing precisely defined states of consciousness, navigating within these levels, and developing our cognitive abilities there is an individual journey.

The experience can be roughly compared to booking a trip without a tour guide, a guidebook, a translation app, and Google Maps. The plane will drop you off in Paris, but finding and recognizing landmarks like the Louvre, the Eiffel Tower, or Montmartre is up to you! The locals speak a different language, and if you don't know French, you'll need to get creative to navigate these unfamiliar surroundings.

The most important basis for the successful application of the Monroe Method is to formulate a clear intention. This reduces the chance of getting lost in meditation or drifting aimlessly.

Just as a tourist in Paris needs a clear intention—whether it's to climb the Eiffel Tower, gaze into the Mona Lisa's eyes, or savor an authentic croissant—you must have a distinct aim for your non-physical journeys.

Most likely, you'll want to return with a record of significant experiences, necessitating a thorough understanding of your perceptual skills to prepare for the journey.

Since the information flow in the matrix's depths is governed by different laws than our usual environment, we need to recalibrate, expand, and fine-tune our "antennas." What we commonly refer to as our "sixth sense" or gut instinct is crucial in this respect.

While some people naturally or spontaneously tap into their intuition, most need to train or refine this ability first.

Our five classic human sensory organs—eyes, ears, nose, taste buds, and skin—are finely tuned to our physical environment. These receptors take in signals and information from our surroundings and quickly transfer them to the brain, where they are processed and interpreted.

Our senses allow us not only to survive in the physical realm but also to experience all its facets consciously.

We feel the texture of objects through our skin, taste flavors like chocolate or pepper on our tongue, hear melodies, see signs and symbols, and smell fragrances. As long as our awareness is centered in physical reality, we can rely on these senses, assuming they function properly.

Even the constant sensory overload that most people are exposed to nowadays is usually not a problem for our five senses. They adapt to the new demands. Technological advancements like hearing aids and glasses can help mitigate the effects of stress and aging.

However, when exploring non-physical environments, it's necessary to disengage from the external noise and calm both body and mind. This involves turning off the physical senses to perceive the much subtler signals from other dimensions.

The aim is to firmly focus one's attention on a non-physical realm without being distracted by external stimuli. The exchange of information in non-physical environments occurs telepathically.

During telepathic communication, the physical senses no longer act as primary receptors. They are only indirectly engaged through the so-called sixth sense, our intuition.

Information that is conveyed to us by spirit guides, deceased individuals, or other intelligent energy forms usually reaches us almost exclusively through this channel. Intuition is defined as the ability to understand or recognize something instantly and without conscious reasoning.

Although intuitive perception often manifests as sudden understanding, it can also take forms similar to physical sensory perception. We see images in our mind's eye or receive auditory impulses that others cannot hear. Intuition can make itself felt through tactile sensations, muscle responses, or even a sense of smell. Beyond sensory perceptions, it often also evokes emotional responses.

Intuitive perception is highly individual. Each person has primary and secondary channels through which they receive information from non-physical dimensions. If you want to enhance your perceptive faculties, you need to start by understanding the ways in which this information reaches you. These pathways can differ greatly from person to person.

Do you see images in your mind's eye? Or do you hear voices in your inner ear? Do you experience emotions or feelings that trigger something inside you? Do you suddenly have knowledge you didn't previously possess? You may even perceive signals through your physical body.

Regular meditation, especially guided meditations, can help you understand your intuitive perceptions as they often target the sixth sense.

It is important not to become fixated on a particular channel of perception during meditation.

Many of my workshop participants become unnecessarily frustrated because they expect to experience clairvoyance. Trying to force visual perceptions often creates barriers and prevents them from noticing important information coming through other perception channels.

Seeing with the mind's eye appears to be the only acceptable form of inner perception for many people. The reason for this is likely that a person with healthy eyes perceives about 80 percent of the environment through visual impressions. Even our dreams are represented as picture sequences. We are biologically conditioned to rely on sight.

The consumption of experiential reports, in which the authors often refer to visual perceptions in non-physical environments, also fosters a corresponding expectation.

For an author, translating supernatural experiences into secular vocabulary is an enormous challenge. When dealing with experiences that have no words, they often resort to using images to convey corresponding impressions to the reader.

Then, editors strive to make the descriptions as clear and concrete as possible, potentially creating the impression that intuitive information must always unfold like a Hollywood movie. However, the reality of these experiences can be vastly different.

Documenting and conveying extrasensory experiences is a very delicate process, extremely prone to distortion.

And finally, the reader applies his own interpretation based on his personal wealth of experience and his own ideas of unfamiliar realities.

Another challenge when exploring non-physical environments is our brain's constant activity.

During waking consciousness, our brain promptly analyzes all incoming information, compares it with prior experiences, and quickly categorizes it as true or false, important or unimportant. Indeed, it is how we have been taught, how we are conditioned. This helps us navigate our complex, fast-paced world.

However, when exploring non-physical environments, this mental hyperactivity can be obstructive. It's crucial not to evaluate or analyze intuitively received signals immediately. As soon as our brain starts its thinking process, we exit the state of expanded awareness and automatically return to waking consciousness.

To illustrate how our brain receives and processes information, I like to use the analogy of receiver and interpreter. The receiver, located in the right hemisphere of the brain, absorbs data without filtering it. The interpreter, in the left hemisphere, retrieves and processes this data as quickly as possible.

The role of the receiver is to align our mental antennas to gather the maximum amount of information possible. Depending on the source of the information, the receiver needs to adjust this alignment continually. Otherwise, we may only pick up background noise, similar to the static from a poorly tuned radio.

The interpreter's job is to constantly retrieve as much data as possible from the receiving end of the brain before it falls into disarray or fades away and becomes unusable.

The interpreter is a pieceworker who, over the years, acquired the additional qualification of an astute curator. He not only translates the information he receives, but also classifies and analyzes it. During the process, the highly motivated interpreter has no consideration whatsoever for the receiver's sensitive task. He takes pride in his work. Once he has completed a job, he calls out:

"Hi! I'm finished. Here's the result. Come on, check it out!"

If we follow his call, we lose our focus, and the receiver's antenna loses its optimum alignment.

The interpreter craves attention. When we ignore him, he instantly feels threatened in his existence and develops new tactics to get through to us. He gets louder, creates more and more connections, and bombards us with irrelevant information.

Let's assume that I am meditating. The picture of a burning candle penetrates the darkness before my mind's eye. This perception is pure and authentic at this stage—the receiver has done an excellent job.

Then, the interpreter takes over, quickly searching the brain's database to assign meaning to this image.

It might connect the candle to my fond memories of lighting candles during the Christmas season. So, he sends the memory of Christmas into my awareness to explain the significance of the candle.

Ideally, after making that connection, the interpreter would step back and allow the receiver to resume its role. But, feeling threatened, the interpreter goes into overdrive.

It starts sending more connections to my awareness—reminding me I haven't bought a Christmas gift for my father yet, which leads to thinking about a potential gift, which leads to thoughts about my father's love for fishing, which leads to thoughts about trout and food, and then considerations about my freezer's electricity consumption.

As these cascading thoughts invade my brain, I lose my focus. The chain of thought spirals out of control, and the original perception—the image of the candle—has long disappeared from my inner vision.

In frustration, I realize I've been drawn back into waking consciousness.

The key is learning to balance the roles of the receiver and the interpreter in our brains to maintain a productive flow of information. This requires the ability to direct our attention swiftly and purposefully between the two.

Ideally, we want to be able to purely receive data while in an expanded state of awareness and then store it in its raw form. We can then later process this data and interpret it at our leisure or pass it along to others in its original form.

Mastering this process requires training and patience.

The perception of experiences in the non-physical occurs in two steps: the intake and processing of information and translating of that information into a physical frame of reference. This process leaves plenty of room for confusion and misinterpretation. It raises the question: How reliable or authentic are our perceptions? A significant factor is our personal reference repertoire.

Every human brain has a unique and limited set of references to process received information, which is based on our individual life experiences.

For example, the brain of an elderly, well-educated gentleman from London, England, who has traveled extensively throughout his lifetime will have a different reference repertoire than that of a young man from the remote Pacific islands who has never left his fishing village and likely has no access to modern media.

Another example: When a deceased person wants to communicate about Mount Everest with a Pacific islander who has never so far in his life seen a snow-covered high mountain range, the brain cannot find a relevant reference point. The experience simply doesn't exist for him.

Because the brain doesn't know what a high mountain range looks like, it can't draw on memory and now looks for the next best point of reference. In the case of the islander, this could be a tall palm tree, the view from up high over the beach, or a feeling of vertigo.

It's then up to that individual to interpret and categorize the information, which always carries a certain risk of distortion.

In my early years of consciousness research, I often felt disappointed and impatient. I frequently disregarded data and signals I received during my Out-of-Body journeys as confused, unclear, or insignificant. I was constantly seeking some extraordinary experience that would eradicate all my doubts.

I might still be waiting for such a life-altering event had I not drastically changed my approach. Now, I embark on my non-physical explorations with relative serenity, aware that I can only somewhat influence how information is transferred.

I have great faith in my own developmental process, particularly because I can now reflect on numerous verifiable experiences.

Much like learning a new language or a musical instrument, some people are naturally gifted and pick it up quickly, while others must practice consistently. Unfortunately, I fall into the latter category and had first to learn how to manage my frustration productively.

When I visit a foreign country, I can't expect the locals to understand my native language. I need to be open to their language, just as they need to find ways to communicate with me if they want to welcome me as a visitor.

I've made it a habit to write down all my perceptions after every meditation, no matter how trivial they seem. I regularly revisit these notes, many of which are years old, because often it's the small details that matter the most. Sometimes, the significance of these notes only becomes clear weeks or months later.

Unfortunately, I undervalued the importance of meticulously documenting my experiences in my early days, something I now regret. For this reason, I urge people to write, write, write!

Another useful tool for capturing important details is the audio recorder app, widely available for all smartphones if not preinstalled. With a bit of practice, you can learn to verbally note your experiences during meditation without being pulled back into waking consciousness.

Here's an example that illustrates how crucial notetaking can be for long-term development: After I established a routine of writing down my experiences, I noticed months later that I frequently mentioned experiencing spontaneous goosebumps during particular meditations.

I had not paid attention to this kinesthetic signal before because it didn't seem significant. However, when I reviewed my notes and saw a pattern, I began to appreciate its importance.

I thought back to when and where I had felt this tingling sensation before and recalled a séance I attended in 2001 in Byron Bay, Australia.

During that event, I felt an undefinable energy coursing through my body, causing my hair to stand on end. The energy seemed to enter through my left arm and spread rapidly throughout my body. All I felt for a few seconds was an electrifying prickle all over my skin.

Each time the sensation seemed to subside, another wave would hit me, causing distinct goosebumps. The intervals between these surges grew shorter, and my initial curiosity turned to intense fear, paralyzing me physically and mentally.

Thankfully, Mary, the medium conducting the séance, noticed what was happening and reacted immediately. I still remember how swiftly she grabbed my hands and directed the energy out of my body.

Mary explained to me later that she occasionally has similar experiences when she contacts entities from the spiritual realm. Over time, she learned to handle this energy productively.

After the séance, Mary gave me precise instructions on preventing a panic attack if the phenomenon were to occur again.

Only a few days later, the energy surges and the associated goosebumps reappeared. This time, I was alone on my patio, enjoying the sunset and the sound of the ocean while sipping a cup of tea.

But instead of panicking, I channeled the energy as Mary had instructed. Though I hardly slept that night, I didn't give much thought to the incident afterward.

When the phenomenon occurred for the third time a few days later, I wasn't worried at all anymore and just dealt with it.

This memory presented a new starting point for my search to explain the tingling. Could the recurring goosebumps possibly be an indication that some entity from the afterlife was trying to make contact? Mary had, after all, reported similar symptoms in the past.

I decided to observe the phenomenon more closely.

My theory seemed to gain support as these inexplicable goosebumps were consistently followed by perceptions that could be interpreted as messages from the afterlife. I felt a mix of elation and anxiety. Was I really prepared to open my inner doors to visitors from other realms?

Several weeks after making this discovery, I accepted an invitation to a barbecue in Venice Beach, California. The host, Laura, a long-time friend, asked me to accompany her on a shopping trip to the grocery store. During a lively discussion about her hometown in Germany, Laura casually mentioned that she had lost her father when she was still a teenager. I wanted to ask about the cause of her father's premature death, but the moment didn't seem appropriate.

Back at her house, Laura started preparing the food. I was leaning against the kitchen door's frame, watching her seasoning the steaks, when I suddenly and totally unexpectedly felt an energy surge and its associated goosebumps.

This time, I didn't dispel the energy at once. Using a special technique I had learned at the Monroe Institute, it only took a single breath to reach the state of expanded awareness.

I promptly saw images of a dark-haired man in a white coat and felt an unpleasant pressure on my chest.

The timing seemed incredibly inappropriate. I wasn't sure how Laura would react if I shared my perceptions with her. Although I had told her about my experiences at the Monroe Institute, she didn't seem to fully grasp my stories. The supernatural had simply not been a part of her life experience and, therefore, not a part of her reality.

Nonetheless, this presented a valuable opportunity to determine if my perceptions were merely figments of my imagination or if I genuinely had a connection to the afterlife.

I drew a deep breath and asked Laura to put the kitchen knife down for a minute.

I then gave her a brief overview of what I had been working on in recent weeks. To my relief, she reacted with surprising calm and even expressed interest. However, she seemed slightly uncomfortable when I hinted that I was sensing a presence in her house.

"Do you know who it is?" she asked tentatively.

I shook my head.

"No, but maybe you'll recognize the person if I describe what I'm sensing."

She hesitated before she nodded.

I then proceeded to describe the man in as much detail as I could muster. It was clear that Laura recognized her father in my description. In addition to his dark hair and white coat, I had also perceived a hospital setting. When I mentioned the pressure on my ribcage, I even felt the tension this man must have experienced shortly before his death.

My mind immediately began to analyze and interpret the information I had received. At that time, I didn't have enough experience to halt this process and simply relayed my perceptions to Laura unfiltered.

In her case, I was fortunate that my interpretations weren't entirely off the mark, though they weren't completely accurate either. According to my interpretation, Laura's father wore a surgical shirt and died at the hospital from a cardiac defect.

In actuality, Laura's father happened to be a cardiologist at a clinic and died from a heart attack while at work.

This example highlights how quickly we can distort perceptions through our own interpretations.

Initially, having my perceptions validated was hugely beneficial. However, relying on external confirmation can soon become a hindrance, leading to insecurity when it is not immediately available.

How can I know if my perception is real and not just based on imagination? Where do the images, feelings, and emotions that present themselves to me come from?

For years I grappled with doubts. I dismissed perceptions that my rational mind couldn't explain as fanciful and purged them from my awareness. My inner skeptic was working overtime.

This only changed when I asked myself what the word imagination actually means and if it truly deserves the bad reputation many people attribute to it.

I realized that imagination is a vital form of perception that should not be overlooked.

I clearly remember the moment my perceptions took a significant leap in clarity. It was the day I consciously decided to set aside my doubts and cultivate trust. From then on, I firmly believed that I was perceiving exactly what was useful and important for me and those close to me at any given moment.

If we allow ourselves to accept a perception that contradicts one of our belief patterns as real, we eradicate that belief and any associated blockages. As a result, the information we receive begins to flow more clearly and distinctly.

Thanks to this newfound trust, I no longer hesitate to articulate my perceptions as long as it is appropriate for the situation.

I find it hugely important to verbalize observations, perceptions, or received information. Alternatively, I also like to artistically express them as paintings, sketches, or drawings. Giving physical expression to these fleeting impressions imbues them with a new, tangible quality.

In the process, further information often spontaneously surfaces that would otherwise remain hidden.

Many people hesitate to share their perceptions, fearing ridicule or the possibility of being wrong. I certainly understand their apprehension. In this case, I find it helpful to examine the authenticity of the personal intent. This step generally saves us from making mistakes.

Placing trust in your own abilities can yield beautiful outcomes. For instance, my wife Anna's grandmother, Hedwig, who passed away at 98 years old, was particularly communicative in the first few months after her death. Almost every day, I sensed her presence or received some form of communication from her.

During our first trip to Germany following her passing, Anna and I visited Hedwig's grave and her apartment.

"I wonder where Granny might be now," Anna mused as we drove.

Almost immediately, the name Otto appeared in my mind, much like a rapid download on a computer screen. I could even visualize the letters. Otto! That's all the information I received, just the name and nothing else.

The name didn't mean anything to me. In the past, I might have disregarded the impression, thinking: If I don't know who Otto is, the information can't be correct.

"Your granny is with Otto," I replied.

Anna was puzzled. The name Otto meant as little to her as it did to me. Even after pondering it for a while, she couldn't recall anybody named Otto in her grandma's life.

Hedwig's husband's name had been Paul, and he'd passed away long before she did. After joking briefly about the possibility of Otto being Hedwig's secret lover, we moved on to another topic.

Had I perhaps just imagined the name Otto?

When we arrived at Hedwig's apartment about an hour later, I distinctly sensed her presence.

"I feel as if she wants to show us something," I explained to Anna, who anxiously trailed me from room to room.

In the bedroom, I had a strong urge to open the nightstand's drawer.

"We don't need to look in there," Anna said. "Mum and I checked it after the funeral. It's empty."

But my intuition was so clear that I felt compelled to follow it. I gently pulled the small wooden knob, revealing an indeed empty drawer, its bottom lined with flower-patterned paper. When I lifted the paper, I found a yellowed envelope.

It was challenging to make out the old German handwriting, but we were astounded when we saw who had signed the letter: Otto!

Suddenly, Anna remembered. Otto had been Hedwig's younger brother. He had perished as a soldier in World War II. This was his last letter from the frontline to his sister, in which he expressed his anticipation for his long overdue leave to come home.

The siblings didn't meet again until seventy years later, in the afterlife.

It seemed that it had been important for Hedwig to clear up the confusion about who she was with.

The communication between the physical and non-physical realms is multifaceted and fascinating. In fact, it should be easy for us to communicate with our spirit guides and deceased relatives. After all, the place where they reside, the afterlife, is in essence, also our home.

Why do we still have such a sense of disconnection from it?

When we incarnate into physical reality, memories of our non-physical existence fade. This is a protective measure because if we could remember our pre-physical existence, we would be plagued by intense longing for our real home.

From early childhood, we are guided to follow certain rhythms and to focus on things pertinent to our new surroundings. We learn reading, writing, math, and physics.

However, we are not taught what could arguably be considered our actual mother tongue: nonverbal communication. Quite the opposite, in fact. Those who don't conform and express an interest in the supernatural often face ridicule.

As a result, we lose conscious contact at an early age with those entities that remain present for us on the other side.

If we find a way to draw on our memories, we can once again get closer to our essence, the higher self, and reawaken our perceptual abilities.

Someone who has gone through this process is the medium Fleur Leussink. When she was eight years old, Fleur and her family emigrated from the Netherlands to the USA. Little did she suspect that she would one day earn her living as an intermediary between the worlds.

As a medium, Fleur conducts both one-on-one sessions and performances for large audiences, as well as offering courses on intuition development. Already in her mid-twenties, she was one of the youngest professionals in her field and also one of the most skilled, as I can personally attest.

I have witnessed Fleur in action multiple times and have even attended one of her workshops in my quest for new insights and inspiration.

We met some time ago to exchange our experiences and understandings of perception and communication with the deceased. While my main goal is to explore various environments of the afterlife, Fleur perceives her role primarily as a messenger, giving voice to those who have passed away.

Our discussion quickly revealed how much our experiences overlap. Fleur's pragmatic approach particularly resonates with me, as she regards her gift as a craft that anyone can learn, given sufficient discipline.

Fleur measures her success at the end of a session by whether she has been able to relay detailed and deeply personal information from the life of a deceased person to her clients.

She first came into contact with the spirit world as a preschooler, seeing the dead as tangibly as the living.

"I always tried to protect myself and suppress my perceptions. As a ten-year-old, I had finally reached the point where I was able to close the door."

It wasn't until her first year of medical school that Fleur began to reacquaint herself with her past and rediscover her unique abilities.

"Even though I've redeveloped my perceptual abilities, I generally don't see the deceased in 3D anymore. And I'm grateful for that," she explains.

Fleur receives signals from the deceased through all her perceptual channels. She can feel and hear them and occasionally see them in her mind.

But much of the information is incomplete and partly encrypted.

"Many people believe that an entity whispers information into a medium's ear, as if someone is reading it aloud or as if the medium is mentally watching a complete movie," says Fleur, "but the reality is different. Every now and then, I receive an image, individual fragments, or symbols. I then must piece these parts together like a jigsaw puzzle."

Fleur calls the entities she communicates with souls. To her, they very much continue to exist. From her experience, communication with these souls happens on a specific frequency spectrum.

"The physical body is nothing more than a mass of atoms and molecules vibrating at a certain frequency. When we die and leave our physical body behind, our frequency changes, and we take on a different density," she explains.

When Fleur wants to communicate with non-physical entities, she consciously increases her vibrational frequency while the deceased entities adjust theirs. In Fleur's words, they meet each other halfway.

"To locate this meeting point is like trying to find a small road leading to a major highway on a map. It's a subtle process, you need to know the area extremely well to pinpoint the exact location," she explains.

According to Fleur, the key to successful communication with the spirit realm lies in practice, dedication, and regular meditation.

"The more frequently you make the journey, the faster you reach that point where the worlds converge," she says.

Fleur believes that every entity has its unique energy signature. Each deceased person operates at an individual frequency which slightly differs from the rest. The more accurately you can adjust to these various frequencies, the clearer and more precise the transmission of information will be.

Fleur encourages beginners not to fear making mistakes. She views errors as an integral part of the learning process, suggesting we can always trace our steps back and try again.

"It's incredibly important to understand how it feels to get it wrong as opposed to getting it right. Recognizing the difference teaches you whether you can trust your perception," she says.

At this point, Fleur trusts her perception nearly one hundred percent.

"If someone tells me my information is incorrect, I can discern whether or not they are right. Sometimes they're simply wrong. I'll then ask them to trust me and verify the information when they get home. But you can only make this distinction if you've been wrong enough times."

I had the chance to witness this precise scenario during one of Fleur's public appearances that I attended with my wife and a mutual acquaintance, Catherine. This was Catherine's first time attending a medium's event.

On stage, Fleur constantly moves, pacing back and forth to maintain a stable energy flow. Depending on the duration of the event, she establishes approximately 10 to 15 connections with the afterlife per evening, known as "links."

Initially, Fleur describes specific features or characteristics of the deceased, along with details from their life and cause of death, until someone in the audience recognizes the deceased as a relative or friend.

That evening, Catherine raised her hand when she thought she recognized her late father from Fleur's description. Fleur then addressed her directly and explained that Catherine's father had died from lung disease and had three children.

Catherine immediately objected, saying that she only had one brother, so it couldn't possibly be her father.

"He's definitely showing me a three," Fleur replied calmly but firmly. "I'm absolutely certain that it is your father. I sense him standing beside me right now."

Catherine continued to reject this assertion, but Fleur wouldn't be swayed.

The entire audience watched the exchange with bated breath. Neither woman would back down. Even as Fleur described additional accurate details from her father's life, Catherine remained unconvinced.

When Fleur eventually moved on to establish a new connection, Catherine suddenly exclaimed, "Oh, my God, you're right! He did have three children. My dad had an adopted daughter from another relationship that we never really accepted."

Fleur sighed with relief and could now continue with the reading. To conclude, she described in detail how Catherine had sat at her father's deathbed, holding his hand in the presence of a nurse.

Even in front of an audience of 70 people, Fleur had not hesitated to stick to her seemingly "incorrect" information. After years of practice, she's confident in her perception channels and maintains them through regular meditation.

"My work requires me to be in a very calm mental state," she explains. "When I'm consistently in a stressful environment, I eventually reach my limits and can't connect with my soul or higher self."

This understanding is key to her abilities, Fleur feels.

"We must first learn to establish a connection with our higher self. Only then can we connect with other souls," she says.

When I asked her if she's ever encountered negative energies, Fleur answered, "Never. I've met many bad people here on Earth, but never a bad soul in the spirit world."

She continues, stating that it's indeed possible for deceased individuals to present themselves through negative energy if they did wrong in life.

"If I would describe a formerly bad guy as a beautiful angel, the other person wouldn't know what I'm talking about. As soon as that person realizes whom I'm describing, the energy changes and the guy on the other side presents himself in his positive essence."

Many people find contacting the dead and astral travel eerie and even potentially dangerous.

Personally, I've never felt threatened, harassed, or attacked by beings in the spiritual world. And until now, I have yet to encounter a single demonic entity.

This could be due to my personal interpretation or perhaps the methodology I employ, but any negative energies I have experienced have always turned out to be manifestations of my own mind.

There have been instances where I initially perceived an energy form as negative. Upon closer examination, however, these perceptions invariably turned out not to be separate entities but projections of my own fears or negative thoughts that had taken shape in a non-physical environment.

Non-physical surroundings are highly thought-responsive. This applies to thoughts we project out of our physical reality in waking consciousness as well as those we project during an OBE.

As such, it is normal and expected that we encounter our own—often unconsciously created—manifestations during Out-of-Body Experiences.

Whenever I perceive a negative energy form, I instantly confront it and ask:

"Who are you? What do you want?"

Typically, the perception fades away at this point. If it doesn't, I engage with the energy, trying to establish its source. I believe it's vitally important to approach your own consciousness research fearlessly and not allow yourself to be unsettled by the horror stories of others.

Our thoughts are potent energy carriers that can trigger immediate consequences. Thus, a controlled approach is crucial when experimenting with Out-of-Body Experiences.

Infiltrating non-physical environments can unpredictably impact those who reside there. Astral travelers who breezily navigate the matrix can be perceived as disruptive.

The analogy could be drawn to a poltergeist, an entity from the non-physical realm that projects itself into physical reality and creates a disturbance.

In my experience, a sense of losing control or unclear impressions serve as warning signs. If your perception during an OBE becomes fuzzy or your ability to navigate with reasonable safety and control diminishes, it's advisable to pull back.

Before delving into the depths of the matrix, I recommend attending a workshop or online course to gain the necessary foundational knowledge.

When we focus our consciousness on non-physical surroundings during an OBE, the familiar physical laws we've internalized as ever-present in our physical environment no longer apply.

Concepts like gravity, space, and time cease to exist. Non-physical worlds are characterized by their breathtaking responsiveness to our intentions, and the immediate consequences of this can sometimes be overwhelming.

In our familiar reality, due to its physical laws, there's a certain density that reacts slowly to impulses. For instance, if you want to build a house, it will take considerable time from the inception of the idea of the new home to the moment you hold the keys in your hand. Before this, you will need planning permissions, architectural drawings, negotiations, cost estimates, official permits, potential headaches, and lots of patience since all of this takes a lot of time.

In many non-physical environments, however, the "make a wish" construction laws apply. The mere thought of a new house is enough to manifest it instantly. But it can also collapse just as quickly. Every intention has immediate consequences.

From my experience, each of our manifestations in the non-physical fades if we don't reinforce them with mental power. Yet, each of our intentions leaves subtle energy traces.

Even though it's difficult for me to ascertain how these intrusions appear to a non-physical being or what they cause, we should be mindful of all potential consequences and act responsibly.

An example from my own field of experience is the Park in Focus 27, the reception area of the afterlife. It has been created and is constantly being shaped by the thought power of billions of individual conscious entities.

I perceive this vibratory level as hyper-flexible and clearly recognize the immediate manifestation of intentions and thoughts.

There's a distinct order within this process. All inhabitants seem to possess a certain degree of maturity and mental clarity. Surprisingly, there's no hint of chaos, even though theoretically, a single individual with a flurry of haphazard manifestations could potentially disrupt the local society.

9

A VISIT TO THE AFTERLIFE

"The eternal and the mortal world are not parallel, rather, they are fused."
John O'Donohue, Irish Author and Poet

On October 6th, 2007, as colorful leaves swirled across the Monroe Institute's parking lot, I retrieved my suitcase from Shaaron's car. I had taken a red-eye flight from Los Angeles just hours after concluding my tour guide season with a seventeen-day bus tour from Denver to San Francisco.

Exhaustion was evident on my face, but despite the sleepless night on a packed airplane, I surprisingly felt quite energetic.

Shaaron had graciously picked me up from the Charlottesville airport and treated me to brunch at her favorite restaurant before dropping me off at Monroe.

It had been three years since my last attendance at the *Heartline* program, and for some time, I had felt the urge to return to Virginia to recharge my paranormal batteries.

I had already postponed attending another course twice due to work commitments, and my resulting credit with the institute was about to expire. So, on a whim, I decided to book the *Lifeline* program, even though the course description hadn't entirely convinced me.

The week's primary subject matter was the exploration of Focus 23-27. While the idea of delving into otherworldly dimensions excited me, *Lifeline* went beyond mere exploration. The program involved the concept of service, teaching participants how to assist the deceased who may not immediately transition to Focus 27 but linger in various realms for different reasons.

I wasn't entirely sure if I was the right person for such a task, as I didn't feel particularly drawn to such undertakings.

Robert Monroe, throughout his years of exploration, had numerous encounters with the deceased and embarked on countless journeys into what the Western world commonly refers to as the afterlife.

He first visited Focus 27 in 1965, discovering a picturesque landscape with lush meadows, vibrant flowers, and towering trees, hence the name Park.

Initially, Monroe didn't feel the need to extensively explore this environment, as death didn't captivate his interest at that time. He found other areas more intriguing.

It was only when his wife Nancy was diagnosed with cancer over 20 years later that he felt compelled to revisit the Park. He was astonished by the remarkable discovery he had made nearly a quarter of a century earlier but had disregarded.

Monroe dedicated subsequent years to in-depth research on the Focus levels 23-27, summarizing his experiences and insights in a book titled "Ultimate Journey".

In his writings, Monroe describes the emotional reunion he experienced in the afterlife with Nancy, his beloved wife who had succumbed to cancer and passed away in the summer of 1992.

*

Even in the 21st century, death continues to be a taboo subject for many people. While discussions about life are embraced, conversations about death are often avoided or considered uncomfortable.

It is nearly ironic that mankind collectively avoids the one aspect of life which is inevitable.

For many individuals, their perception of the afterlife is shaped by the teachings of world religions. They seek guidance from religious organizations that provide them with dogmas and doctrines in the form of stories about heaven, hell, and Judgment Day.

Perhaps the idea of reaching one of these places in the vastness of the universe after death, without the option to return, instills fear.

Would people be less afraid of death if they knew that the afterlife is not drastically different from their present reality? What if they understood it as a vast amusement park with endless possibilities instead of the traditional notions of heaven and hell?

Years of traveling through different levels of consciousness have entirely transformed the image of the afterlife that was conveyed to me as a child by my Protestant family in northern Germany. I have pieced together my experiences and the collected information like parts of a jigsaw puzzle.

However, this puzzle remains far from complete—it continues to grow, and I can only begin to grasp its true extent as each answer and insight leads to new questions.

One thing I can state with absolute certainty is that the afterlife is not a distant place.

Our physical world and the "other side" are intricately intertwined, forming part of a complex matrix. Multiple intersecting levels exist within this overall structure.

How could it otherwise be possible to communicate with individuals in the afterlife?

From our limited human perspective, the reality of this matrix is inconceivable. However, we can approach its attributes through analogies.

I like to envision physical reality as the innermost circle in a set of concentric rings. The transitions between these rings can be likened to a permeable membrane that is easier to penetrate from the outside inward than the other way around.

Another analogy to illustrate the relationship between our everyday perception in physical reality and the perspective from the afterlife is that of a Venetian mirror, also known as a two-way mirror.

When we look into the mirror, we only see our reflection and the physical world. However, from the other side, the mirror appears as a transparent pane of glass that offers an unobstructed view of the world behind it.

But these boundaries I describe only exist within the confines of our everyday consciousness. Once we sharpen our senses, the apparent barriers fade away. The membranes become transparent from our perspective, and the mirror's surface transforms into clear glass.

Now, nothing prevents communication or encounters. When we allow our cognitive abilities to reach their full potential, a new perspective emerges. Death is not the end but a return to our original state of being.

However, as long as our awareness remains focused solely on physical reality, we navigate exclusively within the innermost circle of this model I have described.

After we leave our physical bodies, the process of transition occurs. At this moment, we detach from our physical shell, and our consciousness refocuses, leading to the ultimate Out-of-Body Experience.

What happens next is greatly influenced by the belief systems we acquired during our physical lives as well as by the current state of mind we find ourselves in at the time of our passing.

Our personal experiences shape our path while we are alive, and they continue to shape the environment we encounter immediately after death.

For example, those who firmly believe in being welcomed by St. Peter at the gates of heaven are likely to experience exactly that.

They are in a resonance field that reflects their personal expectations. Although their perception of the environment may appear objective, it is subjective in this phase of their existence in the afterlife, based on the individual interpretation of their impressions.

Those who do not adhere to religious beliefs and believe in the finality of death may find themselves in a sort of vacuum after death. They remain there until an impulse prompts them to move on.

It is difficult to determine the duration of this state, as we exist outside the linear concept of time on Earth after transitioning.

Based on my personal experience, I presume that every human being has a soul that is part of a higher-level soul group or oversoul. The oversoul transmits impulses, often through spirit guides, to awaken the deceased from their relatively stagnant state.

This occurs in the interest of the evolutionary development of the oversoul, which aims to reintegrate all the individual parts into a whole.

Basically, the following applies to the newcomer to the afterlife: The stronger the connection to the Higher Self, the faster the expansion of consciousness.

I like to use the analogy that if the connection to the "server" is weak, the "computer" (the individual) can only download a limited amount of data from the internet. But with a fast and robust connection, the download can occur swiftly.

We can also send impulses to deceased people whose perception is limited, impaired, or tarnished after their transition, so their awareness can expand, and their perception evolve.

To facilitate the process, Robert Monroe designed the *Lifeline* program, where participants can explore various aspects of the afterlife in a safe setting and provide support for the deceased. The aim is to serve both their own well-being and that of others.

When I arrived in Virginia, I had no expectations and was completely unprepared. However, at this stage, I knew that every

Monroe program offered tremendous potential for personal development.

My only concern was that I might end up among a group of grieving individuals seeking to contact their deceased loved ones. But this concern quickly dissolved when I met the fourteen explorers from different parts of the world, each armed with a healthy sense of humor.

Despite their diverse backgrounds, including a medical student from Helsinki, a lawyer from Ohio, and a business coach from Florida, they all shared a common desire to catch a glimpse of the afterlife.

Right from the beginning, the mood among the participants was filled with positive energy, preventing any emotional heaviness.

Having arrived this time with no agenda of my own and no specific expectations, *Lifeline* turned out to be a game-changing experience for me.

My attitude towards Out-of-Body Experiences had significantly changed over the years. I now saw every experience as a gift, regardless of how it manifested.

I no longer felt frustrated when approaching an OBE. My newfound serenity benefited me in all aspects of my waking consciousness and during my explorations through diverse dimensions.

On the first evening, I had the pleasure of meeting Pamela from Florida. She was in her mid-fifties and had recently lost her husband to cancer. Despite this great tragedy, Pam displayed surprising balance and a zest for life.

As we conversed, we discovered commonalities that sparked engaging discussions. Pam worked as a business coach and consultant near Tampa, and we both wondered if *Lifeline* was the right program for us.

"I have no idea what this is truly about," she admitted with a smile, relieved when I confessed to sharing the same uncertainty.

Pam had a hunch that our spirit guides may have played a role in leading us to choose this program.

The following morning, our trainers, Patty Ray Avalon and Lee Stone, prepared us for the course and the upcoming Hemi-Sync exercises.

Thanks to the positive group energy and the trainers' sensitivity, I quickly embraced the subject and the meditations despite my initial doubts.

To my surprise, I found natural and anxiety-free access to the targeted Focus levels beyond physical reality, even if my perceptions were initially vague and imprecise.

Consequently, I eagerly listened to the reports of other participants, some of whom had already received clear impressions and made contact with the deceased on the first day.

Throughout the week, Pam and I regularly met during breaks and meals. Over coffee, she casually mentioned that she had established a connection with her deceased husband.

"I didn't really expect it, but I actually met John during the last meditation."

"I'm delighted for you," I replied.

However, Pam didn't seem entirely happy.

"It may sound a little strange, and of course, I'm very grateful to have met John, but I had hoped to see someone else, to be honest."

Uncertain of how to respond, I began to ask a question, but our conversation was interrupted by another participant who was eager to share. I wished I could have known whom Pam had wanted to contact instead of her husband.

Later in the evening, a journey to Focus 27 was on the program, which is the place that Robert Monroe referred to as the Park. According to his description, this non-physical environment, among other things, encompasses a reception area for newcomers, a planning office, a coordination center, a comprehensive library, and a center for regeneration and healing.

With the intention to explore the healing center, I headed to my CHEC Unit that evening. Filled with trust and relaxation, I allowed the Hemi-Sync frequencies to carry me to the energy field of Focus 27.

Initially, I felt a distinct and uncomfortable pressure on my temples which I attributed to the unfamiliar frequencies. It took a few minutes before I could disregard the pressure and fully focus on the exercise.

Apart from a bright fog, I couldn't perceive a distinct environment at first. So I reinforced my intention to find the healing center and sought assistance from my team.

As soon as I mentally voiced my request, the image in my mind's eye began to clarify.

The following is an excerpt from my notes dating back to 2007:

I find myself standing in front of a glass door, which leads to a building bathed in a pleasant light. I hear voices around me, but I cannot attribute them to anyone in particular. The door opens at the moment I have the thought of wanting to pass through it.

Everywhere I look, there is an abundance of light. There are no shadows to be found.

It takes a moment for me to recognize contrasts in my surroundings.

I move purposefully toward a room at the far end of the corridor and pause in front of the open door. Intuitively, I perceive the room as a treatment room.

"Welcome!" a voice suddenly emerges from nowhere.

I cautiously reply with a greeting, not knowing with whom I am communicating.

In the room, I see a pale figure lying on a bed by the window, while a man with Asian features, whom I perceive as a physician, stands at the foot of the bed.

As a matter of course, he greets me and introduces himself as Dr. Phil. He kindly but firmly requests that I closely observe the treatment he is about to administer to his patient.

Dr. Phil crouches down and places his palms near the soles of the patient's feet without actually touching them. I distinctly sense a powerful energy flow emanating from the physician's hands, streaming into the patient's soles.

The entire room is illuminated, and moments later, the patient begins to move his arms and legs. The two men briefly converse, but I am unable to follow their words. Nonetheless, both appear pleased.

Dr. Phil turns to me and explains that the energy treatment was highly intense and rejuvenating for the patient.

Curious, I ask him if I can learn this type of treatment and apply it on the physical plane.

He responds, "No, a physical body would not withstand it, but I can teach you something that you can readily apply without hesitation."

He beckons me to take his place at the foot of the bed. Intuitively, I place my hands near the patient's feet, feeling a spiral of glowing energy flowing from my palms into the patient's body.

Dr. Phil nods approvingly and says, "Well done. Just like that."

The treatment concludes within seconds.

As I rise, I notice a second doctor in the room. He is a very tall man with striking blue eyes and thick black hair. He seems incredibly delighted about my presence.

"I am David," he introduces himself. "I am now employed here. You can tell her that. I'm doing well, and I love my work."

David exudes a contagious sense of happiness.

Curious, I inquire, "Whom am I supposed to tell?"

Without directly answering, he continues, "Here, we primarily treat new arrivals who were very ill or died in accidents."

David extends his hand to me, revealing a chunky gold ring adorned with an engraved coat of arms.

"She will recognize me through this. Send her my love and tell her that Dr. Dave feels fine and dandy."

Before I can respond, my perception becomes hazy, and darkness envelops me.

Upon returning to waking consciousness, I immediately reached for pen and paper.

The words "Dr. Dave feels fine and dandy" echoed in my mind. It all seemed so absurd. After jotting down my notes, I tried to make sense of what had transpired.

I knew it wasn't a dream, but what exactly was it?

During our group gathering, Pam, who was seated across from me, waved and smiled.

Uncertain if I had fantasized about everything, I mustered the courage to share my experience when the trainers inquired.

I spoke about Dr. Phil and the energy transfer he had allowed me to perform on his patient.

Hesitantly, I added, "And then there was another doctor who called himself Dr. Dave."

After a brief pause, I concluded, "Dr. Dave feels fine and dandy."

Pam struggled to suppress a sharp cry. She abruptly got up and rushed out of the room.

"I'll be back in a minute!" her voice echoed seconds later from the stairs.

Pam was beside herself when she returned soon after, holding a photo in her hands. I couldn't believe my eyes when I saw the image of the blue-eyed man with black hair.

"That's him. That's Dr. Dave," I exclaimed.

Tears welled up in Pam's eyes.

"I know," she sobbed. "He's my brother. David was an oncologist. He died three years ago from a blood disorder. During our last phone conversation, he said: 'Don't worry, sister. Dr. Dave feels fine and dandy'."

I was left speechless. David's words had deeply touched not just Pam, who had hoped for a sign from him, but also me, a total stranger whose worldview had been shaken by the experience.

When I shared with the group about the golden ring that David had shown me, silence enveloped the room. It was his fraternity ring, which he had worn until his passing and bequeathed to Pam in his will.

Now it was clear what encounter Pam had been longing for.

*

Since the *Lifeline* program, I have visited the healing and regeneration center many times. Interestingly, the building takes on different forms during each visit. Sometimes it resembles a typical hospital, while at other times it appears more like a vacation resort.

The description of the healing center may sound like something that could exist in a similar form here on Earth.

However, I am aware that my perceptions are metaphorical. They represent symbolic expressions of information that my brain receives and translates into a language or symbolism that I can comprehend. Without the use of metaphors, our limited human minds would struggle to categorize and integrate non-physical impressions.

I am particularly drawn to the healing center in Focus 27. Perhaps this is why my perceptions there are often more vivid and distinct compared to other locations.

Despite the ever-changing appearance of the building, I frequently encounter individuals I have met during previous visits. Dr. Phil is a prime example of this. Merely thinking of him instantly directs my focus toward him.

Over the years, Dr. Phil has answered many of my questions and assisted me in locating deceased individuals I sought within the healing center.

But why is there a need for a healing center in a realm where the physical body is no longer part of our existence?

Immediately after death, a person's spirit remains in a state similar to that before passing. The speed at which an individual's awareness adjusts to the new situation varies based on numerous factors.

From my understanding, there are individuals who continue to perceive their bodies after death. In cases where the body was afflicted by disease, or the cause of death was a severe injury, the person may still expect or require treatment or regeneration.

The same applies to individuals with mental illness, who undergo an adjustment period and are gently acquainted with their new circumstances.

According to my observations, the inhabitants of Focus 27 can choose their appearance freely. Some prefer to manifest in a human-like form, while others forgo it. Such fluidity is difficult for us to comprehend, but in Focus 27, it is entirely normal.

Every deceased person is welcomed in the Park according to their individual needs, taking into consideration their cultural and religious backgrounds. Consequently, the reception of an indigenous person from the Amazon rainforest would differ significantly from that of someone from Austria, Syria, or China.

The following excerpt from my records describes my initial visit to the reception area:

After going through the preparatory process, it only takes seconds for me to feel the familiar state of Focus 10 distinctly. My body is asleep, while my mind is fully awake.

I can clearly perceive the gradual changes in the Hemi-Sync signals, causing my awareness of the physical surroundings to vanish completely.

At first, I see a warm, yellowish glow, followed by a clear and bright light. From an aerial perspective, I discern indistinct and hazy structures.

As the view becomes clearer, I realize that instead of the expected park with trees and meadows, there is a massive semicircular portal.

In front of it, there is a long line of check-in counters, resembling the organized entrance to an amusement park.

The queues of people waiting seem endless, yet there is an air of calmness without any sign of impatience.

As I fly briefly over the heads of the new arrivals towards the entrance, one man in the crowd points at me and exclaims, "Hey! You're not dead. How did you get here?"

I am taken aback and feel exposed. Without answering him, I swiftly distance myself from the crowd and pass through the check-in area at a safe height.

Beneath me, a huge park area opens up where people are reuniting and embracing each other with joy. I notice children, cats, and dogs among them. While I would love to approach a group, I don't want to interrupt their blissful reunion, so I keep my distance.

Overwhelmed by the multitude of impressions, I leave the Park and feel the need to record my experience. I ask my spirit guides to accompany me and inquire if everyone is welcomed by their loved ones after they pass away.

In response, my team transmits a thought ball—a particular form of telepathic communication that instantly conveys complex knowledge.

The contents of the thought ball are precise: In Focus 27, we are welcomed by those who are spiritually aligned with us and on the same evolutionary path. Typically, these individuals are our relatives and friends. However, they can also be religious figures or angels that the deceased identified with during their lifetime.

Regardless, the purpose of the greeting ceremony is to facilitate the transition from the physical to the non-physical realm for all who return home.

Just like the healing center, I also perceive the immediate reception area in Focus 27 differently on each visit. It is, however, interesting that the area behind the check-in is always a park.

During the *Lifeline* program, nearly everyone in the group shared this observation.

After we had visited the Park several times, the trainers prepared us for a special task.

"This will be your first opportunity to accompany individuals from Focus 23 to Focus 27," Lee explained. "These are people who didn't directly go to the Park after they passed but are lingering in an in-between or transitional level."

The idea is to support individuals in their evolutionary process by paving the way out of Focus 23 to the Park for them. Robert Monroe referred to this process as soul retrieval.

I simply couldn't imagine how this works. I also seriously questioned if I, of all people, would be the right person for the job.

10

RETURNING HOME BY DETOUR

"All things are ready, if our mind be so."
William Shakespeare, English Poet, and Playwright

In Focus 23 reside those who have transitioned to the afterlife with clouded consciousness and consequently limited perceptual abilities. The causes for this condition can be diverse and multifaceted.

Expectations and beliefs held during their physical life may contribute to this state as well as personal attachments to earthly life. But it can also be a consequence of sudden or unexpected death. The circumstances surrounding their transition can impact their ability to fully understand and perceive their new non-physical reality.

Some individuals in Focus 23 deny their death and try to continue participating in earthly affairs for various reasons, such as unresolved matters or a reluctance to separate from familiar energy forms.

Those struggling with addictions may also remain in Focus 23 as they seek resonance with the familiar stimulation they experienced in their physical lives.

However, there are also individuals who voluntarily linger in this in-between level because they don't want to leave grieving loved ones behind. Often, the newly transitioned are held back by the intense suffering of those in the physical world.

In many cases, their spirit guides are unable to reach them due to incompatible vibrational frequencies.

From our vantage point, we have a greater chance of attracting their attention because we are rooted in the physical and, thus, closer to their vibrational frequency.

The process of assisting lost souls follows a simple protocol: First, I ask my spirit team to take me where I am most needed. Once I perceive an individual, I attempt to establish contact and initiate communication in the next step.

Creative approaches are required because the individuals involved usually have limited perceptual abilities. Once contact is established, I strive to gain the trust of the person and gently convey to them that their transition from the physical to the non-physical world has already occurred, and their loved ones are waiting for them elsewhere.

During the conversation, I often sense the presence of one or more entities ready to accompany the individual to the Park. Sometimes, I guide them there myself. At the entrance to the Park, the spirit guides are always present to take over.

The duration of a retrieval varies, ranging from seconds to several minutes, and there are instances where it may not be successful due to a lack of readiness, trust, or denial from the individual in Focus 23.

The trainers at *Lifeline* encouraged us to gather as much information as possible about the deceased individuals as soon as the contact is stable enough, and providing the situation allows for such action. This information, including names, nationalities, details of their death, and other relevant facts, can later be used to verify the experience.

As I prepared myself mentally for the journey, I could feel the weight of responsibility. Lying in my CHEC Unit, I wondered if I would be able to find someone who needed or wanted my assistance. In theory, everything Patty and Lee had explained sounded plausible and easy. But what if I made a mistake?

It soon turned out that my concerns proved unfounded as I quickly encountered a visual impression upon entering the energy field of Focus 23. Before I quote the description of what happened from my journal, I would once again like to point out that I changed the names and locations in these notes out of respect for the families and loved ones of those I met.

I float weightlessly through a vacuum space whose structure appears unfamiliar and can hardly be described in words. I feel neither density nor resistance. I have absolutely no sense of temperature.

It is dark around me, yet I have the impression of being able to see. At first, only vague shapes, but then suddenly, everything becomes very clear.

Right in front of me, I perceive the form of an older woman. She stands in her kitchen at the stove, absentmindedly stirring a pot with a wooden spoon. First clockwise, then counterclockwise. She repeatedly wipes her forehead with the sleeve of her apron.

The woman appears exhausted, her calves bandaged and her well-worn shoes flat.

The kitchen furniture evokes memories of my grandmother's time – bright wooden kitchen cabinets and a gray-mottled countertop. The gas stove looks antique, and the sink is made of tin. The smell of cooked beans with bacon fills the air.

Approaching the old woman, I position myself at her right side. Absorbed in her task, she remains oblivious to my presence.

"Hello," I say softly, cautious not to startle her.

However, she doesn't react. As she tastes the food from the wooden spoon, her hands tremble, and her pale, wrinkled face wears a weary expression. Placing the spoon back into the pot, she turns around and locks eyes with me, causing me to hold my breath.

I step back, startled, as she suddenly moves to the right to open a drawer.

I look down at myself and realize in amazement that I am hovering just above the floor. What is happening here?

I become disoriented momentarily, surrounded by haziness. Then, a distant foghorn sounds, and Robert Monroe's quiet voice echoes in my ear, reminding me of my intention and purpose.

The image of the old woman comes into focus once again, prompting me to find a way to capture her attention.

"Hello!" I assert, with increased determination and volume.

Still, there is no reaction. Deciding to make a bold move, I concentrate my energy on the stove, intending to raise the gas flame.

Shouting as loudly as I can, I exclaim, "Hello, Mrs...."

The gas flame flares up.

Startled, the old woman whispers, "Salm. Else... Salm."

Her voice sounds fragile.

I'm astonished by the clarity with which I hear her.

She adjusts the gas back down.

Curious about my presence, she asks, "Who are you? And how did you get into my apartment?"

In response, I offer, "The front door was open, and the aroma of bean stew was enticing."

It's the best reply I can think of.

Our eyes meet.

"My name is Oliver," I introduce myself. "Oliver Tappe."

"Do we know each other?"

"We don't," I admit truthfully. "I'm new to the area."

"New in Frankfurt?"

"You could say that. I've just arrived. What year is it?"

Confusion appears on her face as she replies, "1976. But why do you ask?"

Feeling anxious, I shrug my shoulders. At this early stage, I can't tell Else Salm why I asked that question.

"Have you seen my husband?" she enquires.

Before I can answer her, she puts the wooden spoon into the sink, wipes her hands on her smock, and turns to face me.

"He's just not coming home," she laments. "I've been waiting and waiting, but he's not returning. I don't understand. Lunch has been ready for a while. I stand here, stirring the stew to prevent it from burning. Where can he be?"

She gazes at me with concern, questioning whether something may have happened to him.

Delicately, I try to determine the best approach, aiming to earn her trust.

"Mrs. Salm, I know where your husband is. I can take you to him," I assert, startled by how effortlessly the words leave my mouth.

How could I possibly know where her husband is? Yet, I cannot let her sense my uncertainty, so I extend my hand to her.

"Come with me," I urge.

She hesitates, unsure.

Encouragingly, I smile, and after a moment's pause, the old lady decides to follow me.

However, she suddenly exclaims, "Wait a minute! The stove! I must turn it off."

Before she can turn away from me, the scene around us shifts abruptly, and we find ourselves standing at the bottom of a magnificent staircase. The grandeur of the wide steps reminds me of the foyer of an old opera house.

Without warning, a male figure appears at the top of the stairs, though his face remains hidden from view. Soon, he stands before us, extending his hand to Mrs. Salm.

Mesmerized, I watch as she accepts his invitation. As their hands touch, the entire backdrop vanishes, and I am once again back in the airless space from before. Within seconds, I open my physical eyes.

Who was that figure? A spirit guide, maybe? Or perhaps even her husband?

And who was Else Salm from Frankfurt anyway? Why did I end up in her kitchen of all places?

So many questions go through my head. None of them can be answered quickly.

I replayed the experience in my mind, and I realized that at the beginning of the episode, I had not perceived any colors. Everything was in black and white until the moment when the grand staircase opened up.

I still don't know the reason for this, but over time I have noticed that similar phenomena occur again and again. My perception of color does not begin until the end of the experience.

Many of the other participants also had impressive experiences during the meditation and brought back very detailed information.

Nonetheless, my inner skeptic was working overtime. It would only be at peace once my gathered data passed verification. I needed confirmation that Else Salm had indeed lived and passed away in Frankfurt in 1976.

As a former journalist, I later contacted the local registration office. A pleasant and extremely helpful employee checked the files and did, in fact, find an entry about the woman's death. Her name, the location, and the year of her death matched. My perception hadn't deceived me.

What initially irritated me was the fact that Mrs. Salm had been continually stirring her stew in Focus 23 since 1976. The idea that something similar could happen to me at some stage began to worry me. Who in their right mind would want to stir the same pot for 31 years?

During later retrievals, I assisted individuals whose physical lifetimes dated back even further.

This may sound alarming from our perspective. But the timespan is irrelevant as Focus 23 is beyond physical reality and, therefore, outside our linear earthly time. Mrs. Salm didn't have any sense of time and didn't feel trapped either.

My concern was based solely on the projection of earthly laws onto Mrs. Salm's non-physical kitchen. From a physical point of view, it would also be incomprehensible why the stew was still spreading its aroma after 31 years on the stove.

Overall, relatively few individuals linger in Focus 23. Most people's consciousness is lucid after their transition, and they go straight to the Park assisted by their spirit team.

Apart from Focus 23, Bob Monroe defined three further levels: Focus 24, 25, and 26. According to him, these environments are occupied by individuals who, while still alive, adopted and internalized strict and specific believe systems regarding their existence after their physical demise.

These include religious groups, indigenous peoples, and individuals caught up in their own beliefs and expectations.

I have made only a few excursions into these planes because I got the impression that intruders were not welcome.

My perception is that the inhabitants feel generally well taken care of. Their evolution has apparently come to a standstill. Only when they become aware of their situation do they turn to their spirit guides and move on.

A sense of time doesn't exist on these levels either. Although from my earthly perspective, it may seem as if these individuals stayed for decades on an in-between level, such temporal contexts do not exist for them.

Personally, I prefer working in Focus 23 as it offers the opportunity to collect verifiable data. I have trusted the process for a long time now, but it is still reassuring to receive additional confirmation.

The following case from the year 2016 particularly touched me and occupied my thoughts for a long time. During a workshop at the Monroe Institute, I had intended to visit the Park in Focus 27, but my spirit team had other plans for me.

I had barely finished my resonant tuning process and mentally voiced my affirmation when I was suddenly transported to an unfamiliar location. As I do in every exercise, I made every effort to perceive and memorize as many details as possible.

I am standing on a grass and tree-lined country road with the wreck of a passenger car diagonally in front of me. About 60 feet away from the car, I perceive a ten to twelve-year-old boy surrounded by a foggy beam of light. As I move towards him, I intuitively know that he didn't survive the accident.

"What's your name?" I ask him.

The boy looks at me in surprise.

"Chris," he replies.

I repeat the question to ensure that I heard him correctly.

"Christopher," he says this time.

He seems apathetic, neither doing well nor badly. He's simply standing there. Even my presence, which he obviously perceives, apparently doesn't surprise him.

I try to look inside the car wreck, but I can't. Yet I intuitively know that at least another two, if not three, people were involved in the accident, including more children.

In my mind, five letters form a surname. I set an anchor for myself to remember the full name later when I return to waking consciousness.

When I turn around to face the boy again, the scene around me briefly changes, and as if in a kind of playback, I see the entire sequence of the accident from the perspective of a bystander: A truck skids and blocks the road. The car Christopher is in speeds toward the truck, slams into it, overturns, and lands on its roof on the side of the road.

I manage to stay calm despite the dramatic images. The scene of the accident fades, and I turn back to the boy. I ask him what year it is and telepathically receive a clear reply.

I invite Christopher to follow me. When I extend my hand to him, he lets me know that he's unable to walk.

I decide to carry him and ask my spirit team to guide us to Focus 27. The scene changes as soon as I hold the boy in my arms, and we float through a cosmic vortex.

Once my perception becomes more distinct again, I recognize a large fun fair with wooden stalls leading to a Ferris wheel.

At this very moment, I hear the speaker's voice of the exercise from a distance:

"It is now time to return. Express your gratitude to those who accompanied and supported you on your mission."

I put Christopher down on the ground. He seems far more relaxed now and even smiles. There's hardly time to say goodbye as the Hemi-Sync signals take me back to waking consciousness.

I try to resist them, but I'm too excited to keep focused. Seconds later, I open my eyes.

I didn't waste any time and picked up my cell phone right away. My perceptions had been clear, and I also had enough information to do some research. My heart was pounding as I Googled Christopher, the surname, and the year I had been given.

Moments later, I was reading an article by a local TV station about a car accident in which Christopher, his brother, and his father had lost their lives.

The surname and the year were correct, as well as the description of the accident, as I had perceived it in Focus 23.

At the time, Christopher and his family had been on their way from a sports event to the fun fair. More than likely, Christopher had been looking forward to the carnival and had high expectations.

This explained why the two of us headed for the Ferris wheel after I'd picked him up. My intention had been to take him to Focus 27, but for Christopher, the reception area was a fun fair.

Christopher's touching fate kept haunting me. I wondered daily what had become of the little boy. Although I had left him in Focus 27 with the best intentions, I had not perceived anyone who had taken care of him.

A few days after returning home from the Monroe Institute, I decided to look for the boy again. I couldn't rest until I was sure that he wasn't alone.

I had just reached the energy field of Focus 27 when I got a surprise. Another boy, who introduced himself as Christopher's brother Nick, approached me to express his gratitude.

I was deeply touched. And then I saw Christopher as well. He was smiling contentedly. Now I knew for certain that he was definitely in the right place.

As I've already mentioned, most people are welcomed by their loved ones in the Park soon after their transition. Why Christopher's consciousness had been anchored elsewhere for a number of years is incomprehensible in retrospect, and perhaps it is not even relevant in the bigger picture. He had not suffered, nor was he aware of a long period of time spent in Focus 23.

In the same way that I reunited with Christopher in Focus 27, anyone can learn to project their consciousness into the Park to spend time with friends or loved ones there.

However, Individuals from the afterlife can also meet us part of the way. Once they lower their vibrational frequency, we can recognize them in a state of expanded awareness. Our perception of them is accordingly subtle. We get the impression of a presence and, for example, sense, feel, or smell the deceased.

Such phenomena are a sign that there's an open communication channel. With a little practice, a stable flow of information can be established from these kinds of situations.

So, there are various ways of making contact, similar to using different apps to communicate with each other in our physical reality.

With the transition from physical to non-physical existence, our energetic vibration changes. We adapt to new environments, which have a much lower density than the physical plane.

Therefore, it is incredibly challenging for the deceased to make themselves physically noticeable to us because of their subtle nature. Yet there are frequent cases where they manipulate matter or electromagnetic waves or even manifest themselves three-dimensionally to give us signs.

To my surprise, it became increasingly apparent during the *Lifeline* program that I could easily establish contact with the inhabitants on the other side even back then.

One specific exercise aimed at gathering as much detailed information as possible about a total stranger.

Each participant in the course wrote the first and last name of a deceased person from their family or circle of acquaintances on a piece of paper and placed it in a bowl. By drawing lots, we then received our subject for the upcoming meditation.

I drew the name Bobby Degman and didn't even know if the individual was male or female.

The trainers had shown us various approaches to solve the task as successfully as possible.

Following the preparatory process, I allowed myself to be guided to Focus 27 by the Hemi-Sync frequencies, of course not without asking for support from my team beforehand through an affirmation.

I'm moving through a milky light and losing any sense of space. Nothing is happening, and I'm about to give up and think about returning to waking consciousness.

But then, I start to discern faint contrasts in the fog. In the distance, I see a large, circular building.

As I get closer, I realize that the sides of the building are open, with no doors or windows. I land directly beside a counter that serves as a kind of reception. I find myself alone in the huge hall.

I shout, "Are you here, Bobby?"

There's no response.

I try again, "Bobby Degman, please talk to me!"

Still, no reply. That's when I notice a service bell on the counter and ring it twice. The sound of the bell echoes through the hall.

Suddenly, as if out of nowhere, a young woman in a dark uniform appears in front of me.

"I'm looking for someone called Bobby Degman."

The lady pauses for a few seconds. She appears to be contemplating intently.

"Bobby can't be contacted at the moment," she says distantly. "Is there anything else I can do for you?"

My mind threatens to take over. The situation is simply too absurd. The reception, the indifferent woman, the large hall …

So I ask, "Could you perhaps provide me with some information about Bobby?"

She looks upward, and at that very moment, I receive various images that do not seem to have any particular connection to each other.

First, I see a typical bungalow with an open-plan kitchen and a spacious living area with white French doors leading to a large patio.

Then, an image of a fenced swimming pool in a relatively small garden appears to me. It is followed by the image of light blue children's shoes lying on a lawn next to the pool.

Inside the house, I perceive a young couple. The woman is standing in the kitchen, and as she opens one of the wall cabinets, numerous small colorful plastic balls come flying out towards her. There are more and more of them, and it seems like the kitchen and the woman are about to be engulfed by the balls.

Before everything around me vanishes in the misty light again, I notice a red toy tractor in the front yard of the house.

I linger in the light and imprint the images in my mind, trying to prevent them from slipping away on the way back to waking consciousness.

Following the meditation, I carefully recorded a list of my perceptions, as Patty and Lee had instructed us not to interpret or distort any of the information we received.

"Just because it doesn't make any sense to you doesn't mean that the information is not important for someone else," Patty had explained.

I strictly focused on the few images that I could consciously remember.

It turned out that Bobby Degman was the nephew of Brenda, an elderly participant from Minnesota. My notes deeply touched her.

"Bobby drowned in his parents' pool when he was two years old in 1973," Brenda tearfully recounted to me.

Apparently, the boy's father had forgotten to close the gate to the pool and had left him unattended for a few moments while preparing dinner. Brenda's brother never forgave himself for that fatal mistake.

The little boy had loved the colorful plastic balls the family kept in a large net in a storeroom. The tractor I had perceived had also been one of Bobby's favorite toys.

Although I never met little Bobby in Focus 27, I had brought back reliable information, and I was extremely satisfied with the result.

Communication with the departed is only possible if both sides are open to it. Loved ones often have a strong desire to contact us after their transition and will seize any opportunity to do so.

Sometimes they simply want us to know that they're okay, while other times they may have specific objectives, like seeking forgiveness or expressing their love for those they left behind.

However, there are situations where a deceased individual may not want any contact, reflecting their reluctance during their lifetime.

By the way, I'm often asked if I can communicate with Michael Jackson or other celebrities in the afterlife. But why would Michael Jackson talk to me after he died if we didn't have a personal relationship during his life?

However, if someone close to Michael Jackson, such as a member of his immediate family or entourage, were to request a medium to act as an intermediary, then an energetic connection would be established, and more than likely, communication could be made.

A crucial factor that can determine success or failure in attempting contact is our own emotional state. Oppressive emotions such as grief, despair, anger, or fear resonate at a very low frequency, making clear perceptions difficult or even impossible.

On the other hand, positive emotions, especially joy, love, and gratitude, create harmony and are very beneficial in establishing contact, as they are much closer to the frequency range of the deceased.

11

DISCOVERIES AND INSIGHTS IN FOCUS 27

"Seeing death as the end of life is like seeing the horizon as the end of the ocean."
David "Doc" Searls, American Author

Participating in the *Lifeline* program considerably enriched my life and gave it a new direction. After the program, I was well able to integrate what I'd learned and continue to apply my newly acquired skills.

I soon noticed that I could easily access Focus 27 even without the corresponding Hemi-Sync signals. Of all the consciousness levels I had experienced thus far, I found myself most drawn to this region.

The Park has become a place I regularly visit in my meditations.

Over the following years, I attended the *Exploration 27* program several times. This program allows for a more in-depth exploration of the Park's various regions. Participants investigate the different facilities both individually and as a group, gathering pertinent data.

The collective expeditions are particularly thrilling because everyone's experiences can be compared afterward. It never ceased to astound me how many details overlapped, despite everyone meditating individually in their CHEC Units.

Following my initial group experience in Focus 27, I discussed the outcomes with my fellow astral traveler Mara. Over the years, she had evolved into a close friend and mentor, consistently offering valuable insights when I reached my own boundaries.

Mara believed that I was now ready for advanced exploration. She proposed to investigate an aspect of my soul I hadn't been aware of before.

What did she mean? During one of her Out-of-Body Experiences, Mara had met an aspect of my greater Self in Focus 27. Initially, her narrative sounded like science fiction to me. She vaguely described this part of me as regularly participating in an activity that somewhat paralleled what I was doing in my physical life.

It all sounded a little cryptic, but Mara had a plan. She proposed to lead me to this part of my soul during a joint OBE in Focus 27.

This excursion would be the first of many journeys into nonphysical environments as a team.

The concept of meeting an unfamiliar aspect of my greater Self or my soul was hard for me to grasp. It provided ample food for thought.

My anticipation heightened as the scheduled day drew closer. We agreed to convene at the Park's entrance at eight in the evening.

I'm having trouble relaxing. It's not working on demand today. I'm doing a breathing exercise from yoga. Finally, my mind is calming down. Hopefully not too late – is Mara already at the agreed-upon location, waiting?

I let the sound frequencies carry me, visualizing the tunnel I've flown through so often to reinforce my intention.

Click-out.

When I regain consciousness, I find myself in a forest clearing. It takes a moment to remember my purpose – Mara!

I need to find Mara. As soon as this thought crosses my mind, the scene changes, and I am suddenly standing by a small body of water.

"I'm glad you made it."

Although the energy behind those words comes from Mara, the figure beside me resembles a giant elf.

"Don't let my appearance irritate you. You also seem different to me than how you perceive yourself.

Evidently, this being can read my thoughts.

"Take my hand," it says.

"How do I know that it's you, Mara?"

Instead of responding, the elf-like figure seizes my arm. I feel restless and anxious.

"Maintain your focus," the entity says sternly.

Within seconds, we're soaring above the water, crossing meadows and treetops towards a large building complex in the heart of the landscape.

I consciously close my mental eyes as we are heading straight toward a rooftop. (Note: Some processes during an OBE may seem irrational to my mind, causing me to snap back to waking consciousness at times. When my thought process starts to become active, I initiate a brief blackout.)

Upon landing, I no longer perceive the elf-like being beside me but Mara in her actual form.

"Where are we?" I ask.

In front of me, there is a long corridor with doors, and behind me, there is a staircase. I have an almost perfect 360-degree view.

Alongside each door is a floor-to-ceiling window several feet wide.

"This is an educational facility," Mara explains as she points at one of the windows. "Take a look inside."

To me, the room resembles a classroom from the '70s. Approximately 40 entities sit at paired desks, listening to a teacher slowly pacing between the rows.

It's only when I fully focus on the man that I recognize him. I'm taken aback.

"That's me!"

"Well spotted," Mara laughs.

"What am I doing?" I ask.

"You can refocus your awareness and adopt his, or rather your other, perspective."

I heed her advice and suddenly find myself speaking, though I can't comprehend my own words. Simultaneously, I see Mara and myself standing behind the window.

My consciousness abruptly snaps back.

"I am a teacher?" I ask, surprised.

"The students in your classroom are new arrivals. You are preparing them for their new opportunities in Focus 27."

I sense my focus threatening to fade.

"Let's go back," Mara suggests, reaching for my arm again.

The return to waking consciousness is gradual but seamless.

The Hemi-Sync recording was still playing when I removed my headphones. It took me a significant amount of time to fully reconnect with my physical body and to document my experience.

I chose not to call Mara that evening, as I wanted to fully process and internalize what had happened before my perception might potentially be influenced by hers.

A surprise awaited me the following day.

"When did you initiate your OBE?" Mara inquired.

"At eight in the evening, as we agreed. Why do you ask?"

"I also began at eight, but eight my time. It was only six o'clock your time."

I gasped. I hadn't considered the time difference between California and Colorado when planning our journey.

"Time is irrelevant in Focus 27," Mara informed me. "By the way, I also work at the education center we visited. We are effectively colleagues."

It was an unbelievable experience the mind finds challenging to comprehend. Mara and I had shared an OBE. We perceived each other as "travel companions", despite embarking on our individual journeys at separate times.

We decided to explore this phenomenon further and arranged regular joint trips to examine our "discovery" in more depth.

Our hypothesis: A specific, aligned intention can result in a shared experience in the non-physical, even if each of us independently decides the timing of our OBE.

Instead of agreeing on a specific day and time, we merely specified a rough time frame of approximately one week. Regardless of the exact day we each selected, we encountered each other multiple times at the agreed-upon locations.

However, not every journey or meeting was successful. In some instances, our perceptions didn't align. Yet, just as many of our experiences confirmed that time is indeed an illusion—at least in non-physical realms.

How else could encounters like these occur?

My travels with Mara imparted an important revelation: Humans are multidimensional beings. I now consider that we exist concurrently in various dimensions. In addition to incarnations on other levels, this might also include so-called reincarnations on Earth.

What we usually refer to as reincarnation is predicated on our limited linear human understanding. I find it more plausible to conceive of reincarnation within a parallel and/or overlapping frame of reference.

*

Every stay in Focus 27 has helped me to regard death and dying from a new and anxiety-free perspective.

Of course, there are times when I wonder what dying might feel like. Some fears can't be easily dismissed. They serve as survival mechanisms in our physical reality, like fear of falling or abrupt, loud noises.

I also experience discomfort when a plane encounters turbulence or when another earthquake rattles Los Angeles. A common fear many of us share is that of an agonizing death.

However, the insights I've received from my spirit team and other intelligent beings on the other side are incredibly comforting.

From their perspective, the awareness of most individuals undergoing what we perceive as a horrific death has already shifted to a non-physical environment at the moment of trauma. In other words, the soul departs the body before the shock is fully felt.

There is no reason for the soul to endure a traumatic transition. This also explains why several of the deceased I have been in contact with have no distinct memory of their passing.

Some didn't even comprehend what had occurred until it was explained to them post-transition or revealed during a life review.

This isn't to suggest that the soul always opts for the path of least resistance. Certain elements of the dying process are an integral part of our earthly incarnation and are consciously experienced—insofar as these elements contribute to or are essential for our growth.

This may include enduring a challenging death.

The thought of having to leave our dear Earth behind when we die fuels numerous fears in most people. In my perspective, these fears are baseless. During the dying process, our consciousness is liberated from the confines of our physical condition, leading to an expansion of our perception.

Dying isn't a shift to another location but rather a transformation.

Even though our energetic density changes after our physical passing, we are still ourselves. And this is precisely how we perceive ourselves post-transition—inclusive of all the experiences gathered during our lifetime.

Without the physical body, we suddenly have the freedom to assume any form that pleases us. Departed individuals often choose to visually present themselves as younger than they were at the time of their passing, especially those who had lived to a ripe old age on Earth.

Being freed from the constraints of physical laws provides us with the ability to lead a completely different existence. However, this doesn't necessarily imply that we disregard Earth after our transition.

From my understanding, four different scenarios can manifest after death:

1. Our awareness remains focused on the physical environment. In that case, we linger in one of the in-between levels until we are reached by impulses that trigger an expansion of consciousness, much like in Mrs. Salm's case.
2. Our awareness entirely shifts to the realm of the afterlife, leading to a loss of interest in the physical world.
3. The focus of our awareness oscillates between the physical and non-physical environments until we are ready to let go fully.
4. We undergo an expansion of our awareness that enables us to perceive and maintain focus across multiple dimensions simultaneously.

*

The question about the fate of people who are considered evil or bad in our society has been bothering me for quite some time, and I am frequently asked about it. What happens to murderers, rapists, or terrorists in the afterlife? Do their actions have consequences? Do they end up in some kind of hell?

Upon leaving the physical body and the corresponding shift in perspective, each person comes to understand what they have inflicted upon others.

However, there is no judgment or punishment in the afterlife. The dominant form of energy is unconditional love. Though, there are beings who initially cannot recognize or accept this love.

Throughout my years of exploration, I've yet to encounter a realm I could label as hell in the traditional sense. But I do occasionally meet individuals who, after their passing, find themselves ensnared in their own anguish. They are unable to see the light, and they are not open to receive the energy of love.

They repeatedly experience the pain they caused to others. From my viewpoint, this resembles a personal hell. Those individuals would most likely be located in what Monroe defined as Focus 26.

I hesitate to speculate how long such individuals remain in this state, and I'm uncertain about how—or if—they can receive assistance from our realm.

It's worth noting that not everyone who has committed a crime or transgression automatically descends into this "personal purgatory." Two circumstances come into play here.

First, a crime may have been part of the life plan for the individuals involved. This implies that the victim and perpetrator made a pre-incarnation agreement to experience certain events.

While this may seem harsh, it can be vitally important for an individual's evolutionary process. Enduring painful experiences often spurs significant growth in people.

Second, some "wrongdoings" occur without deliberate intent. This category includes individuals suffering from psychological disorders, those under the influence, or those manipulated externally.

After their transition, these individuals typically undergo an instant rehabilitation facilitated by their own expanded consciousness. In a dimension dictated by unconditional love, there's no space for thoughts of revenge, hatred, and other negative emotions. This realm is about learning from experiences for one's own good and for the highest good of all.

Ideally, we learn during our lifetime from the positive and negative experiences which will shape our future existence. The self-realization of a person who has made mistakes is already part of the rehabilitation process. Those who are aware of their wrongdoings and subsequently change their intentions and aims evolve enormously, thus serving the whole of creation as well.

However, due to our subjective perception, we're not always aware of the impact our actions and decisions have on our surroundings.

After our transition, we get the opportunity to review the just-finished incarnation and to look at it from different perspectives.

The Life Review is a complex, multi-dimensional process. We become the audience of the blockbuster that was our life and are given the chance to experience certain situations again consciously.

This occurs in parallel from our own perspective as well as that of all those involved. In this way, we become aware of the full extent of our decisions and actions.

It's essential to understand that the life review happens in an environment of loving support. This moment of our evolution is not a "Day of Judgment." There is no condemnation or punishment. The review serves as a learning process, promoting our further growth and development.

We are not alone during this phase. Our spirit guides accompany and support us with compassion.

This also applies to individuals who have chosen their own death. From the afterlife's perspective, suicide is not a tragedy or crime, and hence, it is not met with punishment.

Those who ended their own lives are welcomed into the Park with as much love as anyone else. The person's mental state at the time of their suicide dictates the subsequent events.

Often, suicide is followed by a regeneration phase at the healing center in Focus 27 because those affected have typically been subjected to psychological stress long before their death, leading to impaired consciousness.

My personal interest in this topic was sparked by an unusual experience I had during a weekend retreat I was holding several years ago. It was particularly odd because this was my own Afterlife Workshop, where exploring the beyond was the main theme.

During a Hemi-Sync meditation late in the morning, I suddenly began having trouble breathing, accompanied by a strong urge to cough that I couldn't suppress. One by one, other participants started coughing as well.

Unable to continue with the exercise, we took an unscheduled coffee break. None of us could explain the strange phenomenon.

As planned, I left the event location on the top floor of a residential building in the early evening and headed home.

About half an hour later, my cell phone rang. It was the workshop's organizer.

"Oliver, I've got to talk to you."

I took the next highway exit and pulled into a parking lot.

What I learned on the phone made me shudder.

A woman named Stephanie had taken her own life in an apartment beneath our venue just before noon, coinciding with our meditation. I don't want to go into the specifics of her passing, but I immediately understood what had prompted our collective coughing fit.

During the exercise, our awareness greatly expanded, making us particularly receptive to various impulses, even those beyond our intention.

I instantly questioned if our meditation could have somehow contributed to Stephanie's suicide and if I could have been partially responsible for her death. Had our focus on the afterlife perhaps created an energetic field resonating with her intention?

The guilt weighed on me, justified or not, to the point where I even considered removing the afterlife exploration workshop from my agenda all together.

About a week later, I decided to look for Stephanie. I needed clarity. It was also important for me to know if she had reached the Park or if she was lingering in one of the in-between levels.

My plan was to head to the healing center in Focus 27 and seek Dr. Phil's assistance. In my heightened state of agitation, it took three attempts before I was finally able to perceive the center clearly. To my surprise, Dr. Phil was already waiting at the reception. This time, it had a futuristic appearance.

The doctor greeted me warmly and immediately led me in. There was no need for me to inquire about Stephanie. He was clearly aware of my situation.

My nerves heightened as he opened one of the many doors lining a seemingly infinite corridor and guided me into a room.

Stephanie had never met me before. How would she react to my visit?

The light-filled room reminded me of a luxurious hotel suite. The expansive, floor-to-ceiling windows offered views of a lush, tropical garden.

Stephanie was sitting upright on her bed, a smile on her face. Her strawberry-blonde hair radiated in the sunlight.

"Step a little closer," she encouraged me, waving. "Dr. Phil has already told me quite a bit about you."

Our communication was telepathic.

Stephanie explained that she had been brought to the healing center shortly after her arrival. Before that, she was overjoyed to be greeted by some friends and family members.

On that day, my perception was extremely stable, and I would have loved to ask her tons of questions.

"I know why you're here," she conveyed. "You don't need to feel guilty. My decision to end my life was made long before your workshop took place."

Her words offered immense relief.

"But why did you want to die?" I asked, surprised at my own forwardness.

Stephanie's response was, "I just couldn't stand being in my body anymore. It simply became unbearable. I had to get out of there."

I reflected on the resonance and significance of her words and remained silently beside her.

Her explanation, as brief as it seemed, carried a very special energy, and I suddenly deeply understood her situation. I felt a profound sense of compassion.

There was nothing more to be said.

"You are more than welcome to visit me again if you like," Stephanie said. "Any time you wish."

I nodded, acknowledging that I would accept her offer.

Before I was able to express my gratitude to both Stephanie and Dr. Phil, my perception rapidly faded, and I had no choice but to return to waking consciousness.

Over the following months, I visited Stephanie several times, and to this day, I'm appreciative of her friendly and open way of communicating with me.

Nobody takes their own life without a reason. But it's only after their transition, when their consciousness regains clarity, that they fully realize the impact their suicide has on their loved ones and broader social circles.

Moreover, these individuals often have an intensified desire to communicate. They certainly don't want their loved ones to endure suffering or potential guilt on their account.

I personally know several people who have chosen to exit life prematurely. Their reasons varied greatly and were deeply personal. However, they all shared one thing: They all did their best while they were alive, even though it may not have been sufficient from the viewpoint of those left behind.

Those who remain often grapple with guilt. There's a feeling that you should have or could have prevented that final, devastating act. That you should have been more attentive. And maybe there's also a sense of feeling abandoned and betrayed.

However, peace can be found on both sides if we consider suicide not as an end but as a transition. If we approach the act of suicide with the utmost empathy, if we forgive what needs to be forgiven, both sides can find liberation.

12

NEAR-DEATH EXPERIENCES AND HEALING

"Miracles are not contrary to nature, but only contrary to what we know about nature."
Saint Augustine, Latin Theologian and Philosopher

Some are fortunate to be born twice.

There are numerous people who have consciously experienced their own death and then returned to life. This phenomenon is known as a near-death experience (NDE).

The circumstances surrounding the moment of passing may vary widely: a car crash, a terminal illness, or a failed surgery, to name just a few scenarios. However, the accounts of what happened immediately after clinical death coincide in many cases. Those affected often describe a journey through a tunnel. At the end of it, there appears to be a light that exerts a strong attraction. Most of those who return also recall encounters with deceased relatives and friends.

For centuries, scientists have pondered the true nature of these experiences. Often, they attempt to debunk the reports of NDEs provided by those who claim to have had them.

They put forth theories suggesting that under extreme stress or at the brink of death, the brain produces a flurry of images that are merely an illusion. From a purely scientific standpoint, near-death experiences are seen as implausible.

The prevailing belief is that with clinical death, our ability to experience and remember also ceases. Death, as it is commonly understood, is a one-way journey.

Those who have personally lived through a near-death experience know their truth and are not disconcerted even by scientists. They know firsthand that life goes on even after physical death.

And their fear of dying vanishes and is replaced by a new, liberating outlook on life.

The International Association for Near-Death Studies has meticulously documented and analyzed hundreds of near-death experiences. The findings: Most NDEs are characterized as peaceful and loving, although some are also described as terrifying.

Even though the descriptions of individual components in the transition process are mostly alike, their interpretation and emotional impacts can differ significantly.

The classic components of a near-death experience include:

1. Leaving the physical body. The dying individual often sees their own body left behind, as well as the surroundings, and can later describe this scene in detail.

2. Travelling through a tunnel or darkness, accompanied by wind-like sounds.

3. The ascension into an extremely bright light at the end of the tunnel. This and the following steps are often described as a kind of immersion in unconditional love. The individuals often recognize people, animals, plants, and sometimes even villages or towns.

4. Being greeted by friendly voices, people, or entities, which could be known individuals, strangers, or even religious figures. Information can be shared, and messages can be conveyed.

5. Reviewing the individual's life on earth from birth until death.

6. A warped perception of time and space, with the understanding that worldly dimensions hold no relevance in the non-physical sphere.

7. Expressing disappointment when their physical body survives, often accompanied by a resistance to returning to the density or constraints of the physical body.

Using these criteria, Scott Taylor, a former director of the Monroe Institute, has developed a series of specialized meditations. In these, elements of a classical NDE can be explored without the shock or trauma of spontaneous near-death experiences.

For a number of years, Scott has been teaching a course with the title *Near-Death Experience Intensive* based on his personal experience.

This workshop also utilizes Hemi-Sync frequencies to access specific areas in the non-physical. Unlike classic Monroe programs, Scott refrains from addressing specific Focus levels.

Therefore, people who are not familiar with the Monroe Method and have no previous knowledge can also participate in the program.

For many years, I strictly adhered to the Focus level scale, which assisted my navigation within and between various non-physical environments to the extent that I always knew precisely where I was.

Participating in Scott's program gave me an unexpected insight. I realized that although the scale of Focus levels can provide a helpful map, it also defines the boundaries of the individual levels of consciousness that do not inherently exist.

Both approaches have their pros and cons, and they offer invaluable experiences and fantastic opportunities for exploring our greater existence.

The journeys in *Lifeline* and *Exploration 27* are geographically oriented, specifically targeting areas like in-between levels or the Park. The *Near-Death Experience Intensive* program focuses on the comprehensive exploration and observation of individual elements within the entire spectrum of otherworldly phenomena, regardless of the specific level on which they manifest.

The following excerpt from my Monroe diary describes my first journey through the tunnel and into the light:

I've barely stretched out my legs when I feel my body begin to sink into the familiar state of deep relaxation. I feel a slight chill. My arms are heavy. I can hardly pull the cover over myself, even though the Hemi-Sync signals haven't even started yet. I perceive Scott's voice over the headphones, but I'm already so far gone that I don't even try to follow his instructions.

Instead, I ask my spirit team to assist and guide me: I must find the tunnel!

I can no longer feel my body, and I distinctly sense my awareness expanding.

A dark room opens up in front of me. It has no walls, doors, or windows. A familiar density envelops me like a cloak. I feel safe and, at the same time, free from all earthly limitations.

I am! Without a sense of time and without a destination. Without thoughts and without noise. Eternity.

I resist Scott's voice as it reaches me from an infinite distance.

"Ask your spirit guides to lead you through the tunnel. Try to gather as many impressions as possible and remember them."

Oh, yes… I recall my intention and ask my team to show me the tunnel. It remains dark, but the energy structure surrounding me changes within seconds.

The previously seemingly endless space suddenly takes form. Instead of silence, I now feel a sort of vibration around me accompanied by a sweet sound. The tunnel walls are embedded with stones resembling colorful crystals. They radiate brightly without lighting up the darkness.

Before I can further explore this phenomenon, I notice countless lights zipping by on my right and left at an astonishing speed. They move so quickly that I can't even discern their size or shape.

"Could these be other souls?"

Before I can even fully form the question in my mind, I intuitively know the answer: Yes!

Curious, I decide to follow the lights.

Merely intending to do so provides enough momentum. Before I know it, I'm one of the many lights, all moving in the same direction.

I'm not sure how long I've been traveling when suddenly, an intensely bright light appears before me. A split second later, I'm immersed in it.

"I've arrived!" is my first thought. "Home at last!" is my second.

I'm overwhelmed by the energetic quality of the light. Rational thought is impossible. This light cannot be compared to electric light or sunlight. Not only is it brighter, but it's also filled with pure, unconditional love.

I have no desire to journey further and gather more impressions. I just want to be here, where I am right now. Letting the light flow through me, recharging, feeling safe and secure.

Scott's voice abruptly pulls me out of my bliss. He asks me to return to waking consciousness. I reluctantly comply after expressing my gratitude to my spirit team for this extraordinary experience.

After the meditation, I found it particularly difficult to reconnect with my earthly body and the density of physical reality. Once again, I became aware of how limited and immobile we are in this environment.

I am grateful for the experience and the newfound knowledge and, of course, for knowing that I can revisit this nurturing light whenever I wish.

Most people who have had a near-death experience subsequently report significant shifts in their worldview and their perception of existence.

There are also many accounts from people who experienced spontaneous healing coinciding with their NDE.

Doctors had all but given up on Anita Moorjani in 2006. Her book, *Dying to Be Me,* chronicles how her cancer unexpectedly went into remission following a near-death experience.

Stories like Anita Moorjani's suggest that unimaginable opportunities present themselves in non-physical realms.

Through targeted meditations, in which specific aspects of near-death experiences are consciously experienced, anyone can access this healing potential in the afterlife for themselves.

One of my workshop participants did exactly that and experienced something remarkable.

I first met Larissa in the summer of 2015 at my *Introduction to OBEs* workshop in Hamburg. A little less than a year later, we met again at my *Exploring the Afterlife* program.

Just a few months prior, Larissa had been diagnosed with a highly aggressive type of advanced-stage breast cancer. She was already undergoing chemotherapy when the workshop began.

At the time, I was unaware of her condition. As she later told me, her prognosis was not very promising.

Even though we ventured on a few journeys to otherworldly environments over the course of the weekend, I only briefly mentioned the healing center in Focus 27.

It wasn't until January 2018, when Larissa registered for another workshop that she told me about her serious illness.

Inspired by my teachings and the experiences she'd had during the workshop two years earlier, Larissa visited the healing center in Focus 27 on her own initiative, hoping to find support for her difficult situation.

Larissa shared how she was warmly received at each of her visits over the following months and received therapeutic treatments.

"After a while, everyone there knew me well and was aware of my problem. Everything worked seamlessly. I walked through several energy portals to cleanse my body. There was also a kind of sieve they had me pass through. When I did, I could feel how 'the bad stuff' was left on that sieve."

Larissa admitted that it was difficult to articulate what she had experienced because nothing like it exists in the physical world.

"But it was very real. And my cancer, including the metastases, receded until no more cancer cells were detected. Complete remission."

Larissa became a medical miracle.

"The doctors think I've been incredibly lucky because something like this very rarely happens. But I know what helped me, and I continue to visit the healing center in Focus 27 for follow-up care."

Larissa's experience is encouraging and instills hope in all of us. As invaluable as our conventional treatment options are, it is worthwhile considering complementary and alternative therapies.

In a sense, this story also confirms my own perceptions. Independently and long before Larissa told me about her situation, I witnessed a treatment in Focus 27 that aligns with her description of the purifying sieve.

I generally find the energy field of Focus 27 to be very healing and, as a result, enjoy visiting the Park for my own rejuvenation.

Up until April 2016, when I participated in Scott Taylor's *Near-Death Experience Intensive* program, I hadn't given much thought to the topic of healing work. Perhaps it was because I had not experienced any significant health issues up until then, or maybe because healing appeared to me as a highly complex topic. I was more inclined to use my free time exploring other non-physical phenomena.

However, it was during Scott's workshop that the importance of healing was highlighted to me from the non-physical realm during a meditation. This experience shifted my perspective and emphasized the necessity of incorporating healing not only into my exploration of non-physical phenomena but also into my work.

I am listening to Scott Taylor's pleasantly sonorous voice. Following the guided relaxation, I feel myself gradually detaching from my physical body. Instead of choosing a direction, I am spending a few minutes floating in weightlessness.

I would love to remain in this state for hours, but Scott has other plans. He carefully guides me to the entrance of the tunnel, with a distant light visible at its end.

Since my visual perception is somewhat unstable, I try to feel my surroundings rather than reaching for images at this point.

"What would flying through the tunnel feel like?" I wonder.

Barely have I formulated the question in my mind when I am suddenly swept away by a vortex, losing all sense of orientation.

When the whirlwind finally subsides, I find myself in a stunningly beautiful rose garden bathed in light. Not far from where I stand, I notice a white building, which immediately reminds me of the Sanssouci Palace in Potsdam, Germany.

I allow the vivid colors and strong scent of the roses to envelop my senses until I can no longer resist the pull of the white building.

As I approach, two glass-paned French doors swing open, revealing a spacious and luminous room that instantly reminds me of a yoga studio.

Inside, I see approximately 10 to 12 bald men sitting in a semi-circle on round meditation cushions. They are all attired in white shirts and pants. Upon closer inspection, I notice the presence of a female figure among them, distinguished by her striking black hair that extends to at least shoulder length.

Pondering where I might have landed, a voice in my head responds, "You are in the Park."

I can then clearly sense the slightly electrifying energy of Focus 27.

The entities continue to sit silently, prompting me to wonder about their identity.

"We are the Council," they telepathically reply.

I know that I'm not dreaming or fantasizing. The encounter feels as real as any physical one, if not more so.

Before I can ask more questions, I receive instructions from the "Council." They appear to communicate collectively rather than individually, giving me very detailed directions. They request that I create a new workshop focused on healing, even suggesting specific Hemi-Sync recordings to incorporate.

The Council also indicates which Focus levels I should select for the healing work. Some of the recordings I'll have to design myself, as they don't yet exist in the required form.

This catches me off guard.

"But I've no idea how to do that," I mentally interject and feel a strong resistance towards the assigned task. "I'm really not interested in the subject, and besides, I'm not a healer."

The entities seem unimpressed by my defiance and convey a sense of urgency to me. They seem friendly and loving but very determined.

Then the clarity of my perception begins to fade, and I quickly return to waking consciousness, aided by my ego trying to deny the encounter I have just experienced.

Rarely are my experiences as real and of such visual quality as this one, not to mention the exquisite clarity of our communication, leaving no room for doubt or interpretation.

I wasn't even familiar with the Hemi-Sync recordings the Council had named. But I made a note of their titles because I sensed that the assignment was important, even if my ego still maintained that it didn't fit in with my life plan.

Back in Los Angeles, I immersed myself again in my familiar daily routine. The instructions given by the Council seemed less urgent with each passing day, and I began to suppress the memory of our encounter.

A few months after my return from Virginia, I suddenly felt a stabbing pain in my right shoulder, which worsened from week to week.

On December 8, 2016, I rolled out my yoga mat for the last time. After that, stretching was no longer possible because my shoulder joint had become so immobile.

By mid-January the following year, I saw a doctor and had X-rays as well as a CAT scan. The diagnosis: Frozen Shoulder Syndrome. An inflamed shoulder joint capsule caused stiffness in the joint.

My orthopedist recommended physiotherapy, but my condition only worsened. Extremely frustrated, I quit physio after a few sessions.

Deep inside, I had a hunch about why the energy flow in my body had stagnated. But my ego resisted for weeks to let go and allow the path to healing.

Eventually, I realized that I needed to change my mindset if I wanted to recover.

In the spring, I cautiously began designing the new workshop, setting a firm date for the premiere in Switzerland in July.

With no more excuses, I immersed myself fully in the work, noticing along the way that the inflammation in my shoulder began to recede. The pain lessened, and I felt progressively better, despite the joint's remaining stiffness.

My insecurities and recurring doubts during the workshop preparation led me to question my knowledge about healing and my qualifications to run such a program.

But my authentic intention paved the way, and I learned to trust my inner voice and grow into the role.

The workshop began to take shape, and simultaneously, my shoulder began to show signs of mobility.

Two days before I was due to fly out from Los Angeles, I was invited to a trance healing presentation. During the treatment with a medium, I could clearly perceive powerful energy flowing through my upper body. The result was astonishing: Immediately after the session, my shoulder moved in a range that I hadn't experienced in almost a year.

Thanks to this direct and consciousness-expanding experience, I could now approach my workshop calmly and with positive anticipation.

Nancy "Scooter" McMoneagle, Robert Monroe's stepdaughter and former director of the Institute, aptly defined the term "healing" in words that resonate with me on a deep level:

"The process of invoking and establishing a whole and balanced state of being that is in perfect alignment with our highest purpose and in the greatest interest of all."

Thus, healing doesn't merely involve freedom from physical and psychological symptoms but also promotes the holistic welfare of individuals, their environments, and their communities.

By now, I've held the workshop many times and have come to understand why I was so urgently approached by those non-physical entities. It was time to view Out-of-Body Experiences not just as fun excursions into non-physical realms, but to recognize their benefits and untapped potential as well.

My team was eager to point out a new way of energy work, which serves self-realization and, thus, the well-being of our total self. If we learn to perceive ourselves as multidimensional beings, we can not only support the healing of our physical body but also heal our non-physical aspects.

The non-physical resources available to enhance our lives are diverse, potent, and straightforward to utilize.

For many people, the idea of out-of-body experiences is associated with the hope for great adventures. These adventures certainly await each one of us. However, we must also be aware that this type of self-exploration comes with significant responsibility.

Undeniably, leaving our physical bodies is exciting, but what we bring back from these journeys is even more critical—for our benefit and the benefit of all.

13

THE SEVEN KEYS TO A SUCCESSFUL OBE

"Our greatest weakness lies in giving up. The most certain way to succeed is always to try just one more time."
Thomas Alva Edison, Inventor and Entrepreneur

One of the most common questions I receive is, "Why do some people have incredibly vivid experiences during their OBE-exercises while mine are unspectacular or vague?"

As a trainer and workshop facilitator, I've helped several thousand individuals explore their consciousness over the past twelve years, whether through practicing Out-of-Body Experiences (OBEs), manifesting optimal life conditions, or communicating with non-physical entities.

For years I, too, looked with envy at those who returned from their exploratory journeys with impressive and exciting experiences while I often felt like I was staring at a blank canvas during my exercises. I didn't float out of my body, nor could I report meeting impressive entities from other dimensions.

It wasn't until I adjusted my expectations and changed my perspective that my experiences began to gain vividness.

I learned to gather verifiable information, integrate it into my physical existence, and subsequently improve my quality of life.

To shorten your own path to successful OBEs, I would like to give you some helpful tips and instructions. I believe there are seven aspects that you should internalize if you want to achieve high-quality experiences:

1. Setting the right intention

If you want to undertake journeys into the non-physical, you must be clear about why and with what purpose you embark on these travels. It is important to formulate a clear and positive intention beforehand. It should be based on an authentic desire to explore one's own existence.

It is helpful to formulate this intention carefully in words, ideally handwritten on a sheet of paper. These sentences can then be spoken as affirmations at the beginning of meditations or exercises.

The wording can be modified, refined, or adapted anytime as you progress in your development.

Over time, you will develop a feeling that tells you if your intention is genuinely authentic or driven by ego. A clear, true intention creates a kind of energetic map that guides you to your desired result.

The more detailed and emotionally invested the intention, the more it facilitates the process. It is of utmost importance that you resonate with your chosen words.

Robert Monroe developed the Gateway Affirmation as a declaration of intent to firmly anchor his objective in his consciousness. It can be divided into three sections and can serve as a template for creating your own affirmation.

"I am more than my physical body."

The first and at the same time most important point of the affirmation is a simple yet powerful observation. It is the prerequisite for any experiences in the non-physical.

If you doubt that you are more than just a physical body, you are on shaky ground and have no solid basis for your explorations.

Some people may have hidden doubts. It is advisable to let the above words sink in during a quiet moment or a short meditation. Are your body and mind in resonance with them? Do these words bring you inner peace, or do they prompt questions?

"Because I am more than physical matter, I can perceive that which is greater than the physical world. Therefore, I deeply desire: to expand, to experience, to know, to understand, to control, to use such greater energies and energy systems as may be beneficial and constructive to me and to those who follow me."

In this second section of the Gateway Affirmation, Monroe first describes his desire using very precise words. At the same time, he defines the goal and purpose of fulfilling this wish in great detail. Importantly, Monroe clearly expresses that the experiences he seeks are beneficial not only for himself but also for those with whom he feels connected—both physically and non-physically.

A simplified version of this last part could be "for everyone's highest good."

You are free to articulate specific desires in an affirmation. For instance, if you have a deep, authentic desire for an Out-of-Body Experience, you could phrase it like this:

"I strongly feel that an Out-of-Body Experience would benefit my personal development, and I trust that I will succeed easily and for everyone's highest good."

"Also, I deeply desire the help and cooperation, the assistance, the understanding of those individuals whose wisdom, development and experience are equal or greater than my own."

Monroe maintained a close relationship with his non-physical helpers. They have always played a vital role in the context of his work.

By consciously asking for the support of individuals whose experience was equal to his own or even greater, he created beneficial conditions for his personal growth.

From personal experience, I know how important this form of support is in non-physical environments. In the out-of-body state, away from familiar reality, we move in environments that are not easy to navigate without appropriate experience.

Requesting the help of your spiritual guides is thus a crucial part of any affirmation.

When crafting affirmations, it's vital to focus on positive aspects and avoid negative wording.

Here is an example of how not to word an affirmation:

"I am not afraid of the dark and will not meet any evil spirits."

This negative framing can stimulate the very emotions and experiences you wish to avoid.

Instead, consider using positive phrasing like, "I always move in the light, surrounded by individuals who lovingly and supportively stand by my side."

Finally, every affirmation should conclude with an expression of gratitude. More important than the actual words is the energy behind them. Aim to generate a genuine feeling of thankfulness.

Much like love, gratitude carries a high-energy vibration frequency that can serve as a bridge to the non-physical.

2. Activating energy and directing it in a controlled manner

Energy and consciousness are closely interconnected.

As multidimensional and intelligent beings, it is important for us to optimize and nurture all aspects of the consciousness system. The inner energy is referred to as Chi, Prana, life force, or bioenergy, depending on the philosophical approach, and it manifests in our emotions, various mental states, and our relationships, among other aspects.

Directing this energy purposefully can enhance our vibrational frequency, setting excellent conditions for conscious Out-of-Body Experiences, physical health, and creating optimal living conditions.

A good approach is to learn more about the chakras, the meridians, and the human energy field (the aura). There are various techniques that promote the best possible use of our personal energy field. These also include working with the Resonant Energy Balloon (REBAL) developed by Robert Monroe.

3. Recognizing and eliminating fears

Fear, whether conscious or unconscious, can hinder your intentions. Confronting and dissolving these fears is, therefore, essential.

Unconscious fears can be particularly obstructive.

Persistent failure to achieve certain goals might indicate that suppressed fears are at fault.

There are many reasons why certain emotions are buried deep within the psyche. For example, they may be considered weaknesses, and one might try to maintain the self-image of a strong personality. They could also be associated with painful experiences that have simply been repressed or suppressed.

It requires courage and absolute self-honesty to bring these suppressed emotions to light, but the endeavor is worthwhile.

By overcoming our fears, we unlock our heart's energy, which has tremendous power and is in perfect resonance with our Higher Self.

4. Harnessing the power of imagination

I like to think of imagination as a bridge between the worlds. Imagination helps to move energy and direct it in a certain direction. Like top athletes who visualize their goals, picturing your desired experience in detail can prepare you for attaining it.

Before an exercise, for instance, I picture my energy body detaching from my physical body and moving in a predetermined direction. Or I might visualize a specific encounter with an individual in Focus 27.

5. Inviting perceptions actively

Whenever I don't receive distinct impressions during a meditation or exercise, I mentally ask myself simple questions to activate my non-physical senses.

"What if...?" or "How would it feel if...?" are the two I use most frequently.

For example, if I'm trying to establish conscious contact with a non-physical helper, I mentally say:

"How would it feel if a spirit guide stood right beside me?" and "What if I could feel his hand on my shoulder?"

These simple kinds of questions always work exceptionally well for me and open my perceptive channels.

It is also worthwhile to experiment with commands such as "Perception now!" or "Clarity now!" Don't limit your creativity, and feel free to develop your own questions and commands.

6. Choosing the right time and place

Many people believe that the bed is the best place to have Out-of-Body Experiences. Even though most spontaneous OBEs tend to happen while we're sleeping, the bed isn't always the ideal location for practice. Our bodies and minds associate the bed with sleep, which can make staying awake challenging.

Similarly, the living room couch might not be the best option for everyone. Those accustomed to napping on the couch in the afternoon might find it difficult to stay awake there as well.

I like to use a yoga mat or a garden lounger for practice. I need to lie comfortably, but not too comfortably, to give my body-mind system a clear signal.

For most people, the early morning hours are best suited for practice before they actively engage the mind in daily activities. Those who work shift schedules need to adjust accordingly and practice when they are well-rested.

7. Meditating regularly

Daily meditation, akin to exercising a muscle, sharpens the mind, paving the way to enhanced cognitive abilities.

It is important to develop certain self-discipline and meditate every day, if possible. It's not the length but the quality of the meditation that matters.

I aim to meditate for at least 20 minutes before breakfast every morning. Realistically, I manage to do it five days a week. Whenever I use Hemi-Sync recordings to facilitate longer sessions, I schedule correspondingly more time.

Ideally, you should familiarize yourself with the different states of consciousness and practice achieving them with and without the support of Hemi-Sync. The Monroe Method provides fantastic tools for this.

14

HEMI-SYNC AND THE FOCUS LEVELS

European scientists began investigating binaural beats during the second half of the 19th century. However, Robert Monroe is recognized as the pioneer who conducted comprehensive research into specific sound frequencies and their impacts on the human brain.

A successful businessman and radio program director at the time, Monroe experienced several spontaneous Out-of-Body Experiences in the late 1950s.

In search of answers no one could provide, he established a laboratory on his farm in rural Virginia. There, he collaborated with physicists, psychologists, and other scientists to study the phenomenon of OBEs. Curious neighbors and visitors volunteered as subjects for Monroe's experiments.

Monroe had found a new mission in life and did not only invest his heart and soul but also his private assets. In 1972, his passion led to the establishment of the Monroe Institute and the development of a unique audio technology: Hemi-Sync, which allows both hemispheres of the human brain to work synchronously.

Dr. Lester Fehmi of the Princeton Biofeedback Research Institute, a leading scientist in the field, describes the impact of what is known as brainwave synchrony:

"Synchrony represents the maximum efficiency of information transport through the whole brain."

It is linked to, among other things, vivid imagery, improved memory access, creative insights, and integrative experiences.

It's evident that a highly integrated brain, a brain in which both hemispheres are functioning in symmetry, synchrony, harmony, and unity, is a key to peak states and peak human performance.

Hemi-Sync allows the user to embrace and safely navigate specific states of consciousness deliberately. Monroe called these states Focus levels. To simplify matters, he used numbers to differentiate between the individual levels. The following is an outline of the Focus level spectrum relevant to this book:

F1: Normal waking consciousness. Completely in phase with physical matter reality. Also referred to as C1 Consciousness.

F10: The mind is wide awake; the body is deeply at rest or asleep. A very stable state of deep relaxation.

F12: The state of expanded awareness, no longer limited to perception via the physical senses.

F15: Defined as "state of no time." Perception expands into areas where our linear time structure loses significance. Sometimes referred to as "the void."

F21: The threshold between physical reality and the environments outside time and space. Also referred to as "the bridge."

F22: Level of consciousness of those who are still connected to their physical body but are unconscious, comatose, severely narcotized or suffering from delirium or dementia.

F23: The level of consciousness of individuals who are, in most cases, temporarily unable to detach themselves from the Earth's energies after their physical death due to shock, trauma, or the denial of their demise. Focus 23 is viewed as a kind of transition level.

F24: The first level of the belief systems territories. Here reside those who still follow specific doctrines after their physical death. This area is primarily populated by primitive, religious communities.

F25: The second level of the belief systems territories. This area is a manifestation of larger organized religious communities of more recent physical human history. Clearly separated from each other, Christian, Buddhist, Hindu, Judaic, Islamic, and other belief systems are represented here, including their various offshoots and sects.

F26: The third level of the belief systems territories. Areas that contain structures and knowledge of various, highly individual religions, as well as other beliefs based on direct experience of the self. Unlike F24 and F25, these are extremely small groups of individuals that very precisely define themselves through their beliefs.

F27: The general reception and transfer station to recuperate from traumas of the last physical existence and reorientation. Termed the "Park" by Robert Monroe. This is a versatile, constantly adjusting landscape with various facilities.

*

There is no plausible reason why Monroe selected the term Focus levels. Their order is not hierarchical. The increasing numbers are simply intended to differentiate between individual levels of consciousness. Just because a level has a higher number doesn't mean that it is better, more interesting, or more desirable than a level with a lower number.

I prefer to think of the individual levels as akin to different stations on my car radio. These can range from pop to classical music to news broadcasts. Depending on my personal preference and interest, I can switch stations at will. Each Focus level has its unique characteristics. However, every individual perceives these different levels in a unique way based on their personal experiences, their personal development, and their cultural identity.

EPILOGUE

On the previous pages, I have shared my personal experiences, presented possibilities, and hopefully inspired some to embark on their own quest for answers to life's big questions.

In certain cases, I've drawn tentative conclusions based on the principles of the non-physical realms and entities I've encountered and interacted with.

At this point, I would like to stress once more that this book is not intended to explain human existence or to impose a worldview derived from personal experiences onto my readers.

My goal is to inspire as many people as possible to go out and discover their own truths.

Every society has prevailing belief systems that its members naturally absorb or adapt. Some groups even coerce their members into accepting a rigidly defined worldview, suppressing the desire for self-exploration.

In the Western world, we enjoy the substantial privilege of pursuing our own paths and freely deciding what and whom we believe.

At the onset of his research into Out-of-Body Experiences, Bob Monroe made the radical decision to discard all knowledge and doctrines he'd amassed up until that point in his life. He questioned everything he'd ever learned, enabling groundbreaking insights.

When Monroe made his work available to others, his greatest wish was to uphold the principle of an individual's utmost autonomy over their own truth. He wanted to inspire people not just to believe but to gain knowledge through direct personal experiences.

This approach has also become the sole method for me to discover my truth.

Over thousands of years, humanity has developed diverse methods to expand consciousness and facilitate access to non-physical realities—from traditional meditation and hypnosis to the use of plant medicine or drugs.

Not every approach is suitable for everyone. It's crucial to understand the individual methods, opportunities, and limitations.

Traditional meditation demands patience and determination. Hypnosis provides the opportunity for controlled experiences but needs guidance from a hypnotherapist. In this approach, the nature of the questions asked on the part of the therapist can greatly influence the personal experience.

Drug use can cause an abrupt shift in consciousness and unlock vast potentialities. However, the downside is that experiences usually occur completely uncontrolled. Neither can the duration be predicted, which can lead to unforeseen consequences.

Personally, working with binaural beats strikes a happy medium. I receive strong stimulation via the sound frequencies, yet I maintain full control over the intensity and duration of my experience.

Essentially, each of us can peer behind the curtain of physical reality. We just need to create the time and space to further develop this ability without comparing our individual progress to that of others.

Every stage of development holds value and presents untapped potential. Everyone is perfect just as they are.

* * *

You can find more information about my work at

www.olivertappe.com

GLOSSARY

Arthur Findlay College – College of spiritualism and psychic sciences in Stansted Hall, Stansted Mountfitchet, Essex, England. www.arthurfindlaycollege.org

BodyTalk System™ – Holistic body and soul therapy. www.bodytalksystem.com

CHEC Unit – Abbreviation for Controlled Holistic Environmental Chamber. A wooden enclosure designed by Robert Monroe, furnished with a mattress and a heavy curtain. It contains headphones and speakers, which are used during the meditations. The CHEC Unit also serves as a bed.

Exploration 27 – A Monroe Institute five-day program building on the *Lifeline* program to further explore the "Park" and other afterlife phenomena.

Focus-Level – Robert Monroe named various states of consciousness "Focus levels" and assigned them numbers for the sake of simplicity to help distinguish one from another.

Fox Den – One of several common areas at the Monroe Institute's Nancy Penn Center.

Gateway Voyage – A Monroe Institute five-day program for beginners to become acquainted with and experience Focus levels 10 to 21.

Guidelines – A Monroe Institute five-day program to promote intuitive perception and meet spirit guides.

Heartline – A Monroe Institute five-day program with an emphasis on self-love, trust, and emotional healing.

International Association for Near-Death Studies – Foundation for the investigation of near-death experiences.
https://iands.org

Lifeline – A Monroe Institute five-day program to become acquainted with and experience Focus levels 22 to 27.

Monroe Institute – World's leading institution for the study of human consciousness in Faber, Virginia, founded by Robert Monroe in the early seventies.
www.monroeinstitute.org

Nancy Penn Center – The Monroe Institute's main building where the seminar participants are housed. The building was named after Nancy Penn, Robert Monroe's wife.

Phasing – Explains the process of expanding and refocusing human consciousness.

Point Consciousness – The state of complete inner stillness where the mind no longer focuses on physical reality and the brain doesn't process any information.

PREP-Session – One-on-one session in a soundproof booth with a waterbed at the Monroe Institute's lab, guided by a technician.

Quick Switch-Technique – see *Phasing*.

Remote Viewing – the practice of seeking impressions about a distant or unseen subject or object, purportedly sensing with the mind.

Robert's Mountain Retreat – The Monroe family's former private residence, which was converted into a retreat center after Robert's death.

Stargate Project – A secret U.S. Army unit established in 1978 at Fort Meade, Maryland, by the Defense Intelligence Agency (DIA) to investigate the potential for psychic phenomena in military and domestic intelligence applications.

Trance-Mediumship – A special aspect of mediumship where a medium may channel an entity from the spirit world.

White Carpet Room – Assembly room at the Nancy Penn Center of the Monroe Institute, furnished with a white carpet.

EXPERTS

Dr. Alexander, Eben – Neurosurgeon, author of the bestseller *Proof of Heaven* and *Living in a Mindful Universe*.
www.ebenalexander.com

Buhlman, William – Author, trainer and expert in Out-of-Body Experiences.
www.astralinfo.org

Campbell, Thomas – Physicist, consciousness researcher and author of the *MY Big TOE* trilogy.
www.mybigtoe.com

Cottrell, Lynn – Medium, tutor, spiritual artist.
www.facebook.com/Lynn-Cottrell-Spirit-Art-538820936273542

Dr. Fehmi, Lester – Psychologist, executive director of the Princeton Biofeedback Centre, LLC.
www.openfocus.com

Leussink, Fleur – Psychic medium and Intuition Teacher
www.mediufleur.com

Dr. Lipton, Bruce – Biologist and author of the bestseller *The Biology of Belief*.
www.brucelipton.com

Monroe, Robert – Consciousness researcher and founder of the Monroe Institute. Inventor of the Hemi-Sync® audio technology. www.monroeinstitute.org

Monroe Sound Science – A combination of sound techniques that include binaural beats, as well as frequency, amplitude, and phase modulation.

Dr. Veltheim, John – Originator of the *BodyTalk System*™ and author of several books on the subject. www.bodytalksystem.com

THANK YOU!

Typically, I don't find writing to be a challenge. However, (IN)VISIBLE almost didn't come to fruition due to a chronic shortage of time and several unsuccessful attempts, leaving me with piles of unsorted material.

The pandemic unexpectedly provided the needed time slot in 2020. Unlike writing my previous books, I found the process far from easy.

Without the active support and inspiration from some wonderful individuals, I would have been hopelessly overwhelmed.

I owe my deepest gratitude to my wife, Anna-Barbara, who has offered me unwavering support from the first day of our shared life, continually encouraging me to live my truth. Thank you for your thorough first round of edits and the numerous hours you dedicated to this book. ♡

Many thanks to you, Olaf! Your constructive criticism, your attention to detail, and your expert editing skills of the original German version have enormously enhanced this book.

Thank you, Kim and Sarah, for your awesome support with the English version. I am beyond grateful.

My heartfelt gratitude goes out to my spirit team, who have done an exceptional job guiding me along the way.

Printed in Great Britain
by Amazon

35778614R00110

CW00521081

THE PIT AND THE PENDULUM AND OTHER TALES

Since their first publication in 1830s and 1840s, Edgar Allan Poe's extraordinary Gothic tales have established many of the conventions which still dominate the genre of horror and detective fiction. As well as being highly enjoyable, Poe uses the Gothic to question the integrity of human existence, exposing the misconceptions that make things seem 'mysterious' in the first place. This critical edition selects twenty-four tales and places the most popular alongside less well-known travel narratives, metaphysical essays, and political satires.

EDGAR ALLAN POE was born in Boston in 1809. Deserted by his father, Poe was taken in by the Richmond merchant John Allan on his mother's death in 1811. He entered the University of Virginia in 1826, but despite scholastic success was expelled for gambling debts after one year. To heal the widening breach with Allan, over the next three years Poe served unsuccessfully in the army. He left in 1831 and moved to Baltimore. Having already published two small volumes of poems, he there began his publishing career in earnest with a third volume of poems and his first tales. In Baltimore, Poe set up house with his paternal aunt Maria Clemm, whose daughter Virginia he married five years later. In 1835, he returned with the Clemms to Richmond to edit the *Southern Literary Messenger*. Despite the success of the journal, Poe left at the end of 1936 to pursue his writing career unsuccessfully in New York and more successfully in Philadelphia. In 1838, Harper and Brothers published Poe's first book of fiction, the novel *The Narrative of Arthur Gordon Pym*. Over the next five years Poe wrote the tales for which he is best known today—among them 'Ligeia', 'The Fall of the House of Usher', and his detective fiction. In 1839 he collected his first stories as *Tales of the Grotesque and Arabesque*. In 1944 he moved his family to New York, where the next January he achieved overnight fame with the publication of 'The Raven'. But success came too late. Plagued by unrewarding editorial work, Poe was further tormented by the prolonged illness of his wife, who finally succumbed to tuberculosis in 1847. Devastated, Poe seems to have been worn down by his struggles. He courted a number of women, tried without success to found a literary journal, and in 1848 completed *Eureka* and 'The Poetic Principle'. Shortly before his planned marriage to a former childhood sweetheart, he collapsed in Baltimore where he died in October 1849.

DAVID VAN LEER taught at Cornell and Princeton Universities, and was Professor of English and American Literature at University of California, Davis. A regular contributor to *The New Republic* on American culture from the seventeenth to twentieth centuries, he is the author of *Emerson's Epistemology: The Argument of the Essays* (1986) and *The Queening of America* (1995).

Shutterstock.com

EDGAR ALLAN POE

The Pit and the Pendulum

AND OTHER TALES

Edited with an Introduction and Notes by
DAVID VAN LEER

OXFORD
UNIVERSITY PRESS

Great Clarendon Street, Oxford, OX2 6DP,
United Kingdom

Oxford University Press is a department of the University of Oxford. It furthers the University's objective of excellence in research, scholarship, and education by publishing worldwide. Oxford is a registered trade mark of Oxford University Press in the UK and in certain other countries

First published as an Oxford World's Classics paperback 1998

Reissued 2018

Impression: 1

Published in the United States of America by Oxford University Press
198 Madison Avenue, New York, NY 10016, United States of America

British Library Cataloguing in Publication Data
Data available

Library of Congress Cataloging in Publication Data
Data available

ISBN 978–0–19–882729–0

Printed in Great Britain by
Clays Ltd, Elcograf S.p.A

CONTENTS

INTRODUCTION

EDGAR ALLAN POE is about as famous as an American writer gets. Children encounter him in elementary school, and his stories about mutilated bodies and walled-up corpses are familiar even to those who never read. He long ago passed into US popular imagination as part of the cultural heritage. Classic horror movies spin off from 'The Fall of the House of Usher' and 'The Tell-Tale Heart'; every October that inveterate illiterate Bart Simpson retells 'The Raven' for his Hallowe'en special; and Poe's gloomy portrait broods over a Manhattan coffee bar on the spot where he composed the poem.

Yet Poe is a problem to those who study American literature. Fellow writers turn from him in contempt. Late in life, a forgetful Emerson remembered him as the 'jingle man'. The essayist Paul Elmer More dismissed him as the poet of 'unripe boys and unsound men'. The novelist Henry James, himself incapable of levity, warned that 'to take [Poe] with more than a certain degree of seriousness is to lack seriousness one's self'. The anxiety underlying these rejections was best expressed by the expatriate poet T. S. Eliot. Convinced that Poe's intellect was merely that 'of a highly gifted young person before puberty', Eliot quipped that Poe affected no poet except perhaps the limerick-writer Edward Lear. Immediately afterward, however, regretting his harshness, Eliot confessed, 'And yet one cannot be sure that one's own writing has *not* been influenced by Poe.'

It is tempting to dismiss such rejections as simple jealousy, the inevitable fate of those who achieve 'popular' success in unprestigious literary genres. Yet most adult readers share these writers' discomfort. The first real author Americans read, Poe is the one we most wish to outgrow. Acknowledging the appropriateness of the poet Allan Tate's naming Poe 'our cousin', literary scholars still have trouble tracing the bloodlines. Poe finds no place in the literary history of mid-nineteenth-century American Romanticism, but is buried in a footnote, with only glancing allusions to 'the twins story' or 'the one with the cat'. His success with young readers is assumed to signal the immaturity of his work. Like other talents not conforming to traditional literary paradigms—Cooper, Stevenson, and (formerly) Hawthorne, Twain, and the Brontës—Poe is conveniently pigeon-holed as a children's author, skilful enough but not central to the 'great tradition' in American literature.

Much of our difficulty with Poe begins with his distasteful life. Never a good judge of character, Poe had the misfortune to choose as his literary executor and first biographer a man who vilified him as a charlatan and profligate. Although no one continues to credit Griswold's calumnies, biographers must still admit that Poe's life was something of a mess. Orphaned at three, Poe never subsequently felt at home anywhere, and spent much of his life searching for a kind of parental approval. His futile attempts to impress his remote foster-father John Allan set the pattern for his lifelong wooings and renunciations of powerful men. His hyperbolic attempts to earn Allan's love—through academic and military achievement—inevitably ended in disaster. Repeatedly Allan's failure to respond led the disgruntled Poe to disgrace himself more thoroughly than he had initially succeeded. As a result, history remembers his college gambling but not his prizes; his West Point court martial for neglect of duty and disobedience of orders, but not his rapid rise through the military ranks.

Poe's search in his career for masculine approval was matched in his private life by a yearning after familial affection. Recoiling from the untimely deaths of both his birth mother Eliza Poe and his foster-mother 'Fanny' Allan, Poe sought in women less life-partners than surrogate mothers or sisters. The longest of his female relationships—the sixteen-year *ménage* with his aunt Maria Clemm and her pre-pubescent daughter Virginia—epitomized the idiosyncrasies of Poe's emotional life. It is impossible to agree with those early ill-wishers who read the situation as sexually degenerate. As an economic and living unit, the household was quite successful, and Poe was adored by both his aunt and the cousin he eventually married. Yet the sexual reticence of the arrangement remains disconcerting. Far from degenerate, the relationship was apparently sexless, with the childlike, childless Virginia remaining ill for much of their eleven-year marriage. The emotional aimlessness and the repetitive circularity of his personal relations found a fitting end in Poe's death while travelling to bring his former mother-in-law to his new marriage with a long-lost love from childhood.

Poe's professional life was as untidy as his private one. Although not the habitual dissolute that later writers made of him, Poe did over-indulge occasionally in laudanum and more frequently in alcohol, for which his system had little tolerance. His addictions did not, however, affect his professional accomplishments. He remained a tireless journalist and a canny editor who, in addition to his creative work, produced large quantities of reviews and occasional prose while increasing the circulation of his periodicals as much as fivefold. If anything, his intensity impeded his career more than alcohol did. As exhausting a friend as he was a foe, his enthusiasms for James Russell Lowell and Thomas Chivers were only slightly less discomforting to these patrician poets than was the venom he directed at Henry Wadsworth Longfellow and Margaret Fuller. However engaging, his energy and optimism were seldom grounded in a mature assessment of the literary market-place. Poe's repeated failures to find backing for his collection of interconnected stories 'Tales of the Folio Club' or his literary journal *The Stylus* may mark merely the short-sightedness of mid-century publishing. Yet one can only stand bemused before his final enthusiasm—the foolish belief that *Eureka*, his dense and obscure lecture on Newtonian physics, would be a crowd-pleaser.

The problem of Poe began with his hapless life. Honest but wholly without luck, Poe was never able completely to master his environment or his emotions. Yet the difficulty did not end with his death. His supporters compounded the error by praising his foibles as virtues. Modern readers continue to resist taking Poe seriously in part because of what 'taking him seriously' has meant in the past. Early admirers celebrated the very unsociability that troubled everyone else. To authors as different as D. H. Lawrence, Algernon Swinburne, Fyodor Dostoevsky, Edward Arlington Robinson, Vladimir Nabokov, and Sergei Rachmaninov, Poe's failed life proved his refined sensibilities. Walt Whitman pictured him as a visionary lost in the stormy chaos of mid-century culture:

> On the deck [of a foundering ship] was a slender, slight, beautiful figure, a dim man, apparently enjoying all the terror, the murk, and the dislocation of which he was the centre and the victim. That figure of my lurid dream might stand for Edgar Poe, his spirit, his fortunes, and his poems—themselves all lurid dreams.[1]

[1] Walt Whitman, *Specimen Days* (1882); repr. in Eric W. Carlson (ed.), *The Recognition of Edgar Allan Poe: Selected Criticism Since 1829* (Ann Arbor: University of Michigan Press, 1970), 75.

In the second half of the century, French symbolist poets like Charles Baudelaire, Stéphane Mallarmé, and (later) Paul Valéry expanded Whitman's image of an American Cassandra to view Poe more globally as the *poète maudit*, the cursed truth-teller unwelcome wherever commercialism and bourgeois morality reigned. Such high aesthetic praise added considerably to Poe's reputation. Even the sceptical William Butler Yeats could not dismiss a poet admired by Baudelaire. Yet his sponsors may have done Poe a disservice, promising depths and subtleties that his works could not deliver. As is apparent in Whitman's description, Poe's advocates praised in him what they most admired in themselves. The result was a mythic figure, created in their own image with little concern for historical accuracy. Poe was not a cosmic outcast. His demons were decidedly commonplace—a lack of drawing-room skills and a tendency to tipple. Had he been truly profligate we might enjoy him more. Nor was he, for all his negativity, really a social reformer. Hardly critical of the bourgeoisie, Poe venerated middle-class values. His odd household was not an act of cultural defiance but a measure of how greatly he longed for domesticity, and how little he knew about achieving it.

Later generations of admirers turned from mythic biography back to the works themselves without entirely resisting the temptation to project themselves onto Poe. In response to his preoccupation with extreme mental states, psychoanalytic readers used him to detail the labyrinthine splendours of the mind. Princess Marie Bonaparte and other students of Freud combed the tales for insights into the unconscious. Though stunning demonstrations of the range of dream symbolism, these readings were hard pressed to discover repression in the confessions of Poe's all-too-talkative narrators. Seeking out a shadow plot of sexual misdoing hidden beneath the tales' obvious gothicism, psychoanalytic critics recast the tales as explorations into, virtually creations of, a diseased mind. Even those readings that did not confuse Poe with his unhinged narrators had difficulty explaining why the author was so fixated on a single state of mind. Reducing Poe's extravagances to by-products of mental illness, these early psychologists made the narratives as predictably middle-class as their author.

The recent reinterpretation of psychoanalysis in terms of a more sophisticated understanding of the linguistic structure of the mental has taken Poe's work as one of its major testing-grounds. In his 'seminar' on 'The Purloined Letter', maverick psychoanalyst Jacques

Lacan used the story's unread letter as a model for the ways in which meaning circulates in the mind and in society. Subsequently, aestheticians such as Roland Barthes, Jacques Derrida, and Stanley Cavell explicated semiological implications not only in the deductions of the detective fiction but also in the horror of 'The Black Cat' and 'The Imp of the Perverse'. In their intellectual rigour and respect for Poe's creations, these theoretical readings made it once again safe for grown-ups to think about Poe without feeling guilty.

Linguistic theory brought about a rebirth of scholarly interest in Poe. Yet even these post-modern critics explored his fiction to illustrate analytic paradigms derived from elsewhere. In over-praising Poe's prescience, theorists called attention to how much he left for later generations to articulate. Although anticipating modern trends, Poe is hardly modern. 'The Bells' is not 'Le Bateau ivre', nor ratiocination, deconstruction; and any reader who goes to him looking for Mallarmé or Derrida is bound to be disappointed. The inability of such dazzling analyses to make Poe respectable suggests that perhaps we are trying to defend him in the wrong way. No author wishes to be a precursor—a literary way station on the road to somewhere else. Each aspires to be the word itself. And until we can respect Poe without regard for what his progeny have made of him, we will not be able to appreciate him at all.

Respect for Poe must begin with his ideas. Although his characters are forever burying themselves in 'volumes of forgotten lore', modern readers have trouble imagining Poe himself as an intellectual. Yet in fact Poe's uniqueness rests more with his thought than with his craft. Despite Baudelaire's assertion that he was a pure aesthete, an early proponent of 'art for art's sake', Poe's technical skills were uneven. His language in both the poetry and the prose could be swift and evocative; it could also be ungrammatical, overwrought, relentless. His supposedly innovative use of the *outré* and the perverse was unremarkable, roughly comparable to that in other Gothic fictions of the period. And although we remember the tales as having strong characters and plots, Poe was, as psychoanalytic criticism inadvertently demonstrated, not really very interested in either.

Poe's characters are largely psychic types. However precisely they represent mental disorientation, the tales do not locate these images of insanity within particularized individuals. All Poe's narrators speak roughly the same language. Unconcerned with the ways in which mental states shape personalities or events, Poe treated all disorientation as the same, whether it derived from guilt, anger, fear, or stupidity; and there is little tonal difference between the murderer in 'The Tell-Tale Heart' and the innocent prisoner of 'The Pit and the Pendulum'. The tales show no fascination, as do Freud's case-studies, for how inner turmoil gets expressed differently by individuals, and, in the absence of such personalizing idiosyncrasies, the Usher twins seem much less fully imagined characters than Wolf-Man or Dora.

Poe was no more concerned with plotting than with characterization. According to his celebrated theory about the 'unity of effect', every element of a tale must contribute to the overall purpose. In reviewing Hawthorne's tales, Poe explained:

> in almost all classes of composition, the unity of effect or impression is a point of great importance. . . . [The skilful literary artist] has not fashioned his thoughts to accommodate his incidents; but having conceived, with deliberate care, a certain unique or single *effect* to be wrought out, he then invents such incidents—he then combines such events as may best aid him in establishing this preconceived effect. If his very initial sentence tend not to the outbringing of this effect, then he has failed in his first step. In the whole composition there should be no word written, of which the tendency, direct or indirect, is not to the one pre-established design. And by such means, with such care and skill, a picture is at length painted which leaves in the mind of him who contemplates it with a kindred art, a sense of the fullest satisfaction.

Attempting to professionalize writing, the theory glorified artistic wholeness or 'integrity', by insisting that a work which did not from its very first sentence start doing whatever it intended to do did not deserve the name of 'art'.

The apparent singularity of these 'effects' misled both his readers and occasionally even Poe himself to confuse artistic consistency with narrative surprise. In the very obviousness of their ironic reversals, his endings are often the weakest parts of the tales. His detective stories are compelling in every way *except* as 'whodunits', and in horror tales like 'The Tell-Tale Heart' or 'The Black Cat', the reader is swept along by the psychological or philosophical intensity and simply ignores the moralizing conclusions. Other tales disguise less well the mechanics of their plotting. In tone-poems like 'The Masque of the Red Death', the admirable stylistic unity cannot hide the fact that too much symbolic machinery is expended on the platitude that one cannot cheat Death. And Poe's leisurely pacing can make for slow and attenuated tales: some readers find 'Hop-Frog' preachy and predictable, and the ironies of 'The Cask of Amontillado' can seem more arch with each rereading.

Poe's indifference to character and plot is apparent even in the finest of the moral tales, 'William Wilson'. An immoral man is haunted by a double who shares his name but not his dishonesty. The profligate's hostility to this better self leads him to murder what he at last discovers to be his own conscience. While not a bad narrative idea, the purported 'mystery' of the second Wilson accounts for none of the tale's power. There is no real suspense. Readers guess the double's identity long before its 'revelation' in the final sentence. Nor is the moral particularly compelling. By the end of the tale, we find ourselves siding with the wastrel Wilson, and rejecting his *alter ego* as a tiresome nag. More important, it is hard to figure out exactly what that moral is. Although the name 'Will, son of Will' accuses the protagonist of wilfulness, the charge seems both trivial and a poor description of someone who wanders aimlessly throughout the story. Nor is it clear how his conscience represents a moral advance. Usually in *doppelgänger* stories, the double shows the central figure a new side to himself. In a highly moralistic version like Oscar Wilde's *The Picture of Dorian Gray*, for example, a picture reveals the corruption that the protagonist attempts to hide. In Poe's account, however, the twin teaches the narrator nothing about his inner nature, both because Wilson understands his villainy pretty well from the beginning and because he does not have much of an inner nature to understand. If anything, the tale's allegory discomfortingly suggests that people's desire to be good causes them to be bad. With nothing to illumine, Wilson's conscience turns tattle-tale, driving the bad Wilson on to greater sins if only to escape his own inner dullness.

The moral ambiguities of 'William Wilson' are illumined by Poe's more detailed exploration of 'will' in 'Ligeia'. Here too the tale's triumph lies in neither plot nor character. As Richard Wilbur observed long ago, the story is coherent without making the least bit of sense.[2] A man marries a woman; they study arcane knowledge; she dies. He

[2] Richard Wilbur, *Responses: Prose Pieces 1953–1976* (New York: Harcourt Brace Jovanovich, 1976), 50–1.

marries a second, very different woman; she dies, but arises from her funeral bier in the shape of the first wife. Such a narrative is structurally balanced but devoid of incident or individuals. Rowena has no identity except as second wife, and the narrator lacks even a name. The final character, Ligeia, is explicitly defined in terms of this absence of characteristics —the narrator's inability to remember anything about her except some vague physical features. The two death scenes and the exposition that separates them flesh out the situation without making it more comprehensible. What, after all, is the point of parallels between the two marriages, and especially of the final resurrection of Rowena as Ligeia? Why does so sketchy a plot waste time on detailed descriptions of background material, like Ligeia's relation to astronomy, the oriental decor of Rowena's bridal chamber, and the narrator's fruitless ministrations to her corpse? Psychoanalytic and symbolic readings only compound the confusion by making the narrative too sensible—a lunatic's compulsive confession of killing two wives—or senseless in a different way—a Neoplatonic allegory of cosmic reunification into the Primal One. Such readings prove that the plot does not mean what it says and that it does not mean anything else either.

By discarding characterization and narrative, this stripped-down tale, from its epigraph on, focuses exclusively on Ligeia's stupendous will to life. This preoccupation might have made Ligeia more personable. Will is traditionally considered the quintessential human faculty, what distinguishes us from unselfconscious beasts. But Poe was not interested in anything so sentimental as volition or agency. Like the Puritans before him, he doubted humans' ability to shape their destinies through conscious choice. People fail to get what they want in the tale. Ligeia's will does not prevent her death, and in the farcical final scene, human intentions are treated as pointless, virtually comic. Bobbing up and down on its funeral bier, Rowena's body responds adversely to her husband's caretaking: only when, abandoning all will, he collapses in an unconscious stupor, can the body revive. Still, the tale's scepticism about the efficacy of will should not obscure its recognition that conscious desire is one of the ways humans identify themselves. If will does not control the universe, it does define who we are; and whether or not wishes are fulfilled, Ligeia's personality resides in her 'wild' desire to live, and the narrator's in his 'mad' desire to resurrect her.

Ligeia's will was for Poe only a specific case of a more fundamental problem—the meaning of 'personal identity' itself. By 'identity' he did not mean personal essence, some defining trait or temperament. Identity addressed not who a person *really* was but how a person could be a unit—how we wake up in the morning knowing ourselves to be the same consciousness that went to sleep the night before. In the early 'Morella', the heroine embraces the identity theory of John Locke:

> That identity which is termed personal, Mr Locke, I think, truly defines to consist in the sameness of a rational being. And since by person we understand an intelligent essence having reason, and since there is a consciousness which always accompanies thinking, it is this which makes us all to be that which we call *ourselves*—thereby distinguishing us from other beings that think, and giving us our personal identity.

In *An Essay Concerning Human Understanding*, Locke questioned how persons knew themselves to be the same entity from one moment to the next. The answer could not lie in bodily integrity: all living things change size and shape, constantly losing thousands of dead cells and growing thousands of new ones without any sense of discontinuity. Instead unity had to rest in consciousness itself, especially as measured in terms of memories and of striking moments of self-consciousness, such as exercises of individual will. Yet, Locke wondered, was the unity of consciousness enough to guarantee personhood? If a man were born with Socrates' memories, would he too be Socrates? Was the stability of identity jeopardized by the radical differences of consciousness in the same individual drunk and sober?

The relation between Locke's unifying 'identity' and Ligeia's will is underscored in a companion piece, 'The Man that was Used Up'. Cast in the journalistic form of a celebrity profile, this little-known comic sketch recounts an admirer's attempts to know fully a famous military hero by interviewing both the general and his friends. The narrator discovers finally that the Indian fighter is nothing more than inflated reputation and artificial limbs, a triumph of publicity and prosthetics. Taken on its own, the tale is a delightful (and still timely) satire on imperialist politics and the roles of gossip and the media in popular myth-making. Yet the piece also comments explicitly on the 'Ligeia' narrator's entirely more serious attempt to know his wives. The tales open identically: the one man's tortured confession that he 'cannot, for his soul, remember' where he met Ligeia is deflated by the other's off-hand admission that he 'cannot just now remember' where he met the warrior. The general's literal dismemberment stands emblematically for the philosophical incoherence of personal identity as a concept. Just as the general is exposed to be without his cosmetics only an 'odd looking bundle of something', so all 'self' may be (as Hume feared) merely a random 'bundle' of sensations. When placed alongside its political twin, the psychological 'Ligeia' appears as a similarly bleak meditation on how personal identity works—an exploration of the boundaries not between consciousness and unconsciousness but between self and other. We cannot trust our ability to remember people in their absence, even after their bodies have disappeared. Will and memory maintain Ligeia's integrity no better than reputation held together the general's body parts. The final transformation of one wife into another only concedes the instability of all 'others', and of the perceptions which defined them as separate entities in the first place.

Poe's preoccupation with personhood helps explain the lifelessness of his female characters. Obviously Poe had no concern for gender as such: his famous statement that the most poetic theme was the death of a beautiful woman came dangerously close to claiming that the only good woman was a dead one. Poe's Ligeia is not meant to represent a real individual of whatever gender. She is not even an allegorical figure, like the Red-Cross Knight or Mr Smooth-It-Away, standing for a single moral position. She is less a person than an idea about personhood. In no sense an imitation of life, her story artificially isolates one aspect of personal identity to test the relation between will and personality. The strangeness throughout the 'women' tales—their treatment of people as hypotheses and events as experiments testing those ideas—suggests a model for reading all Poe's characters and plots. Shifting the philosophical focus from ethics to metaphysics, the 'women' tales make clear, as 'William Wilson' did not quite, that Poe's intellectual categories were not primarily moral. It may make some sense to wonder whether or not Wilson was right to cheat at cards. It makes no sense, however, to ask whether one should yank out a lover's teeth or turn one's second wife into one's first. These 'events' do not represent real-life physical situations but approximate a meta-physical condition of disunity. Everywhere in Poe, the Gothic is used to question the integrity of human existence, while twins and doubles blur the distinctions between self and other.

Metaphysical analysis may even redeem 'William Wilson' from the limitations of its moralizing. Although a superficial analysis of the Id and the Super-ego, 'William Wilson' offers an interestingly revisionist account of will and identity. Specifically, the narrator's confusion dramatizes the incoherence of models that represent free will or agency as an internal disagreement over alternative responses—the commonplace belief that one can be 'of two minds' about something. As Jonathan Edwards and Joseph Priestley warned Locke, if such a thing as will existed, the self could assert its freedom only by choosing badly. Were Wilson to accept his double's morality he would become a pale copy of society's conventionalism; to believe in his intellectual independence he must reject logical reasoning as imposed from outside, a kind of doubled 'other'. More generally, the story asks, 'How could you tell if someone was yourself or not?' In terms of so broad a scepticism, the unsatisfactoriness of the tale's conclusion is philosophically astute. The sole solution to such cosmic self-doubt is not to ask the question in the first place, and to his fear that 'he' might be 'me', the narrator can only respond, 'Not any more, he isn't.'

Despite Poe's preference for his poetry, it is the tales, with their leisure to linger over thoughts, that have most impressed subsequent readers. Poe's modern appeal derives most from his ability to give an almost palpable immediacy to abstract questions about will, choice, and personality. Psychoanalytic readers rightly see his explorations of the mental as a kind of proto-psychology, although one concerned more with otherness than with unconsciousness, more with Locke than with Freud. Post-modernists correctly sense that his disinterest in characters or plots avoids the presence and subject-ness that prevent the free play of meaning in traditional writing. For Poe, however, problems of identity did not originate in consciousness but resulted from the foreignness of the environment in which mentality found itself. Minds did not imagine horrors but saw clearly the horribleness of their universe.

Starting with his early prize-winning 'MS. Found in a Bottle', Poe defined minds in terms of the landscape through which they passed. His two most extended works both subordinate people to place. The novel *The Narrative of Arthur Gordon Pym* uses minimal characterization and disjointed plotting to chart a voyage 'southward' into annihilating whiteness. Even more extreme is the late non-fiction *Eureka*, which entirely discards people and plot to cobble together out of scientific treatises by Newton, Laplace, and eighteenth-century natural theologians a 'poetic' account of the formation of the material universe. Such cosmologies and travel narratives only underscore the importance of place or environment throughout the fiction. Poe's very notion of '*other*worldliness' is predicated on a strong sense of *this* one, the physicality of the here and now. In 'The Domain of Arnheim', the particular subsumes the abstract; and Poe depicts an aesthetics of the Beautiful and the individuality of the aesthetician entirely through descriptions of a landscape garden. 'The Fall of the House of Usher' is scarcely less dependent on setting. Naming in its title not the hero Roderick but the 'house' that is both his dwelling and his bloodline, the tale attributes its peculiar 'atmosphere' more to the brooding building and its engulfing tarn than to the tormented inhabitants. Given this preoccupation with place, it is not surprising that one of his final publications, 'Von Kempelen and His Discovery', satirizes the very local phenomenon of the California Gold Rush.

Although it is customary to read setting in Poe as the externalization of mental states, it might be more appropriate to read the mental as an internalization of environment. Paradoxically, Poe's realistic details are often more memorable than his *outré* effects. Setting 'The Pit and the Pendulum' against the backdrop of the Spanish Inquisition may not have made its horror more effective than the less localized Gothicism of 'The Tell-Tale Heart'. It does, however, remind his audience that mental anguish has historical as well as psychological sources. As Walter Benjamin explained, 'The Man in the Crowd' admirably attributed what elsewhere seemed mere 'perverseness' to the alienation and anomie born of industrialization.[3] In juxtaposing the symbolism of 'The Masque of the Red Death' to the social privilege that allowed the elite to flee medieval plagues and nineteenth-century cholera, Poe warns that to emphasize aesthetics over class politics is to repeat as readers that blindness that betrayed Prince Prospero. Even the metaphysics of 'William Wilson' are grounded in social reality; and whatever they say about his schizophrenia, the pages on Wilson's early (mis)development offer great insight into nineteenth-century school-life, fully as moving as anything in *David Copperfield* or *Jane Eyre*.

Traditionally viewed as apathetic or even conservative, Poe was in fact intensely political. He rarely focused on specific events, although his allusions to cholera and to the California Gold Rush did challenge

[3] Walter Benjamin, 'On Some Motifs in Baudelaire', in *Illuminations* (New York: Schocken, 1969), 155–200.

the territorial and class assumptions of his generation. More commonly, Poe explored what we have come to call the politics of knowledge—the ways in which the act of knowing structures and controls what can be known. His travel narratives exposed the imperialist motives behind anthropology; and passages like the Tsalal episode of *Pym* obviously influenced Melville's more extended critiques of racial politics in *Typee* and 'Benito Cereno'. Similarly, his psychological narratives implied the prejudicial character of both what gets known and how it is learned. In his tale of metempsychosis, 'A Tale of the Ragged Mountains', Poe offers first an isolated image of the Orient, and only afterward identifies the moment as a failed attempt at native self-determination. As a result, readers not only find themselves uncomfortably aligned with British colonialism; they are forced to confront the cultural condescension which allowed the West to appropriate Eastern ideas like reincarnation in the first place.

In the even more ambiguous comic tale 'The System of Doctor Tarr and Professor Fether', the desire to know the mind is literalized as a visit to a French insane asylum. As with Delano's racism in 'Benito Cereno', the narrator's assumptions about the nature of madness prevent him from realizing that madmen are running the asylum. Poe's tale, however, goes further to question not only the origins of and cures for madness, but the very project of 'seeing' sanity. The French historian Michel Foucault has shown how the asylum reforms of Phillipe Pinel and William Tuke attempted to 'master' unreason. So, in Poe's tale, the very idea of visiting the insane smacked of the same cultural condescension that marred anthropology. Rejecting as self-deceived the narrator's search for the most efficacious 'system', the tale judges all systems as attempts to control rather than to understand, and asks to what the extent the very science of psychology is merely a species of internal tourism.

Similar reservations about the politics of knowing informed Poe's attitude toward detection. Although Sophocles' *Oedipus Rex* and Shakespeare's *Macbeth* employ some of the suspense techniques associated with contemporary mysteries, Poe wrote the first stories to achieve popularity primarily for their ingenious solutions of puzzles. He also employed many of the motifs still common in such stories—the murder in the locked room, the unjustly accused suspect, analysis by psychological deduction, and the complementary solutions of the least likely person and the most likely place. Most important, Poe created in C. Auguste Dupin a model for the detective that continues to dominate mystery writing. Dupin's eccentric personality and especially his relation to his two foils—a sympathetic but naïve narrator, nameless throughout the series, and an unsympathetic professional investigator, the Prefect of Police Monsieur G.—were explicitly reproduced in such detectives as Arthur Conan Doyle's Sherlock Holmes, Rex Stout's Nero Wolfe, and Agatha Christie's Hercule Poirot.

Yet despite his invention of the genre, Poe's mysteries are not traditional tales of detection. As their lengthy philosophical digressions make clear, Poe is less interested in solving puzzles than in exposing the misconceptions that make things seem 'mysterious' in the first place. For all their obvious interest in the mechanics of problem solving, the tales themselves scarcely offer solutions. By withholding evidence, Poe makes second-guessing impossible. In none of the tales is the reader permitted to solve the mystery along with the detective. Nor do the tales concern crimes in any narrowly legal sense. Only in the first Dupin tale is there even an identifiable murderer. Most important, the tales' solutions lack the moral dimension by which mysteries customarily celebrate the detective's ability to right wrongs or restructure a disordered society. These are not tales of chivalric retribution. The stolen goods of 'The Gold-Bug' are never returned to their rightful owners. In the first two Dupin tales all misdeeds go unpunished, while in the third Dupin's response to the villainous but hardly illegal theft of a love-letter is merely to repeat the original crime in a morally ambiguous way.

Readers were wrong to focus on the cleverness of the stories. 'Where', Poe wondered, 'is the ingenuity of unraveling a web which you yourself [the author] have woven for the express purpose of unraveling?' Far from an unambiguous elucidation of Truth, detection was for Poe merely a specialized way of thinking, and one somewhat at odds with the epistemologies of the other tales. Implicitly ratiocination announces the total explicability of what remains unintelligible everywhere else in Poe. For this very reason it seems unsatisfactory and incomplete. The linguistic literalism Legrand uses to solve the cryptogram in 'The Gold-Bug' marks his intellect as second-rate, no more admirable than his greed. Even Dupin's more imaginative logic clarifies reality by oversimplifying it. In interpreting the Rue Morgue murders, Dupin blithely explains away the very strangeness that the

Gothic tales celebrate. And 'The Purloined Letter', the most sophisticated and non-linear of the detective stories, represses Dupin's support for the kind of aristocratic libertinism and monarchial politics which Poe and his middle-class readership customarily opposed.

The limitations of detection as a way of knowing the world are clearest in what appears the weakest of the detective tales, 'The Mystery of Marie Rogêt'. Trying to explain in fiction the real-life death of shop-girl Mary Rogers, Dupin (and Poe behind him) trade on the right to knowledge afforded them by their culturally privileged position. The comparative failure of their explanations not only challenges that right to know others, it exposes the discriminatory ideologies that make the event inaccessible to them and so gives voice to the very minority identities that privilege seeks to repress. The tale records without comment how the media's manufacture of a culturally acceptable meaning makes class and gender into 'mysteries'. Yet by the most successful of Poe's ironic effects, the implausibility of the 'romantic' explanation of Mary's death makes the realities of class prejudice, sexual harassment, and reproductive politics all the more visible. Marie Rogêt becomes, in her resistance to Dupin, Poe's only gendered character, her narrative his most fully realized world, her murder his sole sexualized event. And in its inability to say the word, the tale stands as our first piece of abortion fiction.

These least known tales show us Poe best. In 'The Murder in the Rue Morgue', Dupin argued that even madmen 'are of some nation'. So too with Poe himself. The extravagance of his narratives encouraged readers to divorce Poe from intellectual and social issues and to imagine that he lived with his characters in some 'ultimate dim Thule', a dream-land 'out of SPACE—out of TIME'. Cut off from his thoughts, Poe not only has no chance of finding a place in our cultural histories. He is robbed of the power to say anything significant to those of us who continue to live within culture. Beyond space and time he is also beyond reach, able to thrill but not to touch us. In this respect our first adolescent reading of Poe may have also been our most courageous. Innocent of subjectivity and unimpressed by symbolism, youths find in Poe's universe the same strangeness that astonishes them in their own. We later teach ourselves to see Poe as otherworldly for fear that what he says about the world might actually be true. Until we can learn once more to read the world back into Poe, we cannot read him seriously at all.

NOTE ON THE TEXT

DESPITE the many printings of Poe's tales, there are few major controversies concerning his texts. This edition reprints from the standard (at present the only) complete edition of Poe: the 'Virginia' edition of *The Complete Works of Edgar Allan Poe*, ed. James A. Harrison, 17 vols. (New York: Thomas Y. Crowell & Co., 1902). I have checked these texts against the magisterial edition of the tales by Thomas Ollive Mabbott, *Collected Works of Edgar Allan Poe*, ii: *Tales and Sketches, 1831–1842*, and iii: *Tales and Sketches, 1843–1849* (Cambridge, Mass.: Harvard University Press, 1978). I have also consulted Patrick Quinn's edition for the Library of America, *Edgar Allan Poe: Poetry and Tales* (New York: Library of America, 1984), which—with its companion, *Edgar Allan Poe: Essays and Reviews*, ed. G. R. Thompson—constitutes the most complete readily available edition. Since this edition is intended as a reading text, I have silently corrected errors in Poe's spelling and punctuation of foreign languages, which previous editors left unchanged. All footnotes within the text are Poe's own.

SELECT BIBLIOGRAPHY

Editions

The Complete Works of Edgar Allan Poe, ed. James A. Harrison, the 'Virginia' edition, 17 vols. (New York: Thomas Y. Crowell & Co., 1902).

Collected Works of Edgar Allan Poe, ed. Thomas Ollive Mabbott, ii: *Tales and Sketches, 1831–1842*, and iii: *Tales and Sketches, 1843–1849* (Cambridge, Mass.: Harvard University Press, 1978).

Edgar Allan Poe: Poetry and Tales, ed. Patrick Quinn (New York: Library of America, 1984).

Edgar Allan Poe: Essays and Reviews, ed. G. R. Thompson (New York: Library of America, 1984).

Biography

Quinn, Arthur Hobson, *Edgar Allan Poe: A Critical Biography* (New York: D. Appleton–Century, 1941).

Silverman, Kenneth, *Edgar A. Poe: Mournful and Never-Ending Remembrance* (New York: Harper Collins, 1991).

Anthologies

Budd, Louis J., and Cady, Edwin H. (eds.), *On Poe: The Best from* American Literature (Durham, NC: Duke University Press, 1993).

Carlson, Eric W. (ed.), *The Recognition of Edgar Allan Poe: Selected Criticism Since 1829* (Ann Arbor: University of Michigan Press, 1970).

Muller, John P., and Richardson, William J. (eds.), *The Purloined Poe: Lacan, Derrida and Psychoanalytic Reading* (Baltimore and London: Johns Hopkins University Press, 1988).

Rosenheim, Shawn, and Rachman, Stephen (eds.), *The American Face of Edgar Allan Poe* (Baltimore and London: Johns Hopkins University Press, 1995).

Silverman, Kenneth (ed.), *New Essays on Poe's Major Tales* (New York: Cambridge University Press, 1993).

Criticism

Benjamin, Walter, 'On Some Motifs in Baudelaire', in *Illuminations* (New York: Schocken, 1969), 155–200.

Byer, Robert, 'Mysteries of the City: A Reading of Poe's "Man in the Crowd" ' in Sacvan Bercovitch and Myra Jehlen (eds.), *Ideology and Classic American Literature* (New York: Cambridge University Press, 1986), 221–46.

Cavell, Stanley, *In Quest of the Ordinary: Lines of Skepticism and Romanticism* (Chicago: University of Chicago Press, 1988); repr. in Rosenheim and Rachman, *The American Face of Edgar Allan Poe*, 3–36.

Davidson, Edward H., *Poe: A Critical Study* (Cambridge, Mass.: Harvard University Press, 1957).

Dayan, Joan, *Fables of Mind: An Inquiry into Poe's Fiction* (New York: Oxford University Press, 1987).

—— 'Romance and Race' in Emory Elliot (ed.), *The Columbia Literary History of the American Novel* (New York: Columbia University Press, 1991), 89–109.

Derrida, Jacques, 'Le Facteur de la Vérité', in *The Post Card: From Socrates to Freud and Beyond*, trans. Alan Bass (Chicago: University of Chicago Press, 1987), 411–96; repr. in Muller and Richardson, *The Purloined Poe*, 173–212.

Foucault, Michel, *Madness and Civilization: A History of Insanity in the Age of Reason* (New York: Vintage Books, 1973).

Hungerford, Edward, 'Poe and Phrenology', *American Literature*, 2 (1930), 209–31.

Irwin, John T., *American Hieroglyphics: The Symbol of Egyptian Hieroglyphics in the American Renaissance* (New Haven: Yale University Press, 1980).

—— *The Mystery to a Solution: Poe, Borges, and the Analytic Story* (Baltimore: Johns Hopkins University Press, 1994).

Jacobs, Robert, *Poe: Journalist and Critic* (Baton Rouge: Louisiana State University Press, 1969).

Johnson, Barbara, 'The Frame of Reference: Poe, Lacan, Derrida', in *The Critical Difference: Essays in the Contemporary Rhetoric of Reading* (Baltimore: Johns Hopkins University Press, 1980), 110–46; repr. in Muller and Richardson, *The Purloined Poe*, 213–51.

Kaplan, Sidney, Introduction to Poe, *The Narrative of Arthur Gordon Pym* (New York: Hill & Wang, 1960), pp. vii–xxv.

Kennedy, J. Gerald, *Poe, Death, and the Life of Writing* (New Haven: Yale University Press, 1987).

Lacan, Jacques, 'Le Séminaire sur "La Lettre volée" ', in *Écrits I* (Paris: Éditions du Seuil, 1966), 7–75; abridged trans. in Muller and Richardson, *The Purloined Poe*, 28–54.

Lind, Sidney, 'Poe and Mesmerism', *PMLA* 62 (1947), 1077–94.

Pease, Donald, *Visionary Compacts: American Renaissance Writings in Cultural Context* (Madison: University of Wisconsin Press, 1987).

Quinn, Patrick, *The French Face of Edgar Allan Poe* (Carbondale, Ill.: Southern Illinois University Press, 1957).

Schueller, Malini Johar, 'Harems, Orientalist Subversions, and the Crisis of Nationalism: The Case of Edgar Allan Poe and "Ligeia" ', *Criticism*, 37 (1995), 601–23.

Thompson, G. R., *Poe's Fiction: Romantic Irony in the Gothic Tales* (Madison: University of Wisconsin Press, 1973).

Van Leer, David, 'Detecting Truth: The World of the Dupin Tales', in Silverman (ed.), *New Essays on Poe's Major Tales*, 65–91.

Wilbur, Richard, *Responses: Prose Pieces 1953–1976* (New York: Harcourt Brace Jovanovich, 1976).

Walsh, John, *Poe the Detective: The Curious Circumstances behind 'The Mystery of Marie Rogêt'* (New Brunswick, NJ: Rutgers University Press, 1968).

A CHRONOLOGY OF EDGAR ALLAN POE

1809 Born 19 January in Boston to the popular actress Eliza Arnold and her less talented husband David Poe. Father abandons family in the autumn the same year.

1811 Mother dies in Richmond, Virginia. Separated from his older brother William and infant sister Rosalie, Poe is taken in (but not formally adopted) by merchant John Allan and his wife Frances.

1815–20 Poe travels with the Allans to Scotland and London, where he attends boarding schools in Chelsea and Stoke Newington.

1820–5 After financial losses, the Allans return to Richmond. In private academies, Poe excels at languages and begins to write. Re-establishes contact with brother and sister, now called Henry and Rose.

1826 Enters the University of Virginia (founded the year before by Thomas Jefferson). Triumphs in Latin and French, but withdraws after one year when Allan refuses to honour his accumulated gambling debts. Returns to Richmond to find his year-old engagement to Elmira Royster broken off by her parents.

1827 In Boston works in newspaper office, publishes anonymously the 40-page *Tamerlane and Other Poems*, and enlists in Army as 'Edgar Perry'. Stationed in South Carolina, Poe soon wishes to leave the military, but to please Allan applies to US Military Academy at West Point.

1829 Frances Allan dies. Allan supports Poe's discharge from Army and application to West Point. In December Poe publishes under his own name *Al Aaraaf, Tamerlane and Minor Poems*, without Allan's financial assistance.

1830 Enters West Point in May. Allan remarries, ending Poe's hope of inheritance.

1831 After Allan's refusal to release him from West Point, Poe in January intentionally neglects academic and military duties until he is expelled. In April he publishes in New York a new volume of *Poems*, including 'To Helen'. In Baltimore lives with his paternal aunt Maria Clemm and her 9-year-old daughter Virginia. Reunited with his brother Henry, who dies in August. Publishes his first tale 'A Dream' in August.

1832–3 Regularly publishes ironic tales, including ones in the projected series 'Tales of the Folio Club'. 'MS. Found in a Bottle' wins prize from the *Baltimore Visiter* [*sic*], where it is published in October.

1835 Travels with Maria and Virginia Clemm to Richmond to assume editorship of *Southern Literary Messenger*. His Gothic tales like 'Berenicë' and incisive reviews increase the *Messenger*'s circulation fivefold.

1836 In Richmond renews acquaintance with sister Rose. Marries the 14-year-old Virginia in May. Leaves editorship in December, although the *Messenger* still publishes over the next two months instalments from his novel *The Narrative of Arthur Gordon Pym*.

1837 Moves to New York and fails to find publisher for 'Tales of the Folio Club'.

1838 Moves to Philadelphia. After a year's delay, Harper and Brothers in July publishes *Pym*, Poe's first book of fiction. Returns to magazine publication, most notably in September with 'Ligeia'.

1839 Assumes editorship of *Burton's Gentleman's Magazine*. Publishes there 'The Man that was Used Up' in August, 'The Fall of the House of Usher' in September, and in December 'The Man of the Crowd'. In December also publishes his first collection of stories, *Tales of the Grotesque and Arabesque*.

1840 After publishing in the *Gentleman's* an attack on Longfellow in February, Poe leaves the magazine in June and immediately begins circulating prospectus for his own journal, the *Penn Magazine*.

1841 Takes position with *Graham's Lady's and Gentleman's Magazine*, the former *Burton's Gentleman's* now under new ownership. Publishes there in March another attack on Longfellow and in April the first detective story, 'The Murders in the Rue Morgue'. Begins to seek a political post under President John Tyler.

1842 In January Virginia ruptures a blood vessel while singing. After increasing the circulation sevenfold, Poe resigns from *Graham's* in April, but publishes there the following month 'The Masque of the Red Death' and his first review of Nathaniel Hawthorne. Money problems and Virginia's continued ill health lead to increased drinking by the end of the year.

1843 His political hopes dashed, Poe tries to extend his literary influence, reviving his prospectus for a journal, now called *The Stylus*, and publishing 'The Tell-Tale Heart' with the Bostonian James Russell Lowell. In June he publishes his prize-winning 'The Gold-Bug', one of the most internationally popular stories ever written. In November begins to lecture on 'The Poetry of America'.

1844 In April moves with Virginia and her mother to New York, where he publishes ephemera in the *Evening Mirror* and the *Democratic Review*. In September publishes 'The Purloined Letter'.

1845 In January publishes in the *Mirror* 'The Raven', an immediate popular success. In March becomes co-editor of *Broadway Journal*, where he reprints earlier work and resumes his attacks on Longfellow's 'plagiarisms'. In June Wiley and Putnam issues a new edition of the *Tales*. In October he takes ownership of the *Journal* and reads 'Al Aaraaf' at the Boston Lyceum without success. In November Wiley issues *The Raven and Other Poems*.

1846 In January the *Journal* folds. Publishes 'The Philosophy of Composition' in April. Moves his family to Turtle Bay, Manhattan, and then in May to nearby Fordham. Between May and October publishes controversial 'Literati' sketches, which result in slanders against Poe.

1847 Virginia dies, 29 January. In February Poe wins libel suit. In December publishes 'Ulalume'.

1848 In February lectures on 'The Universe', published in May as *Eureka*. Courts various women, including his childhood sweetheart Elmira Royster Shelton.

1849 In August and September lectures in Richmond and becomes engaged to Shelton. Dies in Baltimore on 7 October.

SELECTED TALES

MS. FOUND IN A BOTTLE

Qui n'a plus qu'un moment à vivre
N'a plus rien à dissimuler.

Quinault *Atys**

Of my country and of my family I have little to say. Ill usage and length of years have driven me from the one, and estranged me from the other. Hereditary wealth afforded me an education of no common order, and a contemplative turn of mind enabled me to methodise the stores which early study very diligently garnered up. Beyond all things, the works of the German moralists gave me great delight; not from any ill-advised admiration of their eloquent madness, but from the ease with which my habits of rigid thought enabled me to detect their falsities. I have often been reproached with the aridity of my genius; a deficiency of imagination has been imputed to me as a crime; and the Pyrrhonism of my opinions has at all times rendered me notorious. Indeed, a strong relish for physical philosophy has, I fear, tinctured my mind with a very common error of this age—I mean the habit of referring occurrences, even the least susceptible of such reference, to the principles of that science. Upon the whole, no person could be less liable than myself to be led away from the severe precincts of truth by the *ignes fatui* of superstition. I have thought proper to premise thus much, lest the incredible tale I have to tell should be considered rather the raving of a crude imagination, than the positive experience of a mind to which the reveries of fancy have been a dead letter and a nullity.

After many years spent in foreign travel, I sailed in the year 18—, from the port of Batavia, in the rich and populous island of Java, on a voyage to the Archipelago of the Sunda islands. I went as passenger—having no other inducement than a kind of nervous restlessness which haunted me as a fiend.

Our vessel was a beautiful ship of about four hundred tons, copper-fastened, and built at Bombay of Malabar teak. She was freighted with cotton-wool and oil, from the Lachadive islands. We had also on board coir, jaggeree, ghee, cocoa-nuts, and a few cases of opium. The stowage was clumsily done, and the vessel consequently crank.

We got under way with a mere breath of wind, and for many days stood along the eastern coast of Java, without any other incident to beguile the monotony of our course than the occasional meeting with some of the small grabs of the Archipelago to which we were bound.*

One evening, leaning over the taffrail, I observed a very singular, isolated cloud, to the N.W. It was remarkable, as well for its color, as from its being the first we had seen since our departure from Batavia. I watched it attentively until sunset, when it spread all at once to the eastward and westward, girting in the horizon with a narrow strip of vapor, and looking like a long line of low beach. My notice was soon afterwards attracted by the dusky-red appearance of the moon, and the peculiar character of the sea. The latter was undergoing a rapid change, and the water seemed more than usually transparent. Although I could distinctly see the bottom, yet, heaving the lead, I found the ship in fifteen fathoms. The air now became intolerably hot, and was loaded with spiral exhalations similar to those arising from heated iron. As night came on, every breath of wind died away, and a more entire calm it is impossible to conceive. The flame of a candle burned upon the poop without the least perceptible motion, and a long hair, held between the finger and thumb, hung without the possibility of detecting a vibration. However, as the captain said he could perceive no indication of danger, and as we were drifting in bodily to shore, he ordered the sails to be furled, and the anchor let go. No watch was set, and the crew, consisting principally of Malays, stretched themselves deliberately upon deck. I went below—not without a full presentiment of evil. Indeed, every appearance warranted me in apprehending a Simoon.* I told the captain my fears; but he paid no attention to what I said, and left me without deigning to give a reply. My uneasiness, however, prevented me from sleeping, and about midnight I went upon deck. As I placed my foot upon the upper step of the companion-ladder, I was startled by a loud, humming noise, like that occasioned by the rapid revolution of a mill-wheel, and before I could ascertain its meaning, I found the ship quivering to its centre. In the next instant, a wilderness of foam hurled us upon our beam-ends, and, rushing over us fore and aft, swept the entire decks from stem to stern.

The extreme fury of the blast proved, in a great measure, the salvation of the ship. Although completely water-logged, yet, as her masts had gone by the board, she rose, after a minute, heavily from the sea, and, staggering awhile beneath the immense pressure of the tempest, finally righted.

By what miracle I escaped destruction, it is impossible to say. Stunned by the shock of the water, I found myself, upon recovery, jammed in between the stern-post and rudder. With great difficulty I gained my feet, and looking dizzily around, was at first struck with the idea of our being among breakers; so terrific, beyond the wildest imagination, was the whirlpool of mountainous and foaming ocean within which we were ingulfed. After a while, I heard the voice of an old Swede, who had shipped with us at the moment of our leaving port. I hallooed to him with all my strength, and presently he came reeling aft. We soon discovered that we were the sole survivors of the accident. All on deck, with the exception of ourselves, had been swept overboard; the captain and mates must have perished as they slept, for the cabins were deluged with water. Without assistance, we could expect to do little for the security of the ship, and our exertions were at first paralyzed by the momentary expectation of going down. Our cable had, of course, parted like pack-thread, at the first breath of the hurricane, or we should have been instantaneously overwhelmed. We scudded with frightful velocity before the sea, and the water made clear breaches over us. The frame-work of our stern was shattered excessively, and, in almost every respect, we had received considerable injury; but to our extreme joy we found the pumps unchoked, and that we had made no great shifting of our ballast. The main fury of the blast had already blown over, and we apprehended little danger from the violence of the wind; but we looked forward to its total cessation with dismay; well believing, that, in our shattered condition, we should inevitably perish in the tremendous swell which would ensue. But this very just apprehension seemed by no means likely to be soon verified. For five entire days and nights—during which our only subsistence was a small quantity of jaggeree, procured with great difficulty from the forecastle—the hulk flew at a rate defying computation, before rapidly succeeding flaws of wind, which, without equalling the first violence of the Simoon, were still more terrific than any tempest I had before encountered. Our course for the first four days was, with trifling variations, S. E. and by S.; and we must have run down the coast of New Holland.* On the fifth day the cold became extreme, although the wind had hauled round a point more to the northward. The sun arose with a sickly yellow lustre, and clambered a very few degrees above the horizon—emitting no decisive light. There were no clouds apparent, yet the wind was upon the increase, and blew with a fitful and unsteady fury. About noon, as nearly as we could guess, our attention was again arrested by the appearance of the sun. It gave out no light, properly so called, but a dull and sullen glow without reflection, as if all its rays were polarized. Just before sinking within the turgid sea, its central fires suddenly went out, as if hurriedly extinguished by some unaccountable power. It was a dim, silver-like rim, alone, as it rushed down the unfathomable ocean.

We waited in vain for the arrival of the sixth day—that day to me has not arrived—to the Swede, never did arrive. Thenceforward we were enshrouded in pitchy darkness, so that we could not have seen an object at twenty paces from the ship. Eternal night continued to envelop us, all unrelieved by the phosphoric sea-brilliancy to which we had been accustomed in the tropics. We observed too, that, although the tempest continued to rage with unabated violence, there was no longer to be discovered the usual appearance of surf, or foam, which had hitherto attended us. All around were horror, and thick gloom, and a black sweltering desert of ebony. Superstitious terror crept by degrees into the spirit of the old Swede, and my own soul was wrapped up in silent wonder. We neglected all care of the ship, as worse than useless, and securing ourselves, as well as possible, to the stump of the mizen-mast, looked out bitterly into the world of ocean. We had no means of calculating time, nor could we form any guess of our situation. We were, however, well aware of having made farther to the southward than any previous navigators, and felt great amazement at not meeting with the usual impediments of ice. In the meantime every moment threatened to be our last—every mountainous billow hurried to overwhelm us. The swell surpassed anything I had imagined possible, and that we were not instantly buried is a miracle. My companion spoke of the lightness of our cargo, and reminded me of the excellent qualities of our ship; but I could not help feeling the utter hopelessness of hope itself, and prepared myself gloomily for that death which I thought nothing could defer beyond an hour, as, with every knot of way the ship made, the swelling of the black stupendous seas became more dismally appalling. At times we gasped for breath at an elevation beyond the albatross—at times became dizzy with the velocity of our descent into some watery hell, where the air grew stagnant, and no sound disturbed the slumbers of the kraken.

We were at the bottom of one of these abysses, when a quick scream from my companion broke fearfully upon the night. 'See! see!' cried he, shrieking in my ears, 'Almighty God! see! see!' As he spoke, I became aware of a dull, sullen glare of red light which streamed down the sides of the vast chasm where we lay, and threw a fitful brilliancy upon our deck. Casting my eyes upwards, I beheld a spectacle which froze the current of my blood. At a terrific height directly above us, and upon the very verge of the precipitous descent, hovered a gigantic ship, of perhaps four thousand tons. Although upreared upon the summit of a wave more than a hundred times her own altitude, her apparent size still exceeded that of any ship of the line or East Indiaman in existence. Her huge hull was of a deep dingy black, unrelieved by any of the customary carvings of a ship. A single row of brass cannon protruded from her open ports, and dashed from their polished surfaces the fires of innumerable battle-lanterns, which swung to and fro about her rigging. But what mainly inspired us with horror and astonishment, was that she bore up under a press of sail in the very teeth of that supernatural sea, and of that ungovernable hurricane. When we first discovered her, her bows were alone to be seen, as she rose slowly from the dim and horrible gulf beyond her. For a moment of intense terror she paused upon the giddy pinnacle, as if in contemplation of her own sublimity, then trembled and tottered, and—came down.

At this moment, I know not what sudden self-possession came over my spirit. Staggering as far aft as I could, I awaited fearlessly the ruin that was to overwhelm. Our own vessel was at length ceasing from her struggles, and sinking with her head to the sea. The shock of the descending mass struck her, consequently, in that portion of her frame which was already under water, and the inevitable result was to hurl me, with irresistible violence, upon the rigging of the stranger.

As I fell, the ship hove in stays, and went about; and to the confusion ensuing I attributed my escape from the notice of the crew. With little difficulty I made my way, unperceived, to the main hatchway, which was partially open, and soon found an opportunity of secreting myself in the hold. Why I did so I can hardly tell. An indefinite sense of awe, which at first sight of the navigators of the ship had taken hold of my mind, was perhaps the principle of my concealment. I was unwilling to trust myself with a race of people who had offered, to the cursory glance I had taken, so many points of vague novelty, doubt, and apprehension. I therefore thought proper to contrive a hiding-place in the hold. This I did by removing a small portion of the shifting-boards, in such a manner as to afford me a convenient retreat between the huge timbers of the ship.

I had scarcely completed my work, when a footstep in the hold forced me to make use of it. A man passed by my place of concealment with a feeble and unsteady gait. I could not see his face, but had an opportunity of observing his general appearance. There was about it an evidence of great age and infirmity. His knees tottered beneath a load of years, and his entire frame quivered under the burthen. He muttered to himself in a low broken tone, some words of a language which I could not understand, and groped in a corner among a pile of singular-looking instruments, and decayed charts of navigation. His manner was a wild mixture of the peevishness of second childhood and the solemn dignity of a God. He at length went on deck, and I saw him no more.

* * *

A feeling, for which I have no name, has taken possession of my soul—a sensation which will admit of no analysis, to which the lessons of by-gone time are inadequate, and for which I fear futurity itself will offer me no key. To a mind constituted like my own, the latter consideration is an evil. I shall never—I know that I shall never—be satisfied with regard to the nature of my conceptions. Yet it is not wonderful that these conceptions are indefinite, since they have their origin in sources so utterly novel. A new sense—a new entity is added to my soul.

* * *

It is long since I first trod the deck of this terrible ship, and the rays of my destiny are, I think, gathering to a focus. Incomprehensible men! Wrapped up in meditations of a kind which I cannot divine, they pass me by unnoticed. Concealment is utter folly on my part, for the people *will not* see. It was but just now that I passed directly before the eyes of the mate; it was no long while ago that I ventured into the captain's own private cabin, and took thence the materials with which I write, and have written. I shall from time to time continue this journal. It is true that I may not find an opportunity of transmitting it to the world, but I will not fail to make the endeavor. At the last moment I will enclose the MS. in a bottle, and cast it within the sea.

* * *

An incident has occurred which has given me new room for meditation. Are such things the operation of ungoverned chance? I had ventured upon deck and thrown myself down, without attracting any notice, among a pile of ratlin-stuff and old sails, in the bottom of the yawl. While musing upon the singularity of my fate, I unwittingly daubed with a tar-brush the edges of a neatly-folded studding-sail which lay near me on a barrel. The studding-sail is now bent upon the ship, and the thoughtless touches of the brush are spread out into the word DISCOVERY. * * *

I have made many observations lately upon the structure of the vessel. Although well armed, she is not, I think, a ship of war. Her rigging, build, and general equipment, all negative a supposition of this kind. What she *is not*, I can easily perceive; what she *is*, I fear it is impossible to say. I know not how it is, but in scrutinizing her strange model and singular cast of spars, her huge size and overgrown suits of canvass, her severely simple bow and antiquated stern, there will occasionally flash across my mind a sensation of familiar things, and there is always mixed up with such indistinct shadows of recollection, an unaccountable memory of old foreign chronicles and ages long ago. * * *

I have been looking at the timbers of the ship. She is built of a material to which I am a stranger. There is a peculiar character about the wood which strikes me as rendering it unfit for the purpose to which it has been applied. I mean its extreme *porousness*, considered independently of the worm-eaten condition which is a consequence of navigation in these seas, and apart from the rottenness attendant upon age. It will appear perhaps an observation somewhat over-curious, but this wood would have every characteristic of Spanish oak, if Spanish oak were distended by any unnatural means.

In reading the above sentence, a curious apothegm of an old weather-beaten Dutch navigator comes full upon my recollection. 'It is as sure,' he was wont to say, when any doubt was entertained of his veracity, 'as sure as there is a sea where the ship itself will grow in bulk like the living body of the seaman.'

* * *

About an hour ago, I made bold to thrust myself among a group of the crew. They paid me no manner of attention, and, although I stood in the very midst of them all, seemed utterly unconscious of my presence. Like the one I had at first seen in the hold, they all bore about them the marks of a hoary old age. Their knees trembled with infirmity; their shoulders were bent double with decrepitude; their shrivelled skins rattled in the wind; their voices were low, tremulous, and broken; their eyes glistened with the rheum of years; and their gray hairs streamed terribly in the tempest. Around them, on every part of the deck, lay scattered mathematical instruments of the most quaint and obsolete construction. * * *

I mentioned, some time ago, the bending of a studding-sail. From that period, the ship, being thrown dead off the wind, has continued her terrific course due south, with every rag of canvass packed upon her, from her trucks to her lower studding-sail booms, and rolling every moment her top-gallant yard-arms into the most appalling hell of water which it can enter into the mind of man to imagine. I have just left the deck, where I find it impossible to maintain a footing, although the crew seem to experience little inconvenience. It appears to me a miracle of miracles that our enormous bulk is not swallowed up at once and for ever. We are surely doomed to hover continually upon the brink of eternity, without taking a final plunge into the abyss. From billows a thousand times more stupendous than any I have ever seen, we glide away with the facility of the arrowy sea-gull; and the colossal waters rear their heads above us like demons of the deep, but like demons confined to simple threats, and forbidden to destroy. I am led to attribute these frequent escapes to the only natural cause which can account for such effect. I must suppose the ship to be within the influence of some strong current, or impetuous under-tow. * * *

I have seen the captain face to face, and in his own cabin—but, as I expected, he paid me no attention. Although in his appearance there is, to a casual observer, nothing which might bespeak him more or less than man, still, a feeling of irrepressible reverence and awe mingled with the sensation of wonder with which I regarded him. In stature he is nearly my own height; that is, about five feet eight inches. He is of a well-knit and compact frame of body, neither robust nor remarkable otherwise. But it is the singularity of the expression which reigns upon the face—it is the intense, the wonderful, the thrilling evidence of old age, so utter, so extreme, which excites within my spirit a sense—a sentiment ineffable. His forehead, although little wrinkled, seems to bear upon it the stamp of a myriad of years. His gray hairs are records of the past, and his grayer eyes are sybils* of the future. The cabin floor was thickly strewn with strange, iron-clasped folios, and mouldering instruments of science, and obsolete long-forgotten charts. His head was bowed down upon his hands, and he pored, with a fiery, unquiet eye, over a paper which I took to be a commission, and which, at all events, bore the signature of a monarch. He muttered to himself—as did the first seaman whom I saw in the hold—some low peevish syllables of a foreign tongue; and although the speaker was close at my elbow, his voice seemed to reach my ears from the distance of a mile. * * *

The ship and all in it are imbued with the spirit of Eld. The crew glide to and fro like the ghosts of buried centuries; their eyes have an eager and uneasy meaning; and when their figures fall athwart my path in the wild glare of the battle-lanterns, I feel as I have never felt before, although I have been all my life a dealer in antiquities, and have imbibed the shadows of fallen columns at Balbec, and Tadmor, and Persepolis,* until my very soul has become a ruin. * * *

When I look around me, I feel ashamed of my former apprehensions. If I trembled at the blast which has hitherto attended us, shall I not stand aghast at a warring of wind and ocean, to convey any idea of which, the words tornado and simoon are trivial and ineffective? All in the immediate vicinity of the ship is the blackness of eternal night, and a chaos of foamless water; but, about a league on either side of us, may be seen, indistinctly and at intervals, stupendous ramparts of ice, towering away into the desolate sky, and looking like the walls of the universe. * * *

As I imagined, the ship proves to be in a current—if that appellation can properly be given to a tide which, howling and shrieking by the white ice, thunders on to the southward with a velocity like the headlong lashing of a cataract. * * *

To conceive the horror of my sensations is, I presume, utterly impossible; yet a curiosity to penetrate the mysteries of these awful regions, predominates even over my despair, and will reconcile me to the most hideous aspect of death. It is evident that we are hurrying onwards to some exciting knowledge—some never-to-be-imparted secret, whose attainment is destruction. Perhaps this current leads us to the southern pole itself. It must be confessed that a supposition apparently so wild has every probability in its favor.

* * *

The crew pace the deck with unquiet and tremulous step; but there is upon their countenance an expression more of the eagerness of hope than of the apathy of despair.

In the meantime the wind is still in our poop, and, as we carry a crowd of canvass, the ship is at times lifted bodily from out the sea! Oh, horror upon horror!—the ice opens suddenly to the right, and to the left, and we are whirling dizzily, in immense concentric circles, round and round the borders of a gigantic amphitheatre, the summit of whose walls is lost in the darkness and the distance. But little time will be left me to ponder upon my destiny! The circles rapidly grow small—we are plunging madly within the grasp of the whirlpool—and amid a roaring, and bellowing, and thundering of ocean and of tempest, the ship is quivering—oh God! and——going down!

BERENICË

Dicebant mihi sodales, si sepulchrum amicæ visitarem, curas meas aliquantulum fore levatas.

*Ebn Zaiat**

MISERY is manifold. The wretchedness of earth is multiform. Overreaching the wide horizon as the rainbow, its hues are as various as the hues of that arch—as distinct too, yet as intimately blended. Overreaching the wide horizon as the rainbow! How is it that from beauty I have derived a type of unloveliness?—from the covenant of peace, a simile of sorrow? But as, in ethics, evil is a consequence of good so, in fact, out of joy is sorrow born. Either the memory of past bliss is the anguish of to-day, or the agonies which *are* have their origin in the ecstasies which *might have been*.

My baptismal name is Egæus; that of my family I will not mention. Yet there are no towers in the land more time-honored than my gloomy, gray, hereditary halls. Our line has been called a race of visionaries; and in many striking particulars—in the character of the family mansion—in the frescos of the chief saloon—in the tapestries of the dormitories—in the chiselling of some buttresses in the armory—but more especially in the gallery of antique paintings—in the fashion of the library chamber—and, lastly, in the very peculiar nature of the library's contents—there is more than sufficient evidence to warrant the belief.

The recollections of my earliest years are connected with that chamber, and with its volumes—of which latter I will say no more. Here died my mother. Herein was I born. But it is mere idleness to say that I had not lived before—that the soul has no previous existence. You deny it?—let us not argue the matter. Convinced myself, I seek not to convince. There is, however, a remembrance of aerial forms—of spiritual and meaning eyes—of sounds, musical yet sad; a remembrance which will not be excluded; a memory like a shadow—vague, variable, indefinite, unsteady; and like a shadow, too, in the impossibility of my getting rid of it while the sunlight of my reason shall exist.

In that chamber was I born. Thus awaking from the long night of what seemed, but was not, nonentity, at once into the very regions of fairy land—into a palace of imagination—into the wild dominions of monastic thought and erudition—it is not singular that I gazed around me with a startled and ardent eye—that I loitered away my boyhood in books, and dissipated my youth in revery; but it *is* singular, that as years rolled away, and the noon of manhood found me still in the mansion of my fathers—it *is* wonderful what stagnation there fell upon the springs of my life—wonderful how total an inversion took place in the character of my commonest thought. The realities of the world affected me as visions, and as visions only, while the wild ideas of the land of dreams became, in turn, not the material of my every-day existence, but in very deed that existence utterly and solely in itself.

* * *

Berenicë and I were cousins, and we grew up together in my paternal halls. Yet differently we grew—I, ill of health, and buried in gloom—she, agile, graceful, and overflowing with energy; hers, the ramble on the hill-side—mine, the studies of the cloister; I, living within my own heart, and addicted, body and soul, to the most intense and painful meditation—she, roaming carelessly through life, with no thought of the shadows in her path, or the silent flight of the raven-winged hours. Berenicë!—I call upon her name—Berenicë!—and from the gray ruins of memory a thousand tumultuous recollections are startled at the sound! Ah, vividly is her image before me now, as in the early days of her light-heartedness and joy! Oh, gorgeous yet fantastic beauty! Oh, sylph amid the shrubberies of Arnheim! Oh, Naiad among its fountains! And then—then all is mystery and terror, and a tale which should not be told. Disease—a fatal disease, fell like the simoon upon her frame; and, even while I gazed upon her, the spirit of change swept over her, pervading her mind, her habits, and her character, and, in a manner the most subtle and terrible, disturbing even the identity of her person! Alas! the destroyer came and went!—and the victim—where is she? I knew her not—or knew her no longer as Berenicë!

Among the numerous train of maladies superinduced by that fatal and primary one which effected a revolution of so horrible a kind in the moral and physical being of my cousin, may be mentioned as the most distressing and obstinate in its nature, a species of epilepsy not unfrequently terminating in *trance* itself—trance very nearly resembling positive dissolution, and from which her manner of recovery was, in most instances, startlingly abrupt. In the mean time, my own disease—for I have been told that I should call it by no other appellation—my own disease, then, grew rapidly upon me, and assumed finally a monomaniac character of a novel and extraordinary form—hourly and momently gaining vigor—and at length obtaining over me the most incomprehensible ascendency. This monomania, if I must so term it, consisted in a morbid irritability of those properties of the mind in metaphysical science termed the *attentive*. It is more than probable that I am not understood; but I fear, indeed, that it is in no manner possible to convey to the mind of the merely general reader, an adequate idea of that nervous *intensity of interest* with which, in my case, the powers of meditation (not to speak technically) busied and buried themselves, in the contemplation of even the most ordinary objects of the universe.

To muse for long unwearied hours, with my attention riveted to some frivolous device on the margin or in the typography of a book; to become absorbed, for the better part of a summer's day, in a quaint shadow falling aslant upon the tapestry or upon the floor; to lose myself, for an entire night, in watching the steady flame of a lamp, or the embers of a fire; to dream away whole days over the perfume of a flower; to repeat, monotonously, some common word, until the sound, by dint of frequent repetition, ceased to convey any idea whatever to the mind; to lose all sense of motion or physical existence, by means of absolute bodily quiescence long and obstinately persevered in: such were a few of the most common and least pernicious vagaries induced by a condition of the mental faculties, not, indeed, altogether unparalleled, but certainly bidding defiance to anything like analysis or explanation.

Yet let me not be misapprehended. The undue, earnest, and morbid attention thus excited by objects in their own nature frivolous, must not be confounded in character with the ruminating propensity common to all mankind, and more especially indulged in by persons of ardent imagination. It was not even, as might be at first supposed, an extreme condition, or exaggeration of such propensity, but primarily and essentially distinct and different. In the one instance, the dreamer, or enthusiast, being interested by an object usually *not* frivolous, imperceptibly loses sight of this object in a wilderness of deductions and suggestions issuing therefrom, until, at the conclusion of a day-dream *often replete with luxury*, he finds the *incitamentum*, or first cause of his musings, entirely vanished and forgotten. In my case, the primary object was *invariably frivolous*, although assuming, through the medium of my distempered vision, a refracted and unreal importance. Few deductions, if any, were made; and those few pertinaciously returning in upon the original object as a centre. The meditations were *never* pleasurable; and, at the termination of the revery, the first cause, so far from being out of sight, had attained that supernaturally exaggerated interest which was the prevailing feature of the disease. In a word, the powers of mind more particularly exercised were, with me, as I have said before, the *attentive*, and are, with the day-dreamer, the *speculative*.

My books, at this epoch, if they did not actually serve to irritate the disorder, partook, it will be perceived, largely, in their imaginative and inconsequential nature, of the characteristic qualities of the disorder itself. I well remember, among others, the treatise of the noble Italian, Cælius Secundus Curio, '*De Amplitudine Beati Regni Dei*;' St Austin's great work, 'The City of God;' and Tertullian's '*De Carne Christi*,' in which the paradoxical sentence, '*Mortuus est Dei filius; credibile est quia ineptum est; et sepultus resurrexit; certum est quia impossibile est*,' occupied my undivided time, for many weeks of laborious and fruitless investigation.*

Thus it will appear that, shaken from its balance only by trivial things, my reason bore resemblance to that ocean-crag spoken of by Ptolemy Hephestion, which, steadily resisting the attacks of human violence, and the fiercer fury of the waters and the winds, trembled only to the touch of the flower called Asphodel. And although, to a careless thinker, it might appear a matter beyond doubt, that the alteration produced by her unhappy malady, in the *moral* condition of Berenicë, would afford me many objects for the exercise of that intense and abnormal meditation whose nature I have been at some trouble in explaining, yet such was not in any degree the case. In the lucid intervals of my infirmity, her calamity, indeed, gave me pain, and, taking deeply to heart that total wreck of her fair and gentle life, I did not fail to ponder, frequently and bitterly, upon the wonder-working means by which so strange a revolution had been so suddenly brought to pass. But these reflections partook not of the idiosyncrasy of my disease, and were such as would have occurred, under similar circumstances, to the ordinary mass of mankind. True to its own character, my disorder revelled in the less important but more startling changes wrought in the *physical* frame of Berenicë—in the singular and most appalling distortion of her personal identity.

During the brightest days of her unparalleled beauty, most surely I had never loved her. In the strange anomaly of my existence, feelings, with me, *had never been* of the heart, and my passions *always were* of the mind. Through the gray of the early morning—among the trellised shadows of the forest at noonday—and in the silence of my library at night—she had flitted by my eyes, and I had seen her—not as the living and breathing Berenicë, but as the Berenicë of a dream; not as a being of the earth, earthy, but as the abstraction of such a being; not as a thing to admire, but to analyze; not as an object of love, but as the theme of the most abstruse although desultory speculation. And *now*—now I shuddered in her presence, and grew pale at her approach; yet, bitterly lamenting her fallen and desolate condition, I called to mind that she had loved me long, and, in an evil moment, I spoke to her of marriage.

And at length the period of our nuptials was approaching, when, upon an afternoon in the winter of the year—one of those unseasonably warm, calm, and misty days which are the nurse of the beautiful Halcyon,[1]—I sat, (and sat, as I thought, alone,) in the inner apartment of the library. But, uplifting my eyes, I saw that Berenicë stood before me.

Was it my own excited imagination—or the misty influence of the atmosphere—or the uncertain twilight of the chamber—or the gray draperies which fell around her figure—that caused in it so vacillating and indistinct an outline? I could not tell. She spoke no word; and I—not for worlds could I have uttered a syllable. An icy chill ran through my frame; a sense of insufferable anxiety oppressed me; a consuming curiosity pervaded my soul; and, sinking back upon the chair, I remained for some time breathless and motionless, with my eyes riveted upon her person. Alas! its emaciation was excessive, and not one vestige of the former being lurked in any single line of the contour. My burning glances at length fell upon the face.

The forehead was high, and very pale, and singularly placid; and the once jetty hair fell partially over it, and overshadowed the hollow temples with innumerable ringlets, now of a vivid yellow, and jarring discordantly, in their fantastic character, with the reigning melancholy of the countenance. The eyes were lifeless, and lustreless, and seemingly pupilless, and I shrank involuntarily from their glassy stare to the

[1] For as Jove, during the winter season, gives twice seven days of warmth, men have called this clement and temperate time the nurse of the beautiful Halcyon—*Simonides*.

contemplation of the thin and shrunken lips. They parted; and in a smile of peculiar meaning, *the teeth* of the changed Berenicë disclosed themselves slowly to my view. Would to God that I had never beheld them, or that, having done so, I had died!

* * *

The shutting of a door disturbed me, and, looking up, I found that my cousin had departed from the chamber. But from the disordered chamber of my brain, had not, alas! departed, and would not be driven away, the white and ghastly *spectrum* of the teeth. Not a speck on their surface—not a shade on their enamel—not an indenture in their edges—but what that brief period of her smile had sufficed to brand in upon my memory. I saw them *now* even more unequivocally than I beheld them *then*. The teeth!—the teeth!—they were here, and there, and everywhere, and visibly and palpably before me; long, narrow, and excessively white, with the pale lips writhing about them, as in the very moment of their first terrible development. Then came the full fury of my *monomania*, and I struggled in vain against its strange and irresistible influence. In the multiplied objects of the external world I had no thoughts but for the teeth. For these I longed with a frenzied desire. All other matters and all different interests became absorbed in their single contemplation. They—they alone were present to the mental eye, and they, in their sole individuality, became the essence of my mental life. I held them in every light. I turned them in every attitude. I surveyed their characteristics. I dwelt upon their peculiarities. I pondered upon their conformation. I mused upon the alteration in their nature. I shuddered as I assigned to them, in imagination, a sensitive and sentient power, and, even when unassisted by the lips, a capability of moral expression. Of Mademoiselle Sallé it has been well said, '*Que tous ses pas étaient des sentiments*,' and of Berenicë I more seriously believed *que tous ses dents étaient des idées*.* *Des idées!*—ah, here was the idiotic thought that destroyed me! *Des idées!*—ah, *therefore* it was that I coveted them so madly! I felt that their possession could alone ever restore me to peace, in giving me back to reason.

And the evening closed in upon me thus—and then the darkness came, and tarried, and went—and the day again dawned—and the mists of a second night were now gathering around—and still I sat motionless in that solitary room—and still I sat buried in meditation—and still the *phantasma* of the teeth maintained its terrible ascendency, as, with the most vivid and hideous distinctness, it floated about amid the changing lights and shadows of the chamber. At length there broke in upon my dreams a cry as of horror and dismay; and thereunto, after a pause, succeeded the sound of troubled voices, intermingled with many low moanings of sorrow or of pain. I arose from my seat, and, throwing open one of the doors of the library, saw standing out in the ante-chamber a servant maiden, all in tears, who told me that Berenicë was—no more! She had been seized with epilepsy in the early morning, and now, at the closing in of the night, the grave was ready for its tenant, and all the preparations for the burial were completed.

* * *

I found myself sitting in the library, and again sitting there alone. It seemed that I had newly awakened from a confused and exciting dream. I knew that it was now midnight, and I was well aware that since the setting of the sun Berenicë had been interred. But of that dreary period which intervened I had no positive, at least no definite comprehension. Yet its memory was replete with horror—horror more horrible from being vague, and terror more terrible from ambiguity. It was a fearful page in the record of my existence, written all over with dim, and hideous, and unintelligible recollections. I strived to decypher them, but in vain; while ever and anon, like the spirit of a departed sound, the shrill and piercing shriek of a female voice seemed to be ringing in my ears. I had done a deed—what was it? I asked myself the question aloud, and the whispering echoes of the chamber answered me,—'*What was it?*'

On the table beside me burned a lamp, and near it lay a little box. It was of no remarkable character, and I had seen it frequently before, for it was the property of the family physician; but how came it *there*, upon my table, and why did I shudder in regarding it? These things were in no manner to be accounted for, and my eyes at length dropped to the open pages of a book, and to a sentence underscored therein. The words were the singular but simple ones of the poet Ebn Zaiat:—'*Dicebant mihi sodales si sepulchrum amicae visitarem, curas meas aliquantulum fore levatas.*' Why, then, as I perused them, did the hairs of my head erect themselves on end, and the blood of my body become congealed within my veins?

There came a light tap at the library door—and, pale as the tenant of a tomb, a menial entered upon tiptoe. His looks were wild with terror, and he spoke to me in a voice tremulous, husky, and very low. What said he?—some broken sentences I heard. He told of a wild cry disturbing the silence of the night—of the gathering together of the household—of a search in the direction of the sound; and then his tones grew thrillingly distinct as he whispered me of a violated grave—of a disfigured body enshrouded, yet still breathing—still palpitating—*still alive!*

He pointed to my garments; they were muddy and clotted with gore. I spoke not, and he took me gently by the hand: it was indented with the impress of human nails. He directed my attention to some object against the wall. I looked at it for some minutes: it was a spade. With a shriek I bounded to the table, and grasped the box that lay upon it. But I could not force it open; and, in my tremor, it slipped from my hands, and fell heavily, and burst into pieces; and from it, with a rattling sound, there rolled out some instruments of dental surgery, intermingled with thirty-two small, white, and ivory-looking substances that were scattered to and fro about the floor.

MORELLA

Αυτο καθ' αυτο μεθ' αυτου, μονο ειδες αιει ον.

Itself, by itself solely, ONE everlastingly, and single.

PLATO. *Sympos**

WITH a feeling of deep yet most singular affection I regarded my friend Morella. Thrown by accident into her society many years ago, my soul, from our first meeting, burned with fires it had never before known; but the fires were not of Eros, and bitter and tormenting to my spirit was the gradual conviction that I could in no manner define their unusual meaning, or regulate their vague intensity. Yet we met; and fate bound us together at the altar; and I never spoke of passion, nor thought of love. She, however, shunned society, and, attaching herself to me alone, rendered me happy. It is a happiness to wonder;—it is a happiness to dream.

Morella's erudition was profound. As I hope to live, her talents were of no common order—her powers of mind were gigantic. I felt this, and, in many matters, became her pupil. I soon, however, found that, perhaps on account of her Presburg education,* she placed before me a number of those mystical writings which are usually considered the mere dross of the early German literature. These, for what reason I could not imagine, were her favorite and constant study—and that, in process of time they became my own, should be attributed to the simple but effectual influence of habit and example.

In all this, if I err not, my reason had little to do. My convictions, or I forget myself, were in no manner acted upon by the ideal, nor was any tincture of the mysticism which I read, to be discovered, unless I am greatly mistaken, either in my deeds or in my thoughts. Persuaded of this, I abandoned myself implicitly to the guidance of my wife, and entered with an unflinching heart into the intricacies of her studies. And then—then, when, poring over forbidden pages, I felt a forbidden spirit enkindling within me—would Morella place her cold hand upon my own, and rake up from the ashes of a dead philosophy some low, singular words, whose strange meaning burned themselves in upon my memory. And then, hour after hour, would I linger by her side, and dwell upon the music of her voice—until, at length, its melody was tainted with terror,—and there fell a shadow upon my soul—and I grew pale, and shuddered inwardly at those too unearthly tones. And thus, joy suddenly faded into horror, and the most beautiful became the most hideous, as Hinnom became Ge-Henna.*

It is unnecessary to state the exact character of those disquisitions which, growing out of the volumes I have mentioned, formed, for so long a time, almost the sole conversation of Morella and myself. By the learned in what might be termed theological morality they will be readily conceived, and by the unlearned they would, at all events, be little understood. The wild Pantheism of Fichte; the modified *παλιγγενεσια* of the Pythagoreans; and, above all, the doctrines of *Identity* as urged by Schelling, were generally the points of discussion presenting the most of beauty to the imaginative Morella. That identity which is termed personal, Mr Locke, I think, truly defines to consist in the sameness of a rational being. And since by person we understand an intelligent essence having reason, and since there is a consciousness which always accompanies thinking, it is this which makes us all to be that which we call *ourselves*—thereby distinguishing us from other beings that think, and giving us our personal identity. But the *principium individuationis*, the notion of that identity *which at death is or is not lost forever*, was to me, at all times, a consideration of intense interest; not more from the perplexing and exciting nature of its consequences, than from the marked and agitated manner in which Morella mentioned them.*

But, indeed, the time had now arrived when the mystery of my wife's manner oppressed me as a spell. I could no longer bear the touch of her wan fingers, nor the low tone of her musical language, nor the lustre of her melancholy eyes. And she knew all this, but did not upbraid; she seemed conscious of my weakness or my folly, and, smiling, called it Fate. She seemed, also, conscious of a cause, to me unknown, for the gradual alienation of my regard; but she gave me no hint or token of its nature. Yet was she woman, and pined away daily. In time, the crimson spot settled steadily upon the cheek, and the blue veins upon the pale forehead became prominent; and, one instant, my nature melted into pity, but, in the next, I met the glance of her meaning eyes, and then my soul sickened and became giddy with the giddiness of one who gazes downward into some dreary and unfathomable abyss.

Shall I then say that I longed with an earnest and consuming desire for the moment of Morella's decease? I did; but the fragile spirit clung to its tenement of clay for many days—for many weeks and irksome months—until my tortured nerves obtained the mastery over my mind, and I grew furious through delay, and, with the heart of a fiend, cursed the days, and the hours, and the bitter moments, which seemed to lengthen and lengthen as her gentle life declined—like shadows in the dying of the day.

But one autumnal evening, when the winds lay still in heaven, Morella called me to her bed-side. There was a dim mist over all the earth, and a warm glow upon the waters, and, amid the rich October leaves of the forest, a rainbow from the firmament had surely fallen.

'It is a day of days,' she said, as I approached; 'a day of all days either to live or die. It is a fair day for the sons of earth and life—ah, more fair for the daughters of heaven and death!'

I kissed her forehead, and she continued:

'I am dying, yet shall I live.'

'Morella!'

'The days have never been when thou couldst love me—but her whom in life thou didst abhor, in death thou shalt adore.'

'Morella!'

'I repeat that I am dying. But within me is a pledge of that affection—ah, how little!—which thou didst feel for me, Morella. And when my spirit departs shall the child live—thy child and mine, Morella's. But thy days shall be days of sorrow—that sorrow which is the most lasting of impressions, as the cypress is the most enduring of trees. For the hours of thy happiness are over; and joy is not gathered twice in a life, as the roses of Pæstum twice in a year. Thou shalt no longer, then, play the Teian with time, but, being ignorant of the myrtle and the vine, thou shalt bear about with thee thy shroud on earth, as do the Moslemin at Mecca.'*

'Morella!' I cried, 'Morella! how knowest thou this?'—but she turned away her face upon the pillow, and, a slight tremor coming over her limbs, she thus died, and I heard her voice no more.

Yet, as she had foretold, her child—to which in dying she had given birth, and which breathed not until the mother breathed no more—her child, a daughter, lived. And she grew strangely in stature and intellect, and was the perfect resemblance of her who had departed, and I loved her with a love more fervent than I had believed it possible to feel for any denizen of earth.

But, ere long, the heaven of this pure affection became darkened, and gloom, and horror, and grief, swept over it in clouds. I said the child grew strangely in stature and intelligence. Strange indeed was her rapid increase in bodily size—but terrible, oh! terrible were the tumultuous thoughts which crowded upon me while watching the development of her mental being. Could it be otherwise, when I daily discovered in the conceptions of the child the adult powers and faculties of the woman?—when the lessons of experience fell from the lips of infancy? and when the wisdom or the passions of maturity I found hourly gleaming from its full and speculative eye? When, I say, all this became evident to my appalled senses—when I could no longer hide it from my soul, nor throw it off from those perceptions which trembled to receive it—is it to be wondered at that suspicions, of a nature fearful and exciting, crept in upon my spirit, or that my thoughts fell back aghast upon the wild tales and thrilling theories of the entombed Morella? I snatched from the scrutiny of the world a being whom destiny compelled me to adore, and in the rigorous seclusion of my home, watched with an agonizing anxiety over all which concerned the beloved.

And, as years rolled away, and I gazed, day after day, upon her holy, and mild, and eloquent face, and pored over her maturing form, day after day did I discover new points of resemblance in the child to her mother, the melancholy and the dead. And, hourly, grew darker these shadows of similitude, and more full, and more definite, and more perplexing, and more hideously terrible in their aspect. For that her smile was like her mother's I could bear; but then I shuddered at its too perfect *identity*—that her eyes were like Morella's I could endure; but then they too often looked down into the depths of my soul with Morella's own intense and bewildering meaning. And in the contour of the high forehead, and in the ringlets of the silken hair, and in the wan fingers which buried themselves therein, and in the sad musical tones of her speech, and above all—oh, above all—in the phrases and expressions of the dead on the lips of the loved and the living, I found food for consuming thought and horror—for a worm that *would* not die.

Thus passed away two lustra of her life, and, as yet, my daughter remained nameless upon the earth. 'My child' and 'my love' were the designations usually prompted by a father's affection, and the rigid seclusion of her days precluded all other intercourse. Morella's name died with her at her death. Of the mother I had never spoken to the daughter;—it was impossible to speak. Indeed, during the brief period of her existence the latter had received no impressions from the outward world save such as might have been afforded by the narrow limits of her privacy. But at length the ceremony of baptism presented to my mind, in its unnerved and agitated condition, a present deliverance from the terrors of my destiny. And at the baptismal font I hesitated for a name. And many titles of the wise and beautiful, of old and modern times, of my own and foreign lands, came thronging to my lips, with many, many fair titles of the gentle, and the happy, and the good. What prompted me, then, to disturb the memory of the buried dead? What demon urged me to breathe that sound, which, in its very recollection was wont to make ebb the purple blood in torrents from the temples to the heart? What fiend spoke from the recesses of my soul, when, amid those dim aisles, and in the silence of the night, I whispered within the ears of the holy man the syllables—Morella? What more than fiend convulsed the features of my child, and overspread them with hues of death, as, starting at that scarcely audible sound, she turned her glassy eyes from the earth to heaven, and, falling prostrate on the black slabs of our ancestral vault, responded—'I am here!'

Distinct, coldly, calmly distinct, fell those few simple sounds within my ear, and thence, like molten lead, rolled hissingly into my brain. Years—years may pass away, but the memory of that epoch—never! Nor was I indeed ignorant of the flowers and the vine—but the hemlock and the cypress overshadowed me night and day. And I kept no reckoning of time or place, and the stars of my fate faded from heaven, and therefore the earth grew dark, and its figures passed by me, like flitting shadows, and among them all I beheld only—Morella. The winds of the firmament breathed but one sound within my ears, and the ripples upon the sea murmured evermore—Morella. But she died; and with my own hands I bore her to the tomb; and I laughed with a long and bitter laugh as I found no traces of the first, in the charnel where I laid the second—Morella.

LIGEIA

> And the will therein lieth, which dieth not. Who knoweth the mysteries of the will, with its vigor? For God is but a great will pervading all things by nature of its intentness. Man doth not yield himself to the angels, nor unto death utterly, save only through the weakness of his feeble will.
>
> JOSEPH GLANVILL*

I CANNOT, for my soul, remember how, when, or even precisely where, I first became acquainted with the lady Ligeia. Long years have since elapsed, and my memory is feeble through much suffering. Or, perhaps, I cannot *now* bring those points to mind, because, in truth, the character of my beloved, her rare learning, her singular yet placid cast of beauty, and the thrilling and enthralling eloquence of her low musical language, made their way into my heart by paces so steadily and stealthily progressive that they have been unnoticed and unknown. Yet I believe that I met her first and most frequently in some large, old, decaying city near the Rhine. Of her family—I have surely heard her speak. That it is of a remotely ancient date cannot be doubted. Ligeia! Ligeia! Buried in studies of a nature more than all else adapted to deaden impressions of the outward world, it is by that sweet word alone—by Ligeia—that I bring before mine eyes in fancy the image of her who is no more. And now, while I write, a recollection flashes upon me that I have *never known* the paternal name of her who was my friend and my betrothed, and who became the partner of my studies, and finally the wife of my bosom. Was it a playful charge on the part of my Ligeia? or was it a test of my strength of affection, that I should institute no inquiries upon this point? or was it rather a caprice of my own—a wildly romantic offering on the shrine of the most passionate devotion? I but indistinctly recall the fact itself—what wonder that I have utterly forgotten the circumstances which originated or attended it? And, indeed, if ever that spirit which is entitled *Romance*—if ever she, the wan and the misty-winged *Ashtophet** of idolatrous Egypt, presided, as they tell, over marriages ill-omened, then most surely she presided over mine.

There is one dear topic, however, on which my memory fails me not.

It is the *person* of Ligeia. In stature she was tall, somewhat slender, and, in her latter days, even emaciated. I would in vain attempt to portray the majesty, the quiet ease, of her demeanor, or the incomprehensible lightness and elasticity of her footfall. She came and departed as a shadow. I was never made aware of her entrance into my closed study save by the dear music of her low sweet voice, as she placed her marble hand upon my shoulder. In beauty of face no maiden ever equalled her. It was the radiance of an opium dream—an airy and spirit-lifting vision more wildly divine than the phantasies which hovered about the slumbering souls of the daughters of Delos. Yet her features were not of that regular mould which we have been falsely taught to worship in the classical labors of the heathen. 'There is no exquisite beauty,' says Bacon, Lord Verulam, speaking truly of all the forms and *genera* of beauty, 'without some *strangeness* in the proportion.' Yet, although I saw that the features of Ligeia were not of a classic regularity—although I perceived that her loveliness was indeed 'exquisite,' and felt that there was much of 'strangeness' pervading it, yet I have tried in vain to detect the irregularity and to trace home my own perception of 'the strange.' I examined the contour of the lofty and pale forehead—it was faultless—how cold indeed that word when applied to a majesty so divine!—the skin rivalling the purest ivory, the commanding extent and repose, the gentle prominence of the regions above the temples; and then the raven-black, the glossy, the luxuriant and naturally-curling tresses, setting forth the full force of the Homeric epithet, 'hyacinthine!' I looked at the delicate outlines of the nose—and nowhere but in the graceful medallions of the Hebrews had I beheld a similar perfection. There were the same luxurious smoothness of surface, the same scarcely perceptible tendency to the aquiline, the same harmoniously curved nostrils speaking the free spirit. I regarded the sweet mouth. Here was indeed the triumph of all things heavenly—the magnificent turn of the short upper lip—the soft, voluptuous slumber of the under—the dimples which sported, and the color which spoke—the teeth glancing back, with a brilliancy almost startling, every ray of the holy light which fell upon them in her serene and placid, yet most exultingly radiant of all smiles. I scrutinized the formation of the chin—and here, too, I found the gentleness of breadth, the softness and the majesty, the fullness and the spirituality, of the Greek—the contour which the God Apollo revealed but in a dream, to Cleomenes, the son of the Athenian. And then I peered into the large eyes of Ligeia.

For eyes we have no models in the remotely antique. It might have been, too, that in these eyes of my beloved lay the secret to which Lord Verulam alludes. They were, I must believe, far larger than the ordinary eyes of our own race. They were even fuller than the fullest of the gazelle eyes of the tribe of the valley of Nourjahad. Yet it was only at intervals—in moments of intense excitement—that this peculiarity became more than slightly noticeable in Ligeia. And at such moments was her beauty—in my heated fancy thus it appeared perhaps—the beauty of beings either above or apart from the earth—the beauty of the fabulous Houri of the Turk. The hue of the orbs was the most brilliant of black, and, far over them, hung jetty lashes of great length. The brows, slightly irregular in outline, had the same tint. The 'strangeness,' however, which I found in the eyes, was of a nature distinct from the formation, or the color, or the brilliancy of the features, and must, after all, be referred to the *expression*. Ah, word of no meaning! behind whose vast latitude of mere sound we intrench our ignorance of so much of the spiritual. The expression of the eyes of Ligeia! How for long hours have I pondered upon it! How have I, through the whole of a midsummer night, struggled to fathom it! What was it—that something more profound than the well of Democritus—which lay far within the pupils of my beloved? What *was* it? I was possessed with a passion to discover. Those eyes! those large, those shining, those divine orbs! they became to me twin stars of Leda, and I to them devoutest of astrologers.*

There is no point, among the many incomprehensible anomalies of the science of mind, more thrillingly exciting than the fact—never, I believe, noticed in the schools—that, in our endeavors to recall to memory something long forgotten, we often find ourselves *upon the very verge* of remembrance, without being able, in the end, to remember. And thus how frequently, in my intense scrutiny of Ligeia's eyes, have I felt approaching the full knowledge of their expression—felt it approaching—yet not quite be mine—and so at length entirely depart! And (strange, oh strangest mystery of all!) I found, in the commonest objects of the universe, a circle of analogies to that expression. I mean to say that, subsequently to the period when Ligeia's beauty passed into my spirit, there dwelling as in a shrine, I derived, from many existences in the material world, a sentiment such as I felt always aroused within me by her large and luminous orbs. Yet not the more could I define that sentiment, or analyze, or even steadily view it. I recognized it, let me repeat, sometimes in the survey of a rapidly-growing vine—in the contemplation of a moth, a butterfly, a chrysalis, a stream of running water. I have felt it in the ocean; in the falling of a meteor. I have felt it in the glances of unusually aged people. And there are one or two stars in heaven—(one especially, a star of the sixth magnitude, double and changeable, to be found near the large star in Lyra) in a telescopic scrutiny of which I have been made aware of the feeling. I have been filled with it by certain sounds from stringed instruments, and not unfrequently by passages from books. Among innumerable other instances, I well remember something in a volume of Joseph Glanvill, which (perhaps merely from its quaintness—who shall say?) never failed to inspire me with the sentiment;—'And the will therein lieth, which dieth not. Who knoweth the mysteries of the will, with its vigor? For God is but a great will pervading all things by nature of its intentness. Man doth not yield him to the angels, nor unto death utterly, save only through the weakness of his feeble will.'

Length of years, and subsequent reflection, have enabled me to trace, indeed, some remote connection between this passage in the English moralist and a portion of the character of Ligeia. An *intensity* in thought, action, or speech, was possibly, in her, a result, or at least an index, of that gigantic volition which, during our long intercourse, failed to give other and more immediate evidence of its existence. Of all the women whom I have ever known, she, the outwardly calm, the ever-placid Ligeia, was the most violently a prey to the tumultuous vultures of stern passion. And of such passion I could form no estimate, save by the miraculous expansion of those eyes which at once so delighted and appalled me—by the almost magical melody, modulation, distinctness and placidity of her very low voice—and by the fierce energy (rendered doubly effective by contrast with her manner of utterance) of the wild words which she habitually uttered.

I have spoken of the learning of Ligeia; it was immense—such as I have never known in woman. In the classical tongues was she deeply proficient, and as far as my own acquaintance extended in regard to the modern dialects of Europe, I have never known her at fault. Indeed upon any theme of the most admired, because simply the most abstruse of the boasted erudition of the academy, have I *ever* found Ligeia at fault? How singularly—how thrillingly, this one point in the nature of my wife has forced itself, at this late period only, upon my attention! I said her knowledge was such as I have never known in woman—but where breathes the man who has traversed, and successfully, *all* the wide areas of moral, physical, and mathematical science? I saw not then what I now clearly perceive, that the acquisitions of Ligeia were gigantic, were astounding; yet I was sufficiently aware of her infinite supremacy to resign myself, with a child-like confidence, to her guidance through the chaotic world of metaphysical investigation at which I was most busily occupied during the earlier years of our marriage. With how vast a triumph—with how vivid a delight—with how much of all that is ethereal in hope—did I *feel*, as she bent over me in studies but little sought—but less known—that delicious vista by slow degrees expanding before me, down whose long, gorgeous, and all untrodden path, I might at length pass onward to the goal of a wisdom too divinely precious not to be forbidden!

How poignant, then, must have been the grief with which, after some years, I beheld my well-grounded expectations take wings to themselves and fly away! Without Ligeia I was but as a child groping benighted. Her presence, her readings alone, rendered vividly luminous the many mysteries of the transcendentalism in which we were immersed. Wanting the radiant lustre of her eyes, letters, lambent and golden, grew duller than Saturnian lead. And now those eyes shone less and less frequently upon the pages over which I pored. Ligeia grew ill. The wild eyes blazed with a too—too glorious effulgence; the pale fingers became of the transparent waxen hue of the grave, and the blue veins upon the lofty forehead swelled and sank impetuously with the tides of the most gentle emotion. I saw that she must die—and I struggled desperately in spirit with the grim Azrael. And the struggles of the passionate wife were, to my astonishment, even more energetic than my own. There had been much in her stern nature to impress me with the belief that, to her, death would have come without its terrors;—but not so. Words are impotent to convey any just idea of the fierceness of resistance with which she wrestled with the Shadow. I groaned in anguish at the pitiable spectacle. I would have soothed—I would have reasoned; but, in the intensity of her wild desire for life,—for life—*but* for life—solace and reason were alike the uttermost of folly. Yet not until the last instance, amid the most convulsive writhings of her fierce spirit, was shaken the external placidity of her demeanor. Her voice grew more gentle—grew more low—yet I would not wish to dwell upon the wild meaning of the quietly uttered words. My brain reeled as I hearkened, entranced, to a melody more than mortal—to assumptions and aspirations which mortality had never before known.

That she loved me I should not have doubted; and I might have been easily aware that, in a bosom such as hers, love would have reigned no ordinary passion. But in death only, was I fully impressed with the strength of her affection. For long hours, detaining my hand, would she pour out before me the overflowing of a heart whose more than passionate devotion amounted to idolatry. How had I deserved to be so blessed by such confessions?—how had I deserved to be so cursed with the removal of my beloved in the hour of her making them? But upon this subject I cannot bear to dilate. Let me say only, that in Ligeia's more than womanly abandonment to a love, alas! all unmerited, all unworthily bestowed, I at length recognized the principle of her longing with so wildly earnest a desire for the life which was now fleeing so rapidly away. It is this wild longing—it is this eager vehemence of desire for life—*but* for life—that I have no power to portray—no utterance capable of expressing.

At high noon of the night in which she departed, beckoning me, peremptorily, to her side, she bade me repeat certain verses composed by herself not many days before. I obeyed her.—They were these:

Lo! 'tis a gala night
  Within the lonesome latter years!
An angel throng, bewinged, bedight
  In veils, and drowned in tears,
Sit in a theatre, to see
  A play of hopes and fears,
While the orchestra breathes fitfully
  The music of the spheres.

Mimes, in the form of God on high,
  Mutter and mumble low,
And hither and thither fly—
  Mere puppets they, who come and go
At bidding of vast formless things
  That shift the scenery to and fro,
Flapping from out their Condor wings
  Invisible Wo!

That motley drama!—oh, be sure
  It shall not be forgot!
With its Phantom chased forevermore,

By a crowd that seize it not,
Through a circle that ever returneth in
To the self-same spot,
And much of Madness and more of Sin,
And Horror the soul of the plot.

But see, amid the mimic rout,
A crawling shape intrude!
A blood-red thing that writhes from out
The scenic solitude!
It writhes!—it writhes!—with mortal pangs
The mimes become its food,
And the seraphs sob at vermin fangs
In human gore imbued.

Out—out are the lights—out all!
And over each quivering form,
The curtain, a funeral pall,
Comes down with the rush of a storm,
And the angels, all pallid and wan,
Uprising, unveiling, affirm
That the play is the tragedy, 'Man,'
And its hero the Conqueror Worm.*

'O God!' half shrieked Ligeia, leaping to her feet and extending her arms aloft with a spasmodic movement, as I made an end of these lines—'O God! O Divine Father!—shall these things be undeviating so?—shall this Conqueror be not once conquered? Are we not part and parcel in Thee? Who—who knoweth the mysteries of the will with its vigor? Man doth not yield him to the angels, *nor unto death utterly*, save only through the weakness of his feeble will.'

And now, as if exhausted with emotion, she suffered her white arms to fall, and returned solemnly to her bed of Death. And as she breathed her last sighs, there came mingled with them a low murmur from her lips. I bent to them my ear and distinguished, again, the concluding words of the passage in Glanvill—*'Man doth not yield him to the angels, nor unto death utterly, save only through the weakness of his feeble will.'*

She died;—and I, crushed into the very dust with sorrow, could no longer endure the lonely desolation of my dwelling in the dim and decaying city by the Rhine. I had no lack of what the world calls wealth. Ligeia had brought me far more, very far more than ordinarily falls to the lot of mortals. After a few months, therefore, of weary and aimless wandering, I purchased, and put in some repair, an abbey, which I shall not name, in one of the wildest and least frequented portions of fair England. The gloomy and dreary grandeur of the building, the almost savage aspect of the domain, the many melancholy and time-honored memories connected with both, had much in unison with the feelings of utter abandonment which had driven me into that remote and unsocial region of the country. Yet although the external abbey, with its verdant decay hanging about it, suffered but little alteration, I gave way, with a child-like perversity, and perchance with a faint hope of alleviating my sorrows, to a display of more than regal magnificence within. For such follies, even in childhood, I had imbibed a taste, and now they came back to me as if in the dotage of grief. Alas, I feel how much even of incipient madness might have been discovered in the gorgeous and fantastic draperies, in the solemn carvings of Egypt, in the wild cornices and furniture, in the Bedlam patterns of the carpets of tufted gold! I had became a bounden slave in the trammels of opium, and my labors and my orders had taken a coloring from my dreams. But these absurdities I must not pause to detail. Let me speak only of that one chamber, ever accursed, whither in a moment of mental alienation, I led from the altar as my bride—as the successor of the unforgotten Ligeia—the fair-haired and blue-eyed Lady Rowena Trevanion, of Tremaine.*

There is no individual portion of the architecture and decoration of that bridal chamber which is not visibly before me. Where were the souls of the haughty family of the bride, when, through thirst of gold, they permitted to pass the threshold of an apartment *so* bedecked, a maiden and a daughter so beloved? I have said that I minutely remember the details of the chamber—yet I am sadly forgetful on topics of deep moment—and here there was no system, no keeping, in the fantastic display, to take hold upon the memory. The room lay in a high turret of the castellated abbey, was pentagonal in shape, and of capacious size. Occupying the whole southern face of the pentagon was the sole window—an immense sheet of unbroken glass from Venice—a single pane, and tinted of a leaden hue, so that the rays of either the sun or moon, passing through it, fell with a ghastly lustre on the objects within. Over the upper portion of this huge window, extended the trellice-work of an aged vine, which clambered up the massy walls of the turret. The ceiling, of gloomy-looking oak, was excessively lofty, vaulted, and elaborately fretted with the wildest and most grotesque specimens of a semi-Gothic, semi-Druidical device. From out the most central recess of this melancholy vaulting, depended, by a single chain of gold with long links. a huge censer of the same metal, Saracenic in pattern, and with many perforations so contrived that there writhed in and out of them, as if endued with a serpent vitality, a continual succession of parti-colored fires.

Some few ottomans and golden candelabra, of Eastern figure, were in various stations about—and there was the couch, too—the bridal couch—of an Indian model, and low, and sculptured of solid ebony, with a pall-like canopy above. In each of the angles of the chamber stood on end a gigantic sarcophagus of black granite, from the tombs of the kings over against Luxor, with their aged lids full of immemorial sculpture. But in the draping of the apartment lay, alas! the chief phantasy of all. The lofty walls, gigantic in height—even unproportionably so—were hung from summit to foot, in vast folds, with a heavy and massive-looking tapestry—tapestry of a material which was found alike as a carpet on the floor, as a covering for the ottomans and the ebony bed, as a canopy for the bed, and as the gorgeous volutes of the curtains which partially shaded the window. The material was the richest cloth of gold. It was spotted all over, at irregular intervals, with arabesque figures, about a foot in diameter, and wrought upon the cloth in patterns of the most jetty black. But these figures partook of the true character of the arabesque only when regarded from a single point of view. By a contrivance now common, and indeed traceable to a very remote period of antiquity, they were made changeable in aspect. To one entering the room, they bore the appearance of simple monstrosities; but upon a farther advance, this appearance gradually departed; and step by step, as the visitor moved his station in the chamber, he saw himself surrounded by an endless succession of the ghastly forms which belong to the superstition of the Norman, or arise in the guilty slumbers of the monk. The phantasmagoric effect was vastly heightened by the artificial introduction of a strong continual current of wind behind the draperies—giving a hideous and uneasy animation to the whole.

In halls such as these—in a bridal chamber such as this—I passed, with the Lady of Tremaine, the unhallowed hours of the first month of our marriage—passed them with but little disquietude. That my wife dreaded the fierce moodiness of my temper—that she shunned me and loved me but little—I could not help perceiving; but it gave me rather pleasure than otherwise. I loathed her with a hatred belonging more to demon than to man. My memory flew back, (oh, with what intensity of regret!) to Ligeia, the beloved, the august, the beautiful, the entombed. I revelled in recollections of her purity, of her wisdom, of her lofty, her ethereal nature, of her passionate, her idolatrous love. Now, then, did my spirit fully and freely burn with more than all the fires of her own. In the excitement of my opium dreams (for I was habitually fettered in the shackles of the drug) I would call aloud upon her name, during the silence of the night, or among the sheltered recesses of the glens by day, as if, through the wild eagerness, the solemn passion, the consuming ardor of my longing for the departed, I could restore her to the pathway she had abandoned—ah, *could* it be forever?—upon the earth.

About the commencement of the second month of the marriage, the Lady Rowena was attacked with sudden illness, from which her recovery was slow. The fever which consumed her rendered her nights uneasy; and in her perturbed state of half-slumber, she spoke of sounds, and of motions, in and about the chamber of the turret, which I concluded had no origin save in the distemper of her fancy, or perhaps in the phantasmagoric influences of the chamber itself. She became at length convalescent—finally well. Yet but a brief period elapsed, ere a second more violent disorder again threw her upon a bed of suffering; and from this attack her frame, at all times feeble, never altogether recovered. Her illnesses were, after this epoch, of alarming character, and of more alarming recurrence, defying alike the knowledge and the great exertions of her physicians. With the increase of the chronic disease which had thus, apparently, taken too sure hold upon her constitution to be eradicated by human means, I could not fail to observe a similar increase in the nervous irritation of her temperament, and in her excitability by trivial causes of fear. She spoke again, and now more frequently and pertinaciously, of the sounds—of the slight sounds—and of the unusual motions among the tapestries, to which she had formerly alluded.

One night, near the closing in of September, she pressed this distressing subject with more than usual emphasis upon my attention. She had just awakened from an unquiet slumber, and I had been watching, with feelings half of anxiety, half of a vague terror, the workings of her emaciated countenance. I sat by the side of her ebony bed, upon one of the ottomans of India. She partly arose, and spoke, in an earnest low whisper, of sounds which she *then* heard, but which I could not hear—of motions which she *then* saw, but which I could not perceive. The wind was rushing hurriedly behind the tapestries, and I wished to show her (what, let me confess it, I could not *all* believe) that those almost inarticulate breathings, and those very gentle variations of the figures upon the wall, were but the natural effects of that customary rushing of the wind. But a deadly pallor, over-spreading her face, had proved to me that my exertions to reassure her would be fruitless. She appeared to be fainting, and no attendants were within call. I remembered where was deposited a decanter of light wine which had been ordered by her physicians, and hastened across the chamber to procure it. But, as I stepped beneath the light of the censer, two circumstances of a startling nature attracted my attention. I had felt that some palpable although invisible object had passed lightly by my person; and I saw that there lay upon the golden carpet, in the very middle of the rich lustre thrown from the censer, a shadow—a faint, indefinite shadow of angelic aspect—such as might be fancied for the shadow of a shade. But I was wild with the excitement of an immoderate dose of opium, and heeded these things but little, nor spoke of them to Rowena. Having found the wine, I recrossed the chamber, and poured out a goblet-ful, which I held to the lips of the fainting lady. She had now partially recovered, however, and took the vessel herself, while I sank upon an ottoman near me, with my eyes fastened upon her person. It was then that I became distinctly aware of a gentle foot-fall upon the carpet, and near the couch; and in a second thereafter, as Rowena was in the act of raising the wine to her lips, I saw, or may have dreamed that I saw, fall within the goblet, as if from some invisible spring in the atmosphere of the room, three or four large drops of a brilliant and ruby colored fluid. If this I saw—not so Rowena. She swallowed the wine unhesitatingly, and I forbore to speak to her of a circumstance which must, after all, I considered, have been but the suggestion of a vivid imagination, rendered morbidly active by the terror of the lady, by the opium, and by the hour.

Yet I cannot conceal it from my own perception that, immediately subsequent to the fall of the ruby-drops, a rapid change for the worse took place in the disorder of my wife; so that, on the third subsequent night, the hands of her menials prepared her for the tomb, and on the fourth, I sat alone, with her shrouded body, in that fantastic chamber which had received her as my bride. Wild visions, opium-engendered, flitted, shadow-like, before me. I gazed with unquiet eye upon the sarcophagi in the angles of the room, upon the varying figures of the drapery, and upon the writhing of the parti-colored fires in the censer overhead. My eyes then fell, as I called to mind the circumstances of a former night, to the spot beneath the glare of the censer where I had seen the faint traces of the shadow. It was there, however, no longer; and breathing with greater freedom, I turned my glances to the pallid and rigid figure upon the bed. Then rushed upon me a thousand memories of Ligeia—and then came back upon my heart, with the turbulent violence of a flood, the whole of that unutterable wo with which I had regarded *her* thus enshrouded. The night waned; and still, with a bosom full of bitter thoughts of the one only and supremely beloved, I remained gazing upon the body of Rowena.

It might have been midnight, or perhaps earlier, or later, for I had taken no note of time, when a sob, low, gentle, but very distinct, startled me from my revery. I *felt* that it came from the bed of ebony—the bed of death. I listened in an agony of superstitious terror—but there was no repetition of the sound. I strained my vision to detect any motion in the corpse—but there was not the slightest perceptible. Yet I could not have been deceived. I *had* heard the noise, however faint, and my soul was awakened within me. I resolutely and perseveringly kept my attention riveted upon the body. Many minutes elapsed before any circumstance occurred tending to throw light upon the mystery. At length it became evident that a slight, a very feeble, and barely noticeable tinge of color had flushed up within the cheeks, and along the sunken small veins of the eyelids. Through a species of unutterable horror and awe, for which the language of mortality has no sufficiently energetic expression, I felt my heart cease to beat, my limbs grow rigid where I sat. Yet a sense of duty finally operated to restore my self-possession. I could no longer doubt that we had been precipitate in our preparations—that Rowena still lived. It was necessary that some immediate exertion be made; yet the turret was altogether apart from the portion of the abbey tenanted by the servants—there were none within call—I had no means of summoning them to my aid without leaving the room for many minutes—and this I could not venture to do. I therefore struggled alone in my endeavors to call back the spirit still hovering. In a short period it was certain, however, that a relapse had taken place; the color disappeared from both eyelid and cheek, leaving a wanness even more than that of marble; the lips became doubly shrivelled and pinched up in the ghastly expression of death; a repulsive clamminess and coldness overspread rapidly the surface of the body; and all the usual rigorous stiffness immediately supervened. I fell back with a shudder upon the couch from which I had been so startlingly aroused, and again gave myself up to passionate waking visions of Ligeia.

An hour thus elapsed when (could it be possible?) I was a second time aware of some vague sound issuing from the region of the bed. I listened—in extremity of horror. The sound came again—it was a sigh. Rushing to the corpse, I saw—distinctly saw—a tremor upon the lips. In a minute afterward they relaxed, disclosing a bright line of the pearly teeth. Amazement now struggled in my bosom with the profound awe which had hitherto reigned there alone. I felt that my vision grew dim, that my reason wandered; and it was only by a violent effort that I at length succeeded in nerving myself to the task which duty thus once more had pointed out. There was now a partial glow upon the forehead and upon the cheek and throat; a perceptible warmth pervaded the whole frame; there was even a slight pulsation at the heart. The lady *lived*, and with redoubled ardor I betook myself to the task of restoration. I chafed and bathed the temples and the hands, and used every exertion which experience, and no little medical reading, could suggest. But in vain. Suddenly, the color fled, the pulsation ceased, the lips resumed the expression of the dead, and, in an instant afterward, the whole body took upon itself the icy chilliness, the livid hue, the intense rigidity, the sunken outline, and all the loathsome peculiarities of that which has been, for many days, a tenant of the tomb.

And again I sunk into visions of Ligeia—and again, (what marvel that I shudder while I write?) *again* there reached my ears a low sob from the region of the ebony bed. But why shall I minutely detail the unspeakable horrors of that night? Why shall I pause to relate how, time after time, until near the period of the gray dawn, this hideous drama of revivification was repeated; how each terrific relapse was only into a sterner and apparently more irredeemable death; how each agony wore the aspect of a struggle with some invisible foe; and how each struggle was succeeded by I know not what of wild change in the personal appearance of the corpse? Let me hurry to a conclusion.

The greater part of the fearful night had worn away, and she who had been dead, once again stirred—and now more vigorously than hitherto, although arousing from a dissolution more appalling in its utter hopelessness than any. I had long ceased to struggle or to move, and remained sitting rigidly upon the ottoman, a helpless prey to a whirl of violent emotions, of which extreme awe was perhaps the least terrible, the least consuming. The corpse, I repeat, stirred, and now more vigorously than before. The hues of life flushed up with unwonted energy into the countenance—the limbs relaxed—and, save that the eyelids were yet pressed heavily together, and that the bandages and draperies of the grave still imparted their charnel character to the figure, I might have dreamed that Rowena had indeed shaken off, utterly, the fetters of Death. But if this idea was not, even then, altogether adopted, I could at least doubt no longer, when, arising from the bed, tottering, with feeble steps, with closed eyes, and with the manner of one bewildered in a dream, the thing that was enshrouded advanced bodily and palpably into the middle of the apartment.

I trembled not—I stirred not—for a crowd of unutterable fancies connected with the air, the stature, the demeanor of the figure, rushing hurriedly through my brain, had paralyzed—had chilled me into stone. I stirred not—but gazed upon the apparition. There was a mad disorder in my thoughts—a tumult unappeasable. Could it, indeed, be the *living* Rowena who confronted me? Could it indeed be Rowena *at all*—the fair-haired, the blue-eyed Lady Rowena Trevanion of Tremaine? Why, *why* should I doubt it? The bandage lay heavily about the mouth—but then might it not be the mouth of the breathing Lady of Tremaine? And the cheeks—there were the roses as in her noon of life—yes, these might indeed be the fair cheeks of the living Lady of Tremaine. And the chin, with its dimples, as in health, might it not be hers?—but *had she then grown taller since her malady?* What inexpressible madness seized me with that thought? One bound, and I had reached her feet! Shrinking from my touch, she let fall from her head the ghastly cerements which had confined it, and there streamed forth, into the rushing atmosphere of the chamber, huge masses of long and dishevelled hair; *it was blacker than the wings of the midnight!* And now slowly opened *the eyes* of the figure which stood before me. 'Here then, at least,' I shrieked aloud, 'can I never—can I never be mistaken—these are the full, and the black, and the wild eyes—of my lost love—of the lady—of the LADY LIGEIA!'

THE MAN THAT WAS USED UP

A Tale of the Late Bugaboo and Kickapoo Campaign

Pleurez, pleurez, mes yeux, et fondez-vous en eau!
La moitié de ma vie a mis l'autre au tombeau.

Corneille*

I CANNOT just now remember when or where I first made the acquaintance of that truly fine-looking fellow, Brevet Brigadier General John A. B. C. Smith. Some one *did* introduce me to the gentleman, I am sure—at some public meeting, I know very well—held about something of great importance, no doubt—at some place or other, I feel convinced,—whose name I have unaccountably forgotten. The truth is—that the introduction was attended, upon my part, with a degree of anxious embarrassment which operated to prevent any definite impressions of either time or place. I am constitutionally nervous—this, with me, is a family failing, and I can't help it. In especial, the slightest appearance of mystery—of any point I cannot exactly comprehend—puts me at once into a pitiable state of agitation.

There was something, as it were, remarkable—yes, *remarkable*, although this is but a feeble term to express my full meaning—about the entire individuality of the personage in question. He was, perhaps, six feet in height, and of a presence singularly commanding. There was an *air distingué* pervading the whole man, which spoke of high breeding, and hinted at high birth. Upon this topic—the topic of Smith's personal appearance—I have a kind of melancholy satisfaction in being minute. His head of hair would have done honor to a Brutus;—nothing could be more richly flowing, or possess a brighter gloss. It was of a jetty black;—which was also the color, or more properly the no color, of his unimaginable whiskers. You perceive I cannot speak of these latter without enthusiasm; it is not too much to say that they were the handsomest pair of whiskers under the sun. At all events, they encircled, and at times partially overshadowed, a mouth utterly unequalled. Here were the most entirely even, and the most brilliantly white of all conceivable teeth. From between them, upon every proper occasion, issued a voice of surpassing clearness, melody, and strength.

In the matter of eyes, also, my acquaintance was pre-eminently endowed. Either one of such a pair was worth a couple of the ordinary ocular organs. They were of a deep hazel, exceedingly large and lustrous; and there was perceptible about them, ever and anon, just that amount of interesting obliquity which gives pregnancy to expression.

The bust of the General was unquestionably the finest bust I ever saw. For your life you could not have found a fault with its wonderful proportion. This rare peculiarity set off to great advantage a pair of shoulders which would have called up a blush of conscious inferiority into the countenance of the marble Apollo. I have a passion for fine shoulders, and may say that I never beheld them in perfection before. The arms altogether were admirably modelled. Nor were the lower limbs less superb. These were, indeed, the *ne plus ultra* of good legs. Every connoisseur in such matters admitted the legs to be good. There was neither too much flesh, nor too little,—neither rudeness nor fragility. I could not imagine a more graceful curve than that of the *os femoris*, and there was just that due gentle prominence in the rear of the *fibula* which goes to the conformation of a properly proportioned calf. I wish to God my young and talented friend Chiponchipino, the sculptor, had but seen the legs of Brevet Brigadier General John A. B. C. Smith.

But although men so absolutely fine-looking are neither as plenty as reasons* or blackberries, still I could not bring myself to believe that *the remarkable* something to which I alluded just now,—that the odd air of *je ne sais quoi* which hung about my new acquaintance,—lay altogether, or indeed at all, in the supreme excellence of his bodily endowments. Perhaps it might be traced to the *manner*;—yet here again I could not pretend to be positive. There *was* a primness, not to say stiffness, in his carriage—a degree of measured, and, if I may so express it, of rectangular precision, attending his every movement, which, observed in a more diminutive figure, would have had the least little savor in the world, of affectation, pomposity or constraint, but which noticed in a gentleman of his undoubted dimensions, was readily placed to the account of reserve, *hauteur*—of a commendable sense, in short, of what is due to the dignity of colossal proportion.

The kind friend who presented me to General Smith whispered in my ear some few words of comment upon the man. He was a *remarkable* man—a *very* remarkable man—indeed one of the *most* remarkable men of the age. He was an especial favorite, too, with the ladies—chiefly on account of his high reputation for courage.

'In *that* point he is unrivalled—indeed he is a perfect desperado—a downright fire-eater, and no mistake,' said my friend, here dropping his voice excessively low, and thrilling me with the mystery of his tone.

'A downright fire-eater, and *no* mistake. Showed *that*, I should say, to some purpose, in the late tremendous swamp-fight away down South, with the Bugaboo and Kickapoo Indians.' [Here my friend opened his eyes to some extent.] 'Bless my soul!—blood and thunder, and all that!—*prodigies* of valor!—heard of him of course?—you know he's the man—'

'Man alive, how *do* you do? why how *are* ye? *very* glad to see ye, indeed!' here interrupted the General himself, seizing my companion by the hand as he drew near, and bowing stiffly but profoundly, as I was presented. I then thought, (and I think so still,) that I never heard a clearer nor a stronger voice nor beheld a finer set of teeth: but I *must* say that I was sorry for the interruption just at that moment, as, owing to the whispers and insinuations aforesaid, my interest had been greatly excited in the hero of the Bugaboo and Kickapoo campaign.

However, the delightfully luminous conversation of Brevet Brigadier General John A. B. C. Smith soon completely dissipated this chagrin. My friend leaving us immediately, we had quite a long *tête-à-tête*, and I was not only pleased but *really*—instructed. I never heard a more fluent talker, or a man of greater general information. With becoming modesty, he forebore, nevertheless, to touch upon the theme I had just then most at heart—I mean the mysterious circumstances attending the Bugaboo war—and, on my own part, what I conceive to be a proper sense of delicacy forbade me to broach the subject; although, in truth, I was exceedingly tempted to do so. I perceived, too, that the gallant soldier preferred topics of philosophical interest, and that he delighted, especially, in commenting upon the rapid march of mechanical invention. Indeed, lead him where I would, this was a point to which he invariably came back.

'There is nothing at all like it,' he would say; 'we are a wonderful people, and live in a wonderful age. Parachutes and rail-roads—man-traps and spring-guns! Our steam-boats are upon every sea, and the Nassau balloon packet is about to run regular trips (fare either way only twenty pounds sterling) between London and Timbuctoo. And who shall calculate the immense influence upon social life—upon arts—upon commerce—upon literature—which will be the immediate result of the great principles of electro magnetics! Nor, is this all, let me assure you! There is really no end to the march of invention. The most wonderful—the most ingenious—and let me add, Mr—Mr—Thompson, I believe, is your name—let me add, I say, the most *useful*—the most truly *useful* mechanical contrivances, are daily springing up like mushrooms, if I may so express myself, or, more figuratively, like—ah—grasshoppers—like grasshoppers, Mr Thompson—about us and ah—ah—ah—around us!'

Thompson, to be sure, is not my name; but it is needless to say that I left General Smith with a heightened interest in the man, with an exalted opinion of his conversational powers, and a deep sense of the valuable privileges we enjoy in living in this age of mechanical invention. My curiosity, however, had not been altogether satisfied, and I resolved to prosecute immediate inquiry among my acquaintances touching the Brevet Brigadier General himself, and particularly respecting the tremendous events *quorum pars magna fuit*,* during the Bugaboo and Kickapoo campaign.

The first opportunity which presented itself, and which (*horresco referens**) I did not in the least scruple to seize, occurred at the Church of the Reverend Doctor Drummummupp, where I found myself established, one Sunday, just at sermon time, not only in the pew, but by the side, of that worthy and communicative little friend of mine, Miss Tabitha T. Thus seated, I congratulated myself, and with much reason, upon the very flattering state of affairs. If any person knew anything about Brevet Brigadier General John A. B. C. Smith, that person, it was clear to me, was Miss Tabitha T. We telegraphed a few signals, and then commenced, *sotto voce*, a brisk *tête-à-tête*.

'Smith!' said she, in reply to my very earnest inquiry; 'Smith!—why, not General John A. B. C.? Bless me, I thought you *knew* all about *him!* This is a wonderfully inventive age! Horrid affair that!—a bloody set of wretches, those Kickapoos!—fought like a hero—prodigies of valor—immortal renown. Smith!—Brevet Brigadier General John A. B. C.!—why, you know he's the man—'

'Man,' here broke in Doctor Drummummupp, at the top of his voice, and with a thump that came near knocking the pulpit about our ears; 'man that is born of a woman hath but a short time to live; he cometh up and is cut down like a flower!' I started to the extremity of the pew, and perceived by the animated looks of the divine, that the wrath which had nearly proved fatal to the pulpit had been excited by the whispers of the lady and myself. There was no help for it; so I submitted with a good grace, and listened, in all the martyrdom of dignified silence, to the balance of that very capital discourse.

Next evening found me a somewhat late visitor at the Rantipole theatre, where I felt sure of satisfying my curiosity at once, by merely stepping into the box of those exquisite specimens of affability and omniscience, the Misses Arabella and Miranda Cognoscenti. That fine tragedian, Climax, was doing Iago to a very crowded house, and I experienced some little difficulty in making my wishes understood; especially, as our box was next the slips and completely overlooked the stage.

'Smith?' said Miss Arabella, as she at length comprehended the purport of my query; 'Smith?—why, not General John A. B. C.?'

'Smith?' inquired Miranda, musingly. 'God bless me, did you ever behold a finer figure?'

'Never, madam, but *do* tell me—'

'Or so inimitable grace?'

'Never, upon my word!—but pray inform me—'

'Or so just an appreciation of stage effect?'

'Madam!'

'Or a more delicate sense of the true beauties of Shakespeare? Be so good as to look at that leg!'

'The devil!' and I turned again to her sister.

'Smith?' said she, 'why, not General John A. B. C.? Horrid affair that, wasn't it?—great wretches, those Bugaboos—savage and so on—but we live in a wonderful inventive age!—Smith!—O yes! great man!—perfect desperado—immortal renown—prodigies of valor! *Never heard!*' [This was given in a scream.] 'Bless my soul!—why, he's the man—'

> '—mandragora
> Nor all the drowsy syrups of the world
> Shall ever medicine thee to that sweet sleep
> Which thou ow'dst yesterday!'*

here roared out Climax just in my ear, and shaking his fist in my face all the time, in a way that I *couldn't* stand, and I *wouldn't*. I left the Misses Cognoscenti immediately, went behind the scenes forthwith, and gave the beggarly scoundrel such a thrashing as I trust he will remember to the day of his death.

At the *soirée* of the lovely widow, Mrs Kathleen O'Trump, I was confident that I should meet with no similar disappointment. Accordingly, I was no sooner seated at the card-table, with my pretty hostess for a *vis-à-vis*, than I propounded those questions the solution of which had become a matter so essential to my peace.

'Smith?' said my partner, 'why, not General John A. B. C.? Horrid affair that, wasn't it?—diamonds, did you say?—terrible wretches those Kickapoos!—we are playing *whist*, if you please, Mr Tattle—however, this is the age of invention, most certainly *the* age, one may say—*the* age *par excellence*—speak French?—oh, quite a hero—perfect desperado!—*no hearts*, Mr Tattle? I don't believe it!—immortal renown and all that—prodigies of valor! *Never heard!!*—why, bless me, he's the man—'

'Mann?—*Captain* Mann?' here screamed some little feminine interloper from the farthest corner of the room. 'Are you talking about Captain Mann and the duel?—oh, I *must* hear—do tell—go on, Mrs O'Trump!—do now go on!' And go on Mrs O'Trump did—all about a certain Captain Mann, who was either shot or hung, or should have been both shot and hung. Yes! Mrs O'Trump, she went on, and I—I went off. There was no chance of hearing anything farther that evening in regard to Brevet Brigadier General John A. B. C. Smith.

Still I consoled myself with the reflection that the tide of ill luck would not run against me forever, and so determined to make a bold push for information at the rout of that bewitching little angel, the graceful Mrs Pirouette.

'Smith?' said Mrs P., as we twirled about together in a *pas de zéphyr*, 'Smith?—why, not General John A. B. C.? Dreadful business that of the Bugaboos, wasn't it?—terrible creatures, those Indians!—*do* turn out your toes! I really am ashamed of you—man of great courage, poor fellow!—but this is a wonderful age for invention—O dear me, I'm out of breath—quite a desperado—prodigies of valor—*never heard!!*—can't believe it—I shall have to sit down and enlighten you—Smith! why, he's the man—'

'Man-*Fred*, I tell you!' here bawled out Miss Bas-Bleu, as I led Mrs Pirouette to a seat. 'Did ever anybody hear the like? It's Man-*Fred*, I say, and not at all by any means Man-*Friday*.' Here Miss Bas-Bleu beckoned to me in a very peremptory manner; and I was obliged, will I nill I, to leave Mrs P. for the purpose of deciding a dispute touching the title of a certain poetical drama of Lord Byron's. Although I pronounced, with great promptness, that the true title was Man-*Friday*, and not by any means Man-*Fred*, yet when I returned to seek Mrs Pirouette she was not to be discovered, and I made my retreat from the house in a very bitter spirit of animosity against the whole race of the Bas-Bleus.*

Matters had now assumed a really serious aspect, and I resolved to call at once upon my particular friend, Mr Theodore Sinivate; for I knew that here at least I should get something like definite information.

'Smith?' said he, in his well-known peculiar way of drawling out his syllables; 'Smith?—why, not General John A. B. C.? Savage affair that with the Kickapo-o-o-os, wasn't it? Say! don't you think so?—perfect despera-a-ado—great pity, 'pon my honor!—wonderfully inventive age!—pro-o-odigies of valor! By the by, did you ever hear about Captain Ma-a-a-a-n?'

'Captain Mann be d—d!' said I, 'please to go on with your story.'

'Hem!—oh well!—quite *la même cho-o-se*, as we say in France. Smith, eh? Brigadier General John A—B—C.? I say'—[here Mr S. thought proper to put his finger to the side of his nose]—'I say, you don't mean to insinuate now, really and truly, and conscientiously, that you don't know all about that affair of Smith's, as well as I do, eh? Smith? John A—B—C.? Why, bless me, he's the ma-a-an—'

'*Mr* Sinivate,' said I, imploringly, '*is* he the man in the mask?'*

'No-o-o!' said he, looking wise, 'nor the man in the mo-o-on.'

This reply I considered a pointed and positive insult, and so left the house at once in high dudgeon, with a firm resolve to call my friend, Mr Sinivate, to a speedy account for his ungentlemanly conduct and ill-breeding.

In the meantime, however, I had no notion of being thwarted touching the information I desired. There was one resource left me yet. I would go to the fountain-head. I would call forthwith upon the General himself, and demand, in explicit terms, a solution of this abominable piece of mystery. Here, at least, there should be no chance for equivocation. I would be plain, positive, peremptory—as short as pie-crust—as concise as Tacitus or Montesquieu.

It was early when I called, and the General was dressing; but I pleaded urgent business, and was shown at once into his bed-room by an old negro valet, who remained in attendance during my visit. As I entered the chamber, I looked about, of course, for the occupant, but did not immediately perceive him. There was a large and exceedingly odd-looking bundle of something which lay close by my feet on the floor, and, as I was not in the best humor in the world, I gave it a kick out of the way.

'Hem! ahem! rather civil that, I should say!' said the bundle, in one of the smallest, and altogether the funniest little voices, between a squeak and a whistle, that I ever heard in all the days of my existence.

'Ahem! rather civil that, I should observe.'

I fairly shouted with terror, and made off, at a tangent, into the farthest extremity of the room.

'God bless me! my dear fellow,' here again whistled the bundle, 'what—what—what—why, what *is* the matter? I really believe you don't know me at all.'

What *could* I say to all this—what *could* I? I staggered into an arm-chair, and, with staring eyes and open mouth, awaited the solution of the wonder.

'Strange you shouldn't know me though, isn't it?' presently re-squeaked the nondescript, which I now perceived was performing, upon the floor, some inexplicable evolution, very analogous to the drawing on of a stocking. There was only a single leg, however, apparent.

'Strange you shouldn't know me, though, isn't it? Pompey, bring me that leg!' Here Pompey handed the bundle, a very capital cork leg, already dressed, which it screwed on in a trice; and then it stood up before my eyes.

'And a bloody action it *was*,' continued the thing, as if in a soliloquy; 'but then one musn't fight with the Bugaboos and Kickapoos, and think of coming off with a mere scratch. Pompey, I'll thank you now for that arm. Thomas' [turning to me] 'is decidedly the best hand at a cork leg; but if you should ever want an arm, my dear fellow, you must really let me recommend you to Bishop.' Here Pompey screwed on an arm.

'We had rather hot work of it, that you may say. Now, you dog, slip on my shoulders and bosom! Pettitt makes the best shoulders, but for a bosom you will have to go to Ducrow.'

'Bosom!' said I.

'Pompey, will you *never* be ready with that wig? Scalping is a rough process after all; but then you can procure such a capital scratch at De L'Orme's.'*

'Scratch!'

'Now, you nigger, my teeth! For a *good* set of these you had better go to Parmly's at once; high prices, but excellent work. I swallowed some very capital articles, though, when the big Bugaboo rammed me down with the butt end of his rifle.'

'Butt end! ram down!! my eye!!'

'O yes, by-the-by, my eye—here, Pompey, you scamp, screw it in! Those Kickapoos are not so very slow at a gouge; but he's a belied man, that Dr Williams, after all; you can't imagine how well I see with the eyes of his make.'

I now began very clearly to perceive that the object before me was nothing more nor less than my new acquaintance, Brevet Brigadier General John A. B. C. Smith. The manipulations of Pompey had made, I must confess, a very striking difference in the appearance of the personal man. The voice, however, still puzzled me no little; but even this apparent mystery was speedily cleared up.

'Pompey, you black rascal,' squeaked the General, 'I really do believe you would let me go out without my palate.'

Hereupon the negro, grumbling out an apology, went up to his master, opened his mouth with the knowing air of a horse-jockey, and adjusted therein a somewhat singular-looking machine, in a very dexterous manner, that I could not altogether comprehend. The alteration, however, in the entire expression of the General's countenance was instantaneous and surprising. When he again spoke, his voice had resumed all that rich melody and strength which I had noticed upon our original production.

'D—n the vagabonds!' said he, in so clear a tone that I positively started at the change, 'D—n the vagabonds! they not only knocked in the roof of my mouth, but took the trouble to cut off at least seven-eighths of my tongue. There isn't Bonfanti's equal, however, in America, for really good articles of this description. I can recommend you to him with confidence,' [here the General bowed,] 'and assure you that I have the greatest pleasure in so doing.'

I acknowledged his kindness in my best manner, and took leave of him at once, with a perfect understanding of the true state of affairs—with a full comprehension of the mystery which had troubled me so long. It was evident. It was a clear case. Brevet Brigadier General John A. B. C. Smith was the man—was *the man that was used up*.

THE FALL OF THE HOUSE OF USHER*

Son cœur est un luth suspendu;
Sitôt qu'on le touche il résonne.
De Béranger*

DURING the whole of a dull, dark, and soundless day in the autumn of the year, when the clouds hung oppressively low in the heavens, I had been passing alone, on horseback, through a singularly dreary tract of country; and at length found myself, as the shades of the evening drew on, within view of the melancholy House of Usher. I know not how it was—but, with the first glimpse of the building, a sense of insufferable gloom pervaded my spirit. I say insufferable; for the feeling was unrelieved by any of that half-pleasurable, because poetic, sentiment, with which the mind usually receives even the sternest natural images of the desolate or terrible. I looked upon the scene before me—upon the mere house, and the simple landscape features of the domain—upon the bleak walls—upon the vacant eye-like windows—upon a few rank sedges—and upon a few white trunks of decayed trees—with an utter depression of soul which I can compare to no earthly sensation more properly than to the after-dream of the reveller upon opium—the bitter lapse into every-day life—the hideous dropping off of the veil. There was an iciness, a sinking, a sickening of the heart—an unredeemed dreariness of thought which no goading of the imagination could torture into aught of the sublime. What was it—I paused to think—what was it that so unnerved me in the contemplation of the House of Usher? It was a mystery all insoluble; nor could I grapple with the shadowy fancies that crowded upon me as I pondered. I was forced to fall back upon the unsatisfactory conclusion, that while, beyond doubt, there *are* combinations of very simple natural objects which have the power of thus affecting us, still the analysis of this power lies among considerations beyond our depth. It was possible, I reflected, that a mere different arrangement of the particulars of the scene, of the details of the picture, would be sufficient to modify, or perhaps to annihilate its capacity for sorrowful impression; and, acting upon this idea, I reined my horse to the precipitous brink of a black and lurid tarn that lay in unruffled lustre by the dwelling, and gazed down—but with a shudder even more thrilling than before—upon the remodelled and inverted images of the gray sedge, and the ghastly tree-stems, and the vacant and eye-like windows.

Nevertheless, in this mansion of gloom I now proposed to myself a sojourn of some weeks. Its proprietor, Roderick Usher, had been one of my boon companions in boyhood; but many years had elapsed since our last meeting. A letter, however, had lately reached me in a distant part of the country—a letter from him—which, in its wildly importunate nature, had admitted of no other than a personal reply. The MS. gave evidence of nervous agitation. The writer spoke of acute bodily illness—of a mental disorder which oppressed him—and of an earnest desire to see me, as his best, and indeed his only personal friend, with a view of attempting, by the cheerfulness of my society, some alleviation of his malady. It was the manner in which all this, and much more, was said—it was the apparent *heart* that went with his request—which allowed me no room for hesitation; and I accordingly obeyed forthwith, what I still considered a very singular summons.

Although, as boys, we had been even intimate associates, yet I really knew little of my friend. His reserve had been always excessive and habitual. I was aware, however, that his very ancient family had been noted, time out of mind, for a peculiar sensibility of temperament, displaying itself, through long ages, in many works of exalted art, and manifested, of late, in repeated deeds of munificent yet unobtrusive charity, as well as in a passionate devotion to the intricacies, perhaps even more than to the orthodox and easily recognisable beauties, of musical science. I had learned, too, the very remarkable fact, that the stem of the Usher race, all time-honored as it was, had put forth, at no period, any enduring branch; in other words, that the entire family lay in the direct line of descent, and had always, with very trifling and very temporary variation, so lain. It was this deficiency, I considered, while running over in thought the perfect keeping of the character of the premises with the accredited character of the people, and while speculating upon the possible influence which the one, in the long lapse of centuries, might have exercised upon the other—it was this deficiency, perhaps, of collateral issue, and the consequent undeviating transmission, from sire to son, of the patrimony with the name, which had, at length, so identified the two as to merge the original title of the estate in the quaint and equivocal appellation of the 'House of Usher'—an appellation which seemed to include, in the minds of the peasantry who used it, both the family and the family mansion.

I have said that the sole effect of my somewhat childish experiment—that of looking down within the tarn—had been to deepen the first singular impression. There can be no doubt that the consciousness of the rapid increase of my superstition—for why should I not so term it?—served mainly to accelerate the increase itself. Such, I have long known, is the paradoxical law of all sentiments having terror as a basis. And it might have been for this reason only, that, when I again uplifted my eyes to the house itself, from its image in the pool, there grew in my mind a strange fancy—a fancy so ridiculous, indeed, that I but mention it to show the vivid force of the sensations which oppressed me. I had so worked upon my imagination as really to believe that about the whole mansion and domain there hung an atmosphere peculiar to themselves and their immediate vicinity—an atmosphere which had no affinity with the air of heaven, but which had reeked up from the decayed trees, and the gray wall and the silent tarn—a pestilent and mystic vapor, dull, sluggish, faintly discernible, and leaden-hued.

Shaking off from my spirit what *must* have been a dream, I scanned more narrowly the real aspect of the building. Its principal feature seemed to be that of an excessive antiquity. The discoloration of ages had been great. Minute fungi overspread the whole exterior, hanging in a fine tangled web-work from the eaves. Yet all this was apart from an extraordinary dilapidation. No portion of the masonry had fallen; and there appeared to be a wild inconsistency between its still perfect adaptation of parts, and the crumbling condition of the individual stones. In this there was much that reminded me of the specious totality of old wood-work which has rotted for long years in some neglected vault, with no disturbance from the breath of the external air. Beyond this indication of extensive decay, however, the fabric gave little token of instability. Perhaps the eye of a scrutinizing observer might have discovered a barely perceptible fissure, which, extending from the roof of the building in front, made its way down the wall in a zigzag direction, until it became lost in the sullen waters of the tarn.

Noticing these things, I rode over a short causeway to the house. A servant in waiting took my horse, and I entered the Gothic archway of the hall. A valet, of stealthy step, thence conducted me, in silence, through many dark and intricate passages in my progress to the *studio* of his master. Much that I encountered on the way contributed, I know not how, to heighten the vague sentiments of which I have already spoken. While the objects around me—while the carvings of the ceilings, the sombre tapestries of the walls, the ebon blackness of the floors, and the phantasmagoric armorial trophies which rattled as I strode, were but matters to which, or to such as which, I had been accustomed from my infancy—while I hesitated not to acknowledge how familiar was all this—I still wondered to find how unfamiliar were the fancies which ordinary images were stirring up. On one of the staircases, I met the physician of the family. His countenance, I thought, wore a mingled expression of low cunning and perplexity. He accosted me with trepidation and passed on. The valet now threw open a door and ushered me into the presence of his master.

The room in which I found myself was very large and lofty. The windows were long, narrow, and pointed, and at so vast a distance from the black oaken floor as to be altogether inaccessible from within. Feeble gleams of encrimsoned light made their way through the trellised panes, and served to render sufficiently distinct the more prominent objects around; the eye, however, struggled in vain to reach the remoter angles of the chamber, or the recesses of the vaulted and fretted ceiling. Dark draperies hung upon the walls. The general furniture was profuse, comfortless, antique, and tattered. Many books and musical instruments lay scattered about, but failed to give any vitality to the scene. I felt that I breathed an atmosphere of sorrow. An air of stern, deep, and irredeemable gloom hung over and pervaded all.

Upon my entrance, Usher arose from a sofa on which he had been lying at full length, and greeted me with a vivacious warmth which had much in it, I at first thought, of an overdone cordiality—of the constrained effort of the *ennuyé* man of the world. A glance, however, at his countenance, convinced me of his perfect sincerity. We sat down; and for some moments, while he spoke not, I gazed upon him with a feeling half of pity, half of awe. Surely, man had never before so terribly altered, in so brief a period, as had Roderick Usher! It was with difficulty that I could bring myself to admit the identity of the wan being before me with the companion of my early boyhood. Yet the character of his face had been at all times remarkable. A cadaverousness of complexion; an eye large, liquid, and luminous beyond comparison; lips somewhat thin and very pallid, but of a surpassingly beautiful curve; a nose of a delicate Hebrew model, but with a breadth of nostril unusual in similar formations; a finely moulded chin, speaking, in its want of prominence, of a want of moral energy; hair of a more than web-like softness and tenuity; these features, with an inordinate expansion above the regions of the temple, made up altogether a countenance not easily to be forgotten. And now in the mere exaggeration of the prevailing character of these features, and of the expression they were wont to convey, lay so much of change that I doubted to whom I spoke. The now ghastly pallor of the skin, and the now miraculous lustre of the eye, above all things startled and even awed me. The silken hair, too, had been suffered to grow all unheeded, and as, in its wild gossamer texture, it floated rather than fell about the face, I could not, even with effort, connect its Arabesque expression with any idea of simple humanity.

In the manner of my friend I was at once struck with an incoherence—an inconsistency; and I soon found this to arise from a series of feeble and futile struggles to overcome an habitual trepidancy—an excessive nervous agitation. For something of this nature I had indeed been prepared, no less by his letter, than by reminiscences of certain boyish traits, and by conclusions deduced from his peculiar physical conformation and temperament. His action was alternately vivacious and sullen. His voice varied rapidly from a tremulous indecision (when the animal spirits seemed utterly in abeyance) to that species of energetic concision—that abrupt, weighty, unhurried, and hollow-sounding enunciation—that leaden, self-balanced and perfectly modulated guttural utterance, which may be observed in the lost drunkard, or the irreclaimable eater of opium, during the periods of his most intense excitement.

It was thus that he spoke of the object of my visit, of his earnest desire to see me, and of the solace he expected me to afford him. He entered, at some length, into what he conceived to be the nature of his malady. It was, he said, a constitutional and a family evil, and one for which he despaired to find a remedy—a mere nervous affection, he immediately added, which would undoubtedly soon pass. It displayed itself in a host of unnatural sensations. Some of these, as he detailed them, interested and bewildered me; although, perhaps, the terms, and the general manner of the narration had their weight. He suffered much from a morbid acuteness of the senses; the most insipid food was alone endurable; he could wear only garments of certain texture; the odors of all flowers were oppressive; his eyes were tortured by even a faint light; and there were but peculiar sounds, and these from stringed instruments which did not inspire him with horror.

To an anomalous species of terror I found him a bounden slave. 'I shall perish,' said he, 'I *must* perish in this deplorable folly. Thus, thus, and not otherwise, shall I be lost. I dread the events of the future, not in themselves, but in their results. I shudder at the thought of any, even the most trivial, incident, which may operate upon this intolerable agitation of soul. I have, indeed, no abhorrence of danger, except in its absolute effect—in terror. In this unnerved—in this pitiable condition—I feel that the period will sooner or later arrive when I must abandon life and reason together, in some struggle with the grim phantasm, FEAR.'

I learned, moreover, at intervals, and through broken and equivocal hints, another singular feature of his mental condition. He was enchained by certain superstitious impressions in regard to the dwelling which he tenanted, and whence, for many years, he had never ventured forth—in regard to an influence whose supposititious force was conveyed in terms too shadowy here to be re-stated—an influence which some peculiarities in the mere form and substance of his family mansion, had, by dint of long sufferance, he said, obtained over his spirit—an effect which the *physique* of the gray walls and turrets, and of the dim tarn into which they all looked down, had, at length, brought about upon the *morale* of his existence.

He admitted, however, although with hesitation, that much of the peculiar gloom which thus afflicted him could be traced to a more natural and far more palpable origin—to the severe and long-continued illness—indeed to the evidently approaching dissolution—of a tenderly beloved sister—his sole companion for long years—his last and only relative on earth. 'Her decease,' he said, with a bitterness which I can never forget, 'would leave him (him the hopeless and the frail) the last of the ancient race of the Ushers.' While he spoke, the lady Madeline (for so was she called) passed slowly through a remote portion of the apartment, and, without having noticed my presence, disappeared. I regarded her with an utter astonishment not unmingled with dread—and yet I found it impossible to account for such feelings. A sensation of stupor oppressed me, as my eyes followed her retreating steps. When a door, at length, closed upon her, my glance sought instinctively and eagerly the countenance of the brother—but he had buried his face in his hands, and I could only perceive that a far more than ordinary wanness had overspread the emaciated fingers through which trickled many passionate tears.

The disease of the lady Madeline had long baffled the skill of her physicians. A settled apathy, a gradual wasting away of the person, and frequent although transient affections of a partially cataleptical character, were the unusual diagnosis. Hitherto she had steadily borne up against the pressure of her malady, and had not betaken herself finally to bed; but, on the closing in of the evening of my arrival at the house, she succumbed (as her brother told me at night with inexpressible agitation) to the prostrating power of the destroyer; and I learned that the glimpse I had obtained of her person would thus probably be the last I should obtain—that the lady, at least while living, would be seen by me no more.

For several days ensuing, her name was unmentioned by either Usher or myself: and during this period I was busied in earnest endeavors to alleviate the melancholy of my friend. We painted and read together; or I listened, as if in a dream, to the wild improvisations of his speaking guitar. And thus, as a closer and still closer intimacy admitted me more unreservedly into the recesses of his spirit, the more bitterly did I perceive the futility of all attempt at cheering a mind from which darkness, as if an inherent positive quality, poured forth upon all objects of the moral and physical universe, in one unceasing radiation of gloom.

I shall ever bear about me a memory of the many solemn hours I thus spent alone with the master of the House of Usher. Yet I should fail in any attempt to convey an idea of the exact character of the studies, or of the occupations, in which he involved me, or led me the way. An excited and highly distempered ideality threw a sulphureous lustre over all. His long improvised dirges will ring forever in my ears. Among other things, I hold painfully in mind a certain singular perversion and amplification of the wild air of the last waltz of Von Weber.* From the paintings over which his elaborate fancy brooded, and which grew, touch by touch, into vaguenesses at which I shuddered the more thrillingly, because I shuddered knowing not why;—from these paintings (vivid as their images now are before me) I would in vain endeavor to educe more than a small portion which should lie within the compass of merely written words. By the utter simplicity, by the nakedness, of his designs, he arrested and overawed attention. If ever mortal painted an idea, that mortal was Roderick

Usher. For me at least—in the circumstances then surrounding me—there arose out of the pure abstractions which the hypochondriac contrived to throw upon his canvass, an intensity of intolerable awe, no shadow of which felt I ever yet in the contemplation of the certainly glowing yet too concrete reveries of Fuseli.*

One of the phantasmagoric conceptions of my friend, partaking not so rigidly of the spirit of abstraction, may be shadowed forth, although feebly, in words. A small picture presented the interior of an immensely long and rectangular vault or tunnel, with low walls, smooth, white, and without interruption or device. Certain accessory points of the design served well to convey the idea that this excavation lay at an exceeding depth below the surface of the earth. No outlet was observed in any portion of its vast extent, and no torch, or other artificial source of light was discernible; yet a flood of intense rays rolled throughout, and bathed the whole in a ghastly and inappropriate splendor.

I have just spoken of that morbid condition of the auditory nerve which rendered all music intolerable to the sufferer with the exception of certain effects of stringed instruments. It was, perhaps, the narrow limits to which he thus confined himself upon the guitar, which gave birth, in great measure, to the fantastic character of his performances. But the fervid *facility* of his *impromptus* could not so be accounted for. They must have been and were, in the notes, as well as in the words of his wild fantasias (for he not unfrequently accompanied himself with rhymed verbal improvisations), the result of that intense mental collectedness and concentration to which I have previously alluded as observable only in particular moments of the highest artificial excitement. The words of one of these rhapsodies I have easily remembered. I was, perhaps, the more forcibly impressed with it, as he gave it, because, in the under or mystic current of its meaning, I fancied that I perceived, and for the first time, a full consciousness on the part of Usher, of the tottering of his lofty reason upon her throne. The verses, which were entitled 'The Haunted Palace,' ran very nearly, if not accurately, thus:*

I.

In the greenest of our valleys,
   By good angels tenanted,
Once a fair and stately palace—
   Radiant palace—reared its head.
In the monarch Thought's dominion—

It stood there!
Never seraph spread a pinion
Over fabric half so fair.

II.

Banners yellow, glorious, golden,
On its roof did float and flow;
(This—all this—was in the olden
Time long ago)
And every gentle air that dallied,
In that sweet day,
Along the ramparts plumed and pallid,
A winged odor went away.

III.

Wanderers in that happy valley
Through two luminous windows saw
Spirits moving musically
To a lute's well-tunéd law,
Round about a throne, where sitting
(Porphyrogene!)
In state his glory well befitting,
The ruler of the realm was seen.

IV.

And all with pearl and ruby glowing
Was the fair palace door,
Through which came flowing, flowing, flowing,
And sparkling evermore,
A troop of Echoes whose sweet duty
Was but to sing,
In voices of surpassing beauty,
The wit and wisdom of their king.

V.

But evil things, in robes of sorrow,
Assailed the monarch's high estate;
(Ah, let us mourn, for never morrow
Shall dawn upon him, desolate!)
And, round about his home, the glory
That blushed and bloomed
Is but dim-remembered story
Of the old time entombed.

VI.

And travellers now within that valley,
Through the red-litten windows, see
Vast forms that move fantastically
To a discordant melody;
While, like a rapid ghastly river,
Through the pale door,
A hideous throng rush out forever,
And laugh—but smile no more.

I well remember that suggestions arising from this ballad led us into a train of thought wherein there became manifest an opinion of Usher's which I mention not so much on account of its novelty, (for other men[1] have thought thus,) as on account of the pertinacity with which he maintained it. This opinion, in its general form, was that of the sentience of all vegetable things. But, in his disordered fancy, the idea had assumed a more daring character, and trespassed, under certain conditions, upon the kingdom of inorganization. I lack words to express the full extent, or the earnest *abandon* of his persuasion. The belief, however, was connected (as I have previously hinted) with the gray stones of the home of his forefathers. The conditions of the sentience had been here, he imagined, fulfilled in the method of collocation of these stones—in the order of their arrangement, as well as in that of the many *fungi* which overspread them, and of the decayed trees which stood around—above all, in the long undisturbed endurance of this arrangement, and in its reduplication in the still waters of the tarn. Its evidence—the evidence of the sentience—was to be seen, he said (and I here started as he spoke,) in the gradual yet certain condensation of an atmosphere of their own about the waters and the walls. The result was discoverable, he added, in that silent, yet importunate and terrible influence which for centuries had moulded the destinies of his family, and which made *him* what I now saw him—what he was. Such opinions need no comment, and I will make none.

Our books—the books which, for years, had formed no small portion of the mental existence of the invalid—were, as might be supposed, in strict keeping with this character of phantasm. We pored together over such works as the Ververt et Chartreuse of Gresset; the Belphegor of Machiavelli; the Heaven and Hell of Swedenborg; the

[1] Watson, Dr Percival, Spallanzani, and especially the Bishop of Landaff.—See 'Chemical Essays', vol. v.*

Subterranean Voyage of Nicholas Klimm by Holberg; the Chiromancy of Robert Flud, of Jean D'Indaginé, and of De la Chambre; the Journey into the Blue Distance of Tieck; and the City of the Sun of Campanella. One favorite volume was a small octavo edition of the *Directorium Inquisitorum*, by the Dominican Eymeric de Gironne; and there were passages in Pomponius Mela, about the old African Satyrs and Œgipans, over which Usher would sit dreaming for hours. His chief delight, however, was found in the perusal of an exceedingly rare and curious book in quarto Gothic—the manual of a forgotten church—the *Vigiliae Mortuorum secundum Chorum Ecclesiae Maguntinae*.*

I could not help thinking of the wild ritual of this work, and of its probable influence upon the hypochondriac, when, one evening, having informed me abruptly that the lady Madeline was no more, he stated his intention of preserving her corpse for a fortnight, (previously to its final interment,) in one of the numerous vaults within the main walls of the building. The worldly reason, however, assigned for this singular proceeding, was one which I did not feel at liberty to dispute. The brother had been led to his resolution (so he told me) by consideration of the unusual character of the malady of the deceased, of certain obtrusive and eager inquiries on the part of her medical men, and of the remote and exposed situation of the burial-ground of the family. I will not deny that when I called to mind the sinister countenance of the person whom I met upon the staircase, on the day of my arrival at the house, I had no desire to oppose what I regarded as at best but a harmless, and by no means an unnatural, precaution.

At the request of Usher, I personally aided him in the arrangements for the temporary entombment. The body having been encoffined, we two alone bore it to its rest. The vault in which we placed it (and which had been so long unopened that our torches, half smothered in its oppressive atmosphere, gave us little opportunity for investigation) was small, damp, and entirely without means of admission for light; lying, at great depth, immediately beneath that portion of the building in which was my own sleeping apartment. It had been used, apparently, in remote feudal times, for the worst purposes of a donjon-keep, and, in later days, as a place of deposit for powder, or some other highly combustible substance, as a portion of its floor, and the whole interior of a long archway through which we reached it, were carefully sheathed with copper. The door, of massive iron, had been, also, similarly protected. Its immense weight caused an unusually sharp grating sound, as it moved upon its hinges.

Having deposited our mournful burden upon tressels within this region of horror, we partially turned aside the yet unscrewed lid of the coffin, and looked upon the face of the tenant. A striking similitude between the brother and sister now first arrested my attention; and Usher, divining, perhaps, my thoughts, murmured out some few words from which I learned that the deceased and himself had been twins, and that sympathies of a scarcely intelligible nature had always existed between them. Our glances, however, rested not long upon the dead—for we could not regard her unawed. The disease which had thus entombed the lady in the maturity of youth, had left, as usual in all maladies of a strictly cataleptical character, the mockery of a faint blush upon the bosom and the face, and that suspiciously lingering smile upon the lip which is so terrible in death. We replaced and screwed down the lid, and, having secured the door of iron, made our way, with toil, into the scarcely less gloomy apartments of the upper portion of the house.

And now, some days of bitter grief having elapsed, an observable change came over the features of the mental disorder of my friend. His ordinary manner had vanished. His ordinary occupations were neglected or forgotten. He roamed from chamber to chamber with hurried, unequal, and objectless step. The pallor of his countenance had assumed, if possible, a more ghastly hue—but the luminousness of his eye had utterly gone out. The once occasional huskiness of his tone was heard no more; and a tremulous quaver, as if of extreme terror, habitually characterized his utterance. There were times, indeed, when I thought his unceasingly agitated mind was laboring with some oppressive secret, to divulge which he struggled for the necessary courage. At times, again, I was obliged to resolve all into the mere inexplicable vagaries of madness, for I beheld him gazing upon vacancy for long hours, in an attitude of the profoundest attention, as if listening to some imaginary sound. It was no wonder that his condition terrified—that it infected me. I felt creeping upon me, by slow yet certain degrees, the wild influences of his own fantastic yet impressive superstitions.

It was, especially, upon retiring to bed late in the night of the seventh or eighth day after the placing of the lady Madeline within the donjon, that I experienced the full power of such feelings. Sleep came not near my couch—while the hours waned and waned away. I struggled to reason off the nervousness which had dominion over me. I endeavored to believe that much, if not all of what I felt, was due to the bewildering influence of the gloomy furniture of the room—of the dark and tattered draperies, which, tortured into motion by the breath of a rising tempest, swayed fitfully to and fro upon the walls, and rustled uneasily about the decorations of the bed. But my efforts were fruitless. An irrepressible tremor gradually pervaded my frame; and, at length, there sat upon my very heart an incubus of utterly causeless alarm. Shaking this off with a gasp and a struggle, I uplifted myself upon the pillows, and, peering earnestly within the intense darkness of the chamber, harkened—I know not why, except that an instinctive spirit prompted me—to certain low and indefinite sounds which came, through the pauses of the storm, at long intervals, I knew not whence. Overpowered by an intense sentiment of horror, unaccountable yet unendurable, I threw on my clothes with haste (for I felt that I should sleep no more during the night), and endeavored to arouse myself from the pitiable condition into which I had fallen, by pacing rapidly to and fro through the apartment.

I had taken but few turns in this manner, when a light step on an adjoining staircase arrested my attention. I presently recognised it as that of Usher. In an instant afterward he rapped, with a gentle touch, at my door, and entered, bearing a lamp. His countenance was, as usual, cadaverously wan—but, moreover, there was a species of mad hilarity in his eyes—an evidently restrained *hysteria* in his whole demeanor. His air appalled me—but anything was preferable to the solitude which I had so long endured, and I even welcomed his presence as a relief.

'And you have not seen it?' he said abruptly, after having stared about him for some moments in silence—'you have not then seen it?—but, stay! you shall.' Thus speaking, and having carefully shaded his lamp, he hurried to one of the casements, and threw it freely open to the storm.

The impetuous fury of the entering gust nearly lifted us from our feet. It was, indeed, a tempestuous yet sternly beautiful night, and one wildly singular in its terror and its beauty. A whirlwind had apparently collected its force in our vicinity; for there were frequent and violent alterations in the direction of the wind; and the exceeding density of the clouds (which hung so low as to press upon the turrets of the house) did not prevent our perceiving the life-like velocity with which they flew careering from all points against each other, without passing away into the distance. I say that even their exceeding density did not prevent our perceiving this—yet we had no glimpse of the moon or stars—nor was there any flashing forth of the lightning. But the under surfaces of the huge masses of agitated vapor, as well as all terrestrial objects immediately around us, were glowing in the unnatural light of a faintly luminous and distinctly visible gaseous exhalation which hung about and enshrouded the mansion.

'You must not—you shall not behold this!' said I, shudderingly, to Usher, as I led him, with a gentle violence, from the window to a seat. 'These appearances, which bewilder you, are merely electrical phenomena not uncommon—or it may be that they have their ghastly origin in the rank miasma of the tarn. Let us close this casement;—the air is chilling and dangerous to your frame. Here is one of your favorite romances. I will read, and you shall listen;—and so we will pass away this terrible night together.'

The antique volume which I had taken up was the 'Mad Trist' of Sir Launcelot Canning; but I had called it a favorite of Usher's more in sad jest than in earnest; for, in truth, there is little in its uncouth and unimaginative prolixity which could have had interest for the lofty and spiritual ideality of my friend. It was, however, the only book immediately at hand; and I indulged a vague hope that the excitement which now agitated the hypochondriac, might find relief (for the history of mental disorder is full of similar anomalies) even in the extremeness of the folly which I should read. Could I have judged, indeed, by the wild overstrained air of vivacity with which he harkened, or apparently harkened, to the words of the tale, I might well have congratulated myself upon the success of my design.

I had arrived at that well-known portion of the story where Ethelred, the hero of the Trist, having sought in vain for peaceable admission into the dwelling of the hermit, proceeds to make good an entrance by force. Here, it will be remembered, the words of the narrative run thus:

'And Ethelred, who was by nature of a doughty heart, and who was now mighty withal, on account of the powerfulness of the wine which he had drunken, waited no longer to hold parley with the hermit, who, in sooth, was of an obstinate and maliceful turn, but, feeling the rain upon his shoulders, and fearing the rising of the tempest, uplifted his mace outright, and, with blows, made quickly room in the plankings of the door for his gauntleted hand; and now pulling therewith sturdily, he so cracked, and ripped, and tore all asunder, that the noise of the dry and hollow-sounding wood alarummed and reverberated throughout the forest.'

At the termination of this sentence I started, and for a moment, paused; for it appeared to me (although I at once concluded that my excited fancy had deceived me)—it appeared to me that, from some very remote portion of the mansion, there came, indistinctly, to my ears, what might have been, in its exact similarity of character, the echo (but a stifled and dull one certainly) of the very cracking and ripping sound which Sir Launcelot had so particularly described. It was, beyond doubt, the coincidence alone which had arrested my attention; for, amid the rattling of the sashes of the casement, and the ordinary commingled noises of the still increasing storm, the sound, in itself, had nothing, surely, which should have interested or disturbed me. I continued the story:

'But the good champion Ethelred, now entering within the door, was sore enraged and amazed to perceive no signal of the maliceful hermit; but, in the stead thereof, a dragon of a scaly and prodigious demeanor, and of a fiery tongue, which sate in guard before a palace of gold, with a floor of silver; and upon the wall there hung a shield of shining brass with this legend enwritten—

> Who entereth herein, a conqueror hath bin;
> Who slayeth the dragon, the shield he shall win;

And Ethelred uplifted his mace, and struck upon the head of the dragon, which fell before him, and gave up his pesty breath, with a shriek so horrid and harsh, and withal so piercing, that Ethelred had fain to close his ears with his hands against the dreadful noise of it, the like whereof was never before heard.'

Here again I paused abruptly, and now with a feeling of wild amazement—for there could be no doubt whatever that, in this instance, I did actually hear (although from what direction it proceeded I found it impossible to say) a low and apparently distant, but harsh, protracted, and most unusual screaming or grating sound—the exact counterpart of what my fancy had already conjured up for the dragon's unnatural shriek as described by the romancer.

Oppressed, as I certainly was, upon the occurrence of this second and most extraordinary coincidence, by a thousand conflicting sensations, in which wonder and extreme terror were predominant, I still retained sufficient presence of mind to avoid exciting, by any observation, the sensitive nervousness of my companion. I was by no means certain that he had noticed the sounds in question; although, assuredly, a strange alteration had, during the last few minutes, taken place in his demeanor. From a position fronting my own, he had gradually brought round his chair, so as to sit with his face to the door of the chamber; and thus I could but partially perceive his features, although I saw that his lips trembled as if he were murmuring inaudibly. His head had dropped upon his breast—yet I knew that he was not asleep, from the wide and rigid opening of the eye as I caught a glance of it in profile. The motion of his body, too, was at variance with this idea—for he rocked from side to side with a gentle yet constant and uniform sway. Having rapidly taken notice of all this, I resumed the narrative of Sir Launcelot, which thus proceeded:

'And now, the champion, having escaped from the terrible fury of the dragon, bethinking himself of the brazen shield, and of the breaking up of the enchantment which was upon it, removed the carcass from out of the way before him, and approached valorously over the silver pavement of the castle to where the shield was upon the wall; which in sooth tarried not for his full coming, but fell down at his feet upon the silver floor, with a mighty great and terrible ringing sound.'

No sooner had these syllables passed my lips, than—as if a shield of brass had indeed, at the moment, fallen heavily upon a floor of silver—I became aware of a distinct, hollow, metallic, and clangorous, yet apparently muffled reverberation. Completely unnerved, I leaped to my feet; but the measured rocking movement of Usher was undisturbed. I rushed to the chair in which he sat. His eyes were bent fixedly before him, and throughout his whole countenance there reigned a stony rigidity. But, as I placed my hand upon his shoulder, there came a strong shudder over his whole person; a sickly smile quivered about his lips; and I saw that he spoke in a low, hurried and gibbering murmur, as if unconscious of my presence. Bending closely over him, I at length drank in the hideous import of his words.

'Not hear it?—yes, I hear it, and *have* heard it. Long—long—long—many minutes, many hours, many days, have I heard it—yet I dared not—oh, pity me, miserable wretch that I am!—I dared not—I *dared* not speak! *We have put her living in the tomb!* Said I not that my senses were acute? I *now* tell you that I heard her first feeble movements in the hollow coffin. I heard them—many, many days ago—yet I dared not—*I dared not speak!* And now—to-night—Ethelred—ha! ha!—the breaking of the hermit's door, and the death-cry of the dragon, and the clangor of the shield!—say, rather, the rending of her coffin, and the grating of the iron hinges of her prison, and her struggles within the coppered archway of the vault! Oh whither shall I fly? Will she not be here anon? Is she not hurrying to upbraid me for my haste? Have I not heard her footstep on the stair? Do I not distinguish that heavy and horrible beating of her heart? Madman!'—here he sprang furiously to his feet, and shrieked out his syllables, as if in the effort he were giving up his soul—*'Madman! I tell you that she now stands without the door!'*

As if in the superhuman energy of his utterance there had been found the potency of a spell—the huge antique pannels to which the speaker pointed, threw slowly back, upon the instant, their ponderous and ebony jaws. It was the work of the rushing gust—but then without those doors there *did* stand the lofty and enshrouded figure of the lady Madeline of Usher. There was blood upon her white robes, and the evidence of some bitter struggle upon every portion of her emaciated frame. For a moment she remained trembling and reeling to and fro upon the threshold—then, with a low moaning cry, fell heavily inward upon the person of her brother, and in her violent and now final death-agonies, bore him to the floor a corpse, and a victim to the terrors he had anticipated.

From that chamber, and from that mansion, I fled aghast. The storm was still abroad in all its wrath as I found myself crossing the old causeway. Suddenly there shot along the path a wild light, and I turned to see whence a gleam so unusual could have issued; for the vast house and its shadows were alone behind me. The radiance was that of the full, setting, and blood-red moon, which now shone vividly through that once barely-discernible fissure, of which I have before spoken as extending from the roof of the building, in a zigzag direction, to the base. While I gazed, this fissure rapidly widened—there came a fierce breath of the whirlwind—the entire orb of the satellite burst at once upon my sight—my brain reeled as I saw the mighty walls rushing asunder—there was a long tumultuous shouting sound like the voice of a thousand waters—and the deep and dank tarn at my feet closed sullenly and silently over the fragments of the '*House of Usher.*'

WILLIAM WILSON

What say of it? What say of CONSCIENCE grim,
That spectre in my path?

Chamberlayne's *Pharonnida**

LET me call myself, for the present, William Wilson. The fair page now lying before me need not be sullied with my real appellation. This has been already too much an object for the scorn—for the horror—for the detestation of my race. To the uttermost regions of the globe have not the indignant winds bruited its unparalleled infamy? Oh, outcast of all outcasts most abandoned!—to the earth art thou not forever dead? to its honors, to its flowers, to its golden aspirations?—and a cloud, dense, dismal, and limitless, does it not hang eternally between thy hopes and heaven?

I would not, if I could, here or to-day, embody a record of my later years of unspeakable misery, and unpardonable crime. This epoch—these later years—took unto themselves a sudden elevation in turpitude, whose origin alone it is my present purpose to assign. Men usually grow base by degrees. From me, in an instant, all virtue dropped bodily as a mantle. From comparatively trivial wickedness I passed, with the stride of a giant, into more than the enormities of an Elah-Gabalus.* What chance—what one event brought this evil thing to pass, bear with me while I relate. Death approaches; and the shadow which foreruns him has thrown a softening influence over my spirit. I long, in passing through the dim valley, for the sympathy—I had nearly said for the pity—of my fellow men. I would fain have them believe that I have been, in some measure, the slave of circumstances beyond human control. I would wish them to seek out of me, in the details I am about to give, some little oasis of *fatality* amid a wilderness of error. I would have them allow—what they cannot refrain from allowing—that, although temptation may have ere-while existed as great, man was never *thus*, at least, tempted before—certainly, never *thus* fell. And is it therefore that he has never thus suffered? Have I not indeed been living in a dream? And am I not now dying a victim to the horror and the mystery of the wildest of all sublunary visions?

I am the descendant of a race whose imaginative and easily excitable temperament has at all times rendered them remarkable; and, in my earliest infancy, I gave evidence of having fully inherited the family character. As I advanced in years it was more strongly developed; becoming, for many reasons, a cause of serious disquietude to my friends, and of positive injury to myself. I grew self-willed, addicted to the wildest caprices, and a prey to the most ungovernable passions. Weak-minded, and beset with constitutional infirmities akin to my own, my parents could do but little to check the evil propensities which distinguished me. Some feeble and ill-directed efforts resulted in complete failure on their part, and, of course, in total triumph on mine. Thenceforward my voice was a household law; and at an age when few children have abandoned their leading-strings, I was left to the guidance of my own will, and became, in all but name, the master of my own actions.

My earliest recollections of a school-life are connected with a large, rambling, Elizabethan house, in a misty-looking village of England, where were a vast number of gigantic and gnarled trees, and where all the houses were excessively ancient. In truth, it was a dream-like and spirit-soothing place, that venerable old town. At this moment, in fancy, I feel the refreshing chilliness of its deeply-shadowed avenues, inhale the fragrance of its thousand shrubberies, and thrill anew with undefinable delight, at the deep hollow note of the church-bell, breaking, each hour, with sullen and sudden roar, upon the stillness of the dusky atmosphere in which the fretted Gothic steeple lay imbedded and asleep.

It gives me, perhaps, as much of pleasure as I can now in any manner experience, to dwell upon minute recollections of the school and its concerns. Steeped in misery as I am—misery, alas! only too real—I shall be pardoned for seeking relief, however slight and temporary, in the weakness of a few rambling details. These, moreover, utterly trivial, and even ridiculous in themselves, assume, to my fancy, adventitious importance, as connected with a period and a locality when and where I recognise the first ambiguous monitions of the destiny which afterwards so fully over-shadowed me. Let me then remember.

The house, I have said, was old and irregular. The grounds were extensive, and a high and solid brick wall, topped with a bed of mortar and broken glass, encompassed the whole. This prison-like rampart formed the limit of our domain; beyond it we saw but thrice a week—once every Saturday afternoon, when, attended by two ushers, we were permitted to take brief walks in a body through some of the neighboring fields—and twice during Sunday, when we were paraded in the same formal manner to the morning and evening service in the one church of the village. Of this church the principal of our school was pastor. With how deep a spirit of wonder and perplexity was I wont to regard him from our remote pew in the gallery, as, with step solemn and slow, he ascended the pulpit! This reverend man, with countenance so demurely benign, with robes so glossy and so clerically flowing, with wig so minutely powdered, so rigid and so vast,—could this be he who, of late, with sour visage, and in snuffy habiliments, administered, ferule in hand, the Draconian Laws of the academy? Oh, gigantic paradox, too utterly monstrous for solution!

At an angle of the ponderous wall frowned a more ponderous gate. It was riveted and studded with iron bolts, and surmounted with jagged iron spikes. What impressions of deep awe did it inspire! It was never opened save for the three periodical egressions and ingressions already mentioned; then, in every creak of its mighty hinges, we found a plenitude of mystery—a world of matter for solemn remark, or for more solemn meditation.

The extensive enclosure was irregular in form, having many capacious recesses. Of these, three or four of the largest constituted the play-ground. It was level, and covered with fine hard gravel. I well remember it had no trees, nor benches, nor anything similar within it. Of course it was in the rear of the house. In front lay a small parterre, planted with box and other shrubs; but through this sacred division we passed only upon rare occasions indeed—such as a first advent to school or final departure thence, or perhaps, when a parent or friend having called for us, we joyfully took our way home for the Christmas or Midsummer holydays.

But the house!—how quaint an old building was this!—to me how veritably a palace of enchantment! There was really no end to its windings—to its incomprehensible subdivisions. It was difficult, at any given time, to say with certainty upon which of its two stories one happened to be. From each room to every other there were sure to be found three or four steps either in ascent or descent. Then the lateral branches were innumerable—inconceivable—and so returning in upon themselves, that our most exact ideas in regard to the whole mansion were not very far different from those with which we pondered upon infinity. During the five years of my residence here, I was never able to ascertain with precision, in what remote locality lay the little sleeping apartment assigned to myself and some eighteen or twenty other scholars.

The school-room was the largest in the house—I could not help thinking, in the world. It was very long, narrow, and dismally low, with pointed Gothic windows and a ceiling of oak. In a remote and terror-inspiring angle was a square enclosure of eight or ten feet, comprising the *sanctum*, 'during hours,' of our principal, the Reverend Dr Bransby.* It was a solid structure, with massy door, sooner than open which in the absence of the 'Dominie,' we would all have willingly perished by the *peine forte et dure*.* In other angles were two other similar boxes, far less reverenced, indeed, but still greatly matters of awe. One of these was the pulpit of the 'classical' usher, one of the 'English and mathematical.' Interspersed about the room, crossing and recrossing in endless irregularity, were innumerable benches and desks, black, ancient, and time-worn, piled desperately with much-bethumbed books, and so beseamed with intitial letters, names at full length, grotesque figures, and other multiplied efforts of the knife, as to have entirely lost what little of original form might have been their portion in days long departed. A huge bucket with water stood at one extremity of the room, and a clock of stupendous dimensions at the other.

Encompassed by the massy walls of this venerable academy, I passed, yet not in tedium or disgust, the years of the third lustrum of my life. The teeming brain of childhood requires no external world of incident to occupy or amuse it; and the apparently dismal monotony of a school was replete with more intense excitement than my riper youth has derived from luxury, or my full manhood from crime. Yet I must believe that my first mental development had in it much of the uncommon—even much of the *outré*. Upon mankind at large the events of very early existence rarely leave in mature age any definite impression. All is gray shadow—a weak and irregular remembrance—an indistinct regathering of feeble pleasures and phantasmagoric pains. With me this is not so. In childhood I must have felt with the energy of a man what I now find stamped upon memory in lines as vivid, as deep, and as durable as the *exergues* of the Carthaginian medals.*

Yet in fact—in the fact of the world's view—how little was there to remember! The morning's awakening, the nightly summons to bed; the connings, the recitations; the periodical half-holidays, and perambulations; the play-ground, with its broils, its pastimes, its intrigues;—these, by a mental sorcery long forgotten, were made to involve a wilderness of sensation, a world of rich incident, an universe of varied emotion, of excitement the most passionate and spirit-stirring. *'Oh, le bon temps, que ce siècle de fer!'**

In truth, the ardor, the enthusiasm, and the imperiousness of my disposition, soon rendered me a marked character among my school-mates, and by slow, but natural gradations, gave me an ascendancy over all not greatly older than myself;—over all with a single exception. This exception was found in the person of a scholar, who, although no relation, bore the same Christian and surname as myself;—a circumstance, in fact, little remarkable; for, notwithstanding a noble descent, mine was one of those everyday appellations which seem, by prescriptive right, to have been, time out of mind, the common property of the mob. In this narrative I have therefore designated myself as William Wilson,—a fictitious title not very dissimilar to the real. My namesake alone, of those who in school-phraseology constituted 'our set,' presumed to compete with me in the studies of the class—in the sports and broils of the play-ground—to refuse implicit belief in my assertions, and submission to my will—indeed, to interfere with my arbitrary dictation in any respect whatsoever. If there is on earth a supreme and unqualified despotism, it is the despotism of a master-mind in boyhood over the less energetic spirits of its companions.

Wilson's rebellion was to me a source of the greatest embarrassment; the more so as, in spite of the bravado with which in public I made a point of treating him and his pretensions, I secretly felt that I feared him, and could not help thinking the equality which he maintained so easily with myself, a proof of his true superiority; since not to be overcome cost me a perpetual struggle. Yet this superiority—even this equality—was in truth acknowledged by no one but myself; our associates, by some unaccountable blindness, seemed not even to suspect it. Indeed, his competition, his resistance, and especially his impertinent and dogged interference with my purposes, were not more pointed than private. He appeared to be destitute alike of the ambition which urged, and of the passionate energy of mind which enabled me to excel. In his rivalry he might have been supposed actuated solely by a whimsical desire to thwart, astonish, or mortify myself; although there were times when I could not help observing, with a feeling made up of wonder, abasement, and pique, that he mingled with his injuries, his insults, or his contradictions, a certain most inappropriate, and assuredly most unwelcome *affectionateness* of manner. I could only conceive this singular behavior to arise from a consummate self-conceit assuming the vulgar airs of patronage and protection.

Perhaps it was this latter trait in Wilson's conduct, conjoined with our identity of name, and the mere accident of our having entered the school upon the same day, which set afloat the notion that we were brothers, among the senior classes in the academy. These do not usually inquire with much strictness into the affairs of their juniors. I have before said, or should have said, that Wilson was not, in the most remote degree, connected with my family. But assuredly if we *had* been brothers we must have been twins; for, after leaving Dr Bransby's, I casually learned that my namesake was born on the nineteenth of January, 1813—and this is a somewhat remarkable coincidence; for the day is precisely that of my own nativity.*

It may seem strange that in spite of the continual anxiety occasioned me by the rivalry of Wilson, and his intolerable spirit of contradiction, I could not bring myself to hate him altogether. We had, to be sure, nearly every day a quarrel in which, yielding me publicly the palm of victory, he, in some manner, contrived to make me feel that it was he who had deserved it; yet a sense of pride on my part, and a veritable dignity on his own, kept us always upon what are called 'speaking terms,' while there were many points of strong congeniality in our tempers, operating to awake in me a sentiment which our position alone, perhaps, prevented from ripening into friendship. It is difficult, indeed, to define, or even to describe, my real feelings towards him. They formed a motley and heterogeneous admixture;—some petulant animosity, which was not yet hatred, some esteem, more respect, much fear, with a world of uneasy curiosity. To the moralist it will be unnecessary to say, in addition, that Wilson and myself were the most inseparable of companions.

It was no doubt the anomalous state of affairs existing between us, which turned all my attacks upon him, (and they were many, either open or covert) into the channel of banter or practical joke (giving pain while assuming the aspect of mere fun) rather than into a more serious and determined hostility. But my endeavors on this head were by no means uniformly successful, even when my plans were the most wittily concocted; for my namesake had much about him, in character, of that unassuming and quiet austerity which, while enjoying the poignancy of its own jokes, has no heel of Achilles in itself, and absolutely refuses to be laughed at. I could find, indeed, but one vulnerable point, and that, lying in a personal peculiarity, arising, perhaps, from constitutional disease, would have been spared by any antagonist less at his wit's end than myself;—my rival had a weakness in the faucial or guttural organs, which precluded him from raising his voice at any time *above a very low whisper*. Of this defect I did not fail to take what poor advantage lay in my power.

Wilson's retaliations in kind were many; and there was one form of his practical wit that disturbed me beyond measure. How his sagacity first discovered at all that so petty a thing would vex me, is a question I never could solve; but, having discovered, he habitually practised the annoyance. I had always felt aversion to my uncourtly patronymic, and its very common, if not plebeian prænomen. The words were venom in my ears; and when, upon the day of my arrival, a second William Wilson came also to the academy, I felt angry with him for bearing the name, and doubly disgusted with the name because a stranger bore it, who would be the cause of its twofold repetition, who would be constantly in my presence, and whose concerns, in the ordinary routine of the school business, must inevitably, on account of the detestable coincidence, be often confounded with my own.

The feeling of vexation thus engendered grew stronger with every circumstance tending to show resemblance, moral or physical, between my rival and myself. I had not then discovered the remarkable fact that we were of the same age; but I saw that we were of the same height, and I perceived that we were even singularly alike in general contour of person and outline of feature. I was galled, too, by the rumor touching a relationship, which had grown current in the upper forms. In a word, nothing could more seriously disturb me, (although I scrupulously concealed such disturbance,) than any allusion to a similarity of mind, person, or condition existing between us. But, in truth, I had no reason to believe that (with the exception of the matter of relationship, and in the case of Wilson himself), this similarity had ever been made a subject of comment, or even observed at all by our schoolfellows. That *he* observed it in all its bearings, and as fixedly as I, was apparent; but that he could discover in such circumstances so fruitful a field of annoyance, can only be attributed, as I said before, to his more than ordinary penetration.

His cue, which was to perfect an imitation of myself, lay both in words and in actions; and most admirably did he play his part. My dress it was an easy matter to copy; my gait and general manner were, without difficulty, appropriated; in spite of his constitutional defect, even my voice did not escape him. My louder tones were, of course, unattempted, but then the key,* it was identical; *and his singular whisper, it grew the very echo of my own* .

How greatly this most exquisite portraiture harassed me, (for it could not justly be termed a caricature,) I will not now venture to describe. I had but one consolation—in the fact that the imitation, apparently, was noticed by myself alone, and that I had to endure only the knowing and strangely sarcastic smiles of my namesake himself. Satisfied with having produced in my bosom the intended effect, he seemed to chuckle in secret over the sting he had inflicted, and was characteristically disregardful of the public applause which the success of his witty endeavors might have so easily elicited. That the school, indeed, did not feel his design, perceive its accomplishment, and participate in his sneer, was, for many anxious months, a riddle I could not resolve. Perhaps the *gradation* of his copy rendered it not so readily perceptible; or, more possibly, I owed my security to the masterly air of the copyist, who, disdaining the letter, (which in a painting is all the obtuse can see,) gave but the full spirit of his original for my individual contemplation and chagrin.

I have already more than once spoken of the disgusting air of patronage which he assumed toward me, and of his frequent officious interference with my will. This interference often took the ungracious character of advice; advice not openly given, but hinted or insinuated. I received it with a repugnance which gained strength as I grew in years. Yet, at this distant day, let me do him the simple justice to acknowledge that I can recall no occasion when the suggestions of my rival were on the side of those errors or follies so usual to his immature age and seeming inexperience; that his moral sense, at least, if not his general talents and worldly wisdom, was far keener than my own; and that I might, to-day, have been a better, and thus a happier man, had I less frequently rejected the counsels embodied in those meaning whispers which I then but too cordially hated and too bitterly despised.

As it was, I at length grew restive in the extreme under his distasteful supervision, and daily resented more and more openly what I considered his intolerable arrogance. I have said that, in the first years of our connexion as schoolmates, my feelings in regard to him might have been easily ripened into friendship: but, in the latter months of my residence at the academy, although the intrusion of his ordinary manner had, beyond doubt, in some measure, abated, my sentiments, in nearly similar proportion, partook very much of positive hatred. Upon one occasion he saw this, I think, and afterwards avoided, or made a show of avoiding me.

It was about the same period, if I remember aright, that, in an altercation of violence with him, in which he was more than usually thrown off his guard, and spoke and acted with an openness of demeanor rather foreign to his nature, I discovered, or fancied I discovered, in his accent, his air, and general appearance, a something which first startled, and then deeply interested me, by bringing to mind dim visions of my earliest infancy—wild, confused and thronging memories of a time when memory herself was yet unborn. I cannot better describe the sensation which oppressed me, than by saying that I would with difficulty shake off the belief of my having been acquainted with the being who stood before me, at some epoch very long ago—some point of the past even infinitely remote. The delusion, however, faded rapidly as it came; and I mention it at all but to define the day of the last conversation I there held with my singular namesake.

The huge old house, with its countless subdivisions, had several large chambers communicating with each other, where slept the greater number of the students. There were, however, (as must necessarily happen in a building so awkwardly planned,) many little nooks or recesses, the odds and ends of the structure; and these the economic ingenuity of Dr Bransby had also fitted up as dormitories; although, being the merest closets, they were capable of accommodating but a single individual. One of these small apartments was occupied by Wilson.

One night, about the close of my fifth year at the school, and immediately after the altercation just mentioned, finding every one wrapped in sleep, I arose from bed, and, lamp in hand, stole through a wilderness of narrow passages from my own bedroom to that of my rival. I had long been plotting one of those ill-natured pieces of practical wit at his expense in which I had hitherto been so uniformly unsuccessful. It was my intention, now, to put my scheme in operation, and I resolved to make him feel the whole extent of the malice with which I was imbued. Having reached his closet, I noiselessly entered, leaving the lamp, with a shade over it, on the outside. I advanced a step, and listened to the sound of his tranquil breathing. Assured of his being asleep, I returned, took the light, and with it again approached the bed. Close curtains were around it, which, in the prosecution of my plan, I slowly and quietly withdrew, when the bright rays fell vividly upon the sleeper, and my eyes, at the same moment, upon his countenance. I looked;—and a numbness, an iciness of feeling instantly pervaded my frame. My breast heaved, my knees tottered, my whole spirit became possessed with an objectless yet intolerable horror. Gasping for breath, I lowered the lamp in still nearer proximity to the face. Were these,—*these* the lineaments of William Wilson? I saw, indeed, that they were his, but I shook as if with a fit of the ague, in fancying they were not. What *was* there about them to confound me in this manner? I gazed;—while my brain reeled with a multitude of incoherent thoughts. Not thus he appeared—assuredly not *thus*—in the vivacity of his waking hours. The same name! the same contour of person! the same day of arrival at the academy! And then his dogged and meaningless imitation of my gait, my voice, my habits, and my manner! Was it, in truth, within the bounds of human possibility, that *what I now saw* was the result, merely, of the habitual practice of this sarcastic imitation? Awe-stricken, and with a creeping shudder, I extinguished the lamp, passed silently from the chamber, and left, at once, the halls of that old academy, never to enter them again.

After a lapse of some months, spent at home in mere idleness, I found myself a student at Eton.* The brief interval had been sufficient to enfeeble my remembrance of the events at Dr Bransby's, or at least to effect a material change in the nature of the feelings with which I remembered them. The truth—the tragedy—of the drama was no more. I could now find room to doubt the evidence of my senses; and seldom called up the subject at all but with wonder at the extent of human credulity, and a smile at the vivid force of the imagination which I hereditarily possessed. Neither was this species of skepticism likely to be diminished by the character of the life I led at Eton. The vortex of thoughtless folly into which I there so immediately and so recklessly plunged, washed away all but the froth of my past hours, ingulfed at once every solid or serious impression, and left to memory only the veriest levities of a former existence.

I do not wish, however, to trace the course of my miserable profligacy here—a profligacy which set at defiance the laws, while it eluded the vigilance of the institution. Three years of folly, passed without profit, had but given me rooted habits of vice, and added, in a somewhat unusual degree, to my bodily stature, when, after a week of soulless dissipation, I invited a small party of the most dissolute students to a secret carousal in my chambers. We met at a late hour of the night; for our debaucheries were to be faithfully protracted until morning. The wine flowed freely, and there were not wanting other and perhaps more dangerous seductions; so that the gray dawn had already faintly appeared in the east, while our delirious extravagance was at its height. Madly flushed with cards and intoxication, I was in the act of insisting upon a toast of more than wonted profanity, when my attention was suddenly diverted by the violent, although partial unclosing of the door of the apartment, and by the eager voice of a servant from without. He said that some person, apparently in great haste, demanded to speak with me in the hall.

Wildly excited with wine, the unexpected interruption rather delighted than surprised me. I staggered forward at once, and a few steps brought me to the vestibule of the building. In this low and small room there hung no lamp; and now no light at all was admitted, save that of the exceedingly feeble dawn which made its way through the semi-circular window. As I put my foot over the threshold, I became aware of the figure of a youth about my own height, and habited in a white kerseymere morning frock, cut in the novel fashion of the one I myself wore at the moment. This the faint light enabled me to perceive; but the features of his face I could not distinguish. Upon my entering, he strode hurriedly up to me, and, seizing me by the arm with a gesture of petulant impatience, whispered the words 'William Wilson!' in my ear.

I grew perfectly sober in an instant.

There was that in the manner of the stranger, and in the tremulous shake of his uplifted finger, as he held it between my eyes and the light, which filled me with unqualified amazement; but it was not this which had so violently moved me. It was the pregnancy of solemn admonition in the singular, low, hissing utterance; and, above all, it was the character, the tone, *the key*, of those few, simple, and familiar, yet *whispered* syllables, which came with a thousand thronging memories of by-gone days, and struck upon my soul with the shock of a galvanic battery. Ere I could recover the use of my senses he was gone.

Although this event failed not of a vivid effect upon my disordered imagination, yet was it evanescent as vivid. For some weeks, indeed, I busied myself in earnest inquiry, or was wrapped in a cloud of morbid speculation. I did not pretend to disguise from my perception the identity of the singular individual who thus perseveringly interfered with my affairs, and harassed me with his insinuated counsel. But who and what was this Wilson?—and whence came he?—and what were his purposes? Upon neither of these points could I be satisfied—merely ascertaining, in regard to him, that a sudden accident in his family had caused his removal from Dr Bransby's academy on the afternoon of the day in which I myself had eloped. But in a brief period I ceased to think upon the subject, my attention being all absorbed in a contemplated departure for Oxford. Thither I soon went, the uncalculating vanity of my parents furnishing me with an outfit and annual establishment, which would enable me to indulge at will in the luxury already so dear to my heart—to vie in profuseness of expenditure with the haughtiest heirs of the wealthiest earldoms in Great Britain.

Excited by such appliances to vice, my constitutional temperament broke forth with redoubled ardor, and I spurned even the common restraints of decency in the mad infatuation of my revels. But it were absurd to pause in the detail of my extravagance. Let it suffice, that among spendthrifts I out-Heroded Herod, and that, giving name to a multitude of novel follies, I added no brief appendix to the long catalogue of vices then usual in the most dissolute university of Europe.

It could hardly be credited, however, that I had, even here, so utterly fallen from the gentlemanly estate, as to seek acquaintance with the vilest arts of the gambler by profession, and, having become an adept in his despicable science, to practise it habitually as a means of increasing my already enormous income at the expense of the weak-minded among my fellow-collegians. Such, nevertheless, was the fact. And the very enormity of this offence against all manly and honorable sentiment proved, beyond doubt, the main if not the sole reason of the impunity with which it was committed. Who, indeed, among my most abandoned associates, would not rather have disputed the clearest evidence of his senses, than have suspected of such courses, the gay, the frank, the generous William Wilson—the noblest and most liberal commoner at Oxford—him whose follies (said his parasites) were but the follies of youth and unbridled fancy—whose errors but inimitable whim—whose darkest vice but a careless and dashing extravagance?

I had been now two years successfully busied in this way, when there came to the university a young *parvenu* nobleman, Glendinning—rich, said report, as Herodes Atticus—his riches, too, as easily acquired.* I soon found him of weak intellect, and, of course, marked him as a fitting subject for my skill. I frequently engaged him in play, and contrived, with the gambler's usual art, to let him win considerable sums, the more effectually to entangle him in my snares. At length, my schemes being ripe, I met him (with the full intention that this meeting should be final and decisive) at the chambers of a fellow-commoner, (Mr Preston,) equally intimate with both, but who, to do him justice, entertained not even a remote suspicion of my design. To give to this a better coloring, I had contrived to have assembled a party of some eight or ten, and was solicitously careful that the introduction of cards should appear accidental, and originate in the proposal of my contemplated dupe himself. To be brief upon a vile topic, none of the low finesse was omitted, so customary upon similar occasions that it is a just matter for wonder how any are still found so besotted as to fall its victim.

We had protracted our sitting far into the night, and I had at length effected the manœuvre of getting Glendinning as my sole antagonist. The game, too, was my favorite *écarté*. The rest of the company, interested in the extent of our play, had abandoned their own cards, and were standing around us as spectators. The *parvenu*, who had been induced by my artifices in the early part of the evening, to drink deeply, now shuffled, dealt, or played, with a wild nervousness of manner for which his intoxication, I thought, might partially, but could not altogether account. In a very short period he had become my debtor to a large amount, when, having taken a long draught of port, he did precisely what I had been coolly anticipating—he proposed to double our already extravagant stakes. With a well-feigned show of reluctance, and not until after my repeated refusal had seduced him into some angry words which gave a color of *pique* to my compliance, did I finally comply. The result, of course, did but prove how entirely the prey was in my toils: in less than an hour he had quadrupled his debt. For some time his countenance had been losing the florid tinge lent it by the wine; but now, to my astonishment, I perceived that it had grown to a pallor truly fearful. I say, to my astonishment. Glendinning had been represented to my eager inquiries as immeasurably wealthy; and the sums which he had as yet lost, although in themselves vast, could not, I supposed, very seriously annoy, much less so violently affect him. That he was overcome by the wine just swallowed, was the idea which most readily presented itself; and, rather with a view to the preservation of my own character in the eyes of my associates, than from any less interested motive, I was about to insist, peremptorily, upon a discontinuance of the play, when some expressions at my elbow from among the company, and an ejaculation evincing utter despair on the part of Glendinning, gave me to understand that I had effected his total ruin under circumstances which, rendering him an object for the pity of all, should have protected him from the ill offices even of a fiend.

What now might have been my conduct it is difficult to say. The pitiable condition of my dupe had thrown an air of embarrassed gloom over all; and, for some moments, a profound silence was maintained, during which I could not help feeling my cheeks tingle with the many burning glances of scorn or reproach cast upon me by the less abandoned of the party. I will even own that an intolerable weight of anxiety was for a brief instant lifted from my bosom by the sudden and extraordinary interruption which ensued. The wide, heavy folding doors of the apartment were all at once thrown open, to their full extent, with a vigorous and rushing impetuosity that extinguished, as if by magic, every candle in the room. Their light, in dying, enabled us just to perceive that a stranger had entered, about my own height, and closely muffled in a cloak. The darkness, however, was now total; and we could only *feel* that he was standing in our midst. Before any one of us could recover from the extreme astonishment into which this rudeness had thrown all, we heard the voice of the intruder.

'Gentlemen,' he said, in a low, distinct, and never-to-be-forgotten *whisper* which thrilled to the very marrow of my bones, 'Gentlemen, I make no apology for this behavior, because in thus behaving, I am but fulfilling a duty. You are, beyond doubt, uninformed of the true character of the person who has to-night won at *écarté* a large sum of money from Lord Glendinning. I will therefore put you upon an expeditious and decisive plan of obtaining this very necessary information. Please to examine, at your leisure, the inner linings of the cuff of his left sleeve, and the several little packages which may be found in the somewhat capacious pockets of his embroidered morning wrapper.'

While he spoke, so profound was the stillness that one might have heard a pin drop upon the floor. In ceasing, he departed at once, and as abruptly as he had entered. Can I—shall I describe my sensations? Must I say that I felt all the horrors of the damned? Most assuredly I had little time for reflection. Many hands roughly seized me upon the spot, and lights were immediately re-procured. A search ensued. In the lining of my sleeve were found all the court cards essential in *écarté*, and, in the pockets of my wrapper, a number of packs, fac-similes of those used at our sittings, with the single exception that mine were of the species called, technically, *arrondées*; the honors being slightly convex at the ends, the lower cards slightly convex at the sides. In this disposition, the dupe who cuts, as customary, at the length of the pack, will invariably find that he cuts his antagonist an honor; while the gambler, cutting at the breadth, will, as certainly, cut nothing for his victim which may count in the records of the game.

Any burst of indignation upon this discovery would have affected me less than the silent contempt, or the sarcastic composure, with which it was received.

'Mr Wilson,' said our host, stooping to remove from beneath his feet an exceedingly luxurious cloak of rare furs, 'Mr Wilson, this is your property.' (The weather was cold; and, upon quitting my own room, I had thrown a cloak over my dressing wrapper, putting it off upon reaching the scene of play.) 'I presume it is supererogatory to seek here (eyeing the folds of the garment with a bitter smile) for any farther evidence of your skill. Indeed, we have had enough. You will see the necessity, I hope, of quitting Oxford—at all events, of quitting instantly my chambers.'

Abased, humbled to the dust as I then was, it is probable that I should have resented this galling language by immediate personal violence, had not my whole attention been at the moment arrested by a fact of the most startling character. The cloak which I had worn was of a rare description of fur; how rare, how extravagantly costly, I shall not venture to say. Its fashion, too, was of my own fantastic invention; for I was fastidious to an absurd degree of coxcombry, in matters of this frivolous nature. When, therefore, Mr Preston reached me that which he had picked up upon the floor, and near the folding-doors of the apartment, it was with an astonishment nearly bordering upon terror, that I perceived my own already hanging on my arm, (where I had no doubt unwittingly placed it,) and that the one presented me was but its exact counterpart in every, in even the minutest possible particular. The singular being who had so disastrously exposed me, had been muffled, I remember, in a cloak; and none had been worn at all by any of the members of our party, with the exception of myself. Retaining some presence of mind, I took the one offered me by Preston; placed it, unnoticed, over my own; left the apartment with a resolute scowl of defiance; and, next morning ere dawn of day, commenced a hurried journey from Oxford to the continent, in a perfect agony of horror and of shame.

I fled in vain. My evil destiny pursued me as if in exultation, and proved, indeed, that the exercise of its mysterious dominion had as yet only begun. Scarcely had I set foot in Paris, ere I had fresh evidence of the detestable interest taken by this Wilson in my concerns. Years flew, while I experienced no relief. Villain!—at Rome, with how untimely, yet with how spectral an officiousness, stepped he in between me and my ambition! At Vienna, too—at Berlin—and at Moscow! Where, in truth, had I *not* bitter cause to curse him within my heart? From his inscrutable tyranny did I at length flee, panic-stricken, as from a pestilence; and to the very ends of the earth *I fled in vain.*

And again, and again, in secret communion with my own spirit, would I demand the questions 'Who is he?—whence came he?—and what are his objects?' But no answer was there found. And now I scrutinized, with a minute scrutiny, the forms, and the methods, and the leading traits of his impertinent supervision. But even here there was very little upon which to base a conjecture. It was noticeable, indeed, that, in no one of the multiplied instances in which he had of late crossed my path, had he so crossed it except to frustrate those schemes, or to disturb those actions, which, if fully carried out, might have resulted in bitter mischief. Poor justification this, in truth, for an authority so imperiously assumed! Poor indemnity for natural rights of self-agency so pertinaciously, so insultingly denied!

I had also been forced to notice that my tormentor, for a very long period of time, (while scrupulously and with miraculous dexterity maintaining his whim of an identity of apparel with myself,) had so contrived it, in the execution of his varied interference with my will, that I saw not, at any moment, the features of his face. Be Wilson what he might, *this*, at least, was but the veriest of affectation, or of folly. Could he, for an instant, have supposed that, in my admonisher at Eton—in the destroyer of my honor at Oxford,—in him who thwarted my ambition at Rome, my revenge at Paris, my passionate love at Naples, or what he falsely termed my avarice in Egypt,—that in this, my arch-enemy and evil genius, I could fail to recognise the William Wilson of my school-boy days,—the namesake, the companion, the rival,—the hated and dreaded rival at Dr Bransby's? Impossible!—But let me hasten to the last eventful scene of the drama.

Thus far I had succumbed supinely to this imperious domination. The sentiment of deep awe with which I habitually regarded the elevated character, the majestic wisdom, the apparent omnipresence and omnipotence of Wilson, added to a feeling of even terror, with which certain other traits in his nature and assumptions inspired me, had operated, hitherto, to impress me with an idea of my own utter weakness and helplessness, and to suggest an implicit, although bitterly reluctant submission to his arbitrary will. But, of late days, I had given myself up entirely to wine; and its maddening influence upon my hereditary temper rendered me more and more impatient of control. I began to murmur,—to hesitate,—to resist. And was it only fancy which induced me to believe that, with the increase of my own firmness, that of my tormentor underwent a proportional diminution? Be this as it may, I now began to feel the inspiration of a burning hope, and at length nurtured in my secret thoughts a stern and desperate resolution that I would submit no longer to be enslaved.

It was at Rome, during the Carnival of 18—, that I attended a masquerade in the palazzo of the Neapolitan Duke Di Broglio. I had indulged more freely than usual in the excesses of the winetable; and now the suffocating atmosphere of the crowded rooms irritated me beyond endurance. The difficulty, too, of forcing my way through the mazes of the company contributed not a little to the ruffling of my temper; for I was anxiously seeking (let me not say with what unworthy motive) the young, the gay, the beautiful wife of the aged and doting Di Broglio. With a too unscrupulous confidence she had previously communicated to me the secret of the costume in which she would be habited, and now, having caught a glimpse of her person, I was hurrying to make my way into her presence. At this moment I felt a light hand placed upon my shoulder, and that ever-remembered, low, damnable *whisper* within my ear.

In an absolute frenzy of wrath, I turned at once upon him who had thus interrupted me, and seized him violently by the collar. He was attired, as I had expected, in a costume altogether similar to my own; wearing a Spanish cloak of blue velvet, begirt about the waist with a crimson belt sustaining a rapier. A mask of black silk entirely covered his face.

'Scoundrel!' I said, in a voice husky with rage, while every syllable I uttered seemed as new fuel to my fury; 'scoundrel! impostor! accursed villain! you shall not—you *shall not* dog me unto death! Follow me, or

I stab you where you stand!'—and I broke my way from the ball-room into a small ante-chamber adjoining, dragging him unresistingly with me as I went.

Upon entering, I thrust him furiously from me. He staggered against the wall, while I closed the door with an oath, and commanded him to draw. He hesitated but for an instant; then, with a slight sigh, drew in silence, and put himself upon his defence.

The contest was brief indeed. I was frantic with every species of wild excitement, and felt within my single arm the energy and power of a multitude. In a few seconds I forced him by sheer strength against the wainscoting, and thus, getting him at mercy, plunged my sword, with brute ferocity, repeatedly through and through his bosom.

At that instant some person tried the latch of the door. I hastened to prevent an intrusion, and then immediately returned to my dying antagonist. But what human language can adequately portray *that* astonishment, *that* horror which possessed me at the spectacle then presented to view? The brief moment in which I averted my eyes had been sufficient to produce, apparently, a material change in the arrangements at the upper or farther end of the room. A large mirror,—so at first it seemed to me in my confusion—now stood where none had been perceptible before; and, as I stepped up to it in extremity of terror, mine own image, but with features all pale and dabbled in blood, advanced to meet me with a feeble and tottering gait.

Thus it appeared, I say, but was not. It was my antagonist—it was Wilson, who then stood before me in the agonies of his dissolution. His mask and cloak lay, where he had thrown them, upon the floor. Not a thread in all his raiment—not a line in all the marked and singular lineaments of his face which was not, even in the most absolute identity, *mine own*!

It was Wilson; but he spoke no longer in a whisper, and I could have fancied that I myself was speaking while he said:

'You have conquered, and I yield. Yet, henceforward art thou also dead—dead to the World, to Heaven and to Hope! In me didst thou exist—and, in my death, see by this image, which is thine own, how utterly thou hast murdered thyself.'

THE MAN OF THE CROWD

Ce grand malheur, de ne pouvoir être seul.
La Bruyère*

It was well said of a certain German book that *'er lässt sich nicht lesen'*—it does not permit itself to be read. There are some secrets which do not permit themselves to be told. Men die nightly in their beds, wringing the hands of ghostly confessors, and looking them piteously in the eyes—die with despair of heart and convulsion of throat, on account of the hideousness of mysteries which will not *suffer themselves* to be revealed. Now and then, alas, the conscience of man takes up a burthen so heavy in horror that it can be thrown down only into the grave. And thus the essence of all crime is undivulged.

Not long ago, about the closing in of an evening in autumn, I sat at the large bow window of the D— Coffee-House in London. For some months I had been ill in health, but was now convalescent, and, with returning strength, found myself in one of those happy moods which are so precisely the converse of *ennui*—moods of the keenest appetency, when the film from the mental vision departs—the *αχλυζ οζ πριν επηεν**—and the intellect, electrified, surpasses as greatly its every-day condition, as does the vivid yet candid reason of Leibnitz, the mad and flimsy rhetoric of Gorgias.* Merely to breathe was enjoyment; and I derived positive pleasure even from many of the legitimate sources of pain. I felt a calm but inquisitive interest in every thing. With a cigar in my mouth and a newspaper in my lap, I had been amusing myself for the greater part of the afternoon, now in poring over advertisements, now in observing the promiscuous company in the room, and now in peering through the smoky panes into the street.

This latter is one of the principal thoroughfares of the city, and had been very much crowded during the whole day. But, as the darkness came on, the throng momently increased; and, by the time the lamps were well lighted, two dense and continuous tides of population were rushing past the door. At this particular period of the evening I had never before been in a similar situation, and the tumultuous sea of human heads filled me, therefore, with a delicious novelty of emotion.

I gave up, at length, all care of things within the hotel, and became absorbed in contemplation of the scene without.

At first my observations took an abstract and generalizing turn. I looked at the passengers in masses, and thought of them in their aggregate relations. Soon, however, I descended to details, and regarded with minute interest the innumerable varieties of figure, dress, air, gait, visage, and expression of countenance.

By far the greater number of those who went by had a satisfied business-like demeanor, and seemed to be thinking only of making their way through the press. Their brows were knit, and their eyes rolled quickly; when pushed against by fellow-wayfarers they evinced no symptom of impatience, but adjusted their clothes and hurried on. Others, still a numerous class, were restless in their movements, had flushed faces, and talked and gesticulated to themselves, as if feeling in solitude on account of the very denseness of the company around. When impeded in their progress, these people suddenly ceased muttering, but redoubled their gesticulations, and awaited, with an absent and overdone smile upon the lips, the course of the persons impeding them. If jostled, they bowed profusely to the jostlers, and appeared overwhelmed with confusion.—There was nothing very distinctive about these two large classes beyond what I have noted. Their habiliments belonged to that order which is pointedly termed the decent. They were undoubtedly noblemen, merchants, attorneys, tradesmen, stock-jobbers—the Eupatrids* and the common-places of society—men of leisure and men actively engaged in affairs of their own—conducting business upon their own responsibility. They did not greatly excite my attention.

The tribe of clerks was an obvious one and here I discerned two remarkable divisions. There were the junior clerks of flash houses—young gentlemen with tight coats, bright boots, well-oiled hair, and supercilious lips. Setting aside a certain dapperness of carriage, which may be termed *deskism* for want of a better word, the manner of these persons seemed to me an exact facsimile of what had been the perfection of *bon ton* about twelve or eighteen months before. They wore the cast-off graces of the gentry;—and this, I believe, involves the best definition of the class.

The division of the upper clerks of staunch firms, or of the 'steady old fellows,' it was not possible to mistake. These were known by their coats and pantaloons of black or brown, made to sit comfortably, with white cravats and waistcoats, broad solid-looking shoes, and thick hose or gaiters.—They had all slightly bald heads, from which the right ears, long used to pen-holding, had an odd habit of standing off on end. I observed that they always removed or settled their hats with both hands, and wore watches, with short gold chains of a substantial and ancient pattern. Theirs was the affectation of respectability;—if indeed there be an affectation so honorable.

There were many individuals of dashing appearance, whom I easily understood as belonging to the race of swell pick-pockets, with which all great cities are infested. I watched these gentry with much inquisitiveness, and found it difficult to imagine how they should ever be mistaken for gentlemen by gentlemen themselves. Their voluminousness of wristband, with an air of excessive frankness, should betray them at once.

The gamblers, of whom I descried not a few, were still more easily recognisable. They wore every variety of dress, from that of the desperate thimble-rig bully, with velvet waistcoat, fancy neckerchief, gilt chains, and filagreed buttons, to that of the scrupulously inornate clergyman, than which nothing could be less liable to suspicion. Still all were distinguished by a certain sodden swarthiness of complexion, a filmy dimness of eye, and pallor and compression of lip. There were two other traits, moreover, by which I could always detect them;—a guarded lowness of tone in conversation, and a more than ordinary extension of the thumb in a direction at right angles with the fingers.—Very often, in company with these sharpers, I observed an order of men somewhat different in habits, but still birds of a kindred feather. They may be defined as the gentlemen who live by their wits. They seem to prey upon the public in two battalions—that of the dandies and that of the military men. Of the first grade the leading features are long locks and smiles; of the second frogged coats and frowns.

Descending in the scale of what is termed gentility, I found darker and deeper themes for speculation. I saw Jew pedlars, with hawk eyes flashing from countenances whose every other feature wore only an expression of abject humility; sturdy professional street beggars scowling upon mendicants of a better stamp, whom despair alone had driven forth into the night for charity; feeble and ghastly invalids, upon whom death had placed a sure hand, and who sidled and tottered through the mob, looking every one beseechingly in the face, as if in search of some chance consolation, some lost hope; modest young girls returning from long and late labor to a cheerless home, and shrinking more tearfully than indignantly from the glances of ruffians, whose direct contact, even, could not be avoided; women of the town of all kinds and of all ages—the unequivocal beauty in the prime of her womanhood, putting one in mind of the statue in Lucian, with the surface of Parian marble, and the interior filled with filth—the loathsome and utterly lost leper in rags—the wrinkled, bejewelled and paint-begrimed beldame, making a last effort at youth—the mere child of immature form, yet, from long association, an adept in the dreadful coquetries of her trade, and burning with a rabid ambition to be ranked the equal of her elders in vice; drunkards innumerable and indescribable—some in shreds and patches, reeling, inarticulate, with bruised visage and lack-lustre eyes—some in whole although filthy garments, with a slightly unsteady swagger, thick sensual lips, and hearty-looking rubicund faces—others clothed in materials which had once been good, and which even now were scrupulously well brushed—men who walked with a more than naturally firm and springy step, but whose countenances were fearfully pale, whose eyes hideously wild and red, and who clutched with quivering fingers, as they strode through the crowd, at every object which came within their reach; beside these, pie-men, porters, coal-heavers, sweeps; organ-grinders, monkey-exhibiters and ballad mongers, those who vended with those who sang; ragged artizans and exhausted laborers of every description, and all full of a noisy and inordinate vivacity which jarred discordantly upon the ear, and gave an aching sensation to the eye.

As the night deepened, so deepened to me the interest of the scene; for not only did the general character of the crowd materially alter (its gentler features retiring in the gradual withdrawal of the more orderly portion of the people, and its harsher ones coming out into bolder relief, as the late hour brought forth every species of infamy from its den,) but the rays of the gas-lamps, feeble at first in their struggle with the dying day, had now at length gained ascendancy, and threw over every thing a fitful and garish lustre. All was dark yet splendid—as that ebony to which has been likened the style of Tertullian.

The wild effects of the light enchained me to an examination of individual faces; and although the rapidity with which the world of light flitted before the window, prevented me from casting more than a glance upon each visage, still it seemed that, in my then peculiar mental state, I could frequently read, even in that brief interval of a glance, the history of long years.

With my brow to the glass, I was thus occupied in scrutinizing the mob, when suddenly there came into view a countenance (that of a decrepid old man, some sixty-five or seventy years of age,)—a countenance which at once arrested and absorbed my whole attention, on account of the absolute idiosyncracy of its expression. Any thing even remotely resembling that expression I had never seen before. I well remember that my first thought, upon beholding it, was that Retzsch,* had he viewed it, would have greatly preferred it to his own pictural incarnations of the fiend. As I endeavored, during the brief minute of my original survey, to form some analysis of the meaning conveyed, there arose confusedly and paradoxically within my mind, the ideas of vast mental power, of caution, of penuriousness, of avarice, of coolness, of malice, of blood-thirstiness, of triumph, of merriment, of excessive terror, of intense—of supreme despair. I felt singularly aroused, startled, fascinated. 'How wild a history,' I said to myself, 'is written within that bosom!' Then came a craving desire to keep the man in view—to know more of him. Hurriedly putting on an overcoat, and seizing my hat and cane, I made my way into the street, and pushed through the crowd in the direction which I had seen him take; for he had already disappeared. With some little difficulty I at length came within sight of him, approached, and followed him closely, yet cautiously, so as not to attract his attention.

I had now a good opportunity of examining his person. He was short in stature, very thin, and apparently very feeble. His clothes, generally, were filthy and ragged; but as he came, now and then, within the strong glare of a lamp, I perceived that his linen, although dirty, was of beautiful texture; and my vision deceived me, or, through a rent in a closely-buttoned and evidently second-handed *roquelaire* which enveloped him, I caught a glimpse both of a diamond and of a dagger. These observations heightened my curiosity, and I resolved to follow the stranger whithersoever he should go.

It was now fully night-fall, and a thick humid fog hung over the city, soon ending in a settled and heavy rain. This change of weather had an odd effect upon the crowd, the whole of which was at once put into new commotion, and overshadowed by a world of umbrellas. The waver, the jostle, and the hum increased in a tenfold degree. For my own part I did not much regard the rain—the lurking of an old fever in my system rendering the moisture somewhat too dangerously pleasant. Tying a handkerchief about my mouth, I kept on. For half an hour the old man held his way with difficulty along the great thoroughfare;

and I here walked close at his elbow through fear of losing sight of him. Never once turning his head to look back, he did not observe me. By and bye he passed into a cross street, which, although densely filled with people, was not quite so much thronged as the main one he had quitted. Here a change in his demeanor became evident. He walked more slowly and with less object than before—more hesitatingly. He crossed and re-crossed the way repeatedly without apparent aim; and the press was still so thick that, at every such movement, I was obliged to follow him closely. The street was a narrow and long one, and his course lay within it for nearly an hour, during which the passengers had gradually diminished to about that number which is ordinarily seen at noon in Broadway near the Park—so vast a difference is there between a London populace and that of the most frequented American city. A second turn brought us into a square, brilliantly lighted, and overflowing with life. The old manner of the stranger re-appeared. His chin fell upon his breast, while his eyes rolled widly from under his knit brows, in every direction, upon those who hemmed him in. He urged his way steadily and perseveringly. I was surprised, however, to find, upon his having made the circuit of the square, that he turned and retraced his steps. Still more was I astonished to see him repeat the same walk several times—once nearly detecting me as he came round with a sudden movement.

In this exercise he spent another hour, at the end of which we met with far less interruption from passengers than at first. The rain fell fast; the air grew cool; and the people were retiring to their homes. With a gesture of impatience, the wanderer passed into a bye-street comparatively deserted. Down this, some quarter of a mile long, he rushed with an activity I could not have dreamed of seeing in one so aged, and which put me to much trouble in pursuit. A few minutes brought us to a large and busy bazaar, with the localities of which the stranger appeared well acquainted, and where his original demeanor again became apparent, as he forced his way to and fro, without aim, among the host of buyers and sellers.

During the hour and a half, or thereabouts, which we passed in this place, it required much caution on my part to keep him within reach without attracting his observation. Luckily I wore a pair of caoutchouc over-shoes, and could move about in perfect silence. At no moment did he see that I watched him. He entered shop after shop, priced nothing, spoke no word, and looked at all objects with a wild and vacant stare. I was now utterly amazed at his behaviour, and firmly resolved that we should not part until I had satisfied myself in some measure respecting him.

A loud-toned clock struck eleven, and the company were fast deserting the bazaar. A shop-keeper, in putting up a shutter, jostled the old man, and at the instant I saw a strong shudder come over his frame. He hurried into the street, looked anxiously around him for an instant, and then ran with incredible swiftness through many crooked and people-less lanes, until we emerged once more upon the great thoroughfare whence we had started—the street of the D— Hotel. It no longer wore, however, the same aspect. It was still brilliant with gas; but the rain fell fiercely, and there were few persons to be seen. The stranger grew pale. He walked moodily some paces up the once populous avenue, then, with a heavy sigh, turned in the direction of the river, and, plunging through a great variety of devious ways, came out, at length, in view of one of the principal theatres. It was about being closed, and the audience were thronging from the doors. I saw the old man gasp as if for breath while he threw himself amid the crowd; but I thought that the intense agony of his countenance had, in some measure, abated. His head again fell upon his breast; he appeared as I had seen him at first. I observed that he now took the course in which had gone the greater number of the audience—but, upon the whole, I was at a loss to comprehend the waywardness of his actions.

As he proceeded, the company grew more scattered, and his old uneasiness and vacillation were resumed. For some time he followed closely a party of some ten or twelve roisterers; but from this number one by one dropped off, until three only remained together, in a narrow and gloomy lane little frequented. The stranger paused, and, for a moment, seemed lost in thought; then, with every mark of agitation, pursued rapidly a route which brought us to the verge of the city, amid regions very different from those we had hitherto traversed. It was the most noisome quarter of London, where every thing wore the worst impress of the most deplorable poverty, and of the most desperate crime. By the dim light of an accidental lamp, tall, antique, worm-eaten, wooden tenements were seen tottering to their fall, in directions so many and capricious that scarce the semblance of a passage was discernible between them. The paving-stones lay at random, displaced from their beds by the rankly-growing grass. Horrible filth festered in the dammed-up gutters. The whole atmosphere teemed with desolation. Yet, as we proceeded, the sounds of human life revived by sure degrees, and at length large bands of the most abandoned of a London populace were seen reeling to and fro. The spirits of the old man again flickered up, as a lamp which is near its death-hour. Once more he strode onward with elastic tread. Suddenly a corner was turned, a blaze of light burst upon our sight, and we stood before one of the huge suburban temples of Intemperance—one of the palaces of the fiend, Gin.

It was now nearly day-break; but a number of wretched inebriates still pressed in and out of the flaunting entrance. With a half shriek of joy the old man forced a passage within, resumed at once his original bearing, and stalked backward and forward, without apparent object, among the throng. He had not been thus long occupied, however, before a rush to the doors gave token that the host was closing them for the night. It was something even more intense than despair that I then observed upon the countenance of the singular being whom I had watched so pertinaciously. Yet he did not hesitate in his career, but, with a mad energy, retraced his steps at once, to the heart of the mighty London. Long and swiftly he fled, while I followed him in the wildest amazement, resolute not to abandon a scrutiny in which I now felt an interest all-absorbing. The sun arose while we proceeded, and, when we had once again reached that most thronged mart of the populous town, the street of the D— Hotel, it presented an appearance of human bustle and activity scarcely inferior to what I had seen on the evening before. And here, long, amid the momently increasing confusion, did I persist in my pursuit of the stranger. But, as usual, he walked to and fro, and during the day did not pass from out the turmoil of that street. And, as the shades of the second evening came on, I grew wearied unto death, and, stopping fully in front of the wanderer, gazed at him steadfastly in the face. He noticed me not, but resumed his solemn walk, while I, ceasing to follow, remained absorbed in contemplation. 'This old man,' I said at length, 'is the type and the genius of deep crime. He refuses to be alone. *He is the man of the crowd*. It will be in vain to follow; for I shall learn no more of him, nor of his deeds. The worst heart of the world is a grosser book than the "Hortulus Animæ,"[1] and perhaps it is but one of the great mercies of God that "*er lässt sich nicht lesen.*" '

[1] The '*Hortulus Animæ cum Oratiunculis Aliquibus Superadditis*' of Grüninger.*

THE MURDERS IN THE RUE MORGUE

> What song the Syrens sang, or what name Achilles assumed when he hid himself among women, although puzzling questions, are not beyond *all* conjecture.
>
> Sir Thomas Browne*

THE mental features discoursed of as the analytical are, in themselves, but little susceptible of analysis. We appreciate them only in their effects. We know of them, among other things, that they are always to their possessor, when inordinately possessed, a source of the liveliest enjoyment. As the strong man exults in his physical ability, delighting in such exercises as call his muscles into action, so glories the analyst in that moral activity which *disentangles*. He derives pleasure from even the most trivial occupations bringing his talent into play. He is fond of enigmas, of conundrums, of hieroglyphics; exhibiting in his solutions of each a degree of *acumen* which appears to the ordinary apprehension præternatural. His results, brought about by the very soul and essence of method, have, in truth, the whole air of intuition.

The faculty of re-solution is possibly much invigorated by mathematical study, and especially by that highest branch of it which, unjustly, and merely on account of its retrograde operations, has been called, as if *par excellence*, analysis. Yet to calculate is not in itself to analyse. A chess-player, for example, does the one without effort at the other. It follows that the game of chess, in its effects upon mental character, is greatly misunderstood. I am not now writing a treatise, but simply prefacing a somewhat peculiar narrative by observations very much at random; I will, therefore, take occasion to assert that the higher powers of the reflective intellect are more decidedly and more usefully tasked by the unostentatious game of draughts than by all the elaborate frivolity of chess. In this latter, where the pieces have different and *bizarre* motions, with various and variable values, what is only complex is mistaken (a not unusual error) for what is profound. The *attention* is here called powerfully into play. If it flag for an instant, an oversight is committed, resulting in injury or defeat. The possible moves being not only manifold but involute, the chances of such oversights are multiplied; and in nine cases out of ten it is the more concentrative rather than the more acute player who conquers. In draughts, on the contrary, where the moves are *unique* and have but little variation, the probabilities of inadvertence are diminished, and the mere attention being left comparatively unemployed, what advantages are obtained by either party are obtained by superior *acumen*. To be less abstract—Let us suppose a game of draughts where the pieces are reduced to four kings, and where, of course, no oversight is to be expected. It is obvious that here the victory can be decided (the players being at all equal) only by some *recherché* movement, the result of some strong exertion of the intellect. Deprived of ordinary resources, the analyst throws himself into the spirit of his opponent, identifies himself therewith, and not unfrequently sees thus, at a glance, the sole methods (sometimes indeed absurdly simple ones) by which he may seduce into error or hurry into miscalculation.

Whist has long been noted for its influence upon what is termed the calculating power; and men of the highest order of intellect have been known to take an apparently unaccountable delight in it, while eschewing chess as frivolous. Beyond doubt there is nothing of a similar nature so greatly tasking the faculty of analysis. The best chess-player in Christendom *may* be little more than the best player of chess; but proficiency in whist implies capacity for success in all those more important undertakings where mind struggles with mind. When I say proficiency, I mean that perfection in the game which includes a comprehension of *all* the sources whence legitimate advantage may be derived. These are not only manifold but multiform, and lie frequently among recesses of thought altogether inaccessible to the ordinary understanding. To observe attentively is to remember distinctly; and, so far, the concentrative chess-player will do very well at whist; while the rules of Hoyle* (themselves based upon the mere mechanism of the game) are sufficiently and generally comprehensible. Thus to have a retentive memory, and to proceed by 'the book,' are points commonly regarded as the sum total of good playing. But it is in matters beyond the limits of mere rule that the skill of the analyst is evinced. He makes, in silence, a host of observations and inferences. So, perhaps, do his companions; and the difference in the extent of the information obtained lies not so much in the validity of the inference as in the quality of the observation. The necessary knowledge is that of *what* to observe. Our player confines himself not at all; nor, because the game is the object, does he reject deductions from things external to the game. He examines the countenance of his partner, comparing it carefully with that of each of his opponents. He considers the mode of assorting the cards in each hand; often counting trump by trump, and honor by honor, through the glances bestowed by their holders upon each. He notes every variation of face as the play progresses, gathering a fund of thought from the differences in the expression of certainty, of surprise, of triumph, or of chagrin. From the manner of gathering up a trick he judges whether the person taking it can make another in the suit. He recognises what is played through feint, by the air with which it is thrown upon the table. A casual or inadvertent word; the accidental dropping or turning of a card, with the accompanying anxiety or carelessness in regard to its concealment; the counting of the tricks, with the order of their arrangement; embarrassment, hesitation, eagerness or trepidation—all afford, to his apparently intuitive perception, indications of the true state of affairs. The first two or three rounds having been played, he is in full possession of the contents of each hand, and thenceforward puts down his cards with as absolute a precision of purpose as if the rest of the party had turned outward the faces of their own.

The analytical power should not be confounded with simple ingenuity; for while the analyst is necessarily ingenious, the ingenious man is often remarkably incapable of analysis. The constructive or combining power, by which ingenuity is usually manifested, and to which the phrenologists (I believe erroneously) have assigned a separate organ, supposing it a primitive faculty, had been so frequently seen in those whose intellect bordered otherwise upon idiocy, as to have attracted general observation among writers on morals. Between ingenuity and the analytic ability there exists a difference far greater, indeed, than that between the fancy and the imagination, but of a character very strictly analogous. It will be found, in fact, that the ingenious are always fanciful, and the *truly* imaginative never otherwise than analytic.

The narrative which follows will appear to the reader somewhat in the light of a commentary upon the propositions just advanced.

Residing in Paris during the spring and part of the summer of 18—, I there became acquainted with a Monsieur C. Auguste Dupin. This young gentleman was of an excellent—indeed of an illustrious family, but, by a variety of untoward events, had been reduced to such poverty that the energy of his character succumbed beneath it, and he ceased to bestir himself in the world, or to care for the retrieval of his fortunes. By courtesy of his creditors, there still remained in his possession a small remnant of his patrimony; and, upon the income arising from this, he managed, by means of a rigorous economy, to procure the necessaries of life, without troubling himself about its superfluities. Books, indeed, were his sole luxuries, and in Paris these are easily obtained.

Our first meeting was at an obscure library in the Rue Montmartre, where the accident of our both being in search of the same very rare and very remarkable volume brought us into closer communion. We saw each other again and again. I was deeply interested in the little family history which he detailed to me with all that candor which a Frenchman indulges whenever mere self is his theme. I was astonished, too, at the vast extent of his reading; and, above all, I felt my soul enkindled within me by the wild fervor, and the vivid freshness of his imagination. Seeking in Paris the objects I then sought, I felt that the society of such a man would be to me a treasure beyond price; and this feeling I frankly confided to him. It was at length arranged that we should live together during my stay in the city; and as my worldly circumstances were somewhat less embarrassed than his own, I was permitted to be at the expense of renting, and furnishing in a style which suited the rather fantastic gloom of our common temper, a time-eaten and grotesque mansion, long deserted through superstitions into which we did not inquire, and tottering to its fall in a retired and desolate portion of the Faubourg St Germain.

Had the routine of our life at this place been known to the world, we should have been regarded as madmen—although, perhaps, as madmen of a harmless nature. Our seclusion was perfect. We admitted no visitors. Indeed the locality of our retirement had been carefully kept a secret from my own former associates; and it had been many years since Dupin had ceased to know or be known in Paris. We existed within ourselves alone.

It was a freak of fancy in my friend (for what else shall I call it?) to be enamored of the Night for her own sake; and into this *bizarrerie*, as into all his others, I quietly fell; giving myself up to his wild whims with a perfect *abandon*. The sable divinity would not herself dwell with us always; but we could counterfeit her presence. At the first dawn of the morning we closed all the massy shutters of our old building, lighting a couple of tapers which, strongly perfumed, threw out only the ghastliest and feeblest of rays. By the aid of these we then busied our souls in dreams—reading, writing, or conversing, until warned by the clock of the advent of the true Darkness. Then we sallied forth into the streets, arm in arm, continuing the topics of the day, or roaming far and wide until a late hour, seeking, amid the wild lights and shadows of the populous city, that infinity of mental excitement which quiet observation can afford.

At such times I could not help remarking and admiring (although from his rich ideality I had been prepared to expect it) a peculiar analytic ability in Dupin. He seemed, too, to take an eager delight in its exercise—if not exactly in its display—and did not hesitate to confess the pleasure thus derived. He boasted to me, with a low chuckling laugh, that most men, in respect to himself, wore windows in their bosoms, and was wont to follow up such assertions by direct and very startling proofs of his intimate knowledge of my own. His manner at these moments was frigid and abstract; his eyes were vacant in expression; while his voice, usually a rich tenor, rose into a treble which would have sounded petulantly but for the deliberateness and entire distinctness of the enunciation. Observing him in these moods, I often dwelt meditatively upon the old philosophy of the Bi-Part Soul,* and amused myself with the fancy of a double Dupin—the creative and the resolvent.

Let it not be supposed, from what I have just said, that I am detailing any mystery, or penning any romance. What I have described in the Frenchman was merely the result of an excited, or perhaps of a diseased intelligence. But of the character of his remarks at the periods in question an example will best convey the idea.

We were strolling one night down a long dirty street, in the vicinity of the Palais Royal. Being both, apparently, occupied with thought, neither of us had spoken a syllable for fifteen minutes at least. All at once Dupin broke forth with these words:

'He is a very little fellow, that's true, and would do better for the *Théâtre des Variétés.*'

'There can be no doubt of that,' I replied unwittingly, and not at first observing (so much had I been absorbed in reflection) the extraordinary manner in which the speaker had chimed in with my meditations. In an instant afterward I recollected myself, and my astonishment was profound.

'Dupin,' said I, gravely, 'this is beyond my comprehension. I do not hesitate to say that I am amazed, and can scarcely credit my senses. How was it possible you should know I was thinking of—?' Here I paused, to ascertain beyond a doubt whether he really knew of whom I thought.

—'of Chantilly,' said he, 'why do you pause? You were remarking to yourself that his diminutive figure unfitted him for tragedy.'

This was precisely what had formed the subject of my reflections. Chantilly was a *quondam* cobbler of the Rue St Denis, who, becoming stage-mad, had attempted the *rôle* of Xerxes, in Crébillon's tragedy so called, and been notoriously Pasquinaded for his pains.

'Tell me, for Heaven's sake,' I explained, 'the method—if method there is—by which you have been enabled to fathom my soul in this matter.' In fact I was even more startled than I would have been willing to express.

'It was the fruiterer,' replied my friend, 'who brought you to the conclusion that the mender of soles was not of sufficient height for Xerxes *et id genus omne*.'*

'The fruiterer!—you astonish me—I know no fruiterer whomsoever.'

'The man who ran up against you as we entered the street—it may have been fifteen minutes ago.'

I now remembered that, in fact, a fruiterer, carrying upon his head a large basket of apples, had nearly thrown me down, by accident, as we passed from the Rue C— into the thoroughfare where we stood; but what this had to do with Chantilly I could not possibly understand.

There was not a particle of *charlatanerie* about Dupin. 'I will explain,' he said, 'and that you may comprehend all clearly, we will first retrace the course of your meditations, from the moment in which I spoke to you until that of the *rencontre* with the fruiterer in question. The larger links of the chain run thus—Chantilly, Orion, Dr Nichol, Epicurus, Stereotomy, the street stones, the fruiterer.'

There are few persons who have not, at some period of their lives, amused themselves in retracing the steps by which particular conclusions of their own minds have been attained. The occupation is often full of interest; and he who attempts it for the first time is astonished by the apparently illimitable distance and incoherence between the starting-point and the goal. What, then, must have been my amazement when I heard the Frenchman speak what he had just spoken, and when I could not help acknowledging that he had spoken the truth. He continued:

'We had been talking of horses, if I remember aright, just before leaving the Rue C—. This was the last subject we discussed. As we crossed into this street, a fruiterer, with a large basket upon his head, brushing quickly past us, thrust you upon a pile of paving-stones collected at a spot where the causeway is undergoing repair. You stepped upon one of the loose fragments, slipped, slightly strained your ankle, appeared vexed or sulky, muttered a few words, turned to look at the pile, and then proceeded in silence. I was not particularly attentive to what you did; but observation has become with me, of late, a species of necessity.

'You kept your eyes upon the ground—glancing, with a petulant expression, at the holes and ruts in the pavement, (so that I saw you were still thinking of the stones,) until we reached the little alley called Lamartine, which has been paved, by way of experiment, with the overlapping and riveted blocks. Here your countenance brightened up, and, perceiving your lips move, I could not doubt that you murmured the word "stereotomy," a term very affectedly applied to this species of pavement. I knew that you could not say to yourself "stereotomy" without being brought to think of atomies, and thus of the theories of Epicurus; and since, when we discussed this subject not very long ago, I mentioned to you how singularly, yet with how little notice, the vague guesses of that noble Greek had met with confirmation in the late nebular cosmogony,* I felt that you could not avoid casting your eyes upward to the great *nebula* in Orion, and I certainly expected that you would do so. You did look up; and I was now assured that I had correctly followed your steps. But in that bitter *tirade* upon Chantilly, which appeared in yesterday's "*Musée*," the satirist, making some disgraceful allusions to the cobbler's change of name upon assuming the buskin, quoted a Latin line about which we have often conversed. I mean the line

Perdidit antiquum litera prima sonum.*

I had told you that this was in reference to Orion, formerly written Urion; and, from certain pungencies connected with this explanation, I was aware that you could not have forgotten it. It was clear, therefore, that you would not fail to combine the two ideas of Orion and Chantilly. That you did combine them I saw by the character of the smile which passed over your lips. You thought of the poor cobbler's immolation. So far, you had been stooping in your gait; but now I saw you draw yourself up to your full height. I was then sure that you reflected upon the diminutive figure of Chantilly. At this point I interrupted your meditations to remark that as, in fact, he *was* a very little fellow—that Chantilly—he would do better at the *Théâtres des Variétés*.'

Not long after this, we were looking over an evening edition of the 'Gazette des Tribunaux,' when the following paragraphs arrested our attention.

'EXTRAORDINARY MURDERS.—This morning, about three o'clock, the inhabitants of the Quartier St Roch were aroused from sleep by a succession of terrific shrieks, issuing, apparently, from the fourth story of a house in the Rue Morgue, known to be in the sole occupancy of one Madame L'Espanaye, and her daughter, Mademoiselle Camille L'Espanaye. After some delay, occasioned by a fruitless attempt to procure admission in the usual manner, the gateway was broken in with a crowbar, and eight or ten of the neighbors entered, accompanied by two *gendarmes*. By this time the cries had ceased; but, as the party rushed up the first flight of stairs, two or more rough voices, in angry contention, were distinguished, and seemed to proceed from the upper part of the house. As the second landing was reached, these sounds, also, had ceased, and everything remained perfectly quiet. The party spread themselves, and hurried from room to room. Upon arriving at a large back chamber in the fourth story, (the door of which, being found locked, with the key inside, was forced open,) a spectacle presented itself which struck every one present not less with horror than with astonishment.

'The apartment was in the wildest disorder—the furniture broken and thrown about in all directions. There was only one bedstead; and from this the bed had been removed, and thrown into the middle of the floor. On a chair lay a razor, besmeared with blood. On the hearth were two or three long and thick tresses of grey human hair, also dabbled in blood, and seeming to have been pulled out by the roots. On the floor were found four Napoleons, an ear-ring of topaz, three large silver spoons, three smaller of *métal d'Alger*,* and two bags, containing nearly four thousand francs in gold. The drawers of a *bureau*, which stood in one corner, were open, and had been, apparently, rifled, although many articles still remained in them. A small iron safe was discovered under the *bed* (not under the bedstead). It was open, with the key still in the door. It had no contents beyond a few old letters, and other papers of little consequence.

'Of Madame L'Espanaye no traces were here seen; but an unusual quantity of soot being observed in the fire-place, a search was made in the chimney, and (horrible to relate!) the corpse of the daughter, head downward, was dragged therefrom; it having been thus forced up the narrow aperture for a considerable distance. The body was quite warm. Upon examining it, many excoriations were perceived, no doubt occasioned by the violence with which it had been thrust up and disengaged. Upon the face were many severe scratches, and, upon the throat, dark bruises, and deep indentations of finger nails, as if the deceased had been throttled to death.

'After a thorough investigation of every portion of the house, without farther discovery, the party made its way into a small paved yard in the rear of the building, where lay the corpse of the old lady, with her throat so entirely cut that, upon an attempt to raise her, the head fell off.* The body, as well as the head, was fearfully mutilated—the former so much so as scarcely to retain any semblance of humanity.

'To this horrible mystery there is not as yet, we believe, the slightest clew.'

The next day's paper had these additional particulars.

'*The Tragedy in the Rue Morgue*. Many individuals have been examined in relation to this most extraordinary and frightful affair.' [The word "*affaire*" has not yet, in France, that levity of import which it conveys with us,] 'but nothing whatever has transpired to throw light upon it. We give below all the material testimony elicited.

'*Pauline Dubourg*, laundress, deposes that she has known both the deceased for three years, having washed for them during that period. The old lady and her daughter seemed on good terms—very affectionate towards each other. They were excellent pay. Could not speak in regard to their mode or means of living. Believed that Madame L. told fortunes for a living. Was reputed to have money put by. Never met any persons in the house when she called for the clothes or took them home. Was sure that they had no servant in employ. There appeared to be no furniture in any part of the building except in the fourth story.

'*Pierre Moreau*, tobacconist, deposes that he has been in the habit of selling small quantities of tobacco and snuff to Madame L'Espanaye for nearly four years. Was born in the neighborhood, and has always resided there. The deceased and her daughter had occupied the house in which the corpses were found, for more than six years. It was formerly occupied by a jeweller, who under-let the upper rooms to various persons. The house was the property of Madame L. She became dissatisfied with the abuse of the premises by her tenant, and moved into them herself, refusing to let any portion. The old lady was childish. Witness had seen the daughter some five or six times during the six years. The two lived an exceedingly retired life—were reputed to have money. Had heard it said among the neighbors that Madame L. told fortunes—did not believe it. Had never seen any person enter the door except the old lady and her daughter, a porter once or twice, and a physician some eight or ten times.

'Many other persons, neighbors, gave evidence to the same effect. No one was spoken of as frequenting the house. It was not known whether there were any living connexions of Madame L. and her daughter. The shutters of the front windows were seldom opened. Those in the rear were always closed, with the exception of the large back room, fourth story. The house was a good house—not very old.

'*Isidore Musèt, gendarme*, deposes that he was called to the house about three o'clock in the morning, and found some twenty or thirty persons at the gateway, endeavoring to gain admittance. Forced it open, at length, with a bayonet—not with a crowbar. Had but little difficulty in getting it open, on account of its being a double or folding gate, and bolted neither at bottom nor top. The shrieks were continued until the gate was forced—and then suddenly ceased. They seemed to be screams of some person (or persons) in great agony—were loud and drawn out, not short and quick. Witness led the way up stairs. Upon reaching the first landing, heard two voices in loud and angry contention—the one a gruff voice, the other much shriller—a very strange voice. Could distinguish some words of the former, which was that of a Frenchman. Was positive that it was not a woman's voice. Could distinguish the words "*sacré*" and "*diable*." The shrill voice was that of a foreigner. Could not be sure whether it was the voice of a man or of a woman. Could not make out what was said, but believed the language to be Spanish. The state of the room and of the bodies was described by this witness as we described them yesterday.

'*Henri Duval*, a neighbor, and by trade a silver-smith, deposes that he was one of the party who first entered the house. Corroborates the testimony of Musèt in general. As soon as they forced an entrance, they reclosed the door, to keep out the crowd, which collected very fast, notwithstanding the lateness of the hour. The shrill voice, this witness thinks, was that of an Italian. Was certain it was not French. Could not be sure that it was a man's voice. It might have been a woman's. Was not acquainted with the Italian language. Could not distinguish the words, but was convinced by the intonation that the speaker was an Italian. Knew Madame L. and her daughter. Had conversed with both frequently. Was sure that the shrill voice was not that of either of the deceased.

'— *Odenheimer, restaurateur.* This witness volunteered his testimony. Not speaking French, was examined through an interpreter. Is a native of Amsterdam. Was passing the house at the time of the shrieks. They lasted for several minutes—probably ten. They were long and loud—very awful and distressing. Was one of those who entered the building. Corroborated the previous evidence in every respect but one. Was sure that the shrill voice was that of a man—of a Frenchman. Could not distinguish the words uttered. They were loud and quick—unequal—spoken apparently in fear as well as in anger. The voice was harsh—not so much shrill as harsh. Could not call it a shrill voice. The gruff voice said repeatedly "*sacré*," "*diable*," and once "*mon Dieu*."

'*Jules Mignaud*, banker, of the firm of Mignaud et Fils, Rue Deloraine. Is the elder Mignaud. Madame L'Espanaye had some property. Had opened an account with his banking house in the spring of the year — (eight years previously). Made frequent deposits in small sums. Had checked for nothing until the third day before her death, when she took out in person the sum of 4000 francs. This sum was paid in gold, and a clerk sent home with the money.

'*Adolphe Le Bon*, clerk to Mignaud et Fils, deposes that on the day in question, about noon, he accompanied Madame L'Espanaye to her residence with the 4000 francs, put up in two bags. Upon the door being opened, Mademoiselle L. appeared and took from his hands one of the bags, while the old lady relieved him of the other. He then bowed and departed. Did not see any person in the street at the time. It is a bye-street—very lonely.

'*William Bird*, tailor, deposes that he was one of the party who entered the house. Is an Englishman. Has lived in Paris two years. Was one of the first to ascend the stairs. Heard the voices in contention. The gruff voice was that of a Frenchman. Could make out several words, but cannot now remember all. Heard distinctly "*sacré*" and "*mon Dieu*." There was a sound at the moment as if of several persons struggling—a scraping and scuffling sound. The shrill voice was very loud—louder than the gruff one. Is sure that it was not the voice of an Englishman. Appeared to be that of a German. Might have been a woman's voice. Does not understand German.

'Four of the above-named witnesses, being recalled, deposed that the door of the chamber in which was found the body of Mademoiselle L. was locked on the inside when the party reached it. Every thing was perfectly silent—no groans or noises of any kind. Upon forcing the door no person was seen. The windows, both of the back and front room, were down and firmly fastened from within. A door between the two rooms was closed, but not locked. The door leading from the front room into the passage was locked, with the key on the inside. A small room in the front of the house, on the fourth story, at the head of the passage, was open, the door being ajar. This room was crowded with old beds, boxes, and so forth. These were carefully removed and searched. There was not an inch of any portion of the house which was not carefully searched. Sweeps were sent up and down the chimneys. The house was a four story one, with garrets (*mansardes*). A trap-door on the roof was nailed down very securely—did not appear to have been opened for years. The time elapsing between the hearing of the voices in contention and the breaking open of the room door, was variously stated by the witnesses. Some made it as short as three minutes—some as long as five. The door was opened with difficulty.

'*Alfonzo Garcio*, undertaker, deposes that he resides in the Rue Morgue. Is a native of Spain. Was one of the party who entered the house. Did not proceed up stairs. Is nervous, and was apprehensive of the consequences of agitation. Heard the voices in contention. The gruff voice was that of a Frenchman. Could not distinguish what was said. The shrill voice was that of an Englishman—is sure of this. Does not understand the English language, but judges by the intonation.

'*Alberto Montani*, confectioner, deposes that he was among the first to ascend the stairs. Heard the voices in question. The gruff voice was that of a Frenchman. Distinguished several words. The speaker appeared to be expostulating. Could not make out the words of the shrill voice. Spoke quick and unevenly. Thinks it the voice of a Russian. Corroborates the general testimony. Is an Italian. Never conversed with a native of Russia.

'Several witnesses, recalled, here testified that the chimneys of all the rooms on the fourth story were too narrow to admit the passage of a human being. By "sweeps" were meant cylindrical sweeping-brushes, such as are employed by those who clean chimneys. These brushes were passed up and down every flue in the house. There is no back passage by which any one could have descended while the party proceeded up stairs. The body of Mademoiselle L'Espanaye was so firmly wedged in the chimney that it could not be got down until four or five of the party united their strength.

'*Paul Dumas*, physician, deposes that he was called to view the bodies about day-break. They were both then lying on the sacking of the bedstead in the chamber where Mademoiselle L. was found. The corpse of the young lady was much bruised and excoriated. The fact that it had been thrust up the chimney would sufficiently account for these appearances. The throat was greatly chafed. There were several deep scratches just below the chin, together with a series of livid spots which were evidently the impression of fingers. The face was fearfully discolored, and the eye-balls protruded. The tongue had been partially bitten through. A large bruise was discovered upon the pit of the stomach, produced, apparently, by the pressure of a knee. In the opinion of M. Dumas, Mademoiselle L'Espanaye had been throttled to death by some person or persons unknown. The corpse of the mother was horribly mutilated. All the bones of the right leg and arm were more or less shattered. The left *tibia* much splintered, as well as all the ribs of the left side. Whole body dreadfully bruised and discolored. It was not possible to say how the injuries had been inflicted. A heavy club of wood, or a broad bar of iron—a chair—any large, heavy, and obtuse weapon would have produced such results, if wielded by the hands of a very powerful man. No woman could have inflicted the blows with any weapon. The head of the deceased, when seen by witness, was entirely separated from the body, and was also greatly shattered. The throat had evidently been cut with some very sharp instrument—probably with a razor.

'*Alexandre Etienne*, surgeon, was called with M. Dumas to view the bodies. Corroborated the testimony, and the opinions of M. Dumas.

'Nothing farther of importance was elicited, although several other persons were examined. A murder so mysterious, and so perplexing in all its particulars, was never before committed in Paris—if indeed a murder has been committed at all. The police are entirely at fault—an unusual occurrence in affairs of this nature. There is not, however, the shadow of a clew apparent.'

The evening edition of the paper stated that the greatest excitement still continued in the Quartier St Roch—that the premises in question had been carefully re-searched, and fresh examinations of witnesses instituted, but all to no purpose. A postscript, however, mentioned that Adolphe Le Bon had been arrested and imprisoned—although nothing appeared to criminate him, beyond the facts already detailed.

Dupin seemed singularly interested in the progress of this affair—at least so I judged from his manner, for he made no comments. It was only after the announcement that Le Bon had been imprisoned, that he asked me my opinion respecting the murders.

I could merely agree with all Paris in considering them an insoluble mystery. I saw no means by which it would be possible to trace the murderer.

'We must not judge of the means,' said Dupin, 'by this shell of an examination. The Parisian police, so much extolled for *acumen*, are cunning, but no more. There is no method in their proceedings, beyond the method of the moment. They make a vast parade of measures; but, not unfrequently, these are so ill adapted to the objects proposed, as to put us in mind of Monsieur Jourdain's calling for his *robe-de-chambre—pour mieux entendre la musique*.* The results attained by them are not unfrequently surprising, but, for the most part, are brought about by simple diligence and activity. When these qualities are unavailing, their schemes fail. Vidocq,* for example, was a good guesser, and a persevering man. But, without educated thought, he erred continually by the very intensity of his investigations. He impaired his vision by holding the object too close. He might see, perhaps, one or two points with unusual clearness, but in so doing he, necessarily, lost sight of the matter as a whole. Thus there is such a thing as being too profound. Truth is not always in a well. In fact, as regards the more important knowledge, I do believe that she is invariably superficial. The depth lies in the valleys where we seek her, and not upon the mountain-tops where she is found. The modes and sources of this kind of error are well typified in the contemplation of the heavenly bodies. To look at a star by glances—to view it in a side-long way, by turning toward it the exterior portions of the *retina* (more susceptible of feeble impressions of light than the interior), is to behold the star distinctly—is to have the best appreciation of its lustre—a lustre which grows dim just in proportion as we turn our vision *fully* upon it. A greater number of rays actually fall upon the eye in the latter case, but, in the former, there is the more refined capacity for comprehension. By undue profundity we perplex and enfeeble thought; and it is possible to make even Venus herself vanish from the firmament by a scrutiny too sustained, too concentrated, or too direct.

'As for these murders, let us enter into some examinations for ourselves, before we make up an opinion respecting them. An inquiry will afford us amusement,' [I thought this an odd term, so applied, but said nothing] 'and, besides, Le Bon once rendered me a service for which I am not ungrateful. We will go and see the premises with our own eyes. I know G—, the Prefect of Police, and shall have no difficulty in obtaining the necessary permission.'

The permission was obtained, and we proceeded at once to the Rue Morgue. This is one of those miserable thoroughfares which intervene between the Rue Richelieu and the Rue St Roch. It was late in the afternoon when we reached it; as this quarter is at a great distance from that in which we resided. The house was readily found; for there were still many persons gazing up at the closed shutters, with an objectless curiosity, from the opposite side of the way. It was an ordinary Parisian house, with a gateway, on one side of which was a glazed watch-box, with a sliding panel in the window, indicating a *loge de concierge*. Before going in we walked up the street, turned down an alley, and then, again turning, passed in the rear of the building—Dupin, meanwhile, examining the whole neighborhood, as well as the house, with a minuteness of attention for which I could see no possible object.

Retracing our steps, we came again to the front of the dwelling, rang, and, having shown our credentials, were admitted by the agents in charge. We went up stairs—into the chamber where the body of Mademoiselle L'Espanaye had been found, and where both the deceased still lay. The disorders of the room had, as usual, been suffered to exist. I saw nothing beyond what had been stated in the 'Gazette des Tribunaux.' Dupin scrutinized every thing—not excepting the bodies of the victims. We then went into the other rooms, and into the yard; a *gendarme* accompanying us throughout. The examination occupied us until dark, when we took our departure. On our way home my companion stepped in for a moment at the office of one of the daily papers.

I have said that the whims of my friend were manifold, and that *Je les ménageais*:*—for this phrase there is no English equivalent. It was his humor, now, to decline all conversation on the subject of the murder, until about noon the next day. He then asked me, suddenly, if I had observed any thing *peculiar* at the scene of the atrocity.

There was something in his manner of emphasizing the word 'peculiar,' which caused me to shudder, without knowing why.

'No, nothing *peculiar*,' I said; 'nothing more, at least, than we both saw stated in the paper.'

'The "Gazette," ' he replied, 'has not entered, I fear, into the unusual horror of the thing. But dismiss the idle opinions of this print. It appears to me that this mystery is considered insoluble, for the very reason which should cause it to be regarded as easy of solution—I mean for the *outré* character of its features. The police are confounded by the seeming absence of motive—not for the murder itself—but for the atrocity of the murder. They are puzzled, too, by the seeming impossibility of reconciling the voices heard in contention, with the facts that no one was discovered up stairs but the assassinated Mademoiselle L'Espanaye, and that there were no means of egress without the notice of the party ascending. The wild disorder of the room; the corpse thrust, with the head downward, up the chimney; the frightful mutilation of the body of the old lady; these considerations, with those just mentioned, and others which I need not mention, have sufficed to paralyze the powers, by putting completely at fault the boasted *acumen*, of the government agents. They have fallen into the gross but common error of confounding the unusual with the abstruse. But it is by these deviations from the plane of the ordinary, that reason feels its way, if at all, in its search for the true. In investigations such as we are now pursuing, it should not be so much asked "what has occurred", as "what has occurred that has never occurred before." In fact, the facility with which I shall arrive, or have arrived, at the solution of this mystery, is in the direct ratio of its apparent insolubility in the eyes of the police.'

I stared at the speaker in mute astonishment.

'I am now awaiting,' continued he, looking toward the door of our apartment—'I am now awaiting a person who, although perhaps not the perpetrator of these butcheries, must have been in some measure implicated in their perpetration. Of the worst portion of the crimes committed, it is probable that he is innocent. I hope that I am right in this supposition; for upon it I build my expectation of reading the entire riddle. I look for the man here—in this room—every moment. It is true that he may not arrive; but the probability is that he will.

Should he come, it will be necessary to detain him. Here are pistols; and we both know how to use them when occasion demands their use.'

I took the pistols, scarcely knowing what I did, or believing what I heard, while Dupin went on, very much as if in a soliloquy. I have already spoken of his abstract manner at such times. His discourse was addressed to myself; but his voice, although by no means loud, had that intonation which is commonly employed in speaking to some one at a great distance. His eyes, vacant in expression, regarded only the wall.

'That the voices heard in contention,' he said, 'by the party upon the stairs, were not the voices of the women themselves, was fully proved by the evidence. This relieves us of all doubt upon the question whether the old lady could have first destroyed the daughter, and afterward have committed suicide. I speak of this point chiefly for the sake of method; for the strength of Madame L'Espanaye would have been utterly unequal to the task of thrusting her daughter's corpse up the chimney as it was found; and the nature of the wounds upon her own person entirely preclude the idea of self-destruction. Murder, then, has been committed by some third party; and the voices of this third party were those heard in contention. Let me now advert—not to the whole testimony respecting these voices—but to what was *peculiar* in that testimony. Did you observe any thing peculiar about it?'

I remarked that, while all the witnesses agreed in supposing the gruff voice to be that of a Frenchman, there was much disagreement in regard to the shrill, or, as one individual termed it, the harsh voice.

'That was the evidence itself,' said Dupin, 'but it was not the peculiarity of the evidence. You have observed nothing distinctive. Yet there *was* something to be observed. The witnesses, as you remark, agreed about the gruff voice; they were here unanimous. But in regard to the shrill voice, the peculiarity is—not that they disagreed—but that, while an Italian, an Englishman, a Spaniard, a Hollander, and a Frenchman attempted to describe it, each one spoke of it as that *of a foreigner*. Each is sure that it was not the voice of one of his own countrymen. Each likens it—not to the voice of an individual of any nation with whose language he is conversant—but the converse. The Frenchman supposes it the voice of a Spaniard, and "might have distinguished some words *had he been acquainted with the Spanish*." The Dutchman maintains it to have been that of a Frenchman; but we find it stated that "*not understanding French this witness was examined through an interpreter.*" The Englishman thinks it the voice of a German, and "*does not understand German.*" The Spaniard "is sure" that it was that of an Englishman, but "judges by the intonation" altogether, "*as he has no knowledge of the English.*" The Italian believes it the voice of a Russian, but "*has never conversed with a native of Russia.*" A second Frenchman differs, moreover, with the first, and is positive that the voice was that of an Italian; but, *not being cognizant of that tongue*, is, like the Spaniard, "convinced by the intonation." Now, how strangely unusual must that voice have really been, about which such testimony as this *could* have been elicited!—in whose *tones*, even, denizens of the five great divisions of Europe could recognise nothing familiar! You will say that it might have been the voice of an Asiatic—of an African. Neither Asiatics nor Africans abound in Paris; but, without denying the inference, I will now merely call your attention to three points. The voice is termed by one witness "harsh rather than shrill." It is represented by two others to have been "quick and *unequal.*" No words—no sounds resembling words—were by any witness mentioned as distinguishable.

'I know not,' continued Dupin, 'what impression I may have made, so far, upon your own understanding; but I do not hesitate to say that legitimate deductions even from this portion of the testimony—the portion respecting the gruff and shrill voices—are in themselves sufficient to engender a suspicion which should give direction to all farther progress in the investigation of the mystery. I said "legitimate deductions;" but my meaning is not thus fully expressed. I designed to imply that the deductions are the *sole* proper ones, and that the suspicion arises *inevitably* from them as the single result. What the suspicion is, however, I will not say just yet. I merely wish you to bear in mind that, with myself, it was sufficiently forcible to give a definite form—a certain tendency—to my inquiries in the chamber.

'Let us now transport ourselves, in fancy, to this chamber. What shall we first seek here? The means of egress employed by the murderers. It is not too much to say that neither of us believe in præternatural events. Madame and Mademoiselle L'Espanaye were not destroyed by spirits. The doers of the deed were material, and escaped materially. Then how? Fortunately, there is but one mode of reasoning upon the point, and that mode *must* lead us to a definite decision.—Let us examine, each by each, the possible means of egress. It is clear that the assassins were in the room where Mademoiselle L'Espanaye was found, or at least in the room adjoining, when the party ascended the stairs. It is then only from these two apartments that we have to seek issues. The police have laid bare the floors, the ceilings, and the masonry of the walls, in every direction. No *secret* issues could have escaped their vigilance. But, not trusting to *their* eyes, I examined with my own. There were, then, *no* secret issues. Both doors leading from the rooms into the passage were securely locked, with the keys inside. Let us turn to the chimneys. These, although of ordinary width for some eight to ten feet above the hearths, will not admit, throughout their extent, the body of a large cat. The impossibility of egress, by means already stated, being thus absolute, we are reduced to the windows. Through those of the front room no one could have escaped without notice from the crowd in the street. The murderers *must* have passed, then, through those of the back room. Now, brought to this conclusion in so unequivocal a manner as we are, it is not our part, as reasoners, to reject it on account of apparent impossibilities. It is only left for us to prove that these apparent "impossibilities" are, in reality, not such.

'There are two windows in the chamber. One of them is unobstructed by furniture, and is wholly visible. The lower portion of the other is hidden from view by the head of the unwieldy bedstead which is thrust close up against it. The former was found securely fastened from within. It resisted the utmost force of those who endeavored to raise it. A large gimlet-hole had been pierced in its frame to the left, and a very stout nail was found fitted therein, nearly to the head. Upon examining the other window, a similar nail was seen similarly fitted in it; and a vigorous attempt to raise this sash failed also. The police were now entirely satisfied that egress had not been in these directions. And, *therefore*, it was thought a matter of supererogation to withdraw the nails and open the windows.

'My own examination was somewhat more particular, and was so for the reason I have just given—because here it was, I knew, that all apparent impossibilities *must* be proved to be not such in reality.

'I proceeded to think thus—*à posteriori*. The murderers *did* escape from one of these windows. This being so, they could not have refastened the sashes from the inside, as they were found fastened;—the consideration which put a stop, through its obviousness, to the scrutiny of the police in this quarter. Yet the sashes *were* fastened. They *must*, then, have the power of fastening themselves. There was no escape from this conclusion. I stepped to the unobstructed casement, withdrew the nail with some difficulty, and attempted to raise the sash. It resisted all my efforts, as I had anticipated. A concealed spring must, I now knew, exist; and this corroboration of my idea convinced me that my premises, at least, were correct, however mysterious still appeared the circumstances attending the nails. A careful search soon brought to light the hidden spring. I pressed it, and, satisfied with the discovery, forbore to upraise the sash.

'I now replaced the nail and regarded it attentively. A person passing out through this window might have reclosed it, and the spring would have caught—but the nail could not have been replaced. The conclusion was plain, and again narrowed in the field of my investigations. The assassins *must* have escaped through the other window. Supposing, then, the springs upon each sash to be the same, as was probable, there *must* be found a difference between the nails, or at least between the modes of their fixture. Getting upon the sacking of the bedstead, I looked over the head-board minutely at the second casement. Passing my hand down behind the board, I readily discovered and pressed the spring, which was, as I had supposed, identical in character with its neighbor. I now looked at the nail. It was as stout as the other, and apparently fitted in in the same manner—driven in nearly up to the head.

'You will say that I was puzzled; but, if you think so, you must have misunderstood the nature of the inductions. To use a sporting phrase, I had not been once "at fault." The scent had never for an instant been lost. There was no flaw in any link of the chain. I had traced the secret to its ultimate result,—and that result was *the nail.* It had, I say, in every respect, the appearance of its fellow in the other window; but this fact was an absolute nullity (conclusive as it might seem to be) when compared with the consideration that here, at this point, terminated the clew. "There *must* be something wrong," I said, "about the nail." I touched it; and the head, with about a quarter of an inch of the shank, came off in my fingers. The rest of the shank was in the gimlet-hole, where it had been broken off. The fracture was an old one (for its edges were incrusted with rust), and had apparently been accomplished by the blow of a hammer, which had partially imbedded, in the top of the bottom sash, the head portion of the nail. I now carefully replaced this head portion in the indentation whence I had taken it, and the resemblance to a perfect nail was complete—the fissure was invisible. Pressing the spring, I gently raised the sash for a few inches; the head went up with it, remaining firm in its bed. I closed the window, and the semblance of the whole nail was again perfect.

'The riddle, so far, was now unriddled. The assassin had escaped through the window which looked upon the bed. Dropping of its own accord upon his exit (or perhaps purposely closed), it had become fastened by the spring; and it was the retention of this spring which had been mistaken by the police for that of the nail,—farther inquiry being thus considered unnecessary.

'The next question is that of the mode of descent. Upon this point I had been satisfied in my walk with you around the building. About five feet and a half from the casement in question there runs a lightning-rod. From this rod it would have been impossible for any one to reach the window itself, to say nothing of entering it. I observed, however, that the shutters of the fourth story were of the peculiar kind called by Parisian carpenters *ferrades*—a kind rarely employed at the present day, but frequently seen upon very old mansions at Lyons and Bourdeaux. They are in the form of an ordinary door, (a single, not a folding door) except that the upper half is latticed or worked in open trellis—thus affording an excellent hold for the hands. In the present instance these shutters are fully three feet and a half broad. When we saw them from the rear of the house, they were both about half open—that is to say, they stood off at right angles from the wall. It is probable that the police, as well as myself, examined the back of the tenement; but, if so, in looking at these *ferrades* in the line of their breadth (as they must have done), they did not perceive this great breadth itself, or, at all events, failed to take it into due consideration. In fact, having once satisfied themselves that no egress could have been made in this quarter, they would naturally bestow here a very cursory examination. It was clear to me, however, that the shutter belonging to the window at the head of the bed, would, if swung fully back to the wall, reach to within two feet of the lightning-rod. It was also evident that, by exertion of a very unusual degree of activity and courage, an entrance into the window, from the rod, might have been thus effected.—By reaching to the distance of two feet and a half (we now suppose the shutter open to its whole extent) a robber might have taken a firm grasp upon the trellis-work. Letting go, then, his hold upon the rod, placing his feet securely against the wall, and springing boldly from it, he might have swung the shutter so as to close it, and, if we imagine the window open at the time, might even have swung himself into the room.

'I wish you to bear especially in mind that I have spoken of a *very* unusual degree of activity as requisite to success in so hazardous and so difficult a feat. It is my design to show you, first, that the thing might possibly have been accomplished:—but, secondly and *chiefly*, I wish to impress upon your understanding the *very extraordinary*—the almost præternatural character of that agility which could have accomplished it.

'You will say, no doubt, using the language of the law, that "to make out my case," I should rather undervalue, than insist upon a full estimation of the activity required in this matter. This may be the practice in law, but it is not the usage of reason. My ultimate object is only the truth. My immediate purpose is to lead you to place in juxtaposition, that *very unusual* activity of which I have just spoken, with that *very peculiar* shrill (or harsh) and *unequal* voice, about whose nationality no two persons could be found to agree, and in whose utterance no syllabification could be detected.'

At these words a vague and half-formed conception of the meaning of Dupin flitted over my mind. I seemed to be upon the verge of comprehension, without power to comprehend—as men, at times, find themselves upon the brink of remembrance, without being able, in the end, to remember. My friend went on with his discourse.

'You will see,' he said, 'that I have shifted the question from the mode of egress to that of ingress. It was my design to suggest the idea that both were effected in the same manner, at the same point. Let us now revert to the interior of the room. Let us survey the appearances here. The drawers of the bureau, it is said, had been rifled, although many articles of apparel still remained within them. The conclusion here is absurd. It is a mere guess—a very silly one—and no more. How are we to know that the articles found in the drawers were not all these drawers had originally contained? Madame L'Espanaye and her daughter lived an exceedingly retired life—saw no company—seldom went out—had little use for numerous changes of habiliment. Those found were at least of as good quality as any likely to be possessed by these ladies. If a thief had taken any, why did he not take the best—why did he not take all? In a word, why did he abandon four thousand francs in gold to encumber himself with a bundle of linen? The gold *was* abandoned. Nearly the whole sum mentioned by Monsieur Mignaud, the banker, was discovered, in bags, upon the floor. I wish you, therefore, to discard from your thoughts the blundering idea of *motive*, engendered in the brains of the police by that portion of the evidence which speaks of money delivered at the door of the house. Coincidences ten times as remarkable as this (the delivery of the money, and murder committed within three days upon the party receiving it), happen to all of us every hour of our lives, without attracting even momentary notice. Coincidences, in general, are great stumbling-blocks in the way of that class of thinkers who have been educated to know nothing of the theory of probabilities—that theory to which the most glorious objects of human research are indebted for the most glorious of illustration. In the present instance, had the gold been gone, the fact of its delivery three days before would have formed something more than a coincidence. It would have been corroborative of this idea of motive. But, under the real circumstances of the case, if we are to suppose gold the motive of this outrage, we must also imagine the perpetrator so vacillating an idiot as to have abandoned his gold and his motive together.

'Keeping now steadily in mind the points to which I have drawn your attention—that peculiar voice, that unusual agility, and that startling absence of motive in a murder so singularly atrocious as this—let us glance at the butchery itself. Here is a woman strangled to death by manual strength, and thrust up a chimney, head downward. Ordinary assassins employ no such modes of murder as this. Least of all, do they thus dispose of the murdered. In the manner of thrusting the corpse up the chimney, you will admit that there was something *excessively outré*—something altogether irreconcilable with our common notions of human action, even when we suppose the actors the most depraved of men. Think, too, how great must have been that strength which could have thrust the body *up* such an aperture so forcibly that the united vigor of several persons was found barely sufficient to drag it *down!*

'Turn, now, to other indications of the employment of a vigor most marvellous. On the hearth were thick tresses—very thick tresses—of grey human hair. These had been torn out by the roots. You are aware of the great force necessary in tearing thus from the head even twenty or thirty hairs together. You saw the locks in question as well as myself. Their roots (a hideous sight!) were clotted with fragments of the flesh of the scalp—sure token of the prodigious power which had been exerted in uprooting perhaps half a million of hairs at a time. The throat of the old lady was not merely cut, but the head absolutely severed from the body: the instrument was a mere razor. I wish you also to look at the *brutal* ferocity of these deeds. Of the bruises upon the body of Madame L'Espanaye I do not speak. Monsieur Dumas, and his worthy coadjutor Monsieur Etienne, have pronounced that they were inflicted by some obtuse instrument: and so far these gentlemen are very correct. The obtuse instrument was clearly the stone pavement in the yard, upon which the victim had fallen from the window which looked in upon the bed. This idea, however simple it may now seem, escaped the police for the same reason that the breadth of the shutters escaped them—because, by the affair of the nails, their perceptions had been hermetically sealed against the possibility of the windows having ever been opened at all.

'If now, in addition to all these things, you have properly reflected upon the odd disorder of the chamber, we have gone so far as to combine the ideas of an agility astounding, a strength superhuman, a ferocity brutal, a butchery without motive, a *grotesquerie* in horror absolutely alien from humanity, and a voice foreign in tone to the ears of men of many nations, and devoid of all distinct or intelligible syllabification. What result, then, has ensued? What impression have I made upon your fancy?'

I felt a creeping of the flesh as Dupin asked me the question. 'A madman,' I said, 'has done this deed—some raving maniac, escaped from a neighboring *Maison de Santé*.'

'In some respects,' he replied, 'your idea is not irrelevant. But the voices of madmen, even in their wildest paroxysms, are never found to tally with that peculiar voice heard upon the stairs. Madmen are of some nation, and their language, however incoherent in its words, has always the coherence of syllabification. Besides, the hair of a madman is not such as I now hold in my hand. I disentangled this little tuft from the rigidly clutched fingers of Madame L'Espanaye. Tell me what you can make of it.'

'Dupin!' I said, completely unnerved; 'this hair is most unusual—this is no *human* hair.'

'I have not asserted that it is,' said he; 'but, before we decide this point, I wish you to glance at the little sketch I have here traced upon this paper. It is a *fac-simile* drawing of what has been described in one portion of the testimony as "dark bruises, and deep indentations of finger nails," upon the throat of Mademoiselle L'Espanaye, and in another, (by Messrs. Dumas and Etienne,) as a "series of livid spots, evidently the impression of fingers."

'You will perceive,' continued my friend, spreading out the paper upon the table before us, 'that this drawing gives the idea of a firm and fixed hold. There is no *slipping* apparent. Each finger has retained—possibly until the death of the victim—the fearful grasp by which it originally imbedded itself. Attempt, now, to place all your fingers, at the same time, in the respective impressions as you see them.'

I made the attempt in vain.

'We are possibly not giving this matter a fair trial,' he said. 'The paper is spread out upon a plane surface; but the human throat is cylindrical. Here is a billet of wood, the circumference of which is about that of the throat. Wrap the drawing around it, and try the experiment again.'

I did so; but the difficulty was even more obvious than before. 'This,' I said, 'is the mark of no human hand.'

'Read now,' replied Dupin, 'this passage from Cuvier.'*

It was a minute anatomical and generally descriptive account of the large fulvous Ourang-Outang of the East Indian Islands. The gigantic stature, the prodigious strength and activity, the wild ferocity, and the imitative propensities of these mammalia are sufficiently well known to all. I understood the full horrors of the murder at once.

'The description of the digits,' said I, as I made an end of reading, 'is in exact accordance with this drawing. I see that no animal but an Ourang-Outang, of the species here mentioned, could have impressed the indentations as you have traced them. This tuft of tawny hair, too, is identical in character with that of the beast of Cuvier. But I cannot possibly comprehend the particulars of this frightful mystery. Besides, there were *two* voices heard in contention, and one of them was unquestionably the voice of a Frenchman.'

'True; and you will remember an expression attributed almost unanimously, by the evidence, to this voice,—the expression, "*mon Dieu!*" This, under the circumstances, has been justly characterized by one of the witnesses (Montani, the confectioner,) as an expression of remonstrance or expostulation. Upon these two words, therefore, I have mainly built my hopes of a full solution of the riddle. A Frenchman was cognizant of the murder. It is possible—indeed it is far more than probable—that he was innocent of all participation in the bloody transactions which took place. The Ourang-Outang may have escaped from him. He may have traced it to the chamber; but, under the agitating circumstances which ensued, he could never have re-captured it. It is still at large. I will not pursue these guesses—for I have no right to call them more—since the shades of reflection upon which they are based are scarcely of sufficient depth to be appreciable by my own intellect, and since I could not pretend to make them intelligible to the understanding of another. We will call them guesses then, and speak of them as such. If the Frenchman in question is indeed, as I suppose, innocent of this atrocity, this advertisement, which I left last night, upon our return home, at the office of "Le Monde," (a paper devoted to the shipping interest, and much sought by sailors,) will bring him to our residence.'

He handed me a paper, and I read thus:

CAUGHT—*In the Bois de Boulogne, early in the morning of the——inst.*, (the morning of the murder,) *a very large, tawny Ourang-Outang of the Bornese species. The owner, (who is ascertained to be a sailor, belonging to a Maltese vessel,) may have the animal again, upon identifying it satisfactorily, and paying a few charges arising from its capture and keeping. Call at No.——, Rue——,' Faubourg St Germain—au troisième.*

'How was it possible,' I asked, 'that you should know the man to be a sailor, and belonging to a Maltese vessel?'

'I do *not* know it,' said Dupin. 'I am not *sure* of it. Here, however, is a small piece of ribbon, which from its form, and from its greasy appearance, has evidently been used in tying the hair in one of those long *queues* of which sailors are so fond. Moreover, this knot is one which few besides sailors can tie, and is peculiar to the Maltese. I picked the ribbon up at the foot of the lightning-rod. It could not have belonged to either of the deceased. Now if, after all, I am wrong in my induction from this ribbon, that the Frenchman was a sailor belonging to a Maltese vessel, still I can have done no harm in saying what I did in the advertisement. If I am in error, he will merely suppose that I have been misled by some circumstance into which he will not take the trouble to inquire. But if I am right, a great point is gained. Cognizant although innocent of the murder, the Frenchman will naturally hesitate about replying to the advertisement—about demanding the Ourang-Outang. He will reason thus:—"I am innocent; I am poor; my Ourang-Outang is of great value—to one in my circumstances a fortune of itself—why should I lose it through idle apprehensions of danger? Here it is, within my grasp. It was found in the Bois de Boulogne—at a vast distance from the scene of that butchery. How can it ever be suspected that a brute beast should have done the deed? The police are at fault—they have failed to procure the slightest clew. Should they even trace the animal, it would be impossible to prove me cognizant of the murder, or to implicate me in guilt on account of that cognizance. Above all, *I am known*. The advertiser designates me as the possessor of the beast. I am not sure to what limit his knowledge may extend. Should I avoid claiming a property of so great value, which it is known that I possess, I will render the animal at least, liable to suspicion. It is not my policy to attract attention either to myself or to the beast. I will answer the advertisement, get the Ourang-Outang, and keep it close until this matter has blown over." '

At this moment we heard a step upon the stairs.

'Be ready,' said Dupin, 'with your pistols, but neither use them nor show them until at a signal from myself.'

The front door of the house had been left open, and the visiter had entered, without ringing, and advanced several steps upon the staircase. Now, however, he seemed to hesitate. Presently we heard him descending. Dupin was moving quickly to the door, when we again heard him coming up. He did not turn back a second time, but stepped up with decision, and rapped at the door of our chamber.

'Come in,' said Dupin, in a cheerful and hearty tone.

A man entered. He was a sailor, evidently,—a tall, stout, and muscular-looking person, with a certain dare-devil expression of countenance, not altogether unprepossessing. His face, greatly sunburnt, was more than half hidden by whisker and *mustachio*. He had with him a huge oaken cudgel, but appeared to be otherwise unarmed. He bowed awkwardly, and bade us 'good evening,' in French accents, which, although somewhat Neufchatel-ish, were still sufficiently indicative of a Parisian origin.*

'Sit down, my friend,' said Dupin. 'I suppose you have called about the Ourang-Outang. Upon my word, I almost envy you the possession of him; a remarkably fine, and no doubt a very valuable animal. How old do you suppose him to be?'

The sailor drew a long breath, with the air of a man relieved of some intolerable burden, and then replied, in an assured tone:

'I have no way of telling—but he can't be more than four or five years old. Have you got him here?'

'Oh no; we had no conveniences for keeping him here. He is at a livery stable in the Rue Dubourg, just by. You can get him in the morning. Of course you are prepared to identify the property?'

'To be sure I am, sir.'

'I shall be sorry to part with him,' said Dupin.

'I don't mean that you should be at all this trouble for nothing, sir,' said the man. 'Couldn't expect it. Am very willing to pay a reward for the finding of the animal—that is to say, any thing in reason.'

'Well,' replied my friend, 'that is all very fair, to be sure. Let me think!—what should I have? Oh! I will tell you. My reward shall be this. You shall give me all the information in your power about these murders in the Rue Morgue.'

Dupin said the last words in a very low tone, and very quietly. Just as quietly, too, he walked toward the door, locked it, and put the key in his pocket. He then drew a pistol from his bosom and placed it, without the least flurry, upon the table.

The sailor's face flushed up as if he were struggling with suffocation. He started to his feet and grasped his cudgel; but the next moment he fell back into his seat, trembling violently, and with the countenance of death itself. He spoke not a word. I pitied him from the bottom of my heart.

'My friend,' said Dupin, in a kind tone, 'you are alarming yourself unnecessarily—you are indeed. We mean you no harm whatever. I pledge you the honor of a gentleman, and of a Frenchman, that we intend you no injury. I perfectly well know that you are innocent of the atrocities in the Rue Morgue. It will not do, however, to deny that you are in some measure implicated in them. From what I have already said, you must know that I have had means of information about this matter—means of which you could never have dreamed. Now the thing stands thus. You have done nothing which you could have avoided—nothing, certainly, which renders you culpable. You were not even guilty of robbery, when you might have robbed with impunity. You have nothing to conceal. You have no reason for concealment. On the other hand, you are bound by every principle of honor to confess all you know. An innocent man is now imprisoned, charged with that crime of which you can point out the perpetrator.'

The sailor had recovered his presence of mind, in a great measure, while Dupin uttered these words; but his original boldness of bearing was all gone.

'So help me God,' said he, after a brief pause, 'I *will* tell you all I know about this affair;—but I do not expect you to believe one half I say—I would be a fool indeed if I did. Still, I *am* innocent, and I will make a clean breast if I die for it.'

What he stated was, in substance, this. He had lately made a voyage to the Indian Archipelago. A party, of which he formed one, landed at Borneo, and passed into the interior on an excursion of pleasure. Himself and a companion had captured the Ourang-Outang. This companion dying, the animal fell into his own exclusive possession. After great trouble, occasioned by the intractable ferocity of his captive during the home voyage, he at length succeeded in lodging it safely at his own residence in Paris, where, not to attract toward himself the unpleasant curiosity of his neighbors, he kept it carefully secluded, until such time as it should recover from a wound in the foot, received from a splinter on board ship. His ultimate design was to sell it.

Returning home from some sailors' frolic on the night, or rather in the morning of the murder, he found the beast occupying his own bedroom, into which it had broken from a closet adjoining, where it had been, as was thought, securely confined. Razor in hand, and fully lathered, it was sitting before a looking-glass, attempting the operation of shaving, in which it had no doubt previously watched its master through the key-hole of the closet. Terrified at the sight of so dangerous a weapon in the possession of an animal so ferocious, and so well able to use it, the man, for some moments, was at a loss what to do. He had been accustomed, however, to quiet the creature, even in its fiercest moods, by the use of a whip, and to this he now resorted. Upon sight of it, the Ourang-Outang sprang at once through the door of the chamber, down the stairs, and thence, through a window, unfortunately open, into the street.

The Frenchman followed in despair; the ape, razor still in hand, occasionally stopping to look back and gesticulate at its pursuer, until the latter had nearly come up with it. It then again made off. In this manner the chase continued for a long time. The streets were profoundly quiet, as it was nearly three o'clock in the morning. In passing down an alley in the rear of the Rue Morgue, the fugitive's attention was arrested by a light gleaming from the open window of Madame L'Espanaye's chamber, in the fourth story of her house. Rushing to the building, it perceived the lightning-rod, clambered up with inconceivable agility, grasped the shutter, which was thrown fully back against the wall, and, by its means, swung itself directly upon the headboard of the bed. The whole feat did not occupy a minute. The shutter was kicked open again by the Ourang-Outang as it entered the room.

The sailor, in the meantime, was both rejoiced and perplexed. He had strong hopes of now recapturing the brute, as it could scarcely escape from the trap into which it had ventured, except by the rod, where it might be intercepted as it came down. On the other hand, there was much cause for anxiety as to what it might do in the house. This latter reflection urged the man still to follow the fugitive. A lightning-rod is ascended without difficulty, especially by a sailor; but, when he had arrived as high as the window, which lay far to his left, his career was stopped; the most that he could accomplish was to reach over so as to obtain a glimpse of the interior of the room. At this glimpse he nearly fell from his hold through excess of horror. Now it was that those hideous shrieks arose upon the night, which had startled from slumber the inmates of the Rue Morgue. Madame L'Espanaye and her daughter, habited in their night clothes, had apparently been occupied in arranging some papers in the iron chest already mentioned, which had been wheeled into the middle of the room. It was open, and its contents lay beside it on the floor. The victims must have been sitting with their backs toward the window; and, from the time elapsing between the ingress of the beast and the screams, it seems probable that it was not immediately perceived. The flapping-to of the shutter would naturally have been attributed to the wind.

As the sailor looked in, the gigantic animal had seized Madame L'Espanaye by the hair, (which was loose, as she had been combing it,) and was flourishing the razor about her face, in imitation of the motions of a barber. The daughter lay prostrate and motionless; she had swooned. The screams and struggles of the old lady (during which the hair was torn from her head) had the effect of changing the probably pacific purposes of the Ourang-Outang into those of wrath. With one determined sweep of its muscular arm it nearly severed her head from her body. The sight of blood inflamed its anger into phrenzy. Gnashing its teeth, and flashing fire from its eyes, it flew upon the body of the girl, and imbedded its fearful talons in her throat, retaining its grasp until she expired. Its wandering and wild glances fell at this moment upon the head of the bed, over which the face of its master, rigid with horror, was just discernible. The fury of the beast, who no doubt bore still in mind the dreaded whip, was instantly converted into fear. Conscious of having deserved punishment, it seemed desirous of concealing its bloody deeds, and skipped about the chamber in an agony of nervous agitation; throwing down and breaking the furniture as it moved, and dragging the bed from the bedstead. In conclusion, it seized first the corpse of the daughter, and thrust it up the chimney, as it was found; then that of the old lady, which it immediately hurled through the window headlong.

As the ape approached the casement with its mutilated burden, the sailor shrank aghast to the rod, and, rather gliding than clambering down it, hurried at once home—dreading the consequences of the butchery, and gladly abandoning, in his terror, all solicitude about the fate of the Ourang-Outang. The words heard by the party upon the staircase were the Frenchman's exclamations of horror and affright, commingled with the fiendish jabberings of the brute.

I have scarcely anything to add. The Ourang-Outang must have escaped from the chamber, by the rod, just before the breaking of the door. It must have closed the window as it passed through it. It was subsequently caught by the owner himself, who obtained for it a very large sum at the *Jardin des Plantes*.* Le Bon was instantly released, upon our narration of the circumstances (with some comments from Dupin) at the *bureau* of the Prefect of Police. This functionary, however well disposed to my friend, could not altogether conceal his chagrin at the turn which affairs had taken, and was fain to indulge in a sarcasm or two, about the propriety of every person minding his own business.

'Let him talk,' said Dupin, who had not thought it necessary to reply. 'Let him discourse; it will ease his conscience. I am satisfied with having defeated him in his own castle. Nevertheless, that he failed in the solution of this mystery, is by no means that matter for wonder which he supposes it; for, in truth, our friend the Prefect is somewhat too cunning to be profound. In his wisdom is no *stamen*. It is all head and no body, like the pictures of the Goddess Laverna,—or, at best, all head and shoulders, like a codfish. But he is a good creature after all. I like him especially for one master stroke of cant, by which he has attained his reputation for ingenuity, I mean the way he has "*de nier ce qui est, et d'expliquer ce qui n'est pas.*"[1]

[1] Rousseau, *Nouvelle Héloise*.*

ELEONORA

Sub conservatione formæ specificæ salva anima.

Raymond Lully*

I AM come of a race noted for vigor of fancy and ardor of passion. Men have called me mad; but the question is not yet settled, whether madness is or is not the loftiest intelligence—whether much that is glorious—whether all that is profound—does not spring from disease of thought—from *moods* of mind exalted at the expense of the general intellect. They who dream by day are cognizant of many things which escape those who dream only by night. In their grey visions they obtain glimpses of eternity, and thrill, in awaking, to find that they have been upon the verge of the great secret. In snatches, they learn something of the wisdom which is of good, and more of the mere knowledge which is of evil. They penetrate, however rudderless or compassless, into the vast ocean of the 'light ineffable' and again, like the adventurers of the Nubian geographer, '*agressi sunt mare tenebrarum, quid in eo esset exploraturi*.'*

We will say, then, that I am mad. I grant, at least, that there are two distinct conditions of my mental existence—the condition of a lucid reason, not to be disputed, and belonging to the memory of events forming the first epoch of my life—and a condition of shadow and doubt, appertaining to the present, and to the recollection of what constitutes the second great era of my being. Therefore, what I shall tell of the earlier period, believe; and to what I may relate of the later time, give only such credit as may seem due; or doubt it altogether; or, if doubt it ye cannot, then play unto its riddle the Oedipus.*

She whom I loved in youth, and of whom I now pen calmly and distinctly these remembrances, was the sole daughter of the only sister of my mother long departed. Eleonora was the name of my cousin. We had always dwelled together, beneath a tropical sun, in the Valley of the Many-Colored Grass. No unguided footstep ever came upon that vale; for it lay far away up among a range of giant hills that hung beetling around about it, shutting out the sunlight from its sweetest recesses. No path was trodden in its vicinity; and, to reach our happy home, there was need of putting back, with force, the foliage of many thousands of forest trees, and of crushing to death the glories of many millions of fragrant flowers. Thus it was that we lived all alone, knowing nothing of the world without the valley,—I, and my cousin, and her mother.

From the dim regions beyond the mountains at the upper end of our encircled domain, there crept out a narrow and deep river, brighter than all save the eyes of Eleonora; and, winding stealthily about in mazy courses, it passed away, at length, through a shadowy gorge, among hills still dimmer than those whence it had issued. We called it the 'River of Silence:' for there seemed to be a hushing influence in its flow. No murmur arose from its bed, and so gently it wandered along that the pearly pebbles upon which we loved to gaze, far down within its bosom, stirred not at all, but lay in a motionless content, each in its own old station, shining on gloriously forever.

The margin of the river, and of the many dazzling rivulets that glided, through devious ways, into its channel, as well as the spaces that extended from the margins away down into the depths of the streams until they reached the bed of pebbles at the bottom,—these spots, not less than the whole surface of the valley, from the river to the mountains that girdled it in, were carpeted all by a soft green grass, thick, short, perfectly even, and vanilla-perfumed, but so besprinkled throughout with the yellow buttercup, the white daisy, the purple violet, and the ruby-red asphodel, that its exceeding beauty spoke to our hearts, in loud tones, of the love and of the glory of God.

And, here and there, in groves about this grass, like wildernesses of dreams, sprang up fantastic trees, whose tall slender stems stood not upright, but slanted gracefully towards the light that peered at noonday into the centre of the valley. Their bark was speckled with the vivid alternate splendor of ebony and silver, and was smoother than all save the cheeks of Eleonora; so that but for the brilliant green of the huge leaves that spread from their summits in long tremulous lines, dallying with the Zephyrs, one might have fancied them giant serpents of Syria doing homage to their Sovereign the Sun.

Hand in hand about this valley, for fifteen years, roamed I with Eleonora before Love entered within our hearts. It was one evening at the close of the third lustrum of her life, and of the fourth of my own, that we sat, locked in each other's embrace, beneath the serpent-like trees, and looked down within the waters of the River of Silence at our images therein. We spoke no words during the rest of that sweet day;

and our words even upon the morrow were tremulous and few. We had drawn the God Eros from that wave, and now we felt that he had enkindled within us the fiery souls of our forefathers. The passions which had for centuries distinguished our race came thronging with the fancies for which they had been equally noted, and together breathed a delirious bliss over the Valley of the Many-Colored Grass. A change fell upon all things. Strange brilliant flowers, star-shaped, burst out upon the trees where no flowers had been known before. The tints of the green carpet deepened; and when, one by one, the white daisies shrank away, there sprang up, in place of them, ten by ten of the ruby-red asphodel. And life arose in our paths; for the tall flamingo, hitherto unseen, with all gay glowing birds, flaunted his scarlet plumage before us. The golden and silver fish haunted the river, out of the bosom of which issued, little by little, a murmur that swelled, at length, into a lulling melody more divine than that of the harp of Æolus—sweeter than all save the voice of Eleonora. And now, too, a voluminous cloud, which we had long watched in the regions of Hesper, floated out thence, all gorgeous in crimson and gold, and settling in peace above us, sank, day by day, lower and lower, until its edges rested upon the tops of the mountains, turning all their dimness into magnificence, and shutting us up, as if forever, within a magic prison-house of grandeur and of glory.

The loveliness of Eleonora was that of the Seraphim; but she was a maiden artless and innocent as the brief life she had led among the flowers. No guile disguised the fervor of love which animated her heart, and she examined with me its inmost recesses as we walked together in the Valley of the Many-Colored Grass, and discoursed of the mighty changes which had lately taken place therein.

At length, having spoken one day, in tears, of the last sad change which must befall Humanity, she thenceforward dwelt only upon this one sorrowful theme, interweaving it into all our converse, as, in the songs of the bard of Schiraz,* the same images are found occurring, again and again, in every impressive variation of phrase.

She had seen that the finger of Death was upon her bosom—that, like the ephemeron, she had been made perfect in loveliness only to die; but the terrors of the grave, to her, lay solely in a consideration which she revealed to me, one evening at twilight, by the banks of the River of Silence. She grieved to think that, having entombed her in the Valley of the Many-Colored Grass, I would quit forever its happy recesses, transferring the love which now was so passionately her own to some maiden of the outer and every-day world. And, then and there, I threw myself hurriedly at the feet of Eleonora, and offered up a vow, to herself and to Heaven, that I would never bind myself in marriage to any daughter of Earth—that I would in no manner prove recreant to her dear memory, or to the memory of the devout affection with which she had blessed me. And I called the Mighty Ruler of the Universe to witness the pious solemnity of my vow. And the curse which I invoked of *Him* and of her, a saint in Helusion,* should I prove traitorous to that promise, involved a penalty the exceeding great horror of which will not permit me to make record of it here. And the bright eyes of Eleonora grew brighter at my words; and she sighed as if a deadly burthen had been taken from her breast; and she trembled and very bitterly wept; but she made acceptance of the vow, (for what was she but a child?) and it made easy to her the bed of her death. And she said to me, not many days afterwards, tranquilly dying, that, because of what I had done for the comfort of her spirit, she would watch over me in that spirit when departed, and, if so it were permitted her, return to me visibly in the watches of the night; but, if this thing were, indeed, beyond the power of the souls in Paradise, that she would, at least, give me frequent indications of her presence; sighing upon me in the evening winds, or filling the air which I breathed with perfume from the censers of the angels. And, with these words upon her lips, she yielded up her innocent life, putting an end to the first epoch of my own.

Thus far I have faithfully said. But as I pass the barrier in Time's path formed by the death of my beloved, and proceed with the second era of my existence, I feel that a shadow gathers over my brain, and I mistrust the perfect sanity of the record. But let me on.—Years dragged themselves along heavily, and still I dwelled within the Valley of the Many-Colored Grass;—but a second change had come upon all things. The star-shaped flowers shrank into the stems of the trees, and appeared no more. The tints of the green carpet faded; and, one by one, the ruby-red asphodels withered away; and there sprang up, in place of them, ten by ten, dark eye-like violets that writhed uneasily and were ever encumbered with dew. And Life departed from our paths; for the tall flamingo flaunted no longer his scarlet plumage before us, but flew sadly from the vale into the hills, with all the gay glowing birds that had arrived in his company. And the golden and silver fish swam down through the gorge at the lower end of our domain and bedecked the sweet river never again. And the lulling melody that had been softer than the wind-harp of Æolus and more divine than all save the voice of Eleonora, it died little by little away, in murmurs growing lower and lower, until the stream returned, at length, utterly, into the solemnity of its original silence. And then, lastly the voluminous cloud uprose, and, abandoning the tops of the mountains to the dimness of old, fell back into the regions of Hesper,* and took away all its manifold golden and gorgeous glories from the Valley of the Many-Colored Grass.

Yet the promises of Eleonora were not forgotten; for I heard the sounds of the swinging of the censers of the angels; and streams of a holy perfume floated ever and ever about the valley; and at lone hours, when my heart beat heavily, the winds that bathed my brow came unto me laden with soft sighs; and indistinct murmurs filled often the night air; and once—oh, but once only! I was awakened from a slumber like the slumber of death by the pressing of spiritual lips upon my own.

But the void within my heart refused, even thus, to be filled. I longed for the love which had before filled it to overflowing. At length the valley *pained* me through its memories of Eleonora, and I left it forever for the vanities and the turbulent triumphs of the world.

* * * * *

I found myself within a strange city, where all things might have served to blot from recollection the sweet dreams I had dreamed so long in the Valley of the Many-Colored Grass. The pomps and pageantries of a stately court, and the mad clangor of arms, and the radiant loveliness of woman, bewildered and intoxicated my brain. But as yet my soul had proved true to its vows, and the indications of the presence of Eleonora were still given me in the silent hours of the night. Suddenly, these manifestations they ceased; and the world grew dark before mine eyes; and I stood aghast at the burning thoughts which possessed—at the terrible temptations which beset me; for there came from some far, far distant and unknown land, into the gay court of the king I served, a maiden to whose beauty my whole recreant heart yielded at once—at whose footstool I bowed down without a struggle, in the most ardent, in the most abject worship of love. What indeed was my passion for the young girl of the valley in comparison with the fervor, and the delirium, and the spirit-lifting ecstasy of adoration with which I poured out my whole soul in tears at the feet of the ethereal Ermengarde?—Oh bright was the seraph Ermengarde! and in that knowledge I had room for none other.—Oh divine was the angel Ermengarde! and as I looked down into the depths of her memorial eyes I thought only of them—and *of her*.

I wedded;—nor dreaded the curse I had invoked; and its bitterness was not visited upon me. And once—but once again in the silence of the night, there came through my lattice the soft sighs which had forsaken me; and they modelled themselves into familiar and sweet voice, saying:

'Sleep in peace!—for the Spirit of Love reigneth and ruleth, and, in taking to thy passionate heart her who is Ermengarde, thou art absolved, for reasons which shall be made known to thee in Heaven, of thy vows unto Eleonora.'

THE MASQUE OF THE RED DEATH

THE 'Red Death'* had long devastated the country. No pestilence had ever been so fatal, or so hideous. Blood was its Avatar and its seal—the redness and the horror of blood. There were sharp pains, and sudden dizziness, and then profuse bleeding at the pores, with dissolution. The scarlet stains upon the body and especially upon the face of the victim, were the pest ban which shut him out from the aid and from the sympathy of his fellow-men. And the whole seizure, progress and termination of the disease, were the incidents of half an hour.

But the Prince Prospero was happy and dauntless and sagacious. When his dominions were half depopulated, he summoned to his presence a thousand hale and light-hearted friends from among the knights and dames of his court, and with these retired to the deep seclusion of one of his castellated abbeys. This was an extensive and magnificent structure, the creation of the prince's own eccentric yet august taste. A strong and lofty wall girdled it in. This wall had gates of iron. The courtiers, having entered, brought furnaces and massy hammers and welded the bolts. They resolved to leave means neither of ingress or egress to the sudden impulses of despair or of frenzy from within. The abbey was amply provisioned. With such precautions the courtiers might bid defiance to contagion. The external world could take care of itself. In the meantime it was folly to grieve, or to think. The prince had provided all the appliances of pleasure. There were buffoons, there were improvisatori, there were ballet-dancers, there were musicians, there was Beauty, there was wine. All these and security were within. Without was the 'Red Death.'

It was toward the close of the fifth or sixth month of his seclusion, and while the pestilence raged most furiously abroad, that the Prince Prospero entertained his thousand friends at a masked ball of the most unusual magnificence.

It was a voluptuous scene, that masquerade. But first let me tell of the rooms in which it was held. There were seven—an imperial suite. In many palaces, however, such suites form a long and straight vista, while the folding doors slide back nearly to the walls on either hand, so that the view of the whole extent is scarcely impeded. Here the case was very different; as might have been expected from the duke's love of the *bizarre*. The apartments were so irregularly disposed that the vision embraced but little more than one at a time. There was a sharp turn at every twenty or thirty yards, and at each turn a novel effect. To the right and left, in the middle of each wall, a tall and narrow Gothic window looked out upon a closed corridor which pursued the windings of the suite. These windows were of stained glass whose color varied in accordance with the prevailing hue of the decorations of the chamber into which it opened. That at the eastern extremity was hung, for example, in blue—and vividly blue were its windows. The second chamber was purple in its ornaments and tapestries, and here the panes were purple. The third was green throughout, and so were the casements. The fourth was furnished and lighted with orange—the fifth with white—the sixth with violet. The seventh apartment was closely shrouded in black velvet tapestries that hung all over the ceiling and down the walls, falling in heavy folds upon a carpet of the same material and hue. But in this chamber only, the color of the windows failed to correspond with the decorations. The panes here were scarlet—a deep blood color. Now in no one of the seven apartments was there any lamp or candelabrum, amid the profusion of golden ornaments that lay scattered to and fro or depended from the roof. There was no light of any kind emanating from lamp or candle within the suite of chambers. But in the corridors that followed the suite, there stood, opposite to each window, a heavy tripod, bearing a brazier of fire that projected its rays through the tinted glass and so glaringly illumined the room. And thus were produced a multitude of gaudy and fantastic appearances. But in the western or black chamber the effect of the fire-light that streamed upon the dark hangings through the blood-tinted panes, was ghastly in the extreme, and produced so wild a look upon the countenance of those who entered, that there were few of the company bold enough to set foot within its precincts at all.

It was in this apartment, also, that there stood against the western wall, a gigantic clock of ebony. Its pendulum swung to and fro with a dull, heavy, monotonous clang; and when the minute-hand made the circuit of the face, and the hour was to be stricken, there came from the brazen lungs of the clock a sound which was clear and loud and deep and exceedingly musical, but of so peculiar a note and emphasis that, at each lapse of an hour, the musicians of the orchestra were constrained to pause, momentarily, in their performance, to harken to the sound; and thus the waltzers perforce ceased their evolutions; and there was a brief disconcert of the whole gay company; and, while the chimes of the clock yet rang, it was observed that the giddiest grew pale, and the more aged and sedate passed their hands over their brows as if in confessed revery or meditation. But when the echoes had fully ceased, a light laughter at once pervaded the assembly; the musicians looked at each other and smiled as if at their own nervousness and folly, and made whispering vows, each to the other, that the next chiming of the clock should produce in them no similar emotion; and then, after the lapse of sixty minutes, (which embrace three thousand and six hundred seconds of the Time that flies,) there came yet another chiming of the clock, and then were the same disconcert and tremulousness and meditation as before.

But, in spite of these things, it was a gay and magnificent revel. The tastes of the duke were peculiar. He had a fine eye for colors and effects. He disregarded the *decora* of mere fashion. His plans were bold and fiery, and his conceptions glowed with barbaric lustre. There are some who would have thought him mad. His followers felt that he was not. It was necessary to hear and see and touch him to be *sure* that he was not.

He had directed, in great part, the moveable embellishments of the seven chambers, upon occasion of this great *fête*; and it was his own guiding taste which had given character to the masqueraders. Be sure they were grotesque. There were much glare and glitter and piquancy and phantasm—much of what has been since seen in 'Hernani.'* There were arabesque figures with unsuited limbs and appointments. There were delirious fancies such as the madman fashions. There were much of the beautiful, much of the wanton, much of the *bizarre*, something of the terrible, and not a little of that which might have excited disgust. To and fro in the seven chambers there stalked, in fact, a multitude of dreams. And these—the dreams—writhed in and about, taking hue from the rooms, and causing the wild music of the orchestra to seem as the echo of their steps. And, anon, there strikes the ebony clock which stands in the hall of the velvet. And then, for a moment, all is still, and all is silent save the voice of the clock. The dreams are stiff-frozen as they stand. But the echoes of the chime die away—they have endured but an instant—and a light, half-subdued laughter floats after them as they depart. And now again the music swells, and the dreams live, and writhe to and fro more merrily than ever, taking hue from the many tinted windows through which stream the rays from the tripods. But to the chamber which lies most westwardly of the seven, there are now none of the maskers who venture; for the night is waning away; and there flows a ruddier light through the blood-colored panes: and the blackness of the sable drapery appals; and to him whose foot falls upon the sable carpet, there comes from the near clock of ebony a muffled peal more solemnly emphatic than any which reaches *their* ears who indulge in the more remote gaieties of the other apartments.

But these other apartments were densely crowded, and in them beat feverishly the heart of life. And the revel went whirlingly on, until at length there commenced the sounding of midnight upon the clock. And then the music ceased, as I have told; and the evolutions of the waltzers were quieted; and there was an uneasy cessation of all things as before. But now there were twelve strokes to be sounded by the bell of the clock; and thus it happened, perhaps, that more of thought crept, with more of time, into the meditations of the thoughtful among those who revelled. And thus, too, it happened, perhaps, that before the last echoes of the last chime had utterly sunk into silence, there were many individuals in the crowd who had found leisure to become aware of the presence of a masked figure which had arrested the attention of no single individual before. And the rumor of this new presence having spread itself whisperingly around, there arose at length from the whole company a buzz, or murmur, expressive of disapprobation and surprise—then, finally, of terror, of horror, and of disgust.

In an assembly of phantasms such as I have painted, it may well be supposed that no ordinary appearance could have excited such sensation. In truth the masquerade license of the night was nearly unlimited; but the figure in question had out-Heroded Herod, and gone beyond the bounds of even the prince's indefinite decorum. There are chords in the hearts of the most reckless which cannot be touched without emotion. Even with the utterly lost, to whom life and death are equally jests, there are matters of which no jest can be made. The whole company, indeed, seemed now deeply to feel that in the costume and bearing of the stranger neither wit nor propriety existed. The figure was tall and gaunt, and shrouded from head to foot in the habiliments of the grave. The mask which concealed the visage was made so nearly to resemble the countenance of a stiffened corpse that the closest scrutiny must have had difficulty in detecting the cheat. And yet all this might have been endured, if not approved, by the mad revellers around. But the mummer had gone so far as to assume the type of the Red Death. His vesture was dabbled in *blood*—and his broad brow, with all the features of the face, was besprinkled with the scarlet horror.

When the eyes of Prince Prospero fell upon this spectral image (which with a slow and solemn movement, as if more fully to sustain its *role*, stalked to and fro among the waltzers) he was seen to be convulsed, in the first moment with a strong shudder either of terror or distaste; but, in the next, his brow reddened with rage.

'Who dares?' he demanded hoarsely of the courtiers who stood near him—'who dares insult us with this blasphemous mockery?' Seize him and unmask him—that we may know whom we have to hang at sunrise, from the battlements!'

It was in the eastern or blue chamber in which stood the Prince Prospero as he uttered these words. They rang throughout the seven rooms loudly and clearly—for the prince was a bold and robust man, and the music had became hushed at the waving of his hand.

It was in the blue room where stood the prince, with a group of pale courtiers by his side. At first, as he spoke, there was a slight rushing movement of this group in the direction of the intruder, who at the moment was also near at hand, and now, with deliberate and stately step, made closer approach to the speaker. But from a certain nameless awe with which the mad assumptions of the mummer had inspired the whole party, there were found none who put forth hand to seize him; so that, unimpeded, he passed within a yard of the prince's person; and, while the vast assembly, as if with one impulse, shrank from the centres of the rooms to the walls, he made his way uninterruptedly, but with the same solemn and measured step which had distinguished him from the first, through the blue chamber to the purple—through the purple to the green—through the green to the orange—through this again to the white—and even thence to the violet, ere a decided movement had been made to arrest him. It was then, however, that the Prince Prospero, maddening with rage and the shame of his own momentary cowardice, rushed hurriedly through the six chambers, while none followed him on account of a deadly terror that had seized upon all. He bore aloft a drawn dagger, and had approached, in rapid impetuosity, to within three or four feet of the retreating figure, when the latter, having attained the extremity of the velvet apartment, turned suddenly and confronted his pursuer. There was a sharp cry—and the dagger dropped gleaming upon the sable carpet, upon which, instantly afterwards, fell prostrate in death the Prince Prospero. Then, summoning the wild courage of despair, a throng of the revellers at once threw themselves into the black apartment, and, seizing the mummer, whose tall figure stood erect and motionless within the shadow of the ebony clock, gasped in unutterable horror at finding the grave cerements and corpselike mask which they handled with so violent a rudeness, untenanted by any tangible form.

And now was acknowledged the presence of the Red Death. He had come like a thief in the night.* And one by one dropped the revellers in the blood-bedewed halls of their revel, and died each in the despairing posture of his fall. And the life of the ebony clock went out with that of the last of the gay. And the flames of the tripods expired. And Darkness and Decay and the Red Death held illimitable dominion over all.

THE PIT AND THE PENDULUM

Impia tortorum longas hic turba furores
Sanguinis innocui, non satiata, aluit.
Sospite nunc patriâ, fracto nunc funeris antro,
Mors ubi dira fuit, vita salusque patent.

[Quatrain composed for the gates of a market to be erected upon the site of the Jacobin club house at Paris.]*

I WAS sick—sick unto death with that long agony; and when they at length unbound me, and I was permitted to sit, I felt that my senses were leaving me. The sentence—the dread sentence of death—was the last of distinct accentuation which reached my ears. After that, the sound of the inquisitorial voices* seemed merged in one dreamy indeterminate hum. It conveyed to my soul the idea of *revolution*—perhaps from its association in fancy with the burr of a mill-wheel. This only for a brief period; for presently I heard no more. Yet, for a while, I saw; but with how terrible an exaggeration! I saw the lips of the black-robed judges. They appeared to me white—whiter than the sheet upon which I trace these words—and thin even to grotesqueness; thin with the intensity of their expression of firmness—of immoveable resolution—of stern contempt of human torture. I saw that the decrees of what to me was Fate, were still issuing from those lips. I saw them writhe with a deadly locution. I saw them fashion the syllables of my name; and I shuddered because no sound succeeded. I saw, too, for a few moments of delirious horror, the soft and nearly imperceptible waving of the sable draperies which enwrapped the walls of the apartment. And then my vision fell upon the seven tall candles upon the table. At first they wore the aspect of charity, and seemed white slender angels who would save me; but then, all at once, there came a most deadly nausea over my spirit, and I felt every fibre in my frame thrill as if I had touched the wire of a galvanic battery, while the angel forms became meaningless spectres, with heads of flame, and I saw that from them there would be no help. And then there stole into my fancy, like a rich musical note, the thought of what sweet rest there must be in the grave. The thought came gently and stealthily, and it seemed long before it attained full appreciation; but just as my spirit came at length properly to feel and entertain it, the figures of the judges vanished, as if magically, from before me; the tall candles sank into nothingness; their flames went out utterly; the blackness of darkness supervened; all sensations appeared swallowed up in a mad rushing descent as of the soul into Hades. Then silence, and stillness, and night were the universe.

I had swooned; but still will not say that all of consciousness was lost. What of it there remained I will not attempt to define, or even to describe; yet all was not lost. In the deepest slumber—no! In delirium—no! In a swoon—no! In death—no! even in the grave all *is not* lost. Else there is no immortality for man. Arousing from the most profound of slumbers, we break the gossamer web of *some* dream. Yet in a second afterward, (so frail may that web have been) we remember not that we have dreamed. In the return to life from the swoon there are two stages; first, that of the sense of mental or spiritual; secondly, that of the sense of physical, existence. It seems probable that if, upon reaching the second stage, we could recall the impressions of the first, we should find these impressions eloquent in memories of the gulf beyond. And that gulf is—what? How at least shall we distinguish its shadows from those of the tomb? But if the impressions of what I have termed the first stage, are not, at will, recalled, yet, after long interval, do they not come unbidden, while we marvel whence they come? He who has never swooned is not he who finds strange palaces and wildly familiar faces in coals that glow; is not he who beholds floating in mid-air the sad visions that the many may not view; is not he who ponders over the perfume of some novel flower—is not he whose brain grows bewildered with the meaning of some musical cadence which has never before arrested his attention.

Amid frequent and thoughtful endeavors to remember; amid earnest struggles to regather some token of the state of seeming nothingness into which my soul had lapsed, there have been moments when I have dreamed of success; there have been brief, very brief periods when I have conjured up remembrances which the lucid reason of a later epoch assures me could have had reference only to that condition of seeming unconsciousness. These shadows of memory tell, indistinctly, of tall figures that lifted and bore me in silence down—down—still down—till a hideous dizziness oppressed me at the mere idea of the interminableness of the descent. They tell also of a vague horror at my heart, on account of that heart's unnatural stillness. Then comes a sense of sudden motionlessness throughout all things; as if those who bore me (a ghastly train!) had outrun, in their descent, the limits of the limitless, and paused from the wearisomeness of their toil. After this I call to mind flatness and dampness; and then all is *madness*—the madness of a memory which busies itself among forbidden things.

Very suddenly there came back to my soul motion and sound—the tumultuous motion of the heart, and, in my ears, the sound of its beating. Then a pause in which all is blank. Then again sound, and motion, and touch—a tingling sensation pervading my frame. Then the mere consciousness of existence, without thought—a condition which lasted long. Then, very suddenly, *thought*, and shuddering terror, and earnest endeavor to comprehend my true state. Then a strong desire to lapse into insensibility. Then a rushing revival of soul and a successful effort to move. And now a full memory of the trial, of the judges, of the sable draperies, of the sentence, of the sickness, of the swoon. Then entire forgetfulness of all that followed; of all that a later day and much earnestness of endeavor have enabled me vaguely to recall.

So far, I had not opened my eyes. I felt that I lay upon my back, unbound. I reached out my hand, and it fell heavily upon something damp and hard. There I suffered it to remain for many minutes, while I strove to imagine where and *what* I could be. I longed, yet dared not to employ my vision. I dreaded the first glance at objects around me. It was not that I feared to look upon things horrible, but that I grew aghast lest there should be *nothing* to see. At length, with a wild desperation at heart, I quickly unclosed my eyes. My worst thoughts, then, were confirmed. The blackness of eternal night encompassed me. I struggled for breath. The intensity of the darkness seemed to oppress and stifle me. The atmosphere was intolerably close. I still lay quietly, and made effort to exercise my reason. I brought to mind the inquisitorial proceedings, and attempted from that point to deduce my real condition. The sentence had passed; and it appeared to me that a very long interval of time had since elapsed. Yet not for a moment did I suppose myself actually dead. Such a supposition, notwithstanding what we read in fiction, is altogether inconsistent with real existence;—but where and in what state was I? The condemned to death, I knew, perished usually at the *autos-da-fé*, and one of these had been held on the very night of the day of my trial. Had I been remanded to my dungeon, to await the next sacrifice, which would not take place for many months? This I at once saw could not be. Victims had been in immediate demand. Moreover, my dungeon, as well as all the condemned cells at Toledo, had stone floors, and light was not altogether excluded.

A fearful idea now suddenly drove the blood in torrents upon my heart, and for a brief period, I once more relapsed into insensibility. Upon recovering, I at once started to my feet, trembling convulsively in every fibre. I thrust my arms wildly above and around me in all directions. I felt nothing; yet dreaded to move a step, lest I should be impeded by the walls of a *tomb*. Perspiration burst from every pore, and stood in cold big beads upon my forehead. The agony of suspense grew, at length, intolerable, and I cautiously moved forward, with my arms extended, and my eyes straining from their sockets, in the hope of catching some faint ray of light. I proceeded for many paces; but still all was blackness and vacancy. I breathed more freely. It seemed evident that mine was not, at least, the most hideous of fates.

And now, as I still continued to step cautiously onward, there came thronging upon my recollection a thousand vague rumors of the horrors of Toledo. Of the dungeons there had been strange things narrated—fables I had always deemed them—but yet strange, and too ghastly to repeat, save in a whisper. Was I left to perish of starvation in this subterranean world of darkness; or what fate, perhaps even more fearful, awaited me? That the result would be death, and a death of more than customary bitterness, I knew too well the character of my judges to doubt. The mode and the hour were all that occupied or distracted me.

My outstretched hands at length encountered some solid obstruction. It was a wall, seemingly of stone masonry—very smooth, slimy, and cold. I followed it up; stepping with all the careful distrust with which certain antique narratives had inspired me. This process, however, afforded me no means of ascertaining the dimensions of my dungeon; as I might make its circuit, and return to the point whence I set out, without being aware of the fact; so perfectly uniform seemed the wall. I therefore sought the knife which had been in my pocket, when led into the inquisitorial chamber; but it was gone; my clothes had been exchanged for a wrapper of coarse serge. I had thought of forcing the blade in some minute crevice of the masonry, so as to identify my point of departure. The difficulty, nevertheless, was but trivial; although, in the disorder of my fancy, it seemed at first insuperable. I tore a part of the hem from the robe and placed the fragment at full length, and at right angles to the wall. In groping my way around the prison, I could not fail to encounter this rag upon completing the circuit. So, at least I thought: but I had not counted upon the extent of the dungeon, or upon my own weakness. The ground was moist and slippery. I staggered onward for some time, when I stumbled and fell. My excessive fatigue induced me to remain prostrate; and sleep soon overtook me as I lay.

Upon awaking, and stretching forth an arm, I found beside me a loaf and a pitcher with water. I was too much exhausted to reflect upon this circumstance, but ate and drank with avidity. Shortly afterward, I resumed my tour around the prison, and with much toil, came at last upon the fragment of the serge. Up to the period when I fell, I had counted fifty-two paces, and, upon resuming my walk, I had counted forty-eight more—when I arrived at the rag. There were in all, then, a hundred paces; and, admitting two paces to the yard, I presumed the dungeon to be fifty yards in circuit. I had met, however, with many angles in the wall, and thus I could form no guess at the shape of the vault; for vault I could not help supposing it to be.

I had little object—certainly no hope—in these researches; but a vague curiosity prompted me to continue them. Quitting the wall, I resolved to cross the area of the enclosure. At first, I proceeded with extreme caution, for the floor, although seemingly of solid material, was treacherous with slime. At length, however, I took courage, and did not hesitate to step firmly—endeavoring to cross in as direct a line as possible. I had advanced some ten or twelve paces in this manner, when the remnant of the torn hem of my robe became entangled between my legs. I stepped on it, and fell violently on my face.

In the confusion attending my fall, I did not immediately apprehend a somewhat startling circumstance, which yet, in a few seconds afterward, and while I still lay prostrate, arrested my attention. It was this: my chin rested upon the floor of the prison, but my lips and the upper portion of my head, although seemingly at a less elevation than the chin, touched nothing. At the same time, my forehead seemed bathed in a clammy vapor, and the peculiar smell of decayed fungus arose to my nostrils. I put forward my arm, and shuddered to find that I had fallen at the very brink of a circular pit, whose extent, of course, I had no means of ascertaining at the moment. Groping about the masonry just below the margin, I succeeded in dislodging a small fragment, and let it fall into the abyss. For many seconds I hearkened to its reverberations as it dashed against the sides of the chasm in its descent: at length, there was a sullen plunge into water, succeeded by loud echoes. At the same moment, there came a sound resembling the quick opening, and as rapid closing of a door overhead, while a faint gleam of light flashed suddenly through the gloom, and as suddenly faded away.

I saw clearly the doom which had been prepared for me, and congratulated myself upon the timely accident by which I had escaped. Another step before my fall, and the world had seen me no more. And the death just avoided was of that very character which I had regarded as fabulous and frivolous in the tales respecting the Inquisition. To the victims of its tyranny, there was the choice of death with its direst physical agonies, or death with its most hideous moral horrors. I had been reserved for the latter. By long suffering my nerves had been unstrung, until I trembled at the sound of my own voice, and had become in every respect a fitting subject for the species of torture which awaited me.

Shaking in every limb, I groped my way back to the wall—resolving there to perish rather than risk the terrors of the wells, of which my imagination now pictured many in various positions about the dungeon. In other conditions of mind, I might have had courage to end my misery at once, by a plunge into one of these abysses; but now I was the veriest of cowards. Neither could I forget what I had read of these pits—that the *sudden* extinction of life formed no part of their most horrible plan.

Agitation of spirit kept me awake for many long hours; but at length I again slumbered. Upon arousing, I found by my side, as before, a loaf and a pitcher of water. A burning thirst consumed me, and I emptied the vessel at a draught. It must have been drugged—for scarcely had I drunk, before I became irresistibly drowsy. A deep sleep fell upon me—a sleep like that of death. How long it lasted, of course I know not; but when, once again, I unclosed my eyes, the objects around me were visible. By a wild, sulphurous lustre, the origin of which I could not at first determine, I was enabled to see the extent and aspect of the prison.

In its size I had been greatly mistaken. The whole circuit of its walls did not exceed twenty-five yards. For some minutes this fact occasioned me a world of vain trouble; vain indeed—for what could be of less importance, under the terrible circumstances which environed me, than the mere dimensions of my dungeon? But my soul took a wild interest in trifles, and I busied myself in endeavors to account for the error I had committed in my measurement. The truth at length flashed upon me. In my first attempt at exploration, I had counted fifty-two paces, up to the period when I fell: I must then have been within a pace or two of the fragment of serge; in fact, I had nearly performed the circuit of the vault. I then slept—and, upon awaking, I must have returned upon my steps—thus supposing the circuit nearly double what it actually was. My confusion of mind prevented me from observing that I began my tour with the wall to the left, and ended it with the wall to the right.

I had been deceived, too, in respect to the shape of the enclosure. In feeling my way, I had found many angles, and thus deduced an idea of great irregularity; so potent is the effect of total darkness upon one arousing from lethargy or sleep! The angles were simply those of a few slight depressions, or niches, at odd intervals. The general shape of the prison was square. What I had taken for masonry seemed now to be iron, or some other metal, in huge plates, whose sutures or joints occasioned the depressions. The entire surface of this metallic enclosure was rudely daubed in all the hideous and repulsive devices to which the charnel superstition of the monks has given rise. The figures of fiends in aspects of menace, with skeleton forms, and other more really fearful images, overspread and disfigured the walls. I observed that the outlines of these monstrosities were sufficiently distinct, but that the colors seemed faded and blurred, as if from the effects of a damp atmosphere. I now noticed the floor, too, which was of stone. In the centre yawned the circular pit from whose jaws I had escaped; but it was the only one in the dungeon.

All this I saw indistinctly and by much effort—for my personal condition had been greatly changed during slumber. I now lay upon my back, and at full length, on a species of low framework of wood. To this I was securely bound by a long strap resembling a surcingle. It passed in many convolutions about my limbs and body, leaving at liberty only my head, and my left arm to such extent, that I could, by dint of much exertion, supply myself with food from an earthen dish which lay by my side on the floor. I saw, to my horror, that the pitcher had been removed. I say, to my horror—for I was consumed with intolerable thirst. This thirst it appeared to be the design of my persecutors to stimulate—for the food in the dish was meat pungently seasoned.

Looking upward, I surveyed the ceiling of my prison. It was some thirty or forty feet overhead, and constructed much as the side walls.

In one of its panels a very singular figure riveted my whole attention. It was the painted figure of Time as he is commonly represented, save that, in lieu of a scythe, he held what, at a casual glance, I supposed to be the pictured image of a huge pendulum, such as we see on antique clocks. There was something, however, in the appearance of this machine which caused me to regard it more attentively. While I gazed directly upward at it, (for its position was immediately over my own,) I fancied that I saw it in motion. In an instant afterward the fancy was confirmed. Its sweep was brief, and of course slow. I watched it for some minutes, somewhat in fear, but more in wonder. Wearied at length with observing its dull movement, I turned my eyes upon the other objects in the cell.

A slight noise attracted my notice, and, looking to the floor, I saw several enormous rats traversing it. They had issued from the well, which lay just within view to my right. Even then, while I gazed, they came up in troops, hurriedly, with ravenous eyes, allured by the scent of the meat. From this it required much effort and attention to scare them away.

It might have been half an hour, perhaps even an hour, (for I could take but imperfect note of time) before I again cast my eyes upward. What I then saw confounded and amazed me. The sweep of the pendulum had increased in extent by nearly a yard. As a natural consequence, its velocity was also much greater. But what mainly disturbed me was the idea that it had perceptibly *descended*. I now observed—with what horror it is needless to say—that its nether extremity was formed of a crescent of glittering steel, about a foot in length from horn to horn; the horns upward, and the under edge evidently as keen as that of a razor. Like a razor also, it seemed massy and heavy, tapering from the edge into a solid and broad structure above. It was appended to a weighty rod of brass, and the whole *hissed* as it swung through the air.

I could no longer doubt the doom prepared for me by monkish ingenuity in torture. My cognizance of the pit had become known to the inquisitorial agents—*the pit*, whose horrors had been destined for so bold a recusant as myself—*the pit*, typical of hell, and regarded by rumor as the Ultima Thule of all their punishments. The plunge into this pit I had avoided by the merest of accidents, and I knew that surprise, or entrapment into torment, formed an important portion of all the grotesquerie of these dungeon deaths. Having failed to fall, it was no part of the demon plan to hurl me into the abyss; and thus (there being no alternative) a different and a milder destruction awaited me. Milder! I half smiled in my agony as I thought of such application of such a term.

What boots it to tell of the long, long hours of horror more than mortal, during which I counted the rushing oscillations of the steel! Inch by inch—line by line—with a descent only appreciable at intervals that seemed ages—down and still down it came! Days passed—it might have been that many days passed—ere it swept so closely over me as to fan me with its acrid breath. The odor of the sharp steel forced itself into my nostrils. I prayed—I wearied heaven with my prayer for its more speedy descent. I grew frantically mad, and struggled to force myself upward against the sweep of the fearful scimitar. And then I fell suddenly calm, and lay smiling at the glittering death, as a child at some rare bauble.

There was another interval of utter insensibility; it was brief; for, upon again lapsing into life, there had been no perceptible descent in the pendulum. But it might have been long—for I knew there were demons who took note of my swoon, and who could have arrested the vibration at pleasure. Upon my recovery, too, I felt very—oh, inexpressibly—sick and weak, as if through long inanition. Even amid the agonies of that period, the human nature craved food. With painful effort I outstretched my left arm as far as my bonds permitted, and took possession of the small remnant which had been spared me by the rats. As I put a portion of it within my lips, there rushed to my mind a half formed thought of joy—of hope. Yet what business had *I* with hope? It was, as I say, a half formed thought—man has many such, which are never completed. I felt that it was of joy—of hope; but I felt also that it had perished in its formation. In vain I struggled to perfect—to regain it. Long suffering had nearly annihilated all my ordinary powers of mind. I was an imbecile—an idiot.

The vibration of the pendulum was at right angles to my length. I saw that the crescent was designed to cross the region of the heart. It would fray the serge of my robe—it would return and repeat its operations—again—and again. Notwithstanding its terrifically wide sweep, (some thirty feet or more,) and the hissing vigor of its descent, sufficient to sunder these very walls of iron, still the fraying of my robe would be all that, for several minutes, it would accomplish. And at this thought I paused. I dared not go farther than this reflection. I dwelt upon it with a pertinacity of attention—as if, in so dwelling, I could arrest *here* the descent of the steel. I forced myself to ponder upon the sound of the crescent as it should pass across the garment—upon the peculiar thrilling sensation which the friction of cloth produces on the nerves. I pondered upon all this frivolity until my teeth were on edge.

Down—steadily down it crept. I took a frenzied pleasure in contrasting its downward with its lateral velocity. To the right—to the left—far and wide—with the shriek of a damned spirit! to my heart, with the stealthy pace of the tiger. I alternately laughed and howled, as the one or the other idea grew predominant.

Down—certainly, relentlessly down! It vibrated within three inches of my bosom! I struggled violently—furiously—to free my left arm. This was free only from the elbow to the hand. I could reach the latter, from the platter beside me, to my mouth, with great effort, but no farther. Could I have broken the fastenings above the elbow, I would have seized and attempted to arrest the pendulum. I might as well have attempted to arrest an avalanche!

Down—still unceasingly—still inevitably down! I gasped and struggled at each vibration. I shrunk convulsively at its every sweep. My eyes followed its outward or upward whirls with the eagerness of the most unmeaning despair; they closed themselves spasmodically at the descent, although death would have been a relief, oh, how unspeakable! Still I quivered in every nerve to think how slight a sinking of the machinery would precipitate that keen, glistening axe upon my bosom. It was *hope* that prompted the nerve to quiver—the frame to shrink. It was *hope*—the hope that triumphs on the rack—that whispers to the death-condemned even in the dungeons of the Inquisition.

I saw that some ten or twelve vibrations would bring the steel in actual contact with my robe—and with this observation there suddenly came over my spirit all the keen, collected calmness of despair. For the first time during many hours—or perhaps days—I *thought*. It now occurred to me, that the bandage, or surcingle, which enveloped me, was *unique*. I was tied by no separate cord. The first stroke of the razor-like crescent athwart any portion of the band, would so detach it that it might be unwound from my person by means of my left hand. But how fearful, in that case, the proximity of the steel! The result of the slightest struggle, how deadly! Was it likely, moreover, that the minions of the torturer had not foreseen and provided for this possibility? Was it probable that the bandage crossed my bosom in the track of the pendulum? Dreading to find my faint, and, as it seemed, my last hope frustrated, I so far elevated my head as to obtain a distinct view of my breast. The surcingle enveloped my limbs and body close in all directions—*save in the path of the destroying crescent.*

Scarcely had I dropped my head back into its original position, when there flashed upon my mind what I cannot better describe than as the unformed half of that idea of deliverance to which I have previously alluded, and of which a moiety only floated indeterminately through my brain when I raised food to my burning lips. The whole thought was now present—feeble, scarcely sane, scarcely definite—but still entire. I proceeded at once, with the nervous energy of despair, to attempt its execution.

For many hours the immediate vicinity of the low framework upon which I lay, had been literally swarming with rats. They were wild, bold, ravenous—their red eyes glaring upon me as if they waited but for motionlessness on my part to make me their prey. 'To what food,' I thought, 'have they been accustomed in the well?'

They had devoured, in spite of all my efforts to prevent them, all but a small remnant of the contents of the dish. I had fallen into an habitual see-saw, or wave of the hand about the platter; and, at length, the unconscious uniformity of the movement deprived it of effect. In their voracity, the vermin frequently fastened their sharp fangs in my fingers. With the particles of the oily and spicy viand which now remained, I thoroughly rubbed the bandage wherever I could reach it; then, raising my hand from the floor, I lay breathlessly still.

At first the ravenous animals were startled and terrified at the change—at the cessation of movement. They shrank alarmedly back; many sought the well. But this was only for a moment. I had not counted in vain upon their voracity. Observing that I remained without motion, one or two of the boldest leaped upon the frame-work, and smelt at the surcingle. This seemed the signal for a general rush. Forth from the well they hurried in fresh troops. They clung to the wood—they overran it, and leaped in hundreds upon my person. The measured movement of the pendulum disturbed them not at all. Avoiding its strokes, they busied themselves with the anointed bandage. They pressed—they swarmed upon me in ever accumulating heaps. They writhed upon my throat; their cold lips sought my own; I was half stifled by their thronging pressure; disgust, for which the world has no name, swelled my bosom, and chilled, with a heavy clamminess, my heart. Yet one minute, and I felt that the struggle would be over. Plainly I perceived the loosening of the bandage. I knew that in more than one place it must be already severed. With a more than human resolution I lay *still.*

Nor had I erred in my calculations—nor had I endured in vain. I at length felt that I was *free.* The surcingle hung in ribands from my body. But the stroke of the pendulum already pressed upon my bosom. It had divided the serge of the robe. It had cut through the linen beneath. Twice again it swung, and a sharp sense of pain shot through every nerve. But the moment of escape had arrived. At a wave of my hand my deliverers hurried tumultuously away. With a steady movement—cautious, sidelong, shrinking, and slow—I slid from the embrace of the bandage and beyond the reach of the scimitar. For the moment, at least, *I was free.*

Free!—and in the grasp of the Inquisition! I had scarcely stepped from my wooden bed of horror upon the stone floor of the prison, when the motion of the hellish machine ceased, and I beheld it drawn up, by some invisible force, through the ceiling. This was a lesson which I took desperately to heart. My every motion was undoubtedly watched. Free!—I had but escaped death in one form of agony, to be delivered unto worse than death in some other. With that thought I rolled my eyes nervously around on the barriers of iron that hemmed me in. Something unusual—some change which, at first, I could not appreciate distinctly—it was obvious, had taken place in the apartment. For many minutes of a dreamy and trembling abstraction, I busied myself in vain, unconnected conjecture. During this period, I became aware, for the first time, of the origin of the sulphurous light which illumined the cell. It proceeded from a fissure, about half an inch in width, extending entirely around the prison at the base of the walls, which thus appeared, and were completely separated from the floor. I endeavored, but of course in vain, to look through the aperture.

As I arose from the attempt, the mystery of the alteration in the chamber broke at once upon my understanding. I have observed that, although the outlines of the figures upon the walls were sufficiently distinct, yet the colors seemed blurred and indefinite. These colors had now assumed, and were momentarily assuming, a startling and most intense brilliancy, that gave to the spectral and fiendish portraitures an aspect that might have thrilled even firmer nerves than my own. Demon eyes, of a wild and ghastly vivacity, glared upon me in a thousand directions, where none had been visible before, and gleamed with the lurid lustre of a fire that I could not force my imagination to regard as unreal.

Unreal!—Even while I breathed there came to my nostrils the breath of the vapor of heated iron! A suffocating odor pervaded the prison! A deeper glow settled each moment in the eyes that glared at my agonies! A richer tint of crimson diffused itself over the pictured horrors of blood. I panted! I gasped for breath! There could be no doubt of the design of my tormentors—oh! most unrelenting! oh! most demoniac of men! I shrank from the glowing metal to the centre of the cell. Amid the thought of the fiery destruction that impended, the idea of the coolness of the well came over my soul like balm. I rushed to its deadly brink. I threw my straining vision below. The glare from the enkindled roof illumined its inmost recesses. Yet, for a wild moment, did my spirit refuse to comprehend the meaning of what I saw. At length it forced—it wrestled its way into my soul—it burned itself in upon my shuddering reason. Oh! for a voice to speak!—oh! horror!—oh! any horror but this! With a shriek, I rushed from the margin, and buried my face in my hands—weeping bitterly.

The heat rapidly increased, and once again I looked up, shuddering as with a fit of the ague. There had been a second change in the cell—and now the change was obviously in the *form*. As before, it was in vain that I at first endeavoured to appreciate or understand what was taking place. But not long was I left in doubt. The Inquisitorial vengeance had been hurried by my two-fold escape, and there was to be no more dallying with the King of Terrors. The room had been square. I saw that two of its iron angles were now acute—two, consequently, obtuse. The fearful difference quickly increased with a low rumbling or moaning sound. In an instant the apartment had shifted its form into that of a lozenge. But the alteration stopped not here—I neither hoped nor desired it to stop. I could have clasped the red walls to my bosom as a garment of eternal peace. 'Death,' I said, 'any death but that of the pit!' Fool! might I have not known that *into the pit* it was the object of the burning iron to urge me? Could I resist its glow? or if even that, could I withstand its pressure? And now, flatter and flatter grew the lozenge, with a rapidity that left me no time for contemplation. Its centre, and of course, its greatest width, came just over the yawning gulf. I shrank back—but the closing walls pressed me resistlessly onward. At length for my seared and writhing body there was no longer an inch of foothold on the firm floor of the prison. I struggled no more, but the agony of my soul found vent in one loud, long, and final scream of despair. I felt that I tottered upon the brink—I averted my eyes—

There was a discordant hum of human voices! There was a loud blast as of many trumpets! There was a harsh grating as of a thousand thunders! The fiery walls rushed back! An outstretched arm caught my own as I fell, fainting, into the abyss. It was that of General Lasalle. The French army had entered Toledo. The Inquisition was in the hands of its enemies.

THE MYSTERY OF MARIE ROGÊT[1]

A Sequel to 'The Murders in the Rue Morgue'

Es giebt eine Reihe idealischer Begebenheiten, die der Wirklichkeit parallel lauft. Selten fallen sie zusammen. Menschen und Zufälle modificiren gewöhnlich die idealische Begebenheit, so dass sie unvollkommen erscheint, und ihre Folgen gleichfalls unvollkommen sind. So bei der Reformation; statt des Protestantismus kam das Lutherthum hervor.

There are ideal series of events which run parallel with the real ones. They rarely coincide. Men and circumstances generally modify the ideal train of events, so that it seems imperfect, and its consequences are equally imperfect. Thus with the Reformation; instead of Protestantism came Lutheranism.

Novalis (the *nom de plume* of Von Hardenberg),
*Moralische Ansichten**

THERE are few persons, even among the calmest thinkers, who have not occasionally been startled into a vague yet thrilling half-credence in the supernatural, by *coincidences* of so seemingly marvellous a character that, as *mere* coincidences, the intellect has been unable to receive them. Such sentiments—for the half-credences of which I speak have never the full force of *thought*—are seldom thoroughly stifled unless by reference to the doctrine of chance, or, as it is

[1] On the original publication of 'Marie Rogêt,' the foot-notes now appended were considered unnecessary; but the lapse of several years since the tragedy upon which the tale is based, renders it expedient to give them, and also to say a few words in explanation of the general design. A young girl, *Mary Cecilia Rogers*, was murdered in the vicinity of New York; and, although her death occasioned an intense and long-enduring excitement, the mystery attending it had remained unsolved at the period when the present paper was written and published (November, 1842). Herein, under pretence of relating the fate of a Parisian *grisette*,* the author has followed, in minute detail, the essential, while merely paralleling the inessential facts of the real murder of Mary Rogers. Thus all argument founded upon the fiction is applicable to the truth: and the investigation of the truth was the object.

The 'Mystery of Marie Rogêt' was composed at a distance from the scene of the atrocity, and with no other means of investigation than the newspapers afforded. Thus much escaped the writer of which he could have availed himself had he been on the spot, and visited the localities. It may not be improper to record, nevertheless, that the confessions of *two* persons, (one of them the Madame Deluc of the narrative) made, at different periods, long subsequent to the publication, confirmed, in full, not only the general conclusion, but absolutely *all* the chief hypothetical details by which that conclusion was attained.

technically termed, the Calculus of Probabilities. Now this Calculus is, in its essence, purely mathematical; and thus we have the anomaly of the most rigidly exact in science applied to the shadow and spirituality of the most intangible in speculation.

The extraordinary details which I am now called upon to make public, will be found to form, as regards sequence of time, the primary branch of a series of scarcely intelligible *coincidences*, whose secondary or concluding branch will be recognized by all readers in the late murder of MARY CECILIA ROGERS, at New York.

When, in an article entitled 'The Murders in the Rue Morgue,' I endeavoured, about a year ago, to depict some very remarkable features in the mental character of my friend, the Chevalier C. Auguste Dupin, it did not occur to me that I should ever resume the subject. This depicting of character constituted my design; and this design was fulfilled in the train of circumstances brought to instance Dupin's idiosyncrasy. I might have adduced other examples, but I should have proven no more. Late events, however, in their surprising development, have startled me into some farther details, which will carry with them the air of extorted confession. Hearing what I have lately heard, it would be indeed strange should I remain silent in regard to what I both heard and saw so long ago.

Upon the winding up of the tragedy involved in the deaths of Madame L'Espanaye and her daughter, the Chevalier dismissed the affair at once from his attention, and relapsed into his old habits of moody reverie. Prone, at all times, to abstraction, I readily fell in with his humor; and, continuing to occupy our chambers in the Faubourg Saint Germain, we gave the Future to the winds, and slumbered tranquilly in the Present, weaving the dull world around us into dreams.

But these dreams were not altogether uninterrupted. It may readily be supposed that the part played by my friend, in the drama at the Rue Morgue, had not failed of its impression upon the fancies of the Parisian police. With its emissaries, the name of Dupin had grown into a household word. The simple character of those inductions by which he had disentangled the mystery never having been explained even to the Prefect, or to any other individual than myself, of course it is not surprising that the affair was regarded as little less than miraculous, or that the Chevalier's analytical abilities acquired for him the credit of intuition. His frankness would have led him to disabuse every inquirer of such prejudice; but his indolent humor forbade all farther agitation of a topic whose interest to himself had long ceased. It thus happened that he found himself the cynosure of the policial eyes; and the cases were not few in which attempt was made to engage his services at the Prefecture. One of the most remarkable instances was that of the murder of a young girl named Marie Rogêt.

This event occurred about two years after the atrocity in the Rue Morgue. Marie, whose Christian and family name will at once arrest attention from their resemblance to those of the unfortunate 'cigar-girl,' was the only daughter of the widow Estelle Rogêt. The father had died during the child's infancy, and from the period of his death, until within eighteen months before the assassination which forms the subject of our narrative, the mother and daughter had dwelt together in the Rue Pavée Saint Andrée;[1] Madame there keeping a *pension*, assisted by Marie. Affairs went on thus until the latter had attained her twenty-second year, when her great beauty attracted the notice of a perfumer, who occupied one of the shops in the basement of the Palais Royal, and whose custom lay chiefly among the desperate adventurers infesting that neighborhood. Monsieur Le Blanc[2] was not unaware of the advantages to be derived from the attendance of the fair Marie in his perfumery; and his liberal proposals were accepted eagerly by the girl, although with somewhat more of hesitation by Madame.

The anticipations of the shopkeeper were realized, and his rooms soon became notorious through the charms of the sprightly *grisette*. She had been in his employ about a year, when her admirers were thrown into confusion by her sudden disappearance from the shop. Monsieur Le Blanc was unable to account for her absence, and Madame Rogêt was distracted with anxiety and terror. The public papers immediately took up the theme, and the police were upon the point of making serious investigations, when, one fine morning, after the lapse of a week, Marie, in good health, but with a somewhat saddened air, made her re-appearance at her usual counter in the perfumery. All inquiry, except that of a private character, was of course immediately hushed. Monsieur Le Blanc professed total ignorance, as before. Marie, with Madame, replied to all questions, that the last week had been spent at the house of a relation in the country. Thus the affair died away, and was generally forgotten; for the girl, ostensibly to relieve herself from the impertinence of curiosity, soon bade a final

[1] Nassau Street.* [2] Anderson.

adieu to the perfumer, and sought the shelter of her mother's residence in the Rue Pavée Saint Andrée.

It was about three years after this return home, that her friends were alarmed by her sudden disappearance for the second time. Three days elapsed, and nothing was heard of her. On the fourth her corpse was found floating in the Seine,[1] near the shore which is opposite the Quartier of the Rue Saint Andrée, and at a point not very far distant from the secluded neighborhood of the Barrière du Roule.[2]

The atrocity of this murder, (for it was at once evident that murder had been committed,) the youth and beauty of the victim, and, above all, her previous notoriety, conspired to produce intense excitement in the minds of the sensitive Parisians. I can call to mind no similar occurrence producing so general and so intense an effect. For several weeks, in the discussion of this one absorbing theme, even the momentous political topics of the day were forgotten. The Prefect made unusual exertions; and the powers of the whole Parisian police were, of course, tasked to the utmost extent.

Upon the first discovery of the corpse, it was not supposed that the murderer would be able to elude, for more than a very brief period, the inquisition which was immediately set on foot. It was not until the expiration of a week that it was deemed necessary to offer a reward; and even then this reward was limited to a thousand francs. In the mean time the investigation proceeded with vigor, if not always with judgment, and numerous individuals were examined to no purpose; while, owing to the continual absence of all clue to the mystery, the popular excitement greatly increased. At the end of the tenth day it was thought advisable to double the sum originally proposed; and, at length, the second week having elapsed without leading to any discoveries, and the prejudice which always exists in Paris against the Police having given vent to itself in several serious *émeutes*,* the Prefect took it upon himself to offer the sum of twenty thousand francs 'for the conviction of the assassin,' or, if more than one should prove to have been implicated, 'for the conviction of any one of the assassins.' In the proclamation setting forth this reward, a full pardon was promised to any accomplice who should come forward in evidence against his fellow; and to the whole was appended, wherever it appeared, the private placard of a committee of citizens, offering ten thousand francs, in

[1] The Hudson. [2] Weehawken.

addition to the amount proposed by the Prefecture. The entire reward thus stood at no less than thirty thousand francs, which will be regarded as an extraordinary sum when we consider the humble condition of the girl, and the great frequency, in large cities, of such atrocities as the one described.

No one doubted now that the mystery of this murder would be immediately brought to light. But although, in one or two instances, arrests were made which promised elucidation, yet nothing was elicited which could implicate the parties suspected; and they were discharged forthwith. Strange as it may appear, the third week from the discovery of the body had passed, and passed without any light being thrown upon the subject, before even a rumor of the events which had so agitated the public reached the ears of Dupin and myself. Engaged in researches which had absorbed our whole attention, it had been nearly a month since either of us had gone abroad, or received a visiter, or more than glanced at the leading political articles in one of the daily papers. The first intelligence of the murder was brought us by G—, in person. He called upon us early in the afternoon of the thirteenth of July, 18—, and remained with us until late in the night. He had been piqued by the failure of all his endeavors to ferret out the assassins. His reputation—so he said with a peculiarly Parisian air—was at stake. Even his honor was concerned. The eyes of the public were upon him; and there was really no sacrifice which he would not be willing to make for the development of the mystery. He concluded a somewhat droll speech with a compliment upon what he was pleased to term the *tact* of Dupin, and made him a direct, and certainly a liberal proposition, the precise nature of which I do not feel myself at liberty to disclose, but which has no bearing upon the proper subject of my narrative.

The compliment my friend rebutted as best he could, but the proposition he accepted at once, although its advantages were altogether provisional. This point being settled, the Prefect broke forth at once into explanations of his own views, interspersing them with long comments upon the evidence; of which latter we were not yet in possession. He discoursed much, and beyond doubt, learnedly; while I hazarded an occasional suggestion as the night wore drowsily away. Dupin, sitting steadily in his accustomed arm-chair, was the embodiment of respectful attention. He wore spectacles, during the whole interview; and an occasional glance beneath their green glasses, sufficed to convince me that he slept not the less soundly, because silently, throughout the seven or eight leaden-footed hours which immediately preceded the departure of the Prefect.

In the morning, I procured, at the Prefecture, a full report of all the evidence elicited, and, at the various newspaper offices, a copy of every paper in which, from first to last, had been published any decisive information in regard to this sad affair. Freed from all that was positively disproved, this mass of information stood thus:

Marie Rogêt left the residence of her mother, in the Rue Pavée St Andrée, about nine o'clock in the morning of Sunday, June the twenty-second, 18—. In going out, she gave notice to a Monsieur Jacques St Eustache,[1] and to him only, of her intention to spend the day with an aunt who resided in the Rue des Drômes. The Rue des Drômes is a short and narrow but populous thoroughfare, not far from the banks of the river, and at a distance of some two miles, in the most direct course possible, from the *pension* of Madame Rogêt. St Eustache was the accepted suitor of Marie, and lodged, as well as took his meals, at the *pension*. He was to have gone for his betrothed at dusk, and to have escorted her home. In the afternoon, however, it came on to rain heavily; and, supposing that she would remain all night at her aunt's, (as she had done under similar circumstances before,) he did not think it necessary to keep his promise. As night drew on, Madame Rogêt (who was an infirm old lady, seventy years of age,) was heard to express a fear 'that she should never see Marie again;' but this observation attracted little attention at the time.

On Monday, it was ascertained that the girl had not been to the Rue des Drômes; and when the day elapsed without tidings of her, a tardy search was instituted at several points in the city, and its environs. It was not, however, until the fourth day from the period of her disappearance that any thing satisfactory was ascertained respecting her. On this day, (Wednesday, the twenty-fifth of June,) a Monsieur Beauvais,[2] who, with a friend, had been making inquiries for Marie near the Barrière du Roule, on the shore of the Seine which is opposite the Rue Pavée St Andrée, was informed that a corpse had just been towed ashore by some fishermen, who had found it floating in the river. Upon seeing the body, Beauvais, after some hesitation, identified it as that of the perfumery-girl. His friend recognized it more promptly.

[1] Payne. [2] Crommelin.

The face was suffused with dark blood, some of which issued from the mouth. No foam was seen, as in the case of the merely drowned. There was no discoloration in the cellular tissue. About the throat were bruises and impressions of fingers. The arms were bent over on the chest and were rigid. The right hand was clenched; the left partially open. On the left wrist were two circular excoriations, apparently the effect of ropes, or of a rope in more than one volution. A part of the right wrist, also, was much chafed, as well as the back throughout its extent, but more especially at the shoulder-blades. In bringing the body to the shore the fishermen had attached to it a rope; but none of the excoriations had been effected by this. The flesh of the neck was much swollen. There were no cuts apparent, or bruises which appeared the effect of blows. A piece of lace was found tied so tightly around the neck as to be hidden from sight; it was completely buried in the flesh, and was fastened by a knot which lay just under the left ear. This alone would have sufficed to produce death. The medical testimony spoke confidently of the virtuous character of the deceased. She had been subjected, it said, to brutal violence. The corpse was in such condition when found, that there could have been no difficulty in its recognition by friends.

The dress was much torn and otherwise disordered. In the outer garment, a slip, about a foot wide, had been torn upward from the bottom hem to the waist, but not torn off. It was wound three times around the waist, and secured by a sort of hitch in the back. The dress immediately beneath the frock was of fine muslin; and from this a slip eighteen inches wide had been torn entirely out—torn very evenly and with great care. It was found around her neck, fitting loosely, and secured with a hard knot. Over this muslin slip and the slip of lace, the strings of a bonnet were attached; the bonnet being appended. The knot by which the strings of the bonnet were fastened, was not a lady's, but a slip or sailor's knot.

After the recognition of the corpse, it was not, as usual, taken to the Morgue, (this formality being superfluous,) but hastily interred not far from the spot at which it was brought ashore. Through the exertions of Beauvais, the matter was industriously hushed up, as far as possible; and several days had elapsed before any public emotion resulted. A weekly paper,[1] however, at length took up the theme; the corpse was

[1] The 'N. Y. Mercury.'

disinterred, and a re-examination instituted; but nothing was elicited beyond what has been already noted. The clothes, however, were now submitted to the mother and friends of the deceased, and fully identified as those worn by the girl upon leaving home.

Meantime, the excitement increased hourly. Several individuals were arrested and discharged. St Eustache fell especially under suspicion; and he failed, at first, to give an intelligible account of his whereabouts during the Sunday on which Marie left home. Subsequently, however, he submitted to Monsieur G—, affidavits, accounting satisfactorily for every hour of the day in question. As time passed and no discovery ensued, a thousand contradictory rumors were circulated, and journalists busied themselves in *suggestions*. Among these the one which attracted the most notice, was the idea that Marie Rogêt still lived—that the corpse found in the Seine was that of some other unfortunate. It will be proper that I submit to the reader some passages which embody the suggestion alluded to. These passages are *literal* translations from L'Etoile,[1] a paper conducted, in general, with much ability.

'Mademoiselle Rogêt left her mother's house on Sunday morning, June the twenty-second, 18—, with the ostensible purpose of going to see her aunt, or some other connexion, in the Rue des Drômes. From that hour, nobody is proved to have seen her. There is no trace or tidings of her at all. * * * There has no person, whatever, come forward, so far, who saw her at all, on that day, after she left her mother's door. * * * Now, though we have no evidence that Marie Rogêt was in the land of the living after nine o'clock on Sunday, June the twenty-second, we have proof that, up to that hour, she was alive. On Wednesday noon, at twelve, a female body was discovered afloat on the shore of the Barrière du Roule. This was, even if we presume that Marie Rogêt was thrown into the river within three hours after she left her mother's house, only three days from the time she left her home—three days to an hour. But it is folly to suppose that the murder, if murder was committed on her body, could have been consummated soon enough to have enabled her murderers to throw the body into the river before midnight. Those who are guilty of such horrid crimes, choose darkness rather than light. * * * Thus we see that if the body found in the river *was* that of Marie Rogêt, it could only have been in the water two and a half days, or three at the outside. All experience has shown that drowned bodies, or bodies thrown into the water immediately after death by violence, require from six to ten days for sufficient decomposition to take

[1] The 'N. Y. Brother Jonathan,' edited by H. Hastings Weld, Esq.

place to bring them to the top of the water. Even where a cannon is fired over a corpse, and it rises before at least five or six days' immersion, it sinks again, if left alone. Now, we ask, what was there in this case to cause a departure from the ordinary course of nature? * * * If the body had been kept in its mangled state on shore until Tuesday night, some trace would be found on shore of the murderers. It is a doubtful point, also, whether the body would be so soon afloat, even were it thrown in after having been dead two days. And, furthermore, it is exceedingly improbable that any villains who had committed such a murder as is here supposed, would have thrown the body in without weight to sink it, when such a precaution could have so easily been taken.'

The editor here proceeds to argue that the body must have been in the water 'not three days merely, but, at least, five times three days,' because it was so far decomposed that Beauvais had great difficulty in recognizing it. This latter point, however, was fully disproved. I continue the translation:

'What, then, are the facts on which M. Beauvais says that he has no doubt the body was that of Marie Rogêt? He ripped up the gown sleeve, and says he found marks which satisfied him of the identity. The public generally supposed those marks to have consisted of some description of scars. He rubbed the arm and found *hair* upon it—something as indefinite, we think, as can readily be imagined—as little conclusive as finding an arm in the sleeve. M. Beauvais did not return that night, but sent word to Madame Rogêt, at seven o'clock, on Wednesday evening, that an investigation was still in progress respecting her daughter. If we allow that Madame Rogêt, from her age and grief, could not go over, (which is allowing a great deal,) there certainly must have been some one who would have thought it worth while to go over and attend the investigation, if they thought the body was that of Marie. Nobody went over. There was nothing said or heard about the matter in the Rue Pavée St Andrée, that reached even the occupants of the same building. M. St Eustache, the lover and intended husband of Marie, who boarded in her mother's house, deposes that he did not hear of the discovery of the body of his intended until the next morning, when M. Beauvais came into his chamber and told him of it. For an item of news like this, it strikes us it was very coolly received.'

In this way the journal endeavored to create the impression of an apathy on the part of the relatives of Marie, inconsistent with the supposition that these relatives believed the corpse to be hers. Its insinuations amount to this:—that Marie, with the connivance of her friends, had absented herself from the city for reasons involving a charge against her chastity; and that these friends, upon the discovery of a corpse in the Seine, somewhat resembling that of the girl, had availed themselves of the opportunity to impress the public with the belief of her death. But L'Etoile was again overhasty. It was distinctly proved that no apathy, such as was imagined, existed; that the old lady was exceedingly feeble, and so agitated as to be unable to attend to any duty; that St Eustache, so far from receiving the news coolly, was distracted with grief, and bore himself so frantically, that M. Beauvais prevailed upon a friend and relative to take charge of him, and prevent his attending the examination at the disinterment. Moreover, although it was stated by L'Etoile, that the corpse was re-interred at the public expense—that an advantageous offer of private sepulture was absolutely declined by the family—and that no member of the family attended the ceremonial:—although, I say, all this was asserted by L'Etoile in furtherance of the impression it designed to convey—yet *all* this was satisfactorily disproved. In a subsequent number of the paper, an attempt was made to throw suspicion upon Beauvais himself. The editor says:

'Now, then, a change comes over the matter. We are told that, on one occasion, while a Madame B—— was at Madame Rogêt's house, M. Beauvais, who was going out, told her that a *gendarme* was expected there, and that she, Madame B., must not say anything to the *gendarme* until he returned, but let the matter be for him. * * * In the present posture of affairs, M. Beauvais appears to have the whole matter locked up in his head. A single step cannot be taken without M. Beauvais; for, go which way you will, you run against him. * * * For some reason, he determined that nobody shall have any thing to do with the proceedings but himself, and he has elbowed the male relatives out of the way, according to their representations, in a very singular manner. He seems to have been very much averse to permitting the relatives to see the body.'

By the following fact, some color was given to the suspicion thus thrown upon Beauvais. A visiter at his office, a few days prior to the girl's disappearance, and during the absence of its occupant, had observed *a rose* in the key-hole of the door, and the name '*Marie*' inscribed upon a slate which hung near at hand.

The general impression, so far as we were enabled to glean it from the newspapers, seemed to be, that Marie had been the victim of *a gang* of desperadoes—that by these she had been borne across the river, maltreated and murdered. Le Commerciel,[1] however, a print of exten-

[1] N. Y. 'Journal of Commerce.'

sive influence, was earnest in combating this popular idea. I quote a passage or two from its columns:

'We are persuaded that pursuit has hitherto been on a false scent, so far as it has been directed to the Barrière du Roule. It is impossible that a person so well known to thousands as this young woman was, should have passed three blocks without some one having seen her; and any one who saw her would have remembered it, for she interested all who knew her. It was when the streets were full of people, when she went out. * * * It is impossible that she could have gone to the Barrière du Roule, or to the Rue des Drômes, without being recognized by a dozen persons; yet no one has come forward who saw her outside of her mother's door, and there is no evidence, except the testimony concerning her *expressed intentions*, that she did go out at all. Her gown was torn, bound round her, and tied; and by that the body was carried as a bundle. If the murder had been committed at the Barrière du Roule, there would have been no necessity for any such arrangement. The fact that the body was found floating near the Barrière, is no proof as to where it was thrown into the water. * * * A piece of one of the unfortunate girl's petticoats, two feet long and one foot wide, was torn out and tied under her chin around the back of her head, probably to prevent screams. This was done by fellows who had no pocket-handkerchief.'

A day or two before the Prefect called upon us, however, some important information reached the police, which seemed to overthrow, at least, the chief portion of Le Commerciel's argument. Two small boys, sons of a Madame Deluc, while roaming among the woods near the Barrière du Roule, chanced to penetrate a close thicket, within which were three or four large stones, forming a kind of seat, with a back and footstool. On the upper stone lay a white petticoat; on the second a silk scarf. A parasol, gloves, and a pocket-handkerchief were also here found. The handkerchief bore the name 'Marie Rogêt.' Fragments of dress were discovered on the brambles around. The earth was trampled, the bushes were broken, and there was every evidence of a struggle. Between the thicket and the river, the fences were found taken down, and the ground bore evidence of some heavy burthen having been dragged along it.

A weekly paper, Le Soleil,[1] had the following comments upon this discovery—comments which merely echoed the sentiment of the whole Parisian press:

[1] Phil. 'Sat. Evening Post,' edited by C. J. Peterson, Esq.

'The things had all evidently been there at least three or four weeks; they were all mildewed down hard with the action of the rain, and stuck together from mildew. The grass had grown around and over some of them. The silk on the parasol was strong, but the threads of it were run together within. The upper part, where it had been doubled and folded, was all mildewed and rotten, and tore on its being opened. * * * The pieces of her frock torn out by the bushes were about three inches wide and six inches long. One part was the hem of the frock, and it had been mended; the other piece was part of the skirt, not the hem. They looked like strips torn off, and were on the thorn bush, about a foot from the ground. * * * There can be no doubt, therefore, that the spot of this appalling outrage has been discovered.'

Consequent upon this discovery, new evidence appeared. Madame Deluc testified that she keeps a roadside inn not far from the bank of the river, opposite the Barrière du Roule. The neighborhood is secluded—particularly so. It is the usual Sunday resort of blackguards from the city, who cross the river in boats. About three o'clock, in the afternoon of the Sunday in question, a young girl arrived at the inn, accompanied by a young man of dark complexion. The two remained here for some time. On their departure, they took the road to some thick woods in the vicinity. Madame Deluc's attention was called to the dress worn by the girl, on account of its resemblance to one worn by a deceased relative. A scarf was particularly noticed. Soon after the departure of the couple, a gang of miscreants made their appearance, behaved boisterously, ate and drank without making payment, followed in the route of the young man and girl, returned to the inn about dusk, and re-crossed the river as if in great haste.

It was soon after dark, upon this same evening, that Madame Deluc, as well as her eldest son, heard the screams of a female in the vicinity of the inn. The screams were violent but brief. Madame D. recognized not only the scarf which was found in the thicket, but the dress which was discovered upon the corpse. An omnibus-driver, Valence,[1] now also testified that he saw Marie Rogêt cross a ferry on the Seine, on the Sunday in question, in company with a young man of dark complexion. He, Valence, knew Marie, and could not be mistaken in her identity. The articles found in the thicket were fully identified by the relatives of Marie.

The items of evidence and information thus collected by myself,

[1] Adam.

from the newspapers, at the suggestion of Dupin, embraced only one more point—but this was a point of seemingly vast consequence. It appears that, immediately after the discovery of the clothes as above described, the lifeless, or nearly lifeless body of St Eustache, Marie's betrothed, was found in the vicinity of what all now supposed the scene of the outrage. A phial labelled 'laudanum,' and emptied, was found near him. His breath gave evidence of the poison. He died without speaking. Upon his person was found a letter, briefly stating his love for Marie, with his design of self-destruction.

'I need scarcely tell you,' said Dupin, as he finished the perusal of my notes, 'that this is a far more intricate case than that of the Rue Morgue; from which it differs in one important respect. This is an *ordinary*, although an atrocious instance of crime. There is nothing peculiarly *outré* about it. You will observe that, for this reason, the mystery has been considered easy, when, for this reason, it should have been considered difficult, of solution. Thus, at first, it was thought unnecessary to offer a reward. The myrmidons of G—were able at once to comprehend how and why such an atrocity *might have been* committed. They could picture to their imaginations a mode—many modes—and a motive—many motives; and because it was not impossible that either of these numerous modes and motives *could* have been the actual one, they have taken it for granted that one of them *must*. But the ease with which these variable fancies were entertained, and the very plausibility which each assumed, should have been understood as indicative rather of the difficulties than of the facilities which must attend elucidation. I have before observed that it is by prominences above the plane of the ordinary, that reason feels her way, if at all, in her search for the true, and that the proper question in cases such as this, is not so much "what has occurred" as "what has occurred that has never occurred before?" In the investigations at the house of Madame L'Espanaye,[1] the agents of G—were discouraged and confounded by that very *unusualness* which, to a properly regulated intellect, would have afforded the surest omen of success; while this same intellect might have been plunged in despair at the ordinary character of all that met the eye in the case of the perfumery-girl, and yet told of nothing but easy triumph to the functionaries of the Prefecture.

'In the case of Madame L'Espanaye and her daughter, there was, even at the beginning of our investigation, no doubt that murder had

[1] See 'Murders in the Rue Morgue.'

been committed. The idea of suicide was excluded at once. Here, too, we are freed, at the commencement, from all supposition of self-murder. The body found at the Barrière du Roule, was found under such circumstances as to leave us no room for embarrassment upon this important point. But it has been suggested that the corpse discovered, is not that of the Marie Rogêt for the conviction of whose assassin, or assassins, the reward is offered, and respecting whom, solely, our agreement has been arranged with the Prefect. We both know this gentleman well. It will not do to trust him too far. If, dating our inquiries from the body found, and thence tracing a murderer, we yet discover this body to be that of some other individual than Marie; or, if starting from the living Marie, we find her, yet find her unassassinated—in either case we lose our labor; since it is Monsieur G—with whom we have to deal. For our own purpose, therefore, if not for the purpose of justice, it is indispensable that our first step should be the determination of the identity of the corpse with the Marie Rogêt who is missing.

'With the public the arguments of L'Etoile have had weight; and that the journal itself is convinced of their importance would appear from the manner in which it commences one of its essays upon the subject. "Several of the morning papers of the day," it says, "speak of the *conclusive* article in Monday's Etoile." To me, this article appears conclusive of little beyond the zeal of its inditer. We should bear in mind that, in general, it is the object of our newspapers rather to create a sensation—to make a point—than to further the cause of truth. The latter end is only pursued when it seems coincident with the former. The print which merely falls in with ordinary opinion (however well founded this opinion may be) earns for itself no credit with the mob. The mass of the people regard as profound only him who suggests *pungent contradictions* of the general idea. In ratiocination, not less than in literature, it is the *epigram* which is the most immediately and the most universally appreciated. In both, it is of the lowest order of merit.

'What I mean to say is, that it is the mingled epigram and melo-drame of the idea, that Marie Rogêt still lives, rather than any true plausibility in this idea, which have suggested it to L'Etoile, and secured it a favorable reception with the public. Let us examine the heads of this journal's argument; endeavoring to avoid the incoherence with which it is originally set forth.

'The first aim of the writer is to show, from the brevity of the interval between Marie's disappearance and the finding of the floating corpse, that this corpse cannot be that of Marie. The reduction of this interval to its smallest possible dimension, becomes thus, at once, an object with the reasoner. In the rash pursuit of this object, he rushes into mere assumption at the outset. "It is folly to suppose," he says, "that the murder, if murder was committed on her body, could have been consummated soon enough to have enabled her murderers to throw the body into the river before midnight." We demand at once, and very naturally, *why?* Why is it folly to suppose that the murder was committed *within five minutes* after the girl's quitting her mother's house? Why is it folly to suppose that the murder was committed at any given period of the day? There have been assassinations at all hours. But, had the murder taken place at any moment between nine o'clock in the morning of Sunday, and a quarter before midnight, there would still have been time enough "to throw the body into the river before midnight." This assumption, then, amounts precisely to this—that the murder was not committed on Sunday at all—and, if we allow L'Etoile to assume this, we may permit it any liberties whatever. The paragraph beginning "It is folly to suppose that the murder, etc.," however it appears as printed in L'Etoile, may be imagined to have existed actually *thus* in the brain of its inditer—"It is folly to suppose that the murder, if murder was committed on the body, could have been committed soon enough to have enabled her murderers to throw the body into the river before midnight; it is folly, we say, to suppose all this, and to suppose at the same time, (as we are resolved to suppose,) that the body was *not* thrown in until *after* midnight"—a sentence sufficiently inconsequential in itself, but not so utterly preposterous as the one printed.

'Were it my purpose,' continued Dupin, 'merely to *make out a case* against this passage of L'Etoile's argument, I might safely leave it where it is. It is not, however, with L'Etoile that we have to do, but with the truth. The sentence in question has but one meaning, as it stands; and this meaning I have fairly stated: but it is material that we go behind the mere words, for an idea which these words have obviously intended, and failed to convey. It was the design of the journalist to say that, at whatever period of the day or night of Sunday this murder was committed, it was improbable that the assassins would have ventured to bear the corpse to the river before midnight. And herein lies, really, the assumption of which I complain. It is assumed that the murder was committed at such a position, and under such circumstances, that *the bearing it* to the river became necessary. Now, the assassination might have taken place upon the river's brink, or on the river itself; and, thus, the throwing the corpse in the water might have been resorted to, at any period of the day or night, as the most obvious and most immediate mode of disposal. You will understand that I suggest nothing here as probable, or as coincident with my own opinion. My design, so far, has no reference to the *facts* of the case. I wish merely to caution you against the whole tone of L'Etoile's *suggestion*, by calling your attention to its *ex parte* character at the outset.

'Having prescribed thus a limit to suit its own preconceived notions; having assumed that, if this were the body of Marie, it could have been in the water but a very brief time; the journal goes on to say:

> "All experience has shown that drowned bodies, or bodies thrown into the water immediately after death by violence, require from six to ten days for sufficient decomposition to take place to bring them to the top of the water. Even where a cannon is fired over a corpse, and it rises before at least five or six days' immersion, it sinks again if let alone."

'These assertions have been tacitly received by every paper in Paris, with the exception of Le Moniteur.[1] This latter print endeavors to combat that portion of the paragraph which has reference to "drowned bodies" only, by citing some five or six instances in which the bodies of individuals known to be drowned were found floating after the lapse of less time than is insisted upon by L'Etoile. But there is something excessively unphilosophical in the attempt on the part of Le Moniteur, to rebut the general assertion of L'Etoile, by a citation of particular instances militating against that assertion. Had it been possible to adduce fifty instead of five examples of bodies found floating at the end of two or three days, these fifty examples could still have been properly regarded only as exceptions to L'Etoile's rule, until such time as the rule itself should be confuted. Admitting the rule, (and this Le Moniteur does not deny, insisting merely upon its exceptions,) the argument of L'Etoile is suffered to remain in full force; for this argument does not pretend to involve more than a question of the *probability* of the body having risen to the surface in less than three days; and this probability will be in favor of L'Etoile's position until the instances so childishly adduced shall be sufficient in number to establish an antagonistical rule.

[1] The 'N. Y. Commercial Advertiser,' edited by Col. Stone.

'You will see at once that all argument upon this head should be urged, if at all, against the rule itself; and for this end we must examine the *rationale* of the rule. Now the human body, in general, is neither much lighter nor much heavier than the water of the Seine; that is to say, the specific gravity of the human body, in its natural condition, is about equal to the bulk of fresh water which it displaces. The bodies of fat and fleshy persons, with small bones, and of women generally, are lighter than those of the lean and large-boned, and of men; and the specific gravity of the water of a river is somewhat influenced by the presence of the tide from sea. But, leaving this tide out of question, it may be said that *very* few human bodies will sink at all, even in fresh water, *of their own accord*. Almost any one, falling into a river, will be enabled to float, if he suffer the specific gravity of the water fairly to be adduced in comparison with his own—that is to say, if he suffer his whole person to be immersed, with as little exception as possible. The proper position for one who cannot swim, is the upright position of the walker on land, with the head thrown fully back, and immersed; the mouth and nostrils alone remaining above the surface. Thus circumstanced, we shall find that we float without difficulty and without exertion. It is evident, however, that the gravities of the body, and of the bulk of water displaced, are very nicely balanced, and that a trifle will cause either to preponderate. An arm, for instance, uplifted from the water, and thus deprived of its support, is an additional weight sufficient to immerse the whole head, while the accidental aid of the smallest piece of timber will enable us to elevate the head so as to look about. Now, in the struggles of one unused to swimming, the arms are invariably thrown upwards, while an attempt is made to keep the head in its usual perpendicular position. The result is the immersion of the mouth and nostrils, and the inception, during efforts to breathe while beneath the surface, of water into the lungs. Much is also received into the stomach, and the whole body becomes heavier by the difference between the weight of the air originally distending these cavities, and that of the fluid which now fills them. This difference is sufficient to cause the body to sink, as a general rule; but is insufficient in the cases of individuals with small bones and an abnormal quantity of flaccid or fatty matter. Such individuals float even after drowning.

'The corpse, being supposed at the bottom of the river, will there remain until, by some means, its specific gravity again becomes less than that of the bulk of water which it displaces. This effect is brought about by decomposition, or otherwise. The result of decomposition is the generation of gas, distending the cellular tissues and all the cavities, and giving the *puffed* appearance which is so horrible. When this distension has so far progressed that the bulk of the corpse is materially increased without a corresponding increase of *mass* or weight, its specific gravity becomes less than that of the water displaced, and it forthwith makes its appearance at the surface. But decomposition is modified by innumerable circumstances—is hastened or retarded by innumerable agencies; for example, by the heat or cold of the season, by the mineral impregnation or purity of the water, by its depth or shallowness, by its currency or stagnation, by the temperament of the body, by its infection or freedom from disease before death. Thus it is evident that we can assign no period, with any thing like accuracy, at which the corpse shall rise through decomposition. Under certain conditions this result would be brought about within an hour; under others, it might not take place at all. There are chemical infusions by which the animal frame can be preserved *forever* from corruption; the Bi-chloride of Mercury is one. But, apart from decomposition, there may be, and very usually is, a generation of gas within the stomach, from the acetous fermentation of vegetable matter (or within other cavities from other causes) sufficient to induce a distension which will bring the body to the surface. The effect produced by the firing of a cannon is that of simple vibration. This may either loosen the corpse from the soft mud or ooze in which it is imbedded, thus permitting it to rise when other agencies have already prepared it for so doing; or it may overcome the tenacity of some putrescent portions of the cellular tissue; allowing the cavities to distend under the influence of the gas.

'Having thus before us the whole philosophy of this subject, we can easily test by it the assertions of L'Etoile. "All experience shows," says this paper, "that drowned bodies, or bodies thrown into the water immediately after death by violence, require from six to ten days for sufficient decomposition to take place to bring them to the top of the water. Even when a cannon is fired over a corpse, and it rises before at least five or six days' immersion, it sinks again if let alone."

'The whole of this paragraph must now appear a tissue of inconsequence and incoherence. All experience does *not* show that "drowned bodies" *require* from six to ten days for sufficient decomposition to take place to bring them to the surface. Both science and experience show that the period of their rising is, and necessarily must be, indeterminate. If, moreover, a body has risen to the surface through firing cannon, it will *not* "sink again if let alone," until decomposition has so far progressed as to permit the escape of the generated gas. But I wish to call your attention to the distinction which is made between "drowned bodies," and "bodies thrown into the water immediately after death by violence." Although the writer admits the distinction, he yet includes them all in the same category. I have shown how it is that the body of a drowning man becomes specifically heavier than its bulk of water, and that he would not sink at all, except for the struggles by which he elevates his arms above the surface, and his gasps for breath while beneath the surface—gasps which supply by water the place of the original air in the lungs. But these struggles and these gasps would not occur in the body "thrown into the water immediately after death by violence." Thus, in the latter instance, *the body, as a general rule, would not sink at all*—a fact of which L'Etoile is evidently ignorant. When decomposition had proceeded to a very great extent—when the flesh had in a great measure left the bones—then, indeed, but not *till* then, should we lose sight of the corpse.

'And now what are we to make of the argument, that the body found could not be that of Marie Rogêt, because, three days only having elapsed, this body was found floating? If drowned, being a woman, she might never have sunk; or having sunk, might have re-appeared in twenty-four hours, or less. But no one supposes her to have been drowned; and, dying before being thrown into the river, she might have been found floating at any period afterwards whatever.

' "But," says L'Etoile, "if the body had been kept in its mangled state on shore until Tuesday night, some trace would be found on shore of the murderers." Here it is at first difficult to perceive the intention of the reasoner. He means to anticipate what he imagines would be an objection to his theory—viz: that the body was kept on shore two days, suffering rapid decomposition—*more* rapid than if immersed in water. He supposes that, had this been the case, it *might* have appeared at the surface on the Wednesday, and thinks that *only* under such circumstances it could so have appeared. He is accordingly in haste to show that *it was not* kept on shore; for, if so, "some trace would be found on shore of the murderers." I presume you smile at the *sequitur*.* You cannot be made to see how the mere *duration* of the corpse on the shore could operate to *multiply traces* of the assassins. Nor can I.

' "And furthermore it is exceedingly improbable," continues our journal, "that any villains who had committed such a murder as is here supposed, would have thrown the body in without weight to sink it, when such a precaution could have so easily been taken." Observe, here, the laughable confusion of thought! No one—not even L'Etoile—disputes the murder committed *on the body found*. The marks of violence are too obvious. It is our reasoner's object merely to show that this body is not Marie's. He wishes to prove that *Marie* is not assassinated—not that the corpse was not. Yet his observation proves only the latter point. Here is a corpse without weight attached. Murderers, casting it in, would not have failed to attach a weight. Therefore it was not thrown in by murderers. This is all which is proved, if any thing is. The question of identity is not even approached, and L'Etoile has been at great pains merely to gainsay now what it has admitted only a moment before. "We are perfectly convinced," it says, "that the body found was that of a murdered female."

'Nor is this the sole instance, even in this division of his subject, where our reasoner unwittingly reasons against himself. His evident object, I have already said, is to reduce, as much as possible, the interval between Marie's disappearance and the finding of the corpse. Yet we find him *urging* the point that no person saw the girl from the moment of her leaving her mother's house. "We have no evidence," he says, "that Marie Rogêt was in the land of the living after nine o'clock on Sunday, June the twenty-second". As his argument is obviously an *ex parte* one, he should, at least, have left this matter out of sight; for had any one been known to see Marie, say on Monday, or on Tuesday, the interval in question would have been much reduced, and, by his own ratiocination, the probability much diminished of the corpse being that of the *grisette*. It is, nevertheless, amusing to observe that L'Etoile insists upon its point in the full belief of its furthering its general argument.

'Reperuse now that portion of this argument which has reference to the identification of the corpse by Beauvais. In regard to the *hair* upon the arm, L'Etoile has been obviously disingenuous. M. Beauvais, not being an idiot, could never have urged, in identification of the corpse, simply *hair upon its arm*. No arm is *without* hair. The *generality* of the expression of L'Etoile is a mere perversion of the witness' phraseology. He must have spoken of some *peculiarity* in this hair. It must have been a peculiarity of color, of quantity, of length, or of situation.

' "Her foot," says the journal, "was small—so are thousands of feet. Her garter is no proof whatever—nor is her shoe—for shoes and garters are sold in packages. The same may be said of the flowers in her hat. One thing upon which M. Beauvais strongly insists is, that the clasp on the garter found, had been set back to take it in. This amounts to nothing; for most women find it proper to take a pair of garters home and fit them to the size of the limbs they are to encircle, rather than to try them in the store where they purchase." Here it is difficult to suppose the reasoner in earnest. Had M. Beauvais, in his search for the body of Marie, discovered a corpse corresponding in general size and appearance to the missing girl, he would have been warranted (without reference to the question of habiliment at all) in forming an opinion that his search had been successful. If, in addition to the point of general size and contour, he had found upon the arm a peculiar hairy appearance which he had observed upon the living Marie, his opinion might have been justly strengthened; and the increase of positiveness might well have been in the ratio of the peculiarity, or unusualness, of the hairy mark. If, the feet of Marie being small, those of the corpse were also small, the increase of probability that the body was that of Marie would not be an increase in a ratio merely arithmetical, but in one highly geometrical, or accumulative. Add to all this shoes such as she had been known to wear upon the day of her disappearance, and, although these shoes may be "sold in packages," you so far augment the probability as to verge upon the certain. What, of itself, would be no evidence of identity, becomes through its corroborative position, proof most sure. Give us, then, flowers in the hat corresponding to those worn by the missing girl, and we seek for nothing farther. If only *one* flower, we seek for nothing farther—what then if two or three, or more? Each successive one is multiple evidence—proof not *added* to proof, but *multiplied* by hundreds or thousands. Let us now discover, upon the deceased, garters such as the living used, and it is almost folly to proceed. But these garters are found to be tightened, by the setting back of a clasp, in just such a manner as her own had been tightened by Marie, shortly previous to her leaving home. It is now madness or hypocrisy to doubt. What L'Etoile says in respect to this abbreviation of the garter's being an usual occurrence, shows nothing beyond its own pertinacity in error. The elastic nature of the clasp-garter is self-demonstration of the *unusualness* of the abbreviation. What is made to adjust itself, must of necessity require foreign adjustment but rarely. It must have been by an accident, in its strictest sense, that these garters of Marie needed the tightening described. They alone would have amply established her identity. But it is not that the corpse was found to have the garters of the missing girl, or found to have her shoes, or her bonnet, or the flowers of her bonnet, or her feet, or a peculiar mark upon the arm, or her general size and appearance—it is that the corpse had each, and *all collectively*. Could it be proved that the editor of L'Etoile *really* entertained a doubt, under the circumstances, there would be no need, in his case, of a commission *de lunatico inquirendo*.* He has thought it sagacious to echo the small talk of the lawyers, who, for the most part, content themselves with echoing the rectangular precepts of the courts. I would here observe that very much of what is rejected as evidence by a court, is the best of evidence to the intellect. For the court, guiding itself by the general principles of evidence—the recognized and *booked* principles—is averse from swerving at particular instances. And this steadfast adherence to principle, with rigorous disregard of the conflicting exception, is a sure mode of attaining the *maximum* of attainable truth, in any long sequence of time. The practice, *in mass*, is therefore philosophical; but it is not the less certain that it engenders vast individual error.[1]

'In respect to the insinuations levelled at Beauvais, you will be willing to dismiss them in a breath. You have already fathomed the true character of this good gentleman. He is a *busy-body*, with much of romance and little of wit. Any one so constituted will readily so conduct himself, upon occasion of *real* excitement, as to render himself liable to suspicion on the part of the over-acute, or the ill-disposed. M. Beauvais (as it appears from your notes) had some personal interviews with the editor of L'Etoile, and offended him by venturing an opinion that the corpse, notwithstanding the theory of the editor, was, in sober fact that of Marie. "He persists," says the paper, "in asserting the corpse to be that of Marie, but cannot give a circumstance, in addition to those which we have commented upon, to make others believe." Now, without readverting to the fact that stronger evidence "to make

[1] 'A theory based on the qualities of an object, will prevent its being unfolded according to its objects; and he who arranges topics in reference to their causes, will cease to value them according to their results. Thus the jurisprudence of every nation will show that, when law becomes a science and a system, it ceases to be justice. The errors into which a blind devotion to *principles* of classification has led the common law, will be seen by observing how often the legislature has been obliged to come forward to restore the equity its scheme had lost.'—*Landor*.*

others believe," could *never* have been adduced, it may be remarked that a man may very well be understood to believe, in a case of this kind, without the ability to advance a single reason for the belief of a second party. Nothing is more vague than impressions of individual identity. Each man recognizes his neighbor, yet there are few instances in which any one is prepared to *give a reason* for his recognition. The editor of L'Etoile had no right to be offended at M. Beauvais' unreasoning belief.

'The suspicious circumstances which invest him, will be found to tally much better with my hypothesis of *romantic busy-bodyism*, than with the reasoner's suggestion of guilt. Once adopting the more charitable interpretation, we shall find no difficulty in comprehending the rose in the key-hole; the "Marie" upon the slate; the "elbowing the male relatives out of the way;" the "aversion to permitting them to see the body;" the caution given to Madame B—, that she must hold no conversation with the *gendarme* until his return (Beauvais'); and, lastly, his apparent determination "that nobody should have anything to do with the proceedings except himself." It seems to me unquestionable that Beauvais was a suitor of Marie's; that she coquetted with him; and that he was ambitious of being thought to enjoy her fullest intimacy and confidence. I shall say nothing more upon this point; and, as the evidence fully rebuts the assertion of L'Etoile, touching the matter of *apathy* on the part of the mother and other relatives—an apathy inconsistent with the supposition of their believing the corpse to be that of the perfumery-girl—we shall now proceed as if the question of *identity* were settled to our perfect satisfaction.'

'And what,' I here demanded, 'do you think of the opinions of Le Commerciel?'

'That, in spirit, they are far more worthy of attention than any which have been promulgated upon the subject. The deductions from the premises are philosophical and acute; but the premises, in two instances, at least, are founded in imperfect observation. Le Commerciel wishes to intimate that Marie was seized by some gang of low ruffians not far from her mother's door. "It is impossible," it urges, "that a person so well known to thousands as this young woman was, should have passed three blocks without some one having seen her." This is the idea of a man long resident in Paris—a public man—and one whose walks to and fro in the city, have been mostly limited to the vicinity of the public offices. He is aware that *he* seldom passes so far as a dozen blocks from his own *bureau*, without being recognized and accosted. And, knowing the extent of his personal acquaintance with others, and of others with him, he compares his notoriety with that of the perfumery-girl, finds no great difference between them, and reaches at once the conclusion that she, in her walks, would be equally liable to recognition with himself in his. This could only be the case were her walks of the same unvarying, methodical character, and within the same *species* of limited region as are his own. He passes to and fro, at regular intervals, within a confined periphery, abounding in individuals who are led to observation of his person through interest in the kindred nature of his occupation with their own. But the walks of Marie may, in general, be supposed discursive. In this particular instance, it will be understood as most probable, that she proceeded upon a route of more than average diversity from her accustomed ones. The parallel which we imagine to have existed in the mind of Le Commerciel would only be sustained in the event of the two individuals' traversing the whole city. In this case, granting the personal acquaintances to be equal, the chances would be also equal that an equal number of personal rencounters would be made. For my own part, I should hold it not only as possible, but as very far more than probable, that Marie might have proceeded, at any given period, by any one of the many routes between her own residence and that of her aunt, without meeting a single individual whom she knew, or by whom she was known. In viewing this question in its full and proper light, we must hold steadily in mind the great disproportion between the personal acquaintances of even the most noted individual in Paris, and the entire population of Paris itself.

'But whatever force there may still appear to be in the suggestion of Le Commerciel, will be much diminished when we take into consideration *the hour* at which the girl went abroad. "It was when the streets were full of people," says Le Commerciel, "that she went out." But not so. It was at nine o'clock in the morning. Now at nine o'clock of every morning in the week, *with the exception of Sunday*, the streets of the city are, it is true, thronged with people. At nine on Sunday, the populace are chiefly within doors *preparing for church*. No observing person can have failed to notice the peculiarly deserted air of the town, from about eight until ten on the morning of every Sabbath. Between ten and eleven the streets are thronged, but not at so early a period as that designated.

'There is another point at which there seems a deficiency of *observation* on the part of Le Commerciel. "A piece," it says, "of one of the unfortunate girl's petticoats, two feet long, and one foot wide, was torn out and tied under her chin, and around the back of her head, probably to prevent screams. This was done by fellows who had no pocket-handkerchiefs." Whether this idea is, or is not well founded, we will endeavor to see hereafter; but by "fellows who have no pocket-handkerchiefs," the editor intends the lowest class of ruffians. These, however, are the very description of people who will always be found to have handkerchiefs even when destitute of shirts. You must have had occasion to observe how absolutely indispensable, of late years, to the thorough blackguard, has become the pocket-handkerchief.'

'And what are we to think,' I asked, 'of the article in Le Soleil?'

'That it is a pity its inditer was not born a parrot—in which case he would have been the most illustrious parrot of his race. He has merely repeated the individual items of the already published opinion; collecting them, with a laudable industry, from this paper and from that. "The things had all *evidently* been there," he says, "at least, three or four weeks, and there can be *no doubt* that the spot of this appalling outrage has been discovered." The facts here re-stated by Le Soleil, are very far indeed from removing my own doubts upon this subject, and we will examine them more particularly hereafter in connexion with another division of the theme.

'At present we must occupy ourselves with other investigations. You cannot fail to have remarked the extreme laxity of the examination of the corpse. To be sure, the question of identity was readily determined, or should have been; but there were other points to be ascertained. Had the body been in any respect *despoiled*? Had the deceased any articles of jewelry about her person upon leaving home? if so, had she any when found? These are important questions utterly untouched by the evidence; and there are others of equal moment, which have met with no attention. We must endeavor to satisfy ourselves by personal inquiry. The case of St Eustache must be re-examined. I have no suspicion of this person; but let us proceed methodically. We will ascertain beyond a doubt the validity of the *affidavits* in regard to his whereabouts on the Sunday. Affidavits of this character are readily made matter of mystification. Should there be nothing wrong here, however, we will dismiss St Eustache from our investigations. His suicide, however corroborative of suspicion, were there found to be deceit in the affidavits, is, without such deceit, in no respect an unaccountable circumstance, or one which need cause us to deflect from the line of ordinary analysis.

'In that which I now propose, we will discard the interior points of this tragedy, and concentrate our attention upon its outskirts. Not the least usual error, in investigations such as this, is the limiting of inquiry to the immediate, with total disregard of the collateral or circumstantial events. It is the mal-practice of the courts to confine evidence and discussion to the bounds of apparent relevancy. Yet experience has shown, and a true philosophy will always show, that a vast, perhaps the larger portion of truth, arises from the seemingly irrelevant. It is through the spirit of this principle, if not precisely through its letter, that modern science has resolved to *calculate upon the unforeseen*. But perhaps you do not comprehend me. The history of human knowledge has so uninterruptedly shown that to collateral, or incidental, or accidental events we are indebted for the most numerous and most valuable discoveries, that it has at length become necessary, in any prospective view of improvement, to make not only large, but the largest allowances for inventions that shall arise by chance, and quite out of the range of ordinary expectation. It is no longer philosophical to base, upon what has been, a vision of what is to be. *Accident* is admitted as a portion of the substructure. We make chance a matter of absolute calculation. We subject the unlooked for and unimagined, to the mathematical *formulae* of the schools.

'I repeat that it is no more than fact, that the *larger* portion of all truth has sprung from the collateral; and it is but in accordance with the spirit of the principle involved in this fact, that I would divert inquiry, in the present case, from the trodden and hitherto unfruitful ground of the event itself, to the cotemporary circumstances which surround it. While you ascertain the validity of the affidavits, I will examine the newspapers more generally than you have as yet done. So far, we have only reconnoitred the field of investigation; but it will be strange indeed if a comprehensive survey, such as I propose, of the public prints, will not afford us some minute points which shall establish a *direction* for inquiry.'

In pursuance of Dupin's suggestion, I made scrupulous examination of the affair of the affidavits. The result was a firm conviction of their validity, and of the consequent innocence of St Eustache. In the mean time my friend occupied himself, with what seemed to me a minuteness altogether objectless, in a scrutiny of the various newspaper files. At the end of a week he placed before me the following extracts:

'About three years and a half ago, a disturbance very similar to the present, was caused by the disappearance of this same Marie Rogêt, from the *parfumerie* of Monsieur Le Blanc, in the Palais Royal. At the end of the week, however, she re-appeared at her customary *comptoir*, as well as ever, with the exception of a slight paleness not altogether usual. It was given out by Monsieur Le Blanc and her mother, that she had merely been on a visit to some friend in the country; and the affair was speedily hushed up. We presume that the present absence is a freak of the same nature, and that, at the expiration of a week, or perhaps of a month, we shall have her among us again.'—*Evening Paper—Monday, June 23.*[1]

'An evening journal of yesterday, refers to a former mysterious disappearance of Mademoiselle Rogêt. It is well known that, during the week of her absence from Le Blanc's *parfumerie*, she was in the company of a young naval officer, much noted for his debaucheries. A quarrel, it is supposed, providentially led to her return home. We have the name of the Lothario in question, who is, at present, stationed in Paris, but, for obvious reasons, forbear to make it public.'—*Le Mercurie—Tuesday Morning, June 24.*[2]

'An outrage of the most atrocious character was perpetrated near this city the day before yesterday. A gentleman, with his wife and daughter, engaged, about dusk, the services of six young men, who were idly rowing a boat to and fro near the banks of the Seine, to convey him across the river. Upon reaching the opposite shore, the three passengers stepped out, and had proceeded so far as to be beyond the view of the boat, when the daughter discovered that she had left in it her parasol. She returned for it, was seized by the gang, carried out into the stream, gagged, brutally treated, and finally taken to the shore at a point not far from that at which she had originally entered the boat with her parents. The villains have escaped for the time, but the police are upon their trail, and some of them will soon be taken.'—*Morning Paper—June 25.*[3]

'We have received one or two communications, the object of which is to fasten the crime of the late atrocity upon Mennais;[4] but as this gentleman has been fully exonerated by a legal inquiry, and as the arguments of our several correspondents appear to be more zealous than profound, we do not think it advisable to make them public.'—*Morning Paper—June 28.*[5]

[1] 'N. Y. Express.' [2] 'N. Y. Herald.' [3] 'N. Y. Courier and Inquirer.'

[4] Mennais was one of the parties originally suspected and arrested, but discharged through total lack of evidence.

[5] 'N. Y. Courier and Inquirer.'

'We have received several forcibly written communications, apparently from various sources, and which go far to render it a matter of certainty that the unfortunate Marie Rogêt has become a victim of one of the numerous bands of blackguards which infest the vicinity of the city upon Sunday. Our own opinion is decidedly in favor of this supposition. We shall endeavor to make room for some of these arguments hereafter.'—*Evening Paper—Tuesday, June 31.*[1]

'On Monday, one of the bargemen connected with the revenue service, saw an empty boat floating down the Seine. Sails were lying in the bottom of the boat. The bargeman towed it under the barge office. The next morning it was taken from thence, without the knowledge of any of the officers. The rudder is now at the barge office.'— *Le Diligence—Thursday, June 26.*[2]

Upon reading these various extracts, they not only seemed to me irrelevant, but I could perceive no mode in which any one of them could be brought to bear upon the matter in hand. I waited for some explanation from Dupin.

'It is not my present design,' he said, 'to *dwell* upon the first and second of these extracts. I have copied them chiefly to show you the extreme remissness of the police, who, as far as I can understand from the Prefect, have not troubled themselves, in any respect, with an examination of the naval officer alluded to. Yet it is mere folly to say that between the first and second disappearance of Marie, there is no *supposable* connection. Let us admit the first elopement to have resulted in a quarrel between the lovers, and the return home of the betrayed. We are now prepared to view a second *elopement* (if we *know* that an elopement has again taken place) as indicating a renewal of the betrayer's advances, rather than as the result of new proposals by a second individual—we are prepared to regard it as a "making up" of the old *amour*, rather than as the commencement of a new one. The chances are ten to one, that he who had once eloped with Marie, would again propose an elopement, rather than that she to whom proposals of elopement had been made by one individual, should have them made to her by another. And here let me call your attention to the fact, that the time elapsing between the first ascertained, and the second supposed elopement, is a few months more than the general period of the cruises of our men-of-war. Had the lover been interrupted in his first villainy by the necessity of departure to sea, and had he seized the first

[1] 'N. Y. Evening Post.' [2] 'N. Y. Standard.'

moment of his return to renew the base designs not yet altogether accomplished—or not yet altogether accomplished *by him*? Of all these things we know nothing.

'You will say, however, that, in the second instance, there was *no* elopement as imagined. Certainly not—but are we prepared to say that there was not the frustrated design? Beyond St Eustache, and perhaps Beauvais, we find no recognized, no open, no honorable suitors of Marie. Of none other is there any thing said. Who, then, is the secret lover, of whom the relatives (*at least most of them*) know nothing, but whom Marie meets upon the morning of Sunday, and who is so deeply in her confidence, that she hesitates not to remain with him until the shades of the evening descend, amid the solitary groves of the Barrière du Roule? Who is that secret lover, I ask, of whom, at least, *most* of the relatives know nothing? And what means the singular prophecy of Madame Rogêt on the morning of Marie's departure?—"I fear that I shall never see Marie again."

'But if we cannot imagine Madame Rogêt privy to the design of elopement, may we not at least suppose this design entertained by the girl? Upon quitting home, she gave it to be understood that she was about to visit her aunt in the Rue des Drômes, and St Eustache was requested to call for her at dark. Now, at first glance, this fact strongly militates against my suggestion;—but let us reflect. That she *did* meet some companion, and proceed with him across the river, reaching the Barrière du Roule at so late an hour as three o'clock in the afternoon, is known. But in consenting so to accompany this individual, (*for whatever purpose—to her mother known or unknown*,) she must have thought of her expressed intention when leaving home, and of the surprise and suspicion aroused in the bosom of her affianced suitor, St Eustache, when, calling for her, at the hour appointed, in the Rue des Drômes, he should find that she had not been there, and when, moreover, upon returning to the *pension* with this alarming intelligence, he should become aware of her continued absence from home. She must have thought of these things, I say. She must have foreseen the chagrin of St Eustache, the suspicion of all. She could not have thought of returning to brave this suspicion; but the suspicion becomes a point of trivial importance to her, if we suppose her *not* intending to return.

'We may imagine her thinking thus—"I am to meet a certain person for the purpose of elopement, or for certain other purposes known only to myself. It is necessary that there be no chance of interruption—there must be sufficient time given us to elude pursuit—I will give it to be understood that I shall visit and spend the day with my aunt at the Rue des Drômes—I will tell St Eustache not to call for me until dark—in this way, my absence from home for the longest possible period, without causing suspicion or anxiety, will be accounted for, and I shall gain more time than in any other manner. If I bid St Eustache call for me at dark, he will be sure not to call before; but, if I wholly neglect to bid him call, my time for escape will be diminished, since it will be expected that I return the earlier, and my absence will the sooner excite anxiety. Now, if it were my design to return *at all*—if I had in contemplation merely a stroll with the individual in question—it would not be my policy to bid St Eustache call; for, calling, he will be *sure* to ascertain that I have played him false—a fact of which I might keep him for ever in ignorance, by leaving home without notifying him of my intention, by returning before dark, and by then stating that I had been to visit my aunt in the Rue des Drômes. But, as it is my design *never* to return—or not for some weeks—or not until certain concealments are effected—the gaining of time is the only point about which I need give myself any concern."

'You have observed, in your notes, that the most general opinion in relation to this sad affair is, and was from the first, that the girl had been the victim of *a gang* of blackguards. Now, the popular opinion, under certain conditions, is not to be disregarded. When arising of itself—when manifesting itself in a strictly spontaneous manner—we should look upon it as analogous with that *intuition* which is the idiosyncrasy of the individual man of genius. In ninety-nine cases from the hundred I would abide by its decision. But it is important that we find no palpable traces of *suggestion*. The opinion must be rigorously *the public's own*; and the distinction is often exceedingly difficult to perceive and to maintain. In the present instance, it appears to me that this "public opinion," in respect to *a gang*, has been superinduced by the collateral event which is detailed in the third of my extracts. All Paris is excited by the discovered corpse of Marie, a girl young, beautiful and notorious. This corpse is found, bearing marks of violence, and floating in the river. But it is now made known that, at the very period, or about the very period, in which it is supposed that the girl was assassinated, an outrage similar in nature to that endured by the deceased, although less in extent, was perpetrated, by a gang of young ruffians, upon the person of a second young female. Is it wonderful that the one known atrocity should influence the popular judgment in regard to the other unknown? This judgment awaited direction, and the known outrage seemed so opportunely to afford it! Marie, too, was found in the river; and upon this very river was this known outrage committed. The connexion of the two events had about it so much of the palpable, that the true wonder would have been a *failure* of the populace to appreciate and to seize it. But, in fact, the one atrocity, known to be so committed, is, if any thing, evidence that the other, committed at a time nearly coincident, was *not* so committed. It would have been a miracle indeed, if, while a gang of ruffians were perpetrating, at a given locality, a most unheard-of wrong, there should have been another similar gang, in a similar locality, in the same city, under the same circumstances, with the same means and appliances, engaged in a wrong of precisely the same aspect, at precisely the same period of time! Yet in what, if not in this marvellous train of coincidence, does the accidentally *suggested* opinion of the populace call upon us to believe?

'Before proceeding farther, let us consider the supposed scene of the assassination, in the thicket at the Barrière du Roule. This thicket, although dense, was in the close vicinity of a public road. Within were three or four large stones, forming a kind of seat with a back and footstool. On the upper stone was discovered a white petticoat; on the second, a silk scarf. A parasol, gloves, and a pocket-handkerchief, were also here found. The handkerchief bore the name, "Marie Rogêt." Fragments of dress were seen on the branches around. The earth was trampled, the bushes were broken, and there was every evidence of a violent struggle.

'Notwithstanding the acclamation with which the discovery of this thicket was received by the press, and the unanimity with which it was supposed to indicate the precise scene of the outrage, it must be admitted that there was some very good reason for doubt. That it *was* the scene, I may or I may not believe—but there was excellent reason for doubt. Had the *true* scene been, as Le Commerciel suggested, in the neighborhood of the Rue Pavée St Andrée, the perpetrators of the crime, supposing them still resident in Paris, would naturally have been stricken with terror at the public attention thus acutely directed into the proper channel; and, in certain classes of minds, there would have arisen, at once, a sense of the necessity of some exertion to redivert this attention. And thus, the thicket of the Barrière du Roule having been already suspected, the idea of placing the articles where they were found, might have been naturally entertained. There is no real evidence, although Le Soleil so supposes, that the articles discovered had been more than a very few days in the thicket; while there is much circumstantial proof that they could not have remained there, without attracting attention, during the twenty days elapsing between the fatal Sunday and the afternoon upon which they were found by the boys. "They were all *mildewed* down hard," says Le Soleil, adopting the opinions of its predecessors, "with the action of the rain, and stuck together from *mildew*. The grass had grown around and over some of them. The silk of the parasol was strong, but the threads of it were run together within. The upper part, where it had been doubled and folded, was all *mildewed* and rotten, and tore on being opened." In respect to the grass having "grown around and over some of them," it is obvious that the fact could only have been ascertained from the words, and thus from the recollections, of two small boys; for these boys removed the articles and took them home before they had been seen by a third party. But grass will grow, especially in warm and damp weather, (such as was that of the period of the murder,) as much as two or three inches in a single day. A parasol lying upon a newly turfed ground, might, in a week, be entirely concealed from sight by the upspringing grass. And touching that *mildew* upon which the editor of Le Soleil so pertinaciously insists, that he employs the word no less than three times in the brief paragraph just quoted, is he really unaware of the nature of this *mildew*? Is he to be told that it is one of the many classes of *fungus*, of which the most ordinary feature is its upspringing and decadence within twenty-four hours?

'Thus we see, at a glance, that what has been most triumphantly adduced in support of the idea that the articles had been "for at least three or four weeks" in the thicket, is most absurdly null as regards any evidence of that fact. On the other hand, it is exceedingly difficult to believe that these articles could have remained in the thicket specified, for a longer period than a single week—for a longer period than from one Sunday to the next. Those who know any thing of the vicinity of Paris, know the extreme difficulty of finding *seclusion*, unless at a great distance from its suburbs. Such a thing as an unexplored, or even an unfrequently visited recess, amid its woods or groves, is not for a moment to be imagined. Let any one who, being at heart a lover of nature, is yet chained by duty to the dust and heat of this great metropolis—let any such one attempt, even during the weekdays, to slake this thirst for solitude amid the scenes of natural loveliness which immediately surround us. At every second step, he will find the growing charm dispelled by the voice and personal intrusion of some ruffian or party of carousing blackguards. He will seek privacy amid the densest foliage, all in vain. Here are the very nooks where the unwashed most abound—here are the temples most desecrate. With sickness of the heart the wanderer will flee back to the polluted Paris as to a less odious because less incongruous sink of pollution. But if the vicinity of the city is so beset during the working days of the week, how much more so on the Sabbath! It is now especially that, released from the claims of labor, or deprived of the customary opportunities of crime, the town blackguard seeks the precincts of the town, not through love of the rural, which in his heart he despises, but by way of escape from the restraints and conventionalities of society. He desires less the fresh air and the green trees, than the utter *license* of the country. Here, at the road-side inn, or beneath the foliage of the woods, he indulges, unchecked by any eye except those of his boon companions, in all the mad excess of a counterfeit hilarity—the joint offspring of liberty and of rum. I say nothing more than what must be obvious to every dispassionate observer, when I repeat that the circumstance of the articles in question having remained undiscovered, for a longer period than from one Sunday to another, in *any* thicket in the immediate neighborhood of Paris, is to be looked upon as little less than miraculous.

'But there are not wanting other grounds for the suspicion that the articles were placed in the thicket with the view of diverting attention from the real scene of the outrage. And, first, let me direct your notice to the *date* of the discovery of the articles. Collate this with the date of the fifth extract made by myself from the newspapers. You will find that the discovery followed, almost immediately, the urgent communications sent to the evening paper. These communications, although various, and apparently from various sources, tended all to the same point—viz., the directing of attention to *a gang* as the perpetrators of the outrage, and to the neighborhood of the Barrière du Roule as its scene. Now here, of course, the suspicion is not that, in consequence of these communications, or of the public attention by them directed, the articles were found by the boys; but the suspicion might and may well have been, that the articles were not *before* found by the boys, for the reason that the articles had not before been in the thicket; having been deposited there only at so late a period as at the date, or shortly prior to the date of the communications, by the guilty authors of these communications themselves.

'This thicket was a singular—an exceedingly singular one. It was unusually dense. Within its naturally walled enclosure were three extraordinary stones, *forming a seat with a back and footstool.* And this thicket, so full of a natural art, was in the immediate vicinity, *within a few rods*, of the dwelling of Madame Deluc, whose boys were in the habit of closely examining the shrubberies about them in search of the bark of the sassafras. Would it be a rash wager—a wager of one thousand to one—that *a day* never passed over the heads of these boys without finding at least one of them ensconced in the umbrageous hall, and enthroned upon its natural throne? Those who would hesitate at such a wager, have either never been boys themselves, or have forgotten the boyish nature. I repeat—it is exceedingly hard to comprehend how the articles could have remained in this thicket undiscovered, for a longer period than one or two days; and that thus there is good ground for suspicion, in spite of the dogmatic ignorance of Le Soleil, that they were, at a comparatively late date, deposited where found.

'But there are still other and stronger reasons for believing them so deposited, than any which I have as yet urged. And, now, let me beg your notice to the highly artificial arrangement of the articles. On the *upper* stone lay a white petticoat; on the *second* a silk scarf; scattered around, were a parasol, gloves, and a pocket-handkerchief bearing the name, "Marie Rogêt." Here is just such an arrangement as would *naturally* be made by a not-over-acute person wishing to dispose the articles *naturally*. But it is by no means a *really* natural arrangement. I should rather have looked to see the things *all* lying on the ground and trampled under foot. In the narrow limits of that bower, it would have been scarcely possible that the petticoat and scarf should have retained a position upon the stones, when subjected to the brushing to and fro of many struggling persons. "There was evidence," it is said, "of a struggle; and the earth was trampled, the bushes were broken,"—but the petticoat and the scarf are found deposited as if upon shelves. "The pieces of the frock torn out by the bushes were about three inches wide and six inches long. One part was the hem of the frock and it had been mended. They *looked like strips torn off.*" Here, inadvertently, Le Soleil has employed an exceedingly suspicious phrase. The pieces, as described, do indeed "look like strips torn off;" but purposely and by hand. It is one of the rarest of accidents that a piece is "torn off," from any garment such as is now in question, by the agency *of a thorn*. From the very nature of such fabrics, a thorn or nail becoming entangled in them, tears them rectangularly—divides them into two longitudinal rents, at right angles with each other, and meeting at an apex where the thorn enters—but it is scarcely possible to conceive the piece "torn off." I never so knew it, nor did you. To tear a piece *off* from such fabric, two distinct forces, in different directions, will be, in almost every case, required. If there be two edges to the fabric—if, for example, it be a pocket-handkerchief, and it is desired to tear from it a slip, then, and then only, will the one force serve the purpose. But in the present case the question is of a dress, presenting but one edge. To tear a piece from the interior, where no edge is presented, could only be effected by a miracle through the agency of thorns, and no *one* thorn could accomplish it. But, even where an edge is presented, two thorns will be necessary, operating, the one in two distinct directions, and the other in one. And this in the supposition that the edge is unhemmed. If hemmed, the matter is nearly out of the question. We thus see the numerous and great obstacles in the way of pieces being "torn off" through the simple agency of "thorns;" yet we are required to believe not only that one piece but that many have been so torn. "And one part," too, "*was the hem of the frock!*" Another piece was "*part of the skirt, not the hem*,"—that is to say, was torn completely out, through the agency of thorns, from the unedged interior of the dress! These, I say, are things which one may well be pardoned for disbelieving; yet, taken collectedly, they form, perhaps, less of reasonable ground for suspicion, than the one startling circumstance of the articles' having been left in this thicket at all, by any *murderers* who had enough precaution to think of removing the corpse. You will not have apprehended me rightly, however, if you suppose it my design to *deny* this thicket as the scene of the outrage. There might have been a wrong *here*, or, more possibly, an accident at Madame Deluc's. But, in fact, this is a point of minor importance. We are not engaged in an attempt to discover the scene, but to produce the perpetrators of the murder. What I have adduced, notwithstanding the minuteness with which I have adduced it, has been with the view, first, to show the folly of the positive and headlong assertions of Le Soleil, but secondly and chiefly, to bring you, by the most natural route, to a further contemplation of the doubt whether this assassination has, or has not been, the work of *a gang*.

'We will resume this question by mere allusion to the revolting details of the surgeon examined at the inquest. It is only necessary to say that his published *inferences*, in regard to the number of the ruffians, have been properly ridiculed as unjust and totally baseless, by all the reputable anatomists of Paris. Not that the matter *might not* have been as inferred, but that there was no ground for the inference:—was there not much for another?

'Let us reflect now upon "the traces of a struggle;" and let me ask what these traces have been supposed to demonstrate. A gang. But do they not rather demonstrate the absence of a gang? What *struggle* could have taken place—what struggle so violent and so enduring as to have left its "traces" in all directions—between a weak and defenceless girl and the *gang of* ruffians imagined? The silent grasp of a few rough arms and all would have been over. The victim must have been absolutely passive at their will. You will here bear in mind that the arguments urged against the thicket as the scene, are applicable, in chief part, only against it as the scene of an outrage committed by *more than a single individual*. If we imagine but *one* violator, we can conceive, and thus only conceive, the struggle of so violent and so obstinate a nature as to have left the "traces" apparent.

'And again. I have already mentioned the suspicion to be excited by the fact that the articles in question were suffered to remain *at all* in the thicket where discovered. It seems almost impossible that these evidences of guilt have been accidentally left where found. There was sufficient presence of mind (it is supposed) to remove the corpse; and yet a more positive evidence than the corpse itself (whose features might have been quickly obliterated by decay,) is allowed to lie conspicuously in the scene of the outrage—I allude to the handkerchief with the *name* of the deceased. If this was accident, it was not the accident *of a gang*. We can imagine it only the accident of an individual. Let us see. An individual has committed the murder. He is alone with the ghost of the departed. He is appalled by what lies motionless before him. The fury of his passion is over, and there is abundant room in his heart for the natural awe of the deed. His is none of that confidence which the presence of numbers inevitably inspires. He is *alone* with the dead. He trembles and is bewildered. Yet there is a necessity for disposing of the corpse. He bears it to the river, but leaves behind him the other evidences of guilt; for it is difficult, if not impossible to carry all the burthen at once, and it will be easy to return for what is left. But in his toilsome journey to the water his fears redouble within him. The sounds of life encompass his path. A dozen times he hears or fancies the step of an observer. Even the very lights from the city bewilder him. Yet, in time, and by long and frequent pauses of deep agony, he reaches the river's brink, and disposes of his ghastly charge—perhaps through the medium of a boat. But *now* what treasure does the world hold—what threat of vengeance could it hold out—which would have power to urge the return of that lonely murderer over that toilsome and perilous path, to the thicket and its blood-chilling recollections? He returns *not*, let the consequences be what they may. He *could* not return if he would. His sole thought is immediate escape. He turns his back *forever* upon those dreadful shrubberies, and flees as from the wrath to come.

'But how with a gang? Their number would have inspired them with confidence; if, indeed, confidence is ever wanting in the breast of the arrant blackguard; and of arrant blackguards alone are the supposed *gangs* ever constituted. Their number, I say, would have prevented the bewildering and unreasoning terror which I have imagined to paralyze the single man. Could we suppose an oversight in one, or two, or three, this oversight would have been remedied by a fourth. They would have left nothing behind them; for their number would have enabled them to carry *all* at once. There would have been no need of *return*.

'Consider now the circumstance that, in the outer garment of the corpse when found, "a slip, about a foot wide, had been torn upward from the bottom hem to the waist, wound three times round the waist, and secured by a sort of hitch in the back." This was done with the obvious design of affording *a handle* by which to carry the body. But would any *number* of men have dreamed of resorting to such an expedient? To three or four, the limbs of the corpse would have afforded not only a sufficient, but the best possible hold. The device is that of a single individual; and this brings us to the fact that "between the thicket and the river, the rails of the fences were found taken down, and the ground bore evident traces of some heavy burden having been dragged along it!" But would a *number* of men have put themselves to the superfluous trouble of taking down a fence, for the purpose of dragging through it a corpse which they might have *lifted over* any fence in an instant? Would a *number* of men have so *dragged* a corpse at all as to have left evident *traces* of the dragging?

'And here we must refer to an observation of Le Commerciel; an observation upon which I have already, in some measure, commented. "A piece," says this journal, "of one of the unfortunate girl's petticoats was torn out and tied under her chin, and around the back of her head, probably to prevent screams. This was done by fellows who had no pocket-handkerchiefs."

'I have before suggested that a genuine blackguard is never *without* a pocket-handkerchief. But it is not to this fact that I now especially advert. That it was not through want of a handkerchief for the purpose imagined by Le Commerciel, that this bandage was employed, is rendered apparent by the handkerchief left in the thicket; and that the object was not "to prevent screams" appears, also, from the bandage having been employed in preference to what would so much better have answered the purpose. But the language of the evidence speaks of the strip in question as "found around the neck, fitting loosely, and secured with a hard knot." These words are sufficiently vague, but differ materially from those of Le Commerciel. The slip was eighteen inches wide, and therefore, although of muslin, would form a strong band when folded or rumpled longitudinally. And thus rumpled it was discovered. My inference is this. The solitary murderer, having borne the corpse, for some distance, (whether from the thicket or elsewhere) by means of the bandage *hitched* around its middle, found the weight, in this mode of procedure, too much for his strength. He resolved to drag the burthen—the evidence goes to show that it *was* dragged. With this object in view, it became necessary to attach something like a rope to one of the extremities. It could be best attached about the neck, where the head would prevent its slipping off. And, now, the murderer bethought him, unquestionably, of the bandage about the loins. He would have used this, but for its volution about the corpse, the *hitch* which embarrassed it, and the reflection that it had not been "torn off" from the garment. It was easier to tear a new slip from the petticoat. He tore it, made it fast about the neck, and so *dragged* his victim to the brink of the river. That this "bandage," only attainable with trouble and delay, and but imperfectly answering its purpose—that this bandage was employed *at all*, demonstrates that the necessity for its employment sprang from circumstances arising at a period when the handkerchief was no longer attainable—that is to say, arising, as we have imagined, after quitting the thicket, (if the thicket it was), and on the road between the thicket and the river.

'But the evidence, you will say, of Madame Deluc, (!) points especially to the presence of *a gang*, in the vicinity of the thicket, at or about the epoch of the murder. This I grant. I doubt if there were not a *dozen* gangs, such as described by Madame Deluc, in and about the vicinity of the Barrière du Roule at *or about* the period of this tragedy. But the gang which has drawn upon itself the pointed animadversion, although the somewhat tardy and very suspicious evidence of Madame Deluc, is the *only* gang which is represented by that honest and scrupulous old lady as having eaten her cakes and swallowed her brandy, without putting themselves to the trouble of making her payment. *Et hinc illæ iræ?**

'But what *is* the precise evidence of Madame Deluc? "A gang of miscreants made their appearance, behaved boisterously, ate and drank without making payment, followed in the route of the young man and girl, returned to the inn *about dusk*, and recrossed the river as if in great haste."

'Now this "great haste" very possibly seemed *greater* haste in the eyes of Madame Deluc, since she dwelt lingeringly and lamentingly upon her violated cakes and ale—cakes and ale for which she might still have entertained a faint hope of compensation. Why, otherwise, since it was *about dusk*, should she make a point of the *haste?* It is no cause for wonder, surely, that even a gang of blackguards should make *haste* to get home, when a wide river is to be crossed in small boats, when storm impends, and when night *approaches*.

'I say *approaches*; for the night had *not yet arrived*. It was only *about dusk* that the indecent haste of these "miscreants" offended the sober eyes of Madame Deluc. But we are told that it was upon this very evening that Madame Deluc, as well as her eldest son, "heard the screams of a female in the vicinity of the inn." And in what words does Madame Deluc designate the period of the evening at which these screams were heard? "It was *soon after dark*," she says. But "soon *after* dark," is, at least, *dark*; and "*about dusk*" is as certainly daylight. Thus it is abundantly clear that the gang quitted the Barrière du Roule *prior* to the screams overheard (?) by Madame Deluc. And although, in all the many reports of the evidence, the relative expressions in question are distinctly and invariably employed just as I have employed them in this conversation with yourself, no notice whatever of the gross discrepancy has, as yet, been taken by any of the public journals, or by any of the Myrmidons of police.

'I shall add but one to the arguments against *a gang*; but this *one* has, to my own understanding at least, a weight altogether irresistible. Under the circumstances of large reward offered, and full pardon to any King's evidence, it is not to be imagined, for a moment, that some member of *a gang* of low ruffians, or of any body of men, would not long ago have betrayed his accomplices. Each one of a gang so placed, is not so much greedy of reward, or anxious for escape, as *fearful of betrayal.* He betrays eagerly and early that *he may not himself be betrayed.* That the secret has not been divulged, is the very best of proof that it is, in fact, a secret. The horrors of this dark deed are known only to *one*, or two, living human beings, and to God.

'Let us sum up now the meagre yet certain fruits of our long analysis. We have attained the idea either of a fatal accident* under the roof of Madame Deluc, or of a murder perpetrated, in the thicket at the Barrière du Roule, by a lover, or at least by an intimate and secret associate of the deceased. This associate is of swarthy complexion. This complexion, the "hitch" in the bandage, and the "sailor's knot," with which the bonnet-ribbon is tied, point to a seaman. His companionship with the deceased, a gay, but not an abject young girl, designates him as above the grade of the common sailor. Here the well written and urgent communications to the journals are much in the way of corroboration. The circumstance of the first elopement, as mentioned by Le Mercurie, tends to blend the idea of this seaman with that of the "naval officer" who is first known to have led the unfortunate into crime.

'And here, most fitly, comes the consideration of the continued absence of him of the dark complexion. Let me pause to observe that the complexion of this man is dark and swarthy; it was no common swarthiness which constituted the *sole* point of remembrance, both as regards Valence and Madame Deluc. But why is this man absent? Was he murdered by the gang? If so, why are there only *traces* of the assassinated *girl?* The scene of the two outrages will naturally be supposed identical. And where is his corpse? The assassins would most probably have disposed of both in the same way. But it may be said that this man lives, and is deterred from making himself known, through dread of being charged with the murder. This consideration might be supposed to operate upon him now—at this late period—since it has been given in evidence that he was seen with Marie—but it would have had no force at the period of the deed. The first impulse of an innocent man would have been to announce the outrage, and to aid in indentifying the ruffians. This, *policy* would have suggested. He had been seen with the girl. He had crossed the river with her in an open ferry-boat. The denouncing of the assassins would have appeared, even to an idiot, the surest and sole means of relieving himself from suspicion. We cannot suppose him, on the night of the fatal Sunday, both innocent himself and incognizant of an outrage committed. Yet only under such circumstances is it possible to imagine that he would have failed, if alive, in the denouncement of the assassins.

'And what means are ours, of attaining the truth? We shall find these means multiplying and gathering distinctness as we proceed. Let us sift to the bottom this affair of the first elopement. Let us know the full history of "the officer," with his present circumstances, and his whereabouts at the precise period of the murder. Let us carefully compare with each other the various communications sent to the evening paper, in which the object was to inculpate *a gang*. This done, let us compare these communications, both as regards style and MS., with those sent to the morning paper, at a previous period, and insisting so vehemently upon the guilt of Mennais. And, all this done, let us again compare these various communications with the known MSS. of the officer. Let us endeavor to ascertain, by repeated questionings of Madame Deluc and her boys, as well as of the omnibus-driver, Valence, something more of the personal appearance and bearing of the "man of dark complexion." Queries, skilfully directed, will not fail to elicit, from some of these parties, information on this particular point (or upon others)—information which the parties themselves may not even be aware of possessing. And let us now trace *the boat* picked up by the bargeman on the morning of Monday the twenty-third of June, and which was removed from the barge-office, without the cognizance of the officer in attendance, and *without the rudder*, at some period prior to the discovery of the corpse. With a proper caution and perseverance we shall infallibly trace this boat; for not only can the bargeman who picked it up identify it, but the *rudder is at hand*. The rudder *of a sail-boat* would not have been abandoned, without inquiry, by one altogether at ease in heart. And here let me pause to insinuate a question. There was no *advertisement* of the picking up of this boat. It was silently taken to the barge-office, and as silently removed. But its owner or employer—how *happened* he, at so early a period as Tuesday morning, to be informed without the agency of advertisement, of the locality of the boat taken up on Monday, unless we imagine some connexion with the *navy*—some personal permanent connexion leading to cognizance of its minute interests—its petty local news?

'In speaking of the lonely assassin dragging his burden to the shore, I have already suggested the probability of his availing himself *of a boat*. Now we are to understand that Marie Rogêt *was* precipitated from a boat. This would naturally have been the case. The corpse could not have been trusted to the shallow waters of the shore. The peculiar marks on the back and shoulders of the victim tell of the bottom ribs of a boat. That the body was found without weight is also corroborative of the idea. If thrown from the shore a weight would have been attached. We can only account for its absence by supposing the murderer to have neglected the precaution of supplying himself with it before pushing off. In the act of consigning the corpse to the water, he would unquestionably have noticed his oversight; but then no remedy would have been at hand. Any risk would have been preferred to a return to that accursed shore. Having rid himself of his ghastly charge, the murderer would have hastened to the city. There, at some obscure wharf, he would have leaped on land. But the boat—would he have secured it? He would have been in too great haste for such things as securing a boat. Moreover, in fastening it to the wharf, he would have felt as if securing evidence against himself. His natural thought would have been to cast from him, as far as possible, all that had held connection with his crime. He would not only have fled from the wharf, but he would not have permitted *the boat* to remain. Assuredly he would have cast it adrift. Let us pursue our fancies.—In the morning, the wretch is stricken with unutterable horror at finding that the boat has been picked up and detained at a locality which he is in the daily habit of frequenting—at a locality, perhaps, which his duty compels him to frequent. The next night, *without daring to ask for the rudder*, he removes it. Now *where* is that rudderless boat? Let it be one of our first purposes to discover. With the first glimpse we obtain of it, the dawn of our success shall begin. This boat shall guide us, with a rapidity which will surprise even ourselves, to him who employed it in the midnight of the fatal Sabbath. Corroboration will rise upon corroboration, and the murderer will be traced.'

[For reasons which we shall not specify, but which to many readers will appear obvious, we have taken the liberty of here omitting, from the MSS. placed in our hands, such portion as details the *following up* of the apparently slight clew obtained by Dupin. We feel it advisable only to state, in brief, that the result desired was brought to pass; and that the Prefect fulfilled punctually, although with reluctance, the terms of his compact with the Chevalier. Mr Poe's article concludes with the following words.—*Eds.*[1]]

It will be understood that I speak of coincidences *and no more*. What I have said above upon this topic must suffice. In my own heart there dwells no faith in præter-nature. That Nature and its God are two, no man who thinks, will deny. That the latter, creating the former, can, at will, control or modify it, is also unquestionable. I say 'at will;' for the question is of will, and not, as the insanity of logic has assumed, of power. It is not that the Deity *cannot* modify his laws, but that we insult him in imagining a possible necessity for modification. In their origin these laws were fashioned to embrace *all* contingencies which *could* lie in the Future. With God all is *Now*.

I repeat, then, that I speak of these things only as of coincidences. And farther: in what I relate it will be seen that between the fate of the unhappy Mary Cecilia Rogers, so far as that fate is known, and the fate of one Marie Rogêt up to a certain epoch in her history, there has existed a parallel in the contemplation of whose wonderful exactitude the reason becomes embarrassed. I say all this will be seen. But let it not for a moment be supposed that, in proceeding with the sad narrative of Marie from the epoch just mentioned, and in tracing to its *dénouement* the mystery which enshrouded her, it is my covert design to hint at an extension of the parallel, or even to suggest that the measures adopted in Paris for the discovery of the assassin of a grisette, or measures founded in any similar ratiocination, would produce any similar result.

For, in respect to the latter branch of the supposition, it should be considered that the most trifling variation in the facts of the two cases might give rise to the most important miscalculations, by diverting thoroughly the two courses of events; very much as, in arithmetic, an error which, in its own individuality, may be inappreciable, produces, at length, by dint of multiplication at all points of the process, a result enormously at variance with truth. And, in regard to the former branch, we must not fail to hold in view that the very Calculus of Probabilities to which I have referred, forbids all idea of the extension of the parallel:—forbids it with a positiveness strong and decided just in proportion as this parallel has already been long-drawn and exact.

[1] Of the Magazine in which the article was originally published.

This is one of those anomalous propositions which, seemingly appealing to thought altogether apart from the mathematical, is yet one which only the mathematician can fully entertain. Nothing, for example, is more difficult than to convince the merely general reader that the fact of sixes having been thrown twice in succession by a player at dice, is sufficient cause for betting the largest odds that sixes will not be thrown in the third attempt. A suggestion to this effect is usually rejected by the intellect at once. It does not appear that the two throws which have been completed, and which lie now absolutely in the Past, can have influence upon the throw which exists only in the Future. The chance for throwing sixes seems to be precisely as it was at any ordinary time—that is to say, subject only to the influence of the various other throws which may be made by the dice. And this is a reflection which appears so exceedingly obvious that attempts to controvert it are received more frequently with a derisive smile than with anything like respectful attention. The error here involved—a gross error redolent of mischief—I cannot pretend to expose within the limits assigned me at present; and with the philosophical it needs no exposure. It may be sufficient here to say that it forms one of an infinite series of mistakes which arise in the path of Reason through her propensity for seeking truth *in detail.*

THE TELL-TALE HEART

TRUE!—nervous—very, very dreadfully nervous I had been and am; but why *will* you say that I am mad? The disease had sharpened my senses—not destroyed—not dulled them. Above all was the sense of hearing acute. I heard all things in the heaven and in the earth. I heard many things in hell. How, then, am I mad? Hearken! and observe how healthily—how calmly I can tell you the whole story.

It is impossible to say how first the idea entered my brain: but, once conceived, it haunted me day and night. Object there was none. Passion there was none. I loved the old man. He had never wronged me. He had never given me insult. For his gold I had no desire. I think it was his eye! yes, it was this! One of his eyes resembled that of a vulture—a pale blue eye, with a film over it. Whenever it fell upon me, my blood ran cold; and so by degrees—very gradually—I made up my mind to take the life of the old man, and thus rid myself of the eye forever.

Now this is the point. You fancy me mad. Madmen know nothing. But you should have seen *me*. You should have seen how wisely I proceeded—with what caution—with what foresight—with what dissimulation I went to work! I was never kinder to the old man than during the whole week before I killed him. And every night, about midnight, I turned the latch of his door and opened it—oh, so gently! And then, when I had made an opening sufficient for my head, I put in a dark lantern, all closed, closed, so that no light shone out, and then I thrust in my head. Oh, you would have laughed to see how cunningly I thrust it in! I moved it slowly—very, very slowly, so that I might not disturb the old man's sleep. It took me an hour to place my whole head within the opening so far that I could see him as he lay upon his bed. Ha!—would a madman have been so wise as this? And then, when my head was well in the room, I undid the lantern cautiously—oh, so cautiously—cautiously (for the hinges creaked)—I undid it just so much that a single thin ray fell upon the vulture eye. And this I did for seven long nights—every night just at midnight—but I found the eye always closed; and so it was impossible to do the work; for it was not the old man who vexed me, but this Evil Eye. And every morning, when the day broke, I went boldly into the chamber, and spoke courageously to him, calling him by name in a hearty tone, and inquiring how he had passed the night. So you see he would have been a very profound old man, indeed, to suspect that every night, just at twelve, I looked in upon him while he slept.

Upon the eighth night I was more than usually cautious in opening the door. A watch's minute hand moves more quickly than did mine. Never, before that night, had I *felt* the extent of my own powers—of my sagacity. I could scarcely contain my feelings of triumph. To think that there I was, opening the door, little by little, and he not even to dream of my secret deeds or thoughts. I fairly chuckled at the idea; and perhaps he heard me; for he moved on the bed suddenly, as if startled. Now you may think that I drew back—but no. His room was as black as pitch with the thick darkness (for the shutters were close fastened, through fear of robbers,) and so I knew that he could not see the opening of the door, and I kept pushing it on steadily, steadily.

I had my head in, and was about to open the lantern, when my thumb slipped upon the tin fastening, and the old man sprang up in the bed, crying out—'Who's there?'

I kept quite still and said nothing. For a whole hour I did not move a muscle, and in the meantime I did not hear him lie down. He was still sitting up in the bed, listening;—just as I have done, night after night, hearkening to the death-watches in the wall.

Presently I heard a slight groan, and I knew it was the groan of mortal terror. It was not a groan of pain or of grief—oh, no!—it was the low stifled sound that arises from the bottom of the soul when overcharged with awe. I knew the sound well. Many a night, just at midnight, when all the world slept, it has welled up from my own bosom, deepening, with its dreadful echo, the terrors that distracted me. I say I knew it well. I knew what the old man felt, and pitied him, although I chuckled at heart. I knew that he had been lying awake since ever the first slight noise, when he had turned in the bed. His fears had been ever since growing upon him. He had been trying to fancy them causeless, but could not. He had been saying to himself—'It is nothing but the wind in the chimney—it is only a mouse crossing the floor,' or 'it is merely a cricket which has made a single chirp.' Yes, he has been trying to comfort himself with these suppositions: but he had found all in vain. *All in vain*; because Death, in approaching him, had stalked with his black shadow before him, and enveloped the victim. And it was the mournful influence of the unperceived shadow that caused him to feel—although he neither saw nor heard—to *feel* the presence of my head within the room.

When I had waited a long time, very patiently, without hearing him lie down, I resolved to open a little—a very, very little crevice in the lantern. So I opened it—you cannot imagine how stealthily, stealthily—until, at length, a single dim ray, like the thread of the spider, shot from out the crevice and fell upon the vulture eye.

It was open—wide, wide open—and I grew furious as I gazed upon it. I saw it with perfect distinctness—all a dull blue, with a hideous veil over it that chilled the very marrow in my bones; but I could see nothing else of the old man's face or person: for I had directed the ray as if by instinct, precisely upon the damned spot.

And now—have I not told you that what you mistake for madness is but over acuteness of the senses?—now, I say, there came to my ears a low, dull, quick sound, such as a watch makes when enveloped in cotton. I knew *that* sound well, too. It was the beating of the old man's heart. It increased my fury, as the beating of a drum stimulates the soldier into courage.

But even yet I refrained and kept still. I scarcely breathed. I held the lantern motionless, I tried how steadily I could maintain the ray upon the eye. Meantime the hellish tattoo of the heart increased. It grew quicker and quicker, and louder and louder every instant. The old man's terror *must* have been extreme! It grew louder, I say, louder every moment!—do you mark me well? I have told you that I am nervous: so I am. And now at the dead hour of the night, amid the dreadful silence of that old house, so strange a noise as this excited me to uncontrollable terror. Yet, for some minutes longer I refrained and stood still. But the beating grew louder, louder! I thought the heart must burst. And now a new anxiety seized me—the sound would be heard by a neighbor! The old man's hour had come! With a loud yell, I threw open the lantern and leaped into the room. He shrieked once—once only. In an instant I dragged him to the floor, and pulled the heavy bed over him. I then smiled gaily, to find the deed so far done. But, for many minutes, the heart beat on with a muffled sound. This, however, did not vex me; it would not be heard through the wall. At length it ceased. The old man was dead. I removed the bed and examined the corpse. Yes, he was stone, stone dead. I placed my hand upon the heart and held it there many minutes. There was no pulsation. He was stone dead. His eye would trouble me no more.

If still you think me mad, you will think so no longer when I describe the wise precautions I took for the concealment of the body. The night waned, and I worked hastily, but in silence. First of all I dismembered the corpse. I cut off the head and the arms and the legs.

I then took up three planks from the flooring of the chamber, and deposited all between the scantlings. I then replaced the boards so cleverly, so cunningly, that no human eye—not even *his*—could have detected anything wrong. There was nothing to wash out—no stain of any kind—no blood-spot whatever. I had been too wary for that. A tub had caught all—ha! ha!

When I had made an end of these labors, it was four o'clock—still dark as midnight. As the bell sounded the hour, there came a knocking at the street door. I went down to open it with a light heart,—for what had I *now* to fear? There entered three men, who introduced themselves, with perfect suavity, as officers of the police. A shriek had been heard by a neighbor during the night; suspicion of foul play had been aroused; information had been lodged at the police office, and they (the officers) had been deputed to search the premises.

I smiled,—for *what* had I to fear? I bade the gentlemen welcome. The shriek, I said, was my own in a dream. The old man, I mentioned, was absent in the country. I took my visiters all over the house. I bade them search—search *well*. I led them, at length, to *his* chamber. I showed them his treasures, secure, undisturbed. In the enthusiasm of my confidence, I brought chairs into the room, and desired them *here* to rest from their fatigues, while I myself, in the wild audacity of my perfect triumph, placed my own seat upon the very spot beneath which reposed the corpse of the victim.

The officers were satisfied. My *manner* had convinced them. I was singularly at ease. They sat, and while I answered cheerily, they chatted of familiar things. But, ere long, I felt myself getting pale and wished them gone. My head ached, and I fancied a ringing in my ears: but still they sat and still chatted. The ringing became more distinct:—it continued and became more distinct: I talked more freely to get rid of the feeling: but it continued and gained definitiveness—until, at length, I found that the noise was *not* within my ears.

No doubt I now grew *very* pale;—but I talked more fluently, and with a heightened voice. Yet the sound increased—and what could I do? It was *a low, dull, quick sound—much such a sound as a watch makes when enveloped in cotton*. I gasped for breath—and yet the officers heard it not. I talked more quickly—more vehemently; but the noise steadily increased. I arose and argued about trifles, in a high key and with violent gesticulations; but the noise steadily increased. Why *would* they not be gone? I paced the floor to and fro with heavy strides, as if excited to fury by the observations of the men—but the noise steadily increased. Oh God! what *could* I do? I foamed—I raved—I swore! I swung the chair upon which I had been sitting, and grated it upon the boards, but the noise arose over all and continually increased. It grew louder—louder—*louder!* And still the men chatted pleasantly, and smiled. Was it possible they heard not? Almighty God!—no, no! They heard!—they suspected—they *knew!*—they were making a mockery of my horror!—this I thought, and this I think. But anything was better than this agony! Anything was more tolerable than this derision! I could bear those hypocritical smiles no longer! I felt that I must scream or die!—and now—again!—hark! louder! louder! louder! *louder!*—

'Villains!' I shrieked, 'dissemble no more! I admit the deed!—tear up the planks!—here, here!—it is the beating of his hideous heart!'

THE GOLD-BUG

What ho! what ho! this fellow is dancing mad!
He hath been bitten by the Tarantula.

*All in the Wrong**

MANY years ago, I contracted an intimacy with a Mr William Legrand. He was of an ancient Huguenot family, and had once been wealthy; but a series of misfortunes had reduced him to want. To avoid the mortification consequent upon his disasters, he left New Orleans, the city of his forefathers, and took up his residence at Sullivan's Island, near Charleston, South Carolina.

This Island is a very singular one. It consists of little else than the sea sand, and is about three miles long. Its breadth at no point exceeds a quarter of a mile. It is separated from the main land by a scarcely perceptible creek, oozing its way through a wilderness of reeds and slime, a favorite resort of the marsh-hen. The vegetation, as might be supposed, is scant, or at least dwarfish. No trees of any magnitude are to be seen. Near the western extremity, where Fort Moultrie stands, and where are some miserable frame buildings, tenanted, during summer, by the fugitives from Charleston dust and fever, may be found, indeed, the bristly palmetto; but the whole island, with the exception of this western point, and a line of hard, white beach on the seacoast, is covered with a dense undergrowth of the sweet myrtle, so much prized by the horticulturists of England. The shrub here often attains the height of fifteen or twenty feet, and forms an almost impenetrable coppice, burthening the air with its fragrance.

In the inmost recesses of this coppice, not far from the eastern or more remote end of the island, Legrand had built himself a small hut, which he occupied when I first, by mere accident, made his acquaintance. This soon ripened into friendship—for there was much in the recluse to excite interest and esteem. I found him well educated, with unusual powers of mind, but infected with misanthropy, and subject to perverse moods of alternate enthusiasm and melancholy. He had with him many books, but rarely employed them. His chief amusements were gunning and fishing, or sauntering along the beach and through the myrtles, in quest of shells or entomological specimens;—his collection of the latter might have been envied by a Swammerdamm. In these excursions he was usually accompanied by an old negro, called Jupiter, who had been manumitted before the reverses of the family, but who could be induced, neither by threats nor by promises, to abandon what he considered his right of attendance upon the footsteps of his young 'Massa Will.' It is not improbable that the relatives of Legrand, conceiving him to be somewhat unsettled in intellect, had contrived to instil this obstinacy into Jupiter, with a view to the supervision and guardianship of the wanderer.

The winters in the latitude of Sullivan's Island are seldom very severe, and in the fall of the year it is a rare event indeed when a fire is considered necessary. About the middle of October, 18—, there occurred, however, a day of remarkable chilliness. Just before sunset I scrambled my way through the evergreens to the hut of my friend, whom I had not visited for several weeks—my residence being, at that time, in Charleston, a distance of nine miles from the Island, while the facilities of passage and re-passage were very far behind those of the present day. Upon reaching the hut I rapped, as was my custom, and getting no reply, sought for the key where I knew it was secreted, unlocked the door and went in. A fine fire was blazing upon the hearth. It was a novelty, and by no means an ungrateful one. I threw off an overcoat, took an arm-chair by the crackling logs, and awaited patiently the arrival of my hosts.

Soon after dark they arrived, and gave me a most cordial welcome. Jupiter, grinning from ear to ear, bustled about to prepare some marsh-hens for supper. Legrand was in one of his fits—how else shall I term them?—of enthusiasm. He had found an unknown bivalve, forming a new genus, and, more than this, he had hunted down and secured, with Jupiter's assistance, a *scarabæus** which he believed to be totally new, but in respect to which he wished to have my opinion on the morrow.

'And why not to-night?' I asked, rubbing my hands over the blaze, and wishing the whole tribe of *scarabæi* at the devil.

'Ah, if I had only known you were here!' said Legrand, 'but it's so long since I saw you; and how could I foresee that you would pay me a visit this very night of all others? As I was coming home I met Lieutenant G——, from the fort, and, very foolishly, I lent him the bug; so it will be impossible for you to see it until morning. Stay here to-night, and I will send Jup down for it at sunrise. It is the loveliest thing in creation!'

'What?—sunrise?'

'Nonsense! no!—the bug. It is of a brilliant gold color—about the size of a large hickory-nut—with two jet black spots near one extremity of the back, and another, somewhat longer, at the other. The *antennæ* are —'

'Dey aint *no* tin in him, Massa Will, I keep a tellin on you,' here interrupted Jupiter; 'de bug is a goole bug, solid, ebery bit of him, inside and all, sep him wing—neber feel half so hebby a bug in my life.'

'Well, suppose it is, Jup,' replied Legrand, somewhat more earnestly, it seemed to me, than the case demanded, 'is that any reason for your letting the birds burn? The color'—here he turned to me—'is really almost enough to warrant Jupiter's idea. You never saw a more brilliant metallic lustre than the scales emit—but of this you cannot judge till to-morrow. In the mean time I can give you some idea of the shape.' Saying this, he seated himself at a small table, on which were a pen and ink, but no paper. He looked for some in a drawer, but found none.

'Never mind,' said he at length, 'this will answer;' and he drew from his waistcoat pocket a scrap of what I took to be very dirty foolscap, and made upon it a rough drawing with the pen. While he did this, I retained my seat by the fire, for I was still chilly. When the design was complete, he handed it to me without rising. As I received it, a loud growl was heard, succeeded by a scratching at the door. Jupiter opened it, and a large Newfoundland, belonging to Legrand, rushed in, leaped upon my shoulders, and loaded me with caresses; for I had shown him much attention during previous visits. When his gambols were over, I looked at the paper, and, to speak the truth, found myself not a little puzzled at what my friend had depicted.

'Well!' I said, after contemplating it for some minutes, 'this *is* a strange *scarabæus*, I must confess: new to me: never saw anything like it before—unless it was a skull, or a death's-head—which it more nearly resembles than anything else that has come under *my* observation.'

'A death's-head!' echoed Legrand—'Oh—yes—well, it has something of that appearance upon paper, no doubt. The two upper black spots look like eyes, eh? and the longer one at the bottom like a mouth—and then the shape of the whole is oval.'

'Perhaps so,' said I; 'but, Legrand, I fear you are no artist. I must wait until I see the beetle itself, if I am to form any idea of its personal appearance.'

'Well, I don't know,' said he, a little nettled, 'I draw tolerably—

should do it at least—have had good masters, and flatter myself that I am not quite a blockhead.'

'But, my dear fellow, you are joking then,' said I, 'this is a very passable *skull*—indeed, I may say that it is a very *excellent* skull, according to the vulgar notions about such specimens of physiology—and your *scarabæus* must be the queerest *scarabæus* in the world if it resembles it. Why, we may get up a very thrilling bit of superstition upon this hint. I presume you will call the bug *scarabæus caput hominis*,* or something of that kind—there are many similar titles in the Natural Histories. But where are the *antennæ* you spoke of?'

'The *antennæ!*' said Legrand, who seemed to be getting unaccountably warm upon the subject; 'I am sure you must see the *antennæ*. I made them as distinct as they are in the original insect, and I presume that is sufficient.'

'Well, well,' I said, 'perhaps you have—still I don't see them;' and I handed him the paper without additional remark, not wishing to ruffle his temper; but I was much surprised at the turn affairs had taken; his ill humor puzzled me—and, as for the drawing of the beetle, there were positively *no antennæ* visible, and the whole *did* bear a very close resemblance to the ordinary cuts of a death's-head.

He received the paper very peevishly, and was about to crumple it, apparently to throw it in the fire, when a casual glance at the design seemed suddenly to rivet his attention. In an instant his face grew violently red—in another as excessively pale. For some minutes he continued to scrutinize the drawing minutely where he sat. At length he arose, took a candle from the table, and proceeded to seat himself upon a sea-chest in the farthest corner of the room. Here again he made an anxious examination of the paper; turning it in all directions. He said nothing, however, and his conduct greatly astonished me; yet I thought it prudent not to exacerbate the growing moodiness of his temper by any comment. Presently he took from his coat pocket a wallet, placed the paper carefully in it, and deposited both in a writing-desk, which he locked. He now grew more composed in his demeanor; but his original air of enthusiasm had quite disappeared. Yet he seemed not so much sulky as abstracted. As the evening wore away he became more and more absorbed in reverie, from which no sallies of mine could arouse him. It had been my intention to pass the night at the hut, as I had frequently done before, but, seeing my host in this mood, I deemed it proper to take leave. He did not press me to remain, but, as I departed, he shook my hand with even more than his usual cordiality.

It was about a month after this (and during the interval I had seen nothing of Legrand) when I received a visit, at Charleston, from his man, Jupiter. I had never seen the good old negro look so dispirited, and I feared that some serious disaster had befallen my friend.

'Well, Jup,' said I, 'what is the matter now?—how is your master?'

'Why, to speak de troof, massa, him not so berry well as mought be.'

'Not well! I am truly sorry to hear it. What does he complain of?'

'Dar! dat 's it!—him neber plain of notin—but him berry sick for all dat.'

'*Very* sick, Jupiter!—why didn't you say so at once? Is he confined to bed?'

'No, dat he aint!—he aint find nowhar—dat's just whar de shoe pinch—my mind is got to be berry hebby bout poor Massa Will.'

'Jupiter, I should like to understand what it is you are talking about. You say your master is sick. Hasn't he told you what ails him?'

'Why, massa, taint worf while for to git mad bout de matter—Massa Will say noffin at all aint de matter wid him—but den what make him go about looking dis here way, wid he head down and he soldiers up, and as white as a gose? And den he keep a syphon all de time—'

'Keeps a what, Jupiter?'

'Keeps a syphon wid de figgurs on de slate—de queerest figgurs I ebber did see. Ise gittin to be skeered, I tell you. Hab for to keep mighty tight eye pon him noovers. Todder day he gib me slip fore de sun up and was gone de whole ob de blessed day. I had a big stick ready cut for to gib him d—d good beating when he did come—but Ise sich a fool dat I hadn't de heart arter all—he look so berry poorly.'

'Eh?—what?—ah yes!—upon the whole I think you had better not be too severe with the poor fellow—don't flog him, Jupiter—he can't very well stand it—but can you form no idea of what has occasioned this illness, or rather this change of conduct? Has anything unpleasant happened since I saw you?'

'No, massa, dey aint bin noffin onpleasant *since* den—'twas *fore* den I 'm feared—'twas de berry day you was dare.'

'How? what do you mean?'

'Why, massa, I mean de bug—dare now.'

'The what?'

'De bug—I'm berry sartain dat Massa Will bin bit somewhere bout de head by dat goole-bug.'

'And what cause have you, Jupiter, for such a supposition?'

'Claws enuff, massa, and mouff too. I nebber did see sich a d—d bug — he kick and he bite ebery ting what cum near him. Massa Will cotch him fuss, but had for to let him go gin mighty quick, I tell you—den was de time he must ha got de bite. I didn't like de look ob de bug mouff, myself, no how, so I wouldn't take hold ob him wid my finger, but I cotch him wid a piece ob paper dat I found. I rap him up in de paper and stuff piece ob it in he mouff—dat was de way.'

'And you think, then, that your master was really bitten by the beetle, and that the bite made him sick?'

'I don't tink noffin about it—I nose it. What make him dream bout de goole so much, if taint cause he bit by de goole-bug? Ise heerd bout dem goole-bugs fore dis.'

'But how do you know he dreams about gold?'

'How I know? why cause he talk about it in he sleep—dat's how I nose.'

'Well, Jup, perhaps you are right; but to what fortunate circumstance am I to attribute the honor of a visit from you to-day?'

'What de matter, massa?'

'Did you bring any message from Mr Legrand?'

'No, massa, I bring dis here pissel;' and here Jupiter handed me a note which ran thus:

MY DEAR——

Why have I not seen you for so long a time? I hope you have not been so foolish as to take offence at any little *brusquerie* of mine; but no, that is improbable.

Since I saw you I have had great cause for anxiety. I have something to tell you, yet scarcely know how to tell it, or whether I should tell it at all.

I have not been quite well for some days past, and poor old Jup annoys me, almost beyond endurance, by his well-meant attentions. Would you believe it?—he had prepared a huge stick, the other day, with which to chastise me for giving him the slip, and spending the day, *solus*, among the hills on the main land. I verily believe that my ill looks alone saved me a flogging.

I have made no addition to my cabinet since we met.

If you can, in any way, make it convenient, come over with Jupiter. *Do* come. I wish to see you *to-night*, upon business of importance. I assure you that it is of the *highest* importance.

Ever yours,

WILLIAM LEGRAND.

There was something in the tone of this note which gave me great uneasiness. Its whole style differed materially from that of Legrand. What could he be dreaming of? What new crotchet possessed his excitable brain? What 'business of the highest importance' could *he* possibly have to transact? Jupiter's account of him boded no good. I dreaded lest the continued pressure of misfortune had, at length, fairly unsettled the reason of my friend. Without a moment's hesitation, therefore, I prepared to accompany the negro.

Upon reaching the wharf, I noticed a scythe and three spades, all apparently new, lying in the bottom of the boat in which we were to embark.

'What is the meaning of all this, Jup?' I inquired.

'Him syfe, massa, and spade.'

'Very true; but what are they doing here?'

'Him de syfe and de spade what Massa Will sis pon my buying for him in de town, and de debbil's own lot of money I had to gib for em.'

'But what, in the name of all that is mysterious, is your "Massa Will" going to do with scythes and spades?'

'Dat 's more dan *I* know, and debbil take me if I don't blieve 'tis more dan he know, too. But it's all cum ob de bug.'

Finding that no satisfaction was to be obtained of Jupiter, whose whole intellect seemed to be absorbed by 'de bug,' I now stepped into the boat and made sail. With a fair and strong breeze we soon ran into the little cove to the northward of Fort Moultrie, and a walk of some two miles brought us to the hut. It was about three in the afternoon when we arrived. Legrand had been awaiting us in eager expectation. He grasped my hand with a nervous *empressement* which alarmed me and strengthened the suspicions already entertained. His countenance was pale even to ghastliness, and his deep-set eyes glared with unnatural lustre. After some inquiries respecting his health, I asked him, not knowing what better to say, if he had yet obtained the *scarabæus* from Lieutenant G——.

'Oh, yes,' he replied, coloring violently, 'I got it from him the next morning. Nothing should tempt me to part with that *scarabæus*. Do you know that Jupiter is quite right about it?'

'In what way?' I asked, with a sad foreboding at heart.

'In supposing it to be a bug of *real gold*.' He said this with an air of profound seriousness, and I felt inexpressibly shocked.

'This bug is to make my fortune,' he continued, with a triumphant smile, 'to reinstate me in my family possessions. Is it any wonder, then, that I prize it? Since Fortune has thought fit to bestow it upon me, I have only to use it properly and I shall arrive at the gold of which it is the index. Jupiter, bring me that *scarabæus!*'

'What! de bug, massa? I'd rudder not go fer trubble dat bug—you mus git him for your own self.' Hereupon Legrand arose, with a grave and stately air, and brought me the beetle from a glass case in which it was enclosed. It was a beautiful *scarabæus*, and, at that time, unknown to naturalists—of course a great prize in a scientific point of view. There were two round, black spots near one extremity of the back, and a long one near the other. The scales were exceedingly hard and glossy, with all the appearance of burnished gold. The weight of the insect was very remarkable, and, taking all things into consideration, I could hardly blame Jupiter for his opinion respecting it; but what to make of Legrand's agreement with that opinion, I could not, for the life of me, tell.

'I sent for you,' said he, in a grandiloquent tone, when I had completed my examination of the beetle, 'I sent for you, that I might have your counsel and assistance in furthering the views of Fate and of the bug'—

'My dear Legrand,' I cried, interrupting him, 'you are certainly unwell, and had better use some little precautions. You shall go to bed, and I will remain with you a few days, until you get over this. You are feverish and'—

'Feel my pulse,' said he.

I felt it, and, to say the truth, found not the slightest indication of fever.

'But you may be ill and yet have no fever. Allow me this once to prescribe for you. In the first place, go to bed. In the next'—

'You are mistaken,' he interposed, 'I am as well as I can expect to be under the excitement which I suffer. If you really wish me well, you will relieve this excitement.'

'And how is this to be done?'

'Very easily. Jupiter and myself are going upon an expedition into the hills, upon the main land, and, in this expedition, we shall need the aid of some person in whom we can confide. You are the only one we can trust. Whether we succeed or fail, the excitement which you now perceive in me will be equally allayed.'

'I am anxious to oblige you in any way,' I replied; 'but do you mean to say that this infernal beetle has any connection with your expedition into the hills?'

'It has.'

'Then, Legrand, I can become a party to no such absurd proceeding.'

'I am sorry—very sorry—for we shall have to try it by ourselves.'

'Try it by yourselves! The man is surely mad!—but stay!—how long do you propose to be absent?'

'Probably all night. We shall start immediately, and be back, at all events, by sunrise.'

'And will you promise me, upon your honor, that when this freak of yours is over, and the bug business (good God!) settled to your satisfaction, you will then return home and follow my advice implicitly, as that of your physician?'

'Yes; I promise; and now let us be off, for we have no time to lose.'

With a heavy heart I accompanied my friend. We started about four o'clock—Legrand, Jupiter, the dog, and myself. Jupiter had with him the scythe and spades—the whole of which he insisted upon carrying—more through fear, it seemed to me, of trusting either of the implements within reach of his master, than from any excess of industry or complaisance. His demeanor was dogged in the extreme, and 'dat d—d bug' were the sole words which escaped his lips during the journey. For my own part, I had charge of a couple of dark lanterns, while Legrand contented himself with the *scarabæus*, which he carried attached to the end of a bit of whip-cord; twirling it to and fro, with the air of a conjuror, as he went. When I observed this last, plain evidence of my friend's aberration of mind, I could scarcely refrain from tears. I thought it best, however, to humor his fancy, at least for the present, or until I could adopt some more energetic measures with a chance of success. In the mean time I endeavored, but all in vain, to sound him in regard to the object of the expedition. Having succeeded in inducing me to accompany him, he seemed unwilling to hold conversation upon any topic of minor importance, and to all my questions vouchsafed no other reply than 'we shall see!'

We crossed the creek at the head of the island by means of a skiff, and, ascending the high grounds on the shore of the main land, proceeded in a northwesterly direction, through a tract of country excessively wild and desolate, where no trace of a human footstep was to be seen. Legrand led the way with decision; pausing only for an instant, here and there, to consult what appeared to be certain landmarks of his own contrivance upon a former occasion.

In this manner we journeyed for about two hours, and the sun was just setting when we entered a region infinitely more dreary than any yet seen. It was a species of table land, near the summit of an almost inaccessible hill, densely wooded from base to pinnacle, and interspersed with huge crags that appeared to lie loosely upon the soil, and in many cases were prevented from precipitating themselves into the valleys below, merely by the support of the trees against which they reclined. Deep ravines, in various directions, gave an air of still sterner solemnity to the scene.

The natural platform to which we had clambered was thickly overgrown with brambles, through which we soon discovered that it would have been impossible to force our way but for the scythe; and Jupiter, by direction of his master, proceeded to clear for us a path to the foot of an enormously tall tulip-tree, which stood, with some eight or ten oaks, upon the level, and far surpassed them all, and all other trees which I had then ever seen, in the beauty of its foliage and form, in the wide spread of its branches, and in the general majesty of its appearance. When we reached this tree, Legrand turned to Jupiter, and asked him if he thought he could climb it. The old man seemed a little staggered by the question, and for some moments made no reply. At length he approached the huge trunk, walked slowly around it, and examined it with minute attention. When he had completed his scrutiny, he merely said,

'Yes, massa, Jup climb any tree he ebber see in he life.'

'Then up with you as soon as possible, for it will soon be too dark to see what we are about.'

'How far mus go up, massa?' inquired Jupiter.

'Get up the main trunk first, and then I will tell you which way to go—and here—stop! take this beetle with you.'

'De bug, Massa Will!—de goole bug!' cried the negro, drawing back in dismay—'what for mus tote de bug way up de tree? — d—n if I do!'

'If you are afraid, Jup, a great big negro like you, to take hold of a harmless little dead beetle, why you can carry it up by this string—but, if you do not take it up with you in some way, I shall be under the necessity of breaking your head with this shovel.'

'What de matter now, massa?' said Jup, evidently shamed into compliance; 'always want for to raise fuss wid old nigger. Was only funnin any how. *Me* feered de bug! what I keer for de bug?' Here he took cautiously hold of the extreme end of the string, and, maintaining the insect as far from his person as circumstances would permit, prepared to ascend the tree.

In youth, the tulip-tree, or *Liriodendron Tulipiferum*, the most magnificent of American foresters, has a trunk peculiarly smooth, and often rises to a great height without lateral branches; but, in its riper age, the bark becomes gnarled and uneven, while many short limbs make their appearance on the stem. Thus the difficulty of ascension, in the present case, lay more in semblance than in reality. Embracing the huge cylinder, as closely as possible, with his arms and knees, seizing with his hands some projections, and resting his naked toes upon others, Jupiter, after one or two narrow escapes from falling, at length wriggled himself into the first great fork, and seemed to consider the whole business as virtually accomplished. The *risk* of the achievement was, in fact, now over, although the climber was some sixty or seventy feet from the ground.

'Which way mus go now, Massa Will?' he asked.

'Keep up the largest branch—the one on this side,' said Legrand. The negro obeyed him promptly, and apparently with but little trouble; ascending higher and higher, until no glimpse of his squat figure could be obtained through the dense foliage which enveloped it. Presently his voice was heard in a sort of halloo.

'How much fudder is got for go?'

'How high up are you?' asked Legrand.

'Ebber so fur,' replied the negro; 'can see de sky fru de top ob de tree.'

'Never mind the sky, but attend to what I say. Look down the trunk and count the limbs below you on this side. How many limbs have you passed?'

'One, two, tree, four, fibe—I done pass fibe big limb, massa, pon dis side.'

'Then go one limb higher.'

In a few minutes the voice was heard again, announcing that the seventh limb was attained.

'Now, Jup,' cried Legrand, evidently much excited, 'I want you to work your way out upon that limb as far as you can. If you see anything strange, let me know.'

By this time what little doubt I might have entertained of my poor friend's insanity, was put finally at rest. I had no alternative but to conclude him stricken with lunacy, and I became seriously anxious about getting him home. While I was pondering upon what was best to be done, Jupiter's voice was again heard.

'Mos feerd for to ventur pon dis limb berry far—tis dead limb putty much all de way.'

'Did you say it was a *dead* limb, Jupiter?' cried Legrand in a quavering voice.

'Yes, massa, him dead as de door-nail—done up for sartain—done departed dis here life.'

'What in the name of heaven shall I do?' asked Legrand, seemingly in the greatest distress.

'Do!' said I, glad of an opportunity to interpose a word, 'why come home and go to bed. Come now!—that's a fine fellow. It's getting late, and, besides, you remember your promise.'

'Jupiter,' cried he, without heeding me in the least, 'do you hear me?'

'Yes, Massa Will, hear you ebber so plain.'

'Try the wood well, then, with your knife, and see if you think it *very* rotten.'

'Him rotten, massa, sure nuff,' replied the negro in a few moments, 'but not so berry rotten as mought be. Mought ventur out leetle way pon de limb by myself, dat's true.'

'By yourself!—what do you mean?'

'Why I mean de bug. 'Tis *berry* hebby bug. Spose I drop him down fuss, and den de limb won't break wid just de weight ob one nigger.'

'You infernal scoundrel!' cried Legrand, apparently much relieved, 'what do you mean by telling me such nonsense as that? As sure as you let that beetle fall—I'll break your neck. Look here, Jupiter—do you hear me?'

'Yes, massa, needn't hollo at poor nigger dat style.'

'Well! now listen!—if you will venture out on the limb as far as you think safe, and not let go the beetle, I'll make you a present of a silver dollar as soon as you get down.'

'I'm gwine, Massa Will—deed I is,' replied the negro very promptly—'mos out to the eend now.'

'*Out to the end!*' here fairly screamed Legrand, 'do you say you are out to the end of that limb?'

'Soon be to de eend, massa,—o-o-o-o-oh! Lor-gol-a-marcy! what *is* dis here pon de tree?'

'Well!' cried Legrand, highly delighted, 'what is it?'

'Why taint noffin but a skull—somebody bin lef him head up de tree, and de crows done gobble ebery bit ob de meat off.'

'A skull, you say!—very well!—how is it fastened to the limb?—what holds it on?'

'Sure nuff, massa; mus look. Why dis berry curous sarcumstance, pon my word—dare's a great big nail in de skull, what fastens ob it on to de tree.'

'Well now, Jupiter, do exactly as I tell you—do you hear?'

'Yes, massa.'

'Pay attention, then!—find the left eye of the skull.'

'Hum! hoo! dat's good! why dar aint no eye lef at all.'

'Curse your stupidity! do you know your right hand from your left?'

'Yes, I nose dat—nose all bout dat—tis my left hand what I chops de wood wid.'

'To be sure! you are left-handed; and your left eye is on the same side as your left hand. Now, I suppose, you can find the left eye of the skull, or the place where the left eye has been. Have you found it?'

Here was a long pause. At length the negro asked,

'Is de lef eye of de skull pon de same side as de lef hand of de skull, too?—cause de skull aint got not a bit ob a hand at all—nebber mind! I got de lef eye now—here the lef eye! what mus do wid it?'

'Let the beetle drop through it, as far as the string will reach—but be careful and not let go your hold of the string.'

'All dat done, Massa Will; mighty easy ting for to put de bug fru de hole—look out for him dar below!'

During this colloquy no portion of Jupiter's person could be seen; but the beetle, which he had suffered to descend, was now visible at the end of the string, and glistened, like a globe of burnished gold, in the last rays of the setting sun, some of which still faintly illumined the eminence upon which we stood. The *scarabæus* hung quite clear of any branches, and, if allowed to fall, would have fallen at our feet. Legrand immediately took the scythe, and cleared with it a circular space, three or four yards in diameter, just beneath the insect, and, having accomplished this, ordered Jupiter to let go the string and come down from the tree.

Driving a peg, with great nicety, into the ground, at the precise spot where the beetle fell, my friend now produced from his pocket a tape-measure. Fastening one end of this at that point of the trunk of the tree which was nearest the peg, he unrolled it till it reached the peg, and thence farther unrolled it, in the direction already established by the two points of the tree and the peg, for the distance of fifty feet—Jupiter clearing away the brambles with the scythe. At the spot thus attained a second peg was driven, and about this, as a centre, a rude circle, about four feet in diameter, described. Taking now a spade himself, and giving one to Jupiter and one to me, Legrand begged us to set about digging as quickly as possible.

To speak the truth, I had no especial relish for such amusement at any time, and, at that particular moment, would most willingly have declined it; for the night was coming on, and I felt much fatigued with the exercise already taken; but I saw no mode of escape, and was fearful of disturbing my poor friend's equanimity by a refusal. Could I have depended, indeed, upon Jupiter's aid, I would have had no hesitation in attempting to get the lunatic home by force; but I was too well assured of the old negro's disposition, to hope that he would assist me, under any circumstances, in a personal contest with his master. I made no doubt that the latter had been infected with some of the innumerable Southern superstitions about money buried, and that his phantasy had received confirmation by the finding of the *scarabæus*, or, perhaps, by Jupiter's obstinacy in maintaining it to be 'a bug of real gold.' A mind disposed to lunacy would readily be led away by such suggestions—especially if chiming in with favorite preconceived ideas—and then I called to mind the poor fellow's speech about the beetle's being 'the index of his fortune.' Upon the whole, I was sadly vexed and puzzled, but, at length, I concluded to make a virtue of necessity—to dig with a good will, and thus the sooner to convince the visionary, by ocular demonstration, of the fallacy of the opinions he entertained.

The lanterns having been lit, we all fell to work with a zeal worthy a more rational cause; and, as the glare fell upon our persons and implements, I could not help thinking how picturesque a group we composed, and how strange and suspicious our labors must have appeared to any interloper who, by chance, might have stumbled upon our whereabouts.

We dug very steadily for two hours. Little was said; and our chief embarrassment lay in the yelpings of the dog, who took exceeding interest in our proceedings. He, at length, became so obstreperous that we grew fearful of his giving the alarm to some stragglers in the vicinity;—or, rather, this was the apprehension of Legrand;—for myself, I should have rejoiced at any interruption which might have enabled me to get the wanderer home. The noise was, at length, very effectually silenced by Jupiter, who, getting out of the hole with a dogged air of deliberation, tied the brute's mouth up with one of his suspenders, and then returned, with a grave chuckle, to his task.

When the time mentioned had expired, we had reached a depth of five feet, and yet no signs of any treasure became manifest. A general pause ensued, and I began to hope that the farce was at an end. Legrand, however, although evidently much disconcerted, wiped his brow thoughtfully and recommenced. We had excavated the entire circle of four feet diameter, and now we slightly enlarged the limit, and went to the farther depth of two feet. Still nothing appeared. The gold-seeker, whom I sincerely pitied, at length clambered from the pit, with the bitterest disappointment imprinted upon every feature, and proceeded, slowly and reluctantly, to put on his coat, which he had thrown off at the beginning of his labor. In the mean time I made no remark. Jupiter, at a signal from his master, began to gather up his tools. This done, and the dog having been unmuzzled, we turned in profound silence towards home.

We had taken, perhaps, a dozen steps in this direction, when, with a loud oath, Legrand strode up to Jupiter, and seized him by the collar. The astonished negro opened his eyes and mouth to the fullest extent, let fall the spades, and fell upon his knees.

'You scoundrel,' said Legrand, hissing out the syllables from between his clenched teeth—'you infernal black villain!—speak, I tell you!—answer me this instant, without prevarication!—which—which is your left eye?'

'Oh, my golly, Massa Will! aint dis here my lef eye for sartain?' roared the terrified Jupiter, placing his hand upon his *right* organ of vision, and holding it there with a desperate pertinacity, as if in immediate dread of his master's attempt at a gouge.

'I thought so!—I knew it!—hurrah!' vociferated Legrand, letting the negro go, and executing a series of curvets and caracols, much to the astonishment of his valet, who, arising from his knees, looked, mutely, from his master to myself, and then from myself to his master.

'Come! we must go back,' said the latter, 'the game's not up yet;' and he again led the way to the tulip-tree.

'Jupiter,' said he, when we reached its foot, 'come here! was the skull nailed to the limb with the face outward, or with the face to the limb?'

'De face was out, massa, so dat de crows could get at de eyes good, widout any trouble.'

'Well, then, was it this eye or that through which you let the beetle fall?'—here Legrand touched each of Jupiter's eyes.

'Twas dis eye, massa—de lef eye—jis as you tell me,' and here it was his right eye that the negro indicated.

'That will do—we must try it again.'

Here my friend, about whose madness I now saw, or fancied that I saw, certain indications of method, removed the peg which marked the spot where the beetle fell, to a spot about three inches to the westward of its former position. Taking, now, the tape-measure from the nearest point of the trunk to the peg, as before, and continuing the extension in a straight line to the distance of fifty feet, a spot was indicated, removed, by several yards, from the point at which we had been digging.

Around the new position a circle, somewhat larger than in the former instance, was now described, and we again set to work with the spades. I was dreadfully weary, but, scarcely understanding what had occasioned the change in my thoughts, I felt no longer any great aversion from the labor imposed. I had become most unaccountably interested—nay, even excited. Perhaps there was something, amid all the extravagant demeanor of Legrand—some air of forethought, or of deliberation, which impressed me. I dug eagerly, and now and then caught myself actually looking, with something that very much resembled expectation, for the fancied treasure, the vision of which had demented my unfortunate companion. At a period when such vagaries of thought most fully possessed me, and when we had been at work perhaps an hour and a half, we were again interrupted by the violent howlings of the dog. His uneasiness, in the first instance, had been, evidently, but the result of playfulness or caprice, but he now assumed a bitter and serious tone. Upon Jupiter's again attempting to muzzle him, he made furious resistance, and, leaping into the hole, tore up the mould frantically with his claws. In a few seconds he had uncovered a mass of human bones, forming two complete skeletons, intermingled with several buttons of metal, and what appeared to be the dust of decayed woollen. One or two strokes of a spade upturned the blade of a large Spanish knife, and, as we dug farther, three or four loose pieces of gold and silver coin came to light.

At sight of these the joy of Jupiter could scarcely be restrained, but the countenance of his master wore an air of extreme disappointment. He urged us, however, to continue our exertions, and the words were hardly uttered when I stumbled and fell forward, having caught the toe of my boot in a large ring of iron that lay half buried in the loose earth.

We now worked in earnest, and never did I pass ten minutes of more intense excitement. During this interval we had fairly unearthed an oblong chest of wood, which, from its perfect preservation and wonderful hardness, and plainly been subjected to some mineralizing process—perhaps that of the Bi-chloride of Mercury. This box was three feet and a half long, three feet broad, and two and a half feet deep. It was firmly secured by bands of wrought iron, riveted, and forming a kind of trellis-work over the whole. On each side of the chest, near the top, were three rings of iron—six in all—by means of which a firm hold could be obtained by six persons. Our utmost united endeavors served only to disturb the coffer very slightly in its bed. We at once saw the impossibility of removing so great a weight. Luckily, the sole fastenings of the lid consisted of two sliding bolts. These we drew back—trembling and panting with anxiety. In an instant, a treasure of incalculable value lay gleaming before us. As the rays of the lanterns fell within the pit, there flashed upwards from a confused heap of gold and of jewels, a glow and a glare that absolutely dazzled our eyes.

I shall not pretend to describe the feelings with which I gazed. Amazement was, of course, predominant. Legrand appeared exhausted with excitement, and spoke very few words. Jupiter's countenance wore, for some minutes, as deadly a pallor as it is possible, in the nature of things, for any negro's visage to assume. He seemed stupified—thunderstricken. Presently he fell upon his knees in the pit, and, burying his naked arms up to the elbows in gold, let them there remain, as if enjoying the luxury of a bath. At length, with a deep sigh, he exclaimed, as if in a soliloquy,

'And dis all cum ob de goole-bug! de putty goole-bug! de poor little goole-bug, what I boosed in dat sabage kind ob style! Aint you shamed ob yourself, nigger?—answer me dat!'

It became necessary, at last, that I should arouse both master and valet to the expediency of removing the treasure. It was growing late, and it behooved us to make exertion, that we might get every thing housed before daylight. It was difficult to say what should be done;

and much time was spent in deliberation—so confused were the ideas of all. We, finally, lightened the box by removing two thirds of its contents, when we were enabled, with some trouble, to raise it from the hole. The articles taken out were deposited among the brambles, and the dog left to guard them, with strict orders from Jupiter neither, upon any pretence, to stir from the spot, nor to open his mouth until our return. We then hurriedly made for home with the chest; reaching the hut in safety, but after excessive toil, at one o'clock in the morning. Worn out as we were, it was not in human nature to do more just then. We rested until two, and had supper; starting for the hills immediately afterwards, armed with three stout sacks, which, by good luck, were upon the premises. A little before four we arrived at the pit, divided the remainder of the booty, as equally as might be, among us, and, leaving the holes unfilled, again set out for the hut, at which, for the second time, we deposited our golden burthens, just as the first streaks of the dawn gleamed from over the tree-tops in the East.

We were now thoroughly broken down; but the intense excitement of the time denied us repose. After an unquiet slumber of some three or four hours' duration, we arose, as if by preconcert, to make examination of our treasure.

The chest had been full to the brim, and we spent the whole day, and the greater part of the next night, in a scrutiny of its contents. There had been nothing like order or arrangement. Every thing had been heaped in promiscuously. Having assorted all with care, we found ourselves possessed of even vaster wealth than we had at first supposed. In coin there was rather more than four hundred and fifty thousand dollars— estimating the value of the pieces, as accurately as we could, by the tables of the period. There was not a particle of silver. All was gold of antique date and of great variety—French, Spanish, and German money, with a few English guineas, and some counters, of which we had never seen specimens before. There were several very large and heavy coins, so worn that we could make nothing of their inscriptions. There was no American money. The value of the jewels we found more difficulty in estimating. There were diamonds—some of them exceedingly large and fine—a hundred and ten in all, and not one of them small; eighteen rubies of remarkable brilliancy;— three hundred and ten emeralds, all very beautiful; and twenty-one sapphires, with an opal. These stones had all been broken from their settings and thrown loose in the chest. The settings themselves, which we picked out from among the other gold, appeared to have been beaten up with hammers, as if to prevent identification. Besides all this, there was a vast quantity of solid gold ornaments;—nearly two hundred massive finger and ear rings;—rich chains—thirty of these, if I remember;—eighty-three very large and heavy crucifixes;— five gold censers of great value;—a prodigious golden punch-bowl, ornamented with richly chased vine-leaves and Bacchanalian figures; with two sword-handles exquisitely embossed, and many other smaller articles which I cannot recollect. The weight of these valuables exceeded three hundred and fifty pounds avoirdupois; and in this estimate I have not included one hundred and ninety-seven superb gold watches; three of the number being worth each five hundred dollars, if one. Many of them were very old, and as time keepers valueless; the works having suffered, more or less, from corrosion—but all were richly jewelled and in cases of great worth. We estimated the entire contents of the chest, that night, at a million and a half of dollars; and, upon the subsequent disposal of the trinkets and jewels (a few being retained for our own use), it was found that we had greatly undervalued the treasure.

When, at length, we had concluded our examination, and the intense excitement of the time had, in some measure, subsided, Legrand, who saw that I was dying with impatience for a solution of this most extraordinary riddle, entered into a full detail of all the circumstances connected with it.*

'You remember,' said he, 'the night when I handed you the rough sketch I had made of the *scarabæus*. You recollect also, that I became quite vexed at you for insisting that my drawing resembled a death's-head. When you first made this assertion I thought you were jesting; but afterwards I called to mind the peculiar spots on the back of the insect, and admitted to myself that your remark had some little foundation in fact. Still, the sneer at my graphic powers irritated me—for I am considered a good artist—and, therefore, when you handed me the scrap of parchment, I was about to crumple it up and throw it angrily into the fire.'

'The scrap of paper, you mean,' said I.

'No; it had much of the appearance of paper, and at first I supposed it to be such, but when I came to draw upon it, I discovered it, at once, to be a piece of very thin parchment. It was quite dirty, you remember. Well, as I was in the very act of crumpling it up, my glance fell upon the sketch at which you had been looking, and you may imagine my astonishment when I perceived, in fact, the figure of a death's-head just where, it seemed to me, I had made the drawing of the beetle. For a moment I was too much amazed to think with accuracy. I knew that my design was very different in detail from this—although there was a certain similarity in general outline. Presently I took a candle, and seating myself at the other end of the room, proceeded to scrutinize the parchment more closely. Upon turning it over, I saw my own sketch upon the reverse, just as I had made it. My first idea, now, was mere surprise at the really remarkable similarity of outline—at the singular coincidence involved in the fact, that unknown to me, there should have been a skull upon the other side of the parchment, immediately beneath my figure of the *scarabæus*, and that this skull, not only in outline, but in size, should so closely resemble my drawing. I say the singularity of this coincidence absolutely stupified me for a time. This is the usual effect of such coincidences. The mind struggles to establish a connexion—a sequence of cause and effect—and, being unable to do so, suffers a species of temporary paralysis. But, when I recovered from this stupor, there dawned upon me gradually a conviction which startled me even far more than the coincidence. I began distinctly, positively, to remember that there had been *no* drawing on the parchment when I made my sketch of the *scarabæus*. I became perfectly certain of this; for I recollected turning up first one side and then the other, in search of the cleanest spot. Had the skull been then there, of course I could not have failed to notice it. Here was indeed a mystery which I felt it impossible to explain; but, even at that early moment, there seemed to glimmer, faintly, within the most remote and secret chambers of my intellect, a glow-worm-like conception of that truth which last night's adventure brought to so magnificent a demonstration. I arose at once, and putting the parchment securely away, dismissed all farther reflection until I should be alone.

'When you had gone, and when Jupiter was fast asleep, I betook myself to a more methodical investigation of the affair. In the first place I considered the manner in which the parchment had come into my possession. The spot where we discovered the *scarabæus* was on the coast of the main land, about a mile eastward of the island, and but a short distance above high water mark. Upon my taking hold of it, it gave me a sharp bite, which caused me to let it drop. Jupiter, with his accustomed caution, before seizing the insect, which had flown towards him, looked about him for a leaf, or something of that nature, by which to take hold of it. It was at this moment that his eyes, and mine also, fell upon the scrap of parchment, which I then supposed to be paper. It was lying half buried in the sand, a corner sticking up. Near the spot where we found it, I observed the remnants of the hull of what appeared to have been a ship's long boat. The wreck seemed to have been there for a very great while; for the resemblance to boat timbers could scarcely be traced.

'Well, Jupiter picked up the parchment, wrapped the beetle in it, and gave it to me. Soon afterwards we turned to go home, and on the way met Lieutenant G—. I showed him the insect, and he begged me to let him take it to the fort. On my consenting, he thrust it forthwith into his waistcoat pocket, without the parchment in which it had been wrapped, and which I had continued to hold in my hand during his inspection. Perhaps he dreaded my changing my mind, and thought it best to make sure of the prize at once—you know how enthusiastic he is on all subjects connected with Natural History. At the same time, without being conscious of it, I must have deposited the parchment in my own pocket.

'You remember that when I went to the table, for the purpose of making a sketch of the beetle, I found no paper where it was usually kept. I looked in the drawer, and found none there. I searched my pockets, hoping to find an old letter—and then my hand fell upon the parchment. I thus detail the precise mode in which it came into my possession; for the circumstances impressed me with peculiar force.

'No doubt you will think me fanciful—but I had already established a kind of *connexion*. I had put together two links of a great chain. There was a boat lying on a sea-coast, and not far from the boat was a parchment—*not a paper*—with a skull depicted on it. You will, of course, ask "where is the connexion?" I reply that the skull, or death's-head, is the well-known emblem of the pirate. The flag of the death's-head is hoisted in all engagements.

'I have said that the scrap was parchment, and not paper. Parchment is durable—almost imperishable. Matters of little moment are rarely consigned to parchment; since, for the mere ordinary purposes of drawing or writing, it is not nearly so well adapted as paper. This reflection suggested some meaning—some relevancy—in the death's-head. I did not fail to observe, also, the *form* of the parchment. Although one of its corners had been, by some accident, destroyed, it could be seen that the original form was oblong. It was just such a slip, indeed, as might have been chosen for a memorandum—for a record of something to be long remembered and carefully preserved.'

'But,' I interposed, 'you say that the skull was *not* upon the parchment when you made the drawing of the beetle. How then do you trace any connexion between the boat and the skull—since this latter, according to your own admission, must have been designed (God only knows how or by whom) at some period subsequent to your sketching the *scarabæus?*'

'Ah, hereupon turns the whole mystery; although the secret, at this point, I had comparatively little difficulty in solving. My steps were sure, and could afford but a single result. I reasoned, for example, thus: When I drew the *scarabæus*, there was no skull apparent on the parchment. When I had completed the drawing, I gave it to you, and observed you narrowly until you returned it. *You*, therefore, did not design the skull, and no one else was present to do it. Then it was not done by human agency. And nevertheless it was done.

'At this stage of my reflections I endeavored to remember, and *did* remember, with entire distinctness, every incident which occurred about the period in question. The weather was chilly (oh rare and happy accident!), and a fire was blazing on the hearth. I was heated with exercise and sat near the table. You, however, had drawn a chair close to the chimney. Just as I placed the parchment in your hand, and as you were in the act of inspecting it, Wolf, the Newfoundland, entered, and leaped upon your shoulders. With your left hand you caressed him and kept him off, while your right, holding the parchment, was permitted to fall listlessly between your knees, and in close proximity to the fire. At one moment I thought the blaze had caught it, and was about to caution you, but, before I could speak, you had withdrawn it, and were engaged in its examination. When I considered all these particulars, I doubted not for a moment that *heat* had been the agent in bringing to light, on the parchment, the skull which I saw designed on it. You are well aware that chemical preparations exist, and have existed time out of mind, by means of which it is possible to write on either paper or vellum, so that the characters shall become visible only when subjected to the action of fire. Zaffre, digested in *aqua regia*, and diluted with four times its weight of water, is sometimes employed; a green tint results. The regulus of cobalt, dissolved in spirit of nitre, gives a red. These colors disappear at longer or shorter intervals after the material written on cools, but again become apparent upon the re-application of heat.

'I now scrutinized the death's-head with care. Its outer edges—the edges of the drawing nearest the edge of the vellum—were far more *distinct* than the others. It was clear that the action of the caloric had been imperfect or unequal. I immediately kindled a fire, and subjected every portion of the parchment to a glowing heat. At first, the only effect was the strengthening of the faint lines in the skull; but, on persevering in the experiment, there became visible, at the corner of the slip, diagonally opposite to the spot in which the death's-head was delineated, the figure of what I at first supposed to be a goat. A closer scrutiny, however, satisfied me that it was intended for a kid.'

'Ha! ha!' said I, 'to be sure I have no right to laugh at you—a million and a half of money is too serious a matter for mirth—but you are not about to establish a third link in your chain—you will not find any especial connexion between your pirates and a goat—pirates, you know, have nothing to do with goats; they appertain to the farming interest.'

'But I have just said that the figure was *not* that of a goat.'

'Well, a kid then—pretty much the same thing.'

'Pretty much, but not altogether,' said Legrand. 'You may have heard of one *Captain* Kidd.* I at once looked on the figure of the animal as a kind of punning or hieroglyphical signature. I say signature; because its position on the vellum suggested this idea. The death's-head at the corner diagonally opposite, had, in the same manner, the air of a stamp, or seal. But I was sorely put out by the absence of all else—of the body to my imagined instrument—of the text for my context.'

'I presume you expected to find a letter between the stamp and the signature.'

'Something of that kind. The fact is, I felt irresistibly impressed with a presentiment of some vast good fortune impending. I can scarcely say why. Perhaps, after all, it was rather a desire than an actual belief;—but do you know that Jupiter's silly words, about the bug being of solid gold, had a remarkable effect on my fancy? And then the series of accidents and coincidences—these were so *very* extraordinary. Do you observe how mere an accident it was that these events should have occurred on the *sole* day of all the year in which it has been, or may be, sufficiently cool for fire, and that without the fire, or without the intervention of the dog at the precise moment in which he appeared, I should never have become aware of the death's-head, and so never the possessor of the treasure?'

'But proceed—I am all impatience.'

'Well; you have heard, of course, the many stories current—the thousand vague rumors afloat about money buried, somewhere on the Atlantic coast, by Kidd and his associates. These rumors must have had some foundation in fact. And that the rumors have existed so long and so continuously, could have resulted, it appeared to me, only from the circumstance of the buried treasure still *remaining* entombed. Had Kidd concealed his plunder for a time, and afterwards reclaimed it, the rumors would scarcely have reached us in their present unvarying form. You will observe that the stories told are all about money-seekers, not about money-finders. Had the pirate recovered his money, there the affair would have dropped. It seemed to me that some accident—say the loss of a memorandum indicating its locality—had deprived him of the means of recovering it, and that this accident had become known to his followers, who otherwise might never have heard that treasure had been concealed at all, and who, busying themselves in vain, because unguided attempts, to regain it, had given first birth, and then universal currency, to the reports which are now so common. Have you ever heard of any important treasure being unearthed along the coast?'

'Never.'

'But that Kidd's accumulations were immense, is well known. I took it for granted, therefore, that the earth still held them; and you will scarcely be surprised when I tell you that I felt a hope, nearly amounting to certainty, that the parchment so strangely found, involved a lost record of the place of deposit.'

'But how did you proceed?'

'I held the vellum again to the fire, after increasing the heat; but nothing appeared. I now thought it possible that the coating of dirt might have something to do with the failure; so I carefully rinsed the parchment by pouring warm water over it, and, having done this, I placed it in a tin pan, with the skull downwards, and put the pan upon a furnace of lighted charcoal. In a few minutes, the pan having become thoroughly heated, I removed the slip, and, to my inexpressible joy, found it spotted, in several places, with what appeared to be figures arranged in lines. Again I placed it in the pan, and suffered it to remain another minute. On taking it off, the whole was just as you see it now.'

Here Legrand, having re-heated the parchment, submitted it to my inspection. The following characters were rudely traced, in a red tint, between the death's-head and the goat:

53‡‡†305))6*;4826)4‡.)4‡);806*;48†8¶60))85;;]8*;:‡*8†83(88)5*†;46(;
88*96*?;8)*‡(;485);5*†2:*‡(;4956*2(5*–4)8¶8*;4069285);)6†8)4‡‡;1(‡9;4
8081;8:8‡1;48†85;4)485†528806*81(‡9;48;(88;4(‡?34;48)4‡;161;:188;‡?;

'But,' said I, returning him the slip, 'I am as much in the dark as ever. Were all the jewels of Golconda awaiting me on my solution of this enigma, I am quite sure that I should be unable to earn them.'

'And yet,' said Legrand, 'the solution is by no means so difficult as you might be led to imagine from the first hasty inspection of the characters. These characters, as any one might readily guess, form a cipher—that is to say, they convey a meaning; but then, from what is known of Kidd, I could not suppose him capable of constructing any of the more abstruse cryptographs. I made up my mind, at once, that this was of a simple species—such, however, as would appear, to the crude intellect of the sailor, absolutely insoluble without the key.'

'And you really solved it?'

'Readily; I have solved others of an abstruseness ten thousand times greater. Circumstances, and a certain bias of mind, have led me to take interest in such riddles, and it may well be doubted whether human ingenuity can construct an enigma of the kind which human ingenuity may not, by proper application, resolve. In fact, having once established connected and legible characters, I scarcely gave a thought to the mere difficulty of developing their import.

'In the present case—indeed in all cases of secret writing—the first question regards the *language* of the cipher; for the principles of solution, so far, especially, as the more simple ciphers are concerned, depend upon, and are varied by, the genius of the particular idiom. In general, there is no alternative but experiment (directed by probabilities) of every tongue known to him who attempts the solution, until the true one be attained. But, with the cipher now before us, all difficulty is removed by the signature. The pun on the word "Kidd" is appreciable in no other language than the English. But for this consideration I should have begun my attempts with the Spanish and French, as the tongues in which a secret of this kind would most naturally have been written by a pirate of the Spanish main. As it was, I assumed the cryptograph to be English.

'You observe there are no divisions between the words. Had there been divisions, the task would have been comparatively easy. In such case I should have commenced with a collation and analysis of the shorter words, and, had a word of a single letter occurred, as is most likely, (*a* or *I*, for example,) I should have considered the solution as assured. But, there being no division, my first step was to ascertain the predominant letters, as well as the least frequent. Counting all, I constructed a table,* thus:

Of the character 8 there are 33.
; " 26.
4 " 19.
‡) " 16.
* " 13.
5 " 12.
6 " 11.
† 1 " 8.
0 " 6.
9 2 " 5.
: 3 " 4.
? " 3.
¶ " 2.
] —. " 1.

'Now, in English, the letter which most frequently occurs is *e*. Afterwards, the succession runs thus: *a o i d h n r s t u y c f g l m w b k p q x z*. *E*, however, predominates so remarkably that an individual sentence of any length is rarely seen, in which it is not the prevailing character.

'Here, then, we have, in the very beginning, the groundwork for something more than a mere guess. The general use which may be made of the table is obvious—but, in this particular cipher, we shall only very partially require its aid. As our predominant character is 8, we will commence by assuming it as the *e* of the natural alphabet. To verify the supposition, let us observe if the 8 be seen often in couples—for *e* is doubled with great frequency in English—in such words, for example, as "meet," "fleet," "speed," "seen," "been," "agree," &c. In the present instance we see it doubled no less than five times, although the cryptograph is brief.

'Let us assume 8, then, as *e*. Now, of all *words* in the language, "the" is most usual; let us see, therefore, whether there are not repetitions of any three characters, in the same order of collocation, the last of them being 8. If we discover repetitions of such letters, so arranged, they will most probably represent the word "the." On inspection, we find no less than seven such arrangements, the characters being ;48. We may, therefore, assume that the semicolon represents *t*, that 4 represents *h*, and that 8 represents *e*—the last being now well confirmed. Thus a great step has been taken.

'But, having established a single word, we are enabled to establish a vastly important point; that is to say, several commencements and terminations of other words. Let us refer, for example, to the last instance but one, in which the combination ;48 occurs—not far from the end of the cipher. We know that the semicolon immediately ensuing is the commencement of a word, and, of the six characters succeeding this "the," we are cognizant of no less than five. Let us set these characters down, thus, by the letters we know them to represent, leaving a space for the unknown—

t eeth.

'Here we are enabled, at once, to discard the "*th*," as forming no portion of the word commencing with the first *t*; since, by experiment of the entire alphabet for a letter adapted to the vacancy, we perceive that no word can be formed of which this *th* can be a part. We are thus narrowed into

t ee,

and, going through the alphabet, if necessary, as before, we arrive at the word "tree," as the sole possible reading. We thus gain another letter, *r*, represented by (, with the words "the tree" in juxtaposition.

'Looking beyond these words, for a short distance, we again see the combination ;48, and employ it by way of *termination* to what immediately precedes. We have thus this arrangement:

the tree ;4(‡?34 the,

or, substituting the natural letters, where known, it reads thus:

the tree thr‡?3h the.

'Now, if, in place of the unknown characters, we leave blank spaces, or substitute dots, we read thus:

the tree thr...h the,

when the word "*through*" makes itself evident at once. But this discovery gives us three new letters, *o*, *u* and *g*, represented by ‡ ? and 3.

'Looking now, narrowly, through the cipher for combinations of known characters, we find, not very far from the beginning, this arrangement,

83(88, or egree,

which, plainly, is the conclusion of the word "degree," and gives us another letter, *d*, represented by †.

'Four letters beyond the word "degree," we perceive the combination

;46(;88*.

'Translating the known characters, and representing the unknown by dots, as before, we read thus:

th.rtee.

an arrangement immediately suggestive of the word "thirteen," and again furnishing us with two new characters, *i* and *n*, represented by 6 and *.

'Referring, now, to the beginning of the cryptograph, we find the combination,

53‡‡†.

'Translating, as before, we obtain

.good,

which assures us that the first letter is *A*, and that the first two words are "A good."

'To avoid confusion, it is now time that we arrange our key, as far as discovered, in a tabular form. It will stand thus:

5	represents	a
†	"	d
8	"	e
3	"	g
4	"	h
6	"	i
*	"	n
‡	"	o
(	"	r
;	"	t

'We have, therefore, no less than ten of the most important letters represented, and it will be unnecessary to proceed with the details of the solution. I have said enough to convince you that ciphers of this nature are readily soluble, and to give you some insight into the *rationale* of their development. But be assured that the specimen before us appertains to the very simplest species of cryptograph. It now only remains to give you the full translation of the characters upon the parchment, as unriddled. Here it is:

'"*A good glass in the bishop's hostel in the devil's seat twenty-one degrees and thirteen minutes northeast and by north main branch seventh limb east side shoot from the left eye of the death's-head a bee line from the tree through the shot fifty feet out.*"'

'But,' said I, 'the enigma seems still in as bad a condition as ever. How is it possible to extort a meaning from all this jargon about "devil's seats," "death's-heads," and "bishop's hotels?" '

'I confess,' replied Legrand, 'that the matter still wears a serious aspect, when regarded with a casual glance. My first endeavor was to divide the sentence into the natural division intended by the cryptographist.'

'You mean, to punctuate it?'

'Something of that kind.'

'But how was it possible to effect this?'

'I reflected that it had been a *point* with the writer to run his words together without division, so as to increase the difficulty of solution. Now, a not over-acute man, in pursuing such an object, would be nearly certain to overdo the matter. When, in the course of his composition, he arrived at a break in his subject which would naturally require a pause, or a point, he would be exceedingly apt to run his characters, at this place, more than usually close together. If you will observe the MS., in the present instance, you will easily detect five such cases of unusual crowding. Acting on this hint, I made the division thus:

'"*A good glass in the Bishop's hostel in the Devil's seat—twenty-one degrees and thirteen minutes—northeast and by north—main branch seventh limb east side—shoot from the left eye of the death's-head—a bee-line from the tree through the shot fifty feet out.*"'

'Even this division,' said I, 'leaves me still in the dark.'

'It left me also in the dark,' replied Legrand, 'for a few days; during which I made diligent inquiry, in the neighborhood of Sullivan's Island, for any building which went by the name of the "Bishop's Hotel;" for, of course, I dropped the obsolete word "hostel." Gaining no information on the subject, I was on the point of extending my sphere of search, and proceeding in a more systematic manner, when, one morning, it entered into my head, quite suddenly, that this

"Bishop's Hostel" might have some reference to an old family, of the name of Bessop, which, time out of mind, had held possession of an ancient manor-house, about four miles to the northward of the Island. I accordingly went over to the plantation, and re-instituted my inquiries among the older negroes of the place. At length one of the most aged of the women said that she had heard of such a place as *Bessop's Castle*, and thought that she could guide me to it, but that it was not a castle, nor a tavern, but a high rock.

'I offered to pay her well for her trouble, and, after some demur, she consented to accompany me to the spot. We found it without much difficulty, when, dismissing her, I proceeded to examine the place. The "castle" consisted of an irregular assemblage of cliffs and rocks—one of the latter being quite remarkable for its height as well as for its insulated and artificial appearance. I clambered to its apex, and then felt much at a loss as to what should be next done.

'While I was busied in reflection, my eyes fell upon a narrow ledge in the eastern face of the rock, perhaps a yard below the summit on which I stood. This ledge projected about eighteen inches, and was not more than a foot wide, while a niche in the cliff just above it, gave it a rude resemblance to one of the hollow-backed chairs used by our ancestors. I made no doubt that here was the "devil's-seat" alluded to in the MS., and now I seemed to grasp the full secret of the riddle.

'The "good glass," I knew, could have reference to nothing but a telescope; for the word "glass" is rarely employed in any other sense by seamen. Now here, I at once saw, was a telescope to be used, and a definite point of view, *admitting no variation*, from which to use it. Nor did I hesitate to believe that the phrases, "twenty-one degrees and thirteen minutes," and "northeast and by north," were intended as directions for the levelling of the glass. Greatly excited by these discoveries, I hurried home, procured a telescope, and returned to the rock.

'I let myself down to the ledge, and found that it was impossible to retain a seat on it unless in one particular position. This fact confirmed my preconceived idea. I proceeded to use the glass. Of course, the "twenty-one degrees and thirteen minutes" could allude to nothing but elevation above the visible horizon, since the horizontal direction was clearly indicated by the words, "northeast and by north." This latter direction I at once established by means of a pocket-compass; then, pointing the glass as nearly at an angle of twenty-one degrees of elevation as I could do it by guess, I moved it cautiously up or down, until my attention was arrested by a circular rift or opening in the foliage of a large tree that overtopped its fellows in the distance. In the centre of this rift I perceived a white spot, but could not, at first, distinguish what it was. Adjusting the focus of the telescope, I again looked, and now made it out to be a human skull.

'On this discovery I was so sanguine as to consider the enigma solved; for the phrase "main branch, seventh limb, east side," could refer only to the position of the skull on the tree, while "shoot from the left eye of the death's-head" admitted, also, of but one interpretation, in regard to a search for buried treasure. I perceived that the design was to drop a bullet from the left eye of the skull, and that a bee-line, or, in other words, a straight line, drawn from the nearest point of the trunk through "the shot," (or the spot where the bullet fell,) and thence extended to a distance of fifty feet, would indicate a definite point—and beneath this point I thought it at least *possible* that a deposit of value lay concealed.'

'All this,' I said, 'is exceedingly clear, and, although ingenious, still simple and explicit. When you left the Bishop's Hotel, what then?'

'Why, having carefully taken the bearings of the tree, I turned homewards. The instant that I left "the devil's seat," however, the circular rift vanished; nor could I get a glimpse of it afterwards, turn as I would. What seems to me the chief ingenuity in this whole business, is the fact (for repeated experiment has convinced me it *is* a fact) that the circular opening in question is visible from no other attainable point of view than that afforded by the narrow ledge on the face of the rock.

'In this expedition to the "Bishop's Hotel" I had been attended by Jupiter, who had, no doubt, observed, for some weeks past, the abstraction of my demeanor, and took especial care not to leave me alone. But, on the next day, getting up very early, I contrived to give him the slip, and went into the hills in search of the tree. After much toil I found it. When I came home at night my valet proposed to give me a flogging. With the rest of the adventure I believe you are as well acquainted as myself.'

'I suppose,' said I, 'you missed the spot, in the first attempt at digging, through Jupiter's stupidity in letting the bug fall through the right instead of through the left eye of the skull.'

'Precisely. This mistake made a difference of about two inches and a half in the "shot"—that is to say, in the position of the peg nearest the tree; and had the treasure been *beneath* the "shot," the error would have been of little moment; but "the shot," together with the nearest point of the tree, were merely two points for the establishment of a line of direction; of course the error, however trivial in the beginning, increased as we proceeded with the line, and by the time we had gone fifty feet, threw us quite off the scent. But for my deep-seated convictions that treasure was here somewhere actually buried, we might have had all our labor in vain.'

'I presume the fancy of *the skull*, of letting fall a bullet through the skull's eye—was suggested to Kidd by the piratical flag. No doubt he felt a kind of poetical consistency in recovering his money through this ominous insignium.'

'Perhaps so; still I cannot help thinking that common-sense had quite as much to do with the matter as poetical consistency. To be visible from the devil's-seat, it was necessary that the object, if small, should be *white*; and there is nothing like your human skull for retaining and even increasing its whiteness under exposure to all vicissitudes of weather.'

'But your grandiloquence, and your conduct in swinging the beetle—how excessively odd! I was sure you were mad. And why did you insist on letting fall the bug, instead of a bullet, from the skull?'

'Why, to be frank, I felt somewhat annoyed by your evident suspicions touching my sanity, and so resolved to punish you quietly, in my own way, by a little bit of sober mystification. For this reason I swung the beetle, and for this reason I let it fall from the tree. An observation of yours about its great weight suggested the latter idea.'

'Yes, I perceive; and now there is only one point which puzzles me. What are we to make of the skeletons found in the hole?'

'That is a question I am no more able to answer than yourself. There seems, however, only one plausible way of accounting for them—and yet it is dreadful to believe in such atrocity as my suggestion would imply. It is clear that Kidd—if Kidd indeed secreted this treasure, which I doubt not—it is clear that he must have had assistance in the labor. But, the worst of this labor concluded, he may have thought it expedient to remove all participants in his secret. Perhaps a couple of blows with a mattock were sufficient, while his coadjutors were busy in the pit; perhaps it required a dozen—who shall tell?'

THE BLACK CAT

FOR the most wild, yet most homely narrative which I am about to pen, I neither expect nor solicit belief. Mad indeed would I be to expect it, in a case where my very senses reject their own evidence. Yet, mad am I not—and very surely do I not dream. But to-morrow I die, and to-day I would unburthen my soul. My immediate purpose is to place before the world, plainly, succinctly, and without comment, a series of mere household events. In their consequences, these events have terrified—have tortured—have destroyed me. Yet I will not attempt to expound them. To me, they have presented little but Horror—to many they will seem less terrible than *barroques*. Hereafter, perhaps, some intellect may be found which will reduce my phantasm to the common-place—some intellect more calm, more logical, and far less excitable than my own, which will perceive, in the circumstances I detail with awe, nothing more than an ordinary succession of very natural causes and effects.

From my infancy I was noted for the docility and humanity of my disposition. My tenderness of heart was even so conspicuous as to make me the jest of my companions. I was especially fond of animals, and was indulged by my parents with a great variety of pets. With these I spent most of my time, and never was so happy as when feeding and caressing them. This peculiarity of character grew with my growth, and, in my manhood, I derived from it one of my principal sources of pleasure. To those who have cherished an affection for a faithful and sagacious dog, I need hardly be at the trouble of explaining the nature or the intensity of the gratification thus derivable. There is something in the unselfish and self-sacrificing love of a brute, which goes directly to the heart of him who has had frequent occasion to test the paltry friendship and gossamer fidelity of mere *Man*.

I married early, and was happy to find in my wife a disposition not uncongenial with my own. Observing my partiality for domestic pets, she lost no opportunity of procuring those of the most agreeable kind. We had birds, gold-fish, a fine dog, rabbits, a small monkey, and *a cat*.

This latter was a remarkably large and beautiful animal, entirely black, and sagacious to an astonishing degree. In speaking of his intelligence, my wife, who at heart was not a little tinctured with superstition, made frequent allusion to the ancient popular notion, which regarded all black cats as witches in disguise. Not that she was ever *serious* upon this point—and I mention the matter at all for no better reason than that it happens, just now, to be remembered.

Pluto—this was the cat's name—was my favourite pet and playmate. I alone fed him, and he attended me wherever I went about the house. It was even with difficulty that I could prevent him from following me through the streets.

Our friendship lasted, in this manner, for several years, during which my general temperament and character—through the instrumentality of the Fiend Intemperance—had (I blush to confess it) experienced a radical alteration for the worse. I grew, day by day, more moody, more irritable, more regardless of the feelings of others. I suffered myself to use intemperate language to my wife. At length, I even offered her personal violence. My pets, of course, were made to feel the change in my disposition. I not only neglected, but ill-used them. For Pluto, however, I still retained sufficient regard to restrain me from maltreating him, as I made no scruple of maltreating the rabbits, the monkey, or even the dog, when by accident, or through affection, they came in my way. But my disease grew upon me—for what disease is like Alcohol!—and at length even Pluto, who was now becoming old, and consequently somewhat peevish—even Pluto began to experience the effects of my ill temper.

One night, returning home, much intoxicated, from one of my haunts about town, I fancied that the cat avoided my presence. I seized him: when, in his fright at my violence, he inflicted a slight wound upon my hand with his teeth. The fury of a demon instantly possessed me. I knew myself no longer. My original soul seemed, at once, to take its flight from my body; and a more than fiendish malevolence, gin-nurtured, thrilled every fibre of my frame. I took from my waistcoat-pocket a pen-knife, opened it, grasped the poor beast by the throat, and deliberately cut one of its eyes from the socket! I blush, I burn, I shudder, while I pen the damnable atrocity.

When reason returned with the morning—when I had slept off the fumes of the night's debauch—I experienced a sentiment half of horror, half of remorse, for the crime of which I had been guilty; but it was, at best, a feeble and equivocal feeling, and the soul remained untouched. I again plunged into excess, and soon drowned in wine all memory of the deed.

In the meantime the cat slowly recovered. The socket of the lost eye presented, it is true, a frightful appearance, but he no longer appeared to suffer any pain. He went about the house as usual, but, as might be expected, fled in extreme terror at my approach. I had so much of my old heart left, as to be at first grieved by this evident dislike on the part of a creature which had once so loved me. But this feeling soon gave place to irritation. And then came, as if to my final and irrevocable overthrow, the spirit of PERVERSENESS. Of this spirit philosophy takes no account. Yet I am not more sure that my soul lives, than I am that perverseness is one of the primitive impulses of the human heart—one of the indivisible primary faculties, or sentiments, which give direction to the character of Man. Who has not, a hundred times, found himself committing a vile or a silly action, for no other reason than because he knows he should *not*? Have we not a perpetual inclination, in the teeth of our best judgment, to violate that which is *Law*, merely because we understand it to be such? This spirit of perverseness, I say, came to my final overthrow. It was this unfathomable longing of the soul *to vex itself*—to offer violence to its own nature—to do wrong for the wrong's sake only—that urged me to continue and finally to consummate the injury I had inflicted upon the unoffending brute. One morning, in cool blood, I slipped a noose about its neck and hung it to the limb of a tree;—hung it with the tears streaming from my eyes, and with the bitterest remorse at my heart;—hung it *because* I knew that it had loved me, and *because* I felt it had given me no reason of offence;—hung it *because* I knew that in so doing I was committing a sin—a deadly sin that would so jeopardize my immortal soul as to place it—if such a thing were possible—even beyond the reach of the infinite mercy of the Most Merciful and Most Terrible God.

On the night of the day on which this cruel deed was done, I was aroused from sleep by the cry of fire. The curtains of my bed were in flames. The whole house was blazing. It was with great difficulty that my wife, a servant, and myself, made our escape from the conflagration. The destruction was complete. My entire worldly wealth was swallowed up, and I resigned myself thenceforward to despair.

I am above the weakness of seeking to establish a sequence of cause and effect, between the disaster and the atrocity. But I am detailing a chain of fact—and wish not to leave even a possible link imperfect. On the day succeeding the fire, I visited the ruins. The walls, with one exception, had fallen in. This exception was found in a compartment wall, not very thick, which stood about the middle of the house, and against which had rested the head of my bed. The plastering had here, in great measure, resisted the action of the fire—a fact which I attributed to its having been recently spread. About this wall a dense crowd were collected, and many persons seemed to be examining a particular portion of it with very minute and eager attention. The words 'strange!' 'singular!' and other similar expressions, excited my curiosity. I approached and saw, as if graven in *bas relief* upon the white surface, the figure of a gigantic *cat*. The impression was given with an accuracy truly marvellous. There was a rope about the animal's neck.

When I first beheld this apparition—for I could scarcely regard it as less—my wonder and my terror were extreme. But at length reflection came to my aid. The cat, I remembered, had been hung in a garden adjacent to the house. Upon the alarm of fire, this garden had been immediately filled by the crowd—by some one of whom the animal must have been cut from the tree and thrown, through an open window, into my chamber. This had probably been done with the view of arousing me from sleep. The falling of other walls had compressed the victim of my cruelty into the substance of the freshly-spread plaster; the lime of which, with the flames, and the *ammonia* from the carcass, had then accomplished the portraiture as I saw it.

Although I thus readily accounted to my reason, if not altogether to my conscience, for the startling fact just detailed, it did not the less fail to make a deep impression upon my fancy. For months I could not rid myself of the phantasm of the cat; and, during this period, there came back into my spirit a half-sentiment that seemed, but was not, remorse. I went so far as to regret the loss of the animal, and to look about me, among the vile haunts which I now habitually frequented, for another pet of the same species, and of somewhat similar appearance, with which to supply its place.

One night as I sat, half stupified, in a den of more than infamy, my attention was suddenly drawn to some black object, reposing upon the head of one of the immense hogsheads of Gin, or of Rum, which constituted the chief furniture of the apartment. I had been looking steadily at the top of this hogshead for some minutes, and what now caused me surprise was the fact that I had not sooner perceived the object thereupon. I approached it, and touched it with my hand. It was a black cat—a very large one—fully as large as Pluto, and closely resembling him in every respect but one. Pluto had not a white hair upon any portion of his body; but this cat had a large, although indefinite splotch of white, covering nearly the whole region of the breast.

Upon my touching him, he immediately arose, purred loudly, rubbed against my hand, and appeared delighted with my notice. This, then, was the very creature of which I was in search. I at once offered to purchase it of the landlord; but this person made no claim to it—knew nothing of it—had never seen it before.

I continued my caresses, and, when I prepared to go home, the animal evinced a disposition to accompany me. I permitted it to do so; occasionally stooping and patting it as I proceeded. When it reached the house it domesticated itself at once, and became immediately a great favourite with my wife.

For my own part, I soon found a dislike to it arising within me. This was just the reverse of what I had anticipated; but—I know not how or why it was—its evident fondness for myself rather disgusted and annoyed. By slow degrees, these feelings of disgust and annoyance rose into the bitterness of hatred. I avoided the creature; a certain sense of shame, and the remembrance of my former deed of cruelty, preventing me from physically abusing it. I did not, for some weeks, strike, or otherwise violently ill use it; but gradually—very gradually—I came to look upon it with unutterable loathing, and to flee silently from its odious presence, as from the breath of a pestilence.

What added, no doubt, to my hatred of the beast, was the discovery, on the morning after I brought it home, that, like Pluto, it also had been deprived of one of its eyes. This circumstance, however, only endeared it to my wife, who, as I have already said, possessed, in a high degree, that humanity of feeling which had once been my distinguishing trait, and the source of many of my simplest and purest pleasures.

With my aversion to this cat, however, its partiality for myself seemed to increase. It followed my footsteps with a pertinacity which it would be difficult to make the reader comprehend. Whenever I sat, it would crouch beneath my chair, or spring upon my knees, covering me with its loathsome caresses. If I arose to walk it would get between my feet and thus nearly throw me down, or, fastening its long and sharp claws in my dress, clamber, in this manner, to my breast. At such times, although I longed to destroy it with a blow, I was yet withheld from so doing, partly by a memory of my former crime, but chiefly—let me confess it at once—by absolute *dread* of the beast.

This dread was not exactly a dread of physical evil—and yet I should be at a loss how otherwise to define it. I am almost ashamed to own—yes, even in this felon's cell, I am almost ashamed to own—that the terror and horror with which the animal inspired me, had been heightened by one of the merest chimæras it would be possible to conceive. My wife had called my attention, more than once, to the character of the mark of white hair, of which I have spoken, and which constituted the sole visible difference between the strange beast and the one I had destroyed. The reader will remember that this mark, although large, had been originally very indefinite; but by slow degrees—degrees nearly imperceptible, and which for a long time my Reason struggled to reject as fanciful—it had, at length, assumed a rigorous distinctness of outline. It was now the representation of an object that I shudder to name—and for this, above all, I loathed, and dreaded, and would have rid myself of the monster *had I dared*—it was now, I say, the image of a hideous—of a ghastly thing—of the GALLOWS!—oh, mournful and terrible engine of Horror and of Crime—of Agony and of Death!

And now was I indeed wretched beyond the wretchedness of mere Humanity. And *a brute beast*—whose fellow I had contemptuously destroyed—*a brute beast* to work out for *me*—for me a man, fashioned in the image of the High God—so much of insufferable wo! Alas! neither by day nor by night knew I the blessing of Rest any more! During the former the creature left me no moment alone: and, in the latter, I started, hourly, from dreams of unutterable fear, to find the hot breath of *the thing* upon my face, and its vast weight—an incarnate Night-Mare that I had no power to shake off—incumbent eternally upon my *heart!*

Beneath the pressure of torments such as these, the feeble remnant of the good within me succumbed. Evil thoughts became my sole intimates—the darkest and most evil of thoughts. The moodiness of my usual temper increased to hatred of all things and of all mankind; while, from the sudden, frequent, and ungovernable outbursts of a fury to which I now blindly abandoned myself, my uncomplaining wife, alas! was the most usual and the most patient of sufferers.

One day she accompanied me, upon some household errand, into the cellar of the old building which our poverty compelled us to inhabit. The cat followed me down the steep stairs, and, nearly throwing me headlong, exasperated me to madness. Uplifting an axe, and forgetting, in my wrath, the childish dread which had hitherto stayed my hand, I aimed a blow at the animal which, of course, would have proved instantly fatal had it descended as I wished. But this blow was arrested by the hand of my wife. Goaded, by the interference, into a rage more than demoniacal, I withdrew my arm from her grasp and buried the axe in her brain. She fell dead upon the spot, without a groan.

This hideous murder accomplished, I set myself forthwith, and with entire deliberation, to the task of concealing the body. I knew that I could not remove it from the house, either by day or by night, without the risk of being observed by the neighbors. Many projects entered my mind. At one period I thought of cutting the corpse into minute fragments, and destroying them by fire. At another, I resolved to dig a grave for it in the floor of the cellar. Again, I deliberated about casting it in the well in the yard—about packing it in a box, as if merchandize, with the usual arrangements, and so getting a porter to take it from the house. Finally I hit upon what I considered a far better expedient than either of these. I determined to wall it up in the cellar—as the monks of the middle ages are recorded to have walled up their victims.

For a purpose such as this the cellar was well adapted. Its walls were loosely constructed, and had lately been plastered throughout with a rough plaster, which the dampness of the atmosphere had prevented from hardening. Moreover, in one of the walls was a projection, caused by a false chimney, or fireplace, that had been filled up, and made to resemble the rest of the cellar. I made no doubt that I could readily displace the bricks at this point, insert the corpse, and wall the whole up as before, so that no eye could detect any thing suspicious.

And in this calculation I was not deceived. By means of a crowbar I easily dislodged the bricks, and, having carefully deposited the body against the inner wall, I propped it in that position, while, with little trouble, I re-laid the whole structure as it originally stood. Having procured mortar, sand, and hair, with every possible precaution, I prepared a plaster which could not be distinguished from the old, and with this I very carefully went over the new brickwork. When I had finished, I felt satisfied that all was right. The wall did not present the slightest appearance of having been disturbed. The rubbish on the floor was picked up with the minutest care. I looked around triumphantly, and said to myself—'Here at least, then, my labor has not been in vain.'

My next step was to look for the beast which had been the cause of so much wretchedness; for I had, at length, firmly resolved to put it to death. Had I been able to meet with it, at the moment, there could have been no doubt of its fate; but it appeared that the crafty animal had been alarmed at the violence of my previous anger, and forebore to present itself in my present mood. It is impossible to describe, or to imagine, the deep, the blissful sense of relief which the absence of the detested creature occasioned in my bosom. It did not make its appearance during the night—and thus for one night at least, since its introduction into the house, I soundly and tranquilly slept; aye, *slept* even with the burden of murder upon my soul!

The second and the third day passed, and still my tormentor came not. Once again I breathed as a freeman. The monster, in terror, had fled the premises forever! I should behold it no more! My happiness was supreme! The guilt of my dark deed disturbed me but little. Some few inquiries had been made, but these had been readily answered. Even a search had been instituted—but of course nothing was to be discovered. I looked upon my future felicity as secured.

Upon the fourth day of the assassination, a party of the police came, very unexpectedly, into the house, and proceeded again to make rigorous investigation of the premises. Secure, however, in the inscrutability of my place of concealment, I felt no embarrassment whatever. The officers bade me accompany them in their search. They left no nook or corner unexplored. At length, for the third or fourth time, they descended into the cellar. I quivered not in a muscle. My heart beat calmly as that of one who slumbers in innocence. I walked the cellar from end to end. I folded my arms upon my bosom, and roamed easily to and fro. The police were thoroughly satisfied and prepared to depart. The glee at my heart was too strong to be restrained. I burned to say if but one word, by way of triumph, and to render doubly sure their assurance of my guiltlessness.

'Gentlemen,' I said at last, as the party ascended the steps, 'I delight to have allayed your suspicions. I wish you all health, and a little more courtesy. By the bye, gentlemen, this—this is a very well constructed house.' [In the rabid desire to say something easily, I scarcely knew what I uttered at all.]—'I may say an *excellently* well constructed house. These walls—are you going, gentlemen?—these walls are solidly put together;' and here, through the mere phrenzy of bravado, I rapped heavily, with a cane which I held in my hand, upon that very portion of the brick-work behind which stood the corpse of the wife of my bosom.

But may God shield and deliver me from the fangs of the Arch-Fiend! No sooner had the reverberation of my blows sunk into silence, than I was answered by a voice from within the tomb!—by a cry, at first muffled and broken, like the sobbing of a child, and then quickly swelling into one long, loud, and continuous scream, utterly anomalous and inhuman—a howl—a wailing shriek, half of horror and half of triumph, such as might have arisen only out of hell, conjointly from the throats of the damned in their agony and of the demons that exult in the damnation.

Of my own thoughts it is folly to speak. Swooning, I staggered to the opposite wall. For one instant the party upon the stair remained motionless, through extremity of terror and of awe. In the next, a dozen stout arms were toiling at the wall. It fell bodily. The corpse, already greatly decayed and clotted with gore, stood erect before the eyes of the spectators. Upon its head, with red extended mouth and solitary eye of fire, sat the hideous beast whose craft had seduced me into murder, and whose informing voice had consigned me to the hangman. I had walled the monster up within the tomb!

A TALE OF THE RAGGED MOUNTAINS

During the fall of the year 1827, while residing near Charlottesville, Virginia, I casually made the acquaintance of Mr Augustus Bedloe. This young gentleman was remarkable in every respect, and excited in me a profound interest and curiosity. I found it impossible to comprehend him either in his moral or his physical relations. Of his family I could obtain no satisfactory account. Whence he came, I never ascertained. Even about his age—although I call him a young gentleman—there was something which perplexed me in no little degree. He certainly *seemed* young—and he made a point of speaking about his youth—yet there were moments when I should have had little trouble in imagining him a hundred years of age. But in no regard was he more peculiar than in his personal appearance. He was singularly tall and thin. He stooped much. His limbs were exceedingly long and emaciated. His forehead was broad and low. His complexion was absolutely bloodless. His mouth was large and flexible, and his teeth were more wildly uneven, although sound, than I had ever before seen teeth in a human head. The expression of his smile, however, was by no means unpleasing, as might be supposed; but it had no variation whatever. It was one of profound melancholy—of a phaseless and unceasing gloom. His eyes were abnormally large, and round like those of a cat. The pupils, too, upon any accession or diminution of light, underwent contraction or dilation, just such as is observed in the feline tribe. In moments of excitement the orbs grew bright to a degree almost inconceivable; seeming to emit luminous rays, not of a reflected, but of an intrinsic lustre, as does a candle or the sun; yet their ordinary condition was so totally vapid, filmy and dull, as to convey the idea of the eyes of a long-interred corpse.

These peculiarities of person appeared to cause him much annoyance, and he was continually alluding to them in a sort of half explanatory, half apologetic strain, which, when I first heard it, impressed me very painfully. I soon, however, grew accustomed to it, and my uneasiness wore off. It seemed to be his design rather to insinuate than directly to assert that, physically, he had not always been what he was—that a long series of neuralgic attacks had reduced him from a condition of more than usual personal beauty, to that which I saw. For many years past he had been attended by a physician, named Templeton—an old gentleman, perhaps seventy years of age—whom he had first encountered at Saratoga, and from whose attention, while there, he either received, or fancied that he received, great benefit. The result was that Bedloe, who was wealthy, had made an arrangement with Doctor Templeton, by which the latter, in consideration of a liberal annual allowance, had consented to devote his time and medical experience exclusively to the care of the invalid.

Doctor Templeton had been a traveller in his younger days, and, at Paris, had become a convert, in great measure, to the doctrines of Mesmer. It was altogether by means of magnetic remedies that he had succeeded in alleviating the acute pains of his patient; and this success had very naturally inspired the latter with a certain degree of confidence in the opinions from which the remedies had been educed. The Doctor, however, like all enthusiasts, had struggled hard to make a thorough convert of his pupil, and finally so far gained his point as to induce the sufferer to submit to numerous experiments. By a frequent repetition of these, a result had arisen, which of late days has become so common as to attract little or no attention, but which, at the period of which I write, had very rarely been known in America. I mean to say, that between Doctor Templeton and Bedloe there had grown up, little by little, a very distinct and strongly marked *rapport*, or magnetic relation. I am not prepared to assert, however, that this *rapport* extended beyond the limits of the simple sleep-producing power; but this power itself had attained great intensity. At the first attempt to induce the magnetic somnolency, the mesmerist entirely failed. In the fifth or sixth he succeeded very partially, and after long continued effort. Only at the twelfth was the triumph complete. After this the will of the patient succumbed rapidly to that of the physician, so that, when I first became acquainted with the two, sleep was brought about almost instantaneously, by the mere volition of the operator, even when the invalid was unaware of his presence. It is only now, in the year 1845, when similar miracles are witnessed daily by thousands, that I dare venture to record this apparent impossibility as a matter of serious fact.*

The temperament of Bedloe was, in the highest degree, sensitive, excitable, enthusiastic. His imagination was singularly vigorous and creative; and no doubt it derived additional force from the habitual use of morphine, which he swallowed in great quantity, and without which he would have found it impossible to exist. It was his practice to take a very large dose of it immediately after breakfast, each morning—or rather immediately after a cup of strong coffee, for he ate nothing in the forenoon—and then set forth alone, or attended only by a dog, upon a long ramble among the chain of wild and dreary hills that lie westward and southward of Charlottesville, and are there dignified by the title of the Ragged Mountains.

Upon a dim, warm, misty day, towards the close of November, and during the strange *interregnum* of the seasons which in America is termed the Indian Summer, Mr Bedloe departed, as usual, for the hills. The day passed, and still he did not return.

About eight o'clock at night, having become seriously alarmed at his protracted absence, we were about setting out in search of him, when he unexpectedly made his appearance, in health no worse than usual, and in rather more than ordinary spirits. The account which he gave of his expedition, and of the events which had detained him, was a singular one indeed.

'You will remember,' said he, 'that it was about nine in the morning when I left Charlottesville. I bent my steps immediately to the mountains, and, about ten, entered a gorge which was entirely new to me. I followed the windings of this pass with much interest. The scenery which presented itself on all sides, although scarcely entitled to be called grand, had about it an indescribable, and to me, a delicious aspect of dreary desolation. The solitude seemed absolutely virgin. I could not help believing that the green sods and the gray rocks upon which I trod, had been trodden never before by the foot of a human being. So entirely secluded, and in fact inaccessible, except through a series of accidents, is the entrance of the ravine, that it is by no means impossible that I was indeed the first adventurer—the very first and sole adventurer who had ever penetrated its recesses.

'The thick and peculiar mist, or smoke, which distinguishes the Indian Summer, and which now hung heavily over all objects, served, no doubt, to deepen the vague impressions which these objects created. So dense was this pleasant fog, that I could at no time see more than a dozen yards of the path before me. This path was excessively sinuous, and as the sun could not be seen, I soon lost all idea of the direction in which I journeyed. In the meantime the morphine had its customary effect—that of enduing all the external world with an intensity of interest. In the quivering of a leaf—in the hue of a blade of grass—in the shape of a trefoil—in the humming of a bee—in the gleaming of a dew-drop—in the breathing of the wind—in the faint odors that came from the forest—there came a whole universe of suggestion—a gay and motley train of rhapsodical and immethodical thought.

'Busied in this, I walked on for several hours, during which the mist deepened around me to so great an extent, that at length I was reduced to an absolute groping of the way. And now an indescribable uneasiness possessed me—a species of nervous hesitation and tremor. I feared to tread, lest I should be precipitated into some abyss. I remembered, too, strange stories told about these Ragged Hills, and of the uncouth and fierce races of men who tenanted their groves and caverns. A thousand vague fancies oppressed and disconcerted me—fancies the more distressing because vague. Very suddenly my attention was arrested by the loud beating of a drum.

'My amazement was, of course, extreme. A drum in these hills was a thing unknown. I could not have been more surprised at the sound of the trump of the Archangel. But a new and still more astounding source of interest and perplexity arose. There came a wild rattling or jingling sound, as if of a bunch of large keys—and upon the instant a dusky-visaged and half-naked man rushed past me with a shriek. He came so close to my person that I felt his hot breath upon my face. He bore in one hand an instrument composed of an assemblage of steel rings, and shook them vigorously as he ran. Scarcely had he disappeared in the mist, before, panting after him, with open mouth and glaring eyes, there darted a huge beast. I could not be mistaken in its character. It was a hyena.

'The sight of this monster rather relieved than heightened my terrors—for I now made sure that I dreamed, and endeavored to arouse myself to waking consciousness. I stepped boldly and briskly forward. I rubbed my eyes. I called aloud. I pinched my limbs. A small spring of water presented itself to my view, and here, stooping, I bathed my hands and my head and neck. This seemed to dissipate the equivocal sensations which had hitherto annoyed me. I arose, as I thought, a new man, and proceeded steadily and complacently on my unknown way.

'At length, quite overcome by exertion, and by a certain oppressive closeness of the atmosphere, I seated myself beneath a tree. Presently here came a feeble gleam of sunshine, and the shadow of the leaves of he tree fell faintly but definitely upon the grass. At this shadow I azed wonderingly for many minutes. Its character stupified me with stonishment. I looked upward. The tree was a palm.

'I now arose hurriedly, and in a state of fearful agitation—for the ancy that I dreamed would serve me no longer. I saw—I felt that I had erfect command of my senses—and these senses now brought to my oul a world of novel and singular sensation. The heat became all at nce intolerable. A strange odor loaded the breeze. A low continuous nurmur, like that arising from a full, but gently-flowing river, came to ny ears, intermingled with the peculiar hum of multitudinous human oices.

'While I listened in an extremity of astonishment which I need not ttempt to describe, a strong and brief gust of wind bore off the incum-ent fog as if by the wand of an enchanter.

'I found myself at the foot of a high mountain, and looking down nto a vast plain, through which wound a majestic river. On the margin f this river stood an Eastern-looking city, such as we read of in the rabian Tales, but of a character even more singular than any there escribed. From my position, which was far above the level of the own, I could perceive its every nook and corner, as if delineated on a nap. The streets seemed innumerable, and crossed each other irregu-arly in all directions, but were rather long winding alleys than streets, nd absolutely swarmed with inhabitants. The houses were wildly icturesque. On every hand was a wilderness of balconies, of veran-ahs, of minarets, of shrines, and fantastically carved oriels. Bazaars bounded; and in these were displayed rich wares in infinite variety nd profusion—silks, muslins, the most dazzling cutlery, the most nagnificent jewels and gems. Besides these things, were seen, on all ides, banners and palanquins, litters with stately dames close veiled, lephants gorgeously caparisoned, idols grotesquely hewn, drums, anners and gongs, spears, silver and gilded maces. And amid the rowd, and the clamor, and the general intricacy and confusion—amid ne million of black and yellow men, turbaned and robed, and of flow-ng beard, there roamed a countless multitude of holy filleted bulls, while vast legions of the filthy but sacred ape clambered, chattering nd shrieking, about the cornices of the mosques, or clung to the ninarets and oriels. From the swarming streets to the banks of the iver, there descended innumerable flights of steps leading to bathing places, while the river itself seemed to force a passage with difficult through the vast fleets of deeply-burthened ships that far and wid encumbered its surface. Beyond the limits of the city arose, in frequen majestic groups, the palm and the cocoa, with other gigantic and weir trees of vast age; and here and there might be seen a field of rice, th thatched hut of a peasant, a tank, a stray temple, a gypsy camp, or solitary graceful maiden taking her way, with a pitcher upon her head to the banks of the magnificent river.

'You will say now, of course, that I dreamed; but not so. What saw—what I heard—what I felt—what I thought—had about it noth ing of the unmistakeable idiosyncrasy of the dream. All was rigorousl self-consistent. At first, doubting that I was really awake, I entered int a series of tests, which soon convinced me that I really was. Now, whe one dreams, and, in the dream, suspects that he dreams, the suspicio *never fails to confirm itself*, and the sleeper is almost immediatel aroused. Thus Novalis errs not in saying that "we are near wakin when we dream that we dream."* Had the vision occurred to me as describe it, without my suspecting it as a dream, then a dream it migh absolutely have been, but, occurring as it did, and suspected and teste as it was, I am forced to class it among other phenomena.'

'In this I am not sure that you are wrong,' observed Dr Templeton 'but proceed. You arose and descended into the city.'

'I arose,' continued Bedloe, regarding the Doctor with an air of pro found astonishment, 'I arose, as you say, and descended into the city On my way, I fell in with an immense populace, crowding, throug every avenue, all in the same direction, and exhibiting in every actio the wildest excitement. Very suddenly, and by some inconceivabl impulse, I became intensely imbued with personal interest in what wa going on. I seemed to feel that I had an important part to play, withou exactly understanding what it was. Against the crowd which en vironed me, however, I experienced a deep sentiment of animosity. shrank from amid them, and, swiftly, by a circuitous path, reached an entered the city. Here all was the wildest tumult and contention. A small party of men, clad in garments half Indian, half European, an officered by gentlemen in a uniform partly British, were engaged, a great odds, with the swarming rabble of the alleys. I joined the weake party, arming myself with the weapons of a fallen officer, and fightin I knew not whom with the nervous ferocity of despair. We were soo overpowered by numbers, and driven to seek refuge in a species o kiosk. Here we barricaded ourselves, and, for the present, were secure. From a loop-hole near the summit of the kiosk, I perceived a vast crowd, in furious agitation, surrounding and assaulting a gay palace that overhung the river. Presently, from an upper window of this palace, there descended an effeminate-looking person, by means of a string made of the turbans of his attendants. A boat was at hand, in which he escaped to the opposite bank of the river.

'And now a new object took possession of my soul. I spoke a few hurried but energetic words to my companions, and, having succeeded in gaining over a few of them to my purpose, made a frantic sally from the kiosk. We rushed amid the crowd that surrounded it. They retreated, at first, before us. They rallied, fought madly, and retreated again. In the meantime we were borne far from the kiosk, and became bewildered and entangled among the narrow streets of tall overhanging houses, into the recesses of which the sun had never been able to shine. The rabble pressed impetuously upon us, harassing us with their spears, and overwhelming us with flights of arrows. These latter were very remarkable, and resembled in some respects the writhing creese of the Malay. They were made to imitate the body of a creeping serpent, and were long and black, with a poisoned barb. One of them struck me upon the right temple. I reeled and fell. An instantaneous and dreadful sickness seized me. I struggled—I gasped—I died.'

'You will hardly persist *now*,' said I, smiling, 'that the whole of your adventure was not a dream. You are not prepared to maintain that you are dead?'

When I said these words, I of course expected some lively sally from Bedloe in reply; but, to my astonishment, he hesitated, trembled, became fearfully pallid, and remained silent. I looked towards Templeton. He sat erect and rigid in his chair—his teeth chattered, and his eyes were starting from their sockets. 'Proceed!' he at length said hoarsely to Bedloe.

'For many minutes,' continued the latter, 'my sole sentiment—my sole feeling—was that of darkness and nonentity, with the consciousness of death. At length, there seemed to pass a violent and sudden shock through my soul, as if of electricity. With it came the sense of elasticity and of light. This latter I felt—not saw. In an instant I seemed to rise from the ground. But I had no bodily, no visible, audible, or palpable presence. The crowd had departed. The tumult had ceased. The city was in comparative repose. Beneath me lay my corpse, with the arrow in my temple, the whole head greatly swollen and disfigured. But all these things I felt—not saw. I took interest in nothing. Even the corpse seemed a matter in which I had no concern. Volition I had none, but appeared to be impelled into motion, and flitted buoyantly out of the city, retracing the circuitous path by which I had entered it. When I had attained that point of the ravine in the mountains, at which I had encountered the hyena, I again experienced a shock as of a galvanic battery; the sense of weight, of volition, of substance, returned. I became my original self, and bent my steps eagerly homewards—but the past had not lost the vividness of the real—and not now, even for an instant, can I compel my understanding to regard it as a dream.'

'Nor was it,' said Templeton, with an air of deep solemnity, 'yet it would be difficult to say how otherwise it should be termed. Let us suppose only, that the soul of the man of to-day is upon the verge of some stupendous psychal discoveries. Let us content ourselves with this supposition. For the rest I have some explanation to make. Here is a water-colour drawing, which I should have shown you before, but which an unaccountable sentiment of horror has hitherto prevented me from showing.'

We looked at the picture which he presented. I saw nothing in it of an extraordinary character; but its effect upon Bedloe was prodigious. He nearly fainted as he gazed. And yet it was but a miniature portrait—a miraculously accurate one, to be sure—of his own very remarkable features. At least this was my thought as I regarded it.

'You will perceive,' said Templeton, 'the date of this picture—it is here, scarcely visible, in this corner—1780. In this year was the portrait taken. It is the likeness of a dead friend—a Mr Oldeb—to whom I became much attached at Calcutta, during the administration of Warren Hastings.* I was then only twenty years old. When I first saw you, Mr Bedloe, at Saratoga, it was the miraculous similarity which existed between yourself and the painting, which induced me to accost you, to seek your friendship, and to bring about those arrangements which resulted in my becoming your constant companion. In accomplishing this point, I was urged partly, and perhaps principally, by a regretful memory of the deceased, but also, in part, by an uneasy, and not altogether horrorless curiosity respecting yourself.

'In your detail of the vision which presented itself to you amid the hills, you have described, with the minutest accuracy, the Indian city of Benares, upon the Holy River. The riots, the combats, the massacre, were the actual events of the insurrection of Cheyte Sing, which took place in 1780, when Hastings was put in imminent peril of his life.* The man escaping by the string of turbans, was Cheyte Sing himself. The party in the kiosk were sepoys and British officers, headed by Hastings. Of this party I was one, and did all I could to prevent the rash and fatal sally of the officer who fell, in the crowded alleys, by the poisoned arrow of a Bengalee. That officer was my dearest friend. It was Oldeb. You will perceive by these manuscripts,' (here the speaker produced a note-book in which several pages appeared to have been freshly written) 'that at the very period in which you fancied these things amid the hills, I was engaged in detailing them upon paper here at home.'

In about a week after this conversation, the following paragraphs appeared in a Charlottesville paper.

'We have the painful duty of announcing the death of Mr AUGUSTUS BEDLO, a gentleman whose amiable manners and many virtues have long endeared him to the citizens of Charlottesville.

'Mr B., for some years past, has been subject to neuralgia, which has often threatened to terminate fatally; but this can be regarded only as the mediate cause of his decease. The proximate cause was one of especial singularity. In an excursion to the Ragged Mountains, a few days since, a slight cold and fever were contracted, attended with great determination of blood to the head. To relieve this, Dr Templeton resorted to topical bleeding. Leeches were applied to the temples. In a fearfully brief period the patient died, when it appeared that, in the jar containing the leeches, had been introduced, by accident, one of the venomous vermicular sangsues* which are now and then found in the neighboring ponds. This creature fastened itself upon a small artery in the right temple. Its close resemblance to the medicinal leech caused the mistake to be overlooked until too late.

'N.B. The poisonous sangsue of Charlottesville may always be distinguished from the medicinal leech by its blackness, and especially by its writhing or vermicular motions, which very nearly resemble those of a snake.'

I was speaking with the editor of the paper in question, upon the topic of this remarkable accident, when it occurred to me to ask how it happened that the name of the deceased had been given as Bedlo.

'I presume,' said I, 'you have authority for this spelling, but I have always supposed the name to be written with an *e* at the end.'

'Authority?—no,' he replied. 'It is a mere typographical error. The name is Bedlo with an *e*, all the world over, and I never knew it to be spelt otherwise in my life.'

'Then,' said I mutteringly, as I turned upon my heel, 'then indeed has it come to pass that one truth is stranger than any fiction—for Bedlo, without the *e*, what is it but Oldeb conversed? And this man tells me it is a typographical error.'

THE PURLOINED LETTER

Nil sapientiae odiosius acumine nimio.

Seneca*

At Paris, just after dark one gusty evening in the autumn of 18—, I was enjoying the twofold luxury of meditation amd a meerschaum, in company with my friend C. Auguste Dupin, in his little back library, or book-closet, *au troisième,* No. 33, Rue Dunôt, Faubourg St Germain.* For one hour at least we had maintained a profound silence; while each, to any casual observer, might have seemed intently and exclusively occupied with the curling eddies of smoke that oppressed the atmosphere of the chamber. For myself, however, I was mentally discussing certain topics which had formed matter for conversation between us at an earlier period of the evening; I mean the affair of the Rue Morgue, and the mystery attending the murder of Marie Rogêt. I looked upon it, therefore, as something of a coincidence, when the door of our apartment was thrown open and admitted our old acquaintance, Monsieur G—, the Prefect of the Parisian police.

We gave him a hearty welcome; for there was nearly half as much of the entertaining as of the contemptible about the man, and we had not seen him for several years. We had been sitting in the dark, and Dupin now arose for the purpose of lighting a lamp, but sat down again, without doing so, upon G.'s saying that he had called to consult us, or rather to ask the opinion of my friend, about some official business which had occasioned a great deal of trouble.

'If it is any point requiring reflection,' observed Dupin, as he forebore to enkindle the wick, 'we shall examine it to better purpose in the dark.'

'That is another of your odd notions,' said the Prefect, who had a fashion of calling every thing 'odd' that was beyond his comprehension, and thus lived amid an absolute legion of 'oddities.'

'Very true,' said Dupin, as he supplied his visitor with a pipe, and rolled towards him a comfortable chair.

'And what is the difficulty now?' I asked. 'Nothing more in the assassination way, I hope?'

'Oh no; nothing of that nature. The fact is, the business is *very* simple indeed, and I make no doubt that we can manage it sufficiently well ourselves; but then I thought Dupin would like to hear the details of it, because it is so excessively *odd*.'

'Simple and odd,' said Dupin.

'Why, yes; and not exactly that, either. The fact is, we have all been a good deal puzzled because the affair *is* so simple, and yet baffles us altogether.'

'Perhaps it is the very simplicity of the thing which puts you at fault,' said my friend.

'What nonsense you *do* talk!' replied the Prefect, laughing heartily.

'Perhaps the mystery is a little *too* plain,' said Dupin.

'Oh, good heavens! who ever heard of such an idea?'

'A little *too* self-evident.'

'Ha! ha! ha!—ha! ha! ha!—ho! ho! ho!' roared our visiter, profoundly amused. 'Oh, Dupin, you will be the death of me yet!'

'And what, after all, *is* the matter on hand?' I asked.

'Why, I will tell you,' replied the Prefect, as he gave a long, steady, and contemplative puff, and settled himself in his chair. 'I will tell you in a few words; but, before I begin, let me caution you that this is an affair demanding the greatest secrecy, and that I should most probably lose the position I now hold, were it known that I confided it to any one.'

'Proceed,' said I.

'Or not,' said Dupin.

'Well, then; I have received personal information, from a very high quarter, that a certain document of the last importance, has been purloined from the royal apartments. The individual who purloined it is known; this beyond a doubt; he was seen to take it. It is known, also, that it still remains in his possession.'

'How is this known?' asked Dupin.

'It is clearly inferred,' replied the Prefect, 'from the nature of the document, and from the non-appearance of certain results which would at once arise from its passing *out* of the robber's possession;—that is to say, from his employing it as he must design in the end to employ it.'

'Be a little more explicit,' I said.

'Well, I may venture so far as to say that the paper gives its holder a certain power in a certain quarter where such power is immensely valuable.' The Prefect was fond of the cant of diplomacy.

'Still I do not quite understand,' said Dupin.

'No? Well: the disclosure of the document to a third person, who shall be nameless, would bring in question the honor of a personage of most exalted station; and this fact gives the holder of the document an ascendancy over the illustrious personage whose honor and peace was so jeopardized.'

'But this ascendancy,' I interposed, 'would depend upon the robber's knowledge of the loser's knowledge of the robber. Who would dare—'

'The thief,' said G., 'is the Minister D—,* who dares all things, those unbecoming as well as those becoming a man. The method of the theft was not less ingenious than bold. The document in question—a letter, to be frank—had been received by the personage robbed while alone in the royal *boudoir*. During its perusal she was suddenly interrupted by the entrance of the other exalted personage from whom especially it was her wish to conceal it. After a hurried and vain endeavor to thrust it in a drawer, she was forced to place it, open as it was, upon a table. The address, however, was uppermost, and, the contents thus unexposed, the letter escaped notice. At this juncture enters the Minister D—. His lynx eye immediately perceives the paper, recognises the handwriting of the address, observes the confusion of the personage addressed, and fathoms her secret. After some business transactions, hurried through in his ordinary manner, he produces a letter somewhat similar to the one in question, opens it, pretends to read it, and then places it in close juxtaposition to the other. Again he converses, for some fifteen minutes, upon the public affairs. At length, in taking leave, he takes also from the table the letter to which he had no claim. Its rightful owner saw, but, of course, dared not call attention to the act, in the presence of the third personage who stood at her elbow. The minister decamped; leaving his own letter—one of no importance—upon the table.'

'Here, then,' said Dupin to me, 'you have precisely what you demand to make the ascendancy complete—the robber's knowledge of the loser's knowledge of the robber.'

'Yes,' replied the Prefect; 'and the power thus attained has, for some months past, been wielded, for political purposes, to a very dangerous extent. The personage robbed is more thoroughly convinced, every day, of the necessity of reclaiming her letter. But this, of course, cannot be done openly. In fine, driven to despair, she has committed the matter to me.'

'Than whom,' said Dupin, amid a perfect whirlwind of smoke, 'no more sagacious agent could, I suppose, be desired, or even imagined.'

'You flatter me,' replied the Prefect; 'but it is possible that some such opinion may have been entertained.'

'It is clear,' said I, 'as you observe, that the letter is still in possession of the minister; since it is this possession, and not any employment of the letter, which bestows the power. With the employment the power departs.'

'True,' said G.; 'and upon this conviction I proceeded. My first care was to make thorough search of the minister's hotel;* and here my chief embarrassment lay in the necessity of searching without his knowledge. Beyond all things, I have been warned of the danger which would result from giving him reason to suspect our design.'

'But,' said I, 'you are quite *au fait* in these investigations. The Parisian police have done this thing often before.'

'O yes; and for this reason I did not despair. The habits of the minister gave me, too, a great advantage. He is frequently absent from home all night. His servants are by no means numerous. They sleep at a distance from their master's apartment, and, being chiefly Neapolitans, are readily made drunk. I have keys, as you know, with which I can open any chamber or cabinet in Paris. For three months a night has not passed, during the greater part of which I have not been engaged, personally, in ransacking the D— Hotel. My honor is interested, and, to mention a great secret, the reward is enormous. So I did not abandon the search until I had become fully satisfied that the thief is a more astute man than myself. I fancy that I have investigated every nook and corner of the premises in which it is possible that the paper can be concealed.'

'But is it not possible,' I suggested, 'that although the letter may be in possession of the minister, as it unquestionably is, he may have concealed it elsewhere than upon his own premises?'

'This is barely possible,' said Dupin. 'The present peculiar condition of affairs at court, and especially of those intrigues in which D— is known to be involved, would render the instant availability of the document—its susceptibility of being produced at a moment's notice—a point of nearly equal importance with its possession.'

'Its susceptibility of being produced?' said I.

'That is to say, of being *destroyed*,' said Dupin.

'True,' I observed; 'the paper is clearly then upon the premises. As for its being upon the person of the minister, we may consider that as out of the question.'

'Entirely,' said the Prefect. 'He has been twice waylaid, as if by footpads, and his person rigorously searched under my own inspection.'

'You might have spared yourself this trouble,' said Dupin. 'D—, I presume, is not altogether a fool, and, if not, must have anticipated these waylayings, as a matter of course.'

'Not *altogether* a fool,' said G., 'but then he's a poet, which I take to be only one remove from a fool.'

'True,' said Dupin, after a long and thoughtful whiff from his meerschaum, 'although I have been guilty of certain doggrel myself.'

'Suppose you detail,' said I, 'the particulars of your search.'

'Why the fact is, we took our time, and we searched *every where*. I have had long experience in these affairs. I took the entire building, room by room; devoting the nights of a whole week to each. We examined, first, the furniture of each apartment. We opened every possible drawer; and I presume you know that, to a properly trained police agent, such a thing as a *secret* drawer is impossible. Any man is a dolt who permits a "secret" drawer to escape him in a search of this kind. The thing is *so* plain. There is a certain amount of bulk—of space—to be accounted for in every cabinet. Then we have accurate rules. The fiftieth part of a line could not escape us. After the cabinets we took the chairs. The cushions we probed with the fine long needles you have seen me employ. From the tables we removed the tops.'

'Why so?'

'Sometimes the top of a table, or other similarly arranged piece of furniture, is removed by the person wishing to conceal an article; then the leg is excavated, the article deposited within the cavity, and the top replaced. The bottoms and tops of bedposts are employed in the same way.'

'But could not the cavity be detected by sounding?' I asked.

'By no means, if, when the article is desposited, a sufficient wadding of cotton be placed around it. Besides, in our case, we were obliged to proceed without noise.'

'But you could not have removed—you could not have taken to pieces *all* articles of furniture in which it would have been possible to make a deposit in the manner you mention. A letter may be compressed into a thin spiral roll, not differing much in shape or bulk from a large knitting-needle, and in this form it might be inserted into the rung of a chair, for example. You did not take to pieces all the chairs?'

'Certainly not; but we did better—we examined the rungs of every chair in the hotel, and, indeed, the jointings of every description of furniture, by the aid of a most powerful microscope. Had there been any traces of recent disturbance we should not have failed to detect it instantly. A single grain of gimlet-dust, for example, would have been as obvious as an apple. Any disorder in the glueing—any unusual gaping in the joints—would have sufficed to insure detection.'

'I presume you looked to the mirrors, between the boards and the plates, and you probed the beds and the bed-clothes, as well as the curtains and carpets.'

'That of course; and when we had absolutely completed every particle of the furniture in this way, then we examined the house itself. We divided its entire surface into compartments, which we numbered, so that none might be missed; then we scrutinized each individual square inch throughout the premises, including the two houses immediately adjoining, with the microscope, as before.'

'The two houses adjoining!' I exclaimed; 'you must have had a great deal of trouble.'

'We had; but the reward offered is prodigious.'

'You include the *grounds* about the houses?'

'All the grounds are paved with brick. They gave us comparatively little trouble. We examined the moss between the bricks, and found it undisturbed.'

'You looked among D—'s papers, of course, and into the books of the library?'

'Certainly; we opened every package and parcel; we not only opened every book, but we turned over every leaf in each volume, not contenting ourselves with a mere shake, according to the fashion of some of our police officers. We also measured the thickness of every book-*cover*, with the most accurate admeasurement, and applied to each the most jealous scrutiny of the microscope. Had any of the bindings been recently meddled with, it would have been utterly impossible that the fact should have escaped observation. Some five or six volumes, just from the hands of the binder, we carefully probed, longitudinally, with the needles.'

'You explored the floors beneath the carpets?'

'Beyond doubt. We removed every carpet, and examined the boards with the microscope.'

'And the paper on the walls?'

'Yes.'

'You looked into the cellars?'

'We did.'

'Then,' I said, 'you have been making a miscalculation, and the letter is *not* upon the premises, as you suppose.'

'I fear you are right there,' said the Prefect. 'And now, Dupin, what would you advise me to do?'

'To make a thorough re-search of the premises.'

'That is absolutely needless,' replied G—. 'I am not more sure that I breathe than I am that the letter is not at the Hotel.'

'I have no better advice to give you,' said Dupin. 'You have, of course, an accurate description of the letter?'

'Oh yes!'—And here the Prefect, producing a memorandum-book, proceeded to read aloud a minute account of the internal, and especially of the external appearance of the missing document. Soon after finishing the perusal of this description, he took his departure, more entirely depressed in spirits than I had ever known the good gentleman before.

In about a month afterwards he paid us another visit, and found us occupied very nearly as before. He took a pipe and a chair and entered into some ordinary conversation. At length I said,—

'Well, but G—, what of the purloined letter? I presume you have at last made up your mind that there is no such thing as overreaching the Minister?'

'Confound him, say I—yes; I made the re-examination, however, as Dupin suggested—but it was all labor lost, as I knew it would be.'

'How much was the reward offered, did you say?' asked Dupin.

'Why, a very great deal—a *very* liberal reward—I don't like to say how much, precisely; but one thing I *will* say, that I wouldn't mind giving my individual check for fifty thousand francs to any one who could obtain me that letter. The fact is, it is becoming of more and more importance every day; and the reward has been lately doubled. If it were trebled, however, I could do no more than I have done.'

'Why, yes,' said Dupin, drawlingly, between the whiffs of his meerschaum, 'I really—think, G—, you have not exerted yourself—to the utmost in this matter. You might—do a little more, I think, eh?'

'How?—in what way?'

'Why—puff, puff—you might—puff, puff—employ counsel in the matter, eh?—puff, puff, puff. Do you remember the story they tell of Abernethy?'

'No; hang Abernethy!'

'To be sure! hang him and welcome. But, once upon a time, a certain rich miser conceived the design of spunging upon this Abernethy for a medical opinion. Getting up, for this purpose, an ordinary conversation in a private company, he insinuated his case to the physician, as that of an imaginary individual.

'"We will suppose," said the miser, "that his symptoms are such and such; now, doctor, what would *you* have directed him to take?"

'"Take!" said Abernethy, "why, take *advice*, to be sure."'

'But,' said the Prefect, a little discomposed, '*I* am *perfectly* willing to take advice, and to pay for it. I would *really* give fifty thousand francs to any one who would aid me in the matter.'

'In that case,' replied Dupin, opening a drawer, and producing a check-book, 'you may as well fill me up a check for the amount mentioned. When you have signed it, I will hand you the letter.'

I was astounded. The Prefect appeared absolutely thunder-stricken. For some minutes he remained speechless and motionless, looking incredulously at my friend with open mouth, and eyes that seemed starting from their sockets; then, apparently recovering himself in some measure, he seized a pen, and after several pauses and vacant stares, finally filled up and signed a check for fifty thousand francs, and handed it across the table to Dupin. The latter examined it carefully and deposited it in his pocket-book; then, unlocking an *escritoire*, took thence a letter and gave it to the Prefect. This functionary grasped it in a perfect agony of joy, opened it with a trembling hand, cast a rapid glance at its contents, and then, scrambling and struggling to the door, rushed at length unceremoniously from the room and from the house, without having uttered a syllable since Dupin had requested him to fill up the check.

When he had gone, my friend entered into some explanations.

'The Parisian police,' he said, 'are exceedingly able in their way. They are persevering, ingenious, cunning, and thoroughly versed in the knowledge which their duties seem chiefly to demand. Thus, when G— detailed to us his mode of searching the premises at the Hotel

D—, I felt entire confidence in his having made a satisfactory investigation—so far as his labors extended.'

'So far as his labors extended?' said I.

'Yes, said Dupin. 'The measures adopted were not only the best of their kind, but carried out to absolute perfection. Had the letter been deposited within the range of their search, these fellows would, beyond a question, have found it.'

I merely laughed—but he seemed quite serious in all that he said.

'The measures, then,' he continued, 'were good in their kind, and well executed; their defect lay in their being inapplicable to the case, and to the man. A certain set of highly ingenious resources are, with the Prefect, a sort of Procrustean bed to which he forcibly adapts his designs. But he perpetually errs by being too deep or too shallow, for the matter in hand; and many a schoolboy is a better reasoner than he. I knew one about eight years of age, whose success at guessing in the game of "even and odd" attracted universal admiration. This game is simple, and is played with marbles. One player holds in his hand a number of these toys, and demands of another whether that number is even or odd. If the guess is right, the guesser wins one: if wrong, he loses one. The boy to whom I allude won all the marbles of the school. Of course he had some principle of guessing; and this lay in mere observation and admeasurement of the astuteness of his opponents. For example, an arrant simpleton is his opponent, and, holding up his closed hand, asks, "are they even or odd?" Our schoolboy replies, "odd," and loses; but upon the second trial he wins, for he then says to himself, "the simpleton had them even upon the first trial, and his amount of cunning is just sufficient to make him have them odd upon the second; I will therefore guess odd;"—he guesses odd, and wins. Now, with a simpleton a degree above the first, he would have reasoned thus: "This fellow finds that in the first instance I guessed odd, and, in the second, he will propose to himself, upon the first impulse, a simple variation from even to odd, as did the first simpleton; but then a second thought will suggest that this is too simple a variation, and finally he will decide upon putting it even as before. I will therefore guess even;"—he guesses even, and wins. Now this mode of reasoning in the schoolboy, whom his fellows termed "lucky,"—what, in its last analysis, is it?'

'It is merely,' I said, 'an identification of the reasoner's intellect with that of his opponent.'

'It is,' said Dupin; 'and, upon inquiring of the boy by what means he effected the *thorough* identification in which his success consisted, I received answer as follows: "When I wish to find out how wise, or how stupid, or how good, or how wicked is any one, or what are his thoughts at the moment, I fashion the expression of my face, as accurately as possible, in accordance with the expression of his, and then wait to see what thoughts or sentiments arise in my mind or heart, as if to match or correspond with the expression." This response of the schoolboy lies at the bottom of all the spurious profundity which has been attributed to Rochefoucault, to La Bruyère, to Machiavelli, and to Campanella.*

'And the identification,' I said, 'of the reasoner's intellect with that of his opponent, depends, if I understand you aright, upon the accuracy with which the opponent's intellect is admeasured.'

'For its practical value it depends upon this,' replied Dupin; 'and the Prefect and his cohort fail so frequently, first, by default of this identification, and, secondly, by ill-admeasurement, or rather through non-admeasurement, of the intellect with which they are engaged. They consider only their *own* ideas of ingenuity; and, in searching for anything hidden, advert only to the modes in which *they* would have hidden it. They are right in this much—that their own ingenuity is a faithful representative of that of *the mass*; but when the cunning of the individual felon is diverse in character from their own, the felon foils them, of course. This always happens when it is above their own, and very usually when it is below. They have no variation of principle in their investigations; at best, when urged by some unusual emergency—by some extraordinary reward—they extend or exaggerate their old modes of *practice*, without touching their principles. What, for example, in this case of D—, has been done to vary the principle of action? What is all this boring, and probing, and sounding, and scrutinizing with the microscope, and dividing the surface of the building into registered square inches—what is it all but an exaggeration *of the application* of the one principle or set of principles of search, which are based upon the one set of notions regarding human ingenuity, to which the Prefect, in the long routine of his duty, has been accustomed? Do you not see he has taken it for granted that *all* men proceed to conceal a letter,—not exactly in a gimlet-hole bored in a chair-leg—but, at least, in *some* out-of-the-way hole or corner suggested by the same tenor of thought which would urge a man to secrete a letter in a gimlet-hole bored in a chair-leg? And do you not see also, that such *recherchés* nooks for concealment are adapted only for ordinary occasions, and would be adopted only by ordinary intellects; for, in all cases of concealment, a disposal of the article concealed—a disposal of it in this *recherché* manner,—is, in the very first instance, presumable and presumed; and thus its discovery depends, not at all upon the acumen, but altogether upon the mere care, patience, and determination of the seekers; and where the case is of importance—or, what amounts to the same thing in the policial eyes, when the reward is of magnitude,—the qualities in question have *never* been known to fail. You will now understand what I meant in suggesting that, had the purloined letter been hidden any where within the limits of the Prefect's examination—in other words, had the principle of its concealment been comprehended within the principles of the Prefect—its discovery would have been a matter altogether beyond question. This functionary, however, has been thoroughly mystified; and the remote source of his defeat lies in the supposition that the Minister is a fool, because he has acquired renown as a poet. All fools are poets; this the Prefect *feels*; and he is merely guilty of a *non distributio medii* in thence inferring that all poets are fools.'*

'But is this really the poet?' I asked. 'There are two brothers, I know; and both have attained reputation in letters. The Minister I believe has written learnedly on the Differential Calculus. He is a mathematician, and no poet.'

'You are mistaken; I know him well; he is both. As poet *and* mathematician, he would reason well; as mere mathematician, he could not have reasoned at all, and thus would have been at the mercy of the Prefect.'

'You surprise me,' I said, 'by these opinions, which have been contradicted by the voice of the world. You do not mean to set at naught the well-digested idea of centuries. The mathematical reason has long been regarded as *the* reason *par excellence*.'

'"*Il y a à parier,*"' replied Dupin, quoting from Chamfort, '"*que toute idée publique, toute convention reçue, est une sottise, car elle a convenu au plus grand nombre.*"* The mathematicians, I grant you, have done their best to promulgate the popular error to which you allude, and which is none the less an error for its promulgation as truth. With an art worthy a better cause, for example, they have insinuated the term "analysis" into application to algebra. The French are the originators of this particular deception; but if a term is of any importance—if words derive any value from applicability—then "analysis" conveys "algebra" about as much as, in Latin, "*ambitus*" implies "ambition," "*religio*" "religion," or "*homines honesti,*" a set of *honourable* men.'*

'You have a quarrel on hand, I see,' said I, 'with some of the algebraists of Paris; but proceed.'

'I dispute the availability, and thus the value, of that reason which is cultivated in any especial form other than the abstractly logical. I dispute, in particular, the reason educed by mathematical study. The mathematics are the science of form and quantity; mathematical reasoning is merely logic applied to observation upon form and quantity. The great error lies in supposing that even the truths of what is called *pure* algebra, are abstract or general truths. And this error is so egregious that I am confounded at the universality with which it has been received. Mathematical axioms are *not* axioms of general truth. What is true of *relation*—of form and quantity—is often grossly false in regard to morals, for example. In this latter science it is very usually *un*true that the aggregated parts are equal to the whole. In chemistry also the axiom fails. In the consideration of motive it fails; for two motives, each of a given value, have not, necessarily, a value when united, equal to the sum of their values apart. There are numerous other mathematical truths which are only truths within the limits of *relation*. But the mathematician argues, from his *finite truths*, through habit, as if they were of an absolutely general applicability—as the world indeed imagines them to be. Bryant, in his very learned "Mythology," mentions an analogous source of error, when he says that "although the Pagan fables are not believed, yet we forget ourselves continually, and make inferences from them as existing realities."* With the algebraists, however, who are Pagans themselves, the "Pagan fables" *are* believed, and the inferences are made, not so much through lapse of memory, as through an unaccountable addling of the brains. In short, I never yet encountered the mere mathematician who could be trusted out of equal roots, or one who did not clandestinely hold it as a point of his faith that x^2+px was absolutely and unconditionally equal to q. Say to one of these gentlemen, by way of experiment, if you please, that you believe occasions may occur where x^2+px is *not* altogether equal to q, and, having made him understand what you mean, get out of his reach as speedily as convenient, for, beyond doubt, he will endeavor to knock you down.

'I mean to say,' continued Dupin, while I merely laughed at his last observations, 'that if the Minister had been no more than a mathematician, the Prefect would have been under no necessity of giving me this check. I knew him, however, as both mathematician and poet, and my measures were adapted to his capacity, with reference to the circumstances by which he was surrounded. I knew him as a courtier, too, and as a bold *intriguant*. Such a man, I considered, could not fail to be aware of the ordinary policial modes of action. He could not have failed to anticipate—and events have proved that he did not fail to anticipate—the waylayings to which he was subjected. He must have foreseen, I reflected, the secret investigations of his premises. His frequent absences from home at night, which were hailed by the Prefect as certain aids to his success, I regarded only as *ruses*, to afford opportunity for thorough search to the police, and thus the sooner to impress them with the conviction to which G—, in fact, did finally arrive—the conviction that the letter was not upon the premises. I felt, also, that the whole train of thought, which I was at some pains in detailing to you just now, concerning the invariable principle of policial action in searches for articles concealed—I felt that this whole train of thought would necessarily pass through the mind of the Minister. It would imperatively lead him to despise all the ordinary *nooks* of concealment. *He* could not, I reflected, be so weak as not to see that the most intricate and remote recess of his hotel would be as open as his commonest closets to the eyes, to the probes, to the gimlets, and to the microscopes of the Prefect. I saw, in fine, that he would be driven, as a matter of course, to *simplicity*, if not deliberately induced to it as a matter of choice. You will remember, perhaps, how desperately the Prefect laughed when I suggested, upon our first interview, that it was just possible this mystery troubled him so much on account of its being so *very* self-evident.'

'Yes,' said I, 'I remember his merriment well. I really thought he would have fallen into convulsions.'

'The material world,' continued Dupin, 'abounds with very strict analogies to the immaterial; and thus some color of truth has been given to the rhetorical dogma, that metaphor, or simile, may be made to strengthen an argument, as well as to embellish a description. The principle of the *vis inertiæ*, for example, seems to be identical in physics and metaphysics. It is not more true in the former, that a large body is with more difficulty set in motion than a smaller one, and that its subsequent *momentum* is commensurate with this difficulty, than it is, in the latter, that intellects of the vaster capacity, while more forcible, more constant, and more eventful in their movements than those of inferior grade, are yet the less readily moved, and more embarrassed and full of hesitation in the first few steps of their progress. Again: have you ever noticed which of the street signs, over the shopdoors, are the most attractive of attention?'

'I have never given the matter a thought,' I said.

'There is a game of puzzles,' he resumed, 'which is played upon a map. One party playing requires another to find a given word—the name of town, river, state or empire—any word, in short, upon the motley and perplexed surface of the chart. A novice in the game generally seeks to embarrass his opponents by giving them the most minutely lettered names; but the adept selects such words as stretch, in large characters, from one end of the chart to the other. These, like the over-largely lettered signs and placards of the street, escape observation by dint of being excessively obvious; and here the physical oversight is precisely analogous with the moral inapprehension by which the intellect suffers to pass unnoticed those considerations which are too obtrusively and too palpably self-evident. But this is a point, it appears, somewhat above or beneath the understanding of the Prefect. He never once thought it probable, or possible, that the Minister had deposited the letter immediately beneath the nose of the whole world, by way of best preventing any portion of that world from perceiving it.

'But the more I reflected upon the daring, dashing, and discriminating ingenuity of D—; upon the fact that the document must always have been *at hand*, if he intended to use it to good purpose; and upon the decisive evidence, obtained by the Prefect, that it was not hidden within the limits of that dignitary's ordinary search—the more satisfied I became that, to conceal this letter, the Minister had resorted to the comprehensive and sagacious expedient of not attempting to conceal it at all.

'Full of these ideas, I prepared myself with a pair of green spectacles, and called one fine morning, quite by accident, at the Ministerial hotel. I found D— at home, yawning, lounging, and dawdling, as usual, and pretending to be in the last extremity of *ennui*. He is, perhaps, the most really energetic human being now alive—but that is only when nobody sees him.

'To be even with him, I complained of my weak eyes, and lamented the necessity of the spectacles, under cover of which I cautiously and thoroughly surveyed the apartment, while seemingly intent only upon the conversation of my host.

'I paid especial attention to a large writing-table near which he sat, and upon which lay confusedly, some miscellaneous letters and other papers, with one or two musical instruments and a few books. Here, however, after a long and very deliberate scrutiny, I saw nothing to excite particular suspicion.

'At length my eyes, in going the circuit of the room, fell upon a trumpery fillagree card-rack of pasteboard, that hung dangling by a dirty blue ribbon from a little brass knob just beneath the middle of the mantel-piece. In this rack, which had three or four compartments, were five or six visiting cards and a solitary letter. This last was much soiled and crumpled. It was torn nearly in two, across the middle—as if a design, in the first instance, to tear it entirely up as worthless, had been altered, or stayed, in the second. It had a large black seal, bearing the D— cipher *very* conspicuously, and was addressed, in a diminutive female hand, to D—, the minister, himself. It was thrust carelessly, and even, as it seemed, contemptuously, into one of the upper divisions of the rack.

'No sooner had I glanced at this letter, than I concluded it to be that of which I was in search. To be sure, it was, to all appearance, radically different from the one of which the Prefect had read us so minute a description. Here the seal was large and black, with the D— cipher; there it was small and red, with the ducal arms of the S— family. Here, the address, to the Minister, was diminutive and feminine; there the superscription, to a certain royal personage, was markedly bold and decided; the size alone formed a point of correspondence. But, then, the *radicalness* of these differences, which was excessive; the dirt; the soiled and torn condition of the paper, so inconsistent with the *true* methodical habits of D—, and so suggestive of a design to delude the beholder into an idea of the worthlessness of the document; these things, together with the hyperobtrusive situation of this document, full in the view of every visiter, and thus exactly in accordance with the conclusions to which I had previously arrived; these things, I say, were strongly corroborative of suspicion, in one who came with the intention to suspect.

'I protracted my visit as long as possible, and, while I maintained a most animated discussion with the Minister, on a topic which I knew well had never failed to interest and excite him, I kept my attention really riveted upon the letter. In this examination, I committed to memory its external appearance and arrangement in the rack; and also fell, at length, upon a discovery which set at rest whatever trivial doubt I might have entertained. In scrutinizing the edges of the paper, I observed them to be more *chafed* than seemed necessary. They presented the *broken* appearance which is manifested when a stiff paper, having been once folded and pressed with a folder, is refolded in a reversed direction, in the same creases or edges which had formed the original fold. This discovery was sufficient. It was clear to me that the letter had been turned, as a glove, inside out, re-directed, and resealed. I bade the Minister good morning, and took my departure at once, leaving a gold snuff-box upon the table.

'The next morning I called for the snuff-box, when we resumed, quite eagerly, the conversation of the preceding day. While thus engaged, however, a loud report, as if of a pistol, was heard immediately beneath the windows of the hotel, and was succeeded by a series of fearful screams, and the shoutings of a mob. D— rushed to a casement, threw it open, and looked out. In the meantime, I stepped to the card-rack, took the letter, put it in my pocket, and replaced it by a *fac-simile*, (so far as regards externals,) which I had carefully prepared at my lodgings; imitating the D— cipher, very readily, by means of a seal formed of bread.

'The disturbance in the street had been occasioned by the frantic behavior of a man with a musket. He had fired it among a crowd of women and children. It proved, however, to have been without ball, and the fellow was suffered to go his way as a lunatic or a drunkard. When he had gone, D— came from the window, whither I had followed him immediately upon securing the object in view. Soon afterwards I bade him farewell. The pretended lunatic was a man in my own pay.'

'But what purpose had you,' I asked, 'in replacing the letter by a *fac-simile*? Would it not have been better, at the first visit, to have seized it openly, and departed?'

'D—,' replied Dupin, 'is a desperate man, and a man of nerve. His hotel, too, is not without attendants devoted to his interests. Had I made the wild attempt you suggest, I might never have left the Ministerial presence alive. The good people of Paris might have heard of me no more. But I had an object apart from these considerations. You know my political prepossessions. In this matter, I act as a partisan of the lady concerned. For eighteen months the Minister has had her in his power. She has now him in hers; since, being unaware that the letter is not in his possession, he will proceed with his exactions as if it was. Thus will he inevitably commit himself, at once, to his political destruction. His downfall, too, will not be more precipitate than awkward. It is all very well to talk about the *facilis descensus Averni*;* but in all kinds of climbing, as Catalani said of singing, it is far more easy to get up than to come down.* In the present instance I have no sympathy—at least no pity—for him who descends. He is that *monstrum horrendum*, an unprincipled man of genius.* I confess, however, that I should like very well to know the precise character of his thoughts, when, being defied by her whom the Prefect terms "a certain personage," he is reduced to opening the letter which I left for him in the card-rack.'

'How? did you put any thing particular in it?'

'Why—it did not seem altogether right to leave the interior blank—that would have been insulting. D—, at Vienna once, did me an evil turn, which I told him, quite good-humoredly, that I should remember. So, as I knew he would feel some curiosity in regard to the identity of the person who had outwitted him, I thought it a pity not to give him a clue. He is well acquainted with my MS., and I just copied into the middle of the blank sheet the words—

——Un dessein si funeste,
S'il n'est digne d'Atrée, est digne de Thyeste.*

They are to be found in Crébillon's "Atrée." '*

THE SYSTEM OF DOCTOR TARR AND PROFESSOR FETHER

DURING the autumn of 18—, while on a tour through the extreme provinces of France, my route led me within a few miles of a certain *Maison de Santé*, or private Mad House, about which I had heard much, in Paris, from my medical friends.* As I had never visited a place of the kind, I thought the opportunity too good to be lost; and so proposed to my travelling companion, (a gentleman with whom I had made causal acquaintance a few days before,) that we should turn aside, for an hour or so, and look through the establishment. To this he objected—pleading haste, in the first place, and, in the second, a very usual horror at the sight of a lunatic. He begged me, however, not to let any mere courtesy towards himself interfere with the gratification of my curiosity, and said that he would ride on leisurely, so that I might overtake him during the day, or, at all events, during the next. As he bade me good-by, I bethought me that there might be some difficulty in obtaining access to the premises, and mentioned my fears on this point. He replied that, in fact, unless I had personal knowledge of the superintendent, Monsieur Maillard,* or some credential in the way of a letter, a difficulty might be found to exist, as the regulations of these private mad-houses were more rigid than the public hospital laws. For himself, he added, he had, some years since, made the acquaintance of Maillard, and would so far assist me as to ride up to the door and introduce me; although his feelings on the subject of lunacy would not permit of his entering the house.

I thanked him, and, turning from the main-road, we entered a grass-grown by-path, which, in half an hour, nearly lost itself in a dense forest, clothing the base of a mountain. Through this dank and gloomy wood we rode some two miles, when the *Maison de Santé* came in view. It was a fantastic *château*, much dilapidated, and indeed scarcely tenantable through age and neglect. Its aspect inspired me with absolute dread, and, checking my horse, I half resolved to turn back. I soon, however, grew ashamed of my weakness, and proceeded.

As we rode up to the gate-way, I perceived it slightly open, and the visage of a man peering through. In an instant afterward, this man came forth, accosted my companion by name, shook him cordially by the hand, and begged him to alight. It was Monsieur Maillard himself. He was a portly, fine-looking gentleman of the old school, with a polished manner, and a certain air of gravity, dignity, and authority which was very impressive.

My friend, having presented me, mentioned my desire to inspect the establishment, and received Monsieur Maillard's assurance that he would show me all attention, now took leave, and I saw him no more.

When he had gone, the superintendent ushered me into a small and exceedingly neat parlor, containing among other indications of refined taste, many books, drawings, pots of flowers, and musical instruments. A cheerful fire blazed upon the hearth. At a piano, singing an aria from Bellini,* sat a young and very beautiful woman, who, at my entrance, paused in her song, and received me with graceful courtesy. Her voice was low, and her whole manner subdued. I thought, too, that I perceived the traces of sorrow in her countenance, which was excessively, although to my taste, not unpleasingly pale. She was attired in deep mourning, and excited in my bosom a feeling of mingled respect, interest, and admiration.

I had heard, at Paris, that the institution of Monsieur Maillard was managed upon what is vulgarly termed the 'system of soothing'—that all punishments were avoided—that even confinement was seldom resorted to—that the patients, while secretly watched, were left much apparent liberty, and that most of them were permitted to roam about the house and grounds, in the ordinary apparel of persons in right mind.

Keeping these impressions in view, I was cautious in what I said before the young lady; for I could not be sure that she was sane; and, in fact, there was a certain restless brilliancy about her eyes which half led me to imagine she was not. I confined my remarks, therefore, to general topics, and to such as I thought would not be displeasing or exciting even to a lunatic. She replied in a perfectly rational manner to all that I said; and even her original observations were marked with the soundest good sense; but a long acquaintance with the metaphysics of *mania*, had taught me to put no faith in such evidence of sanity, and I continued to practice, throughout the interview, the caution with which I commenced it.

Presently a smart footman in livery brought in a tray with fruit, wine, and other refreshments, of which I partook, the lady soon afterwards leaving the room. As she departed I turned my eyes in an inquiring manner towards my host.

'No,' he said, 'oh, no—a member of my family—my niece, and a most accomplished woman.'

'I beg a thousand pardons for the suspicion,' I replied, 'but of course you will know how to excuse me. The excellent administration of your affairs here is well understood in Paris, and I thought it just possible, you know—'

'Yes, yes—say no more—or rather it is myself who should thank you for the commendable prudence you have displayed. We seldom find so much of forethought in young men; and, more than once, some unhappy *contre-temps* has occurred in consequence of thoughtlessness on the part of our visitors. While my former system was in operation, and my patients were permitted the privilege of roaming to and fro at will, they were often aroused to a dangerous frenzy by injudicious persons who called to inspect the house. Hence I was obliged to enforce a rigid system of exclusion; and none obtained access to the premises upon whose discretion I could not rely.'

'While your *former* system was in operation!' I said, repeating his words—'do I understand you, then, to say that the "soothing system" of which I have heard so much, is no longer in force?'

'It is now,' he replied, 'several weeks since we have concluded to renounce it forever.'

'Indeed! you astonish me!'

'We found it, sir,' he said, with a sigh, 'absolutely necessary to return to the old usages. The *danger* of the soothing system was, at all times, appalling; and its advantages have been much over-rated. I believe, sir, that in this house it has been given a fair trial, if ever in any. We did every thing that rational humanity could suggest. I am sorry that you could not have paid us a visit at an earlier period, that you might have judged for yourself. But I presume you are conversant with the soothing practice—with its details.'

'Not altogether. What I have heard has been at third or fourth hand.'

'I may state the system then, in general terms, as one in which the patients were *ménagés*, humored. We contradicted *no* fancies which entered the brains of the mad. On the contrary, we not only indulged but encouraged them; and many of our most permanent cures have been thus effected. There is no argument which so touches the feeble reason of the madman as the *reductio ad absurdum*.* We have had men, for example, who fancied themselves chickens. The cure was, to insist upon the thing as a fact—to accuse the patient of stupidity in not sufficiently perceiving it to be a fact—and thus to refuse him any other diet for a week than that which properly appertains to a chicken. In this manner a little corn and gravel were made to perform wonders.'

'But was this species of acquiescence all?'

'By no means. We put much faith in amusements of a simple kind, such as music, dancing, gymnastic exercises generally, cards, certain classes of books, and so forth. We affected to treat each individual as if for some ordinary physical disorder; and the word "lunacy" was never employed. A great point was to set each lunatic to guard the actions of all the others. To repose confidence in the understanding or discretion of a madman, is to gain him body and soul. In this way we were enabled to dispense with an expensive body of keepers.'

'And you had no punishments of any kind?'

'None.'

'And you never confined your patients?'

'Very rarely. Now and then, the malady of some individual growing to a crisis, or taking a sudden turn of fury, we conveyed him to a secret cell, lest his disorder should infect the rest, and there kept him until we could dismiss him to his friends—for with the raging maniac we have nothing to do. He is usually removed to the public hospitals.'

'And you have now changed all this—and you think for the better?'

'Decidedly. The system had its disadvantages, and even its dangers. It is now, happily, exploded throughout all the *Maisons de Santé* of France.'

'I am very much surprised,' I said, 'at what you tell me; for I made sure that, at this moment, no other method of treatment for mania existed in any portion of the country.'

'You are young yet, my friend,' replied my host, 'but the time will arrive when you will learn to judge for yourself of what is going on in the world, without trusting to the gossip of others. Believe nothing you hear, and only one half that you see. Now, about our *Maisons de Santé*, it is clear that some ignoramus has misled you. After dinner, however, when you have sufficiently recovered from the fatigue of your ride, I will be happy to take you over the house, and introduce to you a system which, in my opinion, and in that of every one who has witnessed its operation, is incomparably the most effectual as yet devised.'

'Your own?' I inquired—'one of your own invention?'

'I am proud,' he replied, 'to acknowledge that it is—at least in some measure.'

In this manner I conversed with Monsieur Maillard for an hour or two, during which he showed me the gardens and conservatories of the place.

'I cannot let you see my patients,' he said, 'just at present. To a sensitive mind there is always more or less of the shocking in such exhibitions; and I do not wish to spoil your appetite for dinner. We will dine. I can give you some veal *à la St Menehoult*, with cauliflowers in *velouté* sauce—after that a glass of *Clos de Vougeôt*—then your nerves will be sufficiently steadied.'

At six, dinner was announced; and my host conducted me into a large *salle à manger*, where a very numerous company were assembled—twenty-five or thirty in all. They were, apparently, people of rank—certainly of high breeding—although their habiliments, I thought, were extravagantly rich, partaking somewhat too much of the ostentatious finery of the *vieille cour*.* I noticed that at least two-thirds of these guests were ladies; and some of the latter were by no means accoutred in what a Parisian would consider good taste at the present day. Many females, for example, whose age could not have been less than seventy, were bedecked with a profusion of jewelry, such as rings, bracelets, and ear-rings, and wore their bosoms and arms shamefully bare. I observed, too, that very few of the dresses were well made—or, at least, that very few of them fitted the wearers. In looking about, I discovered the interesting girl to whom Monsieur Maillard had presented me in the little parlor; but my surprise was great to see her wearing a hoop and farthingale, with high-heeled shoes, and a dirty cap of Brussels lace, so much too large for her that it gave her face a ridiculously diminutive expression. When I had first seen her, she was attired, most becomingly, in deep mourning. There was an air of oddity, in short, about the dress of the whole party, which, at first, caused me to recur to my original idea of the 'soothing system,' and to fancy that Monsieur Maillard had been willing to deceive me until after dinner, that I might experience no uncomfortable feelings during the repast, at finding myself dining with lunatics; but I remembered having been informed, in Paris, that the southern provincialists were a peculiarly eccentric people, with a vast number of antiquated notions; and then, too, upon conversing with several members of the company, my apprehensions were immediately and fully dispelled.

The dining-room, itself, although perhaps sufficiently comfortable, and of good dimensions, had nothing too much of elegance about it. For example, the floor was uncarpeted; in France however a carpet is frequently dispensed with. The windows, too, were without curtains; the shutters, being shut, were securely fastened with iron bars, applied diagonally, after the fashion of our ordinary shop-shutters. The apartment, I observed, formed, in itself, a wing of the *château*, and thus the windows were on three sides of the parallelogram; the door being at the other. There were no less than ten windows in all.

The table was superbly set out. It was loaded with plate, and more than loaded with delicacies. The profusion was absolutely barbaric. There were meats enough to have feasted the Anakim.* Never, in all my life, had I witnessed so lavish, so wasteful an expenditure of the good things of life. There seemed very little taste, however, in the arrangements; and my eyes, accustomed to quiet lights, were sadly offended by the prodigious glare of a multitude of wax candles, which, in silver *candelabra*, were deposited upon the table, and all about the room, wherever it was possible to find a place. There were several active servants in attendance; and, upon a large table, at the farther end of the apartment, were seated seven or eight people with fiddles, fifes, trombones, and a drum. These fellows annoyed me very much, at intervals, during the repast, by an infinite variety of noises, which were intended for music, and which appeared to afford much entertainment to all present, with the exception of myself.

Upon the whole, I could not help thinking that there was much of the *bizarre* about every thing I saw—but then the world is made up of all kinds of persons, with all modes of thought, and all sorts of conventional customs. I had travelled, too, so much as to be quite an adept in the *nil admirari*,* so I took my seat very coolly at the right hand of my host, and, having an excellent appetite, did justice to the good cheer set before me.

The conversation, in the meantime, was spirited and general. The ladies, as usual, talked a great deal. I soon found that nearly all the company were well educated; and my host was a world of good-humored anecdote in himself. He seemed quite willing to speak of his position as superintendent of a *Maison de Santé*; and, indeed, the topic of lunacy was, much to my surprise, a favorite one with all present. A great many amusing stories were told, having reference to the *whims* of the patients.

'We had a fellow here once,' said a fat little gentleman, who sat at my right—'a fellow that fancied himself a tea-pot; and, by the way, is it not especially singular how often this particular crotchet has entered the brain of the lunatic? There is scarcely an insane asylum in France which cannot supply a human tea-pot. *Our* gentleman was a Britannia-ware tea-pot, and was careful to polish himself every morning with buckskin and whiting.'

'And then,' said a tall man, just opposite, 'we had here, not long ago, a person who had taken it into his head that he was a donkey—which, allegorically speaking, you will say, was quite true. He was a troublesome patient; and we had much ado to keep him within bounds. For a long time he would eat nothing but thistles; but of this idea we soon cured him by insisting upon his eating nothing else. Then he was perpetually kicking out his heel—so—so—'

'Mr De Kock! I will thank you to behave yourself!' here interrupted an old lady, who sat next to the speaker. 'Please keep your feet to yourself! You have spoiled my brocade! Is it necessary, pray, to illustrate a remark in so practical a style? Our friend, here, can surely comprehend you without all this. Upon my word, you are nearly as great a donkey as the poor unfortunate imagined himself. Your acting is very natural, as I live.'

'Mille pardons! Ma'mselle!' replied Monsieur De Kock, thus addressed—'a thousand pardons! I had no intention of offending. Ma'mselle Laplace—Monsieur De Kock will do himself the honor of taking wine with you.'

Here Monsieur De Kock bowed low, kissed his hand with much ceremony, and took wine with Ma'mselle Laplace.

'Allow me, *mon ami*,' now said Monsieur Maillard, addressing myself, 'allow me to send you a morsel of this veal *à la St Menehoult*—you will find it particularly fine.'

At this instant three sturdy waiters had just succeeded in depositing safely upon the table an enormous dish, or trencher, containing what I supposed to be the '*monstrum, horrendum, informe, ingens, cui lumen ademptum*.'* A closer scrutiny assured me, however, that it was only a small calf roasted whole, and set upon its knees, with an apple in its mouth, as is the English fashion of dressing a hare.

'Thank you, no,' I replied; 'to say the truth, I am not particularly partial to veal *à la St*—what is it?—for I do not find that it altogether agrees with me. I will change my plate, however, and try some of the rabbit.'

There were several side-dishes on the table, containing what appeared to be the ordinary French rabbit—a very delicious *morceau*, which I can recommend.

'Pierre,' cried the host, 'change this gentleman's plate, and give him a side-piece of this rabbit *au-chát*.'

'This what?' said I.

'This rabbit *au-chát*.'

'Why, thank you—upon second thoughts, no. I will just help myself to some of the ham.'

There is no knowing what one eats, thought I to myself, at the tables of these people of the province. I will have none of their rabbit *au-chát*—and, for the matter of that, none of their *cat-au-rabbit* either.

'And then,' said a cadaverous-looking personage, near the foot of the table, taking up the thread of the conversation where it had been broken off—'and then, among other oddities, we had a patient, once upon a time, who very pertinaciously maintained himself to be a Cordova cheese, and went about, with a knife in his hand, soliciting his friends to try a small slice from the middle of his leg.'

'He was a great fool, beyond doubt,' interposed some one, 'but not to be compared with a certain individual whom we all know, with the exception of this strange gentleman. I mean the man who took himself for a bottle of champagne, and always went off with a pop and a fizz, in this fashion.'

Here the speaker, very rudely, as I thought, put his right thumb in his left cheek, withdrew it with a sound resembling the popping of a cork, and then, by a dexterous movement of the tongue upon the teeth, created a sharp hissing and fizzing, which lasted for several minutes, in imitation of the frothing of champagne. This behavior, I saw plainly, was not very pleasing to Monsieur Maillard; but that gentleman said nothing, and the conversation was resumed by a very lean little man in a big wig.

'And then there was an ignoramus,' said he, 'who mistook himself for a frog; which, by the way, he resembled in no little degree. I wish you could have seen him, sir,'—here the speaker addressed myself—'it would have done your heart good to see the natural airs that he put on. Sir, if that man was *not* a frog, I can only observe that it is a pity he was not. His croak thus—o-o-o-o-gh—o-o-o-o-gh! was the finest note in the world—B flat; and when he put his elbows upon the table thus—after taking a glass or two of wine—and distended his mouth, thus, and rolled up his eyes, thus, and winked them with excessive rapidity, thus, why then, sir, I take it upon myself to say, positively, that you would have been lost in admiration of the genius of the man.'

'I have no doubt of it,' I said.

'And then,' said somebody else, 'then there was Petit Gaillard, who thought himself a pinch of snuff, and was truly distressed because he could not take himself between his own finger and thumb.'

'And then there was Jules Desoulières, who was a very singular genius, indeed, and went mad with the idea that he was a pumpkin. He persecuted the cook to make him up into pies—a thing which the cook indignantly refused to do. For my part, I am by no means sure that a pumpkin pie *à la Desoulières* would not have been very capital eating, indeed!'

'You astonish me!' said I; and I looked inquisitively at Monsieur Maillard.

'Ha! ha! ha!' said that gentleman—'he! he! he!—hi! hi! hi!—ho! ho! ho!—hu! hu! hu!—very good indeed! You must not be astonished, *mon ami*; our friend here is a wit—*a drôle*—you must not understand him to the letter.'

'And then,' said some other one of the party, 'then there was Bouffon Le Grand—another extraordinary personage in his way. He grew deranged through love, and fancied himself possessed of two heads. One of these he maintained to be the head of Cicero; the other he imagined a composite one, being Demosthenes' from the top of the forehead to the mouth, and Lord Brougham* from the mouth to the chin. It is not impossible that he was wrong; but he would have convinced you of his being in the right; for he was a man of great eloquence. He had an absolute passion for oratory, and could not refrain from display. For example, he used to leap upon the dinner-table thus, and—and—'

Here a friend, at the side of the speaker, put a hand upon his shoulder, and whispered a few words in his ear; upon which he ceased talking with great suddenness, and sank back within his chair.

'And then,' said the friend, who had whispered, 'there was Boullard, the tee-totum. I call him the tee-totum, because, in fact, he was seized with the droll, but not altogether irrational crotchet, that he had been converted into a tee-totum. You would have roared with laughter to see him spin. He would turn round upon one heel by the hour, in this manner—so—'

Here the friend whom he had just interrupted by a whisper, performed an exactly similar office for himself.

'But then,' cried an old lady, at the top of her voice, 'your Monsieur Boullard was a madman, and a very silly madman at best; for who, allow me to ask you, ever heard of a human tee-totum? The thing is absurd. Madame Joyeuse was a more sensible person, as you know. She had a crotchet, but it was instinct with common sense, and gave pleasure to all who had the honor of her acquaintance. She found, upon mature deliberation, that, by some accident, she had been turned into a chicken-cock; but, as such, she behaved with propriety. She flapped her wings with prodigious effect—so—so—so—and, as for her crow, it was delicious! Cock-a-doodle-doo!—cock-a-doodle-doo—cock-a-doodle-de-doo-doo-dooo-do-o-o-o-o-o-o!'

'Madame Joyeuse, I will thank you to behave yourself!' here interrupted our host, very angrily. 'You can either conduct yourself as a lady should do, or you can quit the table forthwith—take your choice.'

The lady, (whom I was much astonished to hear addressed as Madame Joyeuse, after the description of Madame Joyeuse she had just given,) blushed up to the eye-brows, and seemed exceedingly abashed at the reproof. She hung down her head, and said not a syllable in reply. But another and younger lady resumed the theme. It was my beautiful girl of the little parlor!

'Oh, Madame Joyeuse *was* a fool!' she exclaimed; 'but there was really much sound sense, after all, in the opinion of Eugénie Salsafette. She was a very beautiful and painfully modest young lady, who thought the ordinary mode of habiliment indecent, and wished to dress herself, always, by getting outside, instead of inside of her clothes. It is a thing very easily done, after all. You have only to do so—and then so—so—so—and then so—so—so—and then—'

'Mon dieu! Ma'mselle Salsafette!' here cried a dozen voices at once. 'What *are* you about?—forbear!—that is sufficient!—we see, very plainly, how it is done!—hold! hold!' and several persons were already leaping from their seats to withhold Ma'mselle Salsafette from putting herself upon a par with the Medicean Venus,* when the point was very effectually and suddenly accomplished by a series of loud screams, or yells, from some portion of the main body of the château.

My nerves were very much affected, indeed, by these yells; but the rest of the company I really pitied. I never saw any set of reasonable people so thoroughly frightened in my life. They all grew as pale as so many corpses, and, shrinking within their seats, sat quivering and gibbering with terror, and listening for a repetition of the sound. It came again—louder and seemingly nearer—and then a third time *very* loud, and than a fourth time with a vigor evidently diminished. At this apparent dying away of the noise, the spirits of the company were immediately regained, and all was life and anecdote as before. I now ventured to inquire the cause of the disturbance.

'A mere *bagatelle*,' said Monsieur Maillard. 'We are used to these things, and care really very little about them. The lunatics, every now and then, get up a howl in concert; one starting another, as is sometimes the case with a bevy of dogs at night. It occasionally happens, however, that the *concerto* yells are succeeded by a simultaneous effort at breaking loose; when, of course, some little danger is to be apprehended.'

'And how many have you in charge?'

'At present, we have not more than ten, altogether.'

'Principally females, I presume?'

'Oh, no—every one of them men, and stout fellows, too, I can tell you.'

'Indeed! I have always understood that the majority of lunatics were of the gentler sex.'

'It is generally so, but not always. Some time ago, there were about twenty-seven patients here; and, of that number, no less than eighteen were women; but, lately, matters have changed very much, as you see.'

'Yes—have changed very much, as you see,' here interrupted the gentleman who had broken the shins of Ma'mselle Laplace.

'Yes—have changed very much as you see!' chimed in the whole company at once.

'Hold your tongues, every one of you!' said my host, in a great rage. Whereupon the whole company maintained a dead silence for nearly a minute. As for one lady, she obeyed Monsieur Maillard to the letter, and thrusting out her tongue, which was an excessively long one, held it very resignedly, with both hands, until the end of the entertainment.

'And this gentlewoman,' said I, to Monsieur Maillard, bending over and addressing him in a whisper—'this good lady who has just spoken, and who gives us the cock-a-doodle-de-doo—she, I presume, is harmless—quite harmless, eh?'

'Harmless!' ejaculated he, in unfeigned surprise, 'why—why what *can* you mean?'

'Only slightly touched?' said I, touching my head. 'I take it for granted that she is not particularly—not dangerously affected, eh?'

'*Mon Dieu!* what *is* it you imagine? This lady, my particular old friend, Madame Joyeuse, is as absolutely sane as myself. She has her little eccentricities, to be sure—but then, you know, all old women—all *very* old women are more or less eccentric!'

'To be sure,' said I—'to be sure—and then the rest of these ladies and gentlemen—'

'Are my friends and keepers,' interrupted Monsieur Maillard, drawing himself up with *hauteur*—'my very good friends and assistants.'

'What! all of them?' I asked—'the women and all?'

'Assuredly,' he said—'we could not do at all without the women; they are the best lunatic nurses in the world; they have a way of their own, you know; their bright eyes have a marvellous effect;—something like the fascination of the snake, you know.'

'To be sure,' said I—'to be sure! They behave a little odd, eh?—they are a little *queer*, eh?—don't you think so?'

'Odd!—queer!—why, do you *really* think so? We are not very prudish, to be sure, here in the South—do pretty much as we please—enjoy life, and all that sort of thing, you know—'

'To be sure,' said I—'to be sure.'

'And then, perhaps, this *Clos de Vougeôt* is a little heady, you know—a little *strong*—you understand, eh?'

'To be sure,' said I—'to be sure. By-the-by, monsieur, did I understand you to say that the system you have adopted, in place of the celebrated soothing system, was one of very rigorous severity?'

'By no means. Our confinement is necessarily close; but the treatment—the medical treatment, I mean—is rather agreeable to the patients than otherwise.'

'And the new system is one of your own invention?'

'Not altogether. Some portions of it are referable to Professor Tarr, of whom you have, necessarily, heard; and, again, there are modifications in my plan which I am happy to acknowledge as belonging of right to the celebrated Fether, with whom, if I mistake not, you have the honor of an intimate acquaintance.'

'I am quite ashamed to confess,' I replied, 'that I have never even heard the name of either gentleman before.'

'Good Heavens!' ejaculated my host, drawing back his chair abruptly, and uplifting his hands. 'I surely do not hear you aright! You did not intend to say, eh? that you had never *heard* either of the learned Doctor Tarr, or of the celebrated Professor Fether?'

'I am forced to acknowledge my ignorance,' I replied; 'but the truth should be held inviolate above all things. Nevertheless, I feel humbled to the dust, not to be acquainted with the works of these, no doubt, extraordinary men. I will seek out their writings forthwith, and peruse them with deliberate care. Monsieur Maillard, you have really—I must confess it—you have *really*—made me ashamed of myself!'

And this was the fact.

'Say no more, my good young friend,' he said kindly, pressing my hand—'join me now in a glass of Sauterne.'

We drank. The company followed our example, without stint. They chatted—they jested—they laughed—they perpetrated a thousand absurdities—the fiddles shrieked—the drum row-de-dowed—the trombones bellowed like so many brazen bulls of Phalaris*—and the whole scene, growing gradually worse and worse, as the wines gained the ascendancy, became at length a sort of Pandemonium *in petto*.* In the meantime, Monsieur Maillard and myself, with some bottles of Sauterne and Vougeôt between us, continued our conversation at the top of the voice. A word spoken in an ordinary key stood no more chance of being heard than the voice of a fish from the bottom of Niagara Falls.

'And, sir,' said I, screaming in his ear, 'you mentioned something before dinner, about the danger incurred in the old system of soothing. How is that?'

'Yes,' he replied, 'there was, occasionally, very great danger, indeed. There is no accounting for the caprices of madmen; and, in my opinion, as well as in that of Doctor Tarr and Professor Fether, it is *never* safe to permit them to run at large unattended. A lunatic may be "soothed," as it is called, for a time, but, in the end, he is very apt to become obstreperous. His cunning, too, is proverbial, and great. If he has a project in view, he conceals his design with a marvellous wisdom; and the dexterity with which he counterfeits sanity, presents, to the metaphysician, one of the most singular problems in the study of mind. When a madman appears *thoroughly* sane, indeed, it is high time to put him in a straight jacket.'

'But the *danger*, my dear sir, of which you were speaking—in your own experience—during your control of this house—have you had practical reason to think liberty hazardous, in the case of a lunatic?'

'Here?—in my own experience?—why, I may say, yes. For example:—no *very* long while ago, a singular circumstance occurred in this very house. The "soothing system," you know, was then in operation, and the patients were at large. They behaved remarkably well—especially so—any one of sense might have known that some devilish scheme was brewing from that particular fact, that the fellows behaved so *remarkably* well. And, sure enough, one fine morning the keepers found themselves pinioned hand and foot, and thrown into the cells, where they were attended, as if *they* were the lunatics, by the lunatics themselves, who had usurped the offices of the keepers.'

'You don't tell me so! I never heard of anything so absurd in my life!'

'Fact—it all came to pass by means of a stupid fellow—a lunatic—who, by some means, had taken it into his head that he had invented a better system of government than any ever heard of before—of lunatic government, I mean. He wished to give his invention a trial, I suppose—and so he persuaded the rest of the patients to join him in a conspiracy for the overthrow of the reigning powers.'

'And he really succeeded?'

'No doubt of it. The keepers and kept were soon made to exchange places. Not that exactly either—for the madmen had been free, but the keepers were shut up in cells forthwith, and treated, I am sorry to say, in a very cavalier manner.'

'But I presume a counter revolution was soon effected. This condition of things could not have long existed. The country people in the neighborhood—visitors coming to see the establishment—would have given the alarm.'

'There you are out. The head rebel was too cunning for that. He admitted no visitors at all—with the exception, one day, of a very stupid-looking young gentleman of whom he had no reason to be afraid. He let him in to see the place—just by way of variety—to have a little fun with him. As soon as he had gammoned him sufficiently, he let him out, and sent him about his business.'

'And *how* long, then, did the madmen reign?'

'Oh, a very long time, indeed—a month certainly—how much longer I can't precisely say. In the meantime, the lunatics had a jolly season of it—that you may swear. They doffed their own shabby clothes, and made free with the family wardrobe and jewels. The cellars of the *château* were well stocked with wine; and these madmen are just the devils that know how to drink it. They lived well, I can tell you.'

'And the treatment—what was the particular species of treatment which the leader of the rebels put into operation?'

'Why, as for that, a madman is not necessarily a fool, as I have already observed; and it is my honest opinion that his treatment was a much better treatment than that which it superseded. It was a very capital system indeed—simple—neat—no trouble at all—in fact it was delicious—it was—'

Here my host's observations were cut short by another series of yells, of the same character as those which had previously disconcerted us. This time, however, they seemed to proceed from persons rapidly approaching.

'Gracious Heavens!' I ejaculated—'the lunatics have most undoubtedly broken loose.'

'I very much fear it is so,' replied Monsieur Maillard, now becoming excessively pale. He had scarcely finished the sentence, before loud shouts and imprecations were heard beneath the windows; and, immediately afterward, it became evident that some persons outside were endeavoring to gain entrance into the room. The door was beaten with what appeared to be a sledgehammer, and the shutters were wrenched and shaken with prodigious violence.

A scene of the most terrible confusion ensued. Monsieur Maillard, to my excessive astonishment, threw himself under the sideboard. I had expected more resolution at his hands. The members of the orchestra, who, for the last fifteen minutes, had been seemingly too much intoxicated to do duty, now sprang all at once to their feet and to their instruments, and, scrambling upon their table, broke out, with one accord, into 'Yankee Doodle,'* which they performed, if not exactly in tune, at least with an energy superhuman, during the whole of the uproar.

Meantime, upon the main dining-table, among the bottles and glasses, leaped the gentleman, who, with such difficulty, had been restrained from leaping there before. As soon as he fairly settled himself, he commenced an oration, which, no doubt, was a very capital one, if it could only have been heard. At the same moment, the man with the tee-totum predilections, set himself to spinning around the apartment, with immense energy, and with arms outstretched at right angles with his body; so that he had all the air of a tee-totum in fact, and knocked every body down that happened to get in his way.

And now, too, hearing an incredible popping and fizzing of champagne, I discovered at length, that it proceeded from the person who performed the bottle of that delicate drink during dinner. And then, again, the frog-man croaked away as if the salvation of his soul depended upon every note that he uttered. And, in the midst of all this, the continuous braying of a donkey arose over all. As for my old friend, Madame Joyeuse, I really could have wept for the poor lady, she appeared so terribly perplexed. All she did, however, was to stand up in a corner, by the fire-place, and sing out incessantly, at the top of her voice, 'Cock-a-doodle-de-dooooooh!'

And now came the climax—the catastrophe of the drama. As no resistance, beyond whooping and yelling and cock-a-doodleing, was offered to the encroachments of the party without, the ten windows were very speedily, and almost simultaneously, broken in. But I shall never forget the emotions of wonder and horror with which I gazed, when, leaping through these windows, and down among us *pêle-mêle*, fighting, stamping, scratching, and howling, there rushed a perfect army of what I took to be Chimpanzees, Ourang-Outangs, or big black baboons of the Cape of Good Hope.

I received a terrible beating—after which I rolled under a sofa and lay still. After lying there some fifteen minutes, however, during which time I listened with all my ears to what was going on in the room, I came to some satisfactory *dénouement* of this tragedy. Monsieur Maillard, it appeared, in giving me the account of the lunatic who had excited his fellows to rebellion, had been merely relating his own exploits. This gentleman had, indeed, some two or three years before, been the superintendent of the establishment; but grew crazy himself, and so became a patient. This fact was unknown to the travelling companion who introduced me. The keepers, ten in number, having been suddenly overpowered, were first well tarred, then carefully feathered, and then shut up in underground cells. They had been so imprisoned for more than a month, during which period Monsieur Maillard had generously allowed them not only the tar and feathers (which constituted his 'system'), but some bread and abundance of water. The latter was pumped on them daily. At length, one escaping through a sewer, gave freedom to all the rest.

The 'soothing system,' with important modifications, has been resumed at the *château*; yet I cannot help agreeing with Monsieur Maillard, that his own 'treatment' was a very capital one of its kind.

As he justly observed, it was 'simple—neat—and gave no trouble at all—not the least.'

I have only to add that, although I have searched every library in Europe for the works of Doctor *Tarr* and Professor *Fether*, I have, up to the present day, utterly failed in my endeavors at procuring an edition.

THE IMP OF THE PERVERSE

In the consideration of the faculties and impulses—of the *prima mobilia* of the human soul, the phrenologists have failed to make room for a propensity which, although obviously existing as a radical, primitive, irreducible sentiment, has been equally overlooked by all the moralists who have preceded them. In the pure arrogance of the reason, we have all overlooked it. We have suffered its existence to escape our senses, solely through want of belief—of faith;—whether it be faith in Revelation, or faith in the Kabbala. The idea of it has never occurred to us, simply because of its supererogation. We saw no *need* of the impulse—for the propensity. We could not perceive its necessity. We could not understand, that is to say, we could not have understood, had the notion of this *primum mobile* ever obtruded itself;—we could not have understood in what manner it might be made to further the objects of humanity, either temporal or eternal. It cannot be denied that phrenology and, in great measure, all metaphysicianism have been concocted *a priori*. The intellectual or logical man, rather than the understanding or observant man, set himself to imagine designs—to dictate purposes to God. Having thus fathomed, to his satisfaction, the intentions of Jehovah, out of these intentions he built his innumerable systems of mind. In the matter of phrenology, for example, we first determined, naturally enough, that it was the design of the Deity that man should eat. We then assigned to man an organ of alimentiveness, and this organ is the scourge with which the Deity compels man, will-I nill-I, into eating. Secondly, having settled it to be God's will that man should continue his species, we discovered an organ of amativeness, forthwith. And so with combativeness, with ideality, with causality, with constructiveness,—so, in short, with every organ, whether representing a propensity, a moral sentiment, or a faculty of the pure intellect. And in these arrangements of the *principia* of human action, the Spurzheimites, whether right or wrong, in part, or upon the whole, have but followed, in principle, the footsteps of their predecessors; deducing and establishing every thing from the preconceived destiny of man, and upon the ground of the objects of his Creator.*

It would have been wiser, it would have been safer to classify, (if classify we must,) upon the basis of what man usually or occasionally did, and was always occasionally doing, rather than upon the basis of what we took it for granted the Deity intended him to do. If we cannot comprehend God in his visible works, how then in his inconceivable thoughts, that call the works into being? If we cannot understand him in his objective creatures, how then in his substantive moods and phrases of creation?

Induction, *a posteriori*, would have brought phrenology to admit, as an innate and primitive principle of human action, a paradoxical something, which we may call *perverseness*, for want of a more characteristic term. In the sense I intend, it is, in fact, a *mobile* without motive, a motive not *motivirt*. Through its promptings we act without comprehensible object; or, if this shall be understood as a contradiction in terms, we may so far modify the proposition as to say, that through its promptings we act, for the reason that we should *not*. In theory, no reason can be more unreasonable; but, in fact, there is none more strong. With certain minds, under certain conditions, it becomes absolutely irresistible. I am not more certain that I breathe, than that the assurance of the wrong or error of any action is often the one unconquerable *force* which impels us, and alone impels us to its prosecution. Nor will this overwhelming tendency to do wrong for the wrong's sake, admit of analysis, or resolution into ulterior elements. It is a radical, a primitive impulse—elementary. It will be said, I am aware, that when we persist in acts because we feel we should *not* persist in them, our conduct is but a modification of that which ordinarily springs from the *combativeness* of phrenology. But a glance will show the fallacy of this idea. The phrenological combativeness has for its essence, the necessity of self-defence. It is our safeguard against injury. Its principle regards our well-being; and thus the desire to be well is excited simultaneously with its development. It follows, that the desire to be well must be excited simultaneously with any principle which shall be merely a modification of combativeness, but in the case of that something which I term *perverseness*, the desire to be well is not only not aroused, but a strongly antagonistical sentiment exists.

An appeal to one's own heart is, after all, the best reply to the sophistry just noticed. No one who trustingly consults and thoroughly questions his own soul, will be disposed to deny the entire radicalness of the propensity in question. It is not more incomprehensible than distinctive. There lives no man who at some period has not been tormented, for example, by an earnest desire to tantalize a listener by circumlocution. The speaker is aware that he displeases; he has every intention to please; he is usually curt, precise, and clear; the most laconic and luminous language is struggling for utterance upon his tongue; it is only with difficulty that he restrains himself from giving it flow; he dreads and deprecates the anger of him whom he addresses; yet, the thought strikes him, that by certain involutions and parentheses, this anger may be engendered. That single thought is enough. The impulse increases to a wish, the wish to a desire, the desire to an uncontrollable longing, and the longing, (to the deep regret and mortification of the speaker, and in defiance of all consequences,) is indulged.

We have a task before us which must be speedily performed. We know that it will be ruinous to make delay. The most important crisis of our life calls, trumpet-tongued, for immediate energy and action. We glow, we are consumed with eagerness to commence the work, with the anticipation of whose glorious result our whole souls are on fire. It must, it shall be undertaken to-day, and yet we put it off until to-morrow; and why? There is no answer, except that we feel *perverse*, using the word with no comprehension of the principle. To-morrow arrives, and with it a more impatient anxiety to do our duty, but with this very increase of anxiety arrives, also, a nameless, a positively fearful because unfathomable, craving for delay. This craving gathers strength as the moments fly. The last hour for action is at hand. We tremble with the violence of the conflict within us,—of the definite with the indefinite—of the substance with the shadow. But, if the contest have proceeded thus far, it is the shadow which prevails,—we struggle in vain. The clock strikes, and is the knell of our welfare. At the same time, it is the chanticleer-note to the ghost that has so long overawed us. It flies—it disappears—we are free. The old energy returns. We will labor *now*. Alas, it is *too late!*

We stand upon the brink of a precipice. We peer into the abyss—we grow sick and dizzy. Our first impulse is to shrink from the danger. Unaccountably we remain. By slow degrees our sickness, and dizziness, and horror, become merged in a cloud of unnameable feeling. By gradations, still more imperceptible, this cloud assumes shape, as did the vapor from the bottle out of which arose the genius in the Arabian Nights. But out of this *our* cloud upon the precipice's edge, there grows into palpability, a shape, far more terrible than any genius, or any demon of a tale, and yet it is but a thought, although a fearful one, and one which chills the very marrow of our bones with the fierceness of the delight of its horror. It is merely the idea of what would be our sensations during the sweeping precipitancy of a fall from such a height. And this fall—this rushing annihilation—for the very reason that it involves that one most ghastly and loathsome of all the most ghastly and loathsome images of death and suffering which have ever presented themselves to our imagination—for this very cause do we now the most vividly desire it. And because our reason violently deters us from the brink, *therefore*, do we the more impetuously approach it. There is no passion in nature so demoniacally impatient, as that of him, who shuddering upon the edge of a precipice, thus meditates a plunge. To indulge for a moment, in any attempt at *thought*, is to be inevitably lost; for reflection but urges us to forbear, and *therefore* it is, I say, that we *cannot*. If there be no friendly arm to check us, or if we fail in a sudden effort to prostrate ourselves backward from the abyss, we plunge, and are destroyed.

Examine these and similar actions as we will, we shall find them resulting solely from the spirit of the *Perverse*. We perpetrate them merely because we feel that we should *not*. Beyond or behind this, there is no intelligible principle: and we might, indeed, deem this perverseness a direct instigation of the arch-fiend, were it not occasionally known to operate in furtherance of good.

I have said thus much, that in some measure I may answer your question—that I may explain to you why I am here—that I may assign to you something that shall have at least the faint aspect of a cause for my wearing these fetters, and for my tenanting this cell of the condemned. Had I not been thus prolix, you might either have misunderstood me altogether, or, with the rabble, have fancied me mad. As it is, you will easily perceive that I am one of the many uncounted victims of the Imp of the Perverse.

It is impossible that any deed could have been wrought with a more thorough deliberation. For weeks, for months, I pondered upon the means of the murder. I rejected a thousand schemes, because their accomplishment involved a *chance* of detection. At length, in reading some French memoirs, I found an account of a nearly fatal illness that occurred to Madame Pilau, through the agency of a candle accidentally poisoned. The idea struck my fancy at once. I knew my victim's habit of reading in bed. I knew, too, that his apartment was narrow and ill-ventilated. But I need not vex you with impertinent details. I need not describe the easy artifices by which I substituted, in his bed-room candlestand, a wax-light of my own making, for the one which I there found. The next morning he was discovered dead in his bed, and the coroner's verdict was,—'Death by the visitation of God.'

Having inherited his estate, all went well with me for years. The idea of detection never once entered my brain. Of the remains of the fatal taper, I had myself carefully disposed. I had left no shadow of a clue by which it would be possible to convict, or even to suspect me of the crime. It is inconceivable how rich a sentiment of satisfaction arose in my bosom as I reflected upon my absolute security. For a very long period of time, I was accustomed to revel in this sentiment. It afforded me more real delight than all the mere worldly advantages accruing from my sin. But there arrived at length an epoch, from which the pleasurable feeling grew, by scarcely perceptible gradations, into a haunting and harassing thought. It harassed because it haunted. I could scarcely get rid of it for an instant. It is quite a common thing to be thus annoyed with the ringing in our ears, or rather in our memories, of the burthen of some ordinary song, or some unimpressive snatches from an opera. Nor will we be less tormented if the song in itself be good, or the opera air meritorious. In this manner, at last, I would perpetually catch myself pondering upon my security, and repeating, in a low under-tone, the phrase, 'I am safe.'

One day, whilst sauntering along the streets, I arrested myself in the act of murmuring, half aloud, these customary syllables. In a fit of petulance, I re-modelled them thus:—'I am safe—I am safe—yes—if I be not fool enough to make open confession!'

No sooner had I spoken these words, than I felt an icy chill creep to my heart. I had had some experience in these fits of perversity, (whose nature I have been at some trouble to explain,) and I remembered well, that in no instance, I had successfully resisted their attacks. And now my own casual self-suggestion, that I might possibly be fool enough to confess the murder of which I had been guilty, confronted me, as if the very ghost of him whom I had murdered—and beckoned me on to death.

At first, I made an effort to shake off this nightmare of the soul. I walked vigorously—faster—still faster—at length I ran. I felt a maddening desire to shriek aloud. Every succeeding wave of thought overwhelmed me with new terror, for alas! I well, too well understood that, to *think*, in my situation, was to be lost. I still quickened my pace.

I bounded like a madman through the crowded thoroughfares. At length, the populace took the alarm, and pursued me. I felt *then* the consummation of my fate. Could I have torn out my tongue, I would have done it—but a rough voice resounded in my ears—a rougher grasp seized me by the shoulder. I turned—I gasped for breath. For a moment, I experienced all the pangs of suffocation; I became blind, and deaf, and giddy; and then, some invisible fiend, I thought, struck me with his broad palm upon the back. The long-imprisoned secret burst forth from my soul.

They say that I spoke with a distinct enunciation, but with marked emphasis and passionate hurry, as if in dread of interruption before concluding the brief but pregnant sentences that consigned me to the hangman and to hell.

Having related all that was necessary for the fullest judicial conviction, I fell prostrate in a swoon.

But why shall I say more? To-day I wear these chains, and am *here*. To-morrow I shall be fetterless!—*but where*?

THE CASK OF AMONTILLADO

THE thousand injuries of Fortunato I had borne as I best could; but when he ventured upon insult, I vowed revenge. You, who so well know the nature of my soul, will not suppose, however, that I gave utterance to a threat. *At length* I would be avenged; this was a point definitely settled—but the very definitiveness with which it was resolved precluded the idea of risk. I must not only punish, but punish with impunity. A wrong is unredressed when retribution overtakes its redresser. It is equally unredressed when the avenger fails to make himself felt as such to him who has done the wrong.

It must be understood that neither by word nor deed had I given Fortunato cause to doubt my good will. I continued, as was my wont, to smile in his face, and he did not perceive that my smile *now* was at the thought of his immolation.

He had a weak point—this Fortunato—although in other regards he was a man to be respected and even feared. He prided himself on his connoisseurship in wine. Few Italians have the true virtuoso spirit. For the most part their enthusiasm is adopted to suit the time and opportunity—to practise imposture upon the British and Austrian *millionaires*. In painting and gemmary Fortunato, like his countrymen, was a quack—but in the matter of old wines he was sincere. In this respect I did not differ from him materially; I was skilful in the Italian vintages myself, and bought largely whenever I could.

It was about dusk, one evening during the supreme madness of the carnival season, that I encountered my friend. He accosted me with excessive warmth, for he had been drinking much. The man wore motley. He had on a tight-fitting parti-striped dress, and his head was surmounted by the conical cap and bells. I was so pleased to see him that I thought I should never have done wringing his hand.

I said to him—'My dear Fortunato, you are luckily met. How remarkably well you are looking to-day! But I have received a pipe of what passes for Amontillado, and I have my doubts.'*

'How?' said he. 'Amontillado? A pipe? Impossible! And in the middle of the carnival!'

'I have my doubts', I replied; 'and I was silly enough to pay the full

Amontillado price without consulting you in the matter. You were not to be found, and I was fearful of losing a bargain.'

'Amontillado!'

'I have my doubts.'

'Amontillado!'

'And I must satisfy them.'

'Amontillado!'

'As you are engaged, I am on my way to Luchesi. If any one has a critical turn, it is he. He will tell me—'

'Luchesi cannot tell Amontillado from Sherry.'

'And yet some fools will have it that his taste is a match for your own.'

'Come, let us go.'

'Whither?'

'To your vaults.'

'My friend, no; I will not impose upon your good nature. I perceive you have an engagement. Luchesi—'

'I have no engagement;—come.'

'My friend, no. It is not the engagement, but the severe cold with which I perceive you are afflicted. The vaults are insufferably damp. They are encrusted with nitre.'

'Let us go, nevertheless. The cold is merely nothing. Amontillado! You have been imposed upon. And as for Luchesi, he cannot distinguish Sherry from Amontillado.'

Thus speaking, Fortunato possessed himself of my arm. Putting on a mask of black silk, and drawing a *roquelaire* closely about my person, I suffered him to hurry me to my palazzo.

There were no attendants at home; they had absconded to make merry in honor of the time. I had told them that I should not return until the morning, and had given them explicit orders not to stir from the house. These orders were sufficient, I well knew, to insure their immediate disappearance, one and all, as soon as my back was turned.

I took from their sconces two flambeaux, and giving one to Fortunato, bowed him through several suites of rooms to the archway that led into the vaults. I passed down a long and winding staircase, requesting him to be cautious as he followed. We came at length to the foot of the descent, and stood together on the damp ground of the catacombs of the Montresors.

The gait of my friend was unsteady, and the bells upon his cap jingled as he strode.

'The pipe,' said he.

'It is farther on,' said I; 'but observe the white web-work which gleams from these cavern walls.'

He turned towards me, and looked into my eyes with two filmy orbs that distilled the rheum of intoxication.

'Nitre?' he asked, at length.

'Nitre,' I replied. 'How long have you had that cough?'

'Ugh! ugh! ugh!—ugh! ugh! ugh!—ugh! ugh! ugh!—ugh! ugh! ugh!—ugh! ugh! ugh!'

My poor friend found it impossible to reply for many minutes.

'It is nothing', he said, at last.

'Come', I said, with decision, 'we will go back; your health is precious. You are rich, respected, admired, beloved; you are happy, as once I was. You are a man to be missed. For me it is no matter. We will go back; you will be ill, and I cannot be responsible. Besides, there is Luchesi—'

'Enough,' he said; 'the cough is a mere nothing; it will not kill me. I shall not die of a cough.'

'True—true,' I replied; 'and, indeed, I had no intention of alarming you unnecessarily—but you should use all proper caution. A draught of this Medoc will defend us from the damps.'

Here I knocked off the neck of a bottle which I drew from a long row of its fellows that lay upon the mould.

'Drink,' I said, presenting him the wine.

He raised it to his lips with a leer. He paused and nodded to me familiarly, while his bells jingled.

'I drink,' he said, 'to the buried that repose around us.'

'And I to your long life.'

He again took my arm, and we proceeded.

'These vaults,' he said, 'are extensive.'

'The Montresors,' I replied, 'were a great and numerous family.'

'I forget your arms.'

'A huge human foot d'or, in a field azure; the foot crushes a serpent rampant whose fangs are imbedded in the heel.'

'And the motto?'

'*Nemo me inpune lacessit.*'*

'Good!' he said.

The wine sparkled in his eyes and the bells jingled. My own fancy grew warm with the Medoc. We had passed through walls of piled bones, with casks and puncheons intermingling, into the inmost recesses of the catacombs. I paused again, and this time I made bold to seize Fortunato by an arm above the elbow.

'The nitre!' I said; 'see, it increases. It hangs like moss upon the vaults. We are below the river's bed. The drops of moisture trickle among the bones. Come, we will go back ere it is too late. Your cough—'

'It is nothing,' he said; 'let us go on. But first, another draught of the Medoc.'

I broke and reached him a flaçon of De Grâve. He emptied it at a breath. His eyes flashed with a fierce light. He laughed and threw the bottle upwards with a gesticulation I did not understand.

I looked at him in surprise. He repeated the movement—a grotesque one.

'You do not comprehend?' he said.

'Not I,' I replied.

'Then you are not of the brotherhood.'

'How?'

'You are not of the masons.'*

'Yes, yes,' I said, 'yes, yes.'

'You? Impossible! A mason?'

'A mason,' I replied.

'A sign,' he said.

'It is this,' I answered, producing a trowel from beneath the folds of my *roquelaire*.

'You jest,' he exclaimed, recoiling a few paces. 'But let us proceed to the Amontillado.'

'Be it so,' I said, replacing the tool beneath the cloak, and again offering him my arm. He leaned upon it heavily. We continued our route in search of the Amontillado. We passed through a range of low arches, descended, passed on, and descending again, arrived at a deep crypt, in which the foulness of the air caused our flambeaux rather to glow than flame.

At the most remote end of the crypt there appeared another less spacious. Its walls had been lined with human remains, piled to the vault overhead, in the fashion of the great catacombs of Paris. Three sides of this interior crypt were still ornamented in this manner. From the fourth the bones had been thrown down, and lay promiscuously upon the earth, forming at one point a mound of some size. Within the wall thus exposed by the displacing of the bones, we perceived a still interior recess, in depth about four feet, in width three, in height six or seven. It seemed to have been constructed for no especial use within itself, but formed merely the interval between two of the colossal supports of the roof of the catacombs, and was backed by one of their circumscribing walls of solid granite.

It was in vain that Fortunato, uplifting his dull torch, endeavored to pry into the depth of the recess. Its termination the feeble light did not enable us to see.

'Proceed,' I said; 'herein is the Amontillado. As for Luchesi—'

'He is an ignoramus,' interrupted my friend, as he stepped unsteadily forward, while I followed immediately at his heels. In an instant he had reached the extremity of the niche, and finding his progress arrested by the rock, stood stupidly bewildered. A moment more and I had fettered him to the granite. In its surface were two iron staples, distant from each other about two feet, horizontally. From one of these depended a short chain, from the other a padlock. Throwing the links about his waist, it was but the work of a few seconds to secure it. He was too much astounded to resist. Withdrawing the key I stepped back from the recess.

'Pass your hand,' I said, 'over the wall; you cannot help feeling the nitre. Indeed it is *very* damp. Once more let me *implore* you to return. No? Then I must positively leave you. But I must first render you all the little attentions in my power.'

'The Amontillado!' ejaculated my friend, not yet recovered from his astonishment.

'True,' I replied; 'the Amontillado.'

As I said these words I busied myself among the pile of bones of which I have before spoken. Throwing them aside, I soon uncovered a quantity of building stone and mortar. With these materials and with the aid of my trowel, I began vigorously to wall up the entrance of the niche.

I had scarcely laid the first tier of the masonry when I discovered that the intoxication of Fortunato had in a great measure worn off. The earliest indication I had of this was a low moaning cry from the depth of the recess. It was *not* the cry of a drunken man. There was then a long and obstinate silence. I laid the second tier, and the third, and the fourth; and then I heard the furious vibrations of the chain. The noise lasted for several minutes, during which, that I might hearken to it with the more satisfaction, I ceased my labors and sat down upon the bones. When at last the clanking subsided, I resumed the trowel, and finished without interruption the fifth, the sixth, and the seventh tier. The wall was now nearly upon a level with my breast. I again paused, and holding the flambeaux over the mason-work, threw a few feeble rays upon the figure within.

A succession of loud and shrill screams, bursting suddenly from the throat of the chained form, seemed to thrust me violently back. For a brief moment I hesitated—I trembled. Unsheathing my rapier, I began to grope with it about the recess: but the thought of an instant reassured me. I placed my hand upon the solid fabric of the catacombs, and felt satisfied. I reapproached the wall. I replied to the yells of him who clamored. I re-echoed—I aided—I surpassed them in volume and in strength. I did this, and the clamorer grew still.

It was now midnight, and my task was drawing to a close. I had completed the eighth, the ninth, and the tenth tier. I had finished a portion of the last and the eleventh; there remained but a single stone to be fitted and plastered in. I struggled with its weight; I placed it partially in its destined position. But now there came from out the niche a low laugh that erected the hairs upon my head. It was succeeded by a sad voice, which I had difficulty in recognising as that of the noble Fortunato. The voice said—

'Ha! ha! ha!—he! he!—a very good joke indeed—an excellent jest. We will have many a rich laugh about it at the palazzo—he! he! he!—over our wine—he! he! he!'

'The Amontillado!' I said.

'He! he! he!—he! he! he!—yes, the Amontillado. But is it not getting late? Will not they be awaiting us at the palazzo, the Lady Fortunato and the rest? Let us be gone.'

'Yes,' I said, 'let us be gone.'

'For the love of God, Montresor!'

'Yes,' I said, 'for the love of God!'

But to these words I hearkened in vain for a reply. I grew impatient. I called aloud—

'Fortunato!'

No answer. I called again—

'Fortunato!'

No answer still. I thrust a torch through the remaining aperture and let it fall within. There came forth in return only a jingling of the bells.

My heart grew sick—on account of the dampness of the catacombs. I hastened to make an end of my labor. I forced the last stone into its position; I plastered it up. Against the new masonry I re-erected the old rampart of bones. For the half of a century no mortal has disturbed them. *In pace requiescat!*

THE DOMAIN OF ARNHEIM

The garden like a lady fair was cut,
   That lay as if she slumbered in delight,
And to the open skies her eyes did shut.
   The azure fields of Heaven were 'sembled right
   In a large round set with the flowers of light.
The flowers de luce and the round sparks of dew
That hung upon their azure leaves did shew
Like twinkling stars that sparkle in the evening blue.

Giles Fletcher*

FROM his cradle to his grave a gale of prosperity bore my friend Ellison along. Nor do I use the word prosperity in its mere worldly sense. I mean it as synonymous with happiness. The person of whom I speak seemed born for the purpose of foreshadowing the doctrines of Turgot, Price, Priestley and Condorcet—of exemplifying by individual instance what has been deemed the chimera of the perfectionists.* In the brief existence of Ellison I fancy that I have seen refuted the dogma, that in man's very nature lies some hidden principle, the antagonist of bliss. An anxious examination of his career has given me to understand that, in general, from the violation of a few simple laws of humanity arises the wretchedness of mankind—that as a species we have in our possession the as yet unwrought elements of content—and that, even now, in the present darkness and madness of all thought on the great question of the social condition, it is not impossible that man, the individual, under certain unusual and highly fortuitous conditions, may be happy.

With opinions such as these my young friend, too, was fully imbued; and thus it is worthy of observation that the uninterrupted enjoyment which distinguished his life was, in great measure, the result of preconcert. It is, indeed, evident that with less of the instinctive philosophy which, now and then, stands so well in the stead of experience, Mr Ellison would have found himself precipitated, by the very extraordinary success of his life, into the common vortex of unhappiness which yawns for those of pre-eminent endowments. But it is by no means my object to pen an essay on happiness. The ideas of my friend may be summed up in a few words. He admitted but four elementary principles, or, more strictly, conditions, of bliss. That which he considered chief was (strange to say!) the simple and purely physical one of free exercise in the open air. 'The health,' he said, 'attainable by other means is scarcely worth the name.' He instanced the ecstasies of the fox-hunter, and pointed to the tillers of the earth, the only people who, as a class, can be fairly considered happier than others. His second condition was the love of woman. His third, and most difficult of realization, was the contempt of ambition. His fourth was an object of unceasing pursuit; and he held that, other things being equal, the extent of attainable happiness was in proportion to the spirituality of this object.

Ellison was remarkable in the continuous profusion of good gifts lavished upon him by fortune. In personal grace and beauty he exceeded all men. His intellect was of that order to which the acquisition of knowledge is less a labor than an intuition and a necessity. His family was one of the most illustrious of the empire. His bride was the loveliest and most devoted of women. His possessions had been always ample; but, on the attainment of his majority, it was discovered that one of those extraordinary freaks of fate had been played in his behalf which startle the whole social world amid which they occur, and seldom fail radically to alter the moral constitution of those who are their objects.

It appears that, about a hundred years before Mr Ellison's coming of age, there had died, in a remote province, one Mr Seabright Ellison. This gentleman had amassed a princely fortune, and, having no immediate connections, conceived the whim of suffering his wealth to accumulate for a century after his decease. Minutely and sagaciously directing the various modes of investment, he bequeathed the aggregate amount to the nearest of blood, bearing the name Ellison, who should be alive at the end of the hundred years. Many attempts had been made to set aside this singular bequest; their *ex post facto* character rendered them abortive; but the attention of a jealous government was aroused, and a legislative act finally obtained, forbidding all similar accumulations. This act, however, did not prevent young Ellison from entering into possession, on his twenty-first birth-day, as the heir of his ancestor Seabright, of a fortune of *four hundred and fifty millions of dollars.*[1]

[1] An incident, similar in outline to the one here imagined, occurred, not very long ago, in England. The name of the fortunate heir was Thelluson. I first saw an account of this matter in the 'Tour' of Prince Pückler-Muskau, who makes the sum inherited *ninety*

When it had become known that such was the enormous wealth inherited, there were, of course, many speculations as to the mode of its disposal. The magnitude and the immediate availability of the sum bewildered all who thought on the topic. The possessor of any *appreciable* amount of money might have been imagined to perform any one of a thousand things. With riches merely surpassing those of any citizen, it would have been easy to suppose him engaging to supreme excess in the fashionable extravagances of his time—or busying himself with political intrigue—or aiming at ministerial power—or purchasing increase of nobility—or collecting large museums of *virtu*—or playing the munificent patron of letters, of science, of art—or endowing, and bestowing his name upon extensive institutions of charity. But for the inconceivable wealth in the actual possession of the heir, these objects and all ordinary objects were felt to afford too limited a field. Recourse was had to figures, and these but sufficed to confound. It was seen that, even at three per cent., the annual income of the inheritance amounted to no less than thirteen millions and five hundred thousand dollars; which was one million and one hundred and twenty-five thousand per month; or thirty-six thousand nine hundred and eighty-six per day; or one thousand five hundred and forty-one per hour; or six and twenty dollars for every minute that flew. Thus the usual track of supposition was thoroughly broken up. Men knew not what to imagine. There were some who even conceived that Mr Ellison would divest himself of at least one half of his fortune, as of utterly superfluous opulence—enriching whole troops of his relatives by division of his superabundance. To the nearest of these he did, in fact, abandon the very unusual wealth which was his own before the inheritance.

I was not surprised, however, to perceive that he had long made up his mind on a point which had occasioned so much discussion to his friends. Nor was I greatly astonished at the nature of his decision. In regard to individual charities he had satisfied his conscience. In the possibility of any improvement, properly so called, being effected by man himself in the general condition of man, he had (I am sorry to

millions of pounds, and justly observes that 'in the contemplation of so vast a sum, and of the services to which it might be applied, there is something even of the sublime.' To suit the views of this article I have followed the Prince's statement, although a grossly exaggerated one. The germ, and, in fact, the commencement of the present paper was published many years ago—previous to the issue of the first number of Sue's admirable '*Juif Errant*,' which may possibly have been suggested to him by Muskau's account.*

confess it) little faith. Upon the whole, whether happily or unhappily, he was thrown back, in very great measure, upon self.

In the widest and noblest sense he was a poet. He comprehended, moreover, the true character, the august aims, the supreme majesty and dignity of the poetic sentiment. The fullest, if not the sole proper satisfaction of this sentiment he instinctively felt to lie in the creation of novel forms of beauty. Some peculiarities, either in his early education, or in the nature of his intellect, had tinged with what is termed materialism all his ethical speculations; and it was this bias, perhaps, which led him to believe that the most advantageous at least, if not the sole legitimate field for the poetic exercise, lies in the creation of novel moods of purely *physical* loveliness. Thus it happened he became neither musician nor poet—if we use this latter term in its every-day acceptation. Or it might have been that he neglected to become either, merely in pursuance of his idea that in contempt of ambition is to be found one of the essential principles of happiness on earth. Is it not, indeed, possible that, while a high order of genius is necessarily ambitious, the highest is above that which is termed ambition? And may it not thus happen that many far greater than Milton have contentedly remained 'mute and inglorious?'* I believe that the world has never seen—and that, unless through some series of accidents goading the noblest order of mind into distasteful exertion, the world will never see—that full extent of triumphant execution, in the richer domains of art, of which the human nature is absolutely capable.

Ellison became neither musician nor poet; although no man lived more profoundly enamored of music and poetry. Under other circumstances than those which invested him, it is not impossible that he would have become a painter. Sculpture, although in its nature rigorously poetical, was too limited in its extent and consequences, to have occupied, at any time, much of his attention. And I have now mentioned all the provinces in which the common understanding of the poetic sentiment has declared it capable of expatiating. But Ellison maintained that the richest, the truest and most natural, if not altogether the most extensive province, had been unaccountably neglected. No definition had spoken of the landscape-gardener as of the poet; yet it seemed to my friend that the creation of the landscape-garden offered to the proper Muse the most magnificent of opportunities. Here, indeed, was the fairest field for the display of imagination in the endless combining of forms of novel beauty; the elements to enter into combination being, by a vast superiority, the most glorious which the earth could afford. In the multiform and multicolor of the flower and the trees, he recognised the most direct and energetic efforts of Nature at physical loveliness. And in the direction or concentration of this effort—or, more properly, in its adaptation to the eyes which were to behold it on earth—he perceived that he should be employing the best means—laboring to the greatest advantage—in the fulfilment, not only of his own destiny as poet, but of the august purposes for which the Deity had implanted the poetic sentiment in man.

'Its adaptation to the eyes which were to behold it on earth.' In his explanation of this phraseology, Mr Ellison did much toward solving what has always seemed to me an enigma:—I mean the fact (which none but the ignorant dispute) that no such combination of scenery exists in nature as the painter of genius may produce. No such paradises are to be found in reality as have glowed on the canvass of Claude.* In the most enchanting of natural landscapes, there will always be found a defect or an excess—many excesses and defects. While the component parts may defy, individually, the highest skill of the artist, the arrangement of these parts will always be susceptible of improvement. In short, no position can be attained on the wide surface of the *natural* earth, from which an artistical eye, looking steadily, will not find matter of offence in what is termed the 'composition' of the landscape. And yet how unintelligible is this! In all other matters we are justly instructed to regard nature as supreme. With her details we shrink from competition. Who shall presume to imitate the colors of the tulip, or to improve the proportions of the lily of the valley? The criticism which says, of sculpture or portraiture, that here nature is to be exalted or idealized rather than imitated, is in error. No pictorial or sculptural combinations of points of human loveliness do more than approach the living and breathing beauty. In landscape alone is the principle of the critic true; and, having felt its truth here, it is but the headlong spirit of generalization which has led him to pronounce it true throughout all the domains of art. Having, I say, *felt* its truth here; for the feeling is no affectation or chimera. The mathematics afford no more absolute demonstrations than the sentiment of his art yields the artist. He not only believes, but positively knows, that such and such apparently arbitrary arrangements of matter constitute and alone constitute the true beauty. His reasons, however, have not yet been matured into expression. It remains for a more profound analysis than the world has yet seen, fully to investigate and express them. Nevertheless he is confirmed in his instinctive opinions by the voice of all his brethren. Let a 'composition' be defective; let an emendation be wrought in its mere arrangement of form; let this emendation be submitted to every artist in the world; by each will its necessity be admitted. And even far more than this: in remedy of the defective composition, each insulated member of the fraternity would have suggested the identical emendation.

I repeat that in landscape arrangements alone is the physical nature susceptible of exaltation, and that, therefore, her susceptibility of improvement at this one point, was a mystery I had been unable to solve. My own thoughts on the subject had rested in the idea that the primitive intention of nature would have so arranged the earth's surface as to have fulfilled at all points man's sense of perfection in the beautiful, the sublime, or the picturesque; but that this primitive intention had been frustrated by the known geological disturbances—disturbances of form and color-grouping, in the correction or allaying of which lies the soul of art. The force of this idea was much weakened, however, by the necessity which it involved of considering the disturbances abnormal and unadapted to any purpose. It was Ellison who suggested that they were prognostic of *death*. He thus explained:—Admit the earthly immortality of man to have been the first intention. We have then the primitive arrangement of the earth's surface adapted to his blissful estate, as not existent but designed. The disturbances were the preparations for his subsequently conceived deathful condition.

'Now,' said my friend, 'what we regard as exaltation of the landscape may be really such, as respects only the mortal or human *point of view*. Each alternation of the natural scenery may possibly effect a blemish in the picture, if we can suppose this picture viewed at large—in mass—from some point distant from the earth's surface, although not beyond the limits of its atmosphere. It is easily understood that what might improve a closely scrutinized detail, may at the same time injure a general or more distantly observed effect. There *may* be a class of beings, human once, but now invisible to humanity, to whom, from afar, our disorder may seem order—our unpicturesqueness picturesque; in a word, the earth-angels, for whose scrutiny more especially than our own, and for whose death-refined appreciation of the beautiful, may have been set in array by God the wide landscape-gardens of the hemispheres.'

In the course of discussion, my friend quoted some passages from a writer on landscape-gardening, who has been supposed to have well treated his theme:

'There are properly but two styles of landscape-gardening, the natural and the artificial. One seeks to recall the original beauty of the country, by adapting its means to the surrounding scenery; cultivating trees in harmony with the hills or plain of the neighboring land; detecting and bringing into practice those nice relations of size, proportion and color which, hid from the common observer, are revealed everywhere to the experienced student of nature. The result of the natural style of gardening is seen rather in the absence of all defects and incongruities—in the prevalence of a healthy harmony and order—than in the creation of any special wonders or miracles. The artificial style has as many varieties as there are different tastes to gratify. It has a certain general relation to the various styles of building. There are the stately avenues and retirements of Versailles; Italian terraces; and a various mixed old English style, which bears some relation to the domestic Gothic or English Elizabethan architecture. Whatever may be said against the abuses of the artificial landscape-gardening, a mixture of pure art in a garden scene adds to it a great beauty. This is partly pleasing to the eye, by the show of order and design, and partly moral. A terrace, with an old moss-covered balustrade, calls up at once to the eye the fair forms that have passed there in other days. The slightest exhibition of art is an evidence of care and human interest.'*

'From what I have already observed,' said Ellison, 'you will understand that I reject the idea, here expressed, of recalling the original beauty of the country. The original beauty is never so great as that which may be introduced. Of course, everything depends on the selection of a spot with capabilities.* What is said about detecting and bringing into practice nice relations of size, proportion, and color, is one of those mere vaguenesses of speech which serve to veil inaccuracy of thought. The phrase quoted may mean anything, or nothing, and guides in no degree. That the true result of the natural style of gardening is seen rather in the absence of all defects and incongruities than in the creation of any special wonders or miracles, is a proposition better suited to the grovelling apprehension of the herd than to the fervid dreams of the man of genius. The negative merit suggested appertains to that hobbling criticism which, in letters, would elevate Addison into apotheosis. In truth, while that virtue which consists in the mere avoidance of vice appeals directly to the understanding, and can thus be circumscribed in *rule*, the loftier virtue, which flames in creation, can be apprehended in its results alone. Rule applies but to the merits of denial—to the excellencies which refrain. Beyond these, the critical art can but suggest. We may be instructed to build a "Cato," but we are in vain told *how* to conceive a Parthenon or an "Inferno."* The thing done, however; the wonder accomplished; and the capacity for apprehension becomes universal. The sophists of the negative school who, through inability to create, have scoffed at creation, are now found the loudest in applause. What, in its chrysalis condition of principle, affronted their demure reason, never fails, in its maturity of accomplishment, to extort admiration from their instinct of beauty.

'The author's observations on the artificial style,' continued Ellison, 'are less objectionable. A mixture of pure art in a garden scene adds to it a great beauty. This is just; as also is the reference to the sense of human interest. The principle expressed is incontrovertible—but there *may* be something beyond it. There may be an object in keeping with the principle—an object unattainable by the means ordinarily possessed by individuals, yet which, if attained, would lend a charm to the landscape-garden far surpassing that which a sense of merely human interest could bestow. A poet, having very unusual pecuniary resources, might, while retaining the necessary idea of art, or culture, or, as our author expresses it, of interest, so imbue his designs at once with extent and novelty of beauty, as to convey the sentiment of spiritual interference. It will be seen that, in bringing about such result, he secures all the advantages of interest or *design*, while relieving his work of the harshness or technicality of the worldly *art*. In the most rugged of wildernesses—in the most savage of the scenes of pure nature—there is apparent the *art* of a creator; yet this art is apparent to reflection only; in no respect has it the obvious force of a feeling. Now let us suppose this sense of the Almighty design to be *one step depressed*—to be brought into something like harmony or consistency with the sense of human art—to form an intermedium between the two:—let us imagine, for example, a landscape whose combined vastness and definitiveness—whose united beauty, magnificence, and *strangeness*, shall convey the idea of care, or culture, or superintendence, on the part of beings superior, yet akin to humanity—then the sentiment of *interest* is preserved, while the art intervolved is made to assume the air of an intermediate or secondary nature—a nature which is not God, nor an emanation from God, but which still is nature in the sense of the handiwork of the angels that hover between man and God.'

It was in devoting his enormous wealth to the embodiment of a vision such as this—in the free exercise in the open air ensured by the personal superintendence of his plans—in the unceasing object which these plans afforded—in the high spirituality of the object—in the contempt of ambition which it enabled him truly to feel—in the perennial springs with which it gratified, without possibility of satiating, that one master passion of his soul, the thirst for beauty; above all, it was in the sympathy of a woman, not unwomanly, whose loveliness and love enveloped his existence in the purple atmosphere of Paradise, that Ellison thought to find, *and found*, exemption from the ordinary cares of humanity, with a far greater amount of positive happiness than ever glowed in the rapt day-dreams of De Staël.*

I despair of conveying to the reader any distinct conception of the marvels which my friend did actually accomplish. I wish to describe, but am disheartened by the difficulty of description, and hesitate between detail and generality. Perhaps the better course will be to unite the two in their extremes.

Mr Ellison's first step regarded, of course, the choice of a locality; and scarcely had he commenced thinking on this point, when the luxuriant nature of the Pacific Islands arrested his attention. In fact, he had made up his mind for a voyage to the South Seas, when a night's reflection induced him to abandon the idea. 'Were I misanthropic,' he said, 'such a *locale* would suit me. The thoroughness of its insulation and seclusion, and the difficulty of ingress and egress, would in such case be the charm of charms; but as yet I am not Timon.* I wish the composure but not the depression of solitude. There must remain with me a certain control over the extent and duration of my repose. There will be frequent hours in which I shall need, too, the sympathy of the poetic in what I have done. Let me seek, then, a spot not far from a populous city—whose vicinity, also, will best enable me to execute my plans.'

In search of a suitable place so situated, Ellison travelled for several years, and I was permitted to accompany him. A thousand spots with which I was enraptured he rejected without hesitation, for reasons which satisfied me, in the end, that he was right. We came at length to an elevated table-land of wonderful fertility and beauty, affording a panoramic prospect very little less in extent than that of Ætna,* and, in

Ellison's opinion as well as my own, surpassing the far-famed view from that mountain in all the true elements of the picturesque.

'I am aware,' said the traveller, as he drew a sigh of deep delight after gazing on this scene, entranced, for nearly an hour, 'I know that here, in my circumstances, nine-tenths of the most fastidious of men would rest content. This panorama is indeed glorious, and I should rejoice in it but for the excess of its glory. The taste of all the architects I have ever known leads them, for the sake of "prospect," to put up buildings on hill-tops. The error is obvious. Grandeur in any of its moods, but especially in that of extent, startles, excites—and then fatigues, depresses. For the occasional scene nothing can be better—for the constant view nothing worse. And, in the constant view, the most objectionable phase of grandeur is that of extent; the worst phase of extent, that of distance. It is at war with the sentiment and with the sense of *seclusion*—the sentiment and sense which we seek to humor in "retiring to the country." In looking from the summit of a mountain we cannot help feeling *abroad* in the world. The heart-sick avoid distant prospects as a pestilence.'

It was not until toward the close of the fourth year of our search that we found a locality with which Ellison professed himself satisfied. It is, of course, needless to say *where* was the locality. The late death of my friend, in causing his domain to be thrown open to certain classes of visiters, has given to *Arnheim* a species of secret and subdued if not solemn celebrity, similar in kind, although infinitely superior in degree, to that which so long distinguished Fonthill.*

The usual approach to Arnheim was by the river. The visiter left the city in the early morning. During the forenoon he passed between shores of a tranquil and domestic beauty, on which grazed innumerable sheep, their white fleeces spotting the vivid green of rolling meadows. By degrees the idea of cultivation subsided into that of merely pastoral care. This slowly became merged in a sense of retirement—this again in a consciousness of solitude. As the evening approached the channel grew more narrow; the banks more and more precipitous; and these latter were clothed in richer, more profuse, and more sombre foliage. The water increased in transparency. The stream took a thousand turns, so that at no moment could its gleaming surface be seen for a greater distance than a furlong. At every instant the vessel seemed imprisoned within an enchanted circle, having insuperable and impenetrable walls of foliage, a roof of ultra-marine satin, and *no* floor—the keel balancing itself with admirable nicety on that of a phantom bark which, by some accident having been turned upside down, floated in constant company with the substantial one, for the purpose of sustaining it. The channel now became a *gorge*—although the term is somewhat inapplicable, and I employ it merely because the language has no word which better represents the most striking—not the most distinctive—feature of the scene. The character of gorge was maintained only in the height and parallelism of the shores; it was lost altogether in their other traits. The walls of the ravine (through which the clear water still tranquilly flowed) arose to an elevation of a hundred and occasionally of a hundred and fifty feet, and inclined so much toward each other as, in a great measure, to shut out the light of day; while the long plume-like moss which depended densely from the intertwining shrubberies overhead, gave the whole chasm an air of funereal gloom. The windings became more frequent and intricate, and seemed often as if returning in upon themselves, so that the voyager had long lost all idea of direction. He was, moreover, enwrapt in an exquisite sense of the strange. The thought of nature still remained, but her character seemed to have undergone modification; there was a weird symmetry, a thrilling uniformity, a wizard propriety in these her works. Not a dead branch—not a withered leaf—not a stray pebble—not a patch of the brown earth was anywhere visible. The crystal water welled up against the clean granite, or the unblemished moss, with a sharpness of outline that delighted while it bewildered the eye.

Having threaded the mazes of this channel for some hours, the gloom deepening every moment, a sharp and unexpected turn of the vessel brought it suddenly, as if dropped from heaven, into a circular basin of very considerable extent when compared with the width of the gorge. It was about two hundred yards in diameter, and girt in at all points but one—that immediately fronting the vessel as it entered—by hills equal in general height to the walls of the chasm, although of a thoroughly different character. Their sides sloped from the water's edge at an angle of some forty-five degrees, and they were clothed from base to summit—not a perceptible point escaping—in a drapery of the most gorgeous flower-blossoms; scarcely a green leaf being visible among the sea of odorous and fluctuating color. This basin was of great depth, but so transparent was the water that the bottom, which seemed to consist of a thick mass of small round alabaster pebbles, was distinctly visible by glimpses—that is to say, whenever the eye could permit itself *not* to see, far down in the inverted heaven, the duplicate blooming of the hills. On these latter there were no trees, nor even shrubs of any size. The impressions wrought on the observer were those of richness, warmth, color, quietude, uniformity, softness, delicacy, daintiness, voluptuousness, and a miraculous extremeness of culture that suggested dreams of a new race of fairies, laborious, tasteful, magnificent, and fastidious; but as the eye traced upward the myriad-tinted slope, from its sharp junction with the water to its vague termination amid the folds of over-hanging cloud, it became, indeed, difficult not to fancy a panoramic cataract of rubies, sapphires, opals and golden onyxes, rolling silently out of the sky.

The visiter, shooting suddenly into this bay from out the gloom of the ravine, is delighted but astounded by the full orb of the declining sun, which he had supposed to be already far below the horizon, but which now confronts him, and forms the sole termination of an otherwise limitless vista seen through another chasm-like rift in the hills.

But here the voyager quits the vessel which has borne him so far, and descends into a light canoe of ivory, stained with arabesque devices in vivid scarlet, both within and without. The poop and beak of this boat arise high above the water, with sharp points, so that the general form is that of an irregular crescent. It lies on the surface of the bay with the proud grace of a swan. On its ermined floor reposes a single feathery paddle of satin-wood; but no oarsman or attendant is to be seen. The guest is bidden to be of good cheer—that the fates will take care of him. The larger vessel disappears, and he is left alone in the canoe, which lies apparently motionless in the middle of the lake. While he considers what course to pursue, however, he becomes aware of a gentle movement in the fairy bark. It slowly swings itself around until its prow points toward the sun. It advances with a gentle but gradually accelerated velocity, while the slight ripples it creates seem to break about the ivory sides in divinest melody—seem to offer the only possible explanation of the soothing yet melancholy music for whose unseen origin the bewildered voyager looks around him in vain.

The canoe steadily proceeds, and the rocky gate of the vista is approached, so that its depths can be more distinctly seen. To the right arise a chain of lofty hills rudely and luxuriantly wooded. It is observed, however, that the trait of exquisite *cleanness* where the bank dips into the water, still prevails. There is not one token of the usual river *débris*. To the left the character of the scene is softer and more obviously artificial. Here the bank slopes upward from the stream in a very gentle ascent, forming a broad sward of grass of a texture resembling nothing so much as velvet, and of a brilliancy of green which would bear comparison with the tint of the purest emerald. This *plateau* varies in width from ten to three hundred yards; reaching from the river bank to a wall, fifty feet high, which extends, in an infinity of curves, but following the general direction of the river, until lost in the distance to the westward. This wall is of one continuous rock, and has been formed by cutting perpendicularly the once rugged precipice of the stream's southern bank; but no trace of the labor has been suffered to remain. The chiselled stone has the hue of ages and is profusely overhung and overspread with the ivy, the coral honeysuckle, the eglantine, and the clematis. The uniformity of the top and bottom lines of the wall is fully relieved by occasional trees of gigantic height, growing singly or in small groups, both along the *plateau* and in the domain behind the wall, but in close proximity to it; so that frequent limbs (of the black walnut especially) reach over and dip their pendent extremities into the water. Farther back within the domain, the vision is impeded by an impenetrable screen of foliage.

These things are observed during the canoe's gradual approach to what I have called the gate of the vista. On drawing nearer to this, however, its chasm-like appearance vanishes; a new outlet from the bay is discovered to the left—in which direction the wall is also seen to sweep, still following the general course of the stream. Down this new opening the eye cannot penetrate very far; for the stream, accompanied by the wall, still bends to the left, until both are swallowed up by the leaves.

The boat, nevertheless, glides magically into the winding channel; and here the shore opposite the wall is found to resemble that opposite the wall in the straight vista. Lofty hills, rising occasionally into mountains, and covered with vegetation in wild luxuriance, still shut in the scene.

Floating gently onward, but with a velocity slightly augmented, the voyager, after many short turns, finds his progress apparently barred by a gigantic gate or rather door of burnished gold, elaborately carved and fretted, and reflecting the direct rays of the now fast-sinking sun with an effulgence that seems to wreath the whole surrounding forest in flames. This gate is inserted in the lofty wall; which here appears to cross the river at right angles. In a few moments, however, it is seen that the main body of the water still sweeps in a gentle and extensive curve to the left, the wall following it as before, while a stream of considerable volume, diverging from the principal one, makes its way, with a slight ripple, under the door, and is thus hidden from sight. The canoe falls into the lesser channel and approaches the gate. Its ponderous wings are slowly and musically expanded. The boat glides between them, and commences a rapid descent into a vast amphitheatre entirely begirt with purple mountains, whose bases are laved by a gleaming river throughout the full extent of their circuit. Meantime the whole Paradise of Arnheim bursts upon the view. There is a gush of entrancing melody; there is an oppressive sense of strange sweet odor;—there is a dream-like intermingling to the eye of tall slender Eastern trees—bosky shrubberies—flocks of golden and crimson birds—lily-fringed lakes—meadows of violets, tulips, poppies, hyacinths and tuberoses—long intertangled lines of silver streamlets—and, upspringing confusedly from amid all, a mass of semi-Gothic, semi-Saracenic architecture, sustaining itself as if by miracle in mid air; glittering in the red sunlight with a hundred oriels, minarets, and pinnacles; and seeming the phantom handiwork, conjointly, of the Sylphs, of the Fairies, of the Genii, and of the Gnomes.

HOP-FROG

I NEVER knew any one so keenly alive to a joke as the king was. He seemed to live only for joking. To tell a good story of the joke kind, and to tell it well, was the surest road to his favor. Thus it happened that his seven ministers were all noted for their accomplishments as jokers. They all took after the king, too, in being large, corpulent, oily men, as well as inimitable jokers. Whether people grow fat by joking, or whether there is something in fat itself which predisposes to a joke, I have never been quite able to determine; but certain it is that a lean joker is a *rara avis in terris*.*

About the refinements, or, as he called them, the 'ghosts' of wit, the king troubled himself very little. He had an especial admiration for *breadth* in a jest, and would often put up with *length*, for the sake of it. Over-niceties wearied him. He would have preferred Rabelais's 'Gargantua,' to the 'Zadig' of Voltaire:* and, upon the whole, practical jokes suited his taste far better than verbal ones.

At the date of my narrative, professing jesters had not altogether gone out of fashion at court. Several of the great continental 'powers' still retained their 'fools,' who wore motley, with caps and bells, and who were expected to be always ready with sharp witticisms, at a moment's notice, in consideration of the crumbs that fell from the royal table.

Our king, as a matter of course, retained his 'fool.' The fact is, he *required* something in the way of folly—if only to counter-balance the heavy wisdom of the seven wise men who were his ministers—not to mention himself.

His fool, or professional jester, was not *only* a fool, however. His value was trebled in the eyes of the king, by the fact of his being also a dwarf and a cripple. Dwarfs were as common at court, in those days, as fools; and many monarchs would have found it difficult to get through their days (days are rather longer at court than elsewhere) without both a jester to laugh *with*, and a dwarf to laugh *at*. But, as I have already observed, your jesters, in ninety-nine cases out of a hundred, are fat, round and unwieldy—so that it was no small source of self-gratulation with our king that, in Hop-Frog (this was the fool's name,) he possessed a triplicate treasure in one person.

I believe the name 'Hop-Frog' was *not* that given to the dwarf by his sponsors at baptism, but it was conferred upon him, by general consent of the seven ministers, on account of his inability to walk as other men do. In fact, Hop-Frog could only get along by a sort of interjectional gait—something between a leap and a wriggle—a movement that afforded illimitable amusement, and of course consolation, to the king, for (notwithstanding the protuberance of his stomach and a constitutional swelling of the head) the king, by his whole court, was accounted a capital figure.

But although Hop-Frog, through the distortion of his legs, could move only with great pain and difficulty along a road or floor, the prodigious muscular power which nature seemed to have bestowed upon his arms, by way of compensation for deficiency in the lower limbs, enabled him to perform many feats of wonderful dexterity, where trees or ropes were in question, or anything else to climb. At such exercises he certainly much more resembled a squirrel, or a small monkey, than a frog.

I am not able to say, with precision, from what country Hop-Frog originally came. It was from some barbarous region, however, that no person ever heard of—a vast distance from the court of our king. Hop-Frog, and a young girl very little less dwarfish than himself (although of exquisite proportions, and a marvellous dancer,) had been forcibly carried off from their respective homes in adjoining provinces, and sent as presents to the king, by one of his ever-victorious generals.

Under these circumstances, it is not to be wondered at that a close intimacy arose between the two little captives. Indeed, they soon became sworn friends. Hop-Frog, who, although he made a great deal of sport, was by no means popular, had it not in his power to render Trippetta many services; but *she*, on account of her grace and exquisite beauty (although a dwarf,) was universally admired and petted: so she possessed much influence; and never failed to use it, whenever she could, for the benefit of Hop-Frog.

On some grand state occasion—I forget what—the king determined to have a masquerade; and whenever a masquerade, or anything of that kind, occurred at our court, then the talents both of Hop-Frog and Trippetta were sure to be called in play. Hop-Frog, in especial, was so inventive in the way of getting up pageants, suggesting novel characters, and arranging costume, for masked balls, that nothing could be done, it seems, without his assistance.

The night appointed for the *fête* had arrived. A gorgeous hall had been fitted up, under Trippetta's eye, with every kind of device which could possibly give *éclat* to a masquerade. The whole court was in a fever of expectation. As for costumes and characters, it might well be supposed that everybody had come to a decision on such points. Many had made up their minds (as to what *rôles* they should assume) a week, or even a month, in advance; and, in fact, there was not a particle of indecision anywhere—except in the case of the king and his seven ministers. Why *they* hesitated I never could tell, unless they did it by way of a joke. More probably, they found it difficult, on account of being so fat, to make up their minds. At all events, time flew; and, as a last resource, they sent for Trippetta and Hop-Frog.

When the two little friends obeyed the summons of the king, they found him sitting at his wine with the seven members of his cabinet council; but the monarch appeared to be in a very ill humor. He knew that Hop-Frog was not fond of wine; for it excited the poor cripple almost to madness; and madness is no comfortable feeling. But the king loved his practical jokes, and took pleasure in forcing Hop-Frog to drink and (as the king called it) 'to be merry.'

'Come here, Hop-Frog,' said he, as the jester and his friend entered the room: 'swallow this bumper to the health of your absent friends [here Hop-Frog sighed,] and then let us have the benefit of your invention. We want characters—*characters*, man—something novel—out of the way. We are wearied with this everlasting sameness. Come, drink! the wine will brighten your wits.'

Hop-Frog endeavored, as usual, to get up a jest in reply to these advances from the king; but the effort was too much. It happened to be the poor dwarf's birthday, and the command to drink to his 'absent friends' forced the tears to his eyes. Many large, bitter drops fell into the goblet as he took it, humbly, from the hand of the tyrant.

'Ah! ha! ha! ha!' roared the latter, as the dwarf reluctantly drained the beaker. 'See what a glass of good wine can do! Why, your eyes are shining already!'

Poor fellow! his large eyes *gleamed*, rather than shone; for the effect of wine on his excitable brain was not more powerful than instantaneous. He placed the goblet nervously on the table, and looked round upon the company with a half-insane stare. They all seemed highly amused at the success of the king's *'joke.'*

'And now to business,' said the prime minister, a *very* fat man.

'Yes,' said the king; 'come, Hop-Frog, lend us your assistance. Characters, my fine fellow; we stand in need of characters—all of us—ha! ha! ha!' and as this was seriously meant for a joke, his laugh was chorused by the seven.

Hop-Frog also laughed, although feebly and somewhat vacantly.

'Come, come,' said the king, impatiently, 'have you nothing to suggest?'

'I am endeavoring to think of something *novel*,' replied the dwarf, abstractedly, for he was quite bewildered by the wine.

'Endeavoring!' cried the tyrant, fiercely; 'what do you mean by *that?* Ah, I perceive. You are sulky, and want more wine. Here, drink this!' and he poured out another goblet full and offered it to the cripple, who, merely gazed at it, gasping for breath.

'Drink, I say!' shouted the monster, 'or by the fiends—'

The dwarf hesitated. The king grew purple with rage. The courtiers smirked. Trippetta, pale as a corpse, advanced to the monarch's seat, and, falling on her knees before him, implored him to spare her friend.

The tyrant regarded her, for some moments, in evident wonder at her audacity. He seemed quite at a loss what to do or say—how most becomingly to express his indignation. At last, without uttering a syllable, he pushed her violently from him, and threw the contents of the brimming goblet in her face.

The poor girl got up as best she could, and, not daring even to sigh, resumed her position at the foot of the table.

There was a dead silence for about a half a minute, during which the falling of a leaf, or of a feather, might have been heard. It was interrupted by a low, but harsh and protracted *grating* sound which seemed to come at once from every corner of the room.

'What—what—*what* are you making that noise for?' demanded the king, turning furiously to the dwarf.

The latter seemed to have recovered, in great measure, from his intoxication, and looking fixedly but quietly into the tyrant's face, merely ejaculated:

'I—I? How could it have been me?'

'The sound appeared to come from without,' observed one of the courtiers. 'I fancy it was the parrot at the window, whetting his bill upon his cage-wires.'

'True,' replied the monarch, as if much relieved by the suggestion;

'but, on the honor of a knight, I could have sworn that it was the gritting of this vagabond's teeth.'

Hereupon the dwarf laughed (the king was too confirmed a joker to object to any one's laughing), and displayed a set of large, powerful, and very repulsive teeth. Moreover, he avowed his perfect willingness to swallow as much wine as desired. The monarch was pacified; and having drained another bumper with no very perceptible ill effect, Hop-Frog entered at once, and with spirit, into the plans for the masquerade.

'I cannot tell what was the association of idea,' observed he, very tranquilly, and as if he had never tasted wine in his life, 'but *just after* your majesty had struck the girl and thrown the wine in her face—*just after* your majesty had done this, and while the parrot was making that odd noise outside the window, there came into my mind a capital diversion—one of my own country frolics—often enacted among us, at our masquerades: but here it will be new altogether. Unfortunately, however, it requires a company of eight persons, and—'

'Here we *are!*' cried the king, laughing at his acute discovery of the coincidence; 'eight to a fraction—I and my seven ministers. Come! what is the diversion?'

'We call it,' replied the cripple, 'the Eight Chained Ourang-Outangs, and it really is excellent sport if well enacted.'

'*We* will enact it,' remarked the king, drawing himself up, and lowering his eyelids.

'The beauty of the game,' continued Hop-Frog, 'lies in the fright it occasions among the women.'

'Capital!' roared in chorus the monarch and his ministry.

'*I* will equip you as ourang-outangs,' proceeded the dwarf; 'leave all that to me. The resemblance shall be so striking, that the company of masqueraders will take you for real beasts—and of course, they will be as much terrified as astonished.'

'O, this is exquisite!' exclaimed the king. 'Hop-Frog! I will make a man of you.'

'The chains are for the purpose of increasing the confusion by their jangling. You are supposed to have escaped, *en masse*, from your keepers. Your majesty cannot conceive the *effect* produced, as a masquerade, by eight chained ourang-outangs, imagined to be real ones by most of the company; and rushing in with savage cries, among the crowd of delicately and gorgeously habited men and women. The *contrast* is inimitable.'

'It *must* be,' said the king: and the council arose hurriedly (as it was growing late), to put in execution the scheme of Hop-Frog.

His mode of equipping the party as ourang-outangs was very simple, but effective enough for his purposes. The animals in question had, at the epoch of my story, very rarely been seen in any part of the civilized world; and as the imitations made by the dwarf were sufficiently beast-like and more than sufficiently hideous, their truthfulness to nature was thus thought to be secured.

The king and his ministers were first encased in tight-fitting stockinet shirts and drawers. They were then saturated with tar. At this stage of the process, some one of the party suggested feathers; but the suggestion was at once overruled by the dwarf, who soon convinced the eight, by ocular demonstration, that the hair of such a brute as the ourang-outang was much more efficiently represented by *flax*. A thick coating of the latter was accordingly plastered upon the coating of tar. A long chain was now procured. First, it was passed about the waist of the king, *and tied*; then about another of the party, and also tied; then about all successively, in the same manner. When this chaining arrangement was complete, and the party stood as far apart from each other as possible, they formed a circle; and to make all things appear natural, Hop-Frog passed the residue of the chain, in two diameters, at right angles, across the circle, after the fashion adopted, at the present day, by those who capture Chimpanzees, or other large apes, in Borneo.

The grand saloon in which the masquerade was to take place, was a circular room, very lofty, and receiving the light of the sun only through a single window at top. At night (the season for which the apartment was especially designed,) it was illuminated principally by a large chandelier, depending by a chain from the centre of the sky-light, and lowered, or elevated, by means of a counter-balance as usual, but (in order not to look unsightly) this latter passed outside the cupola and over the roof.

The arrangements of the room had been left to Trippetta's superintendence: but, in some particulars, it seems, she had been guided by the calmer judgment of her friend the dwarf. At his suggestion it was that, on this occasion, the chandelier was removed. Its waxen drippings (which, in weather so warm, it was quite impossible to prevent,) would have been seriously detrimental to the rich dresses of the guests, who, on account of the crowded state of the saloon, could not *all* be expected to keep from out its centre—that is to say, from under the chandelier. Additional sconces were set in various parts of the hall, out of the way; and a flambeau, emitting sweet odor, was placed in the right hand of each of the Caryatides that stood against the wall—some fifty or sixty altogether.

The eight ourang-outangs, taking Hop-Frog's advice, waited patiently until midnight (when the room was thoroughly filled with masqueraders) before making their appearance. No sooner had the clock ceased striking, however, than they rushed, or rather rolled in, all together—for the impediment of their chains caused most of the party to fall, and all to stumble as they entered.

The excitement among the masqueraders was prodigious, and filled the heart of the king with glee. As had been anticipated, there were not a few of the guests who supposed the ferocious-looking creatures to be beasts of *some* kind in reality, if not precisely ourang-outangs. Many of the women swooned with affright; and had not the king taken the precaution to exclude all weapons from the saloon, his party might soon have expiated their frolic in their blood. As it was, a general rush was made for the doors; but the king had ordered them to be locked immediately upon his entrance; and, at the dwarf's suggestion, the keys had been deposited with *him*.

While the tumult was at its height, and each masquerader attentive only to his own safety—(for, in fact, there was much *real* danger from the pressure of the excited crowd,)—the chain by which the chandelier ordinarily hung, and which had been drawn up on its removal, might have been seen very gradually to descend, until its hooked extremity came within three feet of the floor.

Soon after this, the king and his seven friends, having reeled about the hall in all directions, found themselves, at length, in its centre, and, of course, in immediate contact with the chain. While they were thus situated, the dwarf, who had followed closely at their heels, inciting them to keep up the commotion, took hold of their own chain at the intersection of the two portions which crossed the circle diametrically and at right angles. Here, with the rapidity of thought, he inserted the hook from which the chandelier had been wont to depend; and, in an instant, by some unseen agency, the chandelier-chain was drawn so far upward as to take the hook out of reach, and, as an inevitable consequence, to drag the ourang-outangs together in close connection, and face to face.

The masqueraders, by this time, had recovered, in some measure, from their alarm; and, beginning to regard the whole matter as a well-contrived pleasantry, set up a loud shout of laughter at the predicament of the apes.

'Leave them to *me!*' now screamed Hop-Frog, his shrill voice making itself easily heard through all the din. 'Leave them to *me*. I fancy *I* know them. If I can only get a good look at them, I can soon tell who they are.'

Here, scrambling over the heads of the crowd, he managed to get to the wall; when, seizing a flambeau from one of the Caryatides, he returned, as he went, to the centre of the room—leaped, with the agility of a monkey, upon the king's head—and thence clambered a few feet up the chain—holding down the torch to examine the group of ourang-outangs, and still screaming, '*I* shall soon find out who they are!'

And now, while the whole assembly (the apes included) were convulsed with laughter, the jester suddenly uttered a shrill whistle; when the chain flew violently up for about thirty feet—dragging with it the dismayed and struggling ourang-outangs, and leaving them suspended in mid-air between the sky-light and the floor. Hop-Frog, clinging to the chain as it rose, still maintained his relative position in respect to the eight maskers, and still (as if nothing were the matter) continued to thrust his torch down towards them, as though endeavoring to discover who they were.

So thoroughly astonished were the whole company at this ascent, that a dead silence, of about a minute's duration, ensued. It was broken by just such a low, harsh, *grating* sound, as had before attracted the attention of the king and his councillors, when the former threw the wine in the face of Trippetta. But, on the present occasion, there could be no question as to *whence* the sound issued. It came from the fang-like teeth of the dwarf, who ground them and gnashed them as he foamed at the mouth, and glared, with an expression of maniacal rage, into the upturned countenance of the king and his seven companions.

'Ah, ha!' said at length the infuriated jester. 'Ah, ha! I begin to see who these people *are*, now!' Here, pretending to scrutinize the king more closely, he held the flambeau to the flaxen coat which enveloped him, and which instantly burst into a sheet of vivid flame. In less than half a minute the whole eight ourang-outangs were blazing fiercely, amid the shrieks of the multitude who gazed at them from below, horror-stricken, and without the power to render them the slightest assistance.

At length the flames, suddenly increasing in virulence, forced the jester to climb higher up the chain, to be out of their reach; and, as he made this movement, the crowd again sank, for a brief instant, into silence. The dwarf seized his opportunity, and once more spoke:

'I now see *distinctly*,' he said, 'what manner of people these maskers are. They are a great king and his seven privy-councillors—a king who does not scruple to strike a defenceless girl, and his seven councillors who abet him in the outrage. As for myself, I am simply Hop-Frog, the jester—and *this is my last jest*.'

Owing to the high combustibility of both the flax and the tar to which it adhered, the dwarf had scarcely made an end of his brief speech before the work of vengeance was complete. The eight corpses swung in their chains, a fetid, blackened, hideous, and indistinguishable mass. The cripple hurled his torch at them, clambered leisurely to the ceiling, and disappeared through the sky-light.

It is supposed that Trippetta, stationed on the roof of the saloon, had been the accomplice of her friend in his fiery revenge, and that, together, they effected their escape to their own country: for neither was seen again.

VON KEMPELEN AND HIS DISCOVERY

AFTER the very minute and elaborate paper by Arago, to say nothing of the summary in 'Silliman's Journal,' with the detailed statement just published by Lieutenant Maury, it will not be supposed, of course, that in offering a few hurried remarks in reference to Von Kempelen's discovery, I have any design to look at the subject in a *scientific* point of view. My object is simply, in the first place, to say a few words of Von Kempelen himself (with whom, some years ago, I had the honor of a slight personal acquaintance,) since everything which concerns him must necessarily, at this moment, be of interest; and, in the second place, to look in a general way, and speculatively, at the *results* of the discovery.

It may be as well, however, to premise the cursory observations which I have to offer, by denying, very decidedly, what seems to be a general impression (gleaned, as usual in a case of this kind, from the newspapers,) viz.: that this discovery, astounding as it unquestionably is, is *unanticipated*.

By reference to the 'Diary of Sir Humphrey Davy,' (Cottle and Munroe, London, pp. 150,) it will be seen at pp. 53 and 82, that this illustrious chemist had not only conceived the idea now in question, but had actually made *no inconsiderable progress, experimentally*, in the very *identical analysis* now so triumphantly brought to an issue by Von Kempelen, who, although he makes not the slightest allusion to it, is, *without doubt* (I say it unhesitatingly, and can prove it, if required,) indebted to the 'Diary' for at least the first hint of his own undertaking. Although a little technical, I cannot refrain from appending two passages from the 'Diary,' with one of Sir Humphrey's equations. [As we have not the algebraic signs necessary, and as the 'Diary' is to be found at the Athenæum Library, we omit here a small portion of Mr Poe's manuscript.—ED.]*

The paragraph from the 'Courier and Enquirer,' which is now going the rounds of the press, and which purports to claim the invention for a Mr Kissam, of Brunswick, Maine, appears to me, I confess, a little apocryphal, for several reasons; although there is nothing either impossible or very improbable in the statement made. I need not go into details. My opinion of the paragraph is founded principally upon its *manner*. It does not *look* true. Persons who are narrating *facts*, are seldom so particular as Mr Kissam seems to be, about day and date and precise location. Besides, if Mr Kissam actually *did* come upon the discovery he says he did, at the period designated—nearly eight years ago—how happens it that he took no steps, *on the instant*, to reap the immense benefits which the merest bumpkin must have known would have resulted to him individually, if not to the world at large, from the discovery? It seems to me quite incredible that any man, of common understanding, could have discovered what Mr Kissam says he did, and yet have subsequently acted so like a baby—so like an owl—as Mr Kissam *admits* that he did. By-the-way, who *is* Mr Kissam? and is not the whole paragraph in the 'Courier and Enquirer' a fabrication got up to 'make a talk?' It must be confessed that it has an amazingly moon-hoax-y air. Very little dependence is to be placed upon it, in my humble opinion; and if I were not well aware, from experience, how very easily men of science are *mystified*, on points out of their usual range of inquiry, I should be profoundly astonished at finding so eminent a chemist as Professor Draper, discussing Mr Kissam's (or is it Mr Quizzem's?) pretensions to this discovery, in so serious a tone.

But to return to the 'Diary' of Sir Humphrey Davy. This pamphlet was *not* designed for the public eye, even upon the decease of the writer, as any person at all conversant with authorship may satisfy himself at once by the slightest inspection of the style. At page 13, for example, near the middle, we read, in reference to his researches about the protoxide of azote:* 'In less than half a minute the respiration being continued, diminished gradually and *were* succeeded by analogous to gentle pressure on all the muscles.' That the *respiration* was not 'diminished,' is not only clear by the subsequent context, but by the use of the plural, 'were.' The sentence, no doubt, was thus intended: 'In less than half a minute, the respiration [being continued, these feelings] diminished gradually, and were succeeded by [a sensation] analogous to gentle pressure on all the muscles.' A hundred similar instances go to show that the MS. so inconsiderately published, was merely a *rough note-book*, meant only for the writer's own eye; but an inspection of the pamphlet will convince almost any thinking person of the truth of my suggestion. The fact is, Sir Humphrey Davy was about the last man in the world to *commit himself* on scientific topics. Not only had he a more than ordinary dislike to quackery, but he was morbidly afraid of *appearing* empirical; so that, however fully he might have been convinced that he was on the right track in the matter now in question, he would never have spoken *out*, until he had everything ready for the most practical demonstration. I verily believe that his last moments would have been rendered wretched, could he have suspected that his wishes in regard to burning this 'Diary' (full of crude speculations) would have been unattended to; as, it seems, they were. I say 'his wishes,' for that he meant to include this note-book among the miscellaneous papers directed 'to be burnt,' I think there can be no manner of doubt. Whether it escaped the flames by good fortune or by bad, yet remains to be seen. That the passages quoted above, with the other similar ones referred to, gave Von Kempelen *the hint*, I do not in the slightest degree question; but I repeat, it yet remains to be seen whether this momentous discovery itself (*momentous* under any circumstances,) will be of service or disservice to mankind at large. That Von Kempelen and his immediate friends will reap a rich harvest, it would be folly to doubt for a moment. They will scarcely be so weak as not to '*realize*,' in time, by large purchases of houses and land, with other property of *intrinsic* value.

In the brief account of Von Kempelen which appeared in the 'Home Journal,' and has since been extensively copied, several misapprehensions of the German original seem to have been made by the translator, who professes to have taken the passage from a late number of the Presburg 'Schnellpost.'* '*Viele*' has evidently been misconceived (as it often is,) and what the translator renders by 'sorrows,' is probably '*lieden,*' which, in its true version, 'sufferings,' would give a totally different complexion to the whole account; but, of course, much of this is merely guess, on my part.

Von Kempelen, however, is by no means 'a misanthrope,' in appearance, at least, whatever he may be in fact. My acquaintance with him was casual altogether; and I am scarcely warranted in saying that I know him at all; but to have seen and conversed with a man of so *prodigious* a notoriety as he has attained, or *will* attain in a few days, is not a small matter, as times go.

'The Literary World' speaks of him, confidently, as a *native* of Presburg (misled, perhaps, by the account in the 'Home Journal,') but I am pleased in being able to state *positively*, since I have it from his own lips, that he was born in Utica, in the State of New York, although both his parents, I believe are of Presburg descent. The family is connected, in some way, with Mäelzel, of Automaton-chess-player memory. [If we are not mistaken, the name of the *inventor* of the chess-player was either Kempelen, Von Kempelen, or something like it.—Ed.]* In person, he is short and stout, with large, *fat*, blue eyes, sandy hair and whiskers, a wide but pleasing mouth, fine teeth, and I think a Roman nose. There is some defect in one of his feet. His address is frank, and his whole manner noticeable for *bonhommie*. Altogether, he looks, speaks and acts as little like 'a misanthrope' as any man I ever saw. We were fellow-sojourners for a week, about six years ago, at Earl's Hotel, in Providence, Rhode Island; and I presume that I conversed with him, at various times, for some three or four hours altogether. His principal topics were those of the day; and nothing that fell from him led me to suspect his scientific attainments. He left the hotel before me, intending to go to New York, and thence to Bremen; it was in the latter city that his great discovery was first made public; or, rather, it was there that he was first suspected of having made it. This is about all that I personally know of the now immortal Von Kempelen; but I have thought that even these few details would have interest for the public.

There can be little question that most of the marvellous rumors afloat about this affair are pure inventions, entitled to about as much credit as the story of Aladdin's lamp; and yet, in a case of this kind, as in the case of the discoveries in California, it is clear that the truth *may be* stranger than fiction. The following anecdote, at least, is so well authenticated, that we may receive it implicitly.

Von Kempelen had never been even tolerably well off during his residence at Bremen; and often, it was well known, he had been put to extreme shifts, in order to raise trifling sums. When the great excitement occurred about the forgery on the house of Gutsmuth & Co., suspicion was directed towards Von Kempelen, on account of his having purchased a considerable property in Gasperitch Lane, and his refusing, when questioned, to explain how he became possessed of the purchase money. He was at length arrested, but nothing decisive appearing against him, was in the end set at liberty. The police, however, kept a strict watch upon his movements, and thus discovered that he left home frequently, taking always the same road, and invariably giving his watchers the slip in the neighborhood of that labyrinth of narrow and crooked passages known by the flash-name of the 'Dondergat.' Finally, by dint of great perseverance, they traced him to a garret in an old house of seven stories, in an alley called Flätplatz; and, coming upon him suddenly, found him, as they imagined, in the midst of his counterfeiting operations. His agitation is represented as so excessive that the officers had not the slightest doubt of his guilt. After hand-cuffing him, they searched his room, or rather rooms; for it appears he occupied all the *mansarde*.

Opening into the garret where they caught him was a closet, ten feet by eight, fitted up with some chemical apparatus, of which the object has not yet been ascertained. In one corner of the closet was a very small furnace, with a glowing fire in it, and on the fire a kind of duplicate crucible—two crucibles connected by a tube. One of these crucibles was nearly full of *lead* in a state of fusion, but not reaching up to the aperture of the tube, which was close to the brim. The other crucible had some liquid in it, which, as the officers entered, seemed to be furiously dissipating in vapor. They relate that, on finding himself taken, Von Kempelen seized the crucibles with both hands (which were encased in gloves that afterwards turned out to be asbestic), and threw the contents on the tiled floor. It was now that they hand-cuffed him; and, before proceeding to ransack the premises, they searched his person, but nothing ususual was found about him, excepting a paper parcel, in his coat pocket, containing what was afterwards ascertained to be a mixture of antimony and some *unknown substance*, in nearly, but not quite, equal proportions. All attempts at analyzing the unknown substance have, so far, failed, but that it will ultimately be analyzed, is not to be doubted.

Passing out of the closet with their prisoner, the officers went through a sort of ante-chamber, in which nothing material was found, to the chemist's sleeping-room. They here rummaged some drawers and boxes, but discovered only a few papers, of no importance, and some good coin, silver and gold. At length, looking under the bed, they saw *a large, common hair trunk, without hinges, hasp, or lock,* and with the top lying carelessly *across* the bottom portion. Upon attempting to draw this trunk out from under the bed, they found that, with their united strength (there were three of them, all powerful men), they 'could not stir it one inch.' Much astonished at this, one of them crawled under the bed, and looking into the trunk, said:

'No wonder we couldn't move it—why, it's full to the brim of old bits of brass!'

Putting his feet, now, against the wall, so as to get a good purchase, and pushing with all his force, while his companions pulled with all theirs, the trunk, with much difficulty, was slid out from under the bed, and its contents examined. The supposed brass with which it was filled was all in small, smooth pieces, varying from the size of a pea to that of a dollar; but the pieces were irregular in shape, although all more or less flat—looking, upon the whole 'very much as lead looks when thrown upon the ground in a molten state, and there suffered to grow cool.' Now, not one of these officers for a moment suspected this metal to be anything *but* brass. The idea of its being *gold* never entered their brains, of course; how *could* such a wild fancy have entered it? And their astonishment may be well conceived, when next day it became known, all over Bremen, that the 'lot of brass' which they had carted so contemptuously to the police office, without putting themselves to the trouble of pocketing the smallest scrap, was not only gold—real gold—but gold far finer than any employed in coinage—gold, in fact, absolutely pure, virgin, without the slightest appreciable alloy!

I need not go over the details of Von Kempelen's confession (as far as it went) and release, for these are familiar to the public. That he has actually realized, in spirit and in effect, if not to the letter, the old chimera of the philosopher's stone, no sane person is at liberty to doubt. The opinions of Arago are, of course, entitled to the greatest consideration; but he is by no means infallible; and what he says of *bismuth*, in his report to the academy, must be taken *cum grano salis*. The simple truth is, that up to this period, *all* analysis has failed; and until Von Kempelen chooses to let us have the key to his own published enigma, it is more than probable that the matter will remain, for years, *in statu quo*. All that as yet can fairly be said to be known, is, that '*pure gold can be made at will, and very readily, from lead, in connection with certain other substances, in kind and in proportions, unknown.*'

Speculation, of course, is busy as to the immediate and ultimate results of this discovery—a discovery which few thinking persons will hesitate in referring to an increased interest in the matter of gold generally, by the late developments in California;* and this reflection brings us inevitably to another—the exceeding *inopportuneness* of Von Kempelen's analysis. If many were prevented from adventuring to California, by the mere apprehension that gold would so materially diminish in value, on account of its plentifulness in the mines there, as to render the speculation of going so far in search of it a doubtful one—what impression will be wrought *now*, upon the minds of those about to emigrate, and especially upon the minds of those actually in the mineral region, by the announcement of this astounding discovery of Von Kempelen? a discovery which declares, in so many words, that beyond its intrinsic worth for manufacturing purposes, (whatever that worth may be), gold now is, or at least soon will be (for it cannot be supposed that Von Kempelen can *long* retain his secret) of no greater *value* than lead, and of far inferior value to silver. It is, indeed, exceedingly difficult to speculate prospectively upon the consequences of the discovery; but one thing may be positively maintained—that the announcement of the discovery six months ago would have had material influence in regard to the settlement of California.

In Europe, as yet, the most noticeable results have been a rise of two hundred per cent. in the price of lead, and nearly twenty-five per cent. in that of silver.

EXPLANATORY NOTES

POE'S tales abound in recondite references, some of which seem chosen primarily for their mellifluous obscurity. I have, in general, annotated only those allusions which seem to underscore themes in the tales. In preparing these notes, I have relied on the exemplary editions of T. O. Mabbott for Harvard and Patrick F. Quinn for the Library of America.

MS. Found in a Bottle

This early tale won a fiction prize from the *Baltimore Saturday Visiter*, where it was subsequently printed on 15 June 1833. It was collected in *Tales of the Grotesque and Arabesque* (1840).

3 *Qui n'a . . .*: 'He who has only a moment to live no longer has anything to dissemble'; from Philippe Quinault, *Atys*, I. vi. 15–16.

4 *grabs*: small coasting vessels, with two or three masts.

Simoon: literally sirocco, a hot desert wind; here, a tropical storm.

5 *New Holland*: Australia.

10 *sybils*: long-lived prophetesses.

11 *Balbec . . . Persepolis*: famous ruined cities. Ba'albek, called Heliopolis by the Greeks, was a centre of sun-worship. Tadmor, also called Tamar and Palmyra, was built by Solomon. Persepolis was the capital of ancient Persia.

Berenicë

One of Poe's earliest explorations of the death of a beautiful woman, this tale was published in the *Southern Literary Messenger* for March 1835. It was collected in *Tales of the Grotesque and Arabesque* (1840).

13 *Dicebant mihi . . .*: 'My companions told me I might find some little alleviation of my misery, in visiting the grave of my beloved'; Poe's English translation, from the Latin, of an elegy of second-century Baghdad poet Ben Zaïat. In the nineteenth century the name 'Berenice' had four syllables, rhyming with 'icy'.

16 *the treatise . . . impossibile est*: Curio's *On the size of the Blessed Kingdom of God*, Augustine's *City of God*, and Tertullian's *On the Flesh of Christ* all deal with the mysterious relation between the material and the spiritual worlds. According to Tertullian's famous paradox, 'The Son of God has died, it is to be believed because it is incredible; and, buried, He is risen, it is sure because it is impossible.'

18 *Mademoiselle Sallé . . . des idées*: in the eighteenth century Marie Sallé was said to dance so expressively that all her steps were feelings; the narrator adapts this praise to claim that all Berenicë's teeth were ideas.

Morella

First published in the *Southern Literary Messenger* for April 1835, this early exploration of metempsychosis was collected in *Tales of the Grotesque and Arabesque* (1840).

21 *Sympos.*: at the climax of Plato's *Symposium* (211*b*), Socrates recalled his teacher Diotima's vision of unity as the 'soul of beauty'. The translation is Poe's own.

Presburg: because of its ancient university, Pressburg in Hungary (now Bratislava in Slovakia) was rumoured to be a centre of black magic.

22 *Hinnom became Ge-Henna*: Hinnom was, according to Jeremiah 19: 5, a place near Jerusalem where children were sacrificed to the pagan god Moloch. In its generalized form as 'Gehenna', the name means simply 'hell'.

The wild Pantheism . . . mentioned them: the paragraph alludes to various theories of the self. Johann Gottlieb Fichte (1762–1814) treated as substantial the consciousness that Kant had insisted was only a logical presupposition of thought. While not truly pantheistic, the resulting Fichtean 'Ego' was like God ubiquitous and omniscient. Fichte's disciple Friedrich Schelling (1775–1854) extended these theories, especially with respect to Nature. According to his theory of identity, subjectivity and objectivity together constituted the Universe, making the Real and the Ideal one in the Absolute. The Pythagoreans, followers of the Greek mathematician from the sixth century BC, believed among other things in *palingenesia* or reincarnation. The sentences on John Locke summarize arguments from Bk. 2, ch. 27 of *An Essay Concerning Human Understanding* (1690).

23 *the Teian . . . Mecca*: the references imply the triumph of mortality. Unlike Morella, the Greek poet Anacreon of Teos sang optimistically of love's victory over time. Pilgrims to Mecca were traditionally buried in clothes worn on their pilgrimage.

Ligeia

The greatest of the 'women' tales and Poe's personal favourite among his short fiction, 'Ligeia' was first published in the Baltimore *American Museum* for September 1838. It was collected in *Tales of the Grotesque and Arabesque* (1840).

26 *Glanvill*: although the seventeenth-century Neoplatonist Joseph Glanvill believed strongly in the power of the will, the motto has not been found in his writings and may be Poe's invention. The name 'Ligeia' is used variously by Virgil and Milton.

Ashtophet: a goddess of the Sidonians related to Ashtoreth, Astarte, Aphrodite, and Venus.

28 *There is one dear topic . . . astrologers*: in describing Ligeia, the narrator ranges widely through literature and myth. The most important allusions are to: Francis Bacon's 'Of Beauty'; the statue Venus de Medici, falsely attributed to Cleomenes; Democritus' purported claim that truth is as deep as a well; and Castor and Pollux, the twin stars of the constellation Leda.

32 *Lo! . . . Worm*: published on its own in 1843, the poem 'The Conqueror Worm' was two years later added to a revised version of 'Ligeia'.

33 *the fair-haired . . . Tremaine*: Rowena is the fairer of the two heroines in Sir Walter Scott's *Ivanhoe*.

The Man that was Used Up

First published in *Burton's Gentleman's Magazine* for August 1839, this satire was collected in *Tales of the Grotesque and Arabesque* (1840).

40 *Pleurez, pleurez . . .*: Poe translated the motto, 'Weep, weep, my eyes! It is no time to laugh | For half myself has buried the other half'; from *Le Cid*, III. iii. 7–8. The 'used up' of the title can mean 'badly treated', as well as 'exhausted'. The Kickapoo tribe was among those fighting in the Florida Indian Wars of 1839.

41 *reasons*: pronounced 'raisins' in Poe's joke.

43 *quorum pars magna fuit*: 'of which he was a great part'; from Virgil, *Aeneid*, ii. 6.

horresco referens: 'I shudder recalling it'; ibid. ii. 204.

44 *mandragora . . . yesterday*: Shakespeare, *Othello*, III. iii. 330–3.

46 *Man-Fred . . . Bas-Bleus*: the excess of Byron's romantic *Manfred* was both admired and parodied. A Man Friday is a devoted aide, after the native in Defoe's *Robinson Crusoe*. *Bas-Bleu* is French for 'bluestocking', a derogatory term for women interested in the arts.

man in the mask: the Man in the Iron Mask was a political prisoner in the Bastille. With his identity hidden, his aristocratic origins were the subject of popular speculation, especially in the novel of Alexandre Dumas.

47 *scratch*: a kind of wig. Although De L'Orme is a fiction, many of those named in this section were real Philadelphia tradespeople.

The Fall of the House of Usher

First published in *Burton's Gentleman's Magazine*, for September 1839, this famous tale was collected in both *Tales of the Grotesque and Arabesque* (1840) and *Tales* (1845).

49 *Usher*: the source of the protagonist's family name is uncertain. Poe's mother acted with a couple named Usher, whose children were neurotic. Elsewhere, Poe alludes to Archbishop James Ussher, the respected though pedantic seventeenth-century biblical scholar, best remembered for dating Creation precisely in 4004 BC.

Son cœur . . .: 'His heart is a suspended lute; it sounds as soon as it is touched'; adapted from the nineteenth-century lyricist Pierre-Jean de Béranger.

55 *Von Weber*: the early nineteenth-century German composer Carl Maria von Weber was best known for his representations of the supernatural, as in the Wolf Glen scene of his gothic opera *Der Freischütz*. His so-called 'last waltz' was actually by his friend Karl Gottlieb Reissiger.

56 *Fuseli*: the Swiss-born English painter John Henry Fuseli was best known for his depictions of the unconscious, as in *The Nightmare* (1785–90).

'The Haunted Palace': published separately in April 1839, the poem was

included in all editions of the tale. According to Poe the central image is of 'a mind haunted by phantoms—a disordered brain'.

58 n. 1 *Watson ... vol. v*: Poe's 'authenticating' note draws on the collected works of Richard Watson, Professor of Chemistry at Cambridge in the eighteenth century. Watson cites the works of Dr Thomas Percival and Abbé Lazzaro Spallanzani, and is himself the Bishop of Llandaff.

59 *We pored . . . Maguntinae*: all the books in Usher's library, except the 'Mad Trist', are real, although many are so rare that Poe could have known them only second- or third-hand. Gresset, Machiavelli, Holberg, Tieck, and Campanella offer allegorical tales with optimistic and pessimistic views about contemporary society; Swedenborg's vision of heaven and hell and Pomponius Mela's geography are similarly Utopian, though both claim to be true. The palmistries of Robert Fludd, Joannes ab Indagine, and Marin Cureau de la Chambre involve Renaissance traditions of fortune-telling. The *Directorium* of Eymeric of Gironne instructs priests during the Spanish Inquisition, especially concerning forbidden books. The *Vigiliae* describes the vigils for the dead used in Mainz in 1500.

William Wilson

This tale first appeared in *The Gift: a Christmas and New Year's Present for 1840*, which was actually issued earlier, in 1839. It was collected in *Tales of the Grotesque and Arabesque* (1840).

66 *Pharonnida*: the motto is not from the named work of William Chamberlayne, though the seventeenth-century playwright does speak of conscience in another of his plays.

Elah-Gabalus: the homosexual Roman emperor Elagabalus or Heliogabalus was renowned for his cruelty.

69 *Dr Bransby*: at Stoke Newington near London, Poe himself studied at Manor House School under the Reverend John Bransby. Here and elsewhere in the tale, the details of Wilson's life parallel those of Poe's own.

peine forte et dure: literally 'strong and hard penalty', the legal term sentencing a person to be crushed to death.

Carthaginian medals: the *exergue* is the lower part of the emblem on the reverse of a coin. Poe seems to believe, from his misreading of a French encyclopaedia, that this part of the design lasts longer.

70 *Oh, le bon temps...*: 'Oh, what a good time it was, that age of iron'; from Voltaire, 'Le Mondain'.

71 *the nineteenth ... own nativity*: Poe's birthday was 19 January; and although born in 1809, to make himself seem younger he sometimes gave 1813 (or 1811) as the year of his birth.

73 *key*: here, tone or pitch of voice.

75 *Eton*: as Poe had no first-hand experience of this famous English public school, Wilson's years there are less fully described than his earlier schooling.

78 *Herodes Atticus*: Tiberius Claudius Atticus Herodes was a second-century rhetorician who, like his friend the emperor Hadrian, spent his wealth liberally on public buildings.

The Man of the Crowd

The tale appeared in both *The Casket* and *[Burton's] Gentleman's Magazine* for December 1839. It was collected in *Tales* (1845).

84 *Ce grand malheur*...: 'That great misfortune, not to be able to be alone'; from *Les Caractères*, by the seventeenth-century moralist Jean de la Bruyère.

αχλυς . . . : 'the mist that previously was upon them'; adapted from Homer, *Iliad*, v. 127.

Leibnitz... *Gorgias*: Poe's opinion elsewhere varied on Leibniz, the seventeenth-century rationalist and co-inventor of calculus. The sophist Gorgias represents faulty rhetoric in the Socratic dialogue bearing his name.

85 *Eupatrids*: well-born, after hereditary nobles of Athens.

88 *Retzsch*: Friedrich Retzsch, nineteenth-century German artist, famous for his illustrations of Goethe's *Faust*.

91 n. 1 *Hortulus Animæ*...: the rare sixteenth-century *Ortulus anime cum oratiunculis* of Johanna Grüninger, whose illustrations Isaac D'Israeli judged indecent.

The Murders in the Rue Morgue

Arguably the first detective story, this tale was published in *Graham's Magazine* for April 1841. It was collected in *Tales* (1845).

92 *Browne*: from chapter V of *Urn Burial* by the seventeenth-century doctor and polymath. The first version of this extensively revised tale omitted the motto, but opened with a learned paragraph on the phrenological organ of 'analysis', similar to the discussion of phrenology at the beginning of 'The Imp of the Perverse'.

93 *Hoyle*: in the eighteenth century, Edmund Hoyle published widely on the rules of card-playing. In revised forms, his books remain in print.

96 *Bi-Part Soul*: since as early as Plato's *Symposium*, philosophers have argued for the duality of the soul. One variation accounts for the *Doppelgänger* motive, common in Poe.

97 *et id genus omne*: 'and all of that kind'. The whole discussion of the fictitious effeminate Chantilly suggests the narrator's fears about the sexual ambiguity of his relation to Dupin; see David Van Leer, 'Detecting Truth: The World of the Dupin Tales', in Silverman (ed.), *New Essays on Poe's Major Tales*, 69–79.

98 *Epicurus . . . nebular cosmogony*: in *Eureka*, his late essay on the universe, Poe associated the atomic theory of the ancient Greek philosopher with William Herschel's eighteenth-century explanation of the universe in terms of the Orion nebula.

Perdidit...: 'the first letter has lost its original sound'; from Ovid, *Fasti*, v.

99 *métal d'Alger*: an inexpensive alloy used in place of silver. Napoleons are 20-franc gold pieces.

100 *the head fell off*: earlier versions continue 'and rolled to some distance'. Most other of Poe's many revisions to the description of the crime are less gruesome and concern only minor details.

105 *Monsieur Jourdain*: in Act I, scene ii of Molière's *Le Bourgeois Gentilhomme*, the middle-class hero affects gentlemanly airs by calling for his dressing-gown (*robe de chambre*), 'better to hear the [chamber] music'.

Vidocq: in the nineteenth century, the reformed criminal François-Eugène Vidocq headed the intelligence service under Napoleon, and later founded the first private detective agency. His 1828 *Memoires* whetted readers' appetite for crime novels, and Vidocq's own moral ambiguity made him the model for the tortured avenger of subsequent detective fiction.

106 *Je les ménageais*: 'I dealt with them tactfully'.

116 *Cuvier*: Georges Cuvier, nineteenth-century French natural historian.

118 *Neufchatel-ish*: countrified, after a remote French province.

122 *Jardin des Plantes*: the great Parisian Botanical Garden whose zoological displays anticipated evolutionary theory.

122n. 1 "*de nier* . . .": 'to deny what is, and to explain what is not'; from Part VI, letter xi of Rousseau's *Julie, or The New Héloïse*, an eighteenth-century novel exploring the female inner conscience. The phallic implications of the paragraph's 'stamens' and 'codfish' emasculate the Prefect.

Eleonora

The last of Poe's 'women' tales, 'Eleonora' appeared in *The Gift: A Christmas and New Year's Present for 1842*, available in autumn 1841.

123 *Lully*: 'Under the protection of a specific form, the soul is safe.' The reference, quoted in Victor Hugo's *Notre-Dame de Paris*, is to the trials of the biblical Job, as explicated by the thirteenth-century Spanish mystic Ramon Llull.

'*agressi* . . . *exploraturi*': 'they were come into the sea of shades [Atlantic Ocean], to find out what is in it'. From *Geographia Nubiensis*, the Latin translation of the twelfth-century travel narrative of Arab scientist Al-Idrisi.

Oedipus: on arriving at Thebes, the Greek hero Oedipus solved the riddle of the sphinx, which refers to the stages of human maturation.

125 *bard of Schiraz*: the fourteenth-century Persian poet Shams ud-din Muhammad, known as Hafiz.

126 *Helusion*: variant for Elysium.

127 *Hesper*: Hesperia, the western region dominated by Hesperus, the evening star.

The Masque of the Red Death

This brief masterpiece first appeared in *Graham's Magazine* for May 1842.

129 *Red Death*: although its name recalls the Black Plague of the Middle Ages, the

Red Death is imaginary. Cholera, however, was a pressing reality in the nineteenth century, and the United States suffered two serious outbreaks during Poe's lifetime.

131 *'Hernani'*: Victor Hugo's 1830 play of political and romantic intrigue in the reign of Charles V of Spain.

134 *a thief in the night*: Christ in His second coming will reappear like a thief in the night: 1 Thessalonians 5: 2.

The Pit and the Pendulum

This tale first appeared in *The Gift: A Christmas and New Year's Present, MDCCCXLIII*, available earlier in 1842.

135 *Impia . . . at Paris*: the motto reads: 'Here the wicked mob, unappeased, long cherished a hatred of blood. Now that the fatherland is saved, and the cave of death demolished, where grim death has been, life and health appear.' In the French Revolution, the Jacobins were extreme radicals responsible for the excesses of the Reign of Terror. Their liberal politics were the opposite of those of the reactionary Spanish Inquisition.

inquisitorial voices: Poe draws on American anti-Catholic paranoia in the nineteenth century, especially about the long-standing 'inquisitions' by which the Church searched out heresy. Although not historically precise, the tale correctly suggests that the Inquisition was particularly harsh in Spain, where it was centred in Toledo, and was halted temporarily in 1808 by Napoleonic troops under General Colbert, Comte de Lasalle.

The Mystery of Marie Rogêt

This second of the Dupin tales appeared in William Snowden's *Ladies' Companion* in three instalments—November and December 1842, and February 1843. It was collected in his 1845 *Tales*. Poe's use of a fictional character to solve a real-life murder affords the tale its special interest, and led Dorothy Sayers to declare it his finest work. The facts were essentially as Poe indicated. In July 1841 the shop-girl Mary Rogers was found floating dead in the Hudson River. Sensationalizing journalists converted this commonplace incident into a media event by emphasizing its mysterious elements, implying that Rogers was the victim of gang violence. When Poe began his account, the death remained unexplained. His early instalments reprinted various newspaper articles in an edited but fairly accurate form to expose their faulty logic and implicit xenophobia. While he was preparing his final instalment—in which Dupin exposed the complicity of Rogers's secret lover—the innkeeper Mrs Loss (called Madame Deluc by Poe) confessed on her death-bed to having assisted in the abortion during which Rogers died. Faced with this new evidence, Poe quickly altered his final instalment and revised the whole tale more extensively for its republication in book form. As a result, the tale offers fundamentally two explanations: the favoured is Poe's original solution involving the secret lover; the second, barely sketched in, transforms the lover into the abortionist of Mrs Loss's account, without ever actually mentioning her confession or what it implied about Rogers's death. For a detailed account of Poe's use of his sources, see John Walsh, *Poe the Detective: The*

Curious Circumstances behind 'The Mystery of Marie Rogêt' (New Brunswick, NJ: Rutgers University Press, 1968).

149 *Novalis*: the late eighteenth-century German romantic writer, Friedrich von Hardenberg.

grisette: French term for a seamstress, identified by her grey (*gris*) smock. By assuming the sexual immorality of such a class of women, the term can also mean, more colloquially, 'prostitute'.

151 n. 1 *Nassau Street*: Poe's Paris is not geographically accurate. Although his notes provide the real names for most of the characters, they do not do so for Madame Deluc, the guilty innkeeper who actually arranged for the disposal of Mary's body after the failed abortion.

152 *émeutes*: French for tumults or uprisings, in particular the revolutionary activity of 1830.

167 *sequitur*: Latin for 'it follows', most commonly in the phrase *non sequitur*.

170 *de lunatico inquirendo*: the Latin name for the legal writ calling for a jury inquiry into the defendant's sanity.

170 n. 1 *Landor*: William Landor, pseudonym of Horace Binney Wallace. The quotation is from Wallace's anonymous novel *Stanley* (1838).

187 *Et hinc illæ iræ?*: Latin for 'And hence this anger?'

188 *fatal accident*: the reference to the possibility of death at Deluc's inn is one of Poe's late additions, trying to adjust his original solution to the real-life fact of the fatal abortion. On Poe and abortion, see Van Leer, 'Detecting Truth'.

The Tell-Tale Heart

The tale first appeared in January 1843 in James Russell Lowell's *The Pioneer*. It was frequently reprinted, but not collected by Poe himself.

The Gold-Bug

Poe's tale won a contest sponsored by the Philadelphia *Dollar Newspaper*, in which it first appeared in two instalments on 21 and 28 June 1843. It was frequently reprinted and collected in *Tales* (1845).

198 *All in the Wrong*: the motto is Poe's own, and not, as claimed, from Arthur Murphy's eighteenth-century comedy.

199 *scarabæus*: Latin for scarab, a family of beetles, whose sacred image ancient Egyptians frequently used as ornaments.

201 *scarabæus caput hominis*: scarab with a human head.

216 *connected with it*: end of first newspaper instalment.

220 *Captain Kidd*: the buried treasure of the Scottish pirate William Kidd (*c.*1645–1701) was a popular legend in mid-nineteenth-century America. It is alluded to as well in works by Irving, Thoreau, and Melville.

223 *a table*: although Poe's tabulations are not correct, his cryptography is fundamentally sound.

The Black Cat

The tale first appeared in August 1843 in the Philadelphia magazine *The United States Saturday Post*, later renamed *The Saturday Evening Post*. It was collected in *Tales* (1845).

A Tale of the Ragged Mountains

The tale first appeared in *Godey's Magazine and Lady's Book* for April 1844.

240 *serious fact*: the Swiss-German physician Franz Anton Mesmer (1733–1815) popularized the therapeutic potential of hypnotism, which he called 'animal magnetism'. Part of a more general spiritualist revival in mid-nineteenth-century America, the fascination with mesmerism was also treated in novels by Nathaniel Hawthorne, Oliver Wendell Holmes, and Henry James. On Poe and mesmerism, see Sidney Lind, 'Poe and Mesmerism', *PMLA* 62 (1947), 1077–94.

244 *dream*: Novalis, 'Fragmente, Paralipomen zum Blütenstaub', no. 121.

246 *Warren Hastings*: the British governor charged with putting down the Benares insurrection. Poe drew many of his details from T. B. Macaulay's review of G. R. Gleig's biography of Hastings.

247 *The riots . . . his life*: Poe's fundamentally accurate account of Cheyte Sing's insurrection of 1781 derives from Macaulay's essay. On orientalism in Poe, see Malini Johar Schueller, 'Harems, Orientalist Subversions, and the Crisis of Nationalism: The Case of Edgar Allan Poe and "Ligeia" ', *Criticism*, 37 (1995), 601–23, and more generally John T. Irwin, *American Hieroglyphics: The Symbol of Egyptian Hieroglyphics in the American Renaissance* (New Haven: Yale University Press, 1980).

sangsues: French for leeches; the poisonous variety is Poe's invention.

The Purloined Letter

This third and final Dupin tale first appeared in *The Gift: A Christmas, New Year, and Birthday Present*, dated 1845 but issued in September 1844. It was collected in *Tales* (1845).

249 *Nil sapientiae . . .*: Latin for 'Nothing is more hateful to wisdom than cleverness.' The source of the passage, ascribed to the Roman philosopher Seneca, has not been identified.

au troisième: on the third, or what Americans today call the fourth, floor.

251 *the Minister D—*: the similarity between the minister's name and Dupin's own has led some critics to posit a symbolic and even a biological relation between the two characters.

252 *hotel*: used in the French sense, where *hôtel* can mean 'private mansion' as well as 'public hostelry'.

258 *Rochefoucault . . . Campanella*: La Rochefoucauld and La Bruyère were French moral philosophers, famous for their 'maxims'. Machiavelli and Campanella were Italian political philosophers, the former ruthlessly practical, the latter

dreamily Utopian. The famous discussion of 'evens and odds' has been of considerable interest to modern theorists, who compare it to the *fort/da* episode in Freud's *Beyond the Pleasure Principle*. See Jacques Lacan, 'Le Séminaire sur "La Lettre volée" ', in *Écrits I* (Paris: Éditions du Seuil, 1966), 7–75; Jacques Derrida, 'Le Facteur de la Vérité' in *The Post Card: From Socrates to Freud and Beyond*, trans. Alan Bass (Chicago: University of Chicago Press, 1987), 411–96; Barbara Johnson, 'The Frame of Reference: Poe, Lacan, Derrida', in *The Critical Difference: Essays in the Contemporary Rhetorica of Reading* (Baltimore: Johns Hopkins University Press, 1980), 110–46; and especially Stanley Cavell, *In Quest of the Ordinary: Lines of Skepticism and Romanticism* (Chicago: University of Chicago Press, 1988).

259 *non distributio medii*: the fallacy of the undistributed middle mistakenly argues from a premiss—if *a* then *b* (all fools are poets)—to its converse—if *b* then *a* (all poets are fools). In so doing it fails to acknowledge the middle possibility—some *b*s are not *a*s (some poets are wise).

"*Il y a à parier . . .*": 'One can bet that any popular idea, every accepted convention, is a foolishness, since it has convinced the majority of people'; from the *Maximes et Penseés* of the eighteenth-century French author Sebastien-Roch Nicolas, who wrote under the name of Chamfort.

260 *ambitus . . . honesti*: despite the similarity to English terms, in Latin *ambitus* literally means 'seeking office' and *religio* 'superstition', while *homines honesti* is Cicero's term for men of his own party.

Bryant . . .: Jacob Bryant, *A New System of Antient Mythology* (1807).

265 *facilis descensus Averni*: 'The descent to Hades is easy'; from Virgil, *Aeneid*, vi. 126.

as Catalani said: Angelica Catalani, nineteenth-century Italian opera star. The source of her comment is unidentified.

monstrum horrendum: a terrifying monster, according to Virgil, *Aeneid*, iii. 658.

Un dessein si funeste . . .: 'So deadly a scheme, if not worthy of Atreus [the avenger], is deserved by Thyestes [the criminal]'; from *Atrée et Thyeste* (1707) by Prosper-Jolyot de Crébillon. For Poe's use of the passage, see Johnson, 'The Frame of Reference'.

The System of Doctor Tarr and Professor Fether

The tale was first published in *Graham's Magazine* for November 1845.

266 *the autumn of* 18—: the temporal setting refers to the widespread prison reforms after the great revolutions in both America and France. According to Foucault, the great symbolic act in this reconceptualization of punishment was Pinel's removal in 1794 of the chains from inmates at Bicêtre.

Monsieur Maillard: some of the characters' names seem ironic. Stanislas-Marie Maillard led in the overthrow of the Bastille. Paul de Kock was a French novelist who sensationalized city life. Pierre-Simon, Marquis de Laplace was the astronomer whose nebular theory Poe celebrated in his cosmology *Eureka*. 'Petit Gaillard' means a hearty little fellow. 'Desoulières' alludes to *souliers* or shoes, which would not cook well into a pumpkin pie. Georges-Louis Leclerc de Buffon was a famous naturalist; although 'Bouffon le Grand' means 'the great idiot'.

267 *Bellini*: the great opera composer Vincenzo Bellini represented his heroines' descents into madness through a beautiful, but dramatically inappropriate lyricism. Finding the composer's personal demeanour as tepid as his characters' psychologies, the poet Heine dismissed Bellini as 'a sigh in dancing-pumps'.

268 *reductio ad absurdum*: a rhetorical strategy which disproves an argument by demonstrating the absurdity of its more extreme cases.

270 *vieille cour*: literally 'old court'; the phrase often refers to the aristocratic regime before the French Revolution.

271 *the Anakim*: the giant sons of Anak; Numbers 13: 33.

nil admirari: Latin for 'to be astonished at nothing'; from Horace, *Epistles*, I. vi. 1.

272 *monstrum, horrendum, informe* . . .: 'a horrible, malformed, huge monster, deprived of light'; from Virgil, *Aeneid*, iii. 658, where it refers to the Cyclops blinded by Ulysses. Poe quotes part of the passage near the end of 'The Purloined Letter'.

274 *Demosthenes' . . . Brougham*: Henry Lord Brougham was a nineteenth-century polemicist and Lord Chancellor of England. Although he quoted from the Athenian orator Demosthenes, he could not be said to look like a Greek from the fourth century BC, of whom no representations survive.

275 *the Medicean Venus*: a statue notorious for its nude depiction of the goddess.

278 *bulls of Phalaris*: a hollow brass statue of a bull in which the king Phalaris burned people to death. As they died, their screams sounded like the roarings of the bull.

Pandemonium in petto: Pandemonium is the assembly hall of hell, where the devils noisily (and foolishly) debate in the opening books of Milton's *Paradise Lost*; *in petto* means 'in the breast' or 'private'.

280 *Yankee Doodle*: though now degenerated into a children's song, 'Yankee Doodle' originally embodied the impudence of the colonies, and is here linked with the antitraditionalism of post-revolutionary France.

The Imp of the Perverse

This tale first appeared in *Graham's Magazine* for July 1845.

283 *Spurzheimites*: Poe casts his tale as a revision of phrenology, which associated personality traits with the shape of an individual's skull. In addition to cranial lobes marking hunger ('alimentiveness') or self-defence ('combativeness'), Poe's narrator isolates a new organ of 'perverseness'. Dr Johann Gaspar Spurzheim was one of the discoverers of phrenology and its chief advocate in the United States. The references to 'moral sentiment', 'pure intellect', and 'the *principia* of human action', however, connect the particular pseudo-science of phrenology to eighteenth-century faculty psychology in general, alluding to Isaac Newton, John Locke, and Immanuel Kant. On phrenology, see Edward

Hungerford, 'Poe and Phrenology', *American Literature*, 2 (1930), 209–31; on the philosophical implications of perverseness, see Cavell, *In Quest of the Ordinary*.

The Cask of Amontillado

This tale first appeared in *Godey's Magazine and Lady's Book* for November 1846.

289 *Amontillado*: a light-coloured Spanish sherry, not the finest of wines. Throughout the tale, Poe probably chooses specific wines for the sound of their names and not their alcoholic character.

291 '*Nemo me* . . .': 'No one provokes me with impunity.'

292 *masons*: Freemasonry is a private fraternal organization that arose in the seventeenth century and continues to exist today. In the nineteenth century Americans feared its secret rituals, and the Masons were frequent victims of mob violence. Although many Masonic rituals refer back symbolically to the organization's origins in stonemasonry, Montresor's claim to be a Mason is purely ironic.

The Domain of Arnheim

This tale, an expansion of 'The Landscape Garden' (1842), was published in the New York *Columbian Lady's and Gentleman's Magazine* for March 1847. It has as its sequel 'Landor's Cottage' (1849).

296 *Giles Fletcher*: from 'Christ's Victorie on Earth' (1610).

perfectionists: Poe here associates the doctrine of the perfectibility of man with numerous eighteenth-century thinkers: the French statesman Anne-Robert-Jacques Turgot; the English common-sense philosopher Richard Price; the English empiricist Joseph Priestley; and the French mathematician Marie-Jean Caritat, Marquis de Condorcet. Since Poe is elsewhere sceptical about man's perfectibility, this reference (and many others in the story) may be ironic and mark Poe's reservations about Ellison's aestheticism. See Joan Dayan, *Fables of Mind: An Inquiry into Poe's Fiction* (New York: Oxford University Press, 1987).

298 n. 1 *Muskau's account*: the story of the inheritance exists largely as Poe describes it in Prince Hermann Pückler-Muskau, *Tour in England, Ireland, and France* (1833). Poe rightly notes that a similar inheritance, secretly invested for heirs a century and a half later, lies at the centre of Eugène Sue's *The Wandering Jew* (1844–5).

299 *mute and inglorious*: adapted from Gray, 'Elegy in a Country Churchyard'.

300 *Claude*: seventeenth-century French landscape painter Claude Lorrain.

302 '*There are properly . . . human interest*': the paragraph is quoted from an anonymous review of a book on *American Landscape Gardening* in a contemporary New York magazine.

capabilities: a reference to Launcelot 'Capability' Brown, the eighteenth-century landscape gardener who popularized the term to describe an uncultivated setting's potential for development.

303 *Addison... 'Inferno'*: *Cato* is by the eighteenth-century playwright Joseph Addison, who is more famous for his *Spectator* essays. By comparing Addison's play to the first part of Dante's masterly *Commedia* and to the sublime symmetry of the ancient Greek temple, the narrator differentiates skilful fabrication from true inspiration, which transcends all learning.

304 *De Staël*: the eighteenth-century German writer Anne Louise Germaine Necker, better known as Madame de Staël, introduced German Romanticism to England and America.

Timon: in Shakespeare's *Timon of Athens*, the misanthropic hero rejects society and lives in a cave.

Ætna: Mt. Etna in Sicily was celebrated by Romantics for its vistas.

305 *Fonthill*: the picturesque home of the extravagant eighteenth-century writer William Beckford, author of the oriental Gothic novel *Vathek*.

Hop-Frog

This story, Poe's last full-length narrative, was published in Boston's *The Flag of Our Union* on 17 March 1849. It derives from an anecdote in Froissart's *Chronicles*.

310 *rara avis in terris*: 'a rare bird in the world'; Juvenal, *Satires*, vi. 165.

Rabelais . . . Voltaire: Poe contrasts the effusive, bawdy sixteenth-century humour of Rabelais with the more restrained eighteenth-century satire of Voltaire.

Von Kempelen and his Discovery

This late satiric essay was published in Boston's *The Flag of Our Union* on 14 April 1849.

319 '*Diary of Sir Humphrey Davy*': although Davy and many others named in the story are real, the publications are all fictitious. The 'editorial' brackets throughout are Poe's own.

320 *protoxide of azote*: laughing-gas.

321 *Presburg*: for the association of Pressburg, Hungary with magic, see note to p. 21 above. The ironic tone of the essay suggests that Von Kempelen's birthplace may also be a pun, and indicate his origin in the hyperbole of the media or 'press'.

322 *Mäelzel*: the automated chess-player of Wolfgang von Kempelen, exhibited in the United States by J. N. Mäelzel, is the subject of Poe's 'Maelzel's Chess-Player' (1836). On the importance of Mäelzel in Poe's detective fiction, see John T. Irwin, *The Mystery to a Solution: Poe, Borges, and the Analytic Story* (Baltimore: Johns Hopkins University Press, 1994), 104–14.

324 *late developments in California*: the 'Rush' to California after John Sutter's discovery of gold in 1848.